# GERMAN
# CONVERSATION-GRAMMAR

A

## NEW AND PRACTICAL METHOD OF LEARNING THE GERMAN LANGUAGE

BY

## D<sup>R.</sup> EMIL OTTO,

PROFESSOR OF MODERN LANGUAGES AND LECTURER AT THE UNIVERSITY
OF HEIDELBERG, AUTHOR OF THE 'FRENCH CONVERSATION
GRAMMAR' AND SOME OTHER CLASS-BOOKS

### TWENTY-FOURTH EDITION.

**LONDON.**
DAVID NUTT, 270 Strand.
DULAU & Co., 37 Soho Square.
SAMPS LOW & Co., St. Dunstan's House, Fetter Lane, Fleet Street.

AGENCIES FOR AMERICA:

NEW YORK.
STEIGER E. & Co.,
25 Park Place.
THE INTERNATIONAL
NEWS COMPANY.
29 and 31 Beckman Street.

CHICAGO.
MUHLBAUER & BEHRLE,
41 La Salle Sreet

BOSTON.
CHARLES SCHÖNHOF
144 Tremont Street.

HEIDELBERG.
JULIUS GROOS.
1888.

# Preface to the first edition.

Within the last few years, the study of the German language in England has become so universal, that the appearance of another German grammar in addition to the comparatively few that have hitherto been published, will scarcely excite surprise, especially as the book mostly in use with the English student, viz: 'Ollendorff's New Method of learning German', is in reality no grammar, but only a book of exercises, affording the pupil no systematic and connected view of the grammatical rules, necessarily to be observed in German. The difficulties of the language are not removed by Ollendorff's Exercises, they are simply avoided. However a *mere* grammar, i. e. an assemblage of grammatical rules, without practical application, is equally unfitted to satisfy the pupil desirous not only of comprehending and reading, but also of *writing* and *speaking* the language. The present 'German Grammar' will conduce to the attainment of *all* these objects. It is based on the so-called *Conversational Method*, first applied by the author of this book in his 'French Conversation-Grammar', which work has met with great success in Germany, and has distinctly shown that this method is the easiest, quickest, and the best calculated to assist the pupil in overcoming the difficulties of a language.

*

This 'German Conversation-Grammar' combines the grammatical and logical exposition of the German language with the constant application of the different forms and rules to *writing* and *speaking*.

The book is divided into Lessons, each complete in itself, and containing in systematic arrangement a portion of the grammar, followed by a German *Reading exercise* in which the different forms are applied the whole sentences. An *Exercise for translation* into German comes next: the lesson being concluded by an easy and familiar *Conversation*, re-embodying the matter introduced in the previous exercises.

It is impossible to conceive a more practical method of acquiring the art of *speaking* German, than for the pupil to be questioned in German by his teacher on subjects already familiar to him by translation, and then to endeavour to give a fitting reply. In a short time the ear becomes so familiarized with the strange accents, that the teacher is understood, the tongue at the same time acquiring a fluency, to be attained by none of the other methods. The author's practical experience in teaching his mother-tongue to foreigners, warrants him fully in making this assertion.

The advantage of *conversational* exercises is evident. Whoever has occupied himself with the study of modern languages, is aware that by far the most difficult thing is, to comprehend the foreign idiom. Accustomed from the very beginning to understand the easy questions the teacher addresses to him in German, and to answer in the same language on subjects already known to him from the foregoing Reading exercise and translation, the learner exercises equally his *ear* and *tongue*, and will in a short time be enabled to express his thoughts fluently and correctly in the foreign idiom.

The book is divided into two *Parts* or *Courses;* the *First Part* contains the complete Etymology, that is, the ten *parts of speech,* considered in their nature and inflections, including the irregular verbs, with only the plainest syntactical rules requisite for translating the exercises.

The *Second Part* contains the complete Syntax and the more difficult and idiomatical parts of the grammar. This part, as the most essential, has been systematically explained in clear and accurate rules, all of which are illustrated by the necessary examples, and followed by fitting *Exercises* and *German Reading-lessons,* both with the requisite words. *Free Exercises, Materials for conversation* and a few German *dialogues* conclude the Grammar.

Lastly, a few Specimens of German *poetical literature,* some of which may be advantageously commited to memory, are introduced in the 'Appendix'.

In respect to the mode of employing this Grammar, the author begs that he may be allowed to offer teachers and pupils a few suggestions. The rules with their examples and the 'Words' should be first learned by heart, and the German 'Reading Exercise' read and translated into English. This done, the *'Conversation'* should be read, then the Exercise for translation (Aufgabe) put into German and, when corrected, written out fairly and gone through again. Finally the *'Conversation'* should be read or committed to memory. The pupil may commence with the Reading lessons and with the easier poems in the 'Appendix' as soon as the teacher considers him sufficiently advanced even though he should not have gone through the whole of the first Part.

HEIDELBERG, September 1856.

## DR. EMIL OTTO.

# Preface to the eighteenth, nineteenth and twentieth editions.

The method followed in this grammar*) and the improvements made in the preceding editions having been so much approved by the public as to cause it to be adopted by many schools and private families, as 'the best German Grammar' and 'one of the most useful class-books', the author as well as the publisher have spared no trouble to make it as perfect as possible. They flatter themselves that by this new edition, carefully revised and more elegantly printed, it will be found more deserving of the increasing patronage it has hitherto experienced, and they trust that it will materially contribute towards promoting the study of the German language in England and America.

The author takes this accasion to inform those who wish to learn German that he has written also a smaller grammar, entitled: '*An elementary Grammar of the German language*, combined with Exercises, Readings and Conversations (price only two marks) which retains exactly the same method as this larger one, and is destined for first beginners. Further also in connection with it another little book which is much needed: viz. '*German-*

---

*) Explained in the Preface to the first edition.

*English Conversation. A new methodical guide for learning to speak German'.*

He begs leave to mention also that he has recently published: **Supplementary Exercises** to the German Grammar and further two little volumes: '**Materials for translating English into German** with grammatical notes and a Vocabulary, first†) and second Part, intended for proficient learners. When they have gone through the grammar, the use of these little works will certainly prove useful in giving them a greater facility not only in *writing* but also in *speaking* German correctly.

A **Key,** containing the translations of the English Exercises into German, the necessary notes and translations of the pieces of German literature contained in the 'Appendix', and some specimens of German letter-writing, has been published††) for the convenience of those who are unable to procure an efficient teacher. The new edition of it exactly agrees with this edition of the Grammar. Further the author begs leave to say, that he has published a '**First German Book**'*) for the use of younger pupils who are to acquire a slight *practical* knowledge of the elements of the German language, before commencing a regular grammatical course; likewise a **German Reader** the *first* part of which contains: *Easy Readings*, *fables*, *little stories* etc., the second: Select Reading in German literature; the third: *German plays*, each with notes and a Vocabulary, all three in new editions.

HEIDELBERG, March 1878.

DR. EMIL OTTO.

---

†) 5th edition 1882. — ††) 15th ed. 1882. — *) 7th ed. 1887.

# Preface to the Twenty-second Edition.

Referring the student of this grammar to the contents of the Prefaces to the First, Eighteenth, Nineteenth and Twentieth editions, we may state that the present Edition has been most carefully revised, corrected and in every essential way amended by *Herr Prof. Dr. H. Müller of Heidelberg.*

A careful observer, on comparing this edition with the foregoing, will soon notice that not only the new Orthography, adopted in the meanwhile by all the German governments, has been introduced, but also that many other useful and more or less important corrections and additions have been made.

A résumé of the Accidence will appear as an Appendix, in the hope that it may prove useful to those who wish to revise quickly the Accidence as given in Part I.

HEIDELBEGR, July 1886.

The Editor.

# Corrections.

Page 32 near bottom of page for foll read *fool.*
- » 52 omit note 2.
- » 57 bottom of page omit "in which words the final *e* is only added for euphony."
- » 60 3rd line from bottom for wen read *when.*
- » 120 5th line from bottom for feeble read *weak.*

# Extract
from "Rochester Daily Union".

---

## Heidelberg, Germany.

*To the American Student coming to Germany.*

One of the most difficult questions for the American student to get properly answered, when he is about to start for Europe for purposes of study is, where to find the best place to set himself to work. Many waste a good part of their time before they find they have not been properly advised on this point. It makes a vast difference where the student of German pursues his studies, not only as to the purity of the language spoken, but as to the ability of those who lecture on the topics he may wish to hear . . . .

It is a singular fact, but an undeniable one, that the most difficult thing to find in Germany is a good teacher of the German language. The want of a good system of text books, and the fact of having been instructed orally, and by lectures, renders the native German teacher incapable of following a system of instruction that the better disciplined mind of the American student demands.

It must not be supposed that German teachers are deficient in knowledge. On the contrary their attainments

are a matter of wonder. They speak several foreign
languages with as much ease and fluency as their own.
But they acquire languages much more readily than the
American student, and therefore fail to comprehend the
difficulties which a foreigner finds in their own. They
almost invariably use English and French methods in teaching their own language, and these do not meet the neces-
sities of the case. I have often had occasion to remark
that, until some German linguist took the trouble to put
himself in the position of the English scholar, and to
comprehend the difficulties, which the German language
presents to the foreigner, well enough to perfect a system
of instruction adopted to the case, the correct comprehension of the spirit and letter of the German would be the
lot of a very small proportion of those who study it.
Woodbury's method, which is mostly used in America, is
found to be very faulty, when any one tries to use what
they have learned from it in intercourse with Germans.
The German is not pure, and many of the classifications
are wholly incorrect, therefore half the time spent in
learning it, is wasted. Ahn's method is better German,
but it is *neither systematically nor progressively arranged.*
Having been perplexed by the defects of the various systems and text books in use for the English pupils, and
the want of systematic and thorough teachers, it has been
a source of great satisfaction to have found here at the
University of Heidelberg, in the person of one of the
professors, **Dr. Otto,** a teacher who has comprehended and
solved *satisfactorily* the difficulties which his own language
presents to the foreigner. He has been a close student
of languages, and has not only made many interesting
discoveries in German, and originated a most useful system of classification of words, but he has so clearly

comprehended the spirit of the English language as to be able to adapt his discoveries and classifications successfully to it.

As a result of his researches and studies he has published a **grammar*** ) for the English student, which, in my opinion, **is better than any heretofore published in Europe or America;** and I earnestly recommend it to all who wish to learn German. Twelve months' trial with other Teachers and systems, added to my own experience in teaching, may justify me in speaking on thi point with more assurance than I otherwise would.

My conviction is that the student will do better to spend his first four or six months in the beautiful town of Heidelberg. No teacher whom I have found, can take him on so understandingly and so fast as **Dr. Otto.** His systematic application of the rules and principles of his **superior grammar,** and his extensive acquaintance with German literature and German history render his instructions invaluable to the student of German. . . . . .

**Prof. Peck.**

---

*) The full title is: **German Conversation-Grammar.** A *new and practical* method of learning the German language by **Dr. Emil Otto,** Prof. of modern languages and Lecturer at the University of Heidelberg. **22ⁿᵈ Edition.** Published by Julius Groos, Heidelberg.

# CONTENTS.

## First Part. — Etymology.

**

# Appendix.

A few specimens of German poetical literature.

# GENERAL INDEX.

A.

Ab, separable prefix 207.

aber, sondern, allein 246.

About, how rendered 359.

Above, how rendered 359.

Accent of words 12.

Accessory sentence, its arrangement of words 372; with separ. verbs 210

Accusative 339; governed by prepositions 45, 259—263; — with the infinitive 326; governed by adj. 339.

Active verbs 119.

Adjectives determinative 71 ..; demonstrative 71; interrogative 72; possessive 73; indefinite 74; predicative 96; Declension of adj with the definite article 97; with the indefin. article 98; without either article 100. Compar. of adj. 105; government of adj. 339; with prepositions 341; adj. with suffixes 102; adj. used as nouns 103.

Adverbs of place 236; — of time 237; — of quantity and comparison 240; — of affirmation and negation 241; — of interrogation 241, order 242; — their comparison 107, 242; their position in a sentence 366; inversion of their position 370.

All, with the article 74; without it 283; meaning "whole" 304.

All, when not declined 304.

Allein, as conjunction 245.

Als, conjunction 248, 249.

Als wenn, als ob, 254; followed by the subjunctive mood 313.

An, separable particle 207.

An, prep., its significations 354.

Anderthalb, used for zweithalb 117.

Any, how rendered 158, 305.

Apposition 65.

Arrangement of words 79, 366 ...

Article, the definite 20; the indef. 23; contracted with prepositions 47; special use

## German Writing Alphabet

a, b, c, d, e, f, g, h, i, j, k,

l, m, n, o, p, q, r, s, u,

t, u, v, w, x, y, z.

## Compound Consonants

## Capital Letters

A, B, C, D, E, F, G, H,

I, J, K, L, M, N, O,

P, Q, R, S, T, U, V,

W, X, Y, Z.

1, 2, 3, 4, 5, 6, 7, 8, 9, 0.

# Part I.

# ETYMOLOGY:

comprehending

the elements of the language.

# On Pronunciation.

## Letters of the Alphabet.

The German Alphabet consists of 26 letters, which are represented as follows:

| Characters. | Name. | Characters. | Name. |
|---|---|---|---|
| 𝔄, a = a | ah*) (au). | 𝔑, n = n | enn. |
| 𝔅, b = b | bey. | 𝔒, o = o | ō. |
| ℭ, c = c | tsey. | 𝔓, p = p | pey. |
| 𝔇, d = d | dey. | 𝔔, q = q | koo.***) |
| 𝔈, e = e | ey. | 𝔑, r = r | airr. |
| 𝔉, f = f | eff. | 𝔖, ſ, s = s | ess. |
| 𝔊, g = g | gay | 𝔗, t = t | tey. |
| 𝔥, h = h | hah.*) | 𝔘, u = u | oo.***) |
| 𝔍, i = i | ee. | 𝔙, v = v | fow (fou).†) |
| 𝔍, j = j | yŏt.**) | 𝔚, w = w | vey. |
| 𝔎, k = k | kah.*) | 𝔛, x = x | iks. |
| 𝔏, l = l | ell. | 𝔜, y = y | ypsilon. |
| 𝔐, m = m | em | 𝔷, z = z | tset. |

Of these, a, e, i, o, u, y are simple vowels, the others are simple consonants.

Besides these, there are in German *double vowels, modified vowels, diphthongs* and *compound consonants:*

### Double vowels.

| 𝔄a, aa | — ee | — oo. |
|---|---|---|

### Modified vowels.

| Ä, ä, or 𝔄e. | Ö, ö, or 𝔒e. | Ü, ü, or 𝔘e. |
|---|---|---|

### Diphthongs.

| 𝔄i, ai. | 𝔈i, ei. | 𝔈u, eu. |
|---|---|---|
| 𝔄u, au. | 𝔈y, ey. | Äu, äu or 𝔄eu. |

---

*) ah = a in *hard, are.*
**) o = o in *not, got.*
***) oo = oo in *fool, stool.*
†) ow (ou) = ow in *fowl, owl.*

1*

### Double and compound Consonants.

Ch, ch, ch. — chs = x.          Sp, sp, sp.
Sch, sch, sh. — ck = ck. — ss, ß, ss. St, st, st.
Qu, qu, qu. — ng = ng. — tz = tz. Th, th = t.

Several of these letters are very much alike; we therefore recommend them to the attention of beginners, as they may easily be confounded with each other. To prevent such mistakes, we give them here:
B and B; C and C; N, N and K; O and O.
b and h; ſ and f; v and y; r and r.

## Pronunciation of the vowels.

### 1. Simple and double vowels.

#### A, a.

A, a has always the same sound, and is pronounced like *a* in the English words: *farthing, father, are;* never like *a* in *ball*, or *name* or *hat*. Ex.: ab*), hat, ha-be, Aſ-ſe, Mann, Bad, la-ben.

Aa, aa is pronounced in the same manner, but longer·
Aas, Haar, Saal.

#### E, e.

E, e has three different sounds, the two first of which may be either long or short.

1) The broad e is like *a* in the English word *share:* ter, wer, wert, Schwert, Mehl; — short as in the word *shell:* hell, denn, wenn, End, Ente, Feld.

2) The acute e sounds like the French *é* and the *ey* in the words *they, grey* or in *hate*, as: eb-en, Reh, geht, lehrt, E-ſel (in the first syllable). This is also the sound of the double ee, as: Heer, Meer, Kaf-fee, See.

When the e is followed by two consonants or a double one, it is considered to be short; this being the case with all the vowels. —**)

3) e at the end of a word or in an unaccented prefix or final syllable, is very short and has rather on obtuse sound nearly like a short ö. be-te, Dede, Elle, Stelle, stellen, lobte, Verein, bezahlen ꝛc.

---

*) The consonants used in connection with these vowels are pronounced as in English.
**) The only exception is, when in conjugation, after a single consonant, an e has been dropped before the t or ſt of the termination, p. e. du lebſt, er lebt, du läßt, er läßt

## 3, i.

3, i has only one sound, the same as in *field*, *sister*, *milk*, never like *i* in *wise*, as: in, im, im=mer, mir, Lippe, mild, Tiſch, Kind ꝛc. — This vowel appears in some words lengthened by e *mute* after it, as in *field*: bie = *dee*, hier (here), vier (four), Lie=be, Wien, Dieb, bie=ſer.

In some words however the letter i belongs to the first syllable and e to the following; in this case i and e are of course pronounced separately: Spa=nien = Spā= ni=ĕn, Lilie = Li=li=ĕ (three syllables). — This does not take place in the final syllable of foreign words, where the accent falls on the last syllable: Melobi'e = melodee; Harmoni'e.

3, i is also made long by the insertion of h mute, in the following personal and possessive pronouns with their derivatives: pers. ihm, ihr, ihn, ihnen, Ihnen; possess. ihr, ihre, ihr, ber, bie, baß ihrige, Ihrige.

## D, o.

D, o when long, has the sound of the *o* in the English words *stone*, *alone*: D=fen, Hof, Boben, Rohr, Roſe, loß. When followed by two consonants, it is short and sounds nearly like the English *o* in *off*, *loss*: Gott, kommen, ſoll, offen. — Double o (oo) is always long and has the first sound ō: Mooß = mose, Moor (Sumpflanb) = more, Boot.

## U, u.

U, u sounds in long syllables like the English *u* in *rule*, *soup*, or the *oo* in *food*: Blut, Hut, nun, Ruhe, ru=fen; a little shorter, when followed by two consonants, as in *full* or *good*: Null, Bunb, Hulb, Hunb. — Double u does not occur.

## Y, y.

Y, y appears as a simple vowel only in foreign words, where its sound does not differ from that of the i, as Cy=pern, Ly=ſiaß ꝛc. — Preceded by e, it will be mentioned with the diphtongs. The German y is never used as a consonant.

## 2. Modified vowels.

The vowels ä, ö, ü are properly speaking simple ones as well, as the foregoing; but as a peculiar character for them is wanting, they are repiesented as modified a, o

and u's, and printed with a small e above, as ꞗ ꞗ ꞗ or
ä, ö, ü. At the beginning of words the capital letters,
are either modified with two dots or followed by the e,
as: Ä, or Ae, Ö, Oe, Ü, Ue. — In writing, the e over the
small letters has long since been corrupted into two dots,
as ä, ö, ü, which has now also obtained in printing.

### Ä, ä or Ae.

The sound of this vowel, when long, is nearly the
same as in *fair* (the French ê), as. Käse, grämen, Bäter,
wählen. — When short, the sound becomes rather slender,
as in *fell*, as: Fälle, Kälte, Bälde, Hände, Apfel or Aepfel.

### Ö, ö or Oe.

When sharp, this vowel *approaches* the English sound
in *murderer;* it is very like the French *eu* in *seul* or
*jeune*, as: Hölle, öfter, Götter, können. — When long, there
is no sound answering to it in the English language;
the nearest to it is perhaps *bird*, *heard* etc.; it resembles
the French *eu* in *feu*, as· Ofen or Oefen, Köhler, Höhle,
Oede, Bögen.

### Ü, ü or Ue.

The English have nothing corresponding to this sound.
It is exactly the French *u* in *russe*, *sur etc.*, as: über, für,
Übel or Uebel, Hütte, führen, füllen.

## 3. Diphthongs.
### Ai, ai. Au, au. Äu, äu or Aeu.

Ai, which occurs only in a few substantives, is pronounced almost like the Englisch *i* or *y* in *fire*, *sky*, but a
little broader, the a predominating: Kaiser, Waise, Hain,
Mai, Main. —

ay is no longer used in German, except in a few
proper names.

Au, like the *ou* in *house*, *sound*, as: Haus, aus, auf,
Baum, Raum, glauben, faul.

Äu, äu *resembles somewhat* the English *oy* in *boy;*
but whilst here the o predominates, in the German äu
the a is more heard; again the second half is not so
open as i, but more like the ü (French *u*), as Häuser,
Bäume, träumen, Bräute (as if spelled Häüser, Bäüme).

## Ei, ei (ey).

Ei has always the sound of the English *i* in *mind*, as: mein, dein, Bein, klein, Rei=me, heilen, Ei, Eier.*)

ey was formerly used instead of ei at the end of words, and in order to distinguish the two different words of the same sound: fein (*his*) and feyn (*to be*). This practice is now abolished, and all German words having the sound of ei in any one of their syllables are now written with ei, as einer=lei, Ei, Eier, bei, bei=legen. —

## Eu, eu.

Eu, eu has in fact the same sound now as äu, whilst formerly the latter one was somewhat broader; it is not quite so broad as the English *oi*, as: neu, Leute, heute, treu.

## Pronunciation of the consonants.

### 1. Simple consonants.

B, b and D, d, as in English; but when they end a word or even a syllable followed by another consonant, they are somewhat harder and approach the sound of p and t: Ball, Birne, breit, ab, Grab, El=be, ab=legen; Damm, der, mild, Tab=ler, Kind=lein, Abend.

C, c. This letter by itself, appears only in foreign words and is pronounced, before ä, e, i and y, like *ts* (the same as z), as: Cä=far, Ceder, Citrone, Cypern; — before the other vowels and consonants, hard like k, as. Catilina, Cato, Cortez, Claudius, Clölia. In many words formerly written with C or c we are now writing K or k and z, as Konzert, Köln, Kultur inst. of Concert, Cöln, Cultur 2c.

F, f; L, l; M, m; N, n; P, p; T, t and X, x are quite the same as in English, as: fin=den, auf, Affe, frei; Liebe, loben, fallen, fiel, Falke; Mann, mir, im, Hammer, nimmt; Tafel, Traum, Bett, betreffen; Xaver, Axe, Exempel.

t in words ending in ion, which are taken from the Latin, sounds like z (*ts*), according to our pronunciation of this language, as: Lektion = Lek=zion, Portion = Porzion, Nation, Emigration etc.

*) This diphthong ei is not to be confounded with ie (long i) which is not a diphthong (see p. 4, i). Compare the two words: beinen and bienen (= binen); Wein (*wine*) and Wien (*Vienna*).

𝔊, g ought always to have the hard sound like the English *g* in *garden*, *glad*, *pig*, as: Gar=ten, geben, gegen, Glas, Kragen, Flagge, Berg, genug; except in words ending in the unaccented final syllable ig, and their derivatives, where it sounds like ich, as: König (= Königch), giftig (= giftich), gütig, wenig, königlich, reinigen.

It must however be mentioned, that in a part of Germany the g after each vowel is pronounced soft, sounding like ch (see that letter p. 8). legen = leechen, Lage = Laa=che, genug = genuch, Heidelberg = Heidel=berch. Yet this is by no ways recommendable.

g with an n before it (ng) see p. 9.

ℌ, h, at the beginning of words, is aspirated as in English or even more· haben, Held, Hort, hören, Hut, hundert. — Between two vowels the aspiration is so slight as to be scarcely heard: Höhe, sehen, Schuhe, blühen, ziehen. — Before a consonant and at the end of words it is mute, but it indicates in this position that the vowel before it, is long: Ohr, Hahn, roh, Floh, Stroh, eh=ren, Zähne, Mohr, Uhr.

ℑ, j (yot) corresponds with *y* (consonant) in *you*, as: Ja, Jahr, jeder, jung, Jude, be=jahrt.

𝔎, k is like the English *k*, as: kahl, kalt, Kreuz, Klee, Balken; it is never mute before n, as: Knie, Knabe.

ℜ, r is pronounced shriller and with more emphasis than in English. Its being placed at the beginning, middle or end makes no difference: Rad, Ruhm, Erde, bergen, Burg, her, Haar, Flur, Führer.

𝔖, s, s has the *hard* sound (like the English *s* in *son*): 1) at the beginning of words; 2) in the inner part of words, when following the letters b, p, d, t, ch, k, und k; 3) before a consonant; as: satt, sein; Erbse, Lotse, wach=sam, durch=sehen, murksen, mucksen, Häcksel; du hast, bist; 4) likewise at the end of words, and in the inner part of words, when the syllable, which it ends, constitutes a *root*; in which latter cases it is written s· es, Haus, Bosheit, aus=gehen, Haus=thür, Gläs=chen, Häus=chen. — It sounds like the English soft *s* in *rose*: in the interior of words between two vowels, and before c after n, m, r: lesen, Rose, Riese, Linse, Hirse, Gemse.

𝔙, v. The sound of this letter is in fact mostly about the same as that of the German f, as: von, Vater, ver=

loren, Vetter, viel, Frevel, Sklave = son, Fater, fer=loren, Fetter, fiel, Fresel, Sklase, although we must say this is an abuse, and not only theoretically, but as well practically the ꝟ ought to be always pronounced perceptibly softer than the f, and be therefoie much more similar to the English *v*, especially in words of foreign oiigin. For *v*, a ieal *semivowel* (*u* consonant), which has more and more crept into the German alphabets only in the mediaeval times, has been introduced into them from Latin and Greek for the veiy purpose to maik in writing the *softer* sound of the labial spiians, and to distinguish it from the *harder* one, for which *f* has been kept — Comp.: Jacob. Grimm, Germ. Dict. letter f, and J. Giimm, Germ. Gram. (2nd ed., 1869) p. 48 and p. p. 110—113. —

W, w answers to the English and French *v*, but is somewhat more open, the lips being less contracted than in pronouncing the English *v*. This sound requires particular attention Wein = *vine*, wer, wann, wo, wild, ewig.

w is never silent nor used at the end of words.

Z, z is pronounced as *ts* in *gets* or *uits*, as: zehn, zu, dazu, zwei, Zahl, Zoll, au=ziehen.

The sounds of the English *j*, *w* or *wh* and *th* do not occur in German.

## 2. Double and compound consonants.

Ch, ch. There is nothing, corresponding to this in English. It has two different sounds:

1) When placed after a, o, u and au, its sound is a guttural one and resembles the Scotch *ch* in *Loch*. It is impossible to define it clearer. The pupil must therefore refer to his teacher for the correct pronunciation, as: Bach, lachen, Loch, tochen, Buch, Kuchen, auch, Rauch.

2) The other sound which occurs after e, i, ei, ä, ö, äu, eu and ü, and after any consonant is a soft *"palatic aspirate"*, as: ich, Licht, ieich, recht, Bäche, Löcher, räu= chern, heu=cheln, Bücher, welche, Händ=chen.

At the beginning of words, Ch is pronounced like K, as: Christ = Krist, Christian, Chor, except before e and i, as in Chemie, chemisch, Chirurg, Chili, China ꝛc., where it is soft. In words taken from French like Charlatan, Char= lotte, Chaussee it keeps its French pronunciation like *sh* or German sch = Scharlatan, Scharlotte, Schossee.

ᚦ§. When ᚦ is followed by § or ſ, they are pronounced together like *ks* or *x*, as· Wachſ = Waſs or Wax;
thus: Ochs, Ochſen, Fuchs, Füchſe, Achſel, wachſen.

This however cannot be done in compound words
when ᚦ and § belong to different syllables: wachſam =
wach-ſam, nachſuchen = nach-ſuchen, nach-ſetzen, durch-ſehen,
— or when the § is abridged from es, especially in the
Genitive case· des Buchs, for Buches or Buch's; des Dachs
for Daches or Dach's; er ſprach's.

ᚦ appears at the end or in the middle of a word
after a short vowel with the sound of a double f, as in
English, as: Stock, Pack, Stecken, Glocke, Nacken, drücken;
— ᚦ is never allowed after a consonant. To write ſtarck,
Werck, Banck ꝛc. would be incorrect; they must be spelt·
ſtark, Werk, Bank ꝛc.

There are a few compound words in which even ᚦ
and f occur together, as: Rück-kehr, Druckkoſten, Dickkopf.

ng sounds like the English *ng* in *long*, as: lang, Ring,
Geſang. — The same pronunciation is retained, when ng
is followed by a vowel, as: lange = lang-e (not lan-ge),
hangen, Finger, bringen, ſingen, gelungen. — In compound
words, when the first ends in n and the other begins
with g, each is pronounced separately, as: an-genehm, an-
gefang-en, Un-geduld.

Qu, qu; q is always joined with u; together they
have then the sound of kw as in the English word *quire*.
In German qu is found in few words only: Quarz, quer,
Quirl, Qual, Quelle.

ſſ or ß*); the former is used as double s in the
middle of a word after a short vowel· laſſen, beſſer,
müſſen; the latter in the middle of a word after a long
vowel, and as final double s (not z) at the end of words
and syllables· — grüßen, fließen, daß (= dass), Haß,
Schloß, muß-te.

Ph, ph has the same sound as f, and occurs mostly
in words of Greek origin: Epheu, Philoſophie, Geographie,
Adolph**).

---

*) This letter is not compounded, as it appears in print, of
ſ and z, but of ſ and § (final s, = ſs; it sounds like ss (not sz).
**) In the new orthography: Adolf.

**Pf, pf.** Here the two letters p and f are united in one sound, uttered with compressed lips: Pfahl, Pfeil, Apfel, Pferd.

**Sch, sch** like the English *sh* in *ship*, as. Schiff, schaffen, Busch, Asche, wischen, kindisch.

**Sp, sp,** and **St, st** as in English, with the only difference, that the sound of S before p and t in the *greater* part of Germany somewhat *approaches* that of *sh = sht* and *shp*, as often as it occurs in the *beginning* of words and syllables (im Anlaut), as. Spiel, Sparren, Spieß, Spule, an-sprechen, verspielen, Stall, Stein, Stroh, be-stehen 2c. To do the same also at the end of words or syllables (im Auslaut), like Ast = Asht or Bürs-te = Bursh-te, is only the custom in the Suabian and Alemanic parts of Germany, and therefore to be avoided by the foreigner

*Obs.* Whether for the „Anlaut" he will follow the usage of the *majority*, or rather that of the *minority* which is found in *some* parts of North-Germany, as Hannover, Hamburg, Bremen etc., viz to pronounce Spiel = Sspiel, Stein = Sstein etc, may be completely left to his own liking The best decision, we think, would be for everybody, not to exaggerate neither the one nor the other method so far as to make the pronunciation hard and disagreeable to the dissenting part of the nation, but to take the „golden medium" as their rule. For English and American students the usage of the *minority*, of course is *easier*, because corresponding with their own custom. Therefore, at least in the *beginning*, we think, they are justified to prefer it, though in a later time they may find it more convenient to adopt the pronunciation of the majority. —

**Th, th** must not be pronounced otherwise than as simple t; it has never the sound of the English *th*, as: That, like Tät; Thor, thun, Thaler = Tor, tun, Taler. — Wherever in the new orthography it is still admitted in German words, it indicates the length of a following simple vowel, like in That, Thor 2c. Before diphthongs and in the middle or at the end of words and syllables it is no longer admitted, except in such words of *foreign* origin the *foreign* spelling of which is not yet altered by usage. Therefore do no more write: theuer, rathen, Roth, Armuth, Athem, Reichthum 2c., but teuer, raten, Rot, Armut, Atem, Reichtum 2c. Theater, Thräne, Thee and other foreign words keep their *th*.

**tz = zz.** When the sound of z is to be doubled, which must be done after each vowel, except in compound words, then t is prefixed to z = tz, equivalent to ʒʒ = *ts*, as: Taʒe, Bliʒ, troʒen, Müʒe. — ʒ is never admitted after a consonant, as: Lenʒ, tanʒen, Herʒ, ſtürʒen; but not: Lenʒ, tanʒen, ſtürʒen ꝛc.

---

### Remark.

To give here any *orthographical rules* in addition to the few preceding remarks about C and K, ph and f, th and t, necessitated by our new orthography, would be entirely useless for the beginner, as they depend mostly on etymology and derivation, some previous knowledge of the language being indispensable. The only rule, the beginner wants, is, that all substantives and other words employed substantively, are written with a capital letter. Many examples have been given in the foregoing pages.

The same rule is applicable to proper names: Ludwig, Albert, Schiller, Müller, Wieland, Cicero, Julius Cäſar. Of the pronouns, only Sie and Ihr are written with capitals, when they answer to the English *you* and *your*. The personal pronoun ich requires always a small i, not a capital, as in the English *I*.

The *signs of punctuation*, being the same as in English, need no further explanation.

The characters for German *handwriting*, differing greatly from the printed letters, have been annexed in two tables and should be carefully copied and practised. The pupil is advised at once to begin writing his exercises in the German character.

---

# On the Accent.

As in other languages with words of more than one syllable, in the German tongue the *accent* is indispensable to the art of speaking. The verbal accent produces the rhythm; without rhythm the language would be too monotonous, it would offend the ear and the innate feeling of harmony. However as the accentuation of words was not originally laid down according to fixed rules, but was rather the consequence of an undefined feeling and tact, some irregularities are necessarily found, which do not quite agree with the rules determined at a later period.

All the beginner requires, to enable him to read correctly, may be simply reduced to the following rules:

1) The pupil must distinguish *simple* words and *compound* words.

2) *Simple* words, which are either *monosyllabic roots*, or *derivative words*, have (generally) o n e accent, as: groß, klein, géb=en, fáh=ren.

3) *Compound* ones have two or more, as: 2ín'fang'.

4) With monosyllables, no mistake can occur: auf, bei, nur, wenn, doch, Mann, Frau, Kind, Haus, Dach, lieb.

5) When a simple word is not monosyllabic, it consists of a *root* or *principal syllable* (Stammsilbe) and of one or more *accessory syllables* (Nebensilben), and is called a *derivative*. The latter are partly *prefixes*, partly *suffixes*, which are never used alone and appear only in connection with roots. They are

*a*) Such as are placed *before* the root, *prefixes* (Vorsilben): be, emp, ent, er, ge, ver, zer.

*b*) Such as are placed *after*, *suffixes* (Nachsilben): e, el, en, end, er, ern, es, est, et, ig, icht, in, isch, lich, ung, igen.

These syllables under *a*) and *b*) are all u n a c c e n t e d.

6' Hence the first chief-rule: *All derivative German words have the accent on their root or chief-syllable, but never on either of the accessory syllables.*

### Examples with prefixes.

Bĕ=rúf, Ĕmp=fáng, ĕnt=gíeng, ĕrfúhr, Gĕbraúch, Vĕr=múnft.

### Examples with suffixes.

Líe=bĕ, Mítt=ĕl, lóbĕn, Túgĕnd, Bíldĕr, steíuĕrn, Gútes, rédĕst, bíttĕt, ártig, hólzicht, Lówin, hérrlich, kíndisch, Bäúm=chĕn, Wóhnúngĕn, heíligĕn.

### Examples with both.

Bĕ=rúf=ĕn, Ĕmpfángĕr, Ĕrfáhrúng, Ĕrfáhrúngĕn, gĕbraúchlich, vĕrlórĕn, ĕntspréchĕn, Zĕrlégúng, Vĕrwúnschúngĕn.

*Note.* Nouns taken from foreign languages, having been *germanised*, do not come under this rule. These mostly receive the accent on the *last* syllable, as: Stúdént, Próphét, Kúltúr, Próvínz, Mórást, Fígúr, Rĕlígíón,

Spinát, Regent, Kämel, Franzós, Sólcát, Offizier, Májór, Generál; Hómér, Sállúst, Kórnél, Ovio, Hóráz ꝛc. *Proper names* however, which have the accent in the original on the first syllable, when used in German in their *original* form, remain unaltered, as: Cáto, Cícěró, Pincár, Cónón, Cánning, Sháïěspeáre, Býron, Rácíne ꝛc.

7) Besides the *simple words* (which are not to be mistaken for monosyllables), there are a great many *compound words* which have an accent on *each of the components*. The first however is the strongest. To avoid any misconception, we must distinctly state, that this term not only embraces *compound substantives*, as for ex.: Hauptwort, Landmann ꝛc.; — but *all combinations of independent words used by themselves and conveying an idea*. Thus · An'fang (*the beginning*) is a compound word as well as Fisch'fang, the first consisting of the two words an (preposition = at) and Fang; the latter of Fisch and Fang.

This definition is the key to all the difficulties, which as yet could not be resolved by the two theories adopted by grammarians, one of which says: 'The *radical syllable* of a word always takes the chief-accent'; the other: 'It must be taken by that which has most meaning and signification'. Both principles are deficient, as seen above in the word Anfang Here the radical syllable is fang, yet it does not bear the chief-accent, which lies on An; nor is the first syllable, which does bear it, that which has most meaning and signification.

8) Compound words may consist of substantives, verbs, adjectives, pronouns, adverbs, prepositions, the prefixes miß, un,*) or the final syllables: bar, haft, ling, fal, schaft, nis, sam, tum, lein, ei, heit, at and ut,*) the accent of which is somewhat less strong. For all words thus compounded, the following is the principal rule; *Each component, even when combined, keeps its accent on its radical syllable.* Hence it follows *that every compound word is pronounced with two or more accents* according to the number of components. Euphony however requires, that the latter loses something of its value and weight, so that the first receives *rather more stress*. This has probably been the reason why other gramma-

_____

*) Antiquated words which are no more used by themselves now.

rians have adopted a *full accent* and a *demi-accent*. Ex.:
Höſthor, Vórhóf, Eingang, Mittág, Náchrichten, uúſicher,
Ofenróhr, Régenbógen, fúrchtbár.

9) Therefore the second chief rule about German
accent is· **Compound words have an accent on
each of the components.**

*Note.* It must however be observed that compound
*particles* have only one accent, *viz.* on their *second* syllable, as, for example, compounded
 with h i n: hín=áb, hín=aúf, hínaús, hínein, hínzú.
 with h e r: hĕr=áb, hĕr=aúf, hĕraús, hĕrein, hĕrzú, hĕrúm,
    úmhér.
 with d a: dămít, dărín, dăzú, dăvón, dăraús, dăzwíſchĕn ꝛc.
 with z u: zúrück.

*Promiscuous examples.*

Óſtwínd (Óſt=wind), Múnd=lóch, Aúftrág, geíſtreích, Mít=
leíd, Nótdúrſt, Úmgáng, Männlein, Freúndſcháft, Aúsfúhr,
Zúkúnſt, frúchtbár, Freíheít, Júngling, Lábſál, Allmácht, Fínſter=
nís, mít=leídig, aúf=hóren, bĕ=mít=leíden, hínaúf=ſáhrĕn, hĕreín=
kómmĕn, úm=gánglich, aús=geſúhrt, zúkünſtig, Júnglíngs=álter,
Reíchtúm, Reíchtúmer, baúfällig, Abendrót, liebkóſen, Aber=
glaúbe, tótesmútig. Räúbereí, Sónnenſcheín, Úhren=ſchlúſſel,
Féderméſſer, Féldzúg, Féldzeúgmeíſter, Kríegszáhlámt, Un=über=
tréfflichkeít, Liebenswúrdigkeít, Maúlbéerbäúme, zuſámmen=
kómmen, úngerécht, zurückkéhren, dazwíſchen=légen.

----

## Reading Exercise.

**Die Bie-ne und die Tau-be. The bee and the dove.**

Ei-ne Bie-ne war dur-ſtig; ſie ſlog zu ei-ner
A      bee      was    thirsty;  she flew to     a

Quel-le, um zu trin-ken, a-ber ſie wur-de von dem
well,   in order to drink,   but   she  was     by  the

ſtrö-men-den Waſ-ſer fort-ge-riſ-ſen, und wä-re
sreaming    water  carried away    and  was

bei-na-he er-trun-ken.
nearly   drowned.

Ei-ne Tau-be, wel-che die-ses be-merk-te, pick-te
A    dove     which    this    perceived,     picked

ein Baum-blatt ab, und warf es in das Was-ser. Die
a   (tree-)leaf   off,   and threw it into the    water.    The

Bie-ne er-griff es und ret-te-te sich.
bee    seized   it   and    saved herself.

Nicht lang-e nach-her' saß die Tau-be auf ei-nem
Not    long   afterwards sat   the   dove    on    a

Baum und be-merk-te nicht, daß ein Jä-ger mit sei-
tree,   and   perceived   not   that   a   hunter with   his

ner Flin-te auf sie ziel-te. Die dank-ba-re Bie-ne,
gun   at   her   aimed.   The    thankful    bee,

wel-che die Ge-fahr er-kann-te, in wel-cher ih-re Wohl-
which   the   danger   recognised,   in which    her   bene-

thä-te-rin sich be-fand, flog hin-zu', und stach den
factress   herself found,   flew   near    and stung the

Jä-ger in die Hand. Der Schuß ging da-ne'-ben,
hunter   in   the   hand.   The   shot    went    aside,

und die Tau-be war ge-ret-tet.
and the   dove   was    saved.

---

## Die drei Freun-de.    The three friends.

1) Ein Mann hat-te drei Freun-de. Zwei von
A    man    had   three   friends.   Two   of

ih-nen lieb-te er sehr; der drit-te war ihm gleich-gül-tig,
them   loved he much, the   third   was to him indifferent,

ob-gleich die-ser sein be-ster Freund war. Einst wur-de
though this one his   best    friend was.   Once   was

er vor den Rich-ter ge-for-dert, wo er, — ob-schon
he before the   judge   summoned where he, —   though

un-schul-dig —, doch hart ver-klagt war. — „Wer
innocent —,    yet   hard   accused was. — „Who

un-ter euch," sag-te er zu sei-nen Freun-den, „will mit
among you,"   said he to   his    friends,    „will with

mir ge-hen und für mich zeu-gen? Denn ich bin un=
me    go    and   for   me   witness?    for   I   am   un-

ge-recht ver-klagt, und der Kö-nig zürnt."
justly   accused,    and the   king   is angry."

2) Der er-ste sei-ner Freun-de ent-schul'-dig-te sich
The   first   of his   friends    excused    himself

so-gleich und sag-te, er kön-ne nicht mit ihm ge-hen
immediately and   said,   he   could   not   with him   go

we-gen an-de-rer Ge-schäf-te. Der zwei-te be-glei-te-te
on account of other   business.   The   second    accompanied

ihn bis zu der Thü-re des Richt-hau-ses; dann wand-te
him as far as the   door of the   tribunal;    then   turned

er sich um und ging zu-rück, aus Furcht vor dem
he (himself) and   went   back,    for   fear   of   the

zor-ni-gen Rich-ter. Der drit-te, auf wel-chen er am
angry   judge.   The   third    on   whom   he the

we'-nig-sten ge-baut hat-te, ging hin-ein, re'-de-te für
least    relied   had,   went   in,    spoke   for

ihn und zeug-te von sei-ner Un-schuld so freu-dig,
him and gave evidence of   his    innocence   so   cheerfully,

daß der Rich-ter ihn los-ließ und be-schenk-te.
that the   judge   him   liberated and    rewarded.

3) Drei Freun-de hat der Mensch in die-ser Welt;
Three   friends   has    man    in   this    world;

wie be-tra-gen sie sich in der Stun-de des To-des,
how   behave   they   in   the   hour   of   death,

wenn Gott ihn vor sein Ge-richt for-dert? — Das
when   God   him before his   tribunal   summons?   —   The

Geld, sein er-ster Freund, ver-läßt ihn zu-erst und
money,   his   first   friend,   leaves   him   first   and

geht nicht mit ihm. Sei-ne Ver-wand-ten und
goes   not   with him.   His    relations    and

Freun-de be-glei-ten ihn bis zu der Thü-re des
friends    accompany   him   unto   the   door of the

Gra-bes, und keh-ren dann zu-rück in ih-re Häu-ser.
grave,   and   return   then   back   to   their   houses.

Der drit-te, den er im Le-ben am öf-te-sten ver-gaß,
The      third,   whom he in   life   the  oftenest  forgot,

sind sei-ne gu-ten Wer-fe.  Sie al-lein be-glei-ten
are   his   good   works.  They alone  accompany

ihn bis zu dem Thron des Rich-ters; sie gehen
him as far as  the  throne of the  judge,   they  go

vor-an', spre-chen für ihn, und fin-den Barm-her-zig-feit
before,   speak   for him, and   find        mercy

und Gna-de.
and  grace.

_____

# Etymology.

### Preliminary notions.   Parts of speech.

There are in the German language *ten* parts of speech:

1) The article, der Artifel or das Geschlechtswort.
2) The noun *or* substantive, das Hauptwort.
3) The determinative adjective *or* adjective pronoun,
   das Bestimmungswort.
   (including the indefinite numeral adjectives and
   the numbers, das unbestimmte und bestimmte
   Zahlwort.)
4) The (qualifying) adjective, das Eigenschaftswort.
5) The pronoun, das Fürwort.
6) The verb, das Zeitwort.
7) The adverb, das Umstandswort.
8) The preposition, das Vorwort.
9) The conjunction, das Bindewort.
10) The interjection, das Ausrufswort.

The first six are variable, the four last invariable.

The change which the first five undergo by means
of *terminations*, is called *declension;* it refers to *gender,*
*number* and *case.*

There are in German three *genders:* the *masculine*
(das männliche), the *feminine* (das weibliche) and the *neuter*
gender (das sächliche Geschlecht). The rules concerning the
gender will be found in the 10th lesson.

There are also two *numbers*: *Singular* (Einzahl) and *Plural* (Mehrzahl), and four *cases*, expressing the different relations of words to each other, namely: the *nominative*, *genitive*, *dative* and *accusative*.

The nominative case (Werfall) or the *subject* answers the question: *who?* or *what?* Ex.: Who is learning? *The boy* (Latin: puer).

The genitive or possessive case (Wessenfall) answers the question. *whose?* or *of which?* Ex.: Whose book? *The boy's* book (pueri).

The dative (Wemfall) answers the question *to whom?* Ex· To whom shall I give it? *To the boy* (puero).

The accusative or *objective* case (Wenfall) marks the object of an action and answers the question: *whom?* or *what?* Ex.: Whom *or* what do you see? I see *the boy* (puerum), *the house* (domum).

*Note.* For the *vocative case* there is no particular form in German; if required, the *nominative* serves for it in all the declensions.

# First Lesson.

(Crfte Leftion.)

## On the definite Article.

(Der beſtimmte Artikel.)

There are two articles in German as in English.
the *definite* and the *indefinite*.

The *definite article*, answering to the English *the*, is
used to indicate the gender of substantives, and has for
each gender in the singular a particular form, viz.:

*masc.* der, *fem.* die, *neut.* das, as:

der Mann the man.
die Frau the woman.
das Kind the child.

The plural for all three genders is die, as:

die Knaben the boys.

It is varied by four cases: the *nominative*, *genitive*, .
*dative* and *accusative*. It will be observed that the *accusative singular* of the feminine and neuter gender, and
the *accusative plural* are always like the *nominative*.

### Declension of the definite article.

| | *Singular.* | | | *Plural* |
|---|---|---|---|---|
| | *masc.* | *fem.* | *neuter.* | *for all genders.* |
| *Nom.* | der | die | das the | die the |
| *Gen.* | des | der | des of the | der of the |
| *Dat* | dem | der | dem to the | den to the |
| *Acc.* | den | die | das the. | die the. |

In the same manner, the following words are declined, which are often substituted for the *definite* article, viz.:

| | *Singular.* | | | *Plural* |
|---|---|---|---|---|
| *masc.* | *fem.* | *neuter.* | | *for all genders.* |
| dieſer | dieſe | dieſes this, that | | dieſe these |
| jener | jene | jenes that | | jene those |
| welcher | welche | welches which? | | welche which? |
| jeder | jede | jedes every. | | — — |

## Declension.

| | Singular. | | | Plural |
|---|---|---|---|---|
| | *masc.* | *fem.* | *neuter.* | *for all genders.* |
| N. | dieſer | dieſe | dieſes this (that) | dieſe these |
| G. | dieſes | dieſer | dieſes of this | dieſer of these |
| D. | dieſem | dieſer | dieſem to this | dieſen to these |
| A. | dieſen | dieſe | dieſes this. | dieſe these. |

### Examples.

| | |
|---|---|
| Dieſer Mann this man. | Jeder Mann every man. |
| Dieſe Frau this woman. | Welchen Stock (*Acc.*) which stick? |
| Jene Frau that woman. | Jedes Kind every child. |

## Words (Wörter).*)

*masc.*

Der König the king.
der Vater the father.
der Mann the man, husband.
der Sohn the son.
der Garten the garden.
der Wein the wine.
der Stock the stick.
der Hund the dog, hound.
der Teller the plate.

*fem.*

Die Königin the queen.

die Mutter the mother.
die Frau the woman, wife.
die Tochter the daughter.
die Feder the pen, feather.
die Katze the cat.

*neuter.*

Das Schloß the castle, palace.
das Kind the child.
das Haus the house.
das Buch the book.
das Waſſer the water.

und and. Ja yes. Nein no. nicht not.

| S. | Ich habe | I have | Habe ich? | have I? |
|---|---|---|---|---|
| | du haſt | thou hast | haſt du? | hast thou? |
| | er hat | he has | hat er? | has he? |
| | ſie hat | she has | hat ſie? | has she? |
| | es hat | it has | hat es? | has it? |

### Reading Exercise (Übung). 1.

Der Vater und der Sohn. Die Mutter und das Kind. Der Garten und das Haus. Jener Garten, jenes Haus. Ich habe den Stock.**) Du haſt das Waſſer. Der König hat das Schloß.

---

*) In this and the following lists of words the article precedes each substantive, that it may be learnt *at the same time.* It may also be observed here, once for all, that these words preceding the Exercises, are to be well committed to memory, as their signification is seldom repeated when appearing in subsequent Exercises.

**) The noun governed by the verb haben (to have), and by all *transitive* verbs must be in the Accusative. — All German monosyllabic substantives of whatever gender are alike in the Accusative and Nominative.

Der Vater hat den Wein. Welchen Wein hat er? Welches
Wasser? Dieser Hund. Diese Katze. Das Kind dieser (of this)
Frau. Welches Kind? Jedes Kind. Welche Frau? Welcher
Mann hat den Hund? Welchen Stock hat der Mann? Er hat
diesen Stock.

### Aufgabe. 2.
#### Exercise for translation.

1. The king and the queen. The son and the daughter.
The father and the mother. The child has the book. The
daughter has the book. The man has the (*Acc.* den) stick.
I have the wine. The man has the water. This father. This
woman. This house. The king has the castle. The queen
has the book. Which book? Which house? Which pen?
This book; that pen. Every man. I have the (*Acc.*) dog.

2.*) I have not the stick. The child has the stick.
That wine and this water. This man has not the book.
Which castle has the (*Nom.*) king? He has that castle.
That mother has the child. The woman has the house. The
castle *of the* queen.**) Has the man the book? Which plate?
This plate. The son of the queen. The daughter has the
pen. Every mother. Every book.

### Conversation (Sprechübung).

| | |
|---|---|
| Habe ich die Feder? | Ja, du hast die Feder. |
| Hast du das Buch? | Nein, ich habe das Buch nicht. |
| Hat der Vater den Wein? | Er hat den Wein. |
| Hat die Frau die Katze? | Ja, sie hat die Katze. |
| Welche Katze hat sie? | Sie hat die junge (young) Katze. |
| Hat das Kind den Stock? | Nein, der Vater hat den Stock. |
| Welches Schloß hat die Königin? | Sie hat dieses Schloß. |
| Hat diese Frau das Kind? | Nein, jene Frau hat es (it). |
| Hat der Mann den Hund? | Der Mann hat den Hund nicht; er hat die Katze. |
| Welches Buch hat der Sohn? | Er hat das Buch der Mutter. |
| Hat die Mutter das Buch? | Nein, die Tochter hat das Buch. |
| Welche Feder hat das Kind? | Es hat die Feder der Frau. |
| Hat der Vater das Wasser? | Nein, er hat den Wein. |
| Welches Haus hat der Mann? | Er hat das Haus der Mutter. |

---

*) All the Exercises are divided into two parts. The second
part need not be translated at once, but when the pupil repeats,
which should be done regularly after 10 or 12 lessons.

**) Feminine nouns have all the cases in the singular like
the nominative: thus, only the article is declined, *G.* = der Königin.

# Second Lesson.
## (Zweite Lektion.)
### On the indefinite Article.
(Der unbestimmte Artikel.)

The indefinite article is *masc.* ein, *fem.* eine, *neut.* ein;
it is equivalent to the English *a* or *an*, and has also
three genders; but in the nominative, the masculine and
neuter are alike, viz.:

ein Mann a man; eine Frau a woman; ein Kind a child.

It has the four cases, of course only the singular,
as, from its nature, it can have no plural.

### Declension of the indefinite article.

|    | *masc.* | *fem.* | *neuter.* |  |
|----|---------|--------|-----------|--|
| N. | ein     | eine   | ein       | a *or* an |
| G. | eines   | einer  | eines     | of a |
| D. | einem   | einer  | einem     | to a |
| A  | einen   | eine   | ein       | a. |

The following words, which occasionally take the
place of the article, are declined in the same way, and
have a plural:

| *masc.* | *fem.* | *neuter.* |  | | *masc.* | *fem.* | *neuter.* | |
|---------|--------|-----------|--|--|---------|--------|-----------|--|
| kein    | keine  | kein      | no*) | | unser | unsere | unser | our |
| mein    | meine  | mein      | my | | Ihr | Ihre | Ihr | your |
| dein    | deine  | dein      | thy | | ihr | ihre | ihr | {her {their |
| sein    | seine  | sein      | his, its. | | | | | |

### Declension.

|    | Singular. | | | | Plural for all genders |  |
|----|-----------|--------|---------|--------|-------|-----|
|    | *masc.*   | *fem.* | *neuter* | | | |
| N. | mein      | meine  | mein    | my  | meine | my |
| G. | meines    | meiner | meines  | of my | meiner | of my |
| D. | meinem    | meiner | meinem  | to my | meinen | to my |
| A  | meinen    | meine  | mein    | my. | meine | my. |

### Examples.

Mein Bruder my brother.
Kein Brot no bread.
Unser Vater our father.
Ihr Buch (*n*) your book

Meine Schwester my sister.
Unsre Mutter our mother.
Sein Pferd (*n*.) his horse.
Ihre Feder her pen.

---

*) no followed by a noun is kein.

## Words.

Ein Freund *m.* a friend.
ein Apfel *m.* an apple
ein Baum *m.* a tree.
ein Hut *m.* a hat.
ein Löffel *m.* a spoon.
ein Rod *m.* a coat.
ein Bruder *m.* a brother.

Eine Blume *f.* a flower.
eine Birne *f.* a pear.
eine Rose *f.* a rose.
eine Stadt *f.* a town.

eine Frucht *f.* a fruit.
eine Gabel *f.* a fork.

Ein Messer *n.* a knife.
ein Federmesser *n.* a penknife.
ein Kleid *n.* a dress.
ein Pferd *n.* a horse.
ein Tier *n.* an animal.

schön fine, beautiful.
alt old. sehr very.
jung young.
gesehen seen.
geben Sie mir give me.

ist is. wer? who? was? what? oder or.
auch also. wo? where?

*Pl.* Wir haben    we have
ihr habt     } ye have
(Sie haben) } you have
sie haben    they have.

Haben wir?    have we?
habt ihr?     } have ye?
(haben Sie)? } have you?
haben sie?    have they?

### Reading Exercise. 3.

Ich habe eine Blume. Hast du meine Blume? Wir haben einen Freund. Haben Sie auch einen Freund? Dieser Mann ist mein Freund. Sie (sie) hat kein Brot. Sie (sie) haben keinen Apfel. Mein Kind hat eine Birne; es (it) hat auch eine Rose. Ihr Sohn und Ihre Tochter haben jenen Baum gesehen.[1] Die Katze ist ein Tier. Die Rose ist eine Blume. Geben Sie mir dieses Buch. Geben Sie mir auch eine Blume. Dieses Haus ist nicht schön. Unsre Stadt ist sehr alt.

### Aufgabe. 4.

1. I have a rose. She has a book. You have a[2] stick. My brother has a pear. My sister has a apple. His child has a knife. We have no bread. Give me a rose. The father has no horse. A dog is an animal. Which pen has the child? The son has a hat. Who has a flower? My daughter has a flower. Where is your mother? That child has no[2] apple. I have no (*Acc. m.*) spoon. That house is old.[3] Her house is beautiful. My horse is young. Have you seen[1] the castle?

2. Give (Geben Sie) this stick to[4] my brother. Give this penknife to[4] your sister. The apple is a fruit. The

---

1) In compound tenses the participle past comes *last.*
2) *Accusative masc.* einen — keinen ꝛc. (see the foot-note ** p. 21).
3) Adjectives, when placed *after* their noun, remain unchanged.
4) The word 'to' indicating the dative, must not be translated.

rose is no fruit, the rose is a flower. You have no hat.
Where is your hat? Wo has ³seen ¹my ²hat? Give me
a knife. Give me also a fork and a spoon. He has not his
coat They have no horse. Where is my brother? Where
is the rose of my (*Gen. f.*) sister? Not every horse is fine;
this horse is young.

### Conversation.

Was haben Sie?
Haben Sie eine Rose?
Haben Sie ein Pferd?

Ich habe eine Blume.
Ja, ich habe eine Rose.
Nein, ich habe kein Pferd, ich
habe einen Hund.

Hat das Kind kein Brot?
Wer (who) hat mein Buch?
Wo ist meine Feder?
Welches Haus haben Sie?
Ist Ihr Sohn jung?
Wo ist mein Federmesser?
Hat unsre Mutter eine Rose?
Welches Messer hat mein Kind?
Ist die Rose eine Frucht?
Welchen Stock haben Sie?
Wer hat mein Buch?
Haben Sie Wasser?

Das Kind hat kein Brot.
Deine Schwester hat dein Buch.
Sie (it) ist nicht da (there).
Ich habe dieses Haus.
Er ist sehr jung.
Ihr Bruder hat es (it).
Nein, sie hat keine Rose
Es hat sein Messer.
Nein, die Rose ist eine Blume.
Ich habe meinen Stock.
Das Kind hat Ihr Buch.
Wir haben kein Wasser; aber (but)
wir haben Wein.

Ist die Katze ein Tier?
Hat Ihre Mutter einen Bruder?

Ja, die Katze ist ein Tier.
Meine Mutter hat keinen Bruder,
aber sie hat eine Schwester.

# Third Lesson.
## (Dritte Lektion.)
### Declension of Substantives.
#### (Deklination der Hauptwörter)

The German grammarians are not yet agreed on
the division of the nouns substantive into declensions,
and on the number of these. Some adopt 6, others 5,
others again 4 or 3, and even 2 declensions only. This
distribution, however, is quite arbitrary; indeed, in this
matter there is much irregularity in German. The reason
is, that the language was practised and cultivated by
different tribes in various ways before a grammar existed.
So they where obliged to accept matters as they were,
and to make the best of them. Notwithstanding, there

are three fundamental ideas, on which declension is prin-
cipally founded, viz. the *gender*, the *termination*, and the
*number of syllables*, and though this system presents occasionally also some deviations and exceptions, it offers
really far less difficulty than any other distribution.*)

We state therefore that each of the three genders
has its own mode of inflexion, and further that the masculine gender admits of three different forms of declension,
the feminine of one, and the neuter also of one.

Hence we adopt **five** declensions, the three first of
which comprise the *masculine*, the fourth the *feminine*,
the fifth the *neuter* nouns, a few exceptions not included.

Our division has the great advantage of enabling the
learner, on seeing any substantive, accompanied by its
article, to refer it to its proper declension. This is not
to be attained by any other system.

In consequence we state as follows:

1) The first declension comprehends all *masculine*
and *neuter* nouns ending in **el, en, er, chen** and **lein**.

2) The second comprehends all *masculine* nouns ending in **e**, and most foreign masculine substantives having
the accent on the last syllable.

3) The third contains all *monosyllabic masculine* nouns
and those of two syllables ending in **ich, ig** and **ling,**
and a few words of foreign origin.

4) To the fourth belong all the *feminine* substantives.

5) To the fifth all *neuter* substantives not ending in
**el, en, er, chen** and **lein** (see 1).

### Table of the endings of the five declensions.

#### *Singular.*

|  | masculine. | | | feminine. | | neuter |
|---|---|---|---|---|---|---|
|  | I. | II. | III. | IV. | | V. |
| N. | — . | — e | — | — . | singular | — (-) |
| G. | — s | — en | — es (s) | — . | no | — es (s) |
| D. | — . | — en | — (e) | — . | change | — (e) |
| A. | — . | — en | — | — . | at all | — . |

---

*) Most German grammarians adopt only *two* declensions, the
so-called *strong declension* and the *weak one*, the former comprising
all nouns having in the genitive case **s**, the latter those having
in the genitive and all other cases **en**. Despite the great difference in the plurals, this arrangement may suffice for Germans,
who know from habit the inflexion of each word; but it is in-

## Plural.

| | I. | II. | III. | IV. | | | V. |
|---|---|---|---|---|---|---|---|
| N. | „- | — en | „e | „e | —n or en | — e | „er |
| G. | „- | — en | „e | „e | —n or en | — e | „er |
| D. | „-n | — en | „en | „en | —n or en | — en | „ern |
| A. | „- | — en | „e | „e | —n or en | — e | „er |

These marks „ indicate the *modified* vowels, ä, ö, ü.

## Remarks.

Before we present the declensions themselves, we think it well to give the following general hints, which may facilitate their study.

1) The genitive case in the **singular** of all *masculine* nouns (except those of the 2nd decl.) and of **all** *neuter* nouns without any exception ends in ß*) (or eß).

2) The *accusative* singular of feminine and neuter words is always like the nominative.

3) The accusative singular of the masculine nouns not ending in e is also like the nominative case.

4) The *vocative* case, in either number, is always understood to be like the nominative without the article; it will therefore be mentioned only once.

5) In the **plural** the *nominative*, *genitive* and *accusative* are always alike.

6) The *dative* plural of all declinable words terminates in n.

7) All root-nouns (i. e. without the prefix Ge-) ending in e form their plural in en without modifying their vowel.

8) All *feminine* substantives remain unchanged in the singular.

9) Most *monosyllables* having a, o, u, or au in their root, modify in the plural this vowel into ä, ö, ü, or äu.

10) In all *compound nouns* only the **last** component is declined according to the declension it belongs to.

## First declension.

To the first declension belong all *masculine* and *neuter* nouns ending in el, en and er, besides all diminutives in djen and lein, which are all of the neuter gender.

The only change of termination which nouns belonging to this declension undergo, consists in taking ß for

---

sufficient for foreigners, as it does not enable them to ascertain the inflexion of the other cases.

*) In a simple ß, when polysyllabic, in eß when monosyllabic.

the genitive singular, and ꞑ for the dative plural. This termination ꞑ however is common to all declensions ın the dative plural. Words terminating in ꞑ do not require an additional ꞑ.

In the plural, most words belonging to the 1st declension modify the three vowels a, o, ꞑ into ä, ö, ü. Nouns with other vowels or diphthongs remain unchanged.

### 1) Examples of masculine nouns.

| Singular. | | | Plural. | |
|---|---|---|---|---|
| N. | der Bruder | the brother | die **Brüder** | the brothers |
| G. | des Bruder=8 | of the brother | der Brüder | of the brothers |
| D. | dem Bruder | to the brother | den Brüder=n | to the brothers |
| A. | den Bruder | the brother | die Brüder | the brothers |
| Voc. | o Bruder! | o brother! | o Brüder! | o brothers! |

| | | | | |
|---|---|---|---|---|
| N. | der Garten | the garden | die **Gärten** | the gardens |
| G. | des Gartens | of the garden | der Gärten | of the gardens |
| D. | dem Garten | to the garden | den Gärten | to the gardens |
| A. | den Garten | the garden. | die Gärten | the gardens. |

In the same manner are declined:

| | | | |
|---|---|---|---|
| Der Vater | the father. | der Teller | the plate. |
| der Apfel | the apple. | der Hammer | the hammer. |
| der Schlüssel | the key | der Vogel | the bird |
| der Flügel | the wing. | der Schneider | the tailor. |
| der Löffel | the spoon. | der Schwager | the brother-in-law. |
| der Engel | the angel. | der Engländer | the Englishman. |
| der Himmel | (the) heaven. | der Römer | the Roman. |
| der Lehrer | the teacher. | *der Adler*) | the eagle. |
| der Schüler | the pupil. | *der Tropfen | the drop. |
| der Spiegel | the looking-glass. | *der Kuchen | the cake. |
| der Regen | the rain. | *der Maler | the painter. |
| der Stiefel | the boot. | *der Amerikaner | the American. |

Plur. die Väter, die Äpfel, die Schlüssel, die Schüler, die Stiefel, die Teller, die Vögel, die Engländer, die Amerikaner.

### 2) Examples of neuter nouns.

| Singular. | | | Plural. | |
|---|---|---|---|---|
| N. | das Fenster | the window | die **Fenster** | the windows |
| G. | des Fensters | of the window | der Fenster | of the windows |
| D. | dem Fenster | to the window | den Fenstern | to the windows |
| A. | das Fenster | the window. | die Fenster | the windows |

---

*) Those marked with ᵛ do not modify their vowel in the plural, as: the eagles, die Adler, die Kuchen, die Maler ꞇc.

### Declension of diminutives

| *Singular.* | *Plural* |
|---|---|
| N. bas Bäumchen the little tree | bie Bäumchen the little trees |
| G  bes Bäumchens of the little tr. | ber Bäumchen of the little trees |
| D  bem Bäumchen to the little tr. | ben Bäumchen to the little trees |
| A. bas Bäumchen the little tree. | bie Bäumchen the little trees. |

Such neuter nouns are:

| | |
|---|---|
| bas Feuer the fire. | *bas Kupfer (the) copper. |
| bas Messer the knife. | bas Kloster the convent. |
| bas Wetter the weather. | bas Mittel the means. |
| *bas Wasser the water | bas Veilchen the violet. |
| bas Silber (the) silver. | bas Mädchen the girl, maiden. |

3) Declension with the indefinite article.

| *masc* | *neuter.* |
|---|---|
| N. ein Diener a man-servant | mein Zimmer     my room |
| G. eines Dieners of a servant | meines Zimmers of my room |
| D. einem Diener to a servant | meinem Zimmer to my room |
| A. einen Diener a servant. | mein Zimmer     my room. |

Compound nouns of the 1st declension (see p. 27, § 10).

Der Groß'vater the grandfather.  *Gen.* bes Großvaters ꝛc.
bas Feder'messer the penknife.  *Gen.* bes Federmessers.
ber Sprach'lehrer the master of languages.
ber Haus'schlüssel the house-key.
ber Zug'vogel the bird of passage.  *Pl.* bie Zugvögel.
bas Schlaf'zimmer the bed-room.  *Pl.* bie Schlafzimmer.

### Observations.

1) The following 10 words originally terminating in en, now very often used without n, belong also to the first declension; in the plural they do not change their vowel.

| | |
|---|---|
| ber Namen or Name the name. | ber Frieden or Friede (the) peace. |
| ber Glauben or Glaube the faith. | ber Willen or Wille the will. |
| ber Funken or Funke the spark. | ber Felsen or Fels the rock |
| ber Haufen or Haufe the heap. | ber Samen or Same the seed. |
| ber Gedanken or Gedanke the thought. | ber Buchstabe**) (Buchstaben) the letter of the alphabet. |

### Declension.

| N. ber Namen or Name the name | *Pl.* bie Namen the names |
|---|---|
| G  bes Namens of the name | ber Namen of the names |
| D. bem Namen to the name | ben Namen to the names |
| A. ben Namen the name. | bie Namen the names. |

2) The following words are declined in the singular according to this declension, but form their plural in n. See the 9th lesson.

---

**) The form 'Buchstaben' has now become quite obsolete.

Der Bauer the peasant.
der Bayer the Bavarian.
der Vetter the cousin.
der Nachbar the neighbour.
der Stachel the sting.
der Pantoffel the slipper.

der Gevatter the fellow-god-
    father.
der Muskel the muscle.
der Profeſſor the professor.
der Dok'tor the doctor.

*Gen.* des Bauers, des Vetters, des Nachbars, des Dok'tors.
*Plur.* die Bauern, die Vettern, die Nachbarn, die Dokto'ren.

## Words.

Gott God.
der Europä'er the European.
der Spanier the Spaniard.
der Sänger the singer.
der Schöpfer the creator.
    sind are. zwei two.

das Gold (the) gold.
die Wohl'that the benefit.
krant ill. gut good.
klein little, small. ſehr very.
groß large, great, tall.
in in. hier here.

## Reading Exercise. 5.

Der Bruder des Vaters. Der Garten des Bruders. Das Bäumchen des Gartens. In\*) (*with the dative,* in) dem Garten. In dem Zimmer. In den Zimmern. Die Fenster (*pl.*) des Zimmers. Der Diener des Amerikaners. Die Tropfen des Regens. Geben Sie dieſe Apfel den Schülern. Dem Lehrer. Mein Schwager. Deine Brüder. Deine Schlüſſel (*pl.*). Ich habe den Schlüſſel des Zimmers. Er hat das Meſſer ſeines Bruders. Die Adler ſind Vögel. Die Apfel ſind auf (on) dem Teller. Das Mädchen iſt in einem Kloſter. Wo iſt der Schneider? Er iſt nicht hier.

## Aufgabe. 6.

1. The garden of the father. The gardens of my brother.
I have two spoons. The Englishman has two servants. We
are in the room (*Dat.*). My father is in the garden. Our teacher
is old. The man has two hammers. Is your brother-in-law
a doctor? These cakes are not good. Where are the birds?
They are in the garden. Give me your (*Acc.*) plate. A bird
has two wings. The wings of the birds. The angels of (the)\*\*)
heaven. Have you seen †) the rooms of the American?

2. The castle has [a]\*\*) hundred (hundert) windows. The
book of the pupil. The plate of the girl. We are Americans.
You are Europeans. The violets are in the gardens. The
pupils are at school (in der Schule). The rooms of my father.
I have no silver and no gold. Give me the key of my room.

---

\*) Germ. „In" with dative indicates rest, or repose = Engl.
'in' with accusative, motion or direction = Engl. 'into'. See p. 46, 3.
\*\*) Observe that a parenthesis (. .) encloses a word *to be trans-
lated* or an annotation, whereas *brackets* [...] signify »leave out«.
†) See the foot-note 1) p. 24.

The name of the painter   The benefit of (the) peace. The
house of my teacher.   We have no fire.   God is the creator
of the heaven and (of the) earth (unb ber Erbe).

## Conversation.

Welches (what) ist der Name   Sein Name ist Schmidt.
dieses Engländers?
Haben Sie die Vögel gesehen?   Ja, ich habe sie (them) gesehen.
Ist das (that) Ihr Garten?   Es ist der Garten meines Nachbars.
Wo sind die Schlüssel meines   Hier sind sie.
Zimmers?
Wer (who) ist dieses Mädchen?   Sie ist die Tochter eines Eng=
   länders.
Wer ist dieser junge Mann?   Er ist der Sohn meines Vetters.
Sind Sie ein Maler?   Nein, ich bin (I am) kein Maler;
   ich bin ein Sänger.
Ist er ein Europäer?   Ja, er ist ein Spanier.
Wer ist in dem Garten?   Die Tochter meines Lehrers.
Habe ich das Buch Ihres Vaters?   Ja, Sie haben es (it).
Haben Sie den Stock meines   Nein, ich habe ihn (it) nicht.
Bruders?
Haben Sie das Haus des Spa=   Nein, ich habe sein Haus nicht
niers gesehen?   gesehen.
Wer ist krank?   Der Diener des Malers ist krank.
Ist der Spiegel klein?   Nein, er (it) ist groß und schön.

---

# Fourth Lesson.
## (Vierte Lektion.)
### Second declension.

This declension contains another series of *masculine*
words, viz.:

1) all those ending in **e**. Its inflection is very simple.
All the cases, both of the singular and plural, are formed
by adding **n**, without altering the vowel in the plural:

### Example.

| Singular. | Plural |
|---|---|
| *N.* der Knabe   the boy | die Knaben the boys |
| *G.* des Knaben  of the boy | der Knaben of the boys |
| *D.* dem Knaben  to the boy | den Knaben to the boys |
| *A.* den Knaben  the boy. | die Knaben the boys |

Thus are declined·

| | |
|---|---|
| Der Affe the monkey. | der Löwe the lion |
| der Ochse (Ochs) the ox. | der Falke the falcon. |

| | |
|---|---|
| der Bote the messenger. | der Hafe the hare. |
| der Erbe the heir. | der Rabe the raven. |
| der Neffe the nephew. | der Gatte the husband |
| der Riefe the giant. | der Bediente the man-servant. |
| der Sflave the slave. | der Franzofe the Frenchman. |
| der Jude the Jew. | der Sachfe the Saxon. |
| der Pate the godfather, godchild. | der Ruffe the Russian. |
| der Hirte (Hiit) the herdsman. | der Preuße the Prussian. |
| der Heide the Heathen. | der Türke the Turc. |

(See the 12th lesson. § 9.)

*Plur.* die Affen, die Ochfen, die Löwen, die Raben, die Reffen, die Hafen, die Franzofen, die Ruffen, die Preußen etc.

*Note* Further all *adjectives* used substantively when preceded by the definite article:

| | |
|---|---|
| Der Alte the old man. | der Kranke the patient (sick man). |
| der Reifende the traveller. | der Gelehrte the learned man. |

*Gen :* des Alten, des Kranken, des Reifenden, *pl* die Gelehrten

2) The following words, though monosyllabic, are also subject to this mode of inflexion, doubtless because in course of time they have dropped the letter e.

### Example.

| Singular. | Plural |
|---|---|
| *N.* der Graf[1] the count, earl | die Grafen the counts |
| *G.* des Grafen of the count | der Grafen of the counts |
| *D.* dem Grafen to the count | den Grafen to the counts |
| *A.* den Grafen the count. | die Grafen the counts. |

Thus:

| | | Singular. | Plural. |
|---|---|---|---|
| Der Held[2] the hero. | *Gen.* | des Helden x. | die Helden x. |
| der Fürst[3] the prince. | " | des Fürsten x. | die Fürsten x. |
| der Herr[1] the master, Mr. gentleman. | " | des Herrn x. | die Herren x. |
| der Narr / der Thor the foll. | " | des Narren x des Thoren x. | die Narren x die Thoren x. |
| der Bär the bear. | " | des Bären x. | die Bären x. |
| der Menfch man, mankind | " | des Menfchen. | die Menfchen x. |

3) All masculine nouns from other languages, not ending in al, an, aft or r,[4] and having the accent on the last syllable, are declined according to this mode of inflexion:

---

1) Old German: der Grabe — der Herre.
2) Anglo-Saxon *haeleth* (dissyllabic).
3) der Fürst is like the English root first = der Erfte.
4) Such as der General', Offizier', x, which belong to the 3rd declension, see p 37, 4.

## Example

| Singular. | | Plural. | |
|---|---|---|---|
| N. der Student' | the student | die Studen'ten | the students |
| G. des Studen'ten | of the student | der Studenten | of the students |
| D. dem Studenten | to the student | den Studenten | to the students |
| A. den Studenten | the student. | die Studenten | the students. |

Such are:

| | |
|---|---|
| Der Advokat' the advocate (lawyer). | der Präsident' the president. |
| der Kamerab' the comrade. | der Tyrann' the tyrant. |
| der Kandidat' the candidate. | der Jesuit' the Jesuit. |
| der Philosoph' the philosopher. | der Regent' the regent. |
| der Dukat' the ducat. | der Elefant' the elephant. |
| der Soldat' the soldier. | der Diamant' the diamond. |
| der Monarch' the monarch. | der Poet' the poet. |
| der Komet' the comet. | der Christ the Christian. |
| der Planet' the planet. | der Prinz the prince. |

*Plur.* die Advokaten, die Soldaten, die Christen 2c.

### Words.

| | |
|---|---|
| Der Kaiser the emperor. | der Brief the letter. |
| die Herde the herd, flock. | der Esel (1st decl.) the ass. |
| die Tante the aunt. | kennen Sie? do you know? |
| der Körper the body. | ich gebe I give. |
| der Grieche the Greek. | war was; hatte had. |
| der Kosak the Cossack. | |

| S. | | | |
|---|---|---|---|
| Ich bin I am | Bin ich am I? | | |
| du bist thou art | bist du art thou? | | |
| er ist he is | ist er is he? | | |
| sie ist she is | ist sie is she? | | |
| Pl. wir sind we are | sind wir are we? | | |
| Sie sind } you are | sind Sie } are you? | | |
| (ihr seid) } ye are | (seid ihr) } | | |
| sie sind they are. | sind sie are they? | | |

### Reading Exercise. 7.

Das Messer des Knaben *) Ich gebe dem Knaben das Brot. Kennen Sie den Knaben? Das Buch eines Studenten. Der Körper eines Elefanten. Die Flügel der Adler und der Falken. Die Soldaten des Kaisers. Die Raben sind Vögel. Die Knaben haben zwei Raben und drei Hasen. Die Türken haben Sklaven. Die Kosaken des Kaisers sind Russen. Das Gold des Grafen. Der Brief des Fürsten. Die Menschen sind sterblich (mortal). Der Bruder des Prinzen Albert.

### Aufgabe. 8.

1. The brothers of the boy. These boys are brothers. The name of the student. The sister of the count. The aunt

---

*) Or „des Knaben Messer, eines Studenten Buch" etc in the same order as in the Saxon genitive in English.

of the prince. The knife of the soldier. The letter of the
president. The emperors Caligula and Nero were (waren)
tyrants. Do you know the princes? The child has a raven.
The Americans have a president. I have seen the diamonds of
the prince. The old (alten) Greeks had (hatten) slaves. Give
the gold to*) the Jew.

2. We have seen a comet. Are you Saxons or Prussians?
The body of a giant is very large. These two boys are my
nephews. Those soldiers are Russians. The Turks are no
heathens. We are Christians. These boys are Jews. My
comrades are ill. We have no oxen, we have two asses.
Give this (Acc.) letter to*) the messenger (Dat.) of the count.

### Conversation.

| | |
|---|---|
| Haben Sie den Elefanten ge= sehen? | Wir haben ihn (it) heute (to-day) gesehen. |
| Haben die Knaben den Löwen, den Tiger und den Bären ge= sehen? | Unsre Knaben haben den Löwen und den Bären gesehen; aber (but) nicht den Tiger. |
| Wer ist dieser Mann? | Er ist der Bruder des Präsiden'ten. |
| Ist dieser Student ein Preuße? | Nein, er ist ein Sachse. |
| Wer ist sein Vater? | Sein Vater ist ein Advokat'. |
| Lieben Sie (do you like) die Affen? | Nein, ich liebe die Affen nicht. |
| Kennen Sie diese Soldaten? | Ich kenne sie (know them) nicht. |
| Haben Sie einen Hasen? | Ja, ich habe drei Hasen. |
| Ist der Bediente des Grafen ein Franzose? | Nein, er ist ein Engländer |
| Haben Sie einen Neffen? | Ich habe zwei Neffen. |
| Sind diese Knaben Juden? | Nein, sie sind Christen. |
| Wo sind Ihre Kameraden? | Sie sind nicht hier (here), sie sind zu Hause (at home). |
| Haben die Falken Flügel? | Ja, alle (all the) Vögel haben Flügel. |
| War der Held ein Russe? | Nein, er war ein Grieche. |

# Fifth Lesson.
## (Fünfte Lektion.)
### Third declension.

This declension contains the greatest number of the
masculine substantives. In the *Singular*, the Genitive is
formed by adding es or s to the nominative; in the da-

---

*) *to* is not to be translated, the dative is meant.

tive, the word remains either unchanged or takes an e; the accustive is like the nominative. All the Plural cases take e, and the dative an n, besides the e. Moreover, most of them having a, o, u or au in the root, modify it into ä, ö, ü or äu. To this declension belong
1) *all masculine monosyllabic nouns.*

### Examples.

| Singular. | | Plural. | |
|---|---|---|---|
| N. der Fiſch | the fish | die Fiſche | the fishes |
| G. des Fiſches | of the fish | der Fiſche | of the fishes |
| D. dem Fiſch(e) | to the fish | den Fiſchen | to the fishes |
| A. den Fiſch | the fish. | die Fiſche | the fishes. |

| | | | |
|---|---|---|---|
| N. der Sohn | the son | die Söhne | the sons |
| G. des Sohn(e)s | of the son | der Söhne | of the sons |
| D. dem Sohn(e) | to the son | den Söhnen | to the sons. |
| A. den Sohn | the son. | die Söhne | the sons. |

| | | | |
|---|---|---|---|
| N. der Baum | the three | die Bäume | the trees |
| G. des Baum(e)s | of the tree | der Bäume | of the trees |
| D. dem Baum(e) | to the tree | den Bäumen | to the trees |
| A. den Baum | the tree. | die Bäume | the trees. |

*Note.* Concerning the inflexion of the genitive and dative singular, es and e, we may remark that the e is only euphonical and in common conversation often omitted, especially in the dative. We may say des Sohns for des Sohnes, dem Sohn for dem Sohne, one sounds as well as the other, but we never say des Fiſchs, des Pfabs or des Platzs, this being intolerably harsh Observe however that with monosyllables the *Gen.* es is preferred.

Such are:

| | |
|---|---|
| Der Tiſch the table. | der Zahn the tooth. |
| der Stuhl the chair. | der Hahn the cock. |
| der Berg the hill. | der Sturm the storm |
| der Hut the hat. | der Turm the tower. |
| der Ring the ring. | der Traum the dream. |
| der Freund the friend. | der Wall the rampart. |
| der Feind the enemy, foe. | der Kopf the head. |
| der Aſt the branch. | der Ton the sound, tone. |
| der Gaſt the guest | der Lohn the reward. |
| der Fuß the foot. | der Rock the coat. |
| der Fluß the river. | der Stock the stick. |
| der Fuchs the fox. | der Tanz the dance |
| der Wolf the wolf. | der Brief the letter &c. |

*Plur.* die Tiſche, die Stühle, die Zähne, die Berge, die Freunde, die Flüſſe, die Stöcke, die Briefe ꝛc.

*Note.* The following nouns do not modify their vowel in the plural:

Der Arm the arm.      der Lachs the salmon.
der Tag the day.      der Aal the eel.
der Hund the dog, hound.      der Huf the hoof.
der Schuh the shoe.      der Pfad the path.
der Grad the degree.      der Stoff the stuff.
der Dachs the badger.      der Punkt the point.

*Plur.* die Arme, die Tage, die Hunde, die Schuhe ꝛc.

2) When such masculine *roots* have a *prefix* before them, they are declined in the same manner as if they were simple; but it must be observed that, being no longer monosyllabic, the euphonical e in the genitive and dative singular is generally omitted. This is also the case with *compound nouns* of this declension.

## Examples.

| *Singular.* | *Singular.* |
|---|---|
| *N.* der Be-fehl' the order | der Apfel-baum the apple-tree |
| *G* des Befehls of the order | des Apfelbaums of the apple-tree |
| *D* dem Befehl to the order | dem Apfelbaum to the apple-tree |
| *A* den Befehl the order. | den Apfelbaum the apple-tree. |
| *Plural.* | *Plural.* |
| *N.* die Befehle the orders | die Apfelbäume\*) the apple-trees |
| *G.* der Befehle of the orders | der Apfelbäume of the apple-tr. |
| *D.* den Befehlen to the orders | den Apfelbäumen to the apple-tr. |
| *A* die Befehle the orders | die Apfelbäume the apple-tr. |

Such are:

Der Gesang the song, air.      der Ohrring the ear-ring.
der Gebrauch custom, use.      der Handschuh the glove.
der Vorhang the curtain.      der Strohhut the straw-hat.
der Unfall the accident.      der Überrock the great-coat.
der Ausgang the issue.      der Feiertag the holiday.

*Gen.* des Gesangs, des Vorhangs, des Ausgangs ꝛc.
*Plur.* die Vorhänge, die Gebräuche, die Handschuhe ꝛc.

3) This third declension comprehends further the *masculine derivatives* ending in ig, ich at and ling, as:

| *Singular.* | *Plural.* |
|---|---|
| *N.* der König the king | die Könige the kings |
| *G.* des Königs of the king | der Könige of the kings |
| *D.* dem König to the king | den Königen to the king |
| *A* den König the king. | die Könige the kings. |

---

\*) not Äpfelbäume

Such are:

Der Käfig the cage.     der Pfirsich the peach.
der Teppich the carpet.     der Mo'nat the month.
der Essig the vinegar.     der Jüngling the youth.
der Honig (the) honey.     der Hering the herring.

*Plur.* die Käfige, die Mo'nate, die Jünglinge, die Heringe :c.

4) Further some nouns of foreign origin ending in al, an, ar, ast, ier, or and on, as:

| | *Singular.* | | *Plural.* | |
|---|---|---|---|---|
| *N.* | der Palast' | the palace | die Palä'ste | the palaces |
| *G.* | des Palastes | of the palace | der Paläste | of the palaces |
| *D.* | dem Palast | to the palace | den Palästen | to the palaces |
| *A* | den Palast | the palace. | die Paläste | the palaces. |

Such are:

Der General' the general.     der Morast' the swamp.
der Kardinal' the cardinal.     der Altar' the altar.
der Admiral' the admiral.     der Offizier' the officer.
*der Vokal' the vowel.     der Grenadier' the grenadier
der Kaplan' the chaplain.     *der Postillion' the postillion.

*Plur.* die Generä'le, die Vokale, die Altäre, die Offizie're :c.

---

### Words.

Der Wald the forest, wood.   die Nahrung the food.
der Schlaf sleep. der Tod death.   der Storch the stork
der Vetter the cousin.   der Winter winter.
der Frosch the frog.   weiß white   lang long
drei three. vier four. mit (*dat.*) with. aber but.

### Reading Exercise. 9.

Die Söhne des Vaters. Die Fische des Flusses. Auf (on) dem Tisch(e). Auf den Bäumen. Die Bäume des Waldes. Die Vögel sind in dem Wald. Die Zähne des Löwen. Mit dem Stock(e). Mit den Füßen. Diese Stühle sind alt. Ich hatte einen Traum. Die Soldaten sind auf den Wällen. Die Füße der Hähne haben Sporen (spurs)*). Die Paläste der Könige sind groß. Wir haben die Teppiche des Königs gesehen. Haben Sie die Wölfe und Füchse nicht gesehen? Die Freunde meines Vaters sind hier. Die Hunde deines Vetters. Der Schlaf ist das Bild (image) des Todes. Hier sind Ihre Schuhe. Wo sind meine Handschuhe?

### Aufgabe. 10.

1. The tables and the chairs of the room. The trees of the wood. The ramparts of the enemies. The rings of the girl. The letters of my friends. With the son (*Dat.*) of my brother. With the sons of the count. Do you know my

---

*) The regular form „die Spornen" has now more and more become obsolete.

guests? The fishes are in the rivers. We have a table, but no chairs. I give the dogs to the sons of the Englishman. The days are long. The trees have branches. I have no stick. We have no sticks. The curtains of my room are white. The frogs are the food of (the) storks.

2. The storms of (the) winter are over (vorüber). On the (auf dem) chair of the president. The gloves are on the table. The fish(es) have no feet. The fish(es) have no teeth. The birds are on the trees. My sons have seen two ravens and four storks. Three months and two days. The banks (die Ufer) of the rivers. The name of the officer. The herrings are fishes. Do you know those two generals? Yes, I know them (ich kenne sie). The windows of the palace. In the palace of the king.

### Conversation.

| | |
|---|---|
| Wo sind die Fische? | Sie sind in den Flüssen. |
| Wo sind meine drei Söhne? | Sie sind in dem Garten oder (or) in dem Hof (yard). |
| Welche Röcke hat der Schneider? | Er hat die Röcke des Offiziers. |
| Sind diese Stühle alt? | Diese Stühle sind neu (new). |
| Von wem sprechen Sie? (Of whom do you speak?) | Wir sprechen von unsern Freunden. |
| Wieviele (how many) Monate? | Drei Monate. |
| Wieviele Tage? | Drei oder vier Tage. |
| Sprechen Sie nicht von (of) dem Sohne des Lehrers? | Nein, wir sprechen von seinen Schülern. |
| Wieviele Türme hat die Stadt? | Diese Stadt hat drei Türme. |
| Welchen Stock haben Sie? | Ich habe den Stock des Grafen. |
| Haben Sie keine Freunde? | Ich hatte (had) zwei Freunde, aber sie sind tot (dead). |
| Wieviele Füße hat ein Hund? | Ein Hund hat vier Füße. |
| Was haben Sie gesehen? | Ich habe die Füchse und die Wölfe gesehen. |
| Haben die Schüler einen Feiertag? | Sie haben zwei Feiertage. |
| Wo ist der General? | Er ist in dem Palast des Königs. |

# Sixth Lesson.

## FEMININE SUBSTANTIVES.

### Fourth declension.

The 4th declension comprises all the substantives of the *feminine* gender.

In the singular, feminine words remain *unchanged* in all the cases. In the plural, they take either e, or n or en.

1) The *true monosyllables* take e in the *plural*, at the same time softening their vowel.

### Example.

| Singular. | | Plural. | |
|---|---|---|---|
| *N. y A.* | die Hand the hand | die Hände the hands |
| *Gen.* | der Hand of the hand | der Hände of the hands |
| *Dat.* | der Hand to the hand. | den Händen to the hands. |

The other *true monosyllables* are the following 28:

| | |
|---|---|
| Die Axt the axe. | die Laus the louse. |
| die Angst fear, anxiety. | die Luft the air. |
| die Bank the bench. | die Lust the pleasure, desire. |
| die Braut the bride. | die Magd the maid-servant. |
| die Brust the breast. | die Macht the power. |
| die Faust the fist. | die Maus the mouse. |
| die Frucht the fruit. | die Nacht the night. |
| die Gans the goose. | die Not the distress. |
| die Gruft the vault. | die Nuß the walnut. |
| die Haut the skin. | die Sau the sow. |
| die Kluft the cleft. | die Stadt the town, city. |
| die Kraft the force, strength. | die Schnur the string. |
| die Kuh the cow. | die Wand the wall. |
| die Kunst the art. | die Wurst the sausage. |

*Plur.* die Äxte, die Bänke, die Früchte, die Gänse, die Kühe, die Künste, die Mäuse, die Nächte, die Nüsse, die Städte ec.

*Note.* There are other monosyllabic words of the feminine gender, which do not follow this mode of forming their plural, because they were originally *dissyllabic*, and dropped their e: as: Die Frau, old German die Fraue; die Post and die Form from the French: *la poste, la forme &c.* — They belong therefore to the following class and take en in the plural, as: die Frauen ec. A list of them will be found in the 9th Lesson.

2) The dissyllabic and polysyllabic feminine nouns take n or en in the plural, *without changing* the *vowel*, for all the cases. Words ending in l or r have no e before n.

### Examples.

| Singular. | | Singular. | |
|---|---|---|---|
| *N. y A.* | die Blume the flower | die Schwester the sister |
| *G.* | der Blume of the flower | der Schwester of the sister |
| *D.* | der Blume to the flower. | der Schwester to the sister. |

| Plural. | | Plural. | |
|---|---|---|---|
| *N. A.* | die Blumen the flowers | die Schwestern the sisters |
| *G.* | der Blumen of the flowers | der Schwestern of the sisters |
| *D.* | den Blumen to the flowers. | den Schwestern to the sisters. |

Such are·

Die Rose the rose. | die Feder the pen. feather
die Biene the bee. | die Insel the island.
die Wunde the wound. | die Nadel the needle.
die Stunde the hour, lesson. | die Mauer the wall.
die Brücke the bridge. | die Absicht the intention.
die Kirche the church. | die Schmeichelei' (the) flattery.
die Kirsche the cherry. | die Schönheit the beauty.
die Tasche the pocket. | die Krankheit the disease.
die Pflanze the plant. | die Freiheit liberty, freedom.
die Schule the school. | die Wissenschaft the science
die Birne the pear. | die Freundschaft the friendship.
die Stirne the forehead. | die Erfahrung experience. •
die Thüre*) the door. | die Hoffnung (the) hope.
die Tante the aunt. | die Fürstin**) the princess.
die Lippe the lip. | die Gräfin the countess.
die Nase the nose. | die Nachbarin the neighbour f.

*NB.* Observe that all derivative substantives ending in
ei, heit, keit, schaft, ung and in are of the feminine gender
(see less. 10, *B*, 3, p. 58), likewise words from foreign languages ending in ie, if, ion' and tät, such as die Melodie',
die Musik', die Nation' (*pl.* Natio'nen), die Universität' ꝛc.

### Exceptions (Ausnahmen).

The following two words are excepted from the mode
of inflexion of this declension, but only in the plural, viz.:
die Mutter and die Tochter.

|  | *Singular.* |  | *Singular.* |
|---|---|---|---|
| *N.* | die Mutter the mother | die Tochter the daughter |
| *G.* | der Mutter of the mother | der Tochter of the daughter |
| *D.* | der Mutter to the mother | der Tochter to the daughter |
| *A.* | die Mutter the mother. | die Tochter the daughter. |
|  | *Plural.* | *Plural.* |
| *N.* | die Mütter the mothers | die Töchter the daughters |
| *G.* | der Mütter of the mothers | der Töchter of the daughters |
| *D.* | den Müttern to the mothers | den Töchtern to the daughters |
| *A.* | die Mütter the mothers. | die Töchter the daughters. |

For the few feminine words ending in nis (*pl. — nisse*) see p. 50,
§ 6, and the foot-note**) p. 43.

---

### Words.

Die Straße the street. | die Liebe (the) love.
die Dame the lady. | die Lilie the lily.
die Farbe the colour. | das Veilchen (*1st decl.*) the violet.

---

*) This word is sometimes used without e: die Thür; but this
is less good.

**) Nouns in in double their n in the plur., as: die Fürstinnen.

der Finger the finger.     die Lampe the lamp.
der Mann the man, husband     ich suche I seek (for).
die Milch the milk.     ich kaufe I buy. reif ripe.
die Taube the pigeon     ich verkaufe I sell.
die Katze the cat    kurz short    ich kenne I know. rot red.
*S.* ich liebe\*) I love *or* like     *Pl.* wir lieben we love *or* like
du liebst thou lovest, likest     (ihr liebet)\ (ye) love *or* like
er liebt he loves, likes     Sie lieben/ you love, you like.
sie liebt she loves *or* likes     sie lieben they love *or* like.
Lieben Sie? do you love *or* like?

### Reading Exercise. 11.

Die Hände des Mädchens. Die Straßen dieser Stadt. Die Federn der Gänse. Die Thüren der Kirche. Die Städte sind groß. Die Farbe der Rose. Die Flügel der Biene sind klein. Der Knabe ist in der Schule. Die Kirchen sind groß. Die Rosen und die Lilien sind schöne (pretty) Blumen. Ich liebe die Birnen.\*\*) Lieben Sie die Nüsse? Die Mädchen lieben die Blumen. Die Vögel haben Federn. Die Finger der Hände sind klein. In (in) dem Winter sind die Nächte lang. Ich liebe die Mäuse nicht; aber (but) ich liebe die Bienen und die Tauben.

### Aufgabe. 12.

1. The hands of the ladies. I like the walnuts. The churches of the town. The boys have no pens. The forehead of the man is high (hoch). I like the roses and violets. The smell (der Geruch) of the roses and violets is sweet (angenehm). Our hopes are vain (eitel). We know (kennen) the love of the mothers. The boys are in (the) school. The ladies are in (the) church. In three hours The soldiers have wounds. Do you know these plants? The cherries are red. I know the daughters of the countess.

2. You know my intentions. The boy has two flowers in his hand. These pens are not good (gut). I love my sisters. The cats catch (fangen) mice. These pears are not ripe. My neighbour sells lamps. The lips are red. We sell our cows and our oxen These two girls are sisters. My [female] neighbour sells potatoes (Kartoffeln). The mothers love their daughters. The girls have no needles. The pears are the fruits of the pear-tree (Birnbaums).

### Conversation.

Kennen Sie den Namen dieser Straße? Es ist die Friedrichsstraße.

---

\*) This is the *present tense* of the verb lieben, and all regular verbs are conjugated in the same manner.

\*\*) Observe, however, that it is better German to say: „Ich esse (eat) Birnen gern (gladly)" 2c To use the verb lieben in the sense of to *like* has only crept into German from the French *aimer* which has both meanings, to *like* and to *love*; the German lieben correctly means only to *love*.

| | |
|---|---|
| Wo sind Ihre Knaben? | Sie sind in der Schule. |
| Wo sind meine Federn? | Sie liegen (lie) auf dem Tisch. |
| Wer fängt (catches) Mäuse? | Die Katzen fangen Mäuse. |
| Wieviele Schwestern hat Ihre Mutter? | Sie hat zwei Schwestern und drei Brüder. |
| Verkaufen Sie Kirschen? | Nein, aber wir verkaufen Birnen. |
| Wie (how) viele Hände hat ein Mensch? | Ein Mensch hat zwei Hände und zwei Füße. |
| Von welcher Farbe sind die Lippen? | Die Lippen sind rot. |
| Hat der Soldat Wunden? | Ja, er hat viele Wunden. |
| Lieben Sie die Katzen? | Ich liebe sie (them) nicht. |
| Wo sind die Damen? | Sie sind in der Kirche. |
| Welche Blumen lieben Sie am meisten (best)? | Ich liebe die Rosen, die Lilien und die Veilchen am meisten. |
| Wieviele Stunden lebte das Kind (did the child live)? | Es lebte drei Stunden. |
| Wie sind die Straßen dieser Stadt? | Sie sind schmutzig (muddy). |
| Wo leben (live) die Fische? | Sie leben in dem Wasser. |
| Wo sind die Gänse? | Die Gänse und die Enten (ducks) sind in dem Hof (yard). |
| Wer verkauft Kartoffeln (potatoes)? | Meine Nachbarin verkauft Kartoffeln. |

# Seventh · Lesson.
## NEUTER SUBSTANTIVES.
### Fifth declension.

It includes merely the nouns of the neuter gender, except those ending in el, en, er, chen and lein, which belong to the 1st declension.

In the singular they borrow the mode of inflexion of the *third* declension, viz. the genitive is formed by adding es or s, the dative by adding e, which may however be omitted in ordinary conversation.

In the plural, a distinction is to be made 1) between words of two and more syllables, and 2) monosyllabic words. The plural of the former ends in e, that of the latter in er with a modified vowel.

### 1) Example of a dissyllable.

| Singular. | | Plural. | |
|---|---|---|---|
| N. das Geschenk' the present | bie Geschenke the presents, gifts |
| G. des Geschenks of the present | der Geschenke of the presents |
| D. dem Geschenk(e) to the present | den Geschenken to the presents |
| A. das Geschenk the present. | die Geschenke the presents. |

Such are:

Das Gesetz the law.  
das Gespräch the conversation.  
das Geschäft the business  
das Gewehr the gun, musket  
das Gebirge*) the mountain.  
das Gemälde*) the picture.  
das Gebäude the building.  
das Zeugnis**) the testimony  
das Geheimnis the secret  
das Bekenntnis the confession.

das Gleichnis the parable.  
das Kamel the camel.  
das Instrument' the instrument.  
das Kompliment' the compliment.  
das Papier' the paper.  
das Metall' the metal.  
das Billet'***) the ticket.  
das Konzert' the concert.  
das Porträt'***) the portrait.  
das Lineal, the ruler

*Plur.* Die Gesetze, die Geschäfte, die Zeugnisse, die Metalle ꝛc.

### 2) Examples of monosyllables.

| *Singular.* | | *Singular.* | |
|---|---|---|---|
| N. das Kind | the child. | das Dorf | the village |
| G. des Kind(e)s | of the child | des Dorf(e)s | of the village |
| D. dem Kind(e) | to the child | dem Dorf(e) | to the village |
| A. das Kind | the child | das Dorf | the village |
| *Plural.* | | *Plural.* | |
| N. die Kinder | the children | die Dörfer | the villages |
| G. der Kinder | of the children | der Dörfer | of the villages |
| D. den Kindern | to the children | den Dörfern | to the villages |
| A. die Kinder | the children | die Dörfer | the villages. |

Such are.

Das Amt the office.  
das Blatt the leaf.  
das Buch the book.  
das Ei the egg.  
das Bild the picture, portrait.  
das Nest the nest.  
das Huhn the hen, fowl.  
das Feld the field  
das Thal the valley.  
das Wort the word.  
das Kalb the calf.

das Lied the song.  
das Schloß the castle, palace.  
das Geld the money.  
das Lamm the lamb.  
das Haus the house.  
das Weib the wife, woman.  
das Dach the roof.  
das Kleid the dress.  
das Land the country, land.  
das Band†) the ribbon.  
das Glas the glass.

*Plur.* die Ämter, die Blätter, die Bücher, die Nester, die Eier, die Wörter, die Häuser, die Hühner, die Länder ꝛc.

---

*) Neuter words which end in the Singular in e, do not add a second e in the plur., as pl. die Gebirge, die Gemälde ꝛc

**) All nouns ending in nis form their plural by adding e, and doubling the s, even two feminine words, as: die Kenntnis, knowledge; pl die Kenntnisse  Die Besorgnis, apprehension, pl. die Besorgnisse.

***) With the two words 'Billet and Porträt' the plural form in s 'die Billets, die Porträts' is preferred now.

†) Der Band m the volume, has its pl. die Bände (3rd decl.).

*Note 1.* The same mode of inflexion is followed by all compound words ending in **tum,** two of which are masculine: Das Kaifertum the empire. | der Reichtum the riches. das Fürftentum the principality. | der Irrtum the error

*Plur.* die Fürftentümer, die Reichtümer, die Irrtümer 2c.

*Note 2.* Some monosyllabic neuter words, especially those ending in r do not take **er** in the plural, but **e** only, nor do they soften their vowel:

Das Haar the hair, *pl.* die Haare.

das Jahr the year; *pl.* die Jahre.

das Meer the sea; *pl.* die Meere.

das Tier the animal, *pl.* die Tiere.

(For the complete list of them see p. 51, § 9)

*Note 3.* The neuter word das Herz (the heart) admits of an irregularity in the singular and plural:

*Sing. Nom. & Acc.* das Herz,   *G.* des Herzens; *D.* dem Herzen.

*Plur.* „ „ „ die Herzen; „ der Herzen; „ den Herzen.

## Words.

Die Aufgabe the exercise.     verloren lost.
das Horn the horn.     leicht easy, light
der Römer the Roman.     rund round.   klein small.
liegen to lie (be laid). ich fehe I see     grün green.   neu new.
finden to find. gefunden found.     schmutzig dirty. hoch high.
fingen to sing     wieviel? how much?
ich kaufe I buy. gekauft bought     viele many
sprechen to speak     die meiften most.

## Reading Exercise 13.

Das Bild des Kindes. Die Bilder der Kinder. Die Farbe des Blattes. Die Blätter der Pflanzen find grün. Die Bäume des Feldes tragen (bear) Früchte. Die Mauern jenes Schloffes find hoch. Der König hat viele Schlöffer. Die Wörter der Auf= gabe find leicht. Ich fuche die Lämmer. Wir haben die Kleider gekauft. In den Neftern der Vögel liegen Eier. Jedes edle Volk (nation) liebt [die] Freiheit. Wo (where) liegen die Eier der Hühner? Sie liegen in den Neftern. Die Ochfen haben Hörner. Der Fürft hat ein Schloß gekauft. Der König hat feine Länder, feine Städte und feine Dörfer verloren. Wir haben unfre Bücher gefunden.

## Aufgabe. 14.

1. This village is small. Those villages are also (auch) small. The laws of the Romans. The fields are large. The flowers of the field. The dresses of the girls are red. I see the roofs of the houses. A brave soldier fights, and, if ne— cessary, dies willingly for the freedom of his country. The children have found a nest. The leaves of the trees are green.

I seek my books. I find the paper in the book. We know the castles of the princes. He is in his house (*Dat*). Our houses are old. The girl sings a song. Have you seen the presents of my aunt? I buy two guns. The president has bought two pictures. 2 The books of the children are not new. These ribbons are red. The doors of the rooms are shut (gefdjloffeu). Those buildings are very old. We speak of (von, *Dat.*) the presents of the king and of the queen. Our father has bought a house and (a) garden. The girls have bought many eggs. I find the words of my exercise very easy. These valleys are beautiful (prädtig). The village lies in a valley. We have bought two fowls. The boy has lost his money.

### Conversation.

| | |
|---|---|
| Kennen Sie die Kinder der Gräfin? | Ja, id) kenne fie (them). |
| Wie (how) finden Sie fie? | Id) finde fie fehr fdjön. |
| Haben die Vögel Nefter? | Ja, die meiften Vögel haben Nefter. |
| Was liegt in dem Nefte? | Id) fehe vier Eier. |
| Lieben Sie die Eier? | Ja, die Eier der Hühner. |
| In welcher Stadt lebt Ihr Vetter (does your cousin live)? | Er lebt in Frankfurt. |
| Wieviel Geld haben Sie? | Id) habe drei Mark (marcs)*). |
| Haben Sie Butter und Eier gekauft? | Id) habe viele Eier gekauft; aber (but) keine Butter. |
| Wie find die Blätter der Bäume? | Sie find grün. |
| Wo find meine Bücher? | Sie find in Ihrem Zimmer. |
| Welches Haus hat Ihr Vater gekauft? | Er hat zwei Häufer gekauft. |
| Hat er aud) einen Garten? | Nein, er hat keinen Garten; aber viele Felder. |
| Wer hat diefe Bilder gemalt (painted)? | Ein deutfdjer (German) Maler. |
| Sind Ihre Bänder rot? | Nein, fie find grün, aber die Bänder meiner Schwefter find rot. |
| Wer hat das alte Schloß gekauft? | Der Sohn des Grafen R. |
| Welche Länder find reid)? | England und Amerika |

# Eighth Lesson.

## Nouns with prepositions.

Very often the cases of substantives are governed by prepositions, which occur so frequently in most sentences, that they should be learned early. Those govern-

---

*) One marc of the new German currency is nearly equal to one shilling English c. —

ing the dative, the accusative, or both, are more used than those which govern the genitive case. For the present, we only give such as are most required. The prepositions are fully treated, lesson 37.

### 1) Prepositions with the dative:

| | |
|---|---|
| **Aus** out of, from. | **feit** since. |
| **bei** near, at, by, (with). | **von** of, from, by. |
| **mit** with. | **zu** to, at. |
| **nach** after, to (*with* the name of a *place*). | **gegen=über** opposite (to). |

#### Examples.

**Aus dem Garten** (*dat. masc.*) from (out of) the garden.
**Aus der Stadt** (*dat. fem.*) from the town.
**Mit einem Stock** (*dat. masc.*) with a stick.
**Mit einer Feder** (*dat. fem.*) with a pen.
- **Nach dem Mittageſſen** (*dat. neut.*) after (the) dinner.
**Nach der Stunde** (*dat. fem.*) after the lesson, &c.

### 2) Prepositions requiring the accusative:

| | |
|---|---|
| **Durch** through, by. | **ohne** without |
| **für** for. | **um** round, about, at (*time*). |
| **gegen** against, towards | *wider* |

#### Examples.

**Durch den Wald** (*acc. masc.*) through the forest (wood).
**Durch die Straße** (*acc. fem.*) through the street.
**Durch das Waſſer** (*acc. neut.*) through the water.
**Für meinen Bruder** (*acc. masc.*) for my brother.
**Für meine Schweſter** (*acc. fem.*) for my sister, etc.

### 3) The following *nine* take the *dative* in answer to the question »*where?*« indicating a state of rest, which is mostly the case. They require however the *accusative* after the question »*whither?*« with a verb denoting a direction or motion from one place to another.

| | | |
|---|---|---|
| **An** (w. *dat.*) at. | **in***) (*dat.*) in, at. | **über** over, across. |
| **an** (w. *acc.*) to. | **in** (w. *acc.*) into. | **unter** (*place*) under. |
| **auf** upon, on. | **neben** beside, near. | **unter**(*number*)among. |
| **hinter** behind. | **vor***) before, ago. | **zwiſchen** between. |

#### Examples with the dative (rest).

**Ich ſtehe an dem Fenſter** (*dat. neut.*) I stand at the window.
**Auf dem Tiſch** (*dat. masc.*) on (upon) the table.
**In dem Hof(e)** (*dat. masc.*) in the (court-)yard.
**In der Stadt** (*dat. fem.*) in (the) town.

---

*) in and vor, when denoting *time*, always take the dative.

Vor dem Fenſter (*dat. neut.*) before the window.
Vor*) einer Stunde (*dat. fem*) an hour ago.

**Examples with the accusative (motion).**

Ich gehe an das Fenſter I go to the window.
Ich gehe über den Fluß I go over the river.
Ich gehe hinter das Haus I go behind the house.
Stellen Sie es vor das Fenſter put it before the window.

### 4) Prepositions with the genitive case:

Während during | ſtatt or anſtatt instead of.
wegen on account of

**Examples**

Während des Regens during the rain.
ſtatt *or* anſtatt eines Briefes instead of a letter.

5) Several of the above prepositions may be contracted with the definite article, in which form they are in very general use.

Am for an dem, as: am Fenſter (rest), at the window.
ans for an das, as: ans Fenſter (motion), to the window.
aufs for auf das, as: aufs Land (motion), into the country.
im for in dem, as: im Winter in winter.
ins for in das, as: ins Waſſer (motion), into the water.
beim for bei dem, as· beim Thor (rest), near the gate.
durchs for durch das, as: durchs Feuer (*acc.*), through the fire.
vom for von dem, as: vom Markt (*dat.*), from the market.
vors for vor das, as: vors Fenſter before the window.
übers for über das, as: übers Meer across the sea.
zum for zu dem, as: zum Vater (I go) to the father.
zur for zu der, as: zur Mutter to the mother.

### Words.

Der Hof the yard. | der Winter (the) winter.
das Dach the roof. | der Mantel the cloak.
der Krieg (the) war. | Wilhelm William.
der Rabe (2. *decl.*) the raven. | gefallen fallen. leben to live.
die Taube the pigeon. | die Nichte the niece.
der Frieden peace. | die Kälte the cold.
das Bett the bed. | ſpielen (to) play.
das Horn the horn. | ich eſſe I eat. fliegen to fly.
das Frühſtück breakfast. | kaufen to buy war was.
das Mittageſſen (the) dinner. | zu Hauſe at home.

### Reading Exercise. 15.

In dem Hofe (im Hof). Aus dem Garten. Auf dem Dach. Die Taube fliegt auf das (aufs) Dach. Im Krieg und im Frieden.

---

*) See the foot-note *) p. 46.

Die Kinder spielen vor dem Hause. Vor der Nacht. Der Vogel sitzt (sits) auf dem Baum. Die Fische leben im Wasser. Mein Hut ist (has) ins Wasser gefallen. Das Federmesser des Knaben liegt auf dem Tisch(e). Der Hund liegt unter dem Bett. Diese Bücher sind für meinen Lehrer. Ihre Tochter ist bei (with) meiner Schwester. Die Soldaten sprechen von dem Krieg. Das (that) war während des Krieges. Ich bleibe (stay) zu Hause wegen des Regens. Das Bett steht (stands) neben der Thüre. Um vier Uhr (at four o'clock) bin ich zu Hause.

## Aufgabe. 16.

1. Out of the room. Near the castle. I eat with a spoon. After the rain. The oxen butt (stoßen) with their horns. We see (sehen) with our eyes (Augen). The boys go (gehen) through the forest. The pupils speak of (von) the school. We speak of (von) the weather. I was in the street during the rain. William is on the tree. Go (gehen Sie) into the yard (*Acc.*). The boy has (ist) fallen into the water. The tree lies in the water. My penknife is in my pocket. Against the door. Put (stecken Sie) your penknife into your pocket. My cloak hangs (hängt) behind the door. I have seen many flowers in the field.

2. The eggs lie in the nests of the (*Gen.*) birds. There (es) was a raven among the pigeons. Before (the) breakfast. We play after (the) dinner. He was in his room. The table stands near the window. Before (the) winter many birds fly (*put:* fly many birds) across the sea. We stay (bleiben) at home on account of the rain. The dog runs (läuft) round the house. Those apples are for my niece, and these pears are for my son. The count was at home at (um) three o'clock. Two days ago.

## Conversation.

| | |
|---|---|
| Wo sitzt der Vogel? | Er sitzt auf dem Dach des Hauses. |
| Wo ist Wilhelm? | Er ist im Garten oder im Hof. |
| Wo ist mein Mantel? | Er hängt hinter der Thüre. |
| Wer hat mein Federmesser? | Es liegt auf dem Tisch. |
| Haben Sie meinen Hut gesehen? | Ja, er ist unter den Tisch gefallen. |
| Woher' (whence) kommen Sie? | Ich komme vom Markt (market). |
| Was haben Sie gekauft? | Ich habe Äpfel und Nüsse gekauft. |
| Wohin' (where) gehen Sie? | Ich gehe auf (to) den Markt. |
| Wohin' fliegen viele Vögel? | Sie fliegen übers Meer. |
| Wann (when) fliegen sie fort (fly off, leave)? | Vor dem Winter. |
| Warum (why) fliegen sie fort? | Wegen der Kälte des Winters. |
| Sind Sie noch (still) im Bett? | Ja, ich bin krank. |
| Wo haben Sie diese Veilchen (*pl.*) gefunden? | Ich habe sie in dem Feld gefunden. |

Haben Sie keine (none) in | Nein, ich kann keine (cannot —
Ihrem Garten? | any) finden
Für wen (whom) sind diese | Sie sind für das Kind meines
Kirschen? | Nachbars.
Von wem haben Sie diese Ge= | Von meinem Vater und von mei=
schenke (pl.) erhalten (received)? | ner Mutter.
Von was sprechen die Soldaten? | Sie sprechen vom Krieg (war).
Ist Ihre Mutter zu Hause? | Nein, sie ist nicht zu Hause, sie
 | ist ausgegangen (gone out).

# Ninth Lesson.*)

## Irregularities in the formation of the plural.

Most of the exceptions, which in other grammars are included amongst the declensions, are irregular only in the plural. We therefore think it proper to range them all under one head.

### I. Irregular plurals of the **first** declension.

§ 1. The following substantives take n in the plural without modifying the vowel:

Der Vater the Bavarian. | der Nachbar the neighbour.
der Bauer the peasant. | der Stachel the sting.
der Vetter the (male) cousin. | der Pantoffel the slipper.
der Gevatter the godfather. | der Muskel the muscle.

*Plur.* Die Baiern, die Bauern, die Vettern, die Nachbarn ꝛc.

*Note.* The word der Charakter has in the *pl.* die Charaktere.

§ 2. Words taken from the Latin in or with the accent on the last syllable but one, form their plural in oren:

Der Doktor the doctor;    *pl.* die Dokto'ren
der Professor the professor;    *pl.* die Professo'ren ꝛc.

*Note.* Der Major' the major; *pl.* die Majo're (3rd decl. 4).

### II. Irregular plurals of the **third** declension.

§ 3. Eight words take in the plural en instead of e:

Der Staat the state. | der Schmerz the pain.
der Strahl the beam, ray. | der Mast the mast.
der Sporn the spur. | der Pfau the pea-cock.
der Dorn the thorn. | der See**) the lake.

*Plur.* Die Staaten, die Strahlen, die Schmerzen, die Seen ꝛc

---

*) The 9th and 10th lessons may be reserved for some weeks later.
**) Notice: There is also a *feminine* word die See the sea
(= das Meer) which has no plural.

§ 4. The following masculine nouns take **er** in the plural, at the same time modifying the vowel ·

| | |
|---|---|
| Der Mann the man, husband. | der Rand the edge. |
| der Wald the forest. | der Gott the God. |
| der Leib the body. | der Ort the place. |
| der Geist the mind, ghost. | der Vormund the guardian. |
| der Wurm the worm. | der Reichtum the riches. |
| | der Irrtum the mistake, error. |

*Plur.* Die **Männer**, die Wälder, die Leiber, die Würmer ꝛc.

## III. Irregularities of the fourth declension.

§ 5. Twenty-nine feminine monosyllables form their plural in **en**, without modifying the vowel:

| | |
|---|---|
| Die Art the kind, species. | die Pflicht the duty. |
| die Bahn the road. | die Post the post-office, post. |
| die Bank the bank. | die Qual the torment, pang. |
| die Bucht the bay. | die Schar the troop. |
| die Burg the old castle, strong hold. · | die Schlacht the battle. |
| die Fahrt the passage. | die Schrift the writing. |
| die Flur the field or fields.*) | die Schuld the debt. |
| die Flut the flood. | die Spur the trace, track. |
| die Form the form. | die That the deed. |
| die Frau the woman. | die Tracht the costume. |
| die Glut the blaze. | die Uhr the watch, clock. |
| die Jagd the chase. | die Wahl the choice, election. |
| die Last the load, weight. | die Welt the world. |
| die Mark the boundary, mark. | die Zahl the number, figure. |
| | die Zeit the time. |

*Plur.* Die **Bahnen** (Eisenbahnen railroads), die Banken, die Frauen, die Lasten, die Pflichten, die Schlachten, die Schulden, die Thaten, die Uhren, die Welten, die Zahlen, die Zeiten.

§ 6. The termination **e** is assumed for the plural by four polysyllabic feminine words ending in **nis** and **sal**:

| | |
|---|---|
| Die Kenntnis knowledge; | *pl.* die Kenntnisse. |
| die Besorgnis fear; | *pl.* die Besorgnisse apprehensions. |
| die Trübsal sorrow; | *pl.* die Trübsale. |
| die Drangsal vexation; | *pl.* die Drangsale miseries etc. |

§ 7. The two words: die **Mutter** (the mother) and die **Tochter** (the daughter) form their plural:

         die **Mütter**.      | die **Töchter** (see p. 40).

---

## Words.

| | |
|---|---|
| Die Sonne *f.* the sun. | leben (or wohnen) to live. |
| das Schlafzimmer the bedroom. | der Heide the heathen. |

---

*) The German word **Flur** mostly means fields and meadows together, the whole of the fields or grounds of a village, township etc.

die Erbe the earth.  
immer always.  
arm poor.  reich rich.

berühmt celebrated.  
hell or klar clear.

## Reading Exercise. 17.

Die Stacheln der Biene. Die Pantoffeln der Gräfin. Die Bauern sind nicht reich. Die Professoren dieser Schule sind berühmt. Die Strahlen der Sonne sind warm. Das Kind leidet (suffers) große Schmerzen. Wer sind diese Männer? Die Würmer leben in der Erde. Diese Uhren sind sehr klein. Ich kenne meine Pflichten. Die Dornen der Rosen sind klein. Dieses Land hat viele Eisenbahnen.

## Aufgabe. 18.

Where are my slippers? Your slippers are in your bedroom. The students praise (loben) their professors, but the professors praise not always their pupils. Those forests are very large. Do you know these men? I have seen two tall (große) men. I know my duties. These women are very poor. The peasants have cows and oxen. The beams of the sun are very warm. The cocks have spurs. The water of the lakes is clear. Do you know the names of the gods of the heathens? The roses have thorns. The united (vereinigten) States of (von) America are very rich.

---

# IV. Irregularities of the fifth declension.

§ 8. Seven neuter words form their plural by taking en:

| | |
|---|---|
| Das Bett the bed; | pl. die Betten. |
| das Hemd the shirt; | pl. die Hemden. |
| das Herz the heart; | pl. die Herzen. |
| das Ohr the ear; | pl. die Ohren. |
| das Auge the eye; | pl. die Augen. |
| das Ende the end; | pl. die Enden. |
| das Insekt the insect; | pl. die Insekten. |

§ 9. A few monosyllabic neuter words do not follow the general rule in forming their plural: they take e instead of er, and do not alter the vowel.

1) Those ending in r; they are eight:

| | |
|---|---|
| das Haar the hair. | das Paar the pair, couple. |
| das Heer the army. | das Rohr the reed. |
| das Jahr the year. | das Tier the animal, beast. |
| das Meer the sea. | das Thor the gate. |

Plur. Die Haare, die Jahre, die Meere, die Tiere ꝛc.

Note. A second r would render the sound too harsh.

4*

2) Those which would be confounded in the plural
with similar words ending in **er***); they are four:

Das Schaf the sheep.          das Seil (Tau) the rope.
das Schiff the ship.          das Spiel the play, game.

*Plur.* Die Schafe, die Schiffe, die Spiele ic.

3) Also the following take **e**\*\*):

Das Bein the leg.             das Netz the net.
das Beil the hatchet.         das Pferd the horse.
das Brot the bread.           das Recht the right.
das Boot the boat.            das Reh the deer, roe.
das Ding the thing.           das Reich the empire, kingdom.
das Fell the hide, skin.      das Roß the horse, steed.
das Pfund the pound.          das Salz the salt.
das Gift the poison.          das Schwein the pig, swine.
das Heft the copy-book.       das Werk the work.
das Joch the yoke.            das Stück the piece.
das Knie the knee.            das Zeug (the) stuff.
das Los the lot, fate.        das Ziel the aim, end, goal.

*Plur.* Die Beine, die Beile, die Pferde, die Werke ic.

§ 10. The following neuter words of *two* syllables
take **er** in the plural:

Das Gemüt the temper.         das Gewand the garment.
das Geschlecht the gender.    das Regiment' the regiment.
das Gemach the apartment.     das Spital' the hospital.

*Plur.* Die Gemüter, die Geschlechter, die Gewänder,
        die Regimenter, die Spitäler ic.

§ 11. A few neuter words terminated in **al** and **ium**
derived from the Latin, take **ien** in the plural:

    das Kapital' the capital, fund;    *pl.* die Kapita'lien.
    das Mineral' the mineral;          *pl.* die Minera'lien.
    das Studium the study,             *pl.* die Stu'dien.

## V. Additional remarks on the plural.

§ 12. Several nouns have a double form of the
plural, when their meaning is different:

---

*) For instance, the plural of Schaf regularly formed should
be Schäfer. Now there is such a word: *pl.* die Schäfer meaning the
*shepherds.* Thus: der Seiler = the rope-maker; der Schiffer the
boatman; der Spieler the player, *pl.* die Spieler the players.
\*\*) Most of them have a double vowel which does not admit
of a modification. Where one has been dropped in the German
orthography, it appears still in the English words, as: Brot from
bread, Pfund from pound, Schaf from sheep etc.

Die Bank = { the bench; *pl.* die Bänfe. <br> { the bank; *pl.* die Banfen.

Das Band\*) = { the ribbon; *pl.* die Bänder. <br> { the bond, tie; *pl.* die Bande.

das Ding the thing; *pl* { die Dinge. <br> { die Dinger (contemptuously or jokingly).

das Geficht { the face; *pl.* die Geficter. <br> { the vision; *pl* die Geficte.

das Wort the word; *pl.* { die Wörter = separate words. <br> { die Worte = expressions.

das Land the country; *pl.* die Länder and (poet.) die Lande.

§ 13. There are a great many German substantives which, from their signification, cannot be used in the plural, whilst others are wanting in the singular. To the first kind (no plural) belong:

1) The names of metals:

Das Gold gold        | das Eifen iron <br>
das Silber silver       | das Blei lead, etc.

2) The names of substances and materials:

Der Honig honey.       | das Mehl meal, flour. <br>
das Wachs wax.        | die Gerfte barley. <br>
das Fleifch meat.       | der Sand sand.

3) General and abstract terms, such as:

Die Liebe love.        | die Jugend youth. <br>
das Glück hapiness     | der Ruhm glory, fame. <br>
die Kälte cold         | der Schlaf sleep. <br>
die Wärme warmth.     | der Hunger hunger

*NB.* The pupil will observe that in German all such names of metals, materials and abstract terms have the article.

§ 14. Others from their signification require a plural, but as they naturally admit of none, the plural must be borrowed from similar compound words:

Das Lob praise; *pl.* die Lobes-Erhebungen. <br>
der Rat advice; *pl.* die Ratfchläge. <br>
der Streit contention, quarrel; *pl.* die Streitigfeiten. <br>
das Unglück misfortune; *pl.* die Unglücksfälle. <br>
die Ehre the honour; *pl* die Ehrenbezeugungen.\*\*) <br>
die Gunft the favour; *pl.* die Gunftbezeugungen. <br>
der Tod death, *pl.* die Todesfälle.

---

\*) Der Band *m.* means the volume, *pl.* die Bände. <br>
\*\*) There is also a plural die Ehren

§ 15.  Masculine and neuter*) nouns indicating *measure*, *weight* and *number*, though having a regular plural, retain the form of the *singular* when preceded by a numeral and followed by an adjective or substantive ·

Der Fuß the foot; as: fünf Fuß (not Füße) lang five feet long.
der Zoll the inch; as: vier Zoll breit four inches wide.
der Grad the degree; as: zwanzig Grad Kälte 20 degrees cold.
das Pfund the pound; as: drei Pfund Zucker three p. *of* sugar.
das Paar**) the pair; as: zwei Paar Schube two pair *of* shoes.
das Dutzend dozen, as. 6 Dutzend Handschuhe six dozen gloves.
das Buch the quire; as: zehn Buch Papier ten quires *of* paper.
der Mann the man, as: fünfhundert Mann Infanterie 500 foot.
das Stück the piece; as: neun Stück Tuch nine pieces *of* cloth.

§ 16.  The following words have no singular:

Die Leute people.
die Kosten ⎰ the expense,
die Unkosten ⎱ the costs.
die Eltern the parents.
die Trümmer the ruins.
die Molken the whey.

die Truppen the troops.
die Einkünfte the revenue
die Ferien the holidays
die Geschwister the brothers and sisters.

§ 17.  Substantives compounded with „mann“ mostly change it in the plural into =leute:***)

Der Hauptmann the captain; *pl* die Hauptleute.
der Handelsmann tradesman; *pl* die Handelsleute.
der Kaufmann the merchant; *pl.* die Kaufleute.
der Schiffmann the sailor; *pl* die Schiffleute.
der Seemann the seaman; *pl* die Seeleute.
der Edelmann the nobleman; *pl* die Edelleute.
der Hofmann the courtier; *pl.* die Hofleute.

---

## Words.

Der Dichter the poet.
schädlich hurtful.  tapfer brave.
französisch French.
der Kranke the sick (man), patient
der Fremde the foreigner, stranger.
der Kaffee coffee.  tief deep.
blau blue.  die Schlacht battle.
die Biene the bee.

stechen to prick (of needles, plants, like roses etc.).
stechen to sting (of insects, like bees, and other animals).
kämpfen (fechten) to fight.
Tiergattung kind (genus) of animals.
gehören to belong.

---

*) Feminine words are used in the plural, as ·
Vier Ellen Tuch four ells *or* yards *of* cloth;
Zehn Flaschen Wein ten bottles *of* wine
**) Ein paar signifies *a few*, as· ein paar Tage a few days.
***) Ehemänner are husbands; Eheleute married people.

## Reading Exercise. 19.

Die Inſekten ſind den Früchten der Bäume ſchädlich  Die Tiere haben Felle.  Die Haare des Mädchens ſind lang  Die franzöſiſchen Heere haben tapfer gefochten (fought bravely)  Die Meere ſind tief.  Die Knaben haben ihre Hefte verloren  Die Werke der Dichter ſind berühmt.  Die Mineralien liegen in der Erde.  Die Kranken ſind in den Spitälern.  Der Fremde hat zwei Paar Stiefel und drei Paar Schuhe.  Viele Kaufleute ſind reich  Ich habe fünf Pfund Zucker und drei Pfund Kaffee gekauft.*)  Ich kenne dieſe Leute nicht  Die Augen des Kindes ſind blau.

## Aufgabe. 20.

These parents have lost all (alle) their children.  We have sheep and pigs.  My neighbour has no horses.  The towns of that country are very small  The rich (reichen) people live in the towns, or in (auf) the country.  The knives and hatchets are sharpened (geſchliffen).  Open (Öffnen Sie) your eyes. We have two ears  In the hearts of the children  The bees are insects.  The salts are minerals.  The boy was five years old (alt).  The sailors have lost four boats.  The ships of the merchants are lost.  In our town [there] are two regiments [of] riflemen (Schützen).  I speak of (von) the battles (*Dat*) of the Romans (Römer).

## Conversation.

| | |
|---|---|
| Kennen Sie meine Nachbarn? | Ich kenne Ihre Nachbarn und Ihre Nachbarinnen. |
| Was verkaufen dieſe Bauern? | Sie verkaufen Kartoffeln. |
| Wo ſind die Pantoffeln meiner Mutter? | Sie ſind in ihrem (her) Schlafzimmer. |
| Wer iſt da (there)? | Die Doktoren ſind da. |
| Lieben Sie Ihre Vettern? | Ich liebe alle meine Vettern |
| Wer ſind dieſe Herren? | Es (they) ſind Kaufleute. |
| Wo ſind die Männer? | Sie ſind im Garten. |
| Womit ſtechen uns die Roſen? | Mit ihren Dornen. |
| Womit kämpfen die Hähne? | Mit ihren Spornen. |
| Wieviele Augen und Ohren hat ein Menſch? | Ein Menſch hat zwei Augen und zwei Ohren. |
| Zu welcher Tiergattung gehören die Bienen? | Sie ſind Inſekten. |
| Sind Ihre Pferde alt? | Nein, ſie ſind jung. |
| Wer ſind dieſe Leute? | Sie (or es) ſind Amerikaner. |

---

*) or '2½ Kilo Zucker und 1½ Kilo Kaffee', one Kilogram or 'Kilo' of the new German weight being equal to two pounds (Pfund) of the old, which in common life is still very much used.

Kennen Sie die Werke dieses Ja, seine Werke sind sehr berühmt.
Dichters?
Sind alle Meere tief?      Nein, nicht alle Meere sind tief.
Leben die Affen in Wäldern oder Sie leben in Wäldern.
in der Ebene?

---

# · Tenth Lesson.

## On the Gender of Substantives.*)

(Bon dem Geschlecht der Hauptwörter.)

The gender of the German nouns substantive having
been established in course of time, not according to fixed
principles, but rather by custom and arbitrary use, general and precise rules cannot be given. This circumstance renders the study of the German language somewhat more difficult than it otherwise would be.

The knowledge of the gender however being indispensable, we recommend the pupil, when learning a German substantive, carefully to acquire at the same time
the article denoting the gender. We shall therefore accompany each with its corresponding article.

The gender of a substantive may be known either
by its *signification*, or by its *termination*.

### A. Masculine (männlich) are·

1) All appellations of men and male animals:

| | |
|---|---|
| Der Bater the father. | der Wolf the wolf. |
| der König the king. | der Bär the bear. |
| der Lehrer the teacher, master. | der Hahn the cock. |
| der Schneider the tailor. | der Adler the eagle. |

*Except* the diminutives in chen and lein, which are all neuter,
as: das Väterchen, das Söhnlein the little son, das Hähnchen chicken
(comp. No. 4).

*Note:* This rule explains why all those substantives of the 2nd
decl. ending in e (see p. 31 and 32), like der Knabe the boy, der
Affe the monkey etc., are of the *masculine* gender. It is because they
denote *male living beings.* •

2) The names of the seasons, months and days:

| | |
|---|---|
| Der Winter winter. | der Montag Monday. |
| der Sommer summer. | der Freitag Friday. |
| der Mai May. | der Morgen the morning. |
| der Juli July. | der Abend the evening. |

---

*) See the footnote *) p. 49.

3) The names of stones.

Der Diamant' the diamond. | der Rubin' the ruby.
der Kiesel the flint. | der Stein the stone.

4) Most words ending in **en** which are neither *diminutives* in **chen** nor substantified *infinitives\**) as:

Der Garten the garden. | der Rücken the back.
der Regen the rain. | der Namen the name.
der Boden the floor, ground. | der Faden the thread.

*Except*: Das Kissen the cushion; das Becken the basin; das Wappen the coat of arms.

5) Five words ending in double **e**:

Der Schnee snow | der Kaffee coffee.
der See\*\*) the lake. | der Thee tea  der Klee clover.

6) All derivatives ending in **ig, ich, ing** and **ling**:

Der König the king. | der Hering\*\*\*) the herring.
der Teppich the carpet. | der Jüngling the youth.

---

## B.  Of the feminine gender (weiblich) are:

1) All female names and appellations: ·

Die Frau the woman. | die Königin the queen.
die Tochter the daughter. | die Amme the nurse.

*Except* the words  Das Weib the wife; das Frauenzimmer a female person, a woman; das Mädchen the girl, and das Fräulein Miss, the two latter because they are *diminutives*, viz. of die Magd (maid) and die Frau (woman).

2) All dissyllabic substantives ending in **e** (not ee), with their compounds, *denoting inanimate objects* (S. p. 56, *Note*):

Die Blume the flower. | die Kirsche the cherry.
die Schule the school. | die Birne the pear.
die Stunde the hour. | die Eiche the oak.
die Straße the street. | die Tanne the fir.
die Erde earth. | die Ehre the honour.
die Liebe love. | die Hilfe†) the help.

*Note 1.*  Hence the *sun* is feminine in German, die Sonne; but the *moon* is always masculine: der Mond.

*Except* the three words  das Auge the eye; das Ende the end, das Erbe the inheritance, in which words the final **e** is only added for euphony, for Aug, End, Erb

---

\*) These both are *neuter*, see C. 4 and 5, p. 59.
\*\*) See the foot-note \*\*) p. 49.
\*\*\*) For more words of this kind see p 37, § 3
†) See also the 4th declension p. 40.

*Note 2.* Words like ber 𝔑ame, ber 𝔖ame ⁊c (see p 29, Obs. 1) cannot be considered exceptions, as their true form ends in en: ber 𝔑amen, ber 𝔖amen ⁊c.

3) All *derivative* nouns formed with the final syllables ei*) (old ei)), ḥeit, feit, ſḍaft, ung and in; and all nouns of foreign origin in ie, ion, if and tät (S. p. 40):

Die Sḍmeiḍelei flattery.   |   bie Überſetzung the translation.
bie Sflaberei slavery.   |   bie Ḥoffnung hope.
bie Freiḥeit liberty.   |   bie Sḍäferin the shepherdess
bie Sḍönḥeit beauty.   |   bie Poeſie' poetry.
bie Freunbſḍaft friendship.   |   bie Perſon' the person.
bie Danfbarfeit gratitude.   |   bie Majeſtät Majesty.

*Except* bas Petſḍaft the seal, and ber Ḥornung, an old word for Februar February.

4) The few nouns ending in aḍt, uḍt, ulb and unſt:

Die Sḍlaḍt the battle.   |   bie Gebulb patience
bie Naḍt the night.   |   bie Sḍulb guilt, debt.
bie Buḍt the bay, gulf.   |   bie Vernunft reason.
bie Ḥulb the favour.   |   bie Anfunft the arrival etc.

---

## C. Of the neuter gender (ſäḍliḍ) are·

1) The letters of the alphabet: bas 𝔅, bas 𝔐, bas 𝖅.

2) The names of metals, *except:* ber Staḥl, the steel, bie Platina platina or platinum, also called 'white gold'; but bas Platin.

Das Golb gold.   |   bas Eiſen iron.
bas Silber silver.   |   bas Blei lead.

3) The names of countries and places (cities, villages, provinces, islands etc.) Franfreiḍ France; 𝔑om Rome. — The article bas however is only used, when an adjective precedes: bas fatḥoliſḍe Spanien Catholic Spain; bas reiḍe Lonbon ⁊c. **)

*Except* bie Sḍweiz Switzerland and all names of countries ending in ei which are *feminine* such as bie Türfei Turkey, bie Mongolei Mongolia, bie Tartarei Tartary, bie Buḍarei Bokhora etc cfr. p. 58, B, 3) and p. 67, 1). Moreover some *masculine* names of provinces and countries as ber Breisgau, ber Sunbgau, ber Vorarl‧berg ⁊c.

---

*) Das Ei the egg; ber Sḍrei or bas Geſḍrei the cry, scream; ber Brei pap, are no *derivatives*, but *roots*.

**) But when the name of a country is masculine or feminine, it takes the article, as: ber Breisgau, bie Pfalz ⁊c.

4) The infinitive mood, when used substantively:

Das Essen eating.
bas Trinken drinking.
bas Leben life.

bas Rauchen smoking.
bas Lesen reading.
bas Vergnügen the pleasure.

5) All diminutives in chen and lein, without exception:

Das Mädchen the girl.
bas Häuschen the little house.

bas Kindlein the baby.
bas Blümchen the little flower.

6) Most collectives beginning with the prefix Ge and which have for their root vowel one of the *thin* vowels e, i, ä, ö, ü, as:

Das Gebirge the mountain.
bas Gemälde the picture.
bas Gewölf the clouds.

bas Gebäude the building.
bas Geschäft the business.
bas Geschenk the present.

*Exception*: die Geschichte history.

*NB* Collectives with Ge having for their root vowel one of the *dark* vowels a, o, u or au mostly are Masc as ber Gebanke the thought, ber Gebrauch the use, ber Geschmad taste, ber Geruch the smell

*Exc* : *Fem* are die Gefahr the danger, bie Geburt birth, bie Gewalt power, bie Gestalt shape, bie Gebulb patience, and a few others

7) Substantives ending in nis are partly neuter, partly feminine; their number however is very small.

*neuter.*

Das Zeugnis the evidence.
Das Begräbnis the funeral.
bas Bedürfnis the want.
bas Gedächtnis the memory, etc.

*feminine.*

die Finsternis the darkness.
die Kenntnis knowledge.
die Betrübnis affliction.
die Erlaubnis permission, etc.

## D. Gender of compound substantives.

The gender of *compound substantives* is generally that of the last component. bie Hausthüre the street-door (from bas Haus and bie Thüre); bas Tintenfaß the ink-stand; ber Kalbsbraten roast veal; bie Winterzeit winter.

*Except*: bie Großmut generosity, bie Sanstmut meekness, and bie Demut humbleness (from ber Mut disposition of mind, courage).

*Note.* Die Antwort the answer, is not a compound word.

## E. Double Gender.

The following nouns have a double gender on account of their different meaning:

| *masc.* | *fem* or *neuter.* |
|---|---|
| Der Band the volume. | Das Band the ribbon, tie, bond. |
| der Bauer the peasant. | das Bauer the bird-cage. |
| der Chor the chorus. | das Chor the choir. |
| der Erbe the heir. | das Erbe the inheritance. |
| der Heide the heathen. | die Heide (or Haide) the heath. |
| der Hut the hat. | die Hut (the) heed, guard. |
| der Kiefer the jaw. | die Kiefer the pine (a sort of fir). |
| der Kunde the customer. | die Kunde knowledge, news. |
| der Leiter the conductor | die Leiter the ladder. |
| der Schild the shield. | das Schild the sign (of an inn). |
| der See the lake. | die See the sea. |
| der Thor the fool. | das Thor the gate. |
| der Verdienst the gain. | das Verdienst merit. |

## F.   Formation of female appellations.

Most appellations of male individuals allow a female appellation to be formed, by adding the syllable **in:**

| *masc.* | *fem.* |
|---|---|
| Der König the king. | die Königin*) the queen. |
| der Fürst ⎫ the prince. | die Fürstin ⎫ the princess. |
| der Prinz ⎰ | die Prinzessin ⎰ |
| der Maler the painter. | die Malerin the female painter. |
| der Nachbar the neighbour. | die Nachbarin the « neighbour. |
| der Künstler the artist | die Künstlerin the female artist. |
| der Engländer the Englishman. | die Engländerin the English lady. |

1) When monosyllables, they modify their vowel.

| | |
|---|---|
| Der Graf the count. | die Gräfin the countess. |
| der Koch the cook. | die Köchin the female cook. |
| der Hund the dog. | die Hündin the bitch. |
| der Wolf the wolf. | die Wölfin the she-wolf etc. |

2) If the masculine ends in e, this letter is rejected:

| | |
|---|---|
| Der Russe the Russian. | die Russin the Russian lady. |
| der Franzose the Frenchman. | die Französin the French lady. |
| der Löwe the lion. | die Löwin the lioness. |

*Exception:* der Deutsche the German, *fem.* die Deutsche the German lady. (See also the *Note* 1, p. 69 )

3) Wen the gender of persons or animals is denoted by different words, the syllable in is not added.

---

*) In the plural all these nouns double their n: Königinnen.

Der Herr { the master, Mr., the gentleman. | Die Frau } the mistress, wife, die Dame } the lady.
der Vater the father. | die Mutter the mother.
der Sohn the son | die Tochter the daughter.
der Bruder the brother. | die Schwester the sister.
der Oheim, Onkel the uncle. | die Tante the aunt.
der Neffe nephew. | die Nichte the niece.
der Vetter the cousin. | die Base (Kousine) the cousin.
der Knabe the boy. | das Mädchen the girl.
der Jüngling the youth. | das Fräulein (the) Miss.
der Junggesell the bachelor. | die Jungfer (Jungfrau) the maid.
der Bräutigam the bridegroom. | die Braut the bride.
der Witwer the widower. | die Witwe the widow.

## Words.

Der Tiger the tiger. | der Gärtner the gardener.
Der Winter (the) winter. | der Schauspieler the actor.
die Zeit (the) time | die Kürze (the) shortness.
die Dichterin the poetess. | der Stein the stone.
ein Schäfer a shepherd. | hatte, hatten had.

### Reading Exercise. 21.

Meine Ehre. Jene Straße. Unsre Hoffnung. Jene Tanne ist hoch. Die Schweiz ist schön. Wilhelm war ein Junggesell. Der Sommer ist warm Wir hatten einen Diamanten. Haben Sie die Fürstin gesehen? Sie ist sehr (very) schön. Dieses Frauenzimmer ist sehr jung Unser Oheim und unsre Tante haben ein Schloß in Spanien (Spain). Der Gärtner hatte eine Rose; die Gärtnerin hatte ein rotes (red) Band. Geben Sie mir diesen Band (m.). Die Frau hatte ein Häuschen und ein Gärtchen.

### Aufgabe. 22.

1. My teacher. His friendship. The count and the countess. This man is a painter. That lady is a princess. My father is your neighbour Your aunt is my neighbour Here is a lion and a lioness, a tiger and a tigress. This woman is a widow. Where is the cook (f.)? My master is old. The baby is young. (The) winter is cold This diamond is beautiful. Here is also a ruby. My sister is a shepherdess This oak is very (sehr) old. Give me a cherry. Which youth (A, 7.) is your son?

2. The friendship of my [female] cousin. The earth is round (rund). The love of the mother. (The) iron is a metal. (The) gold is also a metal. The little house (dim.). The little horse. A little plate. The shortness of (the) time. Have you seen (gesehen) the actor and the actress? My daughter is a poetess I have seen the bridegroom and the bride. My uncle is a bachelor His niece is very young Is it a he-wolf or a she-wolf? It is a he-wolf.

## Conversation.

| | |
|---|---|
| Wo ist mein Neffe? | Hier ist er. |
| Wer hat mein Stöckchen? | Ihr Kind hat es. |
| Wer ist dieser Mann? | Er ist ein Künstler. |
| Wer ist diese Dame? | Sie ist eine Dichterin. |
| Sind Sie ein Sänger? | Nein, ich bin kein Sänger; meine Frau (wife) ist eine Sängerin. |
| Hat Ihr Oheim ein Haus? | Ja, er hat ein Häuschen. |
| Haben Sie die Braut gesehen? | Nein, ich habe die Braut nicht gesehen. Der Bräutigam ist hier. |
| Wo ist die Braut? | Sie ist krank (ill). |
| Ist das Gold ein Stein? | Nein, das Gold ist ein Metall. |
| Hast du den Künstler gesehen? | Ja, und auch die Künstlerin. |
| Ist dieser Winter kalt? | Nein, er ist nicht sehr kalt. |
| Haben Sie einen Hund? | Ich habe einen Hund und eine Hündin. |
| Wer hat ein Schloß? | Die Fürstin hat ein Schloß. |
| Ist Ihr Oheim ein Junggesell? | Nein, er ist ein Witwer. |
| Wer ist hier? | Die Schauspielerin ist hier. |
| Ist dieses Tier eine Löwin? | Nein, es ist eine Tigerin. |
| Hat der Gärtner mein Buch? | Nein, die Gärtnerin hat es. |

---

# Eleventh Lesson.

## Declension of (Personal) Proper Nouns.

### (Eigennamen.)

1) The inflexion of Proper Nouns of *persons* should strictly speaking be formed without the article, and simply by the addition of s for the genitive.

### Examples.

| | | |
|---|---|---|
| *N.* Plato Plato. | Homer' Homer. | Schill'er Schiller. |
| *G.* Platos | Homers | Schillers |
| *D.* Plato | Homer | Schiller |
| *A.* Plato. | Homer | Schiller. |

### Examples of Christian names.

| | |
|---|---|
| *N.* Ludwig Lewis (or der L.). | Friedrich Frederick. |
| *G.* Ludwigs*) (or des Ludwig) | Friedrichs (or des Friedrich) |
| *D.* Ludwig (or dem Ludwig) | Friedrich (or dem Friedrich) |
| *A.* Ludwig (or den Ludwig). | Friedrich (or den Friedrich). |

---

*) now without apostrophe.

Such are:

| | | |
|---|---|---|
| Georg George. | Karl Charles. | Heinrich Henry. |
| Wilhelm William. | Eduard Edward. | Johann John. |

*Note.* The definite article is used before a Proper name, when it is accompanied by an adjective, as:

der arme Heinrich poor Henry; *Gen.* des armen Heinrich.

The learner however must not forget, that the use of the definite article together with the inflexion at the end of the name, is not good German; des armen Heinrichs would be wrong.

2) Masculine names ending in ß, z, tz, x or sch, require in the *genitive*, when used without the article, the termination ens, and in the dative en:

| | | | |
|---|---|---|---|
| *N.* Weiß | Schulz | Max | Fritz |
| *G.* Weißens | Schulzens | Maxens | Fritzens |
| *D.* Weißen. | Schulzen. | Maxen. | Fritzen |

3) The same mode is adopted for the *feminine* names ending in e, and is preferable to the use of the article

| | | |
|---|---|---|
| *N.* Luise Louisa. | Marie' Mary. | Elise Eliza. |
| *G.* Luisens or der Luise | Mari'ens or der M. | Elisens or der Elise |
| *D.* Luisen or der Luise | Mari'en or der M. | Elisen or der Elise |
| *A.* Luise or (die) Luise | Marie or die Marie. | Elise or die Elise. |

Such are.

| | |
|---|---|
| Emi'lie Emily. | Mar'garete Margaret. |
| Ama'lie Amelia. | Lu'cie Lucy. |
| Eli'sabeth Elisabeth | Ka'roline Caroline. |
| Hen'riette Henrietta, Harriet. | Johan'ne Hannchen Jane. |

*Note 1* Feminine names in a take only s in the Genitive and remain unchanged in the two other cases, as:

Emmas, Saras, Annas, Rosas, Lauras, Franziskas

*Note 2.* When *Mary* is the name of a queen or other historical person, it is Maria, as: Maria Stuart, Maria There'sia (empress of Austria) etc *G.* Marias.

4) When foreign names end in a single s, as Alcibi'ades, Eli'as, Augu'stus ec., the article is required for the genitive and sometimes for the two other cases.

| | |
|---|---|
| *N.* Augustus Augustus | *D.* (dem) Augustus to Aug. |
| *G.* des Augustus of Aug. | *A.* (den) Augustus Augustus. |

Examples

Das Leben des Alcibiades the life of Alcibiades.
Der Tod des Augustus the death of Augustus.
Ich bewundre So'krates (or den Sokr.) I admire Socrates.

*Note 1.* Chriſtus always has the Latin genitive Chriſti, and Jeſus has *G.* Jeſu, as:

Das Leben Jeſu the life of Jesus.
Die Lehre Jeſu Chriſti the doctrine of Jesus Christ.

*Note 2.* The word Gott (God) is considered as a proper name and declined without the article, as follows:

*N.* Gott. *G.* Gottes of God. *D.* Gott *A.* Gott.

5) As in English, the proper name in the genitive without the article often precedes the other noun:

Schillers Werke the works of Schiller.
Homer's Iliade the Iliad of Homer.
Emi'liens und Roſas Handſchuhe Emily and Rosa's gloves.

*Note.* The use of the apostrophy before s as the sign of the genitive case is now abolished in Christian names as well as in all other substantives, it is only placed now *instead* of the s in such Christian names which do not form their genitive in s, as for inst. Voß' Luiſe, Rubens' Gemälde, Zedliß' Gedichte (Luisa by Voss, the picture of Rubens, the poems of Zedlitz.

6) In the *dative* case, masculine names generally remain unchanged. We say: bei Homer, von Schiller, zu Göthe, unter Auguſtus ꝛc., not: bei dem Homer, von dem Schiller ꝛc. With *Christian names*, however, the article is often employed; we may say:

Geben Sie dieſes Buch dem Karl, dem Ludwig, dem Friedrich, which is better than the old form. Karln, Ludwigen.

7) The *accusative* of *masculine* names should be used, like the nominative, without the article:

Ich leſe Schiller I read Schiller.
Ich kenne Lamartine I know Lamartine.

*Christian names* however admit of both forms, but the first mode is better:

Rufe (den) Friedrich und Heinrich call Frederick and Henry.
Ich kenne Marie or die Marie I know Mary.
Rufen Sie (die) Sara oder die Katharine call Sarah or Catharine.

8) If a proper name is preceded by a common name, as: (der) Herr Mr.; Frau or Madame Mrs.; Fräulein Miss; or der König, die Königin, der General ꝛc., the latter is declined, while the proper name remains unchanged, as

| | |
|---|---|
| *N.* (der) Herr Schmidt Mr. Smith. | (die) Frau Weber. |
| *G.* des Herrn Schmidt of Mr. S. | der Frau Weber. |
| *D.* dem Herrn Schmidt to Mr. S. | der Frau Weber. |
| *A.* (den) Herrn Schmidt Mr. S. | die Frau Weber. |

Ex.: Die Regierung des Königs Ludwig the reign of king L.

*Note* In the inverted form however, when the proper name is followed by a noun substantive, without the article, the common name preceding remains unchanged, whilst the proper name must be in the genitive, as in English. Ex.:

König Heinrichs Tod king Henry's death (instead of der Tod des Königs Heinrich).
König Ludwigs Regierung.

9) If two or more names appear together, the last only is to be modified:

Friedrich Schillers Werke Frederick Schiller's works.
Karl Friedrichs Ruhm Charles Frederick's renown.
Alexander Humboldts Reisen Alex. Humboldt's travels.

10) When a proper name is followed by an adjective, in form of an apposition, *both* are declined as follows:

N. Karl der Große Charlemagne (Charles the Great).
G. Karls des Großen of Charlemagne.
D. Karl dem Großen to Charlemagne.
A. Karl den Großen Charlemagne.

### Example.

Nach dem Tode Heinrichs des Vierten after the death of Henry IV.

11) In the same way, one noun being in apposition with another noun, both must be in the same case:

Give it to my friend, (the) doctor A.
Geben Sie es meinem Freunde, dem Doktor A.

Likewise: Nach dem Tode des Königs, Heinrichs des Vierten.

*Note 1.* If a plural of proper names is required, it should be indicated only by the article die, without any inflexion, as die Racine, die Schiller, die Rückert ꝛc. — Some however may be declined as common names, viz. with e those of male persons, as: die Heinriche, with en those of females, as: die Wilhelminen, die zwei Marien ꝛc.

*Note 2.* Some Christian names both of the masculine and feminine gender may be changed into a diminutive by adding the syllable chen, as Karlchen, Albertchen, Luischen, Mariechen. — Euphony however will not admit of: Heinrichchen, Ludwigchen.

### Words.

Das Gedicht (*pl* —e) the poem.    das Leben the life.
die Karte the card.    die Iliade the Iliad.
der Sieg the victory    die Tante the aunt
die Regierung the reign.    der Monat the month
das Gesetz (*pl.* —e) the law.    lesen to read. gelesen read.

OTT

erhalten received.
ich denke an I think of.
angekommen arrived.
der fünfte the fifth.

der sechste the sixth.
rufe or rufen Sie call.
gestern yesterday. es it.
war was. auch also

### Reading Exercise. 23.

Der Hut Heinrichs or Heinrichs Hut Die Bücher Wilhelms or Wilhelms Bücher. Lord Broughams Name. Ich liebe Lord Byrons Gedichte. Haben Sie Schiller gelesen? Ich habe Schillers Gedichte gelesen. Ich denke an Luise. Sie denken an Marie. Hier sind Alexander Humboldts Briefe. Saras Mutter ist krank. Friedrich Wilhelms Söhne. Nach dem Tode Karls des Großen. Das Leben Heinrichs des Vierten. Ich habe die Karten des Herrn Hamilton und der Fräulein Schmidt erhalten. Haben Sie (den) Rudolf gesehen? Rufen Sie (den) Robert. Der Sieg des Admirals Nelson bei Trafalgar ist berühmt (celebrated).

### Aufgabe. 24.

1. Frederick's hat. Lewis' books. Mary's sister. The reign of the emperor Augustus. I admire (ich bewundre) Plato Here is the horse of Mr. Stuart. The laws of Solon. The father of poor Charles is arrived Have you read the poems of Goethe? I have read many of them (viele davon). I have bought two hats for George and Edward Henry's books are arrived. I have bought the house of Mr. Smith. We read Cicero. We read also Virgil's Aeneid (Änäi'de) and the Iliad of Homer. Cimon was the son of Miltiades. Victoria is queen of England (von England).

2. The name of Frederick Schiller. The life of Charles the Twelfth (des Zwölften), king (Gen.) of Sweden (von Schweden), was an incessant war (ein beständiger Krieg). The brother of Eliza, and Mary's brother are my friends. Henry the Fifth, king of (von) England, was the son of Henry the Fourth; he married (heira'tete) Catherine, the daughter of Charles the Sixth, king (Gen.) of France (von Frankreich). Give it to my uncle, the doctor (Dat.). The reign of the emperor Charles the Fifth (§ 11). Where is Miss Louisa? She (sie) is with (bei) her aunt, Mrs Walther' (§ 8).

### Conversation.

Wo war Karls Vater gestern? Er war in Frankfurt (Frankfort).
Wo ist Luisens Tante? Sie ist in Hamburg.
Für wen (whom) haben Sie diese Für Karl und Friedrich.
Schuhe gekauft?
Wie heißt die Königin von Sie heißt Viktoria.
England?
Wer war ihr Gemahl (consort)? Prinz Albert.
Wer war Sokrates? Ein berühmter (renowned) Philosoph'.

Wer war der Sieger (conqueror) Der englische Admiral Nelson.
von Trafalgar?
Wer war der Lehrer Alexanders Aristoteles, ein griechischer Welt=
des Großen? weiser (a Grecian philosopher).
Kennen Sie die Gesetze Solons? Ich kenne sie nicht.
Wer war Solon? Ein athenischer Weiser (sage).
Für wen sind diese Bücher? Sie sind für (den) Herrn Maier.
Für wen sind jene Bänder? Sie sind für Madame Walter.
Wem (to whom) geben Sie Ich gebe sie der Luise und der Marie
diese Rosen? (or Luisen und Marien).
Wen rufen Sie? Ich rufe Friedrich und Heinrich.
Haben Sie Miltons „Verlorenes Nein, ich habe es nicht gelesen.
(lost) Paradies" gelesen?

---

# Twelfth Lesson.
## Proper Names of countries, cities etc.

1) Names of countries, cities or towns, villages, provinces and islands have in German, as in English, no
article:

| | |
|---|---|
| Deutschland Germany. | London London. |
| England England. | Berlin' Berlin. Elba Elba. |

*Except:* all *feminine* names of countries, as: die Schweiz
Switzerland, die Türkei' Turkey etc., which are treated as
common names:

G. and D. der Schweiz; *Acc.* die Schweiz (cfr. p. 58, 3,
Exceptions).

Thus also the feminine names of provinces as: die Pfalz
the Palatinate, die Lausitz (Lusatia), die Normandie Normandy
and some few *masculine* names of provinces and countries, as
der Breisgau, Sundgau, Vorarlberg 2c. comp. 10th Less. p. 58,
die Bretagne Britanny 2c.

2) They form their genitive by the addition of s, unless they end in s, z or x:

Die Flüsse Deutschlands the rivers of Germany.
Die Straßen Berlins, Londons 2c.
The streets of Berlin, of London etc.

3) When ending in s, z or x, no termination can be
added, and the genitive is expressed by the preposition
von, as:

Die Straßen von Paris the streets of Paris.

5*

*Note.* The use of the preposition ᵇᵒⁿ is also allowed with other names of countries and towns; but the genitive is better. Thus we may say as well:

Die Produkte von England the products of England.
Die Straßen von London the streets of London.

4) When the proper names of countries, places and months are put in *apposition* with the preceding common name, the preposition *of* is not translated:

Das Königreich Preußen the kingdom *of* Prussia.
Die Stadt London the city *of* London.
Das Dorf Rohrbach the village *of* Rohrbach.
Der Monat Mai the month *of* May.

5) The other cases remain unchanged:

Wir leben in Europa (*dat.*) we live in Europe.
Ich liebe Frankreich (*acc.*) I like France.
Kennen Sie Paris (*acc.*)? do you know Paris?

6) *To* before names of countries and towns must be translated nach, *at* or *in* in*), *from* von or aus, as·

Ich gehe nach Amerika I go *to* America.
Ich schicke Karl nach Wien I send Charles *to* Vienna.
Mein Vater lebt in Paris my father lives *at* Paris.
Ich komme von Brüssel I come *from* Brussels.

7) We subjoin a list of the principal countries:

| | |
|---|---|
| Euro'pa Europe. | Spa'nien Spain. |
| Asien Asia. | Griechenland Greece. |
| Afrika Africa | Preußen Prussia. |
| Ame'rika America. | Sachsen Saxony. |
| Australien Australia. | Baiern Bavaria. |
| Indien India. | Rußland Russia. |
| China China. | Schweden Sweden. |
| Egyp'ten Egypt. | Norwegen Norway. |
| England England. | Dänemark Denmark. |
| Frankreich France. | Holland Holland. |
| Deutschland Germany. | Belgien Belgium. |
| Österreich Austria. | die Schweiz Switzerland. |
| Ita'lien Italy. | die Türkei' Turkey. |

8) The (national) appellations formed of these names of countries end either in er or e.

**a) Appellations ending in er:**

Der Europä'er the European. | der Spa'nier the Spaniard.
der Amerikaner the American. | der Italie'ner the Italian.

---

*) *At* before names of towns is sometimes also expressed with zu. Ex. at Frankfort zu Frankfurt, but in is the best.

der Engländer the Englishman. | der Österreicher the Austrian.
der Schottländer the Scotchman. | der Schweizer the Swiss.
der Irländer the Irishman. | der Römer the Roman, etc.
der Holländer the Dutchman.
These are declined according to the *first* declension.

*b*) The following appellations end in **e**:

Der Deutsche the German. | der Sachse the Saxon.
der Franzose the Frenchman. | der Russe the Russian.
der Grieche the Greek. | der Pole the Pole.
der Preuße the Prussian. | der Türke the Turk.
der Schwede the Swede. | der Däne the Dane.
These follow the *second* declension (like der Knabe).

9) The *feminine* of all these names is formed by the addition of **in**, as: *a*) die Engländerin, die Schweizerin, *b*) die Russin, die Französin, die Türkin 2c. See p. 60, 1 & 2. — The only exception is ·

Die Deutsche the German woman *or* lady.

*Note 1.* The *adjectives* of these names are formed by adding the syllable **isch** instead of **er** or **e**, as. spanisch Spanish; englisch English; französisch French, etc. all spelled with a small letter. See the 18th lesson p. 103, Remark 5.

*Note 2.* The adjectives of names of cities and towns are formed by the addition of **er**, and are invariable. They are used also as nouns as· of Paris Pariser *subst* der Pariser, der Londoner, New-Yorker, Berliner, Heidelberger 2c.

10) The names of rivers, lakes, mountains etc. have always the article, as in English, and are declined as common names according to their respective declensions:

Der Rhein the Rhine. *G.* des Rhein(e)s *D.* dem Rhein(e) 2c.
die Elbe the Elb. *G.* and *D.* der Elbe. *Acc.* die Elbe.
die Pyrenä'en (*pl.*) the Pyrenees *G.* der Pyrenäen *D.* den P. 2c.

11) In English, the names of months and days are considered as proper names, and receive no article; in German both require the definite article, viz.:·

Der Januar January. | der Juli July.
der Februar February. | der August' August.
der März March. | der Septem'ber September.
der April' April. | der Okto'ber October.
der Mai May. | der Novem'ber November.
der Juni June | der Dezem'ber December.
in January etc. is translated im Januar.

der Sonntag Sunday. | der Dienstag Tuesday.
der Montag Monday. | der Mittwoch Wednesday.

der Donnerstag Thursday.     | der Samstag    } Saturday
der Freitag Friday.            | or Sonnabend }
am Sonntag on Sunday.

## Words.

Wien Vienna.                 Köln Cologne.   Paris' Paris.
die Oder the Oder.             die Hauptstadt the capital.
die Donau the Danube       das Gebirge the mountain.
die Insel the island.          das Ufer the bank.   kalt cold.
Frankfurt Frankfort.         kommen to come. gehen to go.

## Reading Exercise. 25.

1 Die Flüsse Rußlands sind groß. Die Thäler der Schweiz
sind schön. Welches (what) sind die Produkte Englands? Die
Straßen Berlins (or von B) sind schön. Napoleon war in Egyp=
ten. Er starb (died) auf der Insel Sankt Helena. Ich war nicht
in Österreich, aber ich war in Preußen. Welches Land ist dieses?
Dieses ist Griechenland. Kennen Sie Philadelphia? Nein, ich
kenne es nicht, ich war nicht in Amerika. Ist dieser Mann ein
Holländer? Nein, er ist ein Irländer; er geht nach Amerika.

2. Ich schicke meinen Sohn nach Paris'. Gu'stav A'dolf
war König von Schweden Kennen Sie die Stadt Frankfurt?
Nein, aber ich kenne die Stadt Köln Der Monat Mai ist der
schönste in Deutschland Der Rhein ist ein großer Fluß Mein
Freund ist im Juni angekommen (arrived). Am Montag oder
Dienstag. Paris ist die Hauptstadt Frankreichs (or von Frankreich).

## Aufgabe. 26.

1. The four largest (größten) rivers of Germany are: the
Rhine, the Elb, the Oder and the Danube The mountains
of Spain are high (hoch). Napoleon was in Russia. The banks
(die Ufer) of the Rhine are beautiful. London is the capital
of England. What (welches) are the productions of Spain?
The streets of Frankfort are narrow (enge). Where do you
come from (Woher' kommen Sie)? I come from England, and
I go *to* France

2 My brothers go *to* Paris. Mr Banks lives (lebt) in
Germany In which town? In the city [*of*] Mainz. (The)
December is cold; July and August are warm. The streets
of Berlin are wide (breit). The houses of the city *of* London
mostly are not high Vienna is the capital of Austria My
nephew (is) arrived in September. The Danube is a very large
(ein sehr großer) river. Come (kommen Sie) on Friday or Saturday.

## Conversation.

Wo waren Sie gestern?       Ich war in Mannheim
Und wo war Ihr Bruder?    Er war in Frankfurt

Welches ist die Hauptstadt von Spanien?
Wo liegt (lies) Hamburg?
Wo sind die Pyrenäen?

Kennen Sie die Schweiz?
Wie heißen (what is the name of) diese zwei Flüsse?
Sind diese Herren (gentlemen) Franzosen?

Wo starb (died) Napoleon?
Welches (what) Land ist dieses?
Waren Sie in Asien?

Woher' (whence) kommen Sie?
Wohin' (where) gehen Sie?
Gehen Sie nach Paris?
Kennen Sie die Türkei?

Wie sind die Straßen Berlins?
In welchem Monat ist Ihr Neffe angekommen?
An (on) welchem Tage?
Wieviele Tage hat der April?
Wieviele Tage hat der Februar?

Madrid ist die Hauptstadt von Spanien.
Hamburg liegt an der Elbe.
Die Pyrenäen liegen zwischen (between) Frankreich und Spanien
Ich kenne die Schweiz und Italien.
Dieser hier ist der Rhein, jener ist die Donau.
Nein, mein Herr, einer von ihnen (of them) ist ein Spanier, der andre (other) ein Russe.
Auf der Insel Sankt Helena.
Dieses ist Frankreich.
Nein, ich war nicht in Asien; aber ich war in Egypten.
Ich komme aus Italien.
Ich gehe nach Rußland.
Ja, nach Paris und nach London.
Ja, ich kenne Griechenland und die Türkei.
Sie sind breit und schön.
Er ist im September angekommen.
Am Donnerstag.
Der April hat dreißig (30) Tage
Der Februar hat nur (only) achtundzwanzig Tage.

---

# Thirteenth Lesson.
## Determinative Adjectives
## or Adjective Pronouns.
### (Bestimmungswörter.)

They are divided into *demonstrative*, *interrogative*, *possessive* and *indefinite numeral adjectives*, and are generally followed by a substantive.

### I. The demonstrative adjectives are:

| Singular. | | | Plural |
| masc. | fem. | neuter. | for all genders. |
|---|---|---|---|
| dieser | diese | dieses this, that. | diese these. |
| jener | jene | jenes that. | jene those. |
| solcher | solche | solches such. | solche such. |
| derselbe | dieselbe | dasselbe the same. | dieselben. |
| der, die, das nämliche the same. | | | die nämlichen. |
| der, die, das andre the other. | | | die andern. |

(For their declension see the first lesson p. 20. The two latter are delined like adjectives, for berfelbe see p. 72, 3.)

1) *That* is generally translated bieſer, bieſe, bieſeß, unless it stands in opposition to *this*, in which case it means jener, jene, jeneß. Ex ·

     Who is that man? wer iſt bieſer Mann?

*Note 1.* *This* and *that*, in immediate connexion with the auxiliary verb to be ſein, and followed by a noun, is translated in the *neuter* form bieſeß or baß, both in the singular and plural (see also the 24th lesson, Obs. 1 and 2) Ex.:

     *This* is my stick bieſeß (not bieſer) or baß iſt mein Stod.
     Are *these* your books ſinb bieſeß (or baß) Jhre Bücher?
     Yes, these are my books ja, bieſeß (or baß) ſinb meine Bücher.

2) Solcher, in the singular, is more used with the indefinite article preceding than alone, and is sometimes followed by it, as in English. Ex.:

     Ein ſolcher Mann (or ſolch' ein Mann) such a man.
     Solche Männer (*pl.*) such men.

3) Derſelbe is declined as follows:

|  | Singular. | | | Plural |
|  | masc. | fem. | neuter. | for all genders. |
| --- | --- | --- | --- | --- |
| N | berſelbe | bieſelbe | baßſelbe. | bieſelben. |
| G. | beßſelben | berſelben | beßſelben. | berſelben. |
| D. | bemſelben | berſelben | bemſelben. | benſelben |
| A. | benſelben | bieſelbe | baßſelbe. | bieſelben |

4) Der nämliche and ber anbre or ein anbrer (*another*) are declined like adjectives (see the 18th lesson). Ex.:

     Die nämlichen Wörter the same words.
     Jch brauche einen anbern Stod I want another stick.

## II. The interrogative adjectives are

1) Welcher? welche? welcheß? which? what?

|  | Singular. | | | Plural |
|  | masc. | fem. | neuter, | for all genders. |
| --- | --- | --- | --- | --- |
| N. | welcher | welche | welcheß which? | welche which? |
| G. | welcheß | welcher | welcheß of which? | welcher of which? |
| D. | welchem | welcher | welchem to which? | welchen to which? |
| A. | welchen | welche | welcheß which? | welche which? |

### Examples.

     Welcher Wein iſt ber beſte? which wine is the best?
     Welchen Weg gehen Sie? which way *do you* go?
     Welche Feder iſt gut? which pen is good?

*Note 2.* What? and which? immediately followed by the auxiliary verb ſein to be, is translated: welches? both in the singular and plural (see the above *Note 1*). Ex.:

What is your name? welches iſt Ihr Name?
What are your terms? welches ſind Ihre Bedingungen?

2) Was für ein, was für eine, was für ein? *what (kind of)?*

Of this, the article ein, eine, ein only is declined and agrees with the following noun. Ex.:

Was für ein Buch (*n*) haben Sie? what book have you?
Was für eine Stadt (*f.*) iſt dieſes? what town is this?

For the plural cases it is only was für? and the substantive follows immediately·

Was für Bücher brauchen Sie? what books *do you* need?
Was für Bäume ſind dieſes? what kind of trees are these?

The same form, was für? without the article is employed before names of materials

Was für Fleiſch kaufen Sie? what sort of meat *do you* buy?
Was für Wein trinken Sie? what kind of wine *do you* drink?

### III.  The **possessive adjectives** are:

| *Singular.* | | | *Plural* |
|---|---|---|---|
| *maso.* | *fem.* | *neuter.* | *for all genders,* |
| mein | meine | mein my. | meine my. |
| dein | deine | dein thy | deine thy |
| ſein | ſeine | ſein his (its). | ſeine his (its). |
| ihr | ihre | ihr her (its). | ihre her (its). |
| unſer | unſre | unſer our. | unſre our. |
| Ihr | Ihre | Ihr } your. | Ihre } your. |
| (euer | eure | euer) | (euere, eure) |
| ihr | ihre | ihr their. | ihre their. |

The declension of the first three is shown in the second lesson. The last five are declined as follows:

| *Singular.* | | | *Plural* |
|---|---|---|---|
| *masc.* | *fem.* | *neuter.* | *for all genders.* |
| *N* unſer | unſre | unſer our | unſre our. |
| *G.* unſres | unſrer | unſres of our | unſrer of our. |
| *D.* unſrem | unſrer | unſrem to our. | unſren to our. |
| *A.* unſren | unſre | unſer our. | unſre our. |
| *N.* Ihr | Ihre | Ihr your. | Ihre your. |
| *G.* Ihres | Ihrer | Ihres of your. | Ihrer of your |
| *D.* Ihrem | Ihrer | Ihrem to your. | Ihren to your. |
| *A* Ihren | Ihre | Ihr your. | Ihre your |

Observe that all these possessive adjectives have no termination added for the *Nom. Sing.* in the masc. and neuter. Ex.:

Our friend unſer Freund (not unſrer Freund).
Your horse Ihr Pferd (not Ihres Pferd) (See also p. 23).

## IV  The indefinite numeral adjectives are:

| *masc.* | *fem.* | *neuter.* | *Plural.* |
|---|---|---|---|
| jeder every, each | jede | jedes. | (*wanting*). |
| aller (all) all | alle | alles (all). | alle all. |
| mancher many a | manche | manches. | manche (some). |
| kein no | keine | kein. | keine no. |
| viel much | viele | viel. | viele many. |
| wenig little | wenige | wenig. | wenige few. |

The following are used in the plural only:

| | |
|---|---|
| beide, *pl* both. | einige, *pl* some, a few. |
| mehrere, *pl.* several. | die meiſten, *pl.* most. |

### Declension.

| *masc.* | *fem.* | *neuter.* | *Plural.* | |
|---|---|---|---|---|
| *N.* aller (all) | alle | alles (all). | alle | einige. |
| *G.* alles | aller | alles. | aller | einiger. |
| *D.* allem | aller | allem. | allen | einigen. |
| *A.* allen | alle | alles (all). | alle | einige. |

### Remarks.

1) When in English the definite article follows the numeral adjective *all*, it must not be translated, as:

All the boys alle Knaben (not alle die Knaben).

2) All before a possessive adjective in the singular, remains in the *masculine* and *neuter* gender unchanged. Ex.:

All our money all unſer Geld (not alles unſer Geld).
With all your money mit all Ihrem Geld (*Dat.*).

3) The article after *both* may either not be translated, or it precedes *both*, as:

Both the sisters beide Schweſtern or die beiden Schweſtern.

4) Possessive adjectives, when joined with beide, must precede, and beibe takes n. Ex.:

Both my sisters meine beiden Schweſtern.
Both our sons unſre beiden Söhne.

5) The word *some* or *any* before a noun in the *singular* is better not translated, as:

I have some bread ich habe Brot.
Have you any cheese? haben Sie Käſe?
No, but here is some butter nein, aber hier iſt Butter.

6) *Some* before a noun in the *plural* should not be left out, but expressed by einige, as:

Lend me some pens leihen Sie mir einige Federn.

7) When, in a reply, *some* is not followed by a substantive, but refers to a preceding noun in the *singular*, it may be expressed by welchen, e, s or davon; when in the *plural*, by einige; frequently however it is not expressed at all. (See the 25th lesson, II, Obs. 4). Ex.:

Have you some wine? Yes, I have *some* (welchen).

---

## Words.

| | |
|---|---|
| Das Gebäude the building. | die Pflanze the plant. |
| die Eltern the parents. | das Schiff (*pl.* —e) the ship. |
| tot dead. reich rich. | der Geldbeutel the purse. |
| das Geld (the) money. | der Bleistift (*pl.* —e) the pencil. |
| der Kaufmann the merchant. | nützlich useful. hoch high. |
| die Base ⎱ the cousin (*fem.*). | heilsam salutary, wholesome. |
| die Kousine ⎰ | das Vergnügen the pleasure. |
| die Regel (*pl.* —n) the rule. | giftig poisonous. |
| der Wagen the carriage. | gehören belong. oft often. |
| der Fehler the mistake, fault. | verkaufen to sell. verkauft sold. |
| bewundern to admire. | schlecht bad. da there. |

## Reading Exercise. 27.

1. Dieser Mann ist reich. Diese Frau ist krank. Diese Kinder haben keine Bücher. Jenes Haus ist sehr alt. Die Früchte jener Bäume sind bitterer (more bitter), als (than) die Früchte dieser Bäume. Meine Eltern sind tot. Unser Oheim (Onkel) ist nicht reich; aber seine Base ist sehr reich. Diese Studenten haben ihr Geld verloren. Wir kennen alle Regeln. Ich kenne keinen solchen Namen. Alle Menschen sind Brüder. Mancher Kaufmann hat sein Geld verloren. Meine Tante hat ihren Ring gefunden.

2. Ich habe die Pferde Ihres Oheims und den Wagen unsres Nachbars gekauft. Jeder Mensch liebt sein Leben (life). Nicht jedes Land ist reich. Sie haben keinen Fehler in Ihrer Aufgabe. Meine beiden Brüder sind angekommen. Alle Häuser dieser Stadt sind hoch. Alle diese Pflanzen sind heilsam. Dieses sind nicht meine Federn. Wir haben einige Vögel gefangen (caught). Was für einen Stock haben Sie da? Mehrere Schiffe sind angekommen.

## Aufgabe. 28.

1. I love my (*Acc.*) father and my mother. We love our parents. You love your sisters. The boys have bought some books. Those flowers are withered (verwelkt). The pupils speak often of (von) their teachers. All men (Menschen)

are like (gleich) before God.  These (I, *Note 1*) are the pencils of my biother.  This man has sold all his houses and
gardens, and all his hoises and carriages.  We admire such
men.  All [the] metals are useful.  What (*sort of*) wine have
you?  Which gloves have you lost?  This lady has lost all
her children.  Our friends (have) (find) ²arrived ¹yesterday.
     2.  We have seen several ships.  I have found your
purse without your money.  We have several friends in Paris.
Not all men (Menschen) are rich.  Each country has its (his)
pleasures.  I have no letters from my son William.  Our
king has several palaces.  No rose without thorns (Dornen)
I will (Ich will) buy some chairs  These dresses are for both
my sisters.  Every bird has two wings.  The boys have eaten
(gegessen) all their apples and pears.  Some plants are poison-
ous.  I give (gebe) these fruits [*to*] my children

### Conversation.

Wer hat meinen Geldbeutel ge-  Ihr Bruder hat ihn (it) gefunden.
    funden?
Sind alle Menschen glücklich?  Nicht alle Menschen sind glücklich.
Was für ein Vogel ist dieses?  Es ist ein Adler (eagle).
Wer hat ihn geschossen (shot *or*  Der Jäger (hunter) hat ihn ge-
    killed)?                          schossen.
Was für eine Blume haben Sie?  Es ist ein Veilchen
Wo sind unsre Hüte?  Ihre Hüte sind in meinem Zimmer.
Habe ich Fehler in meiner Auf-  Ja, Sie haben mehrere Fehler.
    gabe?
Was für Federn haben Sie?  Ich habe Stahl(steel)federn.
Wer ist jener junge Mann?  Er ist der Neffe meines Nachbars.
Warum sind diese Studenten so  Sie haben ihr Geld verloren.
    traurig (sad)?
Haben sie alles Geld verloren?  Nicht alles, aber viel.
Was für Pferde haben Sie ge-  Ich habe zwei Wagenpferde und ein
    kauft?                           Reitpferd (saddle-h) gekauft.
Was haben die Jäger geschossen?  Einige Hasen und Rehe (deer).
Haben Sie einige gute Federn?  Alle meine Federn sind schlecht.
Was für Bücher lesen Sie (do  Ich lese einige englische Bücher.
    you read)?
Was sucht Friedrich (look for)?  Er sucht seinen Bleistift.
Mit wem sind Sie gekommen  Ich bin mit einigen Freunden ge-
    (did you come)?                 kommen.
Haben Sie Briefe von Frank-  Nein, ich habe keinen Brief er-
    furt erhalten (received)?        halten.

# Fourteenth Lesson.
## AUXILIARY VERBS.
(Hilfszeitwörter.)

1) In German there are three complete auxiliary verbs which are not only used by themselves, but are also required for the conjugation of other verbs; they are haben to have; sein (seyn) to be; and werden to become *or* to be.

## Haben (hatte, gehabt) to have.

Indicative Mood. | Subjunctive Mood.

*Present Tense*

Ich habe I have | Ich habe I (may) have
du hast thou hast | du habest thou have
er (sie, es) hat he (she, it) has | er (sie, es) habe he (she, it) have
wir haben we have | wir haben we have
(ihr habt)*) ⎱ ye have | ihr habet ⎱ ye have
Sie haben ⎰ you have | Sie haben ⎰ you have
sie haben they have. | sie haben they have.

*Imperfect* (Preterite).

Ich hatte I had | Ich hätte**) I had
du hattest thou hadst | du hättest thou hadst
er (sie, es) hatte he (she, it) had | er (sie, es) hätte he (she, it) had
wir hatten we had | wir hätten we had
ihr hattet or Sie hatten you had | ihr hättet or Sie hätten you had
sie hatten they had. | sie hätten they had.

*Perfect*

Ich habe . . gehabt I have had | Ich habe gehabt I (may) have had
du hast gehabt thou hast had | du habest gehabt thou have had
er hat gehabt he has had | er habe gehabt he have had
wir haben gehabt we have had | wir haben gehabt we have had
ihr habt gehabt ⎱ ye have had | ihr habet gehabt ⎱ ye have had
Sie haben gehabt ⎰ you have had | Sie haben gehabt ⎰ you have had
sie haben gehabt they have had | sie haben gehabt they have had

*) It may be stated once for all, that the 2nd person Plural of all verbs has two forms ihr and Sie The latter, written with a capital S, to distinguish it from the 3rd person, is the only one to be used by foreigners in conversation

**) This form is chiefly used after wenn (if), as If I had wenn ich . . . hätte (the verb is last) Ex Wenn ich ein Buch hätte.

### Pluperfect.

Ich hatte . . gehabt I had had | Ich hätte gehabt*) I had had
du hattest gehabt thou hadst had | du hättest gehabt thou hadst had
er hatte gehabt he had had | er hätte gehabt he had had
wir hatten gehabt we had had | wir hätten gehabt we had had
 ihr hattet gehabt } ye had had |  ihr hättet gehabt } ye had had
Sie hatten gehabt } you had had | Sie hätten gehabt } you had had
sie hatten gehabt they had had. | sie hätten gehabt they had had.

### First Future.

Ich werde . . haben I shall have | Ich werde haben I shall have
du wirst haben thou wilt have | du werdest haben thou wilt have
er wird haben he will have | er werde haben he will have
wir werden haben we shall have | wir werden haben we shall have
(ihr werdet haben) } ye will have |  ihr werdet haben } ye will have
Sie werden haben } you will h. | Sie werden haben } you will have
sie werden haben they will have. | sie werden haben they will have.

### Second Future (Future Perfect).

Ich werde . . gehabt haben | Ich werde . . gehabt haben
  I shall have had |   I shall have had.

du wirst     thou wilt | du werdest     thou wilt
er wird     he will | er werde     he will
wir werden   gehabt haben   we shall   have had | wir werden   gehabt haben   we shall   have had.
 ihr werdet }   you will |  ihr werdet }   you will
Sie werden   they will | Sie werden   they will
sie werden   they will | sie werden   they will

### First Conditional.

Ich würde . . haben    or ich hätte I should or would have
du würdest haben    or du hättest thou wouldst have
er würde haben    or er hätte he would have
wir würden haben    or wir hätten we should have
ihr würdet haben    or ihr hättet you would have
sie würden haben    or sie hätten they would have.

### Second Conditional (Cond. Perfect).

Ich würde . . gehabt haben   or ich hätte gehabt I should have had
du würdest gehabt haben   or du hättest gehabt thou wouldst   have had.
er würde gehabt haben   or er hätte gehabt he would
wir würden gehabt haben   or wir hätten gehabt we should
ihr würdet gehabt haben   or ihr hättet gehabt you would
sie würden gehabt haben   or sie hätten gehabt they would

---

*) If I had had wenn ich     gehabt hätte.

## Imperative Mood.

Habe have        haben wir   } let us have
er soll haben let him have    lasset uns haben }
sie sollen haben let them have   habet or haben Sie have.

## Infinitive Mood.

*Pres.* haben or zu haben to have.
*Past.* gehabt haben or gehabt zu haben to have had.

## Participles.

*Pres.* habend having.    |   *Past.* gehabt had

2) The negative, interrogative and negative-interro-
gative form of verbs is in German exactly the same as
in English, and requires no further explanation.

### Negative

*Pres.*   Ich habe nicht I have not.
       du hast nicht thou hast not.
       er hat nicht he has not etc.
*Fut.*   Ich werde . . nicht haben I shall not have.
*Perfect.* Ich habe . . nicht gehabt I have not had.
       du hast . . nicht gehabt thou hast not had etc.

### Interrogative.

Habe ich? have I?     |   Haben Sie? have you?
Habe ich . . gehabt? have I had? etc.

### Negative-Interrogative.

Habe ich nicht? have I not? | Hatte ich nicht? had I not?
Habe ich nicht gehabt? have I not had?
Werden wir nicht haben? shall we not have? etc

## Remarks on the German construction.

As the chapter on the ,*Arrangement of words or construction*' cannot be given until all the Parts of speech have
been treated, we may, for the present, remark·

1) That in sentences with *compound tenses* the German
Part· Past must always be at the end. In simple delaratory
clauses (principal propositions) the *subject* comes first; secondly
the auxiliary, thirdly the object (Acc. or Dat.); in the fourth
place the indirect object, the adverb of place and finally the
Participle Past or the Infinitive· This may be called the
*Normal Order.*   Ex.:

Ich habe ein Buch gehabt I have had a book.
Der Knabe hat ein Buch auf der Straße gefunden.
The boy has found a book in the street
Die Mutter wird einen Brief von ihrer Tochter haben.
The mother will have a letter from her daughter.

2) Adverbs of **time** must precede the object:

Der Knabe hat gestern ein Buch gefunden.

The boy found a book yesterday.

3) But when any adverbial expression begins the sentence, then the following verb precedes the subject, as:

Gestern habe ich ein Buch in der Straße gefunden.

Yesterday I found a book in the street.

4) The negation „nicht" follows the direct object (*acc.*) as:

Ich habe das Buch nicht gelesen I have not read the book. *Lit.*: I have the book **not** read.

5) Dependent (or subordinate) clauses take the verb at the very end of the clause. Ex.:

Es ist wahr, daß sie tot ist. (It is true that she *is* dead.)

Du sagst, daß ich das Buch gefunden habe. (that I *found* the book.)

Ich beauftrage dich, ein Buch zu kaufen (to buy a book) etc.

---

## Words.

| | |
|---|---|
| Die Uhr the watch, clock. | das Unglück misfortune. |
| die Butter (the) butter. | die Nadel (*pl* —n) the needle. |
| der Käse (the) cheese. | der Ball the ball   so so. |
| das Fleisch the meat. | keine mehr no more. es it. |
| die Tinte the ink. | der Tod death. daß that. |
| glauben to believe, think. | wenn if. genug enough. |
| die Zeit (the) time. | angenehm agreeable, pleasant. |
| die Gesellschaft company, party. | auf dem Lande in the country. |

### Reading Exercise. 29.

1. Ich habe einen Freund. Hast du auch einen Freund? Haben Sie keine Freunde? Wir haben keine Freunde. Wir hatten Freunde; aber jetzt (now) haben wir keine mehr. Haben Sie Geduld (patience). Haben Sie acht auf (take care of) Ihre Kleider. Ich werde eine neue (new) Uhr haben. Ich habe eine Uhr gehabt; aber ich habe sie (it) verloren. Haben Sie viel Vergnügen gehabt?

2. Wir hatten viele Fische gehabt. Sie werden Gesellschaft gehabt haben. Die Schüler hatten kein Papier. Wenn wir Brot hätten.*) Wenn wir Fleisch gehabt hätten.*) Ihr würdet kein Geld haben. Er würde viel Vergnügen auf dem Lande gehabt haben. Glauben Sie, daß er Geld hat? Glauben Sie, daß wir Wein gehabt haben? Sie werden Wasser gehabt haben.

### Aufgabe. 30.

1. I have butter and cheese. He has bread and meat. We had some birds. The boys had two dogs. I had a watch.

---

*) The conjunction wenn requires the verb at the end; if in a compound tense, the participle is the last word but one

I shall ₃have ₁a ₂picture. I have ₃had ₁two ₂lamps. My
sisters have had many needles. If I had a garden (*Acc.*). If we
had a house and a garden. If you had had some paper.
They will have no ink. Children, take (have) care of (Acht auf,
*acc.*) your books. I have had little wine   She has had much
pleasure at (auf, *dat.*) the ball. I had no time. They would
have a carriage and a horse.

2. We had the [good] fortune (das Glück), to*) have
a faithful friend**). They will have a house in the town.
I should have money enough, if I had not lost my purse.
₃To ₄have*) ₁good (gute) ₂children is agreeable. Do you
wish (Wünschen Sie) to*) have much money? If I had not
had so much misfortune. These young men (jungen Leute)
have had too much (zu viel) pleasure.

## Conversation.

| | |
|---|---|
| Haben Sie meinen Bruder nicht gesehen? | Ja, ich habe ihn in einem Laden (shop) gesehen |
| Hat er etwas (anything) gekauft? | Ja, er hat Handschuhe gekauft. |
| Haben Sie Brot genug? | Nein, wir brauchen (need) mehr |
| Hatten Sie genug Butter und Käse? | Wir hatten Käse genug, aber nicht Butter genug. |
| Haben Sie viel Vergnügen auf dem Lande gehabt? | Wir waren sehr vergnügt(pleased), wir hatten große Gesellschaft |
| Hat dieses arme (poor) Kind keine Eltern mehr? | Es hat seinen Vater verloren; aber seine Mutter lebt noch(still lives) |
| Werden wir schönes Wetter haben? | Ich glaube nicht. |
| Werden Sie Zeit haben, dieses Buch zu lesen? | Ich werde heute (to-day) keine Zeit haben; aber morgen. |
| Hat Karl viel Geld gehabt? | Er hat sehr wenig gehabt. |
| Was für eine Feder hatten Sie? | Ich hatte eine Stahl(steel)feder |
| Werde ich das Vergnügen haben, Ihre Schwester zu sehen? | Sie ist nicht hier, sie ist in Stuttgart. |
| Warum sind Sie so traurig? | Ich habe mein Geld verloren. |
| Wer hat mein Federmesser gehabt? | Ich weiß nicht (I do not know), wer (who) es gehabt hat |

*) When the Infinitive is accompanied by *to*, translate it zu,
till further notice.

**) Translate: a faithful friend to have einen treuen Freund zu
haben. The object of the Infinitive *precedes* the latter in German.

# Fifteenth Lesson.
## SECOND AUXILIARY.
### Sein (war, gewesen) to be.

Indicative. | Subjunctive.

### Present Tense.

Ich bin I am | Ich sei I [may] be
du bist thou art | du seiest thou be
er (sie, es) ist he (she, it) is | er (sie, es) sei he (she, is) be
wir sind we are | wir seien we be
Sie sind ⎱ you are | Sie seien ⎱ you be
(ihr seid) ⎰ ye are | ihr seiet ⎰ ye be
sie sind they are. | sie seien they be.

### Imperfect (Preterite).

Ich war I was | (Wenn)*) ich wäre (if) I were
du warst thou wast | du wärest thou wert
er (sie, es) war he (she, it) was | er (sie, es) wäre he (she, it) were
wir waren we were | wir wären we were
(ihr waret) ⎱ you were | ihr wäret ⎱ you were
Sie waren ⎰ | Sie wären ⎰
sie waren they were. | sie wären they were.

### Perfect.

Ich bin . . gewesen I have been | Ich sei gewesen I (may) have been
du bist gewesen thou hast been | du seiest gewesen thou have been
er ist gewesen he has been | er sei gewesen he have been
wir sind gewesen we have been | wir seien gewesen we have been
(ihr seid gewesen) ⎱ ye have been | (ihr seiet gewesen) ⎱ ye have been
Sie sind gewesen ⎰ you have been | Sie seien gewesen ⎰ you have been
sie sind gewesen they have been. | sie seien gewesen they have been.

### Pluperfect.

Ich war . . gewesen I had been | Ich wäre gewesen I had been *)
du warst gewesen thou hadst b. | du wärest gewesen thou hadst been
er war gewesen he had been | er wäre gewesen he had been
wir waren gewesen we had been | wir wären gewesen we had been
Sie waren gewesen you had been | Sie wären gewesen you had been
sie waren gewesen they had been. | sie wären gewesen they had been.

### First Future.

Ich werde . . sein I shall be | Ich werde sein I shall be
du wirst sein thou wilt be | du werdest sein thou wilt be
er wird sein he will be | er werde sein he will be
wir werden sein we shall be | wir werden sein we shall be
Sie werden sein you will be | Sie werden sein you will be
sie werden sein they will be. | sie werden sein they will be.

---

*) Ex If I was or were rich wenn ich reich wäre.

*Second Future* (Fut. Perfect).

| Jch werde . . geweſen ſein | | Jch werde . . geweſen ſein | |
|---|---|---|---|
| I shall have been. | | I shall have been. | |
| du wirſt | thou wilt | du werdeſt | thou wilt |
| er wird | he will | er werde | he will |
| wir werden | we shall | wir werden | we shall |
| (ihr werdet) | ye will | (ihr werdet) | ye will |
| Sie werden | you will | Sie werden | you will |
| ſie werden | they will | ſie werden | they will |

(geweſen ſein. · have been. | geweſen ſein. · have been.)

### First Conditional.

Jch würde . . ſein (or ich wäre) I should be
du würdeſt ſein (or du wäreſt) thou wouldst be
er würde ſein (or er wäre) he would be
wir würden ſein (or wir wären) we should be
ihr würdet (Sie würden) ſein (or ihr wäret) you would be
ſie würden ſein (or ſie wären) they would be.

*Second Conditional* (Cond. Perfect).

Jch würde geweſen ſein or ich wäre geweſen I should have been
du würdeſt geweſen ſein or du wäreſt geweſen thou wouldst
er würde geweſen ſein or er wäre geweſen he would

wir würden geweſen ſein or wir wären geweſen we should
Sie würden geweſen ſein or Sie wären geweſen you would
ſie würden geweſen ſein or ſie wären geweſen they would

have been.

### Imperative.

Sei be (thou).
er ſoll ſein let him be.
ſie ſollen ſein let them be.

ſeien wir
laſſet uns ſein } let us be.
ſeid or ſeien Sie be (you).

### Infinitive.

*Pres.* ſein or zu ſein to be.
*Past.* geweſen ſein or geweſen zu ſein to have been.

### Participles.

*Pres.* ſeiend being. | *Past.* geweſen been.

*Note 1.* There is and there are answer to the German es
giebt, es iſt, es ſind; there was and there were es gab, es
war or es waren, as:
There are animals etc. es giebt Tiere ꝛc. (See lesson 33.)

*Note 2.* The English *I am to* is translated ich ſoll or muß:
Charles *is to* learn German Karl ſoll Deutſch lernen.

---

*) If I had been wenn ich . . . geweſen wäre.

6*

*Note 3.* The English *to be right* is translated in German recht haben, and *to be wrong* unrecht haben. Ex.:
You *are* right Sie haben recht.
I *am* wrong ich habe unrecht. I *was* wrong ich hatte u.

## Words.

Der Lehrer the master, teacher.   zufrieden contented.
der Großvater the grandfather.   unzufrieden discontented.
das Glas (*pl.* Gläser) the glass.   ruhig quiet.   besser better
glücklich happy   lang(e) long.   gütig kind.   verloren lost.
unglücklich unhappy.   träge idle.   leicht easy.
schön handsome, pretty.   vergnügt pleased.
arm poor.   krank ill, sick.   fleißig industrious, diligent.
unwohl unwell.   zu' too.   aufmerksam attentive.
höflich polite.   immer always.   wünschen to wish
der Wolf (*pl.* Wölfe) the wolf.   gehen to go.   warum why?

### Reading Exercise. 31.

Du bist glücklich. Ich bin unglücklich. Sie ist schön und reich. Wir sind arm und krank. Er war ein guter Vater. Waren Sie gestern in der Kirche? Nein! wir waren zu Hause, wir waren unwohl. Sie werden nicht krank sein. Ich bin bei (at) dem Schneider gewesen, aber mein Rock war [noch] nicht fertig (ready). Ist der Knabe in der Schule gewesen? Wir waren gestern im Theater. Ich würde glücklich sein, wenn ich reich wäre. Karl wird sehr vergnügt sein, wenn (when) er Sie sieht (sees). Sei fleißig, mein Sohn. Seien Sie aufmerksam. Ihr Großvater ist sehr alt gewesen. Meine Großmutter hat recht. Ich habe unrecht. Jung und schön zu sein*) ist angenehm.

### Aufgabe. 32.

1. I am young, you are old. She is very handsome. Our cousin Frederick *has* been in London, but he *has* not been in Paris. Be quiet. Be contented with your situation (Stelle, *f.*). I should be contented, if I were not ill. I should be rich, if I had been in America. My daughters *have* been at the ball (auf dem Ball); they were very happy. It will be better to go out (auszugehen). It would be easy. The parents of these children have been too severe (zu streng). You *are* right, I *am* wrong.

2. I should be contented, if you were not idle. Be polite towards (gegen) your teachers. I wish, she were attentive. *There are* no wolves in England. There were (es waren) no glasses on the table. Be so kind [as] to (zu) give me a glass.

---

*) See the foot-note *) p. 81. Yet the Infinitive here forming the *Subject* of the phrase, the prepos. zu may as well be omitted.

My pupils will not be idle. Miss Caroline was very [much] pleased. The knives were not sharp (ſcharf). We have not bought the butter; it (ſie) was not fresh (friſch). I *am to* go (*Note* 2) to Berlin. *Are we to* learn German? I *was* wrong, my father *was* right.

### Conversation.

| | |
|---|---|
| Sind Sie glücklich? | O ja, ich bin ſehr glücklich. |
| Iſt Ihre Schweſter auch glücklich? | O nein, ſie iſt ſehr unglücklich. |
| Warum iſt ſie unglücklich? | Sie hat alle ihre Kinder verloren. |
| Wo waren Sie geſtern Abend (last night)? | Ich war im Theater. |
| Sind Sie in Stuttgart geweſen? | Nein, ich bin nicht da (there) geweſen. |
| Iſt das Kind lange krank geweſen? | Es iſt ein Jahr (for a year) krank geweſen. |
| Warum war der Lehrer unzufrieden? | Die Schüler waren träge. |
| Iſt er oft (often) unwohl? | Ja, er iſt immer krank |
| Iſt das Mädchen vergnügt? | Ja, ſie iſt ſehr vergnügt. |
| Sind Sie fertig (ready, or have you done)? | Wir werden gleich (directly) fertig ſein. |
| Iſt der Menſch ſterblich (mortal)? | Der Körper iſt ſterblich; aber die Seele (soul) iſt unſterblich. |
| Was ſagte (said) der Lehrer? | Er ſagte. Seien Sie ruhig. |
| Wer hat recht? | Mein Vater hat recht. |
| Hatten Sie auch recht? | Nein, ich hatte unrecht. |

---

# Sixteenth Lesson.
## THIRD AUXILIARY.
### Werden to become, to get (to grow).

| Indicative. | Subjunctive. |
|---|---|

### Present Tense.

| | |
|---|---|
| Ich werde I become, I get | Ich werde I (may) become |
| du wirſt thou becomest | du werdeſt thou become |
| er wird he becomes | er werde he become |
| wir werden we become | wir werden we become |
| Sie werden or ihr werdet y. b. | Sie werden or ihr werdet y. bec. |
| ſie werden they become. | ſie werden they become. |

*Imperfect* (Preterite).

Ich wurde (ich warb)*) I became | Ich würde (if) I became
du wurdeſt (warbſt) th. becamest | du würdeſt thou became
er wurde (warb) he became | er würde he became
wir wurden we became | wir würden we became
Sie wurden or ihr wurdet y. b. | Sie würden or ihr würdet y. bec.
ſie wurden they became. | ſie würden they became.

*Perfect.*

Ich bin .. geworden (or worden) | Ich ſei geworden (or worden) I
I have become (*or* grown) | (may) have become (*or* been)
du biſt geworden thou hast bec. | du ſeiſt geworden (or worden)
er iſt geworden he has bec. | er ſei geworden (or worden)
wir ſind geworden ꝛc. | ꝛc. ꝛc.

*Pluperfect.*

Ich war .. geworden (or worden) | Ich wäre geworden (or worden)
I had become (*or* been) | (if) I had become (*or* been)
du warſt geworden (or worden) | du wäreſt geworden (or worden)
er (ſie, es) war geworden ꝛc. | ꝛc. ꝛc.

*First Future.*

Ich werde .. werden | Ich werde .. werden
I shall become (*or* get) | I shall become
du wirſt .. werden | du werdeſt ⎫
er wird .. werden | er werde ⎬ werden
 | 
wir werden .. ⎫ | wir werden ⎫
Sie werden .. ⎬ werden. | Sie werden ⎬ werden.
ſie werden .. ⎭ | ſie werden ⎭

*Second Future* (Fut. Perfect).

Ich werde geworden (worden) ſein | Ich werde geworden (worden) ſein
I shall have become (been) | I shall have become (been)
du wirſt geworden (worden) ſein | du werdeſt geworden (worden) ſein
ꝛc. ꝛc. | ꝛc. ꝛc.

## First Conditional.

Ich würde .. werden I should *or* would become
du würdeſt werden thou wouldst become
ꝛc. ꝛc.

### Second Conditional.

Ich würde .. geworden (or worden) ſein or ich wäre .. ge‑
worden I should have become *or* been
ꝛc. ꝛc.

---

*) Ich warb is the older form, and getting out of use.

## Imperative.

Werde become (thou).
er soll werden he shall become.
sie sollen werden let them become.

werden wir
laßt uns werden ⎱ let us become
werdet, werden Sie become.
werden Sie nicht do not become.

## Infinitive.

*Pres.* werden or zu werden to become.
*Past* geworden (or worden) sein or zu sein to have become.

## Participles.

*Pres.* werdend becoming.
*Past* geworden (or worden) become (*or* been).

*Note 1.* The verb werden is sometimes translated *to get* or *to grow*, as

Er wird alt he grows old. | Es wird spät it gets late.

*Note 2.* *What has become of* . . .? is translated: Was ist aus . . . geworden?

### Words.

Schläfrig sleepy.
nie or niemals never.
weise wise. spät late.
müde tired. naß wet.
ungeduldig impatient.
die Nachricht the news.
bekannt known träge idle
der Herzog the duke.
plötzlich suddenly.

der Regenschirm the umbrella.
schmutzig dirty. dunkel dark.
der Fleiß industry.
die Sparsamkeit economy.
das Alter old age.
die Leute people. wann? when?
groß tall. grün green.
rein clean. bald soon.
gestern yesterday. jetzt now.

### Reading Exercise. 32a.

Ich werde schläfrig. Sie wird alt. Sie werden niemals weise werden. Meine zwei Kinder wurden krank. Man (a man) wird müde, wenn (when) man viel arbeitet (works). Es wird spät. Ich wurde gestern ungeduldig. Diese Nachricht wurde in der Stadt bekannt. Ich bin jung; aber ich werde alt werden. Sie werden naß werden, denn es regnet (for it rains). Dieses Papier ist schmutzig geworden. Es wird Nacht; es wird dunkel. Diese Knaben werden krank; sie essen (they eat) zu viel. Das Mädchen wurde müde. Durch Fleiß und Sparsamkeit wird man reich. Unser Nachbar ist bald reich geworden. Es regnet; wir werden naß werden. Was ist aus dem Sohn des Schneiders geworden? Er ist Soldat geworden.

### Aufgabe. 32b.

She becomes sleepy. I shall become wise. He *has* become my friend. The duke became suddenly ill. The boys *got* tired

and sleepy. The trees become green in spring (im Frühling).
I am now rich, but I may (kann) ²become ¹poor. We shall
become contented. Do not become impatient. Your children
*have grown* very tall. Old (Alte) people become wise. It *had
grown* dark. I was once (einst) young; but now ²I ¹*have*
grown old. It rains (es regnet), our friends will get wet.
Mr. Brown hopes (hofft) soon ²to (zu) ¹get ¹rich. This man
*has* become [a] soldier. What *has* become *of* his children?
Those boys *have* become men (Männer). I hope (ich hoffe),
you will not become idle.

### Conversation.

| | |
|---|---|
| Warum find Sie geſtern nicht gekommen (did y. not come)? | Ich wurde plötzlich unwohl (unwell). |
| Warum gehen Sie ſchon nach Hauſe (home so soon)? | Es wird ſpät. Ich muß (must) um (at) acht Uhr zu Hauſe ſein. |
| Wann werden die Bäume grün? | Im Frühling |
| Sind Sie Kaufmann geworden? | Nein, ich bin Soldat geworden. |
| Warum (why) iſt dieſes Mädchen krank geworden? | Sie hat zu viel Kuchen gegeſſen (eaten). |
| Sind Sie reich geworden? | Nein, aber (but) ich wünſche reich zu werden. |
| Sind Sie naß geworden? | Ich bin nicht naß geworden; ich hatte einen Regenſchirm. |
| Was iſt aus (of) Ihrem Bruder geworden? | Er iſt in Amerika geſtorben (died). |
| Was iſt aus meinem Buch geworden? | Ich weiß (know) nicht; ich habe es nicht geſehen. |
| Wer wurde träge? | Der Schüler wurde träge. |
| Wer iſt ſchläfrig geworden? | Wilhelm iſt ſchläfrig geworden. |
| Sind die Straßen rein? | Nein, ſie ſind durch den Regen (rain) ſchmutzig geworden. |

# Seventeenth Lesson.
## THE MODAL AUXILIARIES.*)

Besides the three auxiliaries already mentioned, there
are others which convey no full idea in themselves, but
give certain modifications to other verbs, by expressing
the *possibility* or *necessity*, the *lawfulness* or *willingness*
of what is indicated. These *modal* auxiliaries are six**)·

---

*) In German they are called 'Hilfszeitwörter der Art und Weiſe'
(i. Engl auxiliaries of mood or mode, or rather. *modal auxiliaries*).
**) For the verb laſſen See II. Part, Less. 40, III.

Ich kann I can.  ich muß I must
ich will I will.  ich soll I shall *or* am to.
ich mag I may.  ich darf I may *or* dare
While the corresponding English verbs are very defective, these have in German a complete conjugation.

## 1. Können to be able.

| Indicative. | Subjunctive. |
|---|---|

### Present Tense

| | |
|---|---|
| Ich kann I can, I may | Ich könne I may be able |
| du kannst thou canst | du könnest |
| er (sie, es) kann he (she, it) can | er (sie, es) könne |
| man kann one *or* they can | |
| wir können we can *or* may | wir können we may be able |
| (ihr könnt or könnet) ⎱ ye can | ihr könnet ⁊c. |
| Sie können      ⎰ you can | Sie können ⁊c. |
| sie können they can *or* may. | sie können ⁊c |

### Imperfect (Preterite).

| | |
|---|---|
| Ich konnte I could | Ich könnte I might, I could[1] |
| du konntest ⁊c. | du könntest ⁊c |
| er konnte, sie konnte | er könnte ⁊c |
| wir konnten we could | wir könnten ⁊c. |
| Sie konnten you could etc | Sie könnten ⁊c. |

### Perfect.

| | |
|---|---|
| Ich habe gekonnt (or ich habe ..können[2]) I have been able | Ich habe gekonnt (or ich habe . . können) |
| du hast gekonnt ⁊c. | du habest gekonnt ⁊c. |

### Pluperfect.

| | |
|---|---|
| Ich hatte gekonnt (or ich hatte .. können) I had been able. | Ich hätte gekonnt (or ich hätte . . können). |

### First Future.

| | |
|---|---|
| Ich werde können I shall be able | Ich werde können |
| du wirst können ⁊c. | du werdest können ⁊c. |

### Second Future (Fut. Perfect).

Ich werde gekonnt haben I shall have been able.

### First Conditional.

Ich könnte (or ich würde können[3]) I could, I might be able.

### Second Conditional.

Ich hätte gekonnt or können (ich würde gekonnt haben[3]).

---

1) If I could wenn ich . . . könnte
2) See Obs 4, p 94
3) This compound form is not much used. See p 94, Obs. 3.

Infinitive.

*Pres.* können to be able | *Past.* gekonnt haben.

Participle.

*Past* gekonnt been able.

---

## 2. Wollen to be willing, to wish, to like.

| Indicative. | Subjunctive. |
|---|---|
| *Pres.* Ich will I will, I wish | Ich wolle I will |
| du willst thou wishest | du wollest |
| er will he wishes, will | er wolle |
| wir wollen¹) we will, wish | wir wollen |
| ihr wollt or wollet⎱ you' will²) | ⎰ihr wollet |
| Sie wollen ⎰ or like | ⎱Sie wollen |
| sie wollen they will *or* wish. | sie wollen. |

*Imprf.* Ich wollte I was going to, I | Ich wollte I should wish
du wolltest [wished, I would | du wolltest ꝛc.
er wollte | er wollte ꝛc
wir wollten ꝛc. | wir wollten ꝛc.

*Perf.* Ich habe . . gewollt or ich habe | Ich habe gewollt
. . . wollen I have wished
du hast gewollt ꝛc. | du habest gewollt ꝛc.

*Pluprf.* Ich hatte gewollt I had w. | Ich hätte gewollt (or wollen).

*1st Fut.* Ich werde . . wollen | Ich werde wollen
I shall wish
du wirst wollen ꝛc. | du werdest wollen ꝛc.

*2nd Fut.* Ich werde gewollt haben I shall have wished.
*1st Cond.* Ich wollte or ich würde wollen I should wish.
*2nd Cond.* Ich hätte gewollt or wollen (or ich würde gewollt h).³)
*Inf. pres.* Wollen. | *Inf. past.* gewollt haben.
*Part. past.* gewollt.

---

## 3. Sollen.

| | |
|---|---|
| *Pres.* Ich soll I am to*) | *Subj.* Ich solle I' shall |
| du sollst thou shalt | du sollest |
| er soll he is to *or* shall | er solle |
| *Plur.* wir sollen*) we are to | wir sollen |
| ihr sollet ⎱ ye shall | ⎰ihr sollet |
| Sie sollen ⎰ you shall | ⎱Sie sollen |
| sie sollen they are to *or* shall. | sie sollen. |

1) Observe that the plural of these auxiliaries is throughout like the Infinitive mood.
2) You will is mostly Future and translated Sie werden, whereas the interrog.: Will you? is Wollen Sie?
3) This compound form is not much used See p 94, Obs. 3.
*) *I shall* (1st pers.) is translated: ich werde, and the inter-

*Imperf.* Sch follte I should, I was | Sch follte*) I should.
      to *or* I ought to.

*Perf.* Sch habe gefollt or ich habe ... follen | Sch habe gefollt
      du haft gefollt ꝛc. | du habeft gefollt ꝛc.

*Pluperf.* Sch hatte gefollt. | Sch hätte gefollt or follen.

*1st Fut.* Sch werde follen | Sch werde follen
      du wirft follen ꝛc. | du werdeft follen ꝛc.

*2nd Fut.* (Sch werde gefollt haben.)

*1st Cond.* Sch follte I should, I ought to.

*2nd Cond.* Sch hätte — follen I ought to have.

*Inf. pres.* follen.      | *Part. past.* gefollt.

## 4. Müffen to be obliged, to have to.

| *Indicative.* | *Subjunctive.* |
|---|---|

*Pres.* Sch muß I must | Sch müffe I must
      du mußt thou must | du müffeft, er müffe
      er muß he must |

      wir müffen we must | wir müffen
      ihr müffet or müßt} you | ihr müffet
      Sie müffen    } must | Sie müffen
      fie müffen they must. | fie müffen.

*Imperf.* Sch mußte I had to, I was | Sch müßte
      to *or* I was obliged. | I should be obliged.

*Perf.* Sch habe .. gemußt or müffen | Sch habe gemußt
      I have been obliged |
      du haft gemußt ꝛc. | du habeft gemußt ꝛc.

*Pluperf.* Sch hatte gemußt. | Sch hätte gemußt (müffen).

*1st Fut.* Sch werde müffen | Sch werde müffen
      I shall be obliged |
      du wirft müffen ꝛc. | du werdeft müffen ꝛc.

*2nd Fut.* (ich werde gemußt haben.)

*1st Cond.* Sch müßte or würde .. müffen I should be obliged.

*2nd Cond.* Sch hätte gemußt (or — müffen) I should have been

*Inf. pres.* müffen to be obliged          [obliged.

*Part. past.* gemußt.

     *Note.* 'I must *not*' is rendered ich darf nicht.

---

rogative *Shall I:* werde ich? But when '*shall I*' means *am I to?*
it is in German foll ich? — In the same manner in the plural.
*We shall* is = wir werden, but *shall we* (= *are we to*) follen wir?

    **) Observe that ich wollte and ich follte do not modify their
vowel in the Subj. Mood or Conditional. Ex wenn ich .. wollte.

## Words.

Der Bauer (*pl* -n) the peasant.    heute to-day.   nichts nothing.
die Post the post-office.    ab'reifen to depart, set out.
lefen to read.    bezahlen to pay.   mich me.
bleiben to remain, to stay.    strafen to punish.   es it.
aus'gehen to go out.    glauben believe.
schreiben to write.    verstehen to understand.

## Reading Exercise. 33.

Ich kann lefen. Sie können kommen. Ich konnte es nicht glauben. Ich muß ihn (him) sehen. Wir müssen abreifen. Wollen Sie mich bezahlen oder nicht? Ich würde Sie bezahlen, wenn ich könnte. Warum können Sie nicht? Ich habe kein Geld. Man (one) konnte es nicht lefen. Man könnte (might) diefes glauben. Ich muß ausgehen. Karl mußte heute in der Schule bleiben. Wilhelm wird morgen zu Haufe bleiben müssen. Wer (who) wollte (könnte) es glauben? Ich glaube es nicht. Wir werden bleiben müssen. Wir können nicht immer thun (do), was wir wollen. Diefe Schüler follten fleißig fein. Ihr Diener foll den Brief auf die Post tragen (take).

### Aufgabe. 33a.

Can you write? Yes, I can write. He cannot read. We must go out. They must *pay *me (mich) The master should punish the boy.*) He would believe nothing. I will buy it The servant would not (did not wish to) go Thou shalt not steal (stehlen). (The) children should not lie (lügen). I could not**) believe that news (diefe N.). Some peasants cannot read. I will write a letter. Will you take it (ihn . . . tragen) to the (auf die) post-office? They will not come. She should (*or* ought [to]) write to him (an ihn). Children must go to school (in die Schule). I could not**) understand this letter My aunt could not read the book.

## 5. Mögen.

| | |
|---|---|
| *Pres* Ich mag I may (I like) | *Subj.* Ich möge I may |
| du magst thou mayest | du mögest |
| er (fie, es) mag he may | er möge |
| wir mögen we may | wir mögen |
| Sie mögen you may | Sie mögen |
| fie mögen they may. | fie mögen. |
| *Imperf.* Ich mochte I liked | Ich möchte I may, might |
| Ich mochte nicht I did not like or choose. | *or* I should like. |
| *Perf* Ich habe gemocht, du haft xc. | Ich habe gemocht, du habest |
| *Pluperf* Ich hatte gemocht. | Ich hätte gemocht. [xc. |

*) For the position of the Infinitive see the foot-note * p. 80.
**) The negation nicht is to be placed after the object. Translate. I could *that news not* believe (see p. 50, Obs. 4).

*1st Fut.* Ich werde mögen I shall like | Ich werde mögen
du wirst mögen ꝛc. | Du werdest mögen ꝛc.
*1st Cond.* Ich möchte (gern) I should like.
*2nd Cond.* Ich hätte — mögen I should have liked.
*Inf. pres.* Mögen | *Part. past.* gemocht.

*Note 1.* *I may* etc is very often translated können, as:
He may go er kann gehen. — Ich mochte nicht = I did not like.

*Note 2* The interrogative form: may I? etc is rendered·
darf ich? *may we?* dürfen wir? ꝛc.

In the same manner is conjugated vermögen to be able, as:
Ich vermag es nicht zu thun (*Inf.* with zu).

## 6. Dürfen to be allowed, to dare.

*Pres.* Ich darf I may, I dare, | *Subj.* Ich dürfe I may
du darfst [I am allowed. | du dürfest
er darf | er dürfe
wir dürfen we are allowed | wir dürfen
ihr dürft or Sie dürfen | ihr dürfet
sie dürfen. | sie dürfen.

*Imperf.* Ich durfte I was allowed, | Ich dürfte I might
du durftest [I dared. | du dürftest
er durfte he was allowed | er dürfte
wir durften we were allowed | wir dürften
ihr durftet or Sie durften | ihr dürftet
sie durften. | sie dürften.

*Perf.* Ich habe gedurft or . dürfen | Ich habe gedurft
I have been allowed. | du habest ꝛc.

*Pluperf.* Ich hatte gedurft. | Ich hätte gedurft.

*1st Fut.* Ich werde dürfen | Ich werde dürfen
I shall be allowed. | du werdest ꝛc.

*2nd Fut.* Ich werde gedurft haben.
*1st Cond.* Ich dürfte or würde dürfen I should be allowed.
*2nd Cond.* Ich hätte gedurft I should have been allowed.
*Inf. pres.* dürfen. *P past* gedurft. *Inf. past* (gedurft haben).

Negative. Ich darf nicht = I must not.
In the same manner bedürfen to be in need Ich bedarf ꝛc.

---

## Observations.

1) These six auxiliaries are mostly followed by an Infinitive
mood, but they do not admit of zu before the Infinitive.
I can (must, will) read ich kann (muß, will ꝛc.) lesen.
He ought *to* come er sollte kommen.

2) If such an auxiliary is accompanied by *not*, in German the negation nidjt is placed before the following Infinitive:

I *cannot* read the letter idj tann ben Brief nidjt lefen.

3) The *Conditional* seldom occurs in the form idj würde with the Infinitive: idj würde tönnen, idj würde follen 2c.; commonly the Imperfect Subjunctive is used as Conditional: idj tönnte, idj follte, idj müßte, idj wollte, idj mödjte, idj bürfte.

4) The *compound tenses* sometimes appear regularly formed by adding the auxiliary idj Ijabe, Ijatte 2c. to the Participle past, as long as they stand by themselves, as:

Idj Ijabe getonnt, idj Ijabe gemußt 2c.

But when these compound tenses are connected with the *Infinitive* of another verb, which is mostly the case, then they take the form of the Infinitive instead of the Part. past.

Ijaben Sie ben Brief lefen tönnen (instead of lefen getonnt)?
Have you been able *to read* the letter?

Karl Ijat aus'geIjen müffen Charles was obliged *to go out.*

Idj Ijabe es neIjmen müffen.
I was (*or* have been) obliged *to take* it.

Er Ijat fagen wollen (not gewollt).
He (has) wished to say.

5) When in English the auxiliary of mood is in the *Imperfect tense* and the following verb in the *compound* of the Infinitive, the German way of rendering this, greatly differs from the English, viz. the principal verb remains in German in the Infinitive present, and the auxiliary is put in the *Pluperf.* of the *Subjunctive* mood, as:

You *might* or *could (Imp.)* have read the letter.
Sie Ijätten ben Brief lefen tönnen.

He *might* have gone er Ijätte geIjen tönnen.

I *should* have done it or I *ought* to have done it.
Idj Ijätte es tIjun follen.

You *ought* to have written your exercise.
Sie Ijätten Ihre Aufgabe fdjreiben follen.

*Note.* When the auxiliary of mood is in the *Present* tense, the two languages perfectly correspond, as:

You must *have seen* it Sie müffen es gefeIjen Ijaben.
He cannot have seen me er tann midj nidjt gefeIjen Ijaben.

## Remark on the English auxiliary to do.

The frequent use of the veib *to do* in negative and interrogative English sentences might easily induce the English pupil to employ the same mode of expression also in German. It must therefore be stated, that this is not admissible.

1) The negation nid&#7511;t (not) is simply placed after the verb itself and its object, as.

I do not see id&#7511; fe&#7511;e nid&#7511;t (I see not).
We do not want it wir braud&#7511;en e&#223; nid&#7511;t (we w. it not).

2) In the interrogative form, the subject, — be it a personal pronoun or a noun — is simply put after the verb.

Ge&#7511;en Gie? *do* you go? are you going?
Wann fpeifen Gie (ju Mittag)? when *do* you dine?
Rauft der Bater da&#223; Pferd? *does* the father buy the horse?
Gr fauft e&#223; nid&#7511;t he *does* not buy it.
Gagen Gie i&#7511;m nid&#7511;t *do* not tell him.

## Words.

| | |
|---|---|
| Lad&#7511;en to laugh. | da&#223; T&#7511;ea'ter the theatre. |
| die Nad&#7511;rid&#7511;t the news. | die Marf the marc. |
| fpielen to play. | da&#223; Fleifd&#7511; the meat. |
| wa&#7511;r true fe&#7511;en to see. | der Me&#7511;ger ⎱ the butcher. |
| fagen to say. t&#7511;un to do. | der Fleifd&#7511;er ⎰ |

## Reading Exercise. 34.

Gr mag lad&#7511;en. Der Knabe darf nid&#7511;t fpielen Dürfen Gie au&#223;ge&#7511;en? Id&#7511; darf &#7511;eute nid&#7511;t au&#223;ge&#7511;en; aber morgen. Id&#7511; &#7511;abe geftern mein Pferd verfaufen wollen; aber id&#7511; &#7511;abe nid&#7511;t gefonnt. Du magft ge&#7511;en oder nid&#7511;t. Id&#7511; mod&#7511;te nid&#7511;t au&#223;ge&#7511;en. Gr darf nid&#7511;t in den Garten ge&#7511;en. Diefe Nad&#7511;rid&#7511;t mod&#7511;te wa&#7511;r fein. Warum durfte der Knabe nid&#7511;t in die Gd&#7511;ule ge&#7511;en? Gr war franf. Mein Bater &#7511;ätte geftern fein Pferd verfaufen fönnen; aber er &#7511;at nid&#7511;t gewollt. Warum &#7511;at er e&#223; nid&#7511;t verfaufen wollen? Gr braud&#7511;t (wants) e&#223; nod&#7511; (still). Die Kinder &#7511;aben fpielen wollen; fie &#7511;ätten i&#7511;re Aufgabe lernen follen; fie werden bald ju Bette ge&#7511;en müffen.

## Aufgabe. 34a.

You may &#8322;believe &#8321;it (e&#223;).*) *Do* you go to (in *acc.*) the theatre? Do you believe that news? I do not believe it (fie). He may say, what he pleases (wa&#223; er will). *May I* see, what (wa&#223;) you read? I will not go out, it may rain (regnen). Could you &#8323;give &#8321;me (mir) &#8322;two &#8323;marcs? I *would*, but I cannot. The boy must not write. The boys must not write. He *was not allowed to* remain. I *was obliged to* (or *had to*) go to the post-office. The butcher has *been obliged* to sell the meat. You should not believe it. I know (wei&#223;), I *ought to* do it. [I ought to have read (lefen) it. § 5].

*) See the Remarks on G. Constr. p 79 and 80.

### Conversation.

| | |
|---|---|
| Wollen Sie Wein trinken? | Nein, ich will keinen Wein trinken. |
| Wann müssen Sie ausgehen? | Ich muß um acht Uhr (at eight o'clock) ausgehen. |
| Kannst du schreiben und lesen? | Ich kann lesen, aber nicht schreiben. |
| Wollen Sie Butter und Käse? | Nein, ich will Fleisch haben. |
| Soll Albert den Brief auf die Post tragen? | Nein, ich muß selbst (myself) auf die Post gehen. |
| Wollen Sie Ihre Pferde verkaufen? | Nein, ich will sie nicht verkaufen. |
| Warum konnten Sie nicht kommen? | Ich war unwohl und mußte zu Hause bleiben. |
| Warum hat dieser Mann den Brief nicht gelesen? | Er kann nicht lesen. |
| Dürfen Sie ins Theater gehen? | Nein, ich darf nicht. |
| Darf ich Ihnen eine Zigarre geben? | Ich danke Ihnen (I thank you). |
| Warum gehen Sie nicht aus? | Weil (because) es regnet. |
| Darf ich sehen (see), was Sie schreiben? | O ja, Sie dürfen es sehen. |
| Wird er bald (soon) abreisen müssen? | Er wird vielleicht (perhaps) hier bleiben können. |
| Haben Sie die Rechnung (bill) bezahlen müssen? | Ich habe zwei Mark bezahlen müssen. |

# Eighteenth Lesson.
## On the Adjective.

1) The adjective, in German, is either used **predicatively,** to state *how* a thing or a person is. In this case, its place is after the verb, and it requires no alteration at all; it remains the same for the three genders and for both numbers, as in English:

Der Tisch ist rund the table is round.
Das Kleid ist alt the dress is old.
Die Äpfel sind gut the apples are good.
Die Kirschen waren süß the cherries were sweet.

2) Or it is used **attributively,** to qualify a noun. Then it always *precedes* the noun which it qualifies and is varied for the gender, number or case of the substantive, with which it must agree in all these particulars; as: der runde Tisch, *pl.* die runden Tische. The declension of the adjective in its *attributive* use varies according to its being preceded:

I. by the *definite* article (*or* a substitute of it).
II. by the *indefinite* (*or* a substitute of it).
III. by neither of them.

## First form.

1) With the *definite* article, **der, die, das,** every adjective takes the inflexions of the 2nd declension, *viz.* in the nominative case **e,** in all the following cases singular and plural **en,** except in the *accusative singular* of the *fem.* and *neuter* gender, which are always the same as the nominative. With this single deviation the termination of all the cases is the same for all three genders.

### Table of the inflexions of the first form.

| | *masc.* | *fem.* | *neuter.* | *Plural for all.* |
|---|---|---|---|---|
| *Nom* | —e | —e | —e | —en |
| *Gen.* | —en | —en | —en | —en |
| *Dat.* | —en | —en | —en | —en |
| *Acc* | —en | —e | —e | —en. |

### Examples.

| *Singular.*     Masculine. | *Plural.* |
|---|---|
| *N.* der gute Vater the good father | die guten Väter |
| *G.* des guten Vaters of the good father | der guten Väter |
| *D.* dem guten Vater to the good father | den guten Vätern |
| *A.* den guten Vater the good father. | die guten Väter. |

**Feminine.**

| | |
|---|---|
| *N.* die schöne Blume the fine flower | die schönen Blumen |
| *G.* der schönen Blume of the f. fl. | der schönen Blumen |
| *D.* der schönen Blume to the f. fl. | den schönen Blumen |
| *A.* die schöne Blume the f. fl | die schönen Blumen. |

**Neuter.**

| | |
|---|---|
| *N.* das kleine Haus the little house | die kleinen Häuser |
| *G.* des kleinen Hauses of the l. h. | der kleinen Häuser |
| *D.* dem kleinen Hause to the l. h. | den kleinen Häusern |
| *A.* das kleine Haus ⁊c. | die kleinen Häuser. |

*Note 1.* The article before the adjective denoting sufficiently the gender and case of the following noun, these terminations of the *first form* seem to be merely of a euphonical nature.

*Note 2.* Observe that the terminations of the adjective are not the same as those of the article or the noun.

2) The adjectives undergo the same inflexion after these six deteiminative adjectives which have three different forms for the three genders, viz.

| | |
|---|---|
| dieſer, dieſe, dieſes. | mancher, manche, manches. |
| jener, jene, jenes. | derſelbe, dieſelbe, dasſelbe |
| jeder, jebe, jedes (every). | welcher, welche, welches? |

#### Examples.

Dieſer alte Mann this old man; *Gen* dieſes alten Mannes.
Dieſer hohe Baum this high tree; *pl.* dieſe hohen Bäume.
Jenes arme Mädchen that poor girl; *pl.* jene armen Mädchen.
Jedes ſleißige Kind every diligent child.
Von welchem berühmten Manne ſprechen Sie? of which celebrated man are you speaking?

3) When there are two or more adjectives, the inflexion remains the same for both:

| *Singular.* | *Plural.* |
|---|---|
| *N.* der gute, alte Vater. | die ſchönen, kleinen Häuſer. |
| *G.* des guten, alten Vaters ꝛc. | der ſchönen, kleinen Häuſer ꝛc. |

## Second form.

1) With the *indefinite* article ein, eine, ein, the declension is nearly the same as with the definite article, it differs only in the *nominative* case, *masculine* and *neuter*, and in the *accusative neuter*, because in these cases the article ein has no particular termination to indicate the gender. In these cases, the *adjective* must take the termination of the ıespective gender, viz.:

#### Table of the inflexions.

| masc. | neuter. | Plur. |
|---|---|---|
| *Nom.*           —er. | *Nom. & Acc.* —es. | —en. |
| *G. D. & Ac.* —en. | *G. & D.*           —en. | —en. |

#### Declension

*Masc.* *N.* ein armer Mann a poor man
     *G.* eines armen Mannes of a poor man
     *D.* einem armen Mann(e) to a poor man
     *A.* einen armen Mann a poor man.

*Fem.* *N.* eine arme*) Frau a poor woman
     *G.* einer armen Frau of a poor woman
     *D.* einer armen Frau to a poor woman
     *A.* eine arme Frau a poor woman.

*) Observe that the feminine is the same for the *Nom. & Acc.* in all three forms.

*Neut.* *N.* ein armeß Kind a poor child
*G.* eineß armen Kindeß of a poor child
*D* einem armen Kinde to a poor child
*A.* ein armeß Kind a poor child.

2) This mode of inflexion is also used after all determinative adjectives (which are alike in the *masc.* and *neuter*), viz. mein, dein, fein, unfer, Jhr (euer), ihr and fein. Its plural is the same as that of the first form, viz. en in all the cases.

Examples with possessive adj.

*Sing.* Mein kleiner Hund my little dog.
Jhre liebe Tochter your dear daughter.
Unfer neueß Hauß our new house.
*Plur.* Meine kleinen Hunde my little dogs.
Jhre lieben Töchter your dear daughters.
Unfre neuen Häufer our new houses

Declension with a possessive adj.

*Singular.*

*N.* Mein guter Freund my good friend
*G·* meineß guten Freundeß of my good friend
*D* meinem guten Freund to my good fiiend
*A.* meinen guten Freund my good friend.

*Plural.*

*N.* Meine guten Freunde my good friends
*G.* meiner guten Freunde of my good friends
*D* meinen guten Freunden to my good friends
*A.* meine guten Freunde my good friends.

3) If more than one adjective precede a substantive, each adjective must be declined in this manner, as:

*N.* ein armer, alter Mann a poor old man
*G.* eineß armen, alten Manneß of a poor old man
*D.* einem armen, alten Manne to a poor old man
*A.* einen armen, alten, franken Mann a p. old sick man.

---

### Words.

Der Schüler the pupil.
der Maler the painter.
der Geschmack the taste.
der Gesang the song.
der Sommer summer.
das Leben life. lieb dear.
der Berg the hill, mountain.
amerikanisch American.

das Eifen iron.
das Schiff (*pl.* Schiffe) the ship.
lang long. tapfer brave.
bitter bitter.
stehen to stand. sitzen to sit.
die Wunde the wound.
hoch high. stark strong.
treu faithful. geschickt clever.

7*

menſchlich human.
unreif unripe.
warm warm.
hören to hear.

die Nuß (*pl.* Nüſſe) the walnut.
fleißig industrious, diligent.
koſtbar precious.

### Reading Exercise. 35.

Der liebe Bruder. Die liebe Schweſter. Das kleine Mädchen. Ein ſchöner Garten. Eine ſchöne Blume. Ein ſchönes Haus. Der Bruder iſt gut. Die Schweſtern ſind gut. Die ſchönen Gärten. Die neuen Häuſer. Ich liebe die roten Blumen. Die hohen Bäume des grünen Waldes. Ich habe einen treuen Hund. Er hat eine kleine Tochter. Wir kaufen die unreifen Äpfel Dieſe Birnen ſind noch nicht (not yet) reif. Ich ſtehe auf einem hohen Berge. Die Vögel ſitzen in den grünen Bäumen. Ich liebe die kurzen Tage des kalten Winters nicht. Der tapfre Soldat hat eine ſchwere (severe) Wunde. Die engliſchen Schiffe ſind ſehr gut.

### Aufgabe. 36.

1. The river is large. The large river. A large river. The good man. The diligent pupil. The diligent pupils. A faithful sister. A clever painter. I know a (*Acc.*) clever painter. The little child has a new dress Mr. A. is a *) very strong man. (The) iron is a very useful metal. We hear the beautiful song of the little birds. The American ships are very large. The rich count has a beautiful palace.

2. Miss Elizabeth is a diligent little girl (*neut.*). My good old father is ill. The little house stands (ſteht) on (auf *dat.*) a high mountain. We love the good children. We admire (bewundern) the beautiful palace of the rich count. I like the long days of the warm summer. We speak of (von *dat.*) the short human life. The unripe walnuts are not good. I have seen the beautiful large English ships. A good advice (Rat, *m.*) is precious.

---

## Third form.
### Adjectives not preceded by any article.

1) The third form is made use of, when the adjective precedes the substantives *without* any article or substitute (see p. 98, 2 and 99, 2). The gender not being indicated by an article, it must be expressed by the ending of the adjective itself. This form therefore is declined by three genders in the singular; the plural has only one termination for the three genders, like the definite article.

---

☞ With the verb *to be* always use the nominative case.

## Examples.

*Singular.*                                   *Plural.*

**Masculine.**

N. guter Wein good wine | gute Weine good wines
G. guten Weines of good w. | guter Weine
D. gutem Wein(e) | guten Weinen
A. guten Wein. | gute Weine.

**Feminine.**

N. warme Suppe warm soup | warme Suppen warm soups
G. warmer Suppe | warmer Suppen
D. warmer Suppe | warmen Suppen
A. warme Suppe. | warme Suppen.

**Neuter.**

N. frisches Wasser fresh water | neue Bücher new books
G. frischen Wassers | neuer Bücher
D. frischem Wasser | neuen Büchern
A. frisches Wasser | neue Bücher.

*Note* The learner will easily see that these *distinctive* endings of the 3rd form are the terminations of the missing article **der, die, das.** The only case which differs, is the *Gen. sing.*, which should accordingly be: **gutes.** Here an **n** has been substituted for euphony's sake, to avoid the repetition of several s (**s**).

2) When two or more adjectives are placed before the same substantive without an article, they are declined in the same way, as:

N. guter, alter, roter Wein (some) good old red wine
G. guten, alten, roten Weines of good old red wine
D. gutem, altem, rotem Wein to good old red wine
A. guten, alten, roten Wein (some) good old red wine.

N. reiche, gütige Leute rich kind people
G. reicher, gütiger Leute of rich kind people
D. reichen, gütigen Leuten to rich kind people
A. reiche, gütige Leute rich kind people.

3) This third form is also used for the *vocative* case without or with a personal pronoun:

Armer Mann! armes Mädchen! poor man! poor girl!
Ich (du, Sie) armer Mann! I (thou, you) poor man!
Liebes Kind! dear child! | Liebe Kinder! dear children!
Junge Leute or ihr junge Leute! (you) young people!

4) With cardinal numbers and the five numeral adjectives: einige, mehrere, viele, manche and wenige (not alle):

Zehn starke Männer ten strong men.
Viele (wenige) treue Freunde many (few) true friends.
Fünf schöne Pferde five beautiful horses

5) After a *Genitive* this third form is also used:
Heinrichs größtes Vergnügen Henry's greatest pleasure.
Die Mutter, deren kleine Kinder 2c.
The mother whose little children etc.
Herr Bell, mit dessen jüngstem Sohne ich reiste.
Mr. Bell with whose youngest son I travelled.

## Additional remarks.

1) Adjectives ending in **el**, as: edel noble, eitel vain, dunkel dark, mostly lose, when declined, the **e** before **l**:

| | |
|---|---|
| N. der edle Graf (not edele) | die eitle Frau |
| G. des edlen or edeln*) Grafen | der eitlen Frau |
| D. dem edlen   =   =   Grafen | der eitlen Frau |
| A. den edlen   =   =   Grafen. | die eitle Frau. |

2) Those ending in **er** and **en** do not, except sometimes in poetry, require the omission of the **e** in the Nominative, but in the other cases the former take only **n** after **r**, the latter mostly keep their **e**, as

     Ein bitterer Trank a bitter potion,
  G. eines bittern Tranks.
     Eine finstere Nacht a dark night,
  G. & D. einer finstern Nacht.
     Ein offenes Fenster,
  G. eines offenen Fensters.

3) The adjective **hoch** remains unchanged when *after* its noun, but when *before*, it changes in all the cases the **ch** into a simple **h**. We say: Der Baum ist hoch; but.
  N. der hohe Baum, | *pl.* die hohen Bäume the high trees.
  G. des hohen Baumes. | *pl.* hohe Bäume high trees etc.

4) Many adjectives are roots and monosyllables as in English, such as: arm, reich, jung, alt, süß (sweet), rein 2c. But the greater number are *derivatives*, and may be known by the following syllables affixed to a substantive or verb:

= bar: fruchtbar fertile; — kostbar precious.
= en: golden golden, — eichen oaken, — seiden silken.
= ern: hölzern wooden; — eisern iron; — steinern of stone.
= haft: tugend=haft virtuous; — boshaft wicked.
= ig: fleißig diligent; — artig pretty; — prächtig magnificent.
= icht: steinicht stony; — bergicht mountainous, hilly.
= isch: himmlisch heavenly; — kindisch childish.
= lich: herrlich splendid; lieblich lovely; königlich royal, kingly.
= los; grenzenlos boundless; — ehrlos infamous·
= sam: furchtsam timid; — gehorsam obedient; — grausam cruel.

---

*) This other way of declining · des edeln, eiteln, *pl.* die edeln (for edlen) is also sometimes met with.

Likewise with:
=rei ch: finnreich ingenious, fifchreich abounding with fish.
=voll. geiftvoll talented, witty. prachtvoll magnificent.
=würdig. liebenswürdig amiable; ehrwürdig venerable.
=wert: lobenswert praise-worthy; wünfchenswert desirable.

5) Adjectives denoting a *nation* are mostly formed by the termination =ifch, and written with a small letter, as:

| | |
|---|---|
| amerikanifch American. | öfterreichifch Austrian. |
| dänifch Danish. | polnifch Polish. |
| deutfch*) German. | preußifch Prussian. |
| englifch English. | ruffifch Russian. |
| franzöfifch French. | fächfifch Saxon. |
| italienifch Italian. | fchwedifch Swedish. |
| griechifch Greek. | fpanifch Spanish. |
| holländifch Dutch. | türkifch Turkish. |

6) Adjectives and participles may be used substantively. In this case they take the article, and must be written with a capital letter, but retain their inflexion as adjectives. Ex.:

*Adj.* fremd, (strange) reifend, deutfch, gefangen.

First form. **Declension.** Second form.

N. der Fremde the stranger | ein Fremder a stranger
G. des Fremden of the stranger | eines Fremden of a stranger
D. dem Fremden to the stranger | einem Fremden to a stranger
A. den Fremden the stranger. | einen Fremden a stranger.

I. & II. form. *Plural.* III. form.

N. die Fremden the strangers | Fremde strangers
G. der Fremden of the strangers | Fremder of strangers
D. den Fremden to the strangers | Fremden to strangers
A. die Fremden the strangers. | Fremde strangers.

Such are:

Der Reifende the traveller. — ein Reifender a traveller.
der Gelehrte the learned man. — ein Gelehrter a. l. man.
der Bediente the man-servant. — ein Bedienter a man-servant.
der Deutfche the German. — ein Deutfcher a German.
der Gefandte the ambassador. — ein Gefandter an ambassador.
der Gefangene the prisoner. — ein Gefangener a prisoner.

7) Even *neuter* nouns are formed in this manner, as:
Das Schöne the beautiful. | Gutes thun to do good.
Das Neue, das Alte that which is new (old). .

8) After etwas something or anything, nichts nothing, viel, wenig and mehr the adjectives used substantively take the *third* form (—es), as:

*) In deutfch the i has been dropped before fch (from deut=ifch).

Biel Gutes much good | Nichts Neues nothing new (no
Etwas Schlechtes something *or* anything bad.  [news).
Wir sprechen von etwas Nützlichem (*Dat.*).
We are speaking of something useful.

---

### Words.

| | |
|---|---|
| Der Frühling spring. | ein Arbeiter a workman. |
| das Wetter the weather. | die Arbeit the work. |
| das Stück the morsel, piece. | die Gesundheit (the) health. |
| das Bier beer. die Milch milk. | schwach feeble, weak |
| frisch fresh. | angenehm agreeable, pleasant. |
| wohnen to dwell, live. | nützlich useful. |
| wichtig important. süß sweet. | blind blind. |
| die Alpen the Alps. | blau blue. grau grey. |
| die Krankheit the disease. | schwarz black. weiß white. |
| der Becher the cup, goblet. | gefährlich dangerous. |
| die Reise the journey. | vollbringen to perform |
| die Güte the kindness. | immer always. |

### Reading Exercise. 37.

1. Die süßen Kirschen haben einen angenehmen Geschmack
(taste). Der liebliche Frühling ist gekommen. Ich habe die präch=
tigen königlichen Schlösser gesehen. Ich kaufe guten, alten, roten
Wein. Geben Sie mir frisches (new), weißes Brot. Hier ist
schönes rotes Papier. Diese Frau verkauft gute, frische, süße Milch.
Meine liebe, alte, gute Mutter ist sehr krank. Kleine Familien
wohnen in kleinen Häusern.

2. Bei (in) schönem Wetter gehen wir spazieren (take a walk),
bei schlechtem (bad) bleiben wir zu Hause (stay at home). Geben
Sie mir ein Glas süße, frische Milch und ein Stück gutes, weißes
Brot. Neue Freunde sind nicht immer gute Freunde. Ich habe
Ihnen etwas Wichtiges zu sagen. Wissen Sie etwas Neues? Ich
weiß (I know) etwas Neues; aber es ist nichts Angenehmes.

### Aufgabe. 38.

1. Here is sweet milk. Have you [any] good red wine?
Do you like strong beer? The Alps are high mountains. I
want (brauche or wünsche) cold fresh water. The girl sells
beautiful flowers. The brave soldiers have severe (schwere)
wounds. The rich Jews had little old houses. There (da) is
a poor little blind girl. The good mother gives (giebt) ripe
cherries [to] her diligent children. Mr. Asher wears (trägt)
a (*Acc.*) green coat, a blue cloak and a grey hat. A good
book is a*) good and faithful friend. It was on a (in einer)
very dark night. The king had a gold cup in his hand.

---

*) See the foot-note p. 100.

2. The diseases of little children are often dangerous. My good and amiable cousin is ill. I have seen many dear friends during my long journey. They received me (fie em= pfingen mid)) with great kindness. Clever workmen are always sought [for] (gefudit). Feeble women (Frauen) cannot perform this work. I am in good health. Old people, young men and women, and little children walked (gingen . . fpazieren) in the beautiful garden of our kind friend. Read (lefen Sie) something good and useful. The courage (Mut, *m.*) of the brave soldiers was great.

### Conversation.

| | |
|---|---|
| Ift biefer Fluß tief (deep)? | Nein, er ift nidit fehr tief. |
| Ift Karl fleißig? | Ja, er ift ein fleißiger Knabe. |
| Wer hat biefes fdiöne Bild ge= malt (painted)? | Ein berühmter, beutfdier Maler. |
| Weldies ift fein Name? | Er heißt Winterhalter. |
| Wo fino Ihre lieben Kinder? | Sie find in meinem neuen Haufe. |
| Haben Sie einen großen Garten? | Nein, er ift nidit fehr groß. |
| Lieben Sie ben roten Wein? | Ich liebe ben roten und ben weißen. |
| Haben Sie gebratenes1) Fleifch (roasted meat)? | Wir haben gebratenes und ge= kodites1) (boiled). |
| Verkaufen Sie füße Milch? | Ich habe keine füße Milch, aber frifdie Butter. |
| Wo ift mein lieber Arthur? | Er ift in ber Schule. |
| Lieben Sie bie beutfdie Mufit? | O ja; aber ich liebe bie italienifdie mehr (better). |
| Spredien Sie Deutfdi, mein Herr? | Ich spredie ein wenig (a little). |
| Haben Sie beutfdie Stunben (lessons)? | Ja, ich habe jeben Tag eine Stunbe. |
| Wer hat biefen golbenen Ring verloren? | Meine Schwefter Anna hat ihn verloren. |
| Hat ber Bäder (baker) gutes Brot? | Er verkauft immer gutes Brot. |
| Von weldier Farbe find bie Fe= bern ber Raben? | Die Febern ber Raben find fdiwarz. |
| Haben Sie einen fdiwarzen ober einen weißen Hut? | Ich habe zwei Hüte, einen fdiwar= zen und einen weißen. |

# Nineteenth Lesson.

## Degrees of comparison.

1) The comparison, in German as in English, is ef- fected by two degrees, the *comparative* and *superlative*.

---

1) Participles are declined like adjectives.

The comparative degree is formed by the addition of **er,**
or when the adjective ends in **e,** only **r;** the superlative
by adding **ſt** or **ſte,** precisely as in the English language.
Further the vowels **a, o, u** are changed in most monosyllables into **ä, ö, ü** in both degrees.

|  | Comp. | Superlative 1st form. | 2nd form |
|---|---|---|---|
| Reich rich | reicher | der, die, das reichſt=e | or am reichſten. |
| ſchön handsome | ſchöner | ⸗ ⸗ ⸗ ſchönſte | ⸗ am ſchönſten. |
| lang long | länger | ⸗ ⸗ ⸗ längſte | ⸗ am längſten. |
| alt old | älter | ⸗ ⸗ ⸗ ält(e)ſte | ⸗ am älteſten. |
| arm poor | ärmer | ⸗ ⸗ ⸗ ärmſte | ⸗ am ärmſten. |
| ſtark strong | ſtärker | ⸗ ⸗ ⸗ ſtärkſte | ⸗ am ſtärkſten. |
| fromm pious | frömmer | ⸗ ⸗ ⸗ frömmſte | ⸗ am frömmſten. |

2) In the comparative degree of adjectives in **el** (not
**er** or **en**) the **e** is dropped before **l,** as:

edel noble, *Comp.* edler,                     | *Sup.* der edelſte.
bitter bitter, ,,   bitterer (not bittrer), |   ,,   der bitterſte.

3) In the superlative of adjectives ending in three
consonants or in a hissing sound (**z, s, ß, ſch**) an **e** is
often inserted before **ſt** for euphony (**eſte**), as:

|  | Comp. | Superlative degree. |
|---|---|---|
| Schlecht bad | ſchlechter | der ſchlechteſte or am ſchlechteſten. |
| gerecht just | gerechter | ⸗ gerechteſte ⸗ am gerechteſten. |
| kurz short | kürzer | ⸗ kürzeſte ⸗ am kürzeſten |
| ſüß sweet | ſüßer | ⸗ ſüßeſte ⸗ am ſüßeſten. |

*Note 1.* Adjectives ending in **t** with another consonant
before it, may also insert a euphonical **e** in the superlative
degree, as:
    alt, *Sup.* der ältſte as well as der älteſte;
    kalt, *Sup.* der kälteſte or der kältſte.

*Note 2.* Sometimes the word **aller** is prefixed to the superlative, as: der allerſtärkſte meaning the strongest *of all.*

4) The first form of the superlative **der (die, das)**
**reichſte, der (die, das) ſtärkſte ꝛc.** is the *attributive* form of
the superlative, and is only used when followed by a
noun (which however may also be understood), as:
    Der reichſte Mann the richest man.
    Der ſtärkſte Wein the strongest wine.
    Die Roſe iſt die ſchönſte Blume the rose is the finest flower.

5) The second form, **am reichſten, am ſtärkſten ꝛc.**
is invariable, and used, when the adjective is *found
after* the auxiliary verb **ſein** *(to be), the adj. being the
last word of the English sentence,* as:

Dieſer Wein iſt am ſtärkſten this wine is (the) strongest.
Dieſe Roſe iſt am ſchönſten this rose is the most beautiful.
Es iſt am neueſten (ſchönſten) ꝛc. it is the newest, finest etc.

*Note 1* Another adverbial form of the superlative is. Aufs
beſte, aufs ſchönſte ꝛc. in the best, finest etc. *manner*, and a
few superlatives of this kind take nothing but ſt. Such are:
äußerſt extremely; höchſt highly, höflichſt most politely,
ergebenſt most humbly; freundlichſt ꝛc.

*Note 2* The following monosyllabic adjectives change the
vowel neither in the comparative, nor in the superlative:

| | | |
|---|---|---|
| Blaß pale. | knapp close, scarce. | ſanft soft |
| bunt ſpeckled. | lahm lame. | ſchlaff slack |
| falſch false. | matt languid. | ſchlank slender. |
| froh merry. | morſch rotten. | ſtarr stiff. |
| hohl hollow. | nackt naked. | ſtolz proud. |
| hold kind. | platt flat | ſtumpf blunt. |
| kahl bald | plump clumsy. | toll mad. |
| karg scanty. | roh rude. | voll full |
| klar clear | rund round. | zahm tame |

*Note 3.* In like manner the monosyllables ending in au,
as. lau lukewarm; blau blue etc., and all adjectives of two
or more syllables never admit of the modification; as: — blutig
bloody, blutiger (not blüttgen); — fruchtbar, fruchtbarer; artig,
artiger; bekannt, bekannter ꝛc.

6) Some adjectives and adverbs are irregular in the
degrees of comparison, viz.:

| | *Comp* | *Superl* |
|---|---|---|
| Hoch high | höher higher | der höchſte or am höchſten. |
| nahe near | näher nearer | der nächſte, am nächſten. |
| groß great, large | größer greater | der größte, am größten. |
| gut good | beſſer better | der beſte, am beſten the best. |
| viel much | mehr more | der meiſte, am meiſten most. |
| viele *pl* many | mehrere several | die meiſten most. |
| wenig little | { weniger (minder) } less | { am wenigſten (am mindeſten) } the least. |
| weniger *pl* few | wenigere fewer | die wenigſten the fewest. |
| gern willingly | lieber (rather) | am liebſten (I like best). |
| bald soon | eher, früher sooner | am eheſten the soonest. |

*Note.* A few comparative and superlative degrees, originally formed of adverbs or prepositions, have no positive; these
are:

| *Comp.* | *Superl.* |
|---|---|
| Der äußere the exterior (outer); | der äußerſte the extremest, utmost |
| der innere the interior, inner, | der innerſte the innermost. |
| der obere the upper, superior; | der oberſte the uppermost. |
| der untere the lower, inferior, | der unterſte the lowest, undermost. |

| *Comp* | *Superl* |
|---|---|
| der mittlere the middle; | der mittelste the middlemost. |
| der hintere the hinder, hind-; | der hinterste the hindermost. |
| der vordere the front-, fore —, | der vorderste the foremost. |

7) The *declension* of the comparative and superlative degrees is subject to the same rules as the positive form, and depends upon their being preceded by an article, or not, as:

**First form.**          Second form.

*Comp.   Singular (Masc.).*

| | |
|---|---|
| *N.* der höhere Baum the higher tree | ein höherer Baum. |
| *G.* des höheren Baumes of the higher tree | eines höheren Baumes. |
| *D.* dem höheren Baum to the higher tree | einem höheren Baum. |
| *A.* den höheren Baum the higher tree | einen höheren Baum. |

*Plural.*

*N.* and *A.* die höheren Bäume the higher trees | höhere Bäume.

*Comp.   Singular (Fem.).*

| | |
|---|---|
| *N.* die buntere Blume the gayer flower | eine buntere Blume. |
| *G.* der bunteren Blume of the gayer fl. | einer bunteren Blume. |
| *D.* der bunteren Blume to the gayer fl. | einer bunteren Blume. |
| *A.* die buntere Blume the gayer fl. | eine buntere Blume. |

*Plural.*

*N* and *A.* die bunteren Blumen the gayer flowers | —buntere Blumen.

*Comp.   Singular (Neuter).*

| | |
|---|---|
| *N.* das schönere Haus the finer house | ein schöneres Haus. |
| *G.* des schöneren Hauses of the finer house | eines schöneren Hauses. |
| *D.* dem schöneren Hause to the finer house | einem schöneren Hause. |
| *A.* das schönere Haus the finer house | ein schöneres Haus. |

*Plural.*

*N.* & *A.* die schöneren Häuser the finer houses | — schönere Häuser.

When, instead of the indefinite article, one of the possessive or the indefinite numeral adjectives, or the word no (kein) are preceding, the comparative and superlative forms of adjectives take the termination of „en“ in the plural, just as those preceded by the definite article and its resp. substitutes (comp. 1st and 2nd less., pages 20, 21 and 23).

Ex.: meine, unsre, eure, Ihre höheren Bäume; but without neither article *nor substitute* of it, the plural of 'ein höherer Baum' etc. becomes the Third form (see this!) and then is formed 'höhere Bäume, buntere Blumen, schönere Häuser' zc.

*Superlative.*

*N. & A.* das schönfte Haus the finest house
*G.* des schönften Haufes of the finest house
*D* dem schönften Haufe to the finest house.

**Plural.**

*N. & A* die schönften Häufer the finest houses
*G.* der schönften Häufer of the finest houses
*D* den schönften Häufern 2c.

**Third form. Sing.**

*Masc. Nom.* befferer Kaffee, *Acc.* befferen Kaffee better coffee.
*Fem N. & A* schwärzere Tinte blacker ink.
*Neut. N. & A.* schöneres Wetter finer weather.

**Third form. Plur.**

*Plur. N. & A.* schönere Blumen. *G.* schönerer Blumen 2c.

*Note.* We must remark that, when two adjectives are compared with one another, which seldom occurs, this must be done by the word mehr (= rather). Ex.:

Er war mehr glücklich als tapfer.
He was more (rather, successful) than brave.

8, In comparative sentences, *as* followed by an adjective and *as*, is rendered in German by ebenfo — als or wie, and *not so* — *as*, by nicht fo — als or wie. Ex.:

Er ist ebenfo jung als ich or wie ich he is as young as I.
Karl war nicht fo glücklich als fein Freund Wilhelm.
Charles was not so happy as his friend William.

9) *As* — *again* answers to the German noch einmal fo or doppelt fo —. Ex.:

Er ist noch einmal fo alt (or doppelt fo alt) als (or wie) ich.
He is as old again as I.

10) When a relation between two comparatives is expressed, the English *the* — *the* before them is to be translated je — defto. Ex.:

Je höher der Berg, defto tiefer das Thal.
The higher the hill, the deeper the valley.
Je ruhiger ein Leben ist, defto glücklicher ist es.
The quieter a life is, the happier it is.

(See the 36th Lesson on the Conjunctions, 3rd class.)

---

**Words.**

Der See the lake.
das Meer the sea.

ein Veilchen a violet.
der Adler the eagle.

der Flügel the wing
die Kralle the claw
der Platz the square, place.
breit wide, broad.
die Tugend virtue.
der Storch (pl. Störche) the stork.
der Hals (pl. Hälse) the neck.
die Gans (pl. —e) the goose
der Strauß (pl. —e) the ostrich
die Nachbarin the neighbour, f
der Feldherr the general.

das Blei (the) lead
das Kupfer copper.
die Stärke the strength.
der Weg the way.
gefunden found
tief deep.   prächtig beautiful.
leicht light.   scharf sharp
freigebig liberal   streng strict.
unglücklich unfortunate.
ungeschickt unskilful
weit far   als than.

### Reading Exercise. 39.

1. Der breite Fluß. Der breitere See. Das breiteste Meer
Der Fluß ist tief; der See ist tiefer als der Fluß; das Meer ist
am tiefsten. Karl ist stärker als Wilhelm; er ist der stärkste Knabe.
Marie ist fleißiger als Sara. Du hast ein schönes Veilchen gefunden,
aber ich habe ein schöneres   Meine Rose ist schön, die Rose meiner
Schwester ist am schönsten. In den Städten sind die prächtigsten
Häuser. In London leben die reichsten Kaufleute (merchants).
Die reichsten Leute sind nicht immer die freigebigsten.
2. Der Adler ist der stärkste Vogel. Er hat die längsten
Flügel und die schärfsten Krallen. Im Frühling sind die Tage
länger als im Sommer; aber im Winter sind sie am kürzesten.
Das Silber ist kostbarer als das Kupfer. Das Gold ist das kost-
barste Metall. Wein ist besser als Bier. Die spanischen Weine
sind die besten (Weine). Dieser Maler ist nicht so berühmt als
sein Vater, aber seine Bilder sind ebenso (as) schön   Unser Onkel
(Oheim) ist ebenso reich als unser Vetter; aber er ist nicht so glücklich. Der beste Kaffee kommt aus Arabien   Je früher (sooner),
desto besser.

### Aufgabe. 40.

1. The street is wide; the square is wider, the field is
the widest. The apples are sweet; the pears are sweeter,
the cherries are the sweetest. This mountain is high, it is
the highest in this country. The rich are not always the
happiest. (The) money is good, (the) labour is better, (the)
virtue is best. The stork has a longer (*Acc. m.*) neck than
the goose. (The) Ostriches have the longest necks. Mrs. Hunter
is a more industrious woman than my neighbour. She is the
most amiable lady. In spring *the *days *are*) longer than
in winter; in summer *they *are longest  The morning was
warm, the evening was warmer. The old man is feeble; the
sick woman is feebler; the little child is feeblest

---

*) The figures before the words indicate the order in which
the words are to follow in German.

2. Miss Lucy is the handsomest [and loveliest] girl in the town. Napoleon I. (ber Erſte) was the greatest general (The) lead is useful; (the) copper is more useful; (the) iron is the most useful metal. I have a strict master, my cousin has a stricter; the son of the count has the strictest. The strength of the strongest man is far less (weit geringer) than that (die‘) of an elephant. The general was *more\** unfortunate than unskilful. The (Je, § 10) better (the) men are, *the* happier ²they ¹are. Augustus was *more* successful than brave. *The* more, *the* better. It is best We are richest, when (wenn) we ¹are ²most ¹contented. Alexander was *as* ambitious (ehrgeizig) as Cæsar. I am as tall (groß) as you, but my brother is not so tall as you.

### Conversation.

| | |
|---|---|
| Welcher Fluß iſt breiter, der Neckar oder der Rhein? | Der Rhein iſt viel breiter. |
| Iſt Wilhelm ſtärker als Karl? | Ich denke (think), Karl iſt ſtärker. |
| Sind die reichſten Leute immer am glücklichſten? | Das iſt nicht immer der Fall (the case). |
| Welches iſt das koſtbarſte Metall? | Das Gold iſt das koſtbarſte |
| Aber welches iſt am nützlichſten? | Das Eiſen iſt am nützlichſten |
| Welches ſind die beſten Weine? | Die ſpaniſchen Weine |
| Woher‘ kommt der beſte Kaffee? | Der beſteKaffee kommt ausArabien. |
| Welches iſt die ſchönſte Blume? | Ohne Zweifel (no doubt) die Roſe. |
| Iſt Alfred älter als Sie? | Nein, er iſt jünger als ich; er iſt der jüngſte Sohn. |
| Sind dieſe Äpfel reif? | Sie ſind nicht ganz (quite) ſo reif als die Birnen. |
| Welches iſt das ſtärkſte Tier? | Der Elefant iſt das ſtärkſte. |
| Welches iſt der größte Fiſch? | Der Walfiſch (whale) iſt der größte von allen Fiſchen. |
| Haben Sie beſſeres Bier? | Nein, aber ich habe beſſern Wein. |
| Iſt Fräulein Roſa ein ſchönes Mädchen? | Sie iſt ſehr ſchön, ſie iſt die ſchönſte von den drei Schweſtern. |
| Kennen Sie eine ſchönere Blume als die Roſe? | Nein, ich kenne keine ſchönere. |
| Welches iſt der kälteſte Monat in Deutſchland? | Der Monat Januar iſt der kälteſte. |

---

\*) See p 109, *Note.*

# Twentieth Lesson.

## ON THE NUMERALS.

(Zahlwörter.)

The numerals are of two kinds, namely: *Cardinal* and *Ordinal* numbers.

## I. Cardinal numbers. Grundzahlen.

| | |
|---|---|
| Ein, eine, ein or eins one. | sechsundzwanzig twenty-six |
| zwei two | siebenundzwanzig twenty-seven. |
| drei three. | achtundzwanzig twenty-eight |
| vier four. | neununddzwanzig twenty-nine. |
| fünf five. | dreißig thirty. |
| sechs six. | einunddreißig thirty-one etc. |
| sieben seven. | vierzig forty. |
| acht eight. | fünfzig fifty. |
| neun nine. | sechzig sixty. |
| zehn ten | siebzig seventy. |
| elf eleven | achtzig eighty. |
| zwölf twelve | neunzig ninety |
| dreizehn thirteen. | hundert*) a hundred. |
| vierzehn fourteen. | hundert und eins a hundred and |
| fünfzehn fifteen. | zweihundert two hundred. [one |
| sechzehn sixteen | dreihundert three hundred |
| siebzehn seventeen. | vierhundert four hundred |
| achtzehn eighteen. | fünfhundert five hundred etc |
| neunzehn nineteen. | tausend*) a thousand. |
| zwanzig twenty. | zweitausend two thousand. |
| einundzwanzig twenty-one | zehntausend ten thousand. |
| zweiundzwanzig twenty-two. | fünfzigtausend fifty thousand. |
| dreiundzwanzig twenty-three. | hunderttausend a hundred |
| vierundzwanzig twenty-four | thousand |
| fünfundzwanzig twenty-five. | eine Million' a million. |

1800, eintausend achthundert — or achtzehnhundert.

1805, eintausend achthundert(und)fünf — or achtzehnhundertfünf.

1852, eintausend achthundertzweiundfünfzig or achtzehnhundert-
zweiundfünfzig

## Observations.

1) The first number ein, eine, ein (joined to a noun), but einer, eine, eines or eins (when without a noun), is declined like the indefinite article, which is in fact the same word

---

*) *A* hundred and *a* thousand are in German simply hundert and tausend (not ein hundert ꝛc); but the English *one* hundred, *one* thousand is rendered by einhundert and eintausend

When used as a numeral, more stress is employed. The plural is only employed with the definite article: die einen *the ones* or *some*, in which case it is considered as an adjective.

2) We must here observe that the English practice of putting *one* or *ones* after the adjective is not admissible in German. When therefore it occurs in English, it cannot be translated, as: a good *one* = ein guter (*masc.*), or if feminine, eine gute, neuter = ein gutes.

*Note.* The two numbers zwei and drei have an inflexion for the genitive and dative case, when used before a substantive without the article:

Die Gleichheit zweier Dreiecke the equality of two triangles.
Das Bündnis dreier Könige the alliance of three kings.

3) All the numerals up to hundert may take the inflexion en for the dative plural, when not immediately followed by a substantive. It is however better, not to inflect them at all.

Von dreien of *or* from three | mit fünfen with five.
unter zwanzig among twenty.

4) Hundert and Tausend, when nouns, are declined, as:
*N.* and *A.* das Hundert a hundred, die Hunderte the hundreds (die) Tausende (the) thousands.

5) The hours of the day or night are expressed as follows·
What o'clock is it? Wieviel Uhr ist es?
Two o'clock zwei Uhr.
A quarter *past* two ein Viertel nach zwei or auf drei
Half past two halb drei. [(*towards three*).
A quarter *to* three drei Viertel auf drei or 1/4 vor drei.
*At* three o'clock um drei Uhr.

*Note 1.* With minutes we reckon as in English. Ex.:
Ten minutes *to* five zehn Minuten vor (or bis) 5 Uhr.
Five minutes *past* two fünf Minuten nach zwei

*Note 2.* *In* before a year must be translated im Jahr. Ex.:
In 1870 im Jahr 1870.

6) A person's age is expressed as in English. Ex.:
How old are you? Wie alt sind Sie?
I am twenty years old ich bin zwanzig Jahre alt.

7) The numeral adverbs are
Einmal once, zweimal twice; dreimal three times etc.

8) By adding erlei to the cardinals, the *variative* numerals are formed; as: einerlei of one kind, zweierlei of two kinds; dreierlei; viererlei; zehnerlei; mancherlei of several kinds; vielerlei of many kinds; allerlei of all kinds. These words admit of no inflexion and *precede* the noun.

Zeigen Sie mir zweierlei Tuch, blaues und schwarzes.
Show me two kinds (or sorts) of cloth, blue and black.

9) The multiplicatives are formed by adding the syllable **fach** (or **fältig**) to the cardinal numbers; as:

| | |
|---|---|
| einfach simple, single. | dreifach triple, threefold. |
| zweifach \| twofold. | vierfach quadruple. |
| doppelt / double. | zehnfach tenfold etc. |

10) *Single*, meaning *separate*, is translated **einzeln**; but in the sense of *only*, it is **einzig**. Ex.

Single words einzelne Wörter.
Not a single word kein einziges Wort.

11) *Only*, when an adjective, is also rendered **einzig**, as:
My only son mein einziger Sohn.

---

### Words.

| | |
|---|---|
| Die Freundschaft friendship. | der Ballen the bale. |
| das Schaf, *pl.* Schafe, the sheep. | der Feind the enemy. |
| eine Ziege a goat. | geboren born. |
| das Schwein, *pl.* —e, the pig. | der Zucker the sugar. |
| die Kuh, *pl.* Kühe, the cow. | die Meile the mile. |
| der Ochse (*2nd decl.*) the ox. | die Revolution' the revolution. |
| der Einwohner the inhabitant. | eine Insel an island. |
| die Schlacht the battle. | Island Iceland. |
| das Jahr the year. | die Baumwolle cotton. |
| die Woche the week. | der Reisende the traveller. |

leben to live.   mehr als more than.  mal times.

### Reading Exercise. 41.

1. Ich habe nur (only) einen Bruder. Sie haben nur eine Schwester. Die Freundschaft dieser drei Männer. Mein Oheim hatte neun Kinder. Er hat drei Söhne und vier Töchter verloren. Fünf Pferde haben zwanzig Füße; denn (for) jedes Pferd hat vier Füße. Unter (among) dreißig Äpfeln war nicht ein guter (Obs. 2). Eine Woche hat sieben Tage. Ein Tag hat vierundzwanzig Stunden. Dieses Dorf hat achtzehnhundert zweiundzwanzig Einwohner, und dreihundert achtunddreißig Häuser. Zehn und fünfundvierzig machen fünfundfünfzig. 82 und 67 machen 149.

2. Vier mal (times) 8 sind 32. — Sieben mal 9 sind 63. — 21 mal 32 sind 672. Ich bin geboren (was born) im Jahr 1814 und mein jüngster Bruder im Jahr 1818. Mohammed lebte von 571 bis 632, er floh von Mekka nach Medina (Yatreb) im Jahr 622. Im Jahr(e) 1492 hat Kolumbus Amerika entdeckt (discovered). Die Reformation in Deutschland begann im Jahr 1517. (Die Stadt) London hatte am Schlusse des Jahres 1882 schon 2770 Straßen, ungefähr 1140 Kirchen und über vier Millionen

Einwohner. Wir haben 99 Ballen Baumwolle gekauft. Der König hat mehr als zwanzig Schlösser (Paläste). Die Feinde haben mehr als dreißig Kanonen verloren.

### Aufgabe. 42.

1. My neighbour has three houses; I have only one (nur eines). Our cousin has five houses. The peasant has 24 sheep, 18 pigs and 11 goats. He has also 5 horses, 8 cows and one ox. A month has 30 days. February has only 28. A year has 12 months, 52 weeks or 365 days. I am 17 years old; I was (bin) born in the year 1835. My father is 48 years old; he was (ist) born 1822. I have bought 46 pounds (Pfund) [of] sugar and 100 pounds [of] coffee. In the year 1848. — 3 times 9 make (machen) 27. Thirty-five and 42 make 77. I have lost a hundred marks. Is it three o'clock? No, Sir, it is half past three. One German mark is almost equivalent to one English shilling.

2. The city [of] Strasburg had at the end of 1883 about 16,666 houses and more than 200,000 inhabitants. How much is 8 times 15? 8 times 15 are 120. The battle of (bei) Leipsic took place (fand statt) in the year 1813. The French revolution began (begann) in 1789 Iceland is an island; it is 400 miles long and 150 broad. We arrived (sind angekommen) in (im) October 1852, and set out (abgereist) in January 1853. The traveller has seen more than thirty-two towns and ninety-five villages. Show me three kinds [of] paper, blue, green and brown (braun).

---

## II. Ordinal numbers.

These are formed of the cardinals by adding the termination te from two to nineteen, and ste to the remainder, beginning with twenty. The first and third however are irregular, making der erste, der dritte.

They are declined like adjectives.

| | |
|---|---|
| The 1st der, die, das erste. | the 13th der drei'zehn'te. |
| the 2nd der zwei-te. | the 14th der vierzehnte. |
| the 3rd der dritte. | the 15th der fünfzehnte. |
| the 4th der vierte. | the 16th der sechzehnte. |
| the 5th der fünfte. | the 17th der siebzehnte. |
| the 6th der sechste. | the 18th der achtzehnte. |
| the 7th der siebente. | the 19th der neunzehnte. |
| the 8th der achte. | the 20th der zwanzig-ste. |
| the 9th der neunte. | the 21st der einundzwanzigste. |
| the 10th der zehnte. | the 22nd der zweiundzwanzigste |
| the 11th der elfte (eilfte). | the 23rd der dreiundzwanzigste. |
| the 12th der zwölfte. | the 24th der vierundzwanzigste ꝛc. |

| | |
|---|---|
| the 30th der dreißigſte. | the 102nd der hundertunbzweite. |
| the 40th der vierzigſte. | the 120th der hundertunbzwan= |
| the 50th der fünfzigſte. | zigſte ꝛc. |
| the 60th der ſechzigſte | the 200th der zwei'hun'dertſte. |
| the 70th der ſiebenzigſte or ſieb= | the 300th der dreihundertſte ꝛc. |
| the 80th der achtzigſte.   [zigſte. | the 1000th der tauſendſte. |
| the 90th der neunzigſte. | the 2000th der zweitauſendſte. |
| the 100th der hundertſte. | the 10,000th der zehntauſendſte. |
| the 101st der hundertunderſte. | the last der (die, das) letzte. |

the 1255th der zwölfhundertfünfundfünfzigſte or
der tauſendzweihundertfünfundfünfzigſte.

## Observations.

1) In compound numbers, the last only can be an ordinal;
the others remain cardinals, as:

Der hundertvierundzwanzigſte the 124th.

2) The ordinals are declined as adjectives in the three
genders, the form of the declension depends upon their being
preceded by an article, or not, as:

Der zehnte Mann the tenth man.
*Gen.* des zehnten Mannes of the tenth man etc.
Mein drittes Glas my third glass.

3) The date is expressed as follows:

On the tenth *of* May am zehnten Mai or den 10ten Mai.
What is the day of the month = der wievielte iſt heute?
It is the 8th es iſt der achte or wir haben den 8ten.

4) Der erſte and der letzte assume sometimes a comparative
form, when referring to *two* persons or objects: der, die, das
erſtere the former; der, die, das letztere the latter.

5) Of the ordinals are formed the distinctives by the
addition of the termination ens. These are in German:

| | |
|---|---|
| Erſtens (or erſtlich) first(ly) | viertens fourthly etc. |
| zweitens secondly. | zehntens tenthly. |
| drittens thirdly. | elftens eleventhly etc. |

6) The fractional numbers (with the exception of halb
half) are also derived from the ordinals, by adding the word
Teil, which however is commonly abridged into tel, as: ein
Dritteil or Drittel a third; ein Vierteil or Viertel a quarter;
ein Fünftel ꝛc.; ein Zehntel; ein Zwölftel; drei Achtel ³/₈ths;
from nineteen upwards ſtel, derived from ſte of the ordinals:
der zwanzigſte, ein Zwanzigſtel, vier Hundertſtel ⁴/₁₀₀ths; ſieben
Tauſendſtel ⁷/₁₀₀₀ths etc.

7) Halb half and ganz all, whole, are adjectives and
placed *after* the article, as:

Das ganze Jahr all the year, the whole year.
Ein halber Tag half a day.
Eine halbe Stunde half an hour.
Ein halbes Jahr half a year *or* six months.
The *half* means die Hälfte.

*Note* With halb another kind of dimidiative numerals is formed, as: britthalb = 2½; vierthalb = 3½; fünfthalb = 4½ 2c. These expressions mean *two whole ones and of the third the half only etc.* Instead of zweit'halb, which is not usual, we say anderthalb, which signifies *one and a half* and is *undeclined.* Ex.:

Anderthalb Jahre one year and a half.
Vierthalb Ellen three yards and a half.

We may however say with equal propriety: drei und eine halbe Elle or drei Ellen und eine halbe.

---

### Words.

Der Band the volume.
die Flasche the bottle, flask.
das Jahrhun'dert the century.
die Klasse the class.
der Papst the pope.
der Herzog the duke.
der Hase the hare.

vielleicht' perhaps.
er starb he died.
das Alter the age.
der Thee tea. fertig ready.
die Regie'rung the reign.
verhei'ra'tet married.
fleißig industrious, diligent.
Brüssel Brussels.

### Reading Exercise 43.

1. Der erste Monat des dritten Jahres. Der zweite Tag der vierten Woche. Das sechste Fenster des vierten Stocks (story). Herr Robinson war 32 Wochen krank; in der dreiunddreißigsten starb er (he died) Jakob der Zweite (James II.) starb in Frankreich den (or am on the) vierzehnten September 1701. Georg III. (der Dritte) wurde (was) den 22sten September 1761 in der West= minster=Abtei (Abbey) gekrönt (crowned). Er war bei seiner Thron=Besteigung (accession) 22 Jahre alt.

2. Ludwig XIV. (der Vierzehnte) starb im Jahr 1715; Ludwig XV. im Jahre 1774; Ludwig XVI. im Jahre 1783. Drei Achtel sind die Hälfte von drei Viertel. Dieses ist mein fünftes Glas. Die Frau war anderthalb Jahre krank. Hier ist zweierlei Wein, roter und weißer. Wieviel Uhr (what o'clock) ist es? Es ist fünf Uhr oder vielleicht ein Viertel auf sechs. Heinrich der Achte, König von England, war sechsmal verheiratet.

### Aufgabe. 44.

1. The first day. The third year. I have the fifth volume. The second week of the seventh month. This is our sixth bottle. The eighth year of the nineteenth century. The child was a week and a half old. Charles is the twentieth in his

class. March is the third, June is the sixth, and December
the last month of the year. The duke of (von) Marlborough
won (gewann) the battle of (bei) Hochstädt on the 12th [of]
August 1704. He died on the 16th *of* June 1722.
     2. (The) Pope Gregory (Gregor) (*the*) VII. was an enemy
of the emperor Henry IV. (*Gen.*). Edward III. took (nahm)
Calais *on the* 3rd *of* August 1347. I was five t i m e s at (in)
Paris and four times at Brussels. We set out (sind abgereist)
on the 26th [of] November 1850, and we arrived (sind angekommen) on the 14th of April 1851. Peter (Peter) the Great
died at (in) St. Petersburgh on the 8th February 1725, in
the 53rd year of his age and in the 43rd of his reign. Tell
me (sagen Sie mir) *what o'clock it is*. It is four o'clock or
half *past* four. I shall go out at (um) a quarter *to* five.

## Conversation.

| | |
|---|---|
| Wie viele Kinder hat Herr Brown? | Er hat 6 Kinder; 2 Söhne und 4 Töchter. |
| Wie alt ist sein ältester Sohn? | Er ist 18 Jahre alt. |
| Wie alt ist seine jüngste Tochter? | Sie ist fünf Jahre alt |
| In welchem Jahrhundert leben wir? | Wir leben im 19ten Jahrhundert. |
| Wieviel sind 30 und 50? | 30 und 50 sind 80. |
| Wieviel ist 12 mal 12? | 12 mal 12 sind 144. |
| Waren Sie gestern auf der Jagd (out hunting)? | Ja, gestern und heute (to-day). |
| Was haben Sie geschossen (killed)? | Wir haben 13 Hasen geschossen. |
| Welchen Platz (place) hat Georg in der Schule? | Er ist sehr fleißig, er hat immer (always) den ersten Platz. |
| Und sein Bruder Walter? | Walter ist der 26ste in seiner Klasse. |
| Wann wurde Karl V. geboren? | Er wurde geboren im Jahre 1500. |
| Wann starb Peter der Große? | Am (or den) 8ten Februar 1725. |
| Wie alt war er? | Er war 53 Jahre alt. |
| Haben Sie viel Wein getrunken? | Das ist unsre dritte Flasche. |
| Wieviel Thee wünschen Sie? | Ich wünsche drei Viertel Pfund*). |
| Welches ist die Hälfte von 6/8? | Die Hälfte von 6/8 ist 3/8 oder 6/16. |
| Waren Sie lange in Amerika? | 4 Jahre, 2 Monate und 23 Tage. |
| Wieviel Uhr ist es? | Es ist 11 Uhr oder halb zwölf. |
| Können Sie mir sagen, wieviel Uhr es ist? | Ich habe keine Uhr; aber es mag halb zwei Uhr sein. |
| Ist es ein Viertel auf vier? | Es ist drei Viertel auf vier. |
| Um wieviel Uhr speisen Sie? | Ich speise (dine) um 12 Uhr. |
| Um wieviel Uhr gehen Sie zu Bett? | Um 10 Uhr oder halb 11. |

---

*) or drei Achtel Kilo, see p. 55 *).

---

# Twenty-first Lesson.

**T h e  V e r b.**  $\mathfrak{D}\mathfrak{a}\mathfrak{z}$ $\mathfrak{Z}\mathfrak{e}\mathfrak{i}\mathfrak{t}\mathfrak{w}\mathfrak{o}\mathfrak{r}\mathfrak{t}.$

## General Remarks on Verbs.

§ 1.  There are five kinds of verbs, viz.: 1) *active* or *transitive;* 2) *passive;* 3) *neuter* or *intransitive;* 4) *reflective,* and 5) *impersonal verbs.*

1) A verb is *active* or *transitive*, when the action requires an *object* or *person* acted upon:

$\mathfrak{J}\mathfrak{d}$ effe I eat *(what?)* einen $\mathfrak{A}$pfel an apple.
$\mathfrak{J}\mathfrak{d}$ liebe I love *(whom?)* meine $\mathfrak{S}\mathfrak{d}$wefter my sister.

We see that effen and lieben are active or transitive verbs. The object is commonly in the *Accusative,* sometimes in the *Dative.*

2) A verb is considered *passive,* when the action conveyed by the verb, is suffered by the subject itself:

$\mathfrak{M}$eine $\mathfrak{S}\mathfrak{d}$wefter wird von mir geliebt
My sister is loved by me.
$\mathfrak{D}$ie $\mathfrak{A}$pfel werden gegeffen the apples are eaten.

3) A verb is termed *neuter* or *intransitive,* when it implies a state or an action which does not pass over to an object, but remains with the subject

$\mathfrak{J}\mathfrak{d}$ fdlafe I sleep (you cannot say *I sleep something*).
$\mathfrak{J}\mathfrak{d}$ gehe I go (not *I go somebody* or *something*).

4) A verb is *reflective* or *reflected.* when the object to which the action passes over, is the same person as the subject:

$\mathfrak{J}\mathfrak{d}$ unterhalte mich I amuse *myself.*
$\mathfrak{E}$r rettete fich *he* rescued *himself*

5) *Impersonal verbs* are without any relation to a person or thing doing the action expressed by the verb:

$\mathfrak{E}\mathfrak{z}$ fdneit *it* snows.  $\mathfrak{E}\mathfrak{z}$ regnet *it* rains.

§ 2.  With regard to their outer form, they are either **roots** or **derivative** verbs.

*All derivative verbs are regular.*

*Note.* *Prefixes*, of course, do not make a verb *derivative.* Of ergeben or angeben, the radical is not ergeb= or angeb=, but geb, er= and an= before geb= being *prefixes*; hence such verbs are not to be termed *derivative*, but *root-verbs with a prefix* or *compounds*

§ 3. Verbs are inflected by *person*, *number*, *tense* and *mood*. There are *three persons* and *two numbers*. Verbs have *six tenses*, to denote the *time* of the action, viz.: 1) The *Present;* 2) *Imperfect (Preterimperfect);* 3) *Perfect*; 4) *Pluperfect;* 5) *First Future;* 6) *Second Future.*

§ 4. Verbs have *six moods* to denote the different relations of the sentence to the speaker, viz.: 1) *Indicative;* 2) *Subjunctive* (or *Conjunctive*); 3) *Conditional;* 4) *Imperative;* 5) *Infinitive;* 6) *Participle.*

§ 5. There are two different ways of conjugating German verbs; the one is called the *modern* or *regular* form, the other the *ancient* or *irregular* form All the verbs are accordingly divided into *two* great classes:

1) *Regular or modern verbs.*
2) *Irregular or ancient verbs.**)

---

### Regular or modern verbs.

A verb is called *regular* when the vowel or diphthong of the radical syllable remains the same throughout, when the Imperf. ends in **te,** and the Part. in **t.** Ex.:

lob-en — lob-te — gelob-t.

The *modern* or *regular* conjugation comprises, besides many other root-verbs:

1) all those *verbs* whose radical vowel is **o, u** or **eu.** Such are for example:

with **o:**\*\*) holen to fetch; loben to praise; hoffen to hope; klopfen to knock; kochen to boil; sohnen, gehorchen &c.

with **u:**\*\*) suchen to seek, schulden to owe; murren to murmur; summen to hum etc.

with **eu:** beugen to bend; zeugen to witness; scheuen to shun etc.

2) those verbs whose radical vowel is modified, viz.: ä, ö, ü and äu, as: — wärmen to warm; hören to hear; führen to lead; träumen to dream.

---

\*) The conjugation of regular or modern verbs is also called 'feeble (schwache) conjugation', that of irreg. or anc. verbs 'strong (starke) conjugation'.

\*\*) The only *exceptions* to these rules are: 1) with o: kommen to come (see the irregular verbs Nr. 42); stoßen to push (109). — 2) with u: rufen to call (110). (Those figures indicate the number of the irregular verb in their respective lists, Less. 26th to 29th incl.).

*Note.* The following verbs, being irregular, are the only exceptions:

with ä: gebären to bring forth (Nr. 24), gähren to ferment (139).
with ö: ſchwören to swear (148), erlöſchen to become extinct (135).
with ü: lügen to lie (142), betrügen (betriegen) to cheat (113).

3) all verbs ending in ʒen, cken, chten, gnen, eln, ern, igen and ieren, as: tanʒen to dance; packen to pack up; achten to esteem; regnen to rain; ſchmeicheln to flatter; beſſern to improve; ſündigen to sin; ſtudieren to study etc.

*Except:* ſitzen to sit (13), backen to bake (155,), erſchrecken to be frightened (22); fechten to fight (137), and flechten to twist (138)

## Formation of the tenses.

The *Present* tense is formed by detaching the final n from the Infinitive, as: Ich lobe I praise *or* I am praising (from loben to praise); ich ſuche (from ſuchen to seek).

In the *Imperfect* the syllable te (sometimes ete) is added to the radical, as: lob-te from lob-en; hör-te from hör-en; red-ete from red-en.

The *Past participle* is formed by prefixing the syllable ge, and by the addition of t (sometimes et), as: ge-lob-t, ge-hör-t, ge-red-et. All simple and compound verbs (L. 31) take this ge.*)

The *First future* is formed by combining the auxiliary ich werde with the *Infinitive:* ich werde loben, ich werde hören, ich werde reden.

The *Perfect* and *Pluperfect*, by combining the auxiliary ich habe, ich hatte ꝛc. with the *Past Participle*, as: ich habe gelobt, ich habe gehört, ich habe geredet; *Pluperfect* ich hatte gelobt, ich hatte gehört ꝛc. This is quite analogous to the conjugation of the English regular veibs.

The terminations of the different *persons* of the Present and Imperfect tenses are as follows:

| Present. | | Imperfect. | |
|---|---|---|---|
| *Singular.* | *Plural.* | *Singular.* | *Plural.* |
| 1. —e | —en | 1. —te or ete | —ten or eten |
| 2. —ſt or eſt | —t, et or en | 2. —teſt or eteſt | —tet or etet(n) |
| 3. —t or et. | —en. | 3. —te or ete. | —ten or eten. |

---

*) Not those compounded with inseparable particles, where the prefix ge is dropped (see p. 126, 5).

# Conjugation of a regular or modern verb.
## Loben to praise.

| Indicative. | Subjunctive. |
|---|---|

### Present Tense.

Ich lobe*) I praise, I am praising | Ich lobe I [may] praise
du lobst or lobest thou praisest | du lobest thou mayst praise
er (sie, es) lobt he (she, it) praises | er lobe he may praise
man lobt people praise |
wir loben we praise | wir loben we may praise
ihr lobt or lobet ) ye praise | ihr lobet ) ye may praise
Sie loben ) you praise | Sie loben ) you may praise
sie loben they praise. | sie loben they may praise.

### Imperfect.

Ich lobte I praised | Ich lobte**) (if) I praised
du lobtest thou praisedst | du lobtest thou praised
er lobte he praised | er lobte he praised
wir lobten we praised | wir lobten we praised
ihr lobtet ) ye praised | ihr lobtet ) ye praised
Sie lobten ) you praised | Sie lobten ) you praised
sie lobten they praised. | sie lobten they praised.

### Perfect.

Ich habe.. gelobt I have praised | Ich habe gelobt I may have pr.
du hast gelobt thou hast pr. | du habest gelobt thou mayst h. pr.
er hat gelobt he has praised | er habe gelobt he may have pr.
    etc.        etc. |     etc.        etc.

### Pluperfect.

Ich hatte .. gelobt I had praised | Ich hätte gelobt (if) I had praised
du hattest gelobt thou hadst pr. | du hättest gelobt    2c.
er hatte gelobt he had praised. | er hätte gelobt    2c.

### First Future.

Ich werde .. loben I *shall* praise | Ich werde loben I shall praise
du wirst loben thou wilt praise | du werdest loben thou wilt praise
er wird loben he will praise | er werde loben he will praise
wir werden loben we shall pr. | wir werden loben we shall praise
ihr werdet loben ) ye will pr. | ihr werdet loben ) ye will pr.
Sie werden loben ) you will pr. | Sie werden loben ) you will pr
sie werden loben they will pr. | sie werden loben they will praise.

### Second Future.

Ich werde gelobt haben I shall | Ich werde gelobt haben I shall
  have praised | have praised
du wirst gelobt haben 2c. | du werdest gelobt haben    2c.
    2c.        2c. |     2c.        2c.

*) or lob' in the familiar way. — **) or lobete.

### First Conditional.

| Singular. | Plural. |
|---|---|

Ich würde .. loben I should praise · wir würben loben we should pr.
du würdest loben thou *wouldst* p. · ihr würdet loben you *would* pr.
er würde loben he *would* pr · sie würden loben they *would* pr.

In the same manner, conjugated with other auxiliaries of mood:

#### Potential.

| | |
|---|---|
| Ich kann loben I can praise. | Ich konnte loben I could praise. |
| ich muß loben I must praise. | ich sollte loben I ought to praise. |
| ich will loben I will praise | ich wollte loben I would praise ꝛc. |

#### Second Conditional.

Ich würde gelobt haben or hätte gelobt I should have praised
du würdest gelobt haben or hättest gelobt thou *wouldst* have pr. ꝛc.

### Imperative.

Lobe or lob' praise (thou). · loben wir or laßt uns lo= ⎫ let us
er soll loben let him praise · wir wollen loben [ben, ⎰praise.
sie sollen loben let them praise. · lobet or loben Sie praise (you).

### Infinitive.

*Pres* loben or zu loben to praise.
um .. zu loben (in order) to praise.
*Past.* gelobt haben or gelobt zu haben to have praised.

### Participles.

*Pres.* lobend praising. · *Past.* gelobt (gelobet) praised.

*Note 1.* The English mode of conjugating the verb *to be* with the addition of a *Part. pres.* cannot be rendered literally in German, but the corresponding tenses must be given, as:

*Pres.* I am learning ich lerne; he is learning er lernt ꝛc
*Impf.* I was learning ich lernte; he was learning er lernte.
*Perf.* I have been learning ich habe gelernt ꝛc.

*Note 2. Interrogative form* Do I praise? lobe ich? Does he praise? lobt er? Did I praise? lobte ich or habe ich . . . gelobt? Did you praise? lobten Sie or haben Sie gelobt?

*Negative* I do not praise ich lobe . . . nicht, he does not praise er lobt nicht. I did not praise ich lobte . . . nicht or ich habe .. nicht gelobt Do not praise loben Sie nicht.

The inflexion of regular verbs (*Principal parts*), is thus:

ich liebe — lieb-te — ge-liebt.

Such are:

| | |
|---|---|
| Lieben to love, like. | danken (*dat.*) to thank. |
| leben to live, to be alive | kaufen to buy. |
| holen to fetch, to go for. | legen to lay, to put. |
| schicken to send. | suchen to seek, look for. |

machen to make.
lachen to laugh.
weinen to cry, weep.
fragen to ask (a question).
sagen (*dat.*) to say, to tell.
spielen to play.
lehren to teach.
hören to hear.
lernen to learn.
strafen to punish.

stellen to place upright.
zeigen (*dat.*) to show.
leeren to empty.
füllen to fill.
ruhen to rest.
wählen to choose.
dienen to serve.
klagen to complain.
wohnen to live, to dwell.
brauchen to need, to require.
verteidigen to defend.

## Words.

Der Lehrer the teacher, master.
die Aufgabe the exercise, lesson.
der Hahn the cock.
das Ding, *pl.* —e, the thing.
der Handschuh, *pl.* -e, the glove.
die Küche the kitchen.
die Nachtigall the nightingale.
der Metzger the butcher.

niemand nobody.
der Lärm the noise.
das Kalb, *pl.* Kälber, the calf.
träge lazy. bauen to build.
finden to find. liegen to lie.
krähen to crow. tapfer brave.
verdienen to deserve.
diesen Morgen *adv.* this morning.

## Reading Exercise. 45.

1. Ich liebe meinen Bruder. Du liebst deine Schwester.
Die Fische leben im Wasser. Was kaufen Sie? Der König hat
ein Schloß gebaut. Der Knabe lernt. Der Lehrer hat diesen
Schüler gelobt, weil (because) er sehr fleißig ist. Der Knabe hat
seine Aufgabe nicht gelernt. Der Vater straft den trägen Knaben.
Die Mutter spielte mit dem Kind. Die tapfern Soldaten werden
die Stadt verteidigen. Ich sehe (see) das spielende Kind. Die
Mutter würde weinen, wenn das Kind krank wäre.

2. Wir loben den fleißigen Schüler. Sie hatten ihn auch
gelobt. Niemand wird die trägen Schüler loben. Gestern »hörte
»ich schöne Musik. Ich habe sie nicht gehört. Haben die Kinder
gestern gespielt? Sie werden morgen spielen. Hörst du die Nachtigall singen? Hören Sie den Hahn krähen? Der Hahn hat dreimal gekräht. Ich habe ihn nur einmal (only once) gehört. Liebet eure Eltern.

## Aufgabe. 45a.

I seek my hat. He fetches water. I thank you (Ihnen).
The child wept. We hear a great noise. We heard the
cock crow. At (um) what o'clock did it (er) crow? It crowed
at three o'clock this (*Acc.*) morning. Children, hear my words.
Do you not hear what (was) your master says? Do you seek
your cloak? I seek my gloves. Seek and you will find.
The servant sought his knife. Has he sought in the kitchen?
It lies (liegt) in the kitchen. The children will play in the
garden.

## Peculiarities in the conjugation.

1) There are some verbs, in which the **e** after the radical consonant is retained throughout every mood, tense and person. Such are all regular verbs ending in ben, ten, ften, gnen, chnen, thmen, as it would offend the ear to let the termination immediately follow the b, t, m or n, of the radical. For example:

### Reden to talk.
#### Present Tense.

| S. Ich rede I talk | Pl. wir reden we talk |
|---|---|
| du redeft thou talkest | ihr redet } ye talk |
| er redet he talks | Sie reden } you talk |
| man redet people talk | fie reden they talk. |

#### Imperfect.

| S. Ich redete I talked | Pl. wir redeten we talked |
|---|---|
| du redeteft thou talkedst | ihr redetet } ye talked |
| er redete he talked | Sie redeten } you talked |
| fie redete she talked | fie redeten they talked. |

#### Perfect.      Pluperfect.

Ich habe geredet I have talked. | Ich hatte geredet I had talked.

In the same manner are conjugated:

| | |
|---|---|
| Baden to bathe. | mieten to hire, to take. |
| schaden to injure. | fürchten to fear, to be afraid. |
| bilden to form. | töten to kill. |
| landen to land. | schlachten to kill, slaughter. |
| achten to esteem, respect. | retten to save, rescue. |
| antworten to answer. | öffnen to open. |
| beten to pray. | begegnen to meet. |
| warten to wait. | zeichnen to draw. |
| erwarten to expect. | arbeiten to work etc. |

*Imperf.* ich badete, achtete, antwortete, wartete, fürchtete, arbeitete 2c.
*Part. past.* gebadet, geachtet, geantwortet, gewartet, gefürchtet, getötet, geöffnet, begegnet, gerettet, gearbeitet.

2) Verbs ending in sen, ßen, schen or zen retain the **e** only in the *second* person of the singular present.

| | |
|---|---|
| Ich tanze I dance | Ich reise I travel |
| du tanzeft thou dancest | du reifeft thou travellest |
| er tanzt he dances etc. | er reift he travels etc. |

Such are:

| | |
|---|---|
| Wünschen to wish. | fitzen to sit |
| fetzen to put, to place. | haffen to hate. |

3) Verbs ending in **eln,** such as: handeln to act, drop the e before l in the *first* person singular of the Present tense; verbs in **ern** should not omit the e before r.

*Present Tense.*

| | |
|---|---|
| Ich handle (not handele) I act | Ich bewundere I admire |
| du handelst thou actest | du bewunderst thou admirest |
| er handelt he acts | er bewundert he admires |
| wir handeln we act | wir bewundern we admire |
| ihr handelt ) ye act | ihr bewundert ) ye admire |
| Sie handeln / you act | Sie bewundern / you admire |
| sie handeln they act. | sie bewundern they admire. |

*Imperfect*

| | |
|---|---|
| Ich handelte I acted etc. | Ich bewunderte I admired etc. |
| *Part. past.* gehandelt. | \| *Past p.* bewundert. |

Such are:

| | |
|---|---|
| Tadeln to blame. | erwidern to reply. |
| schütteln to shake. | klettern to climb. |

4) Verbs of foreign origin ending in **ieren,** are regularly conjugated; only in the Participle past they do not admit of the prefix ge.

| | | |
|---|---|---|
| Studie'ren to study. *Imp.* | ich studierte. *Perf.* | ich habe studiert. |
| probieren to try. | ich probierte. | ich habe probiert. |
| regie'ren to govern. | ich regierte. | ich habe regiert. |
| †marschie'ren to march. | ich marschierte. | ich bin marschiert. |

5) Verbs having an *unaccented prefix* before them, do not take the syllable ge in their Part. Past. Such prefixes are: **be, emp, ent, er, ver, zer, ge, miß, voll, wider** and **hinter.** Ex.

| | | |
|---|---|---|
| Beloh'nen to reward. *Imp.* | ich belohnte. *Part.* | belohnt.[1] |
| verkaufen to sell. | ich verkaufte. | verkauft. |
| zerstören to destroy. | ich zerstörte. | zerstört. |
| vermieten to let. | • ich vermietete. | vermietet. |

(Further particulars on this class of verbs are given in the Less. 30.)

6) The following verbs and those derived from them, though quite regular in their terminations, change in the *Imperfect* and *Part. past* the root-vowel into a:

| *Infinitive.* | *Present.* | *Imp.* | *Part. past.* |
|---|---|---|---|
| Brennen to burn | ich brenne | ich brannte | gebrannt. |
| Kennen to know[2] | ich kenne | • kannte | gekannt. |
| Nennen to name, call | ich nenne | • nannte | genannt. |

---

1) not gebelohnt. 2) French *connaître.*

| *Infinitive.* | *Present.* | *Imp.* | *Part. past.* |
|---|---|---|---|
| Rennen to run, race | ich renne | ich rannte | gerannt. |
| Senden to send | ich sende | ⸗ sandte¹) | gesandt. |
| Wenden to turn | ich wende | ⸗ wandte²) | gewandt. |
| Denken to think | ich denke | ⸗ **dachte** | **gedacht.** |
| Bringen to bring | ich bringe | ⸗ **brachte** | **gebracht.** |
| Wissen to know³) | ich weiß⁴) | ⸗ wußte | gewußt. |

## Words.

Die Grammatik the grammar.
recht right. unrecht wrong.
der Briefträger the postman.
die Eigenschaft the quality.
prächtig beautiful.
die Stunde the hour.
das Ding, *pl.* —e, the thing.
der Regen the rain.

der Christ, *pl.* -en, the Christian.
der Tod death.
die Köchin the cook, *f.*
die Maus the mouse.
der Fleischer the butcher.
gehorchen to obey.
die Lektion the lesson.
verteidigen to defend.

## Reading Exercise. 46.

Der Mann redet zuviel. Wir redeten über den Krieg (war). Gestern habe ich im Flusse gebadet. Was haben Sie geantwortet? Ich antwortete nichts. Die Schüler arbeiteten nicht viel. Ich handle recht. Du handelst unrecht. Die Dame wollte nicht aus= gehen, sie fürchtete den Regen. Haben Sie Englisch studiert? Nein, ich habe die deutsche Grammatik studiert. Das Schloß ist zerstört. Mein Nachbar hat sein Haus verkauft. Was wün= schen Sie? Ich kannte den Mann nicht. Wir kennen die guten Eigenschaften der Königin. Ich bewundre die schönen Blumen in Ihrem Garten. Wer brachte diesen Brief? Der Briefträger hat ihn gebracht. Ich wußte nicht, daß (that) Sie hier sind.*)

### Aufgabe. 46a.

1. The boy works not much. I answered: Yes, but he answered: No. We have waited an hour. We feared the rain. The woman talks too much. *Do* you admire this beautiful tree? I admire a fine picture. People (man) ⸗al= ways ₁admire (*admires always*) new things. You know the good qualities of that lady. I fear the dog. I feared the cat. A good Christian does not fear (the) death. I have not worked

---

1) In poetry *Imp.* as well sendete. *Part. past.* gesendet.

2) Wenden (to turn) admits of both forms  *Imp.* ich wendete and ich wandte; *Part.* gewendet and gewandt.

3) French *savoir*.

4) The Present tense of wissen is conjugated as follows: ich weiß, du weißt, er weiß; *Plur.* wir wissen, Sie wissen, sie wissen.

*) The conjugation daß throws the verb last.

much. I have studied my lesson. *Did\**) you think (have you thought) of me (an mid)? Fear nothing, I shall defend you.
2. *Did* you think\*) of (an, *acc.*) your poor mother? I shall always think of her (an fie). The president has not esteemed his friends. He *does* not love them (fie). The butcher kills »an ιox ιto-day; yesterday ²he ιkilled two calves. I liked the little girl, but she did not like me (mid). Men (die Menſchen) should love one another (einander). What did\*) the cook (*f*) buy? *She* bought butter and eggs. My nephew has bought two horses. The children have killed a mouse. He saved his life (Leben, *neuter*).

## Conversation.

| | |
|---|---|
| Wer lernt in der Schule? | Die Schüler und Schülerinnen. |
| Wo leben die Fiſche? | Sie leben im Waſſer. |
| Warum achten Sie dieſe Frau? | Ich achte ihre guten Eigenſchaften. |
| Was fürchtet das Mädchen? | Sie fürchtet den Regen. |
| Warum ſtraft der Vater ſeinen Sohn? | Er hat ſeine Aufgabe nicht gelernt. |
| Wer hat die Stadt verteidigt? | Die tapfern (brave) Soldaten. |
| Wer liegt da? | Ein ſchlafendes Kind. |
| Wen (whom) lobt der Lehrer? | Er lobt die fleißigen Schüler. |
| Kann er auch die trägen loben? | Träge Schüler verdienen (deserve) kein Lob (praise). |
| Was verdienen ſie? | Sie verdienen Strafe. |
| Wen ſoll man lieben? | Alle guten Menſchen. |
| Wem ſollen die Kinder gehorchen? | Ihren Eltern und Lehrern. |
| Hat der Hahn gekräht? | Ja, er hat zweimal gekräht. |
| Gehen Sie ins Konzert'? | Nein, ich gehe ins Theater. |
| Was hat das Mädchen gekauft? | Sie hat Brot und Käſe gekauft. |
| Was verkauft dieſe Frau? | Sie verkauft Birnen, Äpfel, Pflaumen (plums) und Nüſſe. |
| Was lehrt dieſer Lehrer? | Er lehrt Franzöſiſch und Engliſch. |
| Hat der Metzger einen Ochſen geſchlachtet? | Nein, er hat zwei Kälber geſchlachtet. |
| Haben Sie die Nachtigall gehört? | Ja, ſie ſingt herrlich (beautifully). |

## Reading-lesson.
### Äſop. Aesop.

Äſop reiſte einmal in eine kleine Stadt. Unterwegs¹ begegnete er einem Reiſenden. Dieſer grüßte² ihn (him) und fragte: „Wie lang muß ich gehen, bis (till or before) ich jene Stadt erreiche (reach), die (which) wir von weitem³ ſehen?"

„Geh" (Go on), antwortete Äſop.

1) on the way. 2) grüßen to bow, to greet. 3) afar.

---

\*) The English *Imperfect tense* is mostly rendered by the German *Perfect tense*, as· I bought it ich habe es gekauft; especially in a question, as *Did* you think? haben Sie ... gedacht?

„Ich weiß wohl" (well), erwiderte (replied) der Reisende, „daß (that) ich gehen muß, um[4] dort[5] anzukommen[4]; aber ich bitte[6] dich, mir zu sagen, in wieviel Zeit ich dort ankommen werde."

„Geh'," wiederholte[7] Äsop.

Ich sehe (see), dachte der Fremde, der Kerl[8] ist ein Narr[9], ich werde ihn nicht mehr[10] fragen, und ging fort (went on). Nach einer Minute rief (cried) Äsop: „He, ein Wort! in zwei Stunden wirst du ankommen."

Der Reisende wandte[11] sich um und sagte: „Wie weißt du es jetzt (now), und warum[12] hast du mir es nicht vorher[13] gesagt?" — Äsop erwiderte: „Wie konnte ich es dir (you) sagen, bevor ich deinen Gang (or Schritt)[14] gesehen hatte?"

4) (in order) to arrive. 5) there. 6) I beg *or* pray thee. — 7) repeated, said again. 8) this fellow. 9) a fool, mad. 10) no more. 11) wandte sich um turned round. 12) why. 13) before. — 14) gait, pace.

# Twenty-second Lesson.

## Passive voice.

The passive Voice, both for the regular and irregular active verbs, is formed by means of the third auxiliary werden with the Past part. of a *transitive* verb.

Geliebt werden to be loved.
Getadelt werden to be blamed.

## Conjugation of a passive verb.

### Gelobt werden to be praised.

Indicative Mood.

| Present. | | Imperfect. | |
|---|---|---|---|
| Ich werde . . gelobt I am*) | | Ich wurde . . gelobt I was | |
| du wirst gelobt thou art | | du wurdest gelobt thou wast | |
| er wird gelobt he is | praised. | er wurde gelobt he was | praised. |
| wir werden gelobt we are | | wir wurden gelobt we·were | |
| ihr werdet gelobt} ye are | | ihr wurdet gelobt} ye were | |
| Sie werden gelobt} you are | | Sie wurden gelobt} you were | |
| sie werden gelobt they are | | sie wurden gelobt they were | |

*Perfect.*

Ich bin . . gelobt worden I have been praised or I *was* praised
du bist gelobt worden thou hast been praised
er ist gelobt worden he has been praised

---

*) *or* I am being praised.

wir find gelobt worden we have been praised
ihr feid gelobt worden ⎫
Sie find gelobt worden ⎰ you (ye) have been praised
fie find gelobt worden they have been praised.

### Pluperfect.

Ich war .. gelobt worden I had been praised
du warst gelobt worden thou hadst been praised
er war gelobt worden he had been praised
wir waren gelobt worden we had been praised etc.

### First Future.

Ich werde .. gelobt werden I shall be praised
du wirst gelobt werden thou wilt be praised
er wird gelobt werden he will be praised
wir werden gelobt werden we shall be praised
ihr werdet gelobt werden ⎫
Sie werden gelobt werden ⎰ you will be praised
fie werden gelobt werden they will be praised.

### Second Future.

Ich werde gelobt worden fein I shall have been praised
du wirst gelobt worden fein thou wilt have been praised
      2c.                        2c.

## Subjunctive Mood.

### Present Tense.

Daß ich gelobt werde that I (may) be praised
  „ du gelobt werdest thou (mayst) be praised
  „ er gelobt werde he (may) be praised
  „ wir gelobt werden that we (may) be praised
      2c.                        2c.

### Imperfect.

Ich würde gelobt (if) I were praised
du würdest gelobt thou wert praised
er würde gelobt he were praised
      2c.                        2c.

### Perfect.

Ich sei gelobt worden I may have been praised
du seiest gelobt worden thou mayst have been praised
er sei gelobt worden he may have been praised
      2c.                        2c.

### Pluperfect.

Wenn ich gelobt worden wäre if I had been praised
wenn du gelobt worden wärest if thou hadst been praised
wenn er gelobt worden wäre if he had been praised
      2c.                        2c.

## First Conditional.

Ich würde gelobt werden I should be praised
du würdest gelobt werden thou wouldst be praised
er würde gelobt werden he would be praised
             2c.               2c.

### Second Conditional.

Ich würde gelobt worden sein } I should have been praised
  or ich wäre gelobt worden }
du würdest gelobt worden sein thou wouldst have been praised
er würde gelobt worden sein he would have been praised
             2c.               2c.

## Imperative.

*Sing.* werde gelobt.*)    *Plur.* werdet gelobt be (ye) praised.

## Infinitive.

*Pres.* gelobt werden or gelobt zu werden to be praised
     um gelobt zu werden in order to be praised.
*Past* gelobt worden sein or zu sein to have-been praised.

## Participle.

*Pres.* zu lobend to be praised.**)

   Such aré:

geſtraft werden to be punished.   zerſtört werden to be destroyed.
getadelt werden to be blamed.   geachtet werden to be respected.
belohnt werden to be rewarded.   verdorben werden to be spoiled.

---

### Words.

Der Arbeiter the workman.    die Hitze the heat.
der Feind the enemy.    Jedermann everybody
der Hof the court.    betrogen(*P.p.*)cheated, deceived.
nachläſſig negligent.    verbeſſert corrected, improved.
artig good.  unartig naughty.    geſprochen (*P. p.*) spoken.
ehrlich honest   weil because.    gerufen (*P. p.*) called.
höflich polite.  ſchlecht bad.    wohlfeil or billig cheap.
gegeben given.    geſtohlen (*P. p.*) stolen.
bezahlen to pay.    von by.  wenn if.
die Sprache the language.    geſchrieben written.

### Reading Exercise. 47.

1. Ich werde von meinem Lehrer gelobt. Du wirſt
nicht von ihm gelobt, denn (for) du biſt nicht fleißig. Der un=

---

*) This Imperative is hardly ever used When a *passive Imperative* is required, it is commonly formed with ſei *pl* ſeid Ex :
   Sei gelobt or gepriesen, o Gott! be praised o God!
**) The Latin laudandus, a, um. This participle stands
before its noun as an adjective, and is declinable, as:
   An action to be praised eine zu lobende Handlung.

artige Knabe wird nicht von seiner Mutter gelobt werden.
Die unartigen Knaben werden von ihren Eltern gestraft wer=
den. Marie wird immer von ihrem Musiklehrer getadelt,
weil sie nachlässig ist. Meine Kousine wird von jedermann ge=
liebt, weil sie immer artig und höflich ist. Die Diener, welche
fleißig sind, werden belohnt werden, und diejenigen, welche träge
sind, werden getadelt werden. Die Stadt wurde von den Fein=
den zerstört. Die Aufgaben wurden von dem Lehrer ver=
bessert. Der arme Mann wurde von dem Fremden betrogen.

2. Karl ist gestraft worden, weil er unartig war. Die
Uhren konnten nicht verkauft werden, weil sie zu (too) schlecht
waren. Die Mädchen, welche ihre Aufgaben gemacht (done) hatten,
sind belohnt worden. Die Arbeiter sind gut bezahlt worden,
weil sie viel gearbeitet haben. Von wem ist diese Aufgabe ver=
bessert worden? Sie (it) ist noch nicht verbessert worden, weil
der Lehrer keine Zeit hatte. Gelobt werden ist besser als ge=
tadelt werden. Dieser arme Knabe muß belohnt werden, weil
er so ehrlich ist. Diese Briefe müssen abgeschrieben (copied) wer=
den, weil sie so schlecht geschrieben (badly written) sind.

### Aufgabe. 48.

1. I *am* loved *by* my brother. This father loves his
children, and he *is* loved *by* them (von ihnen). Mr. Bell *is*
respected by all his pupils. The French language *is* spoken
in (an) all [the] courts of Europe. This ring *was* given me
by my good grand-father. By whom (Von wem) *was* this
letter written? I *was* called out of my room. Frederick
*has been* punished by his teacher. *Have* the young plants
*been* spoiled by the great heat? The roads *have been* spoiled
by the heavy (starken) rain.

2. This boy will *be* punished; he has not done (gemacht)
his exercise. He *was* punished also yesterday. This house
could not *be* sold, were it (wäre es) not so cheap. I *am*
expected at five o'clock; my sisters *are* expected at seven
o'clock A false (falsch) man *is* feared by everybody. This
letter must *be* sent to the post-office (auf die Post). My watch
*has been* stolen. *To be* loved is better than *to be* hated (gehaßt).

---

## Observations on the Passive Voice.

§ 1. The circumstance, that in English 'to be' is
used both for denoting the *passive voice* and the *copula*
with adjective-participles, renders the comprehension
and employment of the German passive voice difficult
for an Englishman; for nothing in his own language in-
forms him, when in a past participle construed with the

auxiliary *to be, a treatment suffered by* the person represented by the subject of the sentence, is indicated. The
pupil therefore must always carefully distinguish, *whether
the past participle construed with* **to be** *expresses either the
endurance of an* **action,** *or the existence in a* **state** *which
is the result of such an action.*

In the first case *to be* must be translated with the
German auxiliary werden, in the second with the auxiliary
fein. For example:

This book *is (being)* much read biefeß Buch wirb viel gelefen.
My friend is convinced mein Freunb ift überzeugt.

### A. When **to be** is translated werden.

§ 2.· Whenever an agent is mentioned, with a *past
participle* and the verb *to be*, it is considered to be the
*passive voice,* and the verb *to be* is rendered werden. Ex.:

*Present* Ich werbe von meinem Bater geliebt
I *am* loved *by* my father. (I am being loved)

*Impf.* Diefeß Schloß wurbe von bem Herzoge erbaut.
This castle *was* built *by* the duke (became built).

*Perf.* Die Stabt ift von ben Feinben verbrannt worben.
The town *has been (was)* burnt by the enemies.

§ 3. When the agent is not mentioned, but *understood, to be* must again be rendered by werben. Ex.:

*Pres.* Die Fifche werben mit Netzen gefangen
(The fish *are* caught with nets (viz. *are in the habit*
of being caught with nets).

*Impf.* Diefeß Schloß wurbe im Jahre 1540 erbaut.
*Perf* Die Stabt ift niebergebrannt worben.

*Note 1.* To ascertain this, the sentence need only be put
in the same tense of the *active voice.* If this can be done
without altering the sense, the use of werben is sure to be
right. Ex.:

1) People catch *(Pres. act)* fish with nets
Man fängt bie Fifche mit Netzen.
2) The duke built *(Impf act)* this castle in 1540.
Der Herzog baute biefeß Schloß im Jahre 1540.
3) The enemies have burnt *(Perf. act)* down the town.
Die Feinbe haben bie Stabt niebergebrannt

All these *active* sentences are quite synonymous with the
above passive sentences.

*Note 2.* In English, this *passive* sense is sometimes indicated by the *Part. pres.* being, added to the *Part past,* or
by the *Part pres.* itself. It may be also renb.red by man.

The house *is being built* or *is building* das Haus wird gebaut
or man baut das Haus.
Breakfast *is preparing* das Frühstück wird (eben = just) gemacht
or man macht eben das Frühstück.

Here the *Pres. tense* of the passive voice denotes an action *in progress or just taking place.* It denotes also *a habit*, as in the above sentence: Die Fische werden mit Netzen gefangen = fish *are (usually) caught* with nets.

**Examples of true passives with werden.**

Alcibiades *was* *) banished from Athens.
Alcibiades wurde aus Athen' verbannt.

This lesson must *be* learned.
Diese Aufgabe muß gelernt werden.

Carthage was destroyed by the Romans.
Karthago wurde von den Römern zerstört.

(The) young trees are planted in spring.
Die jungen Bäume werden im Frühling gepflanzt or
Man pflanzt die jungen Bäume im Frühling.

**B.  When to be is translated sein.**

§ 4. Sometimes the Participle past expresses a *state* or *condition* which the subject has already attained, a property, as it were, of the subject. It is then no longer esteemed as a *verb*, but as an *adjective,* and the auxiliary *to be* which is connected with it, must be translated sein. For instance, when we say: *The lady is dressed*, we do not mean to say: *The lady is being dressed*, but rather: *The lady is ready,* the action of dressing is over; *dressed* therefore has here the value of an *adjective,* and the sentence must be translated:

Die Dame ist angekleidet (*a state*).

*Note.* On the contrary, the English expression: *The lady is being dressed* is rendered in German: Die Dame wird (eben) angekleidet.

*Second example.* — *The glass is broken:* Das Glas ist zerbrochen. To express this in the active voice, the tense must be *changed;* it would then be. Somebody *has broken* the glass. Thus *is broken* has here the meaning of: *has been broken*, but not of *is breaking* or *is being broken.* When therefore *is* or *are* is equal to *has been* or *have been*, they must be rendered ist or sind, and not wird or werden, because they indicate a *state.*

---

*) In French: *Alc. fut banni d'Athènes* (= became banished).

*Third example.* — *The gates of the town* **are** *shut,*
means, they **have been** shut, and are now found closed
(in Latin: *clausæ sunt*), and must be translated:

Die Thore der Stadt sind geschlossen. — Whereas
'The gates *are* shut every day at eight o'clock'
must, according to § 3, be translated: Die Thore werden
jeden Tag um 8 Uhr geschlossen (clauduntur). They *are in
the habit of* being shut every day at 8 o'clock *or* man schließt
die Thore jeden Tag um 8 Uhr.

§ 5. In a similar manner, the Imperfect *was* must
be translated war instead of wurde, when it has the
meaning of *had been.* Ex.:

The glass *was* broken before I came into the room.
Das Glas war zerbrochen, ehe ich ins Zimmer kam.
(In French: *Le verre était cassé.*)

The gates *were* shut (= I found them shut).
Die Thore waren geschlossen.

### Examples of adjective-participles.

I *am* inclined *or* disposed ich bin geneigt.
I am convinced it is true ich bin überzeugt, daß es wahr ist.
We *were* astonished wir waren erstaunt.
The bottles were emptied die Flaschen waren geleert (= leer).
The castle is destroyed das Schloß ist zerstört.
The copy-book is soiled das Heft ist beschmutzt (= schmutzig).

§ 6. In the compound Preterite (Perfect and Pluperfect) the English auxiliary: *I have been etc.* and a Part.
past is *always* translated: Ich bin ... worden. Ex.:

I *have been* invited ich bin eingeladen worden.
The book *has been* found das Buch ist gefunden worden.
You *have been* seen Sie sind gesehen worden.
If they *had been* rewarded wenn sie belohnt worden wären.

§ 7. Active verbs, which govern the *dative,* can
only be employed in the third person singular with es,
in the form of passive impersonal verbs; but not in the
other persons as in English. Ex.:

I *am* allowed { es wird mir erlaubt (not ich werde erlaubt)
{ or man erlaubt mir.
*He is* allowed es wird ihm erlaubt or man erlaubt ihm.
I was allowed es wurde mir erlaubt (man erlaubte mir).
We were allowed es wurde uns erlaubt or man erlaubte uns.

My brother was advised es wurde meinem Bruder geraten or man hat meinem Bruder geraten.

## Words.

| | |
|---|---|
| Der Schmeichler the flatterer. | verwunden to wound. |
| die Verschwörung the conspi- | bewundern to admire. |
| der Sturm the storm.   [racy. | gegeben given. hoffen to hope. |
| die That the deed, action. | eingeladen (*P. p.*) invited. |
| die Treue the fidelity. | verachtet (*P. p.*) despised. |
| die Versammlung the assembly, | entdecken to discover, detect. |
| convention. | belohnen to reward. |
| ehemals (or früher) formerly. | zerstören to destroy. |
| geschickt clever. wieder again. | ermorden to murder. |
| heftig violent. zuerst at first. | vielleicht perhaps. auch also. |

spazieren gehen or einen Spaziergang machen to take a walk.

### Reading Exercise. 49.

1. Mein Sohn Friedrich wird von seinem Lehrer geliebt.
Diese Mädchen werden gelobt und geliebt, weil sie fleißig und
gut sind. Der Soldat ist in der Schlacht verwundet worden.*)
Sie werden morgen von meinem Oheim zum Mittagessen eingeladen werden. Ihr Vetter Paul ist auch eingeladen worden;
aber er wird zu Hause bleiben. Gustav Adolf, König von
Schweden, ist in der Schlacht bei Lützen getötet worden. Wann
ist dieses Haus gebaut worden? Es ist vor (ago) zehn Jahren
gebaut worden. Meine Kleider sind zerrissen (torn).

2. Die Uhr wird nicht verkauft werden. Der verlorne Ring
ist wieder gefunden (found) worden. Dieser Mann ist jetzt all-
gemein (generally) geachtet. Er war früher nicht geachtet. Die
Schmeichler verdienen von jedermann verachtet zu werden. Diese
Arbeit ist sehr (much) bewundert worden. Die Arbeiten der
Fräulein Rosa werden auch bewundert werden. Die Verschwörung
des Katalina wäre vielleicht nicht entdeckt worden, wenn Cicero
nicht Konsul gewesen wäre.

### Aufgabe. 50.

1. I *am* praised by my teacher. We *are* loved by our
father. You *are* esteemed by your neighbour. This house
*has been* sold. The garden will also *be sold*. The enemy *was*
(or has been) beaten (geschlagen..). A new plant *was* much (sehr)
admired by everybody. The picture of Mr. T. will *be* admired. The brave soldiers were praised by the general. *Have*
many soldiers *been* killed? Charles and I are invited to (zu)
a ball. Your sister and your cousin would also *be* invited,
if they were**) here. Such a deed must *be* rewarded. That

---

*) or wurde (was) verwundet —
**) See the foot-note p. 82.

man was formerly not esteemed. The flatterers ought to *be* despised. Carthage (Karthago) *was* destroyed by Scipio Africanus. The house is burnt down (abgebrannt). 2. The child could not *be* saved. The castle *was* built in the year 1622. The stranger *has been* killed in the forest. Many soldiers have been wounded in the last battle. Clever men are always sought [for]. Rome was at first governed by kings. Henry IV. was loved by his people. His name is still esteemed. The industrious will *be* rewarded. Cæsar was murdered by Brutus. Why am I not invited? This is an action to be praised. *) I wish, James (Jakob) may (möchte) be rewarded for his fidelity (Treue, *f.*). The most diligent pupils will be the most (am meisten) praised. At (In) the battle of (bei) Narva ₂the ₃horse of Charles XII. ₁was killed under him.

### Conversation.

Von wem wird Ihr Sohn geliebt?

Er wird von seinen Lehrern geliebt, weil er fleißig ist.

Ist er auch belohnt worden?

Er hat einen Preis bekommen (got).

Welche Soldaten werden gelobt?

Die tapferen.

Wann wurde die Schlacht bei Waterloo geliefert (fought)?

Am 18. Juni 1815.

Wer wurde besiegt (defeated)?

Die Franzosen wurden besiegt.

Wann wird dieses Haus verkauft werden?

Es wurde schon gestern verkauft (or ist . . worden).

Wieviel wurde dafür bezahlt?

Zehntausend vierhundert Mark.

Wird der Garten dazu (with it) gegeben werden?

Nein, dieser (it) wird besonders (separately) verkauft werden.

Wollen Sie diesen Nachmittag einen Spaziergang mit uns machen?

Ich würde mit Ihnen gehen, wenn ich nicht zum Mittagessen (dinner) bei Herrn F. eingeladen wäre.

Von wem ist Karthago zerstört worden?

Von dem römischen Konsul Scipio Africanus.

Warum ist dieser Mann gestraft worden?

Er hat eine goldne Uhr gestohlen (stolen).

Von wem ist Cäsar ermordet worden?

Von Brutus und Cassius, und einigen andern.

Von wem ist die Verschwörung Katalinas entdeckt worden?

Von dem römischen Konsul Cicero.

Ist dieses Haus schon alt?

Es wurde im Jahre 1741 erbaut.

War Heinrich IV. von Frankreich ein guter König?

Ja, er war der beste König und wurde von seinen Unterthanen (subjects) wie ein Vater geliebt.

Wie starb er?

Er wurde von Ravaillac ermordet.

---

*) See the foot-note **) p. 131.

# Twenty-third Lesson.

## ON THE PRONOUNS.

German pronouns are divided into six classes, viz.:
1) *personal*, 2) *interrogative*, 3) *demonstrative*, 4) *possessive*, 5) *relative* and *correlative*, 6) *indefinite pronouns*.

### 1. Personal pronouns.

(Perſönliche Fürwörter.)

§ 1. These are: ich I; bu thou; er he; ſie she; es it; wir we; ihr (Sie) you; ſie they.

They are declined as follows.

#### 1st personal ich I.

| Sing. | | Plur. | |
|---|---|---|---|
| N. | ich I | wir we | |
| G. | meiner*) of me | unſrer (unſer) of us | |
| D. | mir to me, me | uns to us, us | |
| A. | mich me. | uns us. | |

#### 2nd personal bu thou.

| Sing. | | Pl. | |
|---|---|---|---|
| N. | bu thou | ihr (ye) or Sie you | |
| G. | beiner*) of thee | eurer (or) Ihrer of you | |
| D. | bir to thee, thee | euch or Ihnen to you, you | |
| A. | bich thee. | euch or Sie you. | |

#### 3rd personal: er, ſie, es.

| | masc. | | fem. | | neuter. |
|---|---|---|---|---|---|
| N. | er he | ſie she | | es**) it | |
| G. | ſeiner*) of him | ihrer of her | | (ſeiner) of it | |
| D. | ihm to him, him | ihr to her, her | | (ihm) to it | |
| A. | ihn him, it. | ſie her, it. | | es it. | |

*Plural for all three genders.*

N. ſie they
G ihrer of them
D. ihnen (ſich) to them, them
A. ſie them.

#### 4) reflective form ſich.

D. }
Ac. } ſich { himself, herself, itself. }For all genders.
        { yourself, yourselves, themselves. }Sing. and Plur.

---

*) These genitives: meiner, beiner, ſeiner ꝛc. are borrowed from mein, bein, ſein and, in poetry, abridged into mein, bein ꝛc., as. Remember me gebenke mein.

**) es is sometimes contracted with the preceding word, as. baſt bu's, gieb mir's, ich hab's ꝛc. (For the *gen.* and *dat.* see § 5 & 7.)

### Examples.

**1) With the dative.**

Er giebt mir, — dir, — ihm, — ihr.
He gives me, — thee, — him, — her
Er verzeiht uns, — Ihnen, — ihnen.
He pardons us, — you, — them.

**2) With the accusative.**

Sie kennen mich, — dich, — ihn, — sie.
They know me, — thee, — him, — her.
Er liebt uns, — Sie, — sie.
He loves us, — you, — them.

**3) With the reflective form.**

Er kleidet sich he dresses (himself).
Sie (sie) befleißigen sich they apply themselves.

§ 2. The English form of addressing a person in conversation is *you, your;* in German however there are two modes of address, du and Sie. The first implying a certain degree of familiarity, founded upon affection and friendship, is used by relations and intimate friends. Teachers also address their young pupils, and employers their young servants with du. In quarrels and opprobrious language, du is also heard. On the contrary the polite or ceremonial mode of address is Sie, which is, properly speaking, the third person plural, but is distinguished from the same by a capital initial, as:

Wenn Sie wollen (instead of wenn ihr wollt) if you like.
Haben Sie gesehen? (for habt ihr gesehen) have you seen?

In conversational style of the polite or ceremonial form of address, the Imperative is always the Infinitive of the verb followed by the pronoun Sie:

Come kommen Sie (instead of kommet).
Give me geben Sie mir (instead of gebet mir).
Tell him sagen Sie ihm (not saget or saget ihm).

*NB.* The *possessive* pronouns must always be in conformity with the personal pronouns; thus du corresponds with dein, ihr (*ye*) with euer, and Sie (*you*) with Ihr, as· Hast du dein Buch? Habt ihr eure Bücher? Haben Sie Ihre Bücher? He who wishes more ample explanation about this point must be referred to the pages 55—57 (Second Edition) of the "*Key to Dr. E Otto's Materials for translating German into English*, Heid. 1883", where this question is more amply treated and illustrated by a good many examples.

§ 3. In the following expressions the construction of the two languages is diffeient.

| | |
|---|---|
| It is I idj bin eß. | it is we wir ſinb eß. |
| it is he (she) er (ſie) iſt eß. | it is you Sie ſinb eß. |
| It was I idj war eß. | it was you Sie waren eß ꝛc. |

Interrogative.

| | |
|---|---|
| Is it I bin idj eß? | is it we ſinb wir eß? |
| is it he iſt er eß? | is it you ſinb Sie eß? |

### Words.

| | |
|---|---|
| Der Fleiß industry. | fragen to ask (a question). |
| die Nadjridjt news. | braudjen to want. |
| verzeihen (*Dat.*)*) to pardon. | adjten to esteem. |
| benfen (an) to think (of). | leihen (*Dat.*)*) to lend. |
| ſelten seldom. | ſdjiden (*Dat.*) to send |
| idj ſdjreibe I write | |

### Reading Exercise. 51.

Idj liebe didj unb bu liebſt midj. Sie (ſie) lieben unß unb wir lieben ſie. Idj fenne ſie nidjt. Idj verzeihe Ihnen. Idj ver= zeihe ihm nidjt. Er lobte unß. Sie lobten ihn wegen (on ac- count of) ſeineß Fleißeß. Idj werbe morgen einen Brief an ihn ſdjreiben. Idj benfe an (of) didj, — an Sie, — an ſie. Sie benfen immer an unß. Wir ſpredjen ſehr ſelten von ihnen. Idj werbe ſie Ihnen nidjt geben. Er wirb eß unß ſagen. Er erinnert ſidj meiner (he remembers me). Geben Sie ihm bieſeß Budj.

### Aufgabe. 51a.

I ask you. I see him. We know her. She knows me. He esteems us. They want it. You know them. They esteem her. Will you give me (*Dat.*) the letter? Answer me (*Dat.*). She will not pardon*) him (*Dat.*). Does he love them? I write a letter to (an, *acc.*) her. Pray (bitte), lend me your penknife. IIe will lend it [to] you. She does not send it to him. Tell her (*Dat.*) that news. You must buy me (*Dat.*) another stick. He remembers (erinnert ſidj) me (*Gen.*). Our friends do not think of (an) us. Who is there? It (eß) is my father. Is it you? Yes, it is I. It is he. It was she. Tell him and her that (baß) I love them. I will go with you. He goes with us, but not with them.

§ 4. In German, inanimate objects and abstract ideas being either masculine, or feminine, or neuter, the

---

*) For verbs which govern the person in the dative, see the 48th lesson, II. About the *position* of the pronouns in the clause see Syntax, L. 50, No. 6 & 7.

personal pronouns of the *third* person in the singular,
er, fie, es, must be used accordingly, whereas in English *it* serves for all inanimate objects.  For example in
the following sentence  *Where is my hat? It is in your
room*, *it* cannot be translated with es, but with er, because the subject it refers to, viz.: der Hut, is a masculine
noun, as:

1) *Nominative case:* it*) = er, fie, es.

| | |
|---|---|
| Where is my hat? — | *It*\*) is in your room. |
| Wo ist mein Hut (*m.*)? | Er ist in Ihrem Zimmer. |
| Where is my pen? — | *It* lies on the table. |
| Wo ist meine Feder? | Sie liegt auf dem Tisch. |
| Where is my book? — | *It* is there. |
| Wo ist mein Buch (*n.*)? | Es ist da. |

2) *Accusative case:* it**) = ihn, fie, es.

| | |
|---|---|
| Have you my hat? — | Yes, I have it.\*\*) |
| Haben Sie meinen Hut? | Ja, ich habe ihn (*viz.* den Hut). |
| Do you see that flower? | I do not see it. |
| Sehen Sie diese Blume? | Ich sehe sie nicht. |
| Will you buy the house? | Yes, I will buy it. |
| Wollen Sie das Haus kaufen? | Ja, ich will es kaufen |

In the plural it does not change,  as there is only
one form for all three genders, viz *acc.* fie; *dat.* ihnen:

I will see *them* ich will sie sehen.
I give *them* bread ich gebe ihnen Brot

§ 5. The pronoun es, when it expresses a *thing*, is
only used in the *nominative* and *accusative* cases. In the
*genitive* it is replaced by dessen or desselben (see § 8).

Es ist ganz neu it is quite new.
Ich habe es (*Acc.*) gekauft I have bought it.
Ich weiß es (*Acc.*) I know it.
Er bedarf dessen or desselben he requires it.

§ 6. *It is* refering to a *person*, is always es ist. Ex.:
It is my brother es ist mein Bruder.

*They are*, when followed by a noun taken in a
definite sense, is translated. es sind. For example in answer
to the question: *Who are they* wer sind sie? we say:

They are my brothers (sisters) etc.
Es sind meine Brüder (Schwestern) ꝛc.

---

\*) When it stands before the verb, it is Nominative.
\*\*) When it stands after the verb, it is Accusative (masc. = ihn .

§ 7. The pronoun of the third person **e8** etc., either singular or plural, is hardly ever used with a preposition preceding, when it represents an inanimate object or an idea. Commonly the adverb **ba,** which coalesces with the *preposition*, is used instead, both for the dative and accusative, corresponding with the English words *therewith, thereof, therein, thereupon* etc., as:

| | |
|---|---|
| **Damit** with it *or* with them. | **baju** to it *or* to them. |
| **barin** in it *or* in them. | **babei** ⎱ |
| **baburdj** through it *or* them. | **baran** ⎰ at it *or* at them. |
| **babon** of *or* from it *or* them. | **barüber** about *or* over it, them. |
| **barauf** upon it *or* them. | **barunter** among them. |
| **barau8** from it *or* them. | **bafür** for it *or* them. |

### Examples.

**Wir ſinb bamit** (*Dat.*) **jufrieben** we are contented *with it.*
**Wieviele ſinb barin** (*Dat.*) how many are *in it* (therein)?
**Wir werben barüber ſprechen** we will talk *about it.*

*Note.* A similar contraction takes place with the adverb **hier** with prepositions, as· **hiermit** *herewith* or *with this;* **hierin** *in this;* **hierbon,** *of this,* **hierauf, hieraus, hierbei, hierüber** 2c.

§ 8. The pronoun of the third person, **er, ſie, e8,** in all its cases, is sometimes replaced by **berſelbe, bie‧ ſelbe, ba8ſelbe** (*lit. the same*). This is chiefly the case when a misunderstanding might happen, or to avoid employing together two words of similar sound, as: **ihm ihn** or **ihn ihnen.** Ex.:

**Ich habe bieſelben nicht erhalten.**
I have not received *them.*

**Soll ich ihm ben Stod geben?** am I to give him the stick?
**Ja, geben Sie ihm benſelben** (instead of **ihn**).
Yes, give *it* to him.

§ 9. The English words *myself, himself, yourself etc.* are termed *reflective personal pronouns*, when they represent the *same person* as the subject or the nominative. They can only be in the *accusative* and sometimes in the *dative.* In the *accusative* they are rendered by **mich, bich, ſich** 2c.; in the *dative* by **mir, bir, ſich** 2c. Ex.:

*I* wash *myself* **ich waſche mich.**
*He* distinguishes *himself* **er zeichnet ſich au8.**
(For further particulars see the 34th lesson on the Reflective verbs.)

§ 10. If the accusative or dative denotes any other person than the subject, it has no longer a reflective character, and is translated ihn ſelbſt, mir ſelbſt ꝛc.:

I have seen him (himself) (*Acc.*) ich habe ihn ſelbſt geſehen.
He gave it to me (myself) (*Dat.*) er gab es mir ſelbſt.

§ 11. The indefinite pronouns *myself, himself, your-self etc.* preceded by a substantive or another personal pronoun *in the Nominative* case, are rendered only by the word ſelbſt*) without a second pronoun (see the 25th lesson), and must not be confounded with the re-flective personal pronouns. Ex.:

I come myself ich komme ſelbſt (French *moi-même*).
The man himself der Mann ſelbſt.
You say so yourself Sie ſagen es ſelbſt.
We have seen it ourselves wir haben es ſelbſt geſehen.

*Note.* Sometimes both forms occour together, as:

Ich lobe mich (§ 9) ſelbſt I praise myself.
Liebe deinen Nächſten wie dich ſelbſt love thy neighbour as thyself.

### Words.

Die Grammatik the grammar.　der Thee tea.　genommen taken.
der Regenſchirm the umbrella.　das Gebot the command.
gewaſchen washed.　empfehlen to recommend.

### Reading Exercise. 52.

Wo iſt mein Bleiſtift? Hier iſt er. Haben Sie meine Feder genommen? Ich habe ſie nicht genommen. Iſt dieſer Thee gut? Ja, er iſt ſehr gut; ich kann Ihnen denſelben empfehlen. Sind Ihre Bücher in Ihrem Zimmer? Ja, ſie ſind darin. Wollen Sie dieſes Buch leſen? Ich will es Ihnen leihen. Ich habe es [mir] gekauft. Er iſt ſelbſt gekommen. Ich bin es. Iſt ſie es? Ja, ſie iſt es. Karl der Zwölfte kleidete (dressed) ſich ſelbſt (an). Der Knabe hat ſich nicht gewaſchen. Ich dachte nicht daran. Wir ſind damit zufrieden. Der Graf hat es ſelbſt geſagt. Ich weiß Nichts davon.

### Aufgabe. 52a.

Where is my grammar? *It* is not here, I have not seen *it*. Who has taken the apple of the child? I have not taken *it* Have you seen my pencil? I have not seen *it*. Have you lost your stick yourself? No, my son has lost *it*. I will go myself (§ 11). This wine is very good, I can recommend *it*

---

*) Selbſt, placed *before* a noun, answers to the English *even:*
Selbſt die Tiere *even* the animals
Selbſt der König kann es nicht thun even the king cannot do it.

(§ 8) to you  Will she bring it to you? Yes, she will bring
it to me to-morrow.  Jesus has given (gegeben) us the command. »Love thy neigbour as thyself« (§ 11 Note), but many
people do not mind it (achten nicht barauf).  Do you know
anything (wiſſen Sie etwas) *of it?*  We speak *of it.*  They
know nothing *about it.*  Depend (Zählen Sie) *upon it.*

### Conversation.

| | |
|---|---|
| Kennen Sie mich? | Ja, ich kenne Sie. |
| Kennen Sie auch meinen Vater? | Nein, ich kenne ihn nicht. |
| Wer iſt ba? | Es iſt meine Schweſter. |
| Iſt ſie es wirklich (really)? | Ja, ſie iſt es wirklich. |
| Wollen Sie ben Brief ſchreiben? | Nein, mein Sohn wird ihn ſchreiben. |
| Kann ich es ſelbſt thun (do)? | Nein, Sie können es nicht ſelbſt thun, ich muß Ihnen helfen (help) |
| Denkſt bu oft an (of) mich? | Ich benke immer an dich. |
| Haben Sie meinen Regenſchirm geſehen? | Nein, ich habe ihn nicht geſehen. |
| Mit wem gehen Sie ins Theater? | Ich werde mit Ihnen gehen. |
| Geht ſonſt jemanb (anybody else) mit Ihnen? | Meine Nichten (nieces) Emma und Luiſe gehen auch mit mir. |
| Wollen Sie ſo gut (kind) ſein, mir bieſes Buch zu leihen? | Es thut mir leid (I am sorry), ich kann es Ihnen nicht leihen. |
| Warum können Sie es mir nicht leihen? | Weil ich es der Fräulein Grün verſprochen (promised) habe |
| Wer wird uns begleiten (ac-company)? | Unſer Freund A. wird uns be-gleiten |
| Kennen Sie jenen Fremben mit bem grauen Hut? | Ich kenne ihn nicht; ich habe ihn nie (never) geſehen. |

---

# Twenty-fourth Lesson.

## 2. Interrogative pronouns.

(Fragenbe Fürwörter.)

These are: 1) **Wer** who? **Was** what?

### Declension

| | |
|---|---|
| *N.* wer who? | was what? |
| *G.* weſſen whose? | weſſen of what? |
| *D* wem to whom? | was to what? |
| *A.* wen whom? | was what? |

**Wer?** applies to persons without distinction of sex;
**was?** to inanimate objects.  Ex.:

Wer iſt ba? who is there?
Wer hat bieſes gethan? who has done this?

Weſſen Hut iſt das? whose hat is this?
Wem geben Sie dieſen Ring? to whom do you give this ring?
Wen hat er gefragt? whom has he asked?
Was brauchen Sie? what do you want (need)?
Was ſucht er? what is he looking for?
Von was haben Sie geſprochen? of what have you spoken?

*Note.* When such direct questions are placed in dependence on a *preceding verb*, they become »indirect questions«. Then the verb comes last, as:

Wiſſen Sie, wer dieſes geſagt hat? do you know who said this?
Sagen Sie mir, was Sie geſehen haben tell me what you saw.
Zeigen Sie mir, was Sie geleſen haben.
Show me what you have read

2) Welcher? welche? welches (von)? *which (of)?* and
Was für einer, e, s? *what sort?*

The latter is used without a substantive:

Welcher von Ihnen Söhnen? which of your sons?
Welches von dieſen Büchern haben Sie geleſen?
Which of these books have you read?
Hier ſind zwei Raſier'meſſer; welches wollen Sie haben?
Here are two razors, which will you have?
Sie haben einen Stock verloren? Was für einen?
You have lost a stick? What sort of a stick (was it)?

*NB. What* before a *noun* is not a pronoun, but an *interrogative adjective,* and already explained p. 72 & 73; Comp. also 146, 2

## 3. Demonstrative Pronouns.
(Hinweiſende Fürwörter.)

1) The *demonstrative* pronouns are:

| masc. | fem. | neuter. | |
|---|---|---|---|
| Dieſer | dieſe | dieſes this one. | |
| jener | jene | jenes that (that one). | |
| {derjenige | diejenige | dasjenige} that (of), the one. | |
| {der | die | das } (French: celui, celle) | |
| derſelbe | dieſelbe | dasſelbe } the same. | |
| der nämliche | die nämliche | das nämliche } | |
| (ebenderſelbe | ebendieſelbe | ebendasſelbe the very same.) | |
| der andre | die andre | das andre the other | |

2) **Declension of derjenige.**

| | Singular. | | | Plural |
| masc. | fem. | neuter. | | for all genders |
|---|---|---|---|---|
| N. derjenige | diejenige | dasjenige that | ‖ diejenigen those. |
| G. desjenigen | derjenigen | desjenigen of that | ‖ derjenigen of th. |
| D. demjenigen | derjenigen | demjenigen to that | ‖ denjenigen to th. |
| A. denjenigen | diejenige | dasjenige that. | ‖ diejenigen those. |

OTTO ........ ..... ........    10

3) A b r i d g e d   f o r m.

| N. der*) | die | das | that | die | those |
|----------|-----|-----|------|-----|-------|
| G. deſſen | deren | deſſen | of that | derer**) | of those |
| D. dem | der | dem | to that | denen | to those |
| A. den | die | das` | that. | die | those. |

E x a m p l e s.

Mein Stock und derjenige (or der) meines Bruders.
My stick and that of my brother (or and my brother's).
Er hat ſein Geld und dasjenige (or das) ſeines Freundes verloren.
He has lost his (own) money and that of his friend (or
his and his friend's money).

## Observations.

1) When the *demonstrative* pronoun, *this* or *that* is not
immediately followed by its subject, but is separated from it
by the verb *to be*, as for instance: »*this is my hat*«, it takes
in German the *neuter* form of the singular dieſes, with
no regard to the gender or number of the noun. This little
sentence must therefore be translated: dieſes iſt mein Hut,
although Hut is of the masculine gender (see also p. 72,
Note 1)*). It is the same in the *interrogative* form: Iſt dieſes
Ihr Hut? — Instead of dieſes we often abbreviate, and say
dies or das or es. Ex.:

This (*or that*) is my dog dieſes (not dieſer) iſt mein Hund.
This is my daughter dieſes or das iſt meine Tochter.
Are *these* your brothers? ſind dies (das) Ihre Brüder?
These are his gloves das (dies) ſind ſeine Handſchuhe.

2) The same rule applies to the *interrogative which* or *what?*
welches? before ſein, *to be*, both in singular and plural, as:

Which is your pen? welches iſt Ihre Feder?
Which are your pens? welches ſind Ihre Federn?
What is your name? welches iſt Ihr Name?

#### 4.   P o s s e s s i v e   p r o n o u n s.
(Beſitz-anzeigende Fürwörter.)

1) These are formed of the *possessive adjectives*, mein,
dein, ſein, unſer, euer, Ihr, ihr, by adding the termination
ige. With this form, the definite article always precedes.
They are:

---

*) To distinguish this *demonstrative* pronoun from the *definite
article*, more stress must be laid upon it.
**) Sometimes also deren. Ex. Ich habe deren zwei (two of them).
***) But when *this* means *this one*, it agrees. Ex. dieſer iſt Arzt.

| masc. | fem. | neuter. |
|---|---|---|
| der meinige | die meinige | das meinige mine. |
| der deinige | die deinige | das deinige thine. |
| der seinige | die seinige | das seinige his. |
| der ihrige | die ihrige | das ihrige hers. |

*Pl.* die meinigen; die deinigen; die seinigen; die ihrigen.

der, die, das unsrige; *pl.* die unsrigen ours.

der, die, das Ihrige or eurige; *pl.* die Ihrigen yours.

der, die, das ihrige; *pl.* die ihrigen theirs.

They are declined like adjectives with the definite article (*N.* der meinige, *G.* des meinigen, *D.* dem meinigen, *Ac.* den meinigen *Pl.* die meinigen 2c.).

They appear sometimes in the abridged form: der meine, der deine, der seine, der ihre, der unsre, der eure or der Ihre, der ihre, which however is not to be recommended.

2) There is another form unaccompanied by the article, viz.:

| masc. | fem | neuter. | Plural for all genders. | |
|---|---|---|---|---|
| meiner | meine | meines | meine | mine. |
| deiner | deine | deines | deine | thine. |
| seiner | seine | seines | seine | his. |
| ihrer | ihre | ihres | ihre | hers. |
| unsrer | unsre | unsres | unsre | ours. |
| { Ihrer { eurer | Ihre eure | Ihres eures | Ihre } eure } | yours. |
| ihrer | ihre | ihres. | ihre | theirs. |

This latter form is commonly used in conversation and declined like dieser, diese, dieses; viz.:

**Declension.**

| | masc. | fem. | neuter | Plural. |
|---|---|---|---|---|
| *N.* | meiner | meine | meines | meine |
| *G.* | meines | meiner | meines | meiner |
| *D* | meinem | meiner | meinem | meinen |
| *A.* | meinen | meine | meines. | meine. |

**Examples.**

Ist das Ihr Stock? Nein, es ist nicht der meinige (or meiner), es ist der Ihrige (or es ist Ihrer).

Is that your stick? No, it is not mine, it is yours.

Wessen Pferd ist das? Es ist das meinige or meines.

Whose horse is that? It is mine.

Wessen Bücher sind das? Es sind die unsrigen or es sind unsre.

Whose books are these? They are ours.

## Words.

Die Gesundheit the health.
der Körper the body.
der Geist the mind.
die Brieftasche the pocket-book.
tadeln to blame.
klopfen to knock.
das Päckchen the parcel.

der Buchhändler the bookseller.
das Tuch the cloth.
die Tinte the ink.
arbeiten to work.    recht right.
geschrieben written.
finden to find.
nehmen to take.

## Reading Exercise. 53.

Wer geht da? Es ist ein englischer Offizier'. Wessen Uhr ist dieses? Es ist die meines Freundes Arthur. Mit wem wünschen Sie zu sprechen? Ich wünsche mit Ihrem Vater zu sprechen. Welches ist Ihr Hut, dieser oder jener? Dieser ist es. Von welchem Hause sprechen Sie? Wir sprechen von dem (demjenigen) des Herrn Gall. Dieser Garten und der meines Nachbars sind zu verkaufen. Mein Haus ist neu, das Ihrige ist alt. Luisens Kleid ist blau, Ihres (das Ihrige) ist grün. Wer hat dieses Buch gebracht? Ich schreibe an meinen Vater, du schreibst an deinen (den deinigen), Robert schreibt an seinen. Die Gesundheit des Körpers hat großen Einfluß (influence) auf die des Geistes. Was soll ich sagen? Welches von diesen Messern wollen Sie kaufen? Von was (wovon) sprechen Sie?

## Aufgabe. 54.

1. Who comes there? It is my friend Charles. Whose son is he? He is the son of Mr. R. To whom do you send this parcel? I send it [to] the bookseller. Who knocks at the door? To (an, *acc.*) whom have you written a letter? Of (von) whom have you bought this black cloth? Whom do you blame? I blame my servant. To (mit) whom do you speak? Who is that young man? He is my nephew. What have you found in the garden? Which (*m. sing.*) of (von) these three sticks is the longest? This one is longer than that. Here is your pocket-book and *that* (*of*) your brother. That is right.

2. I have lost my [own] book and *that* of my sister. *This* is not my pen; this is my brother's (*that of my br.*). Are these your shoes (Schuhe)? No, they (es) are my cousin's (*those of my c.*). Your coat is old, mine is new. His house is small, yours is very large. My son does not work so much as yours. His ink is not good, ours is much better. Which is the highest mountain of America? Is that your garden? Yes, it is mine; it (*m.*) is not as large as yours. Whose umbrella is this? Is it (es) yours? No, Sir, it is not mine, it is Henry's (*that of H.*). If you do ₁not ₄find ₁your ₂stick, take mine (*Acc.*).

## 6. Relative pronouns.
(Bezügliche Fürwörter.)

These are: 1) welcher, welche, welches (*who*, *which*, *that*) (without a note of interrogation), and 2) der, die, das.

### 1) Declension of welcher, welche, welches.

|  | Singular. | | | Plural |
|---|---|---|---|---|
| *masc.* | *fem.* | *neuter.* | | *for all genders.* |
| N. welcher | welche | welches who, which | | welche |
| G. dessen | deren | dessen whose, of which | | deren |
| D. welchem | welcher | welchem to whom *or* which | | welchen |
| A. welchen | welche | welches whom, which. | | welche. |

### 2) Declension of the relative der, die, das.

| N. der | die | das | who, which, that | die |
|---|---|---|---|---|
| G. dessen | deren | dessen | whose, of which | deren |
| D. dem | der | dem | to whom, to which | denen |
| A. den | die | das | whom, which, that. | die. |

They must agree in gender and number*) with the noun they refer to. Ex.:

Der Mann, welcher or der..., | die Frau, welche or die...,
Das Buch, welches or das..., | die Bücher, welche or die...

It is peculiar to them *to place the verb at the end of the sentence* (or clause). Ex.:

Das Geld, welches ich in der Straße gefunden habe.

## Observations.

1) In English the *relative* pronouns *whom, which, that*, though understood, are sometimes left out after the noun, in German they must always be added, as:

The boy I saw with you yesterday (instead of *whom* I saw).
Der Knabe, den or welchen ich gestern bei Ihnen sah.
Here are the books you have ordered.
Hier sind die Bücher, welche or die Sie bestellt haben.

2) The genitive dessen, deren, dessen, always precedes the word by which it is governed, like *whose* in English:

A tree the branches *of which* are cut off, etc.
Ein Baum, dessen Äste abgehauen sind.

3) In the employment either of welcher, welche, welches or der, die, das, no difference is made between persons, animals or things. The only difference lies in euphony; the former has the advantage of emphasis, as it consists of two syllables; the latter that of brevity, and is to be regarded as an occasional substitute only. Ex.:

---

*) not in *case*.

Hier ist der Wein, den (or welchen) Sie bestellt haben.
Here is the wine you have ordered.

Der Mann, welcher (or der) mir das Buch brachte, das (or welches) er gefunden hatte.
The man who brought me the book (that) he had found.

*Note.* Der, die, das is always used after the personal pronouns, especially when these pronouns, for the sake of emphasis, are repeated after the relative, as:

Ich, der (not welcher) so viel für ihn that.
I who did so much for him.

Wir, die wir jetzt jung sind we who are now young

4) The German relative pronoun welcher or der connected with nicht answers to the English conjunction *but* after a negative sentence, as:

Es giebt keinen Menschen, der nicht seine Fehler hat.
There is no man *but* has his faults.

5) When the relative pronouns are preceded by prepositions, they are often contracted with the latter, so that the pronoun takes the form of wo- or wor- (before a vowel) and the preposition follows it, answering to the English *whereof, whereby, wherefore* etc. The verb goes last. Such are:

| | |
|---|---|
| Wozu to which *or* to what. | woraus from which *or* what. |
| wodurch by which *or* what. | worin in which *or* what. |
| womit with which *or* what. | worüber at (over) which *or* what. |
| wobei at which *or* what. | worauf upon which *or* what. |
| wofür for which *or* what | woran at (to) which *or* what. |
| wovon of which *or* what. | worunter among which. |

Examples

Hier ist der Schlüssel, womit[1] ich die Thüre geöffnet habe.
Here is the key with which I have opened the door.

Die Gläser, woraus[2] wir getrunken haben, sind zerbrochen.
The glasses, out of which we drank, are broken.

Das Zimmer, worin[3] ich schlafe, ist sehr kalt.
The room, in which I sleep, is very cold.

*NB* As we see in the foregoing examples, the relative pronoun, even in its contracted form, requires the verb always *at the end of the clause or sentence.*

6) These contractions *may* also be used interrogatively, as:

Womit (or mit was) haben Sie die Thüre geöffnet?
With what have you opened the door?

Wovon sprechen Sie? of what are you speaking?

---

1) or mit welchem. 2) or aus welchem. 3) or in welchem.

*Note 1.* The real signification of these contracted words depends on the meaning of the preposition governed by a verb, as: What do you think *of*, must be translated· woran denken Sie? because the German verb denken requires the preposition an.

*Note 2* Persons cannot be alluded to in this manner, as Of *whom* are you speaking, must be rendered: Von wem sprechen Sie? not Wovon sprechen Sie?

## Words.

| | |
|---|---|
| Die Grammatik the grammar. | verbessern (*reg. v.*) to correct. |
| das Gedicht (*pl.* —e) the poem. | geliehen lent (*Part. past*). |
| der Schuhmacher the shoemaker. | die Aufgabe the exercise. |
| niemand nobody. | genommen taken. |
| zeigen (*reg. v.*) to show. | letztes Jahr last year. |

## Reading Exercise. 55.

Hier ist der Knabe, welcher sein Buch verloren hat. Da ist das Buch, welches (or das) er verloren hat. Kennen Sie die Herren, welche (or die) gestern bei mir waren? Ja, ich kenne sie. Ist dieses die Dame, welche Ihnen einen Regenschirm geliehen hat? Nein, sie ist es nicht. Der Schüler, welchem Sie Ihre Grammatik geliehen haben, ist sehr fleißig. Welches von diesen Gedichten haben Sie gelernt? Ich habe dieses gelernt. Ich kann nicht mit der Feder schreiben, die Sie mir geschnitten haben (made for me). Können Sie mir sagen, wer meinen Stock genommen hat? Ich weiß es nicht; ich habe niemand gesehen, der Ihren Stock genommen hat.

## Aufgabe. 55a.

Here is the shoemaker who ₈brings ₁your ₂shoes. I have seen the garden, which (*acc.*) you have sold. Is this the exercise which you have written? The rooms (which) my father has taken (gemietet), are not large enough. The pen which you have made (geschnitten) is not good. The pupil whose exercise you *are correcting*, is very lazy. My neighbour whose horse you (have) bought last year, has gone (ist .. gegangen) to America. Do you know the man who has done (gethan) this? I wish to buy the book .. you showed me (*Dat.*) yesterday. The pictures you have sent me, are very beautiful. The traveller to whom (*Dat.*) I have lent a marc, is your friend. The book.. I want, is not to be had (zu haben) here.

## Correlative pronouns.

1) The demonstrative pronouns derjenige ꝛc., when taken in connection with a relative one, are termed *correlative pronouns.* They are:

### Masculine.

Derjenige, welcher; or der, welcher; or derjenige, der = he who.

*Feminine.*

Diejenige, welche; or bie, welche; or biejenige, bie = she who.

*Neuter.*

Dasjenige, welches; or b a 8, welches; or basjenige, bas = that which.

*Plural for all three genders.*

Diejenigen, welche; or bie, welche; {they who, those who,
  or biejenigen, bie        {they which or *acc.* them which.

In the same manner are used:

*Masculine.*

Derselbe or ebenderselbe, welcher (or ber) the same who *or* which.

*Feminine.*

Dieselbe or ebendieselbe, welche (or bie) the same who *or* which.

*Neuter.*

Dasselbe or ebendasselbe, welches (or bas) the same which.

*Plural for all three genders.*

Dieselben or ebendieselben, welche (or bie) the same who *or* which.

Further: Solche, welche such as:

Examples.

Derjenige, welcher (not wer) tugendhaft ist, wirb glücklich sein.
He who is virtuous, will be happy.

Diejenigen, welche tugendhaft leben, sinb weise.
They who live virtuously, are wise.

Diejenigen or solche (*viz.* Tiere), welche im Winter schlafen.
Such (animals) as sleep in the winter-time.

2) Both or either may be declined according to the verb they depend on.

Ich gebe es demjenigen, welchen ich am meisten liebe.
I give it *to him* whom I love most.

Ich kenne benjenigen nicht, b e n (welchen) (*Acc.*) Sie meinen.
I do not know *him* whom you mean.

Ich kenne biejenige (*f.*) nicht, bie (*Nom.*) ben Brief brachte.

3) The expression referring to a preceding neuter noun is in German basjenige, welches that which. Ex.:

Dasjenige (*viz.* Buch), welches ich eben lese.
That which I am reading now.

4) *That which* in a general sense is ba8, wa8. Ex.:

Das, was schön ist, ist nicht immer gut.
That which is fine, is not always good.

5) The *correlative* berjenige, welcher referring to a person, is sometimes contracted into wer, and bas, was into was. Both require the verb at the end of the clause, as:

Wer tugendhaft lebt, ist glücklich.
He who lives virtuously, is happy.
Was schön ist, ist nicht immer gut.
What is fine, is not always good.

6) When wer and was are used in a general sense, they answer also to the English *whoever, whatever*. Ex.:

Wer zuviel bedenkt, wird wenig leisten. (Schiller's W. Tell.)
Who(ever) considers too much, will perform little.
Was gerecht ist, verdient Lob.
Whatever is just, deserves praise.

7) Wer and was are sometimes rendered more emphatic by adding the words immer, auch or auch nur, auch immer, as:

Wer (auch) immer or wer auch nur = (jeder, der) whoever.
Was auch (immer) or was auch (nur) = alles was whatever.
Wer auch immer dieses gesagt hat whoever has said this.
Was Sie auch gesehen haben (mögen).
Whatever you may have seen.

### Words.

| | |
|---|---|
| Die Pflicht the duty | die Wahrheit the truth. |
| erfüllen to fulfil.  wahr true. | verdienen to deserve. |
| ehrlich, rechtschaffen honest. | das Vertrauen the confidence. |
| fluchen to curse. | das Glas the glass |
| segnen to bless. | diesen Morgen *adv.* this morning. |
| hassen to hate.  thun to do. | gebacken baked |
| das Heer the army. | der Weizen the wheat. |
| nachlässig careless.  hart hard. | das Korn, der Roggen the rye. |
| unwissend ignorant. | teuer dear. |

### Reading Exercise. 56.

Derjenige, welcher reich ist, ist nicht immer zufrieden. Diejenigen, welche unzufrieden sind, sind nicht glücklich. Wer seine Pflicht erfüllt, ist ein rechtschaffener Mann. Liebet eure Feinde, segnet die, die euch fluchen, thut Gutes denen, die euch hassen. Er sagte mir, was er wußte. Hier sind einige Federn, welche wollen Sie haben? Ich will die nehmen, welche am härtsten ist. Der König, dessen Heer geschlagen wurde (defeated), ist geflohen (fled). Die Eltern, deren Kinder gestraft wurden, sind nachlässig. Worüber beklagen Sie sich (complain)?

### Aufgabe. 56a.

*He who* ₌will ₁not ₌learn will remain ignorant. What is true to-day, must also be true to-morrow! They who do not speak the truth, deserve no confidence. I will give this book *to him who* is the most industrious. The little girl with whom Mary played yesterday, died (ſtarb) this morning. The boy who found (fand) the gold watch, is honest. The man whose name was written in my pocket-book, is arrived. Here is the glass *out of which* the king has drunk (getrunfen). Who is the happiest man? *He* who is the most contented. The bread on which (wovon) we live, is baked of (aus) wheat and rye.

### Conversation.

| | |
|---|---|
| Wer hat immer genug? | Der zufriedene Menſch. |
| Wen haben Sie getadelt? | Meine träge Schülerin. |
| Was wünſcht der Menſch am meiſten? | Das, was er hofft (hopes). |
| Wer flopft (knocks) an die Thüre? | Es iſt der Schneider, welcher Ihren neuen Rock bringt. |
| Was werden Sie thun? | Ich weiß nicht, was ich thun ſoll. |
| Weſſen Schreibbuch iſt dieſes? | Es iſt das Ihres Schülers. |
| An wen ſchreiben Sie dieſen Brief? | Ich ſchreibe ihn an meinen Lehrer. |
| Iſt Ihr Sohn älter als meiner? Wie alt iſt er? | Nein, der meinige iſt jünger. Er iſt 11 Jahre alt. |
| Hier iſt ein Hut, iſt es der Ihrige (or Ihrer)? | Nein, das iſt nicht der meinige; meiner iſt ganz neu. |
| Sind das Ihre Handſchuhe? | Ja, das ſind meine. |
| Von (on) was leben die Schafe? | Von Gras und Heu (hay). |
| Mit was (womit) haſt du den Knaben geſchlagen (beaten)? | Ich habe ihn mit meinem Stocke geſchlagen. |
| Iſt dieſer Garten zu verfaufen (to be sold)? | Dieſer nicht, aber der meines Nachbars. |
| Was ſagte Ihnen der Bediente? | Er ſagte mir, was er gehört hatte. |
| Welche Menſchen ſind die unglücklichſten? | Diejenigen, welche mit allem unzufrieden ſind. |
| Wo iſt das Glas, aus welchem (woraus) ich getrunfen habe? | Ich habe es in den Schrank (cupboard) geſtellt (put). |
| War es nicht meines? | Nein, es war das des Herrn Grün. |

---

### Reading - lesson.

### Ein teurer Kopf und ein wohlfeiler.

(A dear head and a cheap one.)

Unter der Regie'rung [1] des letzten Königs von Polen brach [2] eine Empörung [3] gegen ihn aus [2]. Einer von den Empörern [4],

1) the reign.  2) broke out, from ausbrechen; *irr. v.* (Nr. 19,.
3) an insurrection, revolt.  4) rebel.

ein polnischer Graf, setzte einen Preis von ungefähr 40,000 Mark*)
auf den Kopf des Königs, und hatte sogar (even) die Frechheit[1],
es dem König selbst zu schreiben, um[2] ihn zu erschrecken Aber
der König schrieb[3] ihm ganz kaltblütig[4] die folgende Antwort:
„Ihren Brief habe ich richtig[5] erhalten[6] und gelesen. Es
hat mir viel Vergnügen gemacht (given), zu sehen, daß mein Kopf
Ihnen so viel wert[7] ist; ich versichere[8] Sie, für den Ihrigen
würde ich keinen Heller[9] geben."

1) impudence. 2) in order to frighten him. 3) wrote, from
schreiben *irr. v.* (82). 4) quite coolly. 5) duly. 6) received. 7) worth.
8) assure. 9) farthing.

# Twenty-fifth Lesson.

## 6. Indefinite pronouns.**)

(Unbestimmte Fürwörter.)

I. They are:

Man one (French: *on*), they, people.
Einander each other, one another.
Jedermann everybody, every one.
Jemand somebody, some one, anybody.
Niemand nobody (not — anybody).
Selbst (selber) . . . self (myself etc.).
Etwas something, anything.
Nichts nothing (not — anything).
Gar nichts nothing at all, nothing whatever.

### Observations.

1) Man, which is expressed in English by *one, they, people*
or by the passive voice, occurs only in the nominative case,
and governs the verb in the singular. Ex.:

Man sagt***) people say, they say.
Wenn man krank ist when one (*or* a man) is ill.
Man hat ihn gelobt he has been praised
Man ist glücklich, wenn man zufrieden ist.
One is happy, when one is contented.

---

*) d. h. in jetziger deutscher Reichswährung (viz. in the German
Currency of our days).

**) All *indefinite pronouns*, as well as all *indefinite numerals*,
are now, as a rule, written with *small* letters as initials, when they
do *not begin* a sentence or clause; even when they are the *grammatical subjects* of phrases, and therefore seem to be used substantively

***) Observe that with man the verb is in the singular.

*Note 1.* When another case is required, it is borrowed from einer, e, 8. Ex.:

Wenn man einen Freund verliert, so thut es einem leib.
When one loses a friend, one is sorry for it.

*Note 2.* *One's* before a substantive, is translated in German with fein (*his*). Ex.:

It is better to lose one's (his) life than one's honour.
Es ist besser, sein Leben als seine Ehre zu verlieren.

*Note 3.* *One's self* is translated sich selbst or only sich, not selbst without sich Ex :

One must not praise one's self man muß sich nicht (selbst) loben.

2) Einander is invariable and both dative and accusative:
Karl und Wilhelm trauen einander (*dat.*).
Charles and William trust one another.

Diese Frauen lieben einander (*acc.*).
These ladies love each other.

3) Selbst or felber is indeclinable, and stands either immediately after a substantive or a personal pronoun, as: der Vater selbst, ich selbst, wir selbst or felber, or nearer the end of the sentence (see the 23rd lesson, § 11). Ex.:

Der Vater brachte seinen Sohn selbst.
The father brought his son himself.

Ich habe es selbst (or felber) gesehen (not mich selbst).
I have seen it myself.

Wir glauben es jetzt selbst (not unserfelbst).*)
We believe it now ourselves.

*Note.* The adverb felbst means *even*, as:
Selbst seine Brüder even his brothers.

4) Jedermann everybody, takes 8 in the genitive, in the other cases it remains unchanged, as:

Gutes thun ist jedermanns Pflicht.
To do good is every one's duty.

Geben Sie jedermann (*Dat.*) was Sie ihm schuldig sind.
Give everybody what you owe him.

5) Jemand and niemand take es or 8 in the genitive; in the dative they may take en or remain unaltered; the accusative is like the nominative, as:

Das ist niemandes (niemands) Geschmack.
That is nobody's taste.

---

*) The personal pronoun with *self* is not repeated in German, as: We ourselves wir selbst.

Mein Nachbar leiht niemand(en) (not niemandem) Geld.
My neighbour lends money to nobody.
Ich habe jemand (— niemand) angetroffen.
I have met somebody (— nobody).

6) *Not — anybody* and *not — anything* are translated nie=
mand and nichts Ex.:

I have not seen anything ich habe nichts gesehen.

---

II. The *indefinite numeral adjectives* are also used as
indefinite *pronouns*, when the substantives are dropped.
We repeat them here:

Jeder, e, s or ein jeder*) each, every one.
Einer, eine, eines one, some one.
Der andre, die andre, das andre the other.
Der eine —. der andre the one —, the other;
    *plur.* die einen —, die andern some —, the others.
Einige some *or* a few.
Einige —, andre some —, others.
Mancher many a man; *plur.* manche some.
Beide both, both of them.
Viel much; *plur.* viele many.
Mehrere several. — Mehr more (is indeclinable).
Die meisten most (of them).
Wenig little; *plur.* wenige few.  (a little ein wenig.)
Alles everything; *plur.* alle all.
Der nämliche (*neut.* das nämliche) the same.
Keiner, keine, keines none, no one.
Irgend einer, e, s any one

## Observations.

1) Jeder, mancher and keiner, e, s, are declined like dieser,
diese, dieses; viz.:

    *G.* Jedes, manches, keines.  *D.* jedem, manchem, keinem.
    *Ac.* Jeden, manchen, keinen.

2) The English pronoun *one*, plur. *ones*, after an adjective
is not expressed in German, the termination of the adjective
being a substitute for it. Ex.:

    I have a grey hat and a black *one*.
    Ich habe einen grauen Hut und einen schwarzen.
    Two old lions and two young *ones*.
    Zwei alte Löwen und zwei junge.

---

*) Jedweder and ein jeglicher (each) are antiquated.

3) Alles, was (or alles das, was) is the English *all that* or only *all.* Ex.:

Das ist alles, was ich habe that is all I have.

*Note.* Alles, was is declined as follows:

*G.* Alles dessen, was ... of all that ...
*D.* Allem (dem), was ... to all that ...
*A.* Alles, was or alles das, was ... all (that) ...

4) The indefinite pronoun *some,* when referring to a preceding substantive, may be translated in different ways. When it replaces a *singular,* we may say in German according to the gender: welchen, welche or welches; in the *plural:* welche, einige or davon. Frequently however it is not expressed at all. Ex.:

Will you have *some* beer? Yes, give me *some.*
Wollen Sie Bier haben? Ja, geben Sie mir welches, or only: geben Sie mir.

Have you bought some tobacco? Yes, I have bought some.
Haben Sie Tabak gekauft? Ja, ich habe (welchen) gekauft.

Have you some *or* any more of these cigars?
Haben Sie noch von diesen Zigarren?

Yes, I have some still (*or* a few more).
Ja, ich habe noch welche (einige davon), or even: ich habe noch.

5) *Any,* in an interrogative sentence, is generally not translated. When equivalent to *every,* it is rendered by jeder:

You will find it in *any* shop.
Sie werden es in jedem Laden finden.

---

## Words.

| | |
|---|---|
| Der Christ the Christian. | der Platz the place. |
| der Fehler the fault, mistake. | gelehrt learned, *adj.* |
| das Gewissen the conscience. | gesprochen spoken. |
| die Stimme the voice. | erhalten (*part.*) received. |
| die Erfahrung experience. | die Welt the world. |
| der Bote the messenger. | beneiden to envy. |
| der Preis the prize. | töten to kill. nie never. |
| ich bin schuldig I owe. | verleumden to calumniate. |
| vor'sichtig cautious. | anwenden to employ. |
| stellen to put (upright). | geschlagen beaten. höflich polite. |

## Reading Exercise. 57.

Man ist glücklich, wenn man zufrieden ist. Man glaubt es nicht, wenn man es nicht sieht (sees). Solche Dinge sieht man nicht jeden Tag. Die zwei Knaben haben einander geschlagen. Bezahlen Sie jedermann, was Sie ihm schuldig sind. Niemand ist so gelehrt, daß er alles weiß (knows). Der wahre Christ beneidet

das Glück niemandes; er verleumdet niemand Klopft jemand?
Ich höre jemandes Stimme. Ich thue nie etwas gegen mein
Gewissen. Beneide nicht das Glück andrer. Jeder (or ein jeder)
hat seine Fehler. Mancher kauft und bezahlt nicht. Mehrere haben
den nämlichen Fehler gemacht Viele von meinen Freunden sind
gestorben (died). Unser Freund spricht von allem. Keiner ist ohne
Fehler. Keiner von uns hat den Preis gewonnen (won).

### Aufgabe. 58.

1. One is unhappy, when one *is ¹discontented. These
young people love each other. (The) animals eat (freſſen)
one another. Be polite to (gegen) everybody. Has the man
killed anybody? No, nobody One should not speak much
of (von) one's self I have seen nobody. Is there (giebt es)
anything prettier (neut.)? I have spoken of nobody Have
you received anything? No, Sir, I have not received anything.
Do (thun Sie) nothing against your conscience. Every one
who knows the world, is cautious. Have you many friends?
I have only a few.

2. Put these books each in (an) its place. The one
goes, the other comes. Some are too (zu) young, the others
are too old. Both are dead. Many a man drinks more than
he wants (bedarf) I know several of (von) them. No one
has helped me (mir geholfen). Do not speak evil (Böses) of
others. Tell me all (II. Obs 3) you know (was Sie wiſſen).
I have sold all One must not kill one's self. The messenger
said the same (neut.). With money *one ¹can do ²much good
(p. 103, § 8) [to] ³one's ⁴fellow-creatures (Nebenmenſchen).

### Conversation.

Wann ist man reich? — Wenn man zufrieden ist
Ist jemand da? — Nein, es ist niemand da.
Was sagte Ihr Freund? — Er sagte nichts.
Giebt es etwas Schöneres als den — Ich kenne nichts Schöneres.
  gestirnten (starry) Himmel?
Haben Sie viele Schüler? — Ich habe mehrere.
Gegen wen soll man höflich sein? — Gegen jedermann.
Was thun diese Leute? — Einige lesen, andre schreiben.
Lieben die Brüder einander? — Ja, sie lieben einander.
Wer ist ohne Fehler? — Keiner (niemand).
Wer will (wishes) glücklich sein? — Jedermann will es (so) sein.
Kennen Sie Herrn Braun oder — Ich kenne beide. Sie wohnen
  Herrn Grün? — beide in meinem Hause.
Wohin' soll ich die Bücher stellen? — Stellen Sie jedes an seinen Platz.
Wer hat das Geld bezahlt? — Einige von unsern Freunden.
Soll man von andern Böses — Man soll von niemand (or von
  (evil) reden? — niemanden) Böses reden.
Von was sprechen Sie? — Wir sprechen von allem.

Wieviele Hüte haben Sie?     Ich habe zwei: einen alten und einen neuen.

Sind Ihre Hüte schwarz oder grau (grey)?     Ich habe einen schwarzen und einen grauen.

Von wem haben Sie diesen Brief erhalten?     Von jemand, den Sie nicht kennen.

---

# Twenty-sixth Lesson.
## IRREGULAR VERBS.
### (Unregelmäßige Zeitwörter.)
#### (Ancient or strong conjugation)

Those verbs are commonly called *irregular* (unregel-mäßig) which deviate from the formation and conjugation of the modern or *regular verbs*. They are indeed sufficiently regular after their own fashion of conjugation. However as the term *irregular* has hitherto been adopted we cannot help using it too. They amount to 163. The deviation from the modern form takes place only in the *Imperfect* and the *Participle Past*; all the other tenses are formed in the same manner.

1) The terminations of the *Present tense* of the irregular verbs are the same as of the regular verbs, but several change, besides, in the second and third persons singular and in the Imperative mood, their radical vowel a into ä, and e into i or ie, as:

Ich schlage, du schlägst; — ich gebe, er giebt (gibt). — Gieb.

2) The peculiar character of the *Imperfect Indicative* of the irregular verbs consists in their *adding no termination at all* to the root, but in *changing its vowel*, as from geben, *Imp.* ich gab. The difference of the vowel causes them to be divided into **four** conjugations, according to the prevailing four vowels a, i, o and u.

1) Those ancient verbs with the vowel a in the Imperfect, compose the *first* conjugation (geben — ich gab);

2) those with i or ie, the *second* (schreiben — ich schrieb);

3) those which take o, the *third* (schießen — ich schoß) and

4) those which take u, the *fourth* (schlagen — ich schlug).

The 3rd pers. sing. of the Imperf. is always like the first.

3) The *Imperfect* of the *Subjunctive* mood is formed by adding **e** to the Imperfect Indicative, and modifying the vowel, when it is **a, o** or **u,** as: Ich gäbe, du gäbest, er gäbe ꝛc. (wenn ich gäbe).

4) The ***Participle past*** of all verbs of the ancient form ends in **en** instead of **t,** as gegeben given; geschrie= ben written etc.; but as the vowel does not always remain the same in the Participle past, the two first conjugations have three subdivisions or classes, according to the prevailing vowel of the Participle past.

## Remarks.

Strictly speaking, only verbs having **a, e, ei** and **i** for their root-vowel can be *ancient* or *irregular* verbs. By anomaly or bad orthography, however, a few verbs with **ä, o, ö, au** and **u** have also crept in.

To facilitate somewhat the study of these verbs, we think it useful to give the following general *hints*, before we enter upon the particulars.

1) Ancient verbs having **a** in their root, retain this vowel in the *Part. past.* The *Imperfect* takes either **ie** or **u,** as:

blasen to blow. *Imp.* blies. *Part* geblasen.
tragen to carry. *Imp.* trug. *Part* getragen.

2) Those having **e** for their root-vowel, take in the *Imperfect* either **a** or **o.** In the *Participle past* the 13 first verbs (p 163, 164 and 165) take **e,** Nr. 14 and 15 **a,** all the others **o,** as:

geben to give; gab — gegeben.
fechten to fight; focht — gefochten.

3) Ancient verbs having **ei** in their root, change it into **i** or **ie,** both in the *Imperfect* and *Part. past,* as:

beißen to bite; biß — gebissen.
bleiben to remain; blieb — geblieben.

4) Ancient verbs having **ie** in their root, change it into **o,** both in the *Imperfect* and *Part. past,*[*] as:

schließen to lock; schloß — geschlossen.

5) Ancient verbs the root of which is **ind, ing** or **ink** have in the *Imperfect* **a** and in the *Part. past* **u,** as:

finden to find; fand — gefunden.
singen to sing; sang — gesungen.

[*] With the exception only of liegen to lie (see Nr. 12, p 165).

## Conjugation of an irregular verb. (1st Conj.)*)
### Imperfect with a.
### Geben to give.

Indicative Mood.        Subjunctive Mood.

*Present Tense.*

| | |
|---|---|
| Ich gebe I give | Ich gebe I (may) give |
| du giebst thou givest | du gebest thou mayst give |
| er giebt he gives | er gebe he may give |
| wir geben we give | wir geben we may give |
| (ihr gebt) } ye give | (ihr gebet) } you may give |
| Sie geben } you give | Sie geben } |
| sie geben they give. | sie geben they may give. |

*Imperfect* (Preterite).

| | |
|---|---|
| Ich gab I gave | Ich gäbe**) I might give, I gave |
| du gabst thou gavest | du gäbest thou mightst give |
| er gab he gave | er gäbe he might give |
| wir gaben we gave | wir gäben we might give |
| ihr gabt } ye gave | (ihr gäbet) } you might give |
| Sie gaben } you gave | Sie gäben } |
| sie gaben they gave. | sie gäben they might give |

*Compound Tenses.*

Perfect.                    Pluperfect.

Ich habe .. gegeben I have given   Ich hatte gegeben I had given
du hast gegeben thou hast given   du hattest gegeben thou hadst given
er hat gegeben he has given        2c.                2c.
  2c.        2c.

*First Future.*

Ich werde . . geben I *shall* give
du wirst geben thou wilt give
er wird geben he will give
wir werden geben we shall give
ihr werdet geben } you will give
Sie werden geben }
sie werden geben they will give.

*Second Future.*

Ich werde . . gegeben haben I shall have given
du wirst gegeben haben thou wilt have given
  2c.        2c.

---

*) Called also die A-Konjugation.
**) Used especially after wenn if. (wenn ich es ihm gäbe)

*First Conditional.*
Ich würde . . geben I should or would give
du würdest geben thou wouldst give
er würde geben he would give
wir würden geben we should or would give
&c. &c.

*Second Conditional.*
Ich würde . . gegeben haben I should have given
du würdest gegeben haben thou wouldst have given
&c. &c.

### Imperative Mood.

Gieb give (thou).
(er soll geben let him give.)
geben wir or laßt uns geben let us give.
gebet or geben Sie give (you).
sie sollen geben let them give.

### Infinitive Mood.

*Pres.* geben or zu geben to give.
*Past.* gegeben haben or gegeben zu haben to have given.

### Participles.

*Pres.* gebend giving.      *Past.* gegeben given.

---

We subjoin now the irregular verbs according to their respective conjugations and classes, numbered in succession from 1 to 163, and followed by an *alphabetical list.*

## First Conjugation.
### Imperfect with a.
### First class: *Past Part.* with e.

| Indicative Present. | Imperative. | Imperfect a | Past Part. e |
|---|---|---|---|
| | | | |

1. Geben to give.

| Indicative Present. | Imperative. | Imperfect a | Past Part. e |
|---|---|---|---|
| Ich gebe, du giebst, er giebt or gibt, wir geben,[1]) ihr gebet (Sie geben), sie geben. | gieb or gib, gebet or geben Sie give. | ich gab, du gabst, er gab, wir gaben &c. *Subj.* ich gäbe. | gegeben given. |

Conjugate in the same manner: aus'geben[2]) *(sep. v.)* to spend (money); vergeben *(insep. v.)* to forgive, *Part. p.* vergeben (not vergegeben); zurück'geben to return, to give back etc.

---

1) The plural is always like the Infinitive.
2) The *compounds* of these verbs are either *separable* or *inseparable*. *Separable* verbs take the augment ge between the preposition and the verb in the *past Part.*, as: ausgegeben (see the 31st lesson); the *inseparable* have no ge in the *past Part.* (see p. 121 and 126, 5).

| Indicative Present. | Imperative. | Imperfect a | Past Part. e |
|---|---|---|---|

### 2. Essen to eat.

Ich esse, du issest, er iß, — esset, | ich aß I ate. | gegessen
ißt, wir essen, ihr esset, essen Sie. | Pl. wir aßen. | eaten.
sie (Sie) essen. | Subj. ich äße.

### 3. Fressen to eat (of animals), to devour.

Ich fresse, du frissest, er friß, | ich fraß. | gefressen
frißt, wir fressen ꝛc. fresset. | Subj. ich fräße. | eaten.

### 4. Messen to measure.

Ich messe, du missest, er miß, messet, | ich maß. | gemessen
mißt, wir messen ꝛc. messen Sie. | Subj. ich mäße. | measured.

Thus is conjugated: ab'messen to measure, to survey.

### 5. Lesen to read.

Ich lese, du liesest, er liest, lies, leset, | ich las. | gelesen
wir lesen ꝛc. lesen Sie. | Subj. ich läse. | read.

Thus: vor'lesen to read to some one.

### 6. Sehen to see, to look.

Ich sehe, du siehst, er sieht, sieh, sehet, | ich sah. | gesehen
wir sehen ꝛc. sehen Sie. | Subj. ich sähe. | seen.

Thus an'sehen to look at; aus'sehen to look (like or — well).

### 7. Treten to kick (also to step, tread).

Ich trete, du trittst, er tritt, tretet, | ich trat. | getreten.
tritt, wir treten ꝛc. treten Sie. | Subj. ich träte

Thus: ab'treten to resign, yield; †eintreten to step in, enter.

### 8. †Genesen*) to recover from illness.

Ich genese, du genesest, er genese, | ich genaß. | genesen
geneset, wir genesen ꝛc. geneset. | Subj. ich genäße. | recovered.

### 9. †Geschehen*) to happen.

Es geschieht, (sie) geschehen. | — | es geschah. | geschehen.

### 10. Vergessen to forget.

Ich vergesse, du vergissest, vergiß, | ich vergaß. | vergessen
er vergißt, wir vergessen. vergesset. | S. ich vergäße. | forgotten.

### 11. Bitten to beg, ask or request.

Ich bitte, du bittest, er bittet, bitte, bittet, | ich bat. | gebeten
wir bitten, ihr bittet ꝛc. bitten Sie. | Subj. ich bäte. | begged.

*) ☞ Verbs marked with † are neuter and form their compound tenses with the auxiliary sein (to be), as: ich bin genesen I have recovered, es ist geschehen it has happened etc. All others are construed with haben.

| Indicative Present. | Imperative. | Imperfect. a | Past Part. e |
|---|---|---|---|

### 12. †Liegen to lie.*)

Ich liege, du liegst, er liegt, | liege, lieget, | ich lag I lay. | gelegen
wir liegen, ihr lieget ꝛc. | liegen Sie. | Subj. ich läge. | lain.

Thus: †unter'liegen to succumb. *Part. p.* unterle'gen.

### 13. †Sitzen to sit.*)

Ich sitze, du sitzest, er sitzt, | sitze, sitzet, | ich saß I sat. | gesessen
wir sitzen, ihr sitzet ꝛc. | sitzen Sie. | Subj. ich säße | sat.

Thus. besitzen to possess. *Imp.* ich besaß; *Perf.* ich habe besessen.

To this class may be added the following three more irregular verbs:

### 14. †Stecken to stick.*)

Ich stecke, du steckst, er steckt, | stecke, stecket, | ich stak. | gesteckt
wir stecken, ihr stecket ꝛc. | stecken Sie. | S. ich stäke. | stuck.

*NB.* The *active* verb stecken (to put) is regular.

### 15. †Stehen to stand.*)

Ich stehe, du stehest or stehst, | stehe, stehet, | ich stand**). | gestanden
er steht, wir stehen ꝛc. | stehen Sie. | Subj. ich stände. | stood.

Thus: †bestehen to consist; †aufstehen to get up, to rise, verstehen to understand. *P. p.* verstanden understood.

### 16. Thun to do, to make.

Ich thue, du thust, er thut, | thue, thuet, | ich that I did. | gethan
wir thun, ihr thut, sie thun. | thun Sie. | Subj. ich thäte. | done.

---

### Words.

Ein Thaler *m.* a German dollar.***)
ein Schilling *m.* a shilling.
der Mensch (*2nd decl.*) mankind.
die Vernunft reason, sense.
Heu *n.* hay. Hafer *m.* oats.
glauben to think, believe.
die Raupe the caterpillar.

der Kuchen the cake.
der Storch the stork.
der Roman' the novel.
der Komet' (*2nd decl.*) the comet.
die Gefahr the danger.
die Mark the marc.
das Ufer the shore, bank.
schwach weak, feeble.

---

*) In Middle- and North-Germany with haben, only in South-Germany with sein.

**) *Old* form ich stund; *Subj.* ich stünde.

***) A German dollar or rather 'thaler' has 3 marcs, an American dollar has 4 marcs.

die Maus the mouse.                    noch keine not yet any.
der Feind the enemy                    der Römer the Roman
leise low.   bald soon.                die Tugend virtue.
noch nicht (nie') not yet (never).

---

## Reading Exercise. 59.

1. Geben Sie mir eine gute Feder. Mein Freund gab
mir einige Thaler. Haben Sie ihm dieselben zurück'gegeben?
Noch nicht. Was ißt jener Knabe da? Er ißt Kirschen. Ich
habe noch keine gegessen. Der Mann aß zu (too) viel. Der
Ochse frißt Gras und Heu. Die Pferde haben allen Hafer
gefressen. Warum messen Sie dieses Tuch? Ich will es
verkaufen. Warum liest der Schüler so leise? Er hat eine
schwache Stimme (voice). Voriges (last) Jahr las er lauter.
Der blinde Mann sieht nichts. Sieh, hier sind deine Bücher.
Haben Sie den Storch gesehen? Wir sahen ihn nicht. Ich
habe noch nie einen Elefanten gesehen.

2. Jemand ist auf meinen Fuß getreten. Der Kranke ist
genesen (8). Vieles geschieht (9) in der Welt (world), was man
nicht verstehen kann. Haben Sie geglaubt, daß dies geschehen
würde? Ich vergaß, Ihnen zu sagen, daß ich Ihren Freund Karl
gesehen habe. Ich hatte das Wort vergessen. Der Bediente stand
an der Thüre; zwei andre Männer standen bei ihm. Der arme
Mann bat mich, ihm zu helfen (help); er hat auch andre Leute
gebeten. Der Rabe saß auf einem hohen Baum, ich weiß nicht,
wie lange er dort (there) saß. Wo lag der Apfel? Er lag im Gras.

## Aufgabe. 60.

1. Give me two marcs. When (wann) will you return
them [to] me? In a few days (Dat.). The countess gave
the poor man (Dat.) a shilling. God (Gott) has given (the)
reason to mankind. I eat bread and cheese. Thou eatest
bread and butter. The children ate cherries. I saw you
eat grapes (Trauben); were they ripe? Eat of (von) this
cake, it*) is for you. The oxen eat (3) grass and hay. The
caterpillars ate (3) all [the] leaves of (von) that tree. The
cat has eaten the (3) mouse. I gave her (Dat.) a flower.
What does Miss Eliza read? She reads a novel by (von) Sir
Walter Scott. Have you read Lord Byron's poems (Gedichte)?
I have not yet read them, but I shall read them soon.

2. Have you ever (je) seen a comet? Yes, I saw a
beautiful comet. The young man does not see the danger in
which he is [placed]. Young lady, read only good books.
Beneath (unter) the sun (Dat.) nothing happens without the

---

*) See p. 141, 1.

will (Willen, *m.*) of God. What *has* (ift) happened? An old man stood on the (am) shore and cried (weinte). Close to him (neben ihm) sat two little children, and a dog lay (12) beside (neben, *Dat.*) them. The poor man begged me, to (zu) give him a few marcs. Fabricius possessed (13) such (fo) great virtues, that (daß) even (felbft) the enemies of the Romans respected him.

---

**Second class:** *Participle* with o.

| *Indicative Present.* | *Imperative.* | *Imperfect.* a | *Past part.* o |
|---|---|---|---|

17. **Befehlen** (*Dat.*)*) to command, to order.

| Ich befehle, du befiehlft, er befiehlt, wir befehlen. | befiehl, befehlet. | ich befahl. S. ich befähle. | befohlen ordered. |
|---|---|---|---|

Thus **empfeh'len** to recommend, *Imp.* empfahl; *P. p.* empfoh'len

18. **Bergen** *or* **verbergen** to hide, to conceal.

| Ich verberge, du verbirgft, er verbirgt, wir verbergen | verbirg, verberget. | ich verbarg. S. ich verbärge. | verborgen hidden. |
|---|---|---|---|

The root **bergen** (to hide) is only used in poetry.

19. †**Berften** to burst

| Ich berfte, du berfteft, er berftet, wir berften ꝛc. | berfte, berftet. | ich barft. S. ich bärfte. | geborften burst. |
|---|---|---|---|

20. **Brechen** to break.

| Ich breche, du brichft, er bricht, wir brechen ꝛc. | brich, brechet. | ich brach. S. ich bräche. | gebrochen broken. |
|---|---|---|---|

Thus: ab'brechen to break off, aus'brechen to break out; unter= bre'chen to interrupt (*P. p.* unterbro'chen), zerbrechen to break to pieces, *Part. p* zerbro'chen.

21. **Drefchen** to thrash.

| Ich drefche, du drifcheft, er drifcht, wir drefchen ꝛc. | drifch, drefchet. | ich drafch. S. ich dräfche. | gedrofchen thrashed. |
|---|---|---|---|

22. † **Erfchrecken** 1) (*neuter*) to be frightened.

| Ich erfchrecke (I am frigh-tened), du erfchrickft, er= erfchrickt, wir erfchrecken. | erfchrick, erfchrecket. | ich erfchrak I was fright-ened. | erfchrocken frightened. |
|---|---|---|---|

*NB.* When erfchrecken¹) is an *active* verb, meaning *to frighten some one*, it is regular, like the simple verb fchrecken.²)

---

*) (*Dat.*) means: The verb governs the *person* in the Dative; to order something means beftellen, reg. v.

1) Pronounce erfchräcken.

2 Pronounce erfchrécken, fchrécken.

| Indicative Present. | Imperative. | Imperfect. a | Past Part. v |
|---|---|---|---|

### 23. Gelten to be worth or estimated.

Ich gelte, du giltst, er | — | ich galt | gegolten.·
gilt, wir gelten ꝛc. | — | S. ich gälte. |

Thus: vergelten to return, to render· P. p. vergolten·

### 24. Gebären to bring forth.

Ich gebäre, du gebierst, sie | — | ich gebar. | geboren
gebiert, wir gebären ꝛc. | — | S. ich gebäre. | born·

### 25. Helfen (Dat.) to help, assist.

Ich helfe, du hilfst, er | hilf, helfet, | ich half. | geholfen
hilft, wir helfen ꝛc. | helfen Sie. | S. ich hälfe. | helped.

### 26. Nehmen to take.

Ich nehme, du nimmst, | nimm, | ich nahm. | genommen
er nimmt, wir nehmen. | nehmen Sie | S. ich nähme. | taken.

Thus: ab'nehmen to take off, an'nehmen to accept; aus'nehmen
to except; heraus'nehmen to take out; unternehmen to undertake (P. p unternom'men), weg'nehmen to take away, zurück'-
nehmen to take back.

### 27. Schelten to scold, chide.

Ich schelte, du schiltst, er | schilt, | ich schalt. | gescholten
schilt, wir schelten ꝛc. | scheltet. | S. ich schälte. | scolded.

### 28. Sprechen to speak.

Ich spreche, du sprichst, er | sprich, | ich sprach. | gesprochen
spricht, wir sprechen ꝛc. | sprechen Sie. | S. ich spräche. | spoken

Thus: aus'sprechen to pronounce; ent'sprechen to correspond;
verspre'chen to promise, Part. p. verspro'chen.

### 29. Stechen to sting, prick.

Ich steche, du stichst, er | stich, | ich stach. | gestochen
sticht, wir stechen ꝛc. | stechet. | S. ich stäche. | stung.

### 30. Stehlen to steal.

Ich stehle, du stiehlst, er | stiehl, | Ich stahl. | gestohlen
stiehlt, wir stehlen ꝛc. | stehlet. | S. ich stähle. | stolen.

### 31. †Sterben to die.

Ich sterbe, du stirbst, er | stirb, | ich starb. | gestorben·
stirbt, wir sterben ꝛc. | sterbet. | S. ich stärbe.*) | died.

---

*) Old form: stürbe, verdürbe.

| Indicative. | Imperative. | Imperfect. a | Past Part. o |
|---|---|---|---|

**32. Verderben to spoil, to ruin.**

Ich verderbe, du verdirbst, | verdirb, | ich verdarb. | verdorben
er verdirbt, wir verderben. | verderbet. | S. ich verdürbe.*) | spoiled.

**33. Werben to enlist, to sue.**

Ich werbe, du wirbst, er | wirb, | ich warb. | geworben.
wirbt, wir werben ꝛc. | werbet. | S. ich würbe. |

Thus. erwerben to acquire. *Imp.* erwarb. *P. p.* erworben

**34. Werfen to throw, fling, cast.**

Ich werfe, du wirfst, er | wirf,  · | ich warf. | geworfen
wirft, wir werfen ꝛc. | werfet. | S. ich würfe. | thrown.

Thus· weg'werfen to throw away; *Imp.* warf..weg; um'werfen
to upset; verwer'fen to reject; vor'werfen to reproach.

**35. Treffen to hit.**

Ich treffe, du triffst, er | triff, | ich traf. | getroffen
trifft, wir treffen ꝛc. | treffet. | S. ich träfe. | hit.

Thus: †ein'treffen to arrive; übertref'fen to excel, surpass.
*Imp* übertraf; *P. p.* übertrof'fen, an'treffen (*Acc.*) and †zu‑
sam'mentreffen (mit) to meet, to have a meeting.

**36. Beginnen to begin.**

Ich beginne, du beginnst, | beginne, | ich begann. | begonnen
er beginnt, w. beginnen ꝛc. | beginnet. | S. ich begänne. | begun.

**37. Gewinnen to win, to gain.**

Ich gewinne, like beginnen.| gewinne. | ich gewann. | gewonnen.

**38. Rinnen to leak, to flow.**

Ich rinne, du rinnst ꝛc. | rinne. | ich rann. | geronnen.

**39. Sinnen to mediate, think.**

Ich sinne, du sinnst ꝛc. | sinne. | ich sann. | gesonnen.

Thus: sich besinnen to reflect, to recollect.

**40. Spinnen to spin.**

Ich spinne, du spinnst ꝛc.| spinne. | ich spann. | gesponnen.

**41. †Schwimmen to swim.**

Ich schwimme ꝛc.     |schwimme. |ich schwamm.|geschwommen

*) See p 168.

| Indicative Present. | Imperative. | Imperfect a | Past Part. e |
|---|---|---|---|

42. †**Kommen** to come.

Ich komme, du kommst, | komme, | ich kam I came.| gekommen
er kommt ꝛc. | kommen Sie | S. ich käme. | come.

Thus: †**an'kommen** to arrive. **Bekommen** to get.

## Words.

Der Feind the enemy.  
der Dieb the thief.  
das Rohr the reed, cane.  
das Eis ice.  
der Matrose the sailor.  
die Tasse the cup. bleich pale.  
der Hauptmann the captain.  
das Gewehr (pl. —e) the musket  
der Schatz the treasure.  
der Mann the husband.  
die Erde the earth.

der Mörder the murderer.  
der Dolch the dagger.  
der Spiegel the looking-glass  
der Stachel the sting.  
das Insekt' (Gen. —s) the insect.  
die Biene the bee.  
die Wunde the wound.  
das Ziel the mark, target, goal.  
der Flachs the flax. tot dead  
laden (irr v.) to load.  
gehorchen to obey.

## Reading Exercise. 61.

1. Wer befiehlt den Soldaten? Die Offiziere befahlen den Soldaten, den Feind an'zugreifen (to attack). Der König hat befohlen, daß ein neuer Palast gebaut werde. Der Dieb hatte sich hinter einer Mauer verborgen. Mein Sohn, warum verbirgst du dein Gesicht (face)? Das Eis ist geborsten. Das Rohr biegt sich (bends); aber es bricht nicht. Der Bediente hat die Tasse zerbrochen. Im Winter drischt man das Getraide (corn). Die Frau erschrak (22), als*) (when) sie ihren Mann so bleich sah. Jedermann war darüber erschrocken. Was haben Sie in der Lotterie gewonnen? Ich habe hundert Mark gewonnen.

2. Wenn du deinem Nachbar hilfst, wird er dir auch wieder helfen. Der Graf hat vielen Armen geholfen. Das Kind hat das Messer genommen. Warum nahmen Sie es nicht weg (away)? Ich begann gerade (just) meine Arbeit, als*) der Fremde eintrat (came in). Die Matrosen schwammen über den Fluß. Die alte Frau hat Flachs gesponnen. Von was haben die Leute gesprochen? Sie sagen, daß der König gestorben ist. Mein Freund ist vom

---

*) When = as with an Imperfect or Pluperfect following is translated als, with other tenses wenn; in both cases the verb stands last.

Pferde gefallen (fallen) und hat den (his) Arm gebrochen Wer hat diesen Stein geworfen? Ein Knabe warf ihn in das Fenster und zerbrach die Scheibe (pane).

### Aufgabe. 62.

1. The general commands, the soldiers must obey. Who has ordered you (*Dat*), ²to (ʒu) ³do ¹this? The captain ordered me ³to load ¹the ²musket. Many treasures are hidden in the earth. The murderer hid his dagger under his coat. Who has broken my looking‑glass? The servant broke *it* (see p 141, 2) this morning We must always return (Nr. 23) good for good (Gutes mit Gutem). The duke was born in the year 1775. Mary *was* (*has been**) stung by a bee The sting of the insect stuck (14) in the wound. Frederick II., king of Prussia, died on the 17th [of] August 1786.

2. »The child is not dead,« said Jesus to (ʒu) its father, »it sleeps (schläft).« The boy spoils (32) his books; he has also spoiled his clothes (Kleider). Of whom have you spoken? We spoke of (von) Columbus. The soldier threw (34) ³away (weg) ¹his ²gun. Who has thrown the stone into the window? I do not know who (wer)** ³has ²thrown ¹it. Have you hit (35) the mark? Yes, I have hit it Can you swim? I swam ²over ³the ⁴river ¹yesterday. Who has spun the flax? My wife (Frau) has spun *it* last winter She began the (*Acc*) day after Christmas (Weihnacht). The unhappy men threw themselves (sich) at the feet (zu den Füßen) of the king.

### Third class : *Past Participle* with u.

The verbs belonging to the third class of the first Conjugation, having the Past participle with u, are easily recognised. All have their root in in followed by d, g or f (ind, ing,*** inf). They are not irregular in the Present tense, nor in the Imperative mood, and consist of the following eighteen (43—60), with their different compounds.

| Indicative Present. | Imperative. | Imperfect. a | Past Part u |
|---|---|---|---|

43. Binden to bind, to die.

| | | | |
|---|---|---|---|
| Ich binde, du bindest, er | binde, | ich band I tied. | gebunden |
| bindet, wir binden ꝛc | bindet, | S ich bände. | bound. |

Thus an'binden¹) to attach; verbinden to oblige, to join, to dress (a wound) (*P. p.* verbunden).

*) Passive voice; see the foot-note 2, p 174
**) See p. 145, *Note.*
***) Bringen is the only one of these verbs that does not belong to this class. Its conjugation occurs p. 126, § 6 and p 127.
1) See the foot-note *) p. 164.

| Indicative Present. | Imperative. | Imperfect. a | Past Part. u |
|---|---|---|---|

**44. Finden to find.**

Jch finde, du findeſt, er | finde. | ich fand. | gefunden
findet, wir finden ꝛc. | | S. ich fände. | found.

Thus erfin'den, erfand, erfunden to invent; empfinden to feel.

**45. †Schwinden to disappear, to vanish.**

Jch ſchwinde. | ſchwinde. | ich ſchwand. | geſchwunden.

Thus: †verſchwin'den to disappear. Part. p. verſchwunden

**46. Winden to wind.**

Jch winde. | winde. | ich wand. | gewunden.

Thus überwinden to overcome, conquer. P. p überwun'den -

**47. †Dringen to force one's way.**

Jch dringe. | dringe. | ich drang. | gedrungen.

Thus †durch'dringen to penetrate, †ein'dringen to enter by force

**48. †Gelingen (impers. with dat.) to succeed.**

Es gelingt mir I succeed, | — | es gelang mir | es iſt mir
es gelingt ihm he suc- | | I succeeded. | gelungen I
ceeds ꝛc. | | S. es gelänge | have succ.

Thus: †mißling'en to fail. P. p. mißlung'en.

**49. Klingen to tinkle, to sound.**

Jch klinge. | klinge. | ich klang. | geklungen.

**50. Ringen to struggle, strive for, wring.**

Jch ringe. | ringe. | ich rang. | gerungen.

Thus erringen to obtain, conquer.
NB. Umring'en to surround, from the noun der Ring, is regular.

**51. Schlingen to sling, to twine.**

Jch ſchlinge. | ſchlinge. | ich ſchlang. | geſchlungen.

Thus. verſchling'en to devour, umſchling'en to embrace.

**52. Schwingen to swing, wave, brandish, wield**

Jch ſchwinge. | ſchwinge. | ich ſchwang. | geſchwungen

**53. Singen to sing**

Jch ſinge. | ſinge. | ich ſang | geſungen.

**54. †Springen to spring, to jump, to crack.**

Jch ſpringe | ſpringe. | ich ſprang. | geſprungen.

Thus: †heraus'ſpringen to jump out, †zerſpring'en to burst.

**55. †Sinken to sink**

Jch ſinke. | ſinke. | ich ſank I sank.| geſunken.

Thus· herab- or hinab'ſinken to sink down; †verſinken to sink

| Indicative Present. | Imperative. | Imperfect. a | Past Part. u |
|---|---|---|---|

56. **Trinken** to drink.

Ich trinke. | trinke. | ich trank. | getrunken.

Thus †er'trinken to be drowned, sich betrink'en to get drunk.

57. **Zwingen** to force, compel

Ich zwinge. | zwinge. | ich zwang. | gezwungen.

Thus: bezwingen to conquer, erzwingen to obtain by force.

*Note.* The three following defective verbs belong also to this class, but are seldom used:

58 **Dingen** to hire a servant. *P. p.* gedungen.
It has also the regular forms *Imp.* dingte, *P.* gedingt.
59. **Schinden** to flay. *P. p.* geschunden
60. **Stinken** to stink, — stank *P. p.* gestunken.

### Words.

Der Gärtner the gardener.
die Kugel the ball, bullet
das Schießpulver gunpowder.
der Blumenkranz the garland.
eine Stecknadel a pin.
der Buchbinder the bookbinder.
der Strick the cord, string.
das Lied the song.
schmücken to decorate, to adorn.
der Jäger the hunter.
die Sängerin the songstress.
das Reh the deer, roe.

der Hag, der Zaun the hedge.
die Brust the chest, breast
die Fahne the flag, standard.
der Kaffee the coffee.
das Elend (the) misery.
die Buchdruckerkunst the art of
das Boot the boat. [printing.
erklingen to resound.
unterhalten to amuse, enjoy.
freiwillig voluntarily.
hübsch pretty, nice, fine.
vorsichtig cautious

### Reading Exercise. 63.

1. Der Gärtner hat das Bäumchen an einen Stock ge= bunden. Man verband die Wunde des Soldaten. Ich fand das Kind schlafend unter einem Baum. Berthold Schwarz, ein Deutscher, erfand das Schießpulver im Jahre 1380. Unter der Regie'rung (reign) Karls VII. (des Siebenten) drangen die Engländer in Frankreich ein, und fanden nur einen schwachen Widerstand (resistance). Die Kugel ist durch die Brust des Offiziers gedrungen. Das Pferd sprang über einen breiten Graben (ditch).

2. Die Trompeten erklangen, die Fahnen wurden geschwungen, als der Kaiser nahte (approached). Sokrates trank den Giftbecher (hemlock-bowl), und starb den Tod des Gerechten (just). Hat er ihn freiwillig getrunken? Man hat ihn gezwungen, dieses zu thun. Das Schiff ist gesunken. Wie haben Sie sich gestern Abend unter= halten? Wir haben gespielt, gesungen und getrunken. Die Mädchen haben Blumenkränze gewunden, um die Häuser zu schmücken (decorate).

### Aufgabe. 64.

1. I do not find my stick. I found these violets in your garden and tied them [together] in a (*Acc.*) bunch (Strauß, *m.*). Where *did*[1]) Louisa find that pin? She (has) found it in the street. They found a purse of (mit) gold. Which bookbinder has bound your pretty book? It was Mr. Long, who ‹lives ›in ₂(the) ₃King-Street. I succeeded (48) in catching (zu fangen) the thief. He *was*[2]) immediately (sogleich) bound with cords. Miss Emma sang an fine song. The songstress has sung admirably (wunderschön). Would you like[3]) to drink a glass [of] wine? I thank you, I have already drunk two cups [of] coffee. The ladies drank tea and ate cake.

2. The cat sprang over the table. A German, called (Namens) Gutenberg, invented the art of printing. The deer *had* (war) sprung over the hedge, when (als) the hunter came. The boat sank before our eyes. She (es) would not *have* (sein) sunk, if the captain *had* been more cautious. Lord Byron swam across the (über den) Hellespont. The poor woman wrung her hands in despair (in Verzweiflung). »(The) misery forced (57) me to steal«, said the thief. Misery *should force* nobody (,) to do wrong (Unrecht). My friends have forced me (,) to become [a] soldier.

### Reading-lesson.

#### Der hungrige Araber. The hungry Arab.

Ein Araber hatte sich in der Wüste (desert) verirrt[1], er hatte seit (for) mehreren Tagen nichts gegessen und fürchtete vor (of) Hunger zu sterben Endlich[2] kam er an einen von (to one of) jenen Brunnen[3], wo die Karawa'nen ihre Kamele tränkten[4], und sah einen ledernen Sack[5] auf dem Sande liegen(v). Er hob (or nahm) ihn auf[6] und befühlte[7] ihn. „Gott sei Dank!" rief[8] er aus, „das[9] sind Datteln[10] oder Haselnüsse."

In dieser süßen Hoffnung[11] beeilte er sich (he hastened), den Sack zu öffnen[12]; aber er fand sich in seiner Erwartung[13] getäuscht (disappointed). Der Sack war mit Perlen[14] gefüllt.

1) wandered, lost his way. 2) at last. 3) well, fountain. 4) to water. 5 a leathern sack *or* bag. 6) auf'heben (141) to pick up, take up. 7) to touch, to feel. 8) aus'rufen (110) to exclaim. 9, see p 146, Obs. 1. 10) dates. 11) sweet hope. 12, to open. 13) expectation. 14) pearls.

1) Translate *has . . found*.
2) Here and in the following 10 Exercises the *Passive Voice* (p. 129) is indicated by printing the verb *to be* in *Italics*.
3) See p. 93, 1st Cond. Möchten Sie . . gern?

Dann wurde er traurig[15] und sank (fell) auf seine Knie und bat Gott, daß er ihn von seiner Not[16] retten (save) und ihm Hilfe[17] schicken möchte (would). Sein Gebet'[18] wurde erhört. Nach einer Stunde kam der Mann zurück,[19] welcher den Sack ver= loren (lost, 125) hatte, auf einem Kamel reitend (riding), um[20] ihn zu suchen. Er war sehr glücklich, ihn wieder[20] zu finden, hatte Mitleid[21] mit dem armen Araber, erquickte[22] ihn mit Speise[23] und Trank, setzte ihn zu sich[24] auf sein Kamel' und kehrte[25] zu der Karawane zurück.

15) sad, sorrowful. 16) distress 17) help. 18) prayer. 19) back.
— 20) again 21) compassion. 22) refreshed, supplied. 23) food.
24) with himself. 25) zurück'kehren to return.

# Twenty-seventh Lesson.
## Second Conjugation.*)
### Imperfect with i or ie.

The second Conjugation is characterized by the sound i in the *Imperfect*, which is either a short i, or a long i spelt ie. The *Past Part.* takes the same vowel i or ie as the *Imperfect;* only in the 3rd class, the vowel of the *Infinitive* is retained. Most verbs of this Conjugation are recognised by the radical diphthong ei.

**First class:** *Imperfect* and *Past Part.* with i.

| Indicative Present. | Imperative. | Imperfect. i | Past Part. i |
|---|---|---|---|
| | | | |

### 61. Beißen to bite.
Ich beiße, du beißest, er | beiße, | ich biß I bit. | gebissen
beißt, wir beißen ꝛc. | beißet. | *Subj.* ich bisse. | bitten.

### 62. Befleißen (sich) to apply one's self.
Ich befleiße mich, du be= | befleiße dich, | ich befliß mich | befliffen
fleißest dich, er befleißt | befleißen | I applied my- | applied.
sich, wir befleißen uns ꝛc. | Sie sich. | self. |
The other form of this verb: sich beflei'ßigen is regular.

### 63. †Erbleichen to turn pale.
Ich erbleiche, du erbleichst, | erbleiche, | ich erblich'. | erblichen.
er erbleicht, wir erbleichen. | erbleichet | S. ich erbliche. |
Thus †verbleichen to fade. P. p verblichen.
The simple verb bleichen (to bleach) is regular.

*) Called also die I-Konjugation.

| Indicative Present. | Imperative. | Imperfect. i | Past Part. i |
|---|---|---|---|

### 64. Greifen to grasp, gripe.

Ich greife, du greifst, er | greife, | ich griff. | gegriffen
greift, wir greifen ꝛc. | greifet. | S. ich griffe. | grasped.

Thus: begrei'fen to understand, to comprehend, ergrei'fen to seize
(P. p ergriffen); an'greifen to attak (P. p. an'gegriffen.

### 65. Gleichen (Dat.) to resemble, to be like.

Ich gleiche, du gleichst, er | gleiche, | ich glich. | geglichen.
gleicht, wir gleichen ꝛc. | gleichet. | S. ich gliche. |

Thus: verglei'chen to compare. Imp. ich verglich. P. p. verglichen.

### 66. †Gleiten or ausgleiten to glide, slide, slip.

Ich gleite, du gleitest, er | gleite, | ich glitt. | geglitten
gleitet, wir gleiten ꝛc. | gleitet. | S. ich glitte. | slipped.

This verb sometimes occurs as regular: Imp. gleitete etc.
NB. begleiten (to accompany) is regular: Imp. ich begleitete,
Past p. begleitet, and takes haben.

### 67. Kneifen to pinch.

Ich kneife, du kneifst, er | kneife, | ich kniff. | gekniffen
kneift, wir kneifen ꝛc. | kneifet. | | pinched.

NB. Another form: kneipen (to pinch) is regular.

### 68. Leiden to suffer.

Ich leide, du leidest, er | leide, | ich litt. | gelitten
leidet, wir leiden ꝛc. | leidet. | S. ich litte. | suffered.

Thus: erleiden to sustain Imp. erlitt, Part. p. erlitten.

### 69. Pfeifen to whistle.

Ich pfeife, du pfeifst, er | pfeife, | ich pfiff. | gepfiffen
pfeift, wir pfeifen ꝛc. | pfeifet. | S. ich pfiffe. | whistled.

### 70. Reißen to rend, tear.

Ich reiße, du reißest, er | reiße, | ich riß I tore. | gerissen
reißt, wir reißen ꝛc. | reißet. | S. ich risse. | torn.

Thus: zerrei'ßen to tear to pieces. Imp. zerriß, P. zerrissen;
entreiß'en to snatch away from.

### 71. †Reiten*) to ride, go on horseback.

Ich reite, du reitest, er | reite, | ich ritt. | geritten.
reitet, wir reiten ꝛc. | reitet. | S. ich ritte. |

Thus: †vorbei'reiten to ride by; †spazieren reiten to take a ride.
NB. bereiten to prepare (from bereit ready), and vor'bereiten
to prepare (before hand), are regular.

---

*) Reiten in an active sense is only used in: ein Pferd reiten,
then it takes haben: Ich habe dieses Pferd geritten.

| Indicative Present. | Imperative | Imperfect. i | Past Part. i |
|---|---|---|---|

**72. Schleifen to sharpen, to grind.**

Ich schleife, du schleifst, er schleift, wir schleifen 2c. | schleife, schleifet. | ich schliff. | geschliffen.

*NB* The verb schleifen to demolish, to drag along, is regular

**73. †Schleichen to sneak or steal into.**

Ich schleiche, du schleichst, er schleicht, wir schleichen | schleiche, schleichet. | ich schlich. | geschlichen.

**74. Streichen to strike, rub (see Nr. 81).**

Ich streiche, du streichst, er streicht, wir streichen 2c. | streiche. | ich strich. | gestrichen.

Thus: aus'streichen to cross out; an'streichen to paint, unter-streichen (*P. p* unterstri'chen) to underline

**75. Schmeißen to fling, to turn out.**

Ich schmeiße, du schmeißest. | schmeiße. | ich schmiß. | geschmissen.

**76. Schneiden to cut.**

Ich schneide, du schneidest, er schneidet, wir schneiden. | schneide. | ich schnitt. | geschnitten.

Thus ab'schneiden to cut off. *P. p.* ab'geschnitten.

**77. †Schreiten to stride, to step.**

Ich schreite, du schreitest 2c. | schreite. | ich schritt. | geschritten.

**78. Streiten to quarrel, dispute, fight.**

Ich streite, du streitest 2c. | streite. | ich stritt. | gestritten.

Thus: bestrei'ten to contest, to dispute.

**79. †Weichen to yield, give way.**

Ich weiche, du weichst 2c. | weiche. | ich wich. | gewichen.

Thus †aus'- or ab'weichen to deviate, †entwei'chen to escape.
*NB.* weichen (to soak) is a regular verb.

---

## Words.

Das Bein the leg, limb.
das Lager the camp.
der Hauptmann the captain.
der Ast the branch.
der Druckfehler the misprint.
der Held the hero.
die Flamme the flame
der Kampf the combat.
begreifen (64) to comprehend.
das Signal' the signal.
das Schwert the sword.

vorbereiten (*reg.*) to prepare.
bemerken (*reg.*) to perceive.
vergleichen (65) to compare.
der Stern the star.
der Bettler the beggar.
die Übersetzung the translation.
legen (*reg.*) to lay, to put.
das Stück' the piece.
das Rasier'messer the razor.
ergreifen (64) to seize.
hinaus'schmeißen to turn out.

## Reading Exercise. 65.

1. Der junge Mann hat sich sehr befliffen, Deutsch zu lernen. Der Hund hat mich in das Bein gebiffen. Das Mäd= chen glitt aus und brach ein Bein. Ich wäre auch ausge= glitten, wenn man mich nicht gehalten (held) hätte. Die Feinde hatten das Lager angegriffen (64). Der Hauptmann ergriff seine Piftolen. Die Tochter gleicht ihrer Mutter. Die armen Gefangenen haben viel gelitten (68). Der Sturm hat viele Äfte von den Bäumen abgeriffen.

2. Meine Schuhe find zerriffen (70). Warum bift du jo schnell geritten? Unsere Soldaten haben wie (like) Helden gestritten; aber fie find endlich dem Feinde gewichen. Der Wind pfiff durch die Bäume. Einige Druckfehler haben sich in das Buch eingeschlichen (crept in). Das Kind hat sich in den Finger geschnitten. Don Duirote schliff sein Schwert und befahl seinem Diener Sancho Panfa, sich zu einem neuen Kampfe vorzubereiten.

## Aufgabe. 66.

1. The dog bit me. He bites everybody. Has he bitten you also? William Tell perceived a large flame; but he could not comprehend whence (woher') this signal came. Day dawns (Es wird Tag); the stars *have* faded. The young gentleman applied himself to learn French. I have compared my translation with yours, and found only two mistakes in it (see p. 142). Our dog *was* torn [to pieces] by a wolf. The traveller cut a piece of meat and laid it on his (*Acc.*) bread. Have you made (*cut*) my pen? Be so kind [as] to *make* it. The hunter strode (77) across (über) the field.

2. Your penknife is not sharpened. The thief opened the door and stole (73) into the house; but he *was* soon seized by a servant and turned out (hinaus=). During my illness ₐI ₐhave suffered much. *Did* you suffer much pain (Schmerzen, *pl.*)? Who has whistled? Charles has whistled with a key. The beggar's coat was quite (ganz) torn. The king rode on a grey horse. Who has sharpened this razor? I do not know who ₐhas ₐsharpened ₐit. The enemy yielded on all sides (auf allen Seiten).

---

## Second class: The *Imperf.* and *Part.* with ie.

80  †Bleiben to remain, stay. *Imp.* ich blieb. *P. p.* geblieben.
Thus: †aus'bleiben to stay away; zurück'bleiben to stay behind.

81. Reiben to rub. *Imp.* ich rieb. *Part.* gerieben.
Thus: auf'reiben to destroy, zerreiben to rub to powder.

82. Schreiben to write. *Imp.* ich schrieb. *Part. p.* geschrieben.
Thus: ab'schreiben to copy; beschreiben to describe, unterschrei'ben to sign (*P. p.* unterschrie'ben).

83. **Treiben** to drive (away). *Imp.* ich trieb. *Part.* getrieben.
Thus: vertrei'ben to expel, übertrei'ben to exaggerate.

84. **Meiden** to shun, avoid. *Imp.* ich mieb. *Part.* gemieden.
Thus: vermei'den to avoid; *P. p.* vermieden

85. **Scheiden** to separate. *Imp.* ich schied. *Part.* geschieden.
Thus entschei'den to decide; unterschei'den to distinguish.

86. †**Gedeihen** to thrive *Imp.* ich gedieh. *Part.* gediehen.

87. **Leihen** to lend. *Imp.* ich lieh. *Part.* geliehen lent.

88. **Schreien** to cry, scream. *Imp.* ich schrie. *Part.* geschrieen.
*Note* An old verb for schreien is kreischen; krisch; *P.* gekrischen.

89. **Speien** to spit. *Imp.* ich spie. *Part.* gespieen.

90. **Verzei'hen** (*dat.*) to pardon. *Imp.* ich verzieh. *P.p.* verziehen.

91. **Preisen** to praise, extol. *Imp.* ich pries. *Part.* gepriesen.

92. **Weisen** to show. *Imp.* ich wies. *Part.* gewiesen.
Thus. bewei'sen to prove, erweisen to show, to do.

93. **Scheinen** 1) to shine; 2) to seem. *Imp.* ich schien. *P.* geschienen.
Thus. †erschei'nen to appear.

94. **Schweigen** to be silent, er schweigt he *is* silent. *Imp.* ich
schwieg I *was* silent. — *Perf.* ich habe geschwiegen
I have been silent.
Thus: verschwei'gen to conceal, to keep secret.

95. †**Steigen** to mount. *Imp.* ich stieg. *P.* gestiegen mounted.
Thus: †ab'steigen to dismount, alight; †hinab'steigen or herab=
steigen to descend, to get down; †hinauf'steigen to mount, to
ascend, ersteigen to mount, to climb up.

96. **Heißen** 1) to bid; 2) to be called. *Imp.* ich hieß I was
called. *Part.* geheißen.
Thus: verheißen to promise. *P. p.* verheißen

---

### Words.

| | |
|---|---|
| Der Verfasser the author. | der Flachs the flax. |
| die Stimme the voice. | der Gipfel the top. |
| die Sonne the sun. | laut loud. |
| die Küste the coast. | hell brightly |
| die Seite the page, side. | beleidigen (*reg. v.*) to offend. |
| die Geschichte history, story. | an'geben to mention. |
| das Billet' or Briefchen a note. | retten to rescue, to save. |
| ein Schäfer a shepherd. | heftig violent, heavy. |
| berühmt famous. nur only. | zornig or böse angry. |
| der Vetter the cousin. | |

### Reading Exercise. 67.

1. Wo blieben Sie so lange? Ich blieb zwei Stunden in dem Kaffeehaus. Wie lange ist Ihr Freund geblieben? Er ist nur eine Stunde geblieben. Wer hat jenes Buch geschrieben? Ich kenne den Verfasser nicht; sein Name ist auf dem Buche nicht angegeben. Warum haben Sie den Umgang (intercourse) mit diesem Manne nicht gemieden? Schreien Sie nicht so laut. Ich habe nicht laut geschrieen. Wie heißen Sie? Ich heiße Friedrich. Wie hieß Ihre Mutter? Sie hieß Elisabeth. Wenn Sie geschwiegen hätten, [so] würden Sie niemand beleidigt haben.

2. Der gerettete Mann pries Gott mit lauter Stimme. Der Reisende war auf den Berg gestiegen; als (when) ich ihn da sah, stieg ich auch hinauf. Die Sonne schien sehr warm, als wir den Berg hinabstiegen. Wer hat Ihnen dieses Geld geliehen? Mein Nachbar lieh es mir unter der Bedingung (condition), daß ich es ihm in acht Tagen (in a week) wieder zurückgebe. Ein heftiger Sturm trieb unser Schiff an die Küste. Wie lange sind Sie auf dem Ball geblieben? Wir blieben bis Mitternacht (till midnight).

### Aufgabe. 68.

1. Remain here till (bis) to-morrow. How long did your cousin stay? He stayed an hour. I write a long letter; yesterday ₂I ₁wrote three pages, to-day ₂I ₁shall write two more (noch zwei). That English history is written by a famous author. I wrote a note to him. The shepherd drove the sheep into the fold (in den Pferch). This year ₂the ₁flax ₁has (ist) not thriven. Why did the boy cry so loud? The son said: »Dear father, pardon me (Dat.) this fault,« and the father pardoned him. The three men (Männer) in the furnace (Feuerofen, m.) praised God with a loud voice.

2. I lent my book [to] some one, but I cannot remember (ich kann mich nicht erinnern) who it was. You have perhaps lent it to (Dat.) Mr. S. That may (kann) be. The sun shone brightly. All animals and plants seem to be created (geschaffen zu sein) for (the) man (mankind). The king seemed to be angry. If he had been silent (geschwiegen) ₂he ₁would not have offended him. Speaking (Inf.) is silver; silence (Schweigen) is gold. How high did the traveller mount? He ascended (mounted) to (bis auf) the top of the mountain.

---

**Third class:** Verbs having a, o, au or u for their radical vowel. They take in the *Imperfect* ie, but retain in the *Past Part.* the vowel or diphthong of their *Infinitive*. In the 2nd and 3rd person of the singular of *Pres. Ind.* they soften their vowel.

| Indicative Present. | Imperative. | Imperfect. ie | Past Part. a |
|---|---|---|---|

### 97. Blasen to blow.

| Ich blase, du bläst, er bläst, wir blasen, ihr blaset, sie blasen. | blase, blaset. | ich blies. S. ich bliese. | geblasen*) blown. |

### 98. Braten to roast.

| Ich brate, du brätst, er brät (or bratet), wir braten, ihr bratet ꝛc. | brate, bratet. | ich briet. S. ich briete. | gebraten roasted. |

### 99. †Fallen to fall.

| Ich falle, du fällst, er fällt, wir fallen ꝛc. | falle, fallet. | ich fiel I fell. S. ich fiele. | gefallen fallen. |

Thus· †herab'fallen to fall down, P. p. herab'gefallen; gefallen to please, †einfallen to occur to the mind, mißfallen to displease; zerfallen to decay.

### 100. Fangen to catch.

| Ich fange, du fängst, er fängt, wir fangen ꝛc. | fange, fanget. | ich fieng or fing. | gefangen caught. |

Thus: an'fangen to begin, Past Part an'gefangen; em-pfan'gen to receive.

### 101. Halten**) to hold, to consider.

| Ich halte, du hältst, er hält, wir halten ꝛc. | halte. | ich hielt I held, took. | gehalten held. |

Thus· ab'halten to prevent, auf'halten to detain; ein'halten to stop; behalten to keep; erhalten to receive (P. p. erhalten).

### 102. †Hangen to hang, to be suspended.

| Ich hange, du hängst, er hängt, wir hangen ꝛc. | hange. | ich hieng I hung. | gehangen hung. |

Thus· ab'hangen or abhängen (von) to depend upon.
NB. Hängen to hang up, is regular. P. p. gehängt.

---

*) Observe that all the irregular verbs which have a or u in their root or infinitive, and most of those which have au or o, retain their root vowels in the Participle past So they do in the Subj mood of Pres. tense Ich blase, du blasest, er blase; ich halte, du haltest, er halte; ich stoße, du stoßest, er stoße ꝛc. The following verbs only make an exception for their Participle past: erschallen, P. p erschollen; saugen, gesogen; saufen, gesoffen; schnauben, geschnoben.

**) Halten with the preposition für answers to the English to consider as, to think, to take for. Ex Ich halte ihn für einen ehrlichen Mann I consider (think) him (to be) an honest man.

| Indicative Present. | Imperative. | Imperfect. ie | Past Part. a |
|---|---|---|---|

### 103 Laſſen to let,*) to leave.

Jch laſſe, du läſſeſt (läßt), | laſſe or laß, | ich ließ I let. | gelaſſen let,
er läßt, wir laſſen 2c | laſſen Sie. | S. ich ließe. | left

Thus: verlaſſen to leave (a place), forsake, quit; *P. p.* verlaſſen; zu'laſſen to admit, aus'laſſen to leave out, zurüd'laſſen to leave behind; hinterlaſ'ſen (*inseparable*) to leave behind (in death). *NB.* Veran'laſſen (to cause) is regular. *Imp.* ich veranlaßte.

### 104. Rathen (*Dat.*)**) to advise.

Jch rathe, du räthſt, er | rathe. | ich rieth | gerathen
rät, wir rathen 2c. | | I advised. | advised.

Thus: erra'ten to guess, ab'rathen to dissuade, verraten to betray.

### 105. Schlafen to sleep.

Jch ſchlafe, du ſchläfſt, er | ſchlafe, | ich ſchlief | geſchlafen
ſchläft, wir ſchlafen 2c. | ſchlafen Sie. | I slept. | slept

Thus. †ein'ſchlafen to fall asleep. *Perf.* ich bin eingeſchlafen.

### 106. †Laufen to run.

Jch laufe, du läufſt, er | laufe. | ich lief | gelaufen
läuft, wir laufen 2c. | | I run. | run.

Thus· †entlau'ſen to run away.

### 107. Hauen to hew, cut down.

Jch haue, du haueſt, er | haue. | ich hieb | gehauen
haut, wir hauen 2c. | | I cut. | hewn.

Thus: ab'hauen to cut off, zerhau'en to cut to pieces.

### 108. †Gehen to go.

Jch gehe, du gehſt, er geht, | gehe, | ich gieng (or†) | gegangen
wir gehen 2c. | gehen Sie | ging' I went. | gone.

Thus· †aus'gehen to go out; †hinein'gehen to go in, to enter; †fort'gehen to go away, to leave; †vergehen to vanish, to pass; †vorbei'gehen to pass by; †zurück'gehen to go back; ſpazieren gehen to take a walk.

### 109. Stoßen to push, thrust.

Jch ſtoße, du ſtößt, er | ſtoße. | ich ſtieß. | geſtoßen.
ſtößt, wir ſtoßen 2c. | | |

Thus: an'ſtoßen to hurt; verſtoßen to reject, cast out, expel.

---

*) To let a *house* means vermieten.
**) See the 22nd lesson, § 7.
†) The spelling 'gieng', which etymologically is the only right one, has now been given up in favour of 'ging' for convenience' sake.

| Indicative Present. | Imperative. | Imperfect. ie | Past Part. |
|---|---|---|---|

### 110. Rufen to call.

Ich rufe, du rufst, er ruft ꝛc. | rufe. | ich rief. | gerufen.

Thus: aus'rufen to exclaim; zurück'rufen to call back.

### Words.

| | |
|---|---|
| Der Wind the wind. | die Mäßigung temperance. |
| der Schwager the brother-in- | die Angel the fishing-rod. |
| der Rat the advice. [law. | das Netz (pl. —e) the net. |
| das Schwert the sword. | kochen (reg. v.) to boil. |
| das Kopfweh the head-ache. | mächtig mighty. bald soon. |
| der Führer the leader. | das Tier (pl. —e) the beast. |
| der Hirsch the stag. | wild wild. schwach feeble. |
| der Bach the brook. | zähmen to tame. |
| die Weisheit wisdom. | befreien to deliver, to release. |
| die Gerechtigkeit justice. | verbannt banished, exiled. |
| die Tugend virtue. | |

### Reading Exercise. 69.

1. Der Wind bläst nicht stark; gestern blies er stärker. Der Koch hat das Fleisch nicht gut (well) gebraten. Der Vogel fiel tot von dem Baum. Mit Speck (bacon) fängt man Mäuse. Ein Löwe wurde in einem Netze gefangen, dann kam eine Maus und befreite ihn. Für wen hältst (take) du mich? Ich erhielt einen Brief von meinem Schwager. Ein Schwert hing über dem Kopf des Damokles. Was raten Sie mir; soll ich bleiben oder gehen? Man riet ihm, hier zu bleiben. Dieses war ein schlechter Rat; es würde besser für ihn gewesen sein, fortzugehen.

2. Der Herr rief seinem Diener. Dieser fragte seinen Herrn (master): „Haben Sie mich gerufen?" Das Kind schläft. Der Tote (Mann) lag da, als wenn (as if) er schliefe. Haben Sie die letzte Nacht gut geschlafen? Ich habe nur wenig geschlafen, weil ich Kopfweh (a head-ache) hatte. Man ließ ihn nicht fortgehen, weil er zu schwach war. Wenn der Knabe noch einmal (again) an den Tisch stößt, [so] wird er bestraft werden. Warum laufen die Leute (people) so zusammen (together)? Man hat einen Dieb gefangen. Sind Sie auch gelaufen? Ich lief mit der Menge (crowd).

### Aufgabe. 70.

1. The wind blows hard (stark); yesterday ‚it ‚blew not so hard. Is this meat boiled or roasted? It is roasted. The gardener fell from the tree. Had (wäre) he not ‚fallen ‚down, ‚he ‚would have caught the bird. Fifty soldiers with their leader were[1] caught. The stag came out of the forest and

1) See the foot-note 2, p. 174.

went to the (an den) brook. The hunter catches the wild
beasts, but he cannot tame them. The Romans considered (101)
wisdom[2]), justice and temperance as (für) the greatest virtues.
2. The fish are[1]) caught with nets and fishing-rods. I
advised him (*Dat.*) to go to America. How long did you
sleep (*Perf.*)? I slept seven hours. The girl ran to (zu) her
mother and told her (ihr) what ₂had[3]) ₁happened (9). The
old man was[1]) pushed out of the house. Cicero left[4]) Rome
(Rom), when (als) he saw, that (daß) his enemies ₂were ₁might-
ier (,) than his friends. Alcibiades *was* banished from Athens
(aus Athen'), but he *was* soon ₂called ₁back.
    1) See the foot-note 2, p. 174. — 2) Put the definite article,
see 38th lesson, § 1. — 3) '*to have*' printed in *Italics* is to be
translated with fein. — 4) to leave a place = verlaffen (not faffen).

### Reading - lesson.
#### Kogzingkog Pferd. Kosciusco's horse.

    Kogzinsto, der eble Pole, wollte (wished) einst[1] einem Geist-
lichen[2] in Solothurn (Soleure) einige Flaschen guten Weines
schicken. Er wählte[3] dazu einen jungen Mann, Namens Zeltner,
und lieh' ihm für die Reise sein eigenes (own) Reitpferd. —
Als Zeltner zurück'tam, sagte er: „Mein Feldherr[4], ich werde Ihr
Pferd nicht wieder[5] reiten, wenn[6] Sie mir nicht[6] zugleich'[7] Ihre
Börse (purse) leihen." — „Wie meinen Sie das" (what do you
mean by that)? fragte Kogzinsto.
    Zeltner antwortete: „Sobald' als (as soon as) ein Armer
auf der Landstraße[8] feinen Hut ab'nahm[9], und um ein Almosen[10]
bat, stand das Pferd augenblicklich[11] still, und ging[12] nicht
von der Stelle[12], bis (till *or* before) der Bettler[13] etwas empfangen (100) hatte; und als ich all mein Geld ausgegeben
(spent) hatte, konnte ich das Pferd nur zufrieden stellen[14] und
vorwärts bringen[15], indem ich mich stellte (by pretending), als
ob ich dem Bettler etwas gäbe. (In English = dem Bettler
etwas zu geben.)
    1) one day. 2) a clergyman. 3) he chose for this purpose.
4) general. 5) again. 6) wenn . . . nicht *conj.* unless. 7) at the
same time. 8) road, highway. 9) abnehmen to take off. 10) for
charity, alms. 11) immediately. 12) von der Stelle gehen to stir
from the spot. 13) beggar. 14) to satisfy, content. 15) get him on.

---

# Twenty-eighth Lesson.
## Third Conjugation.*)
### Imperfect with o.
The third conjugation has both in the *Imperfect* and
*Past participle* o as characterising vowel.

    *) Called also bie O-Konjugation.

**First class:** Such verbs as have ie for their radical vowel:

| Indicative Present. | Imperative. | Imperfect. D | Past Part. D |
|---|---|---|---|

### 111. Biegen to bend.

| Ich biege, du biegst, er biegt, wir biegen ꝛc. | biege. | ich bog I bent. | gebogen bent. |

### 112. Bieten (dat.) to offer.

| Ich biete, du bietest, er bietet, wir bieten ꝛc. | biete. | ich bot I offered. | geboten offered. |

Thus. an'bieten to offer, *P. p.* angeboten; verbie'ten to forbid.

### 113 Betrügen (Betriegen) to cheat, deceive.

| Ichbetrüge, dubetrügst, er betrügt, wir betrügen ꝛc. | betrüge (betriege). | ich betrog. | betrogen deceived. |

*NB.* The simple verb trügen, trog, getrogen is more used in poetry than in prose, except in proverbial expressions, like der Schein trügt (appearance deceives).

### 114. †Fliegen to fly.

| Ich fliege, du fliegst, er fliegt, wir fliegen ꝛc. | fliege. | ich flog I flew. | geflogen flown. |

Thus: †fort'fliegen to fly off; †weg'fliegen to fly away.

### 115. †Fliehen to flee.

| Ich fliehe, du fliehst, er flieht, wir fliehen ꝛc. | fliehe. | ich floh I fled. | geflohen fled. |

Thus: †entfliehen to run away, to escape. *P. p.* entflohen.

### 116. †Fließen to flow.

| Ich fließe, du fließest, er fließt, wir fließen ꝛc. | fließe. | — floß flowed. | geflossen flowed. |

### 117. Frieren to be cold, to freeze.

| Ich friere, du frierst, er friert, wir frieren ꝛc. | — | ich fror I was cold. | gefroren frozen. |

Thus. †gefrie'ren to freeze, †erfrie'ren to freeze to death.

### 118. Genießen to enjoy, to eat.

| Ich genieße, du genießest, er genießt, wir genießen ꝛc. | genieße. | ich genoß I enjoyed. | genossen enjoyed. |

### 119. Gießen to pour (to cast).

| Ich gieße, du gießest, er gießt, wir gießen ꝛc | gieße. | ich goß I poured | gegossen poured. |

Thus: aus'gießen to pour out; begießen to water; sich ergießen to empty one's self, vergie'ßen to shed.

| *Indicative Present.* | *Imperative.* | *Imperfect.* <br> D | *Past Part.* <br> D |
|---|---|---|---|

**120. † Kriechen to creep, to crawl.**

| Ich krieche, du kriechst, er kriecht, wir kriechen ꝛc. | krieche. | ich kroch <br> I crept. | gekrochen <br> crept. |

**121 Riechen to smell.**

| Ich rieche, du riechst, er riecht, wir riechen ꝛc. | rieche. | ich roch <br> I smelled. | gerochen <br> smelled. |

**122. Schießen to shoot, to fire, to kill.**

| Ich schieße, du schießest, er schießt, wir schießen ꝛc. | schieße. | ich schoß <br> I shot. | geschossen <br> shot. |

Thus. beschie'ßen to bombard; erschießen to shoot (to kill).

**123. Schließen to lock.**

| Ich schließe, du schließest, er schließt, wir schließen ꝛc. | schließe. | ich schloß <br> I locked. | geschlossen <br> locked. |

Thus: beschlie'ßen to conclude, resolve; ein'schließen to shut up,
to enclose, aus'schließen to exclude; verschlie'ßen to lock up;
auf'schließen to unlock, zu'schließen to lock.

**124. Verdrießen to vex.**

| Ich verdrieße, du verdrießest, er verdrießt. | verdrieße. | ich verdroß. | verdrossen <br> vexed. |

**125. Verlieren to lose.**

| Ich verliere, du verlierst, er verliert, wir verlieren ꝛc. | verliere. | ich verlor <br> I lost. | verloren <br> lost. |

**126. Wiegen to weigh, to be of weight.**

| Ich wiege, du wiegst, er wiegt, wir wiegen ꝛc. | — | ich wog <br> I weighed. | gewogen <br> weighed. |

The active verbs wägen *(to weigh, to ascertain weight)* and
erwägen *(to consider)* have the Imperf. and Part. past like
wiegen. *Imp.* wog (or wägte). *P.* gewogen, erwogen.
The active verb wiegen *(to rock)* is regular.

**127. Ziehen to pull, to draw.**

| Ich ziehe, du ziehst, er zieht, wir ziehen ꝛc. | ziehe. | ich zog I drew <br> or pulled. | gezogen <br> drawn. |

Thus an'ziehen to put on; aus'ziehen to take off.

**128. Schieben to shove, push.** *Imp.* ich schob. *Part.* geschoben.
Thus: verschieben to put off.

**129. Sieden to boil, to soothe.** *Imp.* ich sott. *Part.* gesotten.

**130. † Sprießen to sprout.** *Imp.* — sproß. *Part.* gesprossen.

131. † Stieben to fly off (sparks). *Imp.* ſtob. *Part.* geſtoben.
132. Triefen to drop, drip. *Imp.* ich troff. *Part.* getrieft (reg).

---

## Words.

| | |
|---|---|
| Der Jude the Jew. | die Laſt the weight, burden. |
| der Frieden peace. | der Schnee (*Gen.* —s) snow. |
| die Kartoffel the potato. | der Storch the stork. |
| der Aſt, *pl.* Äſte, the branch. | der Ofen the stove. recht right. |
| der Kaufmann the merchant. | |

### Reading Exercise. 71.

Wieviel bot der Jude Ihnen für Ihr Pferd? Er hat mir nur zweihundert Mark geboten. Haben Sie meinen Kanarienvogel nicht geſehen? Ja, er iſt über das Haus geflogen. Die Diebe ſind entflohen (115); man konnte ſie nicht fangen. Wir haben lange die Wohlthaten (the benefits) des Friedens genoſſen. Vor einigen Jahren (some y. ago) war der Rhein gefroren. Die Thüre iſt geſchloſſen; ſoll ich ſie aufſchließen? Man ſagt von einem Soldaten, der nie im Kriege war: „Er hat noch kein Pulver (gunpowder) gerochen." Sind die Kartoffeln geſotten (or gekocht)? Nein, ſie ſieden noch; in zehn Minuten werden ſie geſotten ſein. Wieviel Geld verlor Ihr Oheim im Spiel? Er hat nur einige Mark verloren. Ziehen Sie Ihre Stiefel an? Wir haben ſchon unſere Schuhe angezogen. Ich wünſche, daß Sie Ihre Stiefel anziehen.

### Aufgabe. 71a.

Some one has cheated me. The branches are bent under the weight of the snow. The merchant asked (forderte or verlangte) ten shillings. I offered him (*Dat.*) nine. The Jew has offered me (*Dat.*) eighty pounds for my two horses. The storks *have* flown over the sea. It is so cold that the water in the bottle is frozen. The hunter shot, and the bird flew away; he had not hit (35) it. The dog crept behind the stove. Your flowers smell (121) very agreeably. The young plant is frozen. The potatoes are boiled (129); shall I bring them in (herein)? Has the servant locked the door? He locked it at six o'clock. The soldier lost his right arm. Do you know, who *) (has) lost this purse? The tailor has lost it.

---

*) See p. 145, *Note.*

## Second class: Such as have other *root-vowels:*

| Indicative Present. | Imperative. | Imperfect. o | Past Part. o |
|---|---|---|---|

### 133. Bewegen to induce.

Ich bewege, du bewegst, er | bewege | ich bewog | bewogen
bewegt, wir bewegen ꝛc. | | I induced. | induced.

*NB.* When the verb bewegen simply expresses *to move, to put into motion* or *to cause an emotion*, it is regularly inflected. ich be= wege, *Imp.* ich bewegte, *P. p.* bewegt.

### 134. Beklemmen to oppress.

Es beklemmt (*impers.*). | — | es beklomm. | beklommen.

### 135. †Erlöschen to become extinct.

Ich erlösche, — — es | erlisch. | — erlosch | erloschen
erlischt, — sie erlöschen | | became ext. | extinct.

*NB.* The simple verb löschen *(to quench)* and aus'löschen *(to put out)* are regular.

### 136. †Erschallen to resound.

Ich erschalle, du erschallst, | erschalle. | ich erscholl | erschollen
er erschallt, wir erschallen | | and erschallte | (erschallt).

*NB.* The simple verb schallen *(to sound)* is regular, in poetry however the *Imp.* scholl is met with.

### 137. Fechten to fence, to fight.

Ich fechte, du fechtest, er | fechte. | ich focht | gefochten
ficht (or fechtet) ꝛc. | | I fought. | fought.

### 138. Flechten to twist, to plait.

Ich flechte, du flechtest, er | flechte | ich flocht. | geflochten.
flicht, wir flechten ꝛc. | | |

### 139. †Gären to ferment.

Ich gäre, du gärst, er | gäre. | ich gor (also | gegoren.
gärt, wir gären ꝛc. | | reg. gärte). |

### 140. Glimmen to burn faintly, to glimmer.

Ich glimme, du glimmst, | glimme. | — glomm. | geglommen.
er glimmt, sie glimmen. | | |

140a. †Klimmen to climb; *Imp.* klomm; *Part.* geklommen.

### 141. Heben to lift, to raise.

Ich hebe, du hebst, er hebt, | hebe. | ich hob I lif- | gehoben
wir heben ꝛc. | | ted, raised. | raised.

Thus auf'heben to lift up, hold up, to pick up, erheben to raise, to elevate.

| Indicative Present. | Imperative. | Imperfect. ꝺ | Past Part. ꝺ |
|---|---|---|---|

### 142. Lügen to lie, to tell a lie.

Ich lüge, du lügſt, er lügt, wir lügen ꝛc. | lüge | ich log I told a lie. | gelogen lied

### 143. Melfen to milk.

Ich melfe, du melfſt, er melft, wir melfen ꝛc. | melfe. | ich molf and melfte. | gemolfen milked.

### 144. Saugen*) to suck.

Ich ſauge, du ſaugſt, er ſaugt, wir ſaugen ꝛc | ſauge. | ich ſog (or ich ſaugte). | geſogen (or geſaugt).

*NB.* Säugen to suckle, is regular.

### 145. Scheren to shear.

Ich ſchere, du ſcherſt, er ſchert, wir ſcheren ꝛc. | ſchere. | ich ſchor. | geſchoren.

### 146. Schmelzen to smelt, to melt.

Ich ſchmelze, du ſchmelzeſt, er ſchmilzt, wir ſchmelzen. | ſchmelze or ſchmilz. | ich ſchmolz. | geſchmolzen

*NB.* The neuter verb † ſchmelzen *(to melt)* is conjugated in the same manner, but with the auxiliary ſein.

### 147. † Schwellen to swell.

Ich ſchwelle, du ſchwillſt, er ſchwillt, wir ſchwellen | ſchwelle. | ich ſchwoll. | geſchwollen.

### 148. Schwören to swear an oath.

Ich ſchwöre, du ſchwörſt, er ſchwört, wir ſchwören. | ſchwöre. | ich ſchwor (or ich ſchwur). | geſchworen.

Thus beſchwö'ren 1) to confirm by an oath, 2) to conjure, entreat.

### 149. Weben to weave.

Ich webe, du webſt, er webt, wir weben ꝛc. | webe. | ich wob. | gewoben.

The following verbs of this conjugation seldom occur:

150. Erküren (erfieſen) to elect, choose. *Imp.* ich erfor. *Part.* erforen.

151. Pflegen to treat (with).**) *Imp.* ich pflog *Part.* gepflogen.
Ex.: Unterhandlungen pflegen, to negotiate (with).
*NB.* Pflegen is regular, when it signifies *to nurse*, and also in the meaning of gewohnt ſein *to be accustomed.*

---

*) Saugen (to suck) is sometimes used as a regular verb
**) also to foster, entertain (ex.· friendship, der Freundſchaft pflegen *(gen.)*), to indulge in (ex.· in a habit, einer Gewohnheit pflegen, in sleep, des Schlafes pflegen ꝛc.).

152 Quellen to spring forth. *Imp.* quoll. *Part.* gequollen.
153. Saufen*) to drink, lap like brutes. *Imp.* ich foff *Part.* gefoffen
154. Schnauben to snort. *Imp.* ich schnob. *Part* geschnoben.

## Words.

Der Korb the basket.  
der Stein the stone.  
der Tod the death.  
das Feuer fire. freudig joyfully.  
die Magd the maid-servant.  
das Heer or die Armee the army.  
die Asche (*sing.*) the ashes  
das Tuch the cloth  

der Honig honey.  
das Vaterland the country.  
das Licht the light, candle.  
das Bein the leg, limb.  
schwer heavy.  
nie never  
verdienen to deserve.  
tapfer bravely.  

## Reading Exercise. 72.

Was bewog den Maler, die Stadt zu verlassen? Ich weiß nicht, was ihn (dazu) bewogen hat. Das Feuer ist erloschen. Die Athener (the Athenians) haben in der Schlacht bei Marathon tapfer gefochten. Dieser Korb ist schlecht geflochten. Können Sie diesen Stein heben? Ich habe ihn schon aufgehoben. Ich finde ihn nicht so schwer. Der Knabe hat gelogen. Wann werden Ihre Schafe geschoren werden? Im nächsten (next) Monat. Der Schnee ist auf den Bergen geschmolzen. Voriges (last) Jahr schmolz er im Monat Juli. Die jungen Leute zogen (marched) freudig in die Schlacht; sie schworen, zu siegen (to conquer) oder zu sterben.

## Aufgabe. 72a.

The death of my father induced me to leave my country. The light of the sun will never *become extinct* (135). My candle was extinct. Is the fire out (extinct)? Our sheep *have* been shorn twice this year. Has the maid-servant milked the cow? The French army fought (*sing.*) very bravely; not one soldier fled. The fire glimmered long under the ashes. The little bee sucked the honey from (aus) the flowers. He who »has ›once (einmal) ›lied, does not deserve to be trusted (daß man ihm glaube). My leg is swollen. That cloth is very well woven.

## Reading-lesson.
### Die Erfindung des Glases. Discovery of glass.

Einige phönizische[1] Schiffer landeten einst an der Nordküste[2] Afrikas, wo das Flüßchen Belus sich in das Meer ergießt[3].

1) Phenician sailors. 2) the north coast. 3) throws *or* empties itself.

---

*) Saufen is applied only to animals.

Eine weite Sandfläche⁴ lag (12) vor ihren Augen. Sie suchten Steine, um ihre Kessel⁵ und Pfannen über denselben aufzustellen, aber sie fanden keine. Sie waren daher⁶ genötigt⁷, aus ihrem Schiffe einige Salpe'tersteine⁸, die sie als Ladung (cargo) mit sich brachten, zu holen⁹. Sie machten ein Feuer [an], kochten ihre Speisen¹⁰ und genossen (118) dann ihr einfaches Mahl¹¹. Aber o Wunder! Als sie ihre Salpetersteine wieder zu ihrem Schiffe zurücktragen wollten¹², fanden sie, daß dieselben von der Gewalt¹³ des Feuers geschmolzen waren und sich mit der Asche und dem glühenden (glowing) Sand vermischt¹⁴ hatten. Als die flüssige¹⁵ Masse kalt geworden war, lag auf dem Boden (ground) eine helle, durchsichtige¹⁶ Masse: — das war Glas.

So wurden die Phönizier die Erfinder¹⁷ dieses wertvollen¹⁸ Gegenstandes¹⁹, der uns die größten Dienste leistet (renders).

4) a vast plain of sand. 5) kettles and pans. 6) therefore. 7) obliged. 8) saltpeter-stones. 9) to fetch. 10) food, provisions 11) plain meal, dinner. 12) were going. 13) power, heat. 14) mixed themselves 15) liquid. 16) transparent matter. 17) discoverers 18) valuable. 19) material, object, article.

---

# Twenty-ninth Lesson.

## Fourth Conjugation.*)

### Imperfect with u.

This conjugation consists only of nine verbs having a for their radical vowel. Here the distinguishing vowel in the *Imperfect* is u; the *Past participle* retains the radical vowel a of the Infinitive. In the second and third person of the Indicative Present most of them change their a into ä.

| Indicative Present. | Imperative. | Imperfect. u | Past Part. a |
|---|---|---|---|
| 155. Backen to bake. | | | |
| Ich backe, du bäckst (backst), er bäckt (backt), wir backen, ihr backet, sie backen. | backe. | ich buk or reg. ich backte | gebacken baked. |
| 156. †Fahren to drive *or* to go in a carriage *or* boat. | | | |
| Ich fahre, du fährst, er fährt, wir fahren ꝛc. | fahre. | ich fuhr I drove, went. | gefahren driven. |

NB. This verb has also an *active* meaning *to lead the horses:* it then takes haben in the comp. tenses.
Thus· †aus'fahren or †spazieren fahren to take a drive; †ab'-fahren to start, to set out, erfahren to learn. P. p. erfahren

---

*) Called also die U-Konjugation

| Indicative Present. | Imperative. | Imperfect. u | Past Part. a |
|---|---|---|---|

### 157. Graben to dig.

Ich grabe, bu gräbſt, er | grabe. | Ich grub | gegraben
gräbt, wir graben ꝛc. | | I dug. | dug.

Thus: begra'ben to bury. *Imp* ich begrub. *P.p.* begraben buried.

### 158. Laden to load (a gun).

Ich lade, bu ladeſt (läbſt), | lade. | ich lud | geladen*)
er ladet (lädt), wir la⸗ | | I loaded. | loaded.
den ꝛc.

Thus: bela'ben to load; ein'laden to invite (*P.p.* ein'gela'ben).

### 159. Schaffen and erschaffen to create, make

Ich schaffe, bu schaffſt, er | schaffe. | ich schuf (or |geschaffen(or
schafft, wir schaffen ꝛc. | | erschuf). | erschaffen).

*NB.* Schaffen *to work*, which is only used in South-Germany, and its *compounds* are regular, as an'schaffen and beschaffen to get, verschaffen to procure, ab'schaffen to abrogate.

### 160. Schlagen to beat, to strike.

Ich schlage, bu schlägſt, er | schlage. | ich schlug | geschlagen
schlägt, wir schlagen ꝛc. | | I struck. | beaten.

Thus: ab'schlagen 1) to knock off, 2) to refuse; erschla'gen to slay, *Imp.* erschlug, aus'schlagen to decline; zerschla'gen to knock to pieces.

### 161. Tragen to carry, to wear, to take.

Ich trage, bu trägſt, er | trage. | ich trug I | getragen
trägt, wir tragen ꝛc. | | wore, carried. | carried.

Thus: ertra'gen to endure, to bear; sich betra'gen to behave; bei'- tragen to contribute; ab'tragen to clear the table, to wear out; eintragen to note, give a certain rent.

### 162. †Wachsen to grow, wax.

Ich wachse, bu wächſt, er | wachse. | ich wuchs | gewachsen
wächſt, wir wachsen ꝛc. | | I grew. | grown.

### 163. Waschen to wash.

Ich wasche, bu wäſchſt, er | wasche. | ich wusch | gewaschen
wäſcht, wir waschen ꝛc. | | I washed. | washed.

Thus: aus'waschen to wash out.

*) Geladen means *laden* as well as *loaded*.

## Words.

Der Bäcker the baker.
das Dampfboot the steamboat.
die Eisenbahn the railroad.
der Fuchs the fox.
eine Höhle a den, cave.
der Totengräber the gravedigger, sexton.
das Grab the grave.
der Kutscher the coachman.
der Omnibus the omnibus.
der Wagen the carriage, coach.
der Karren the cart.
das Loch the hole
die Wunde the wound.
jeden Tag adv. every day.

das Taschentuch the handkerchief.
der Mufiflehrer the music-master.
das Mittageffen dinner.
der Kriegsminister the minister of war
das Gesicht the face.
das Sprichwort the proverb.
die Eiche the oak. tief deep
die Kanone the gun, cannon.
prächtig elegant,
unartig naughty
schmutzig dirty.
langsam slow, slowly.
unschuldig guiltless, innocent.
pflanzen to plant.

### Reading-Exercise. 73.

1. Heute haben wir Kuchen gebacken. Warum bäckt (backt) Ihr Nachbar kein Brot mehr? Weil er kein Mehl hat. Die nächste Woche wird er wieder backen. Der König fährt mit sechs Pferden. Wohin' fahren Sie? Ich fahre nach Köln. Gestern fuhr mein Freund dahin (there). Ist er mit (by) dem Dampfboot gefahren (gone)? Nein, mit (by) der Eisenbahn. Der Fuchs gräbt sich eine Höhle. Der Totengräber hat ein Grab gegraben. Ein Esel wurde mit vielen Säcken beladen; aber da (as) er die Last (load) nicht tragen konnte, wurde sie auf einen Wagen gelegt (put).

2. Tragen Sie diese Kleider noch? Nein, sie sind abgetragen. Warum schlägt die Mutter das Kind? Weil es so unartig ist; es hat sich nicht gewaschen. Pilatus wusch seine Hände und sprach: „Ich bin unschuldig an dem Blute dieses Gerechten (just man)". Die Theepflanze wächst in China. Früher (formerly) wuchs der Tabak nicht in Deutschland; aber jetzt wird viel Tabak gepflanzt. Dieser Jüngling ist sehr gewachsen, seit (since) ich ihn nicht mehr (last) gesehen habe. Im Anfang schuf Gott Himmel und Erde. Die Welt ist von Gott aus nichts geschaffen worden.

### Aufgabe. 74.

1. The baker has baked no bread to-day; he does not bake every day. The coachman drives too fast (zu schnell). We went (drove) (156) in an omnibus. The prince drove in an elegant carriage with four horses. The fox digs a hole in the ground (Boden, m.). The savages (Wilden) dug a deep hole. A poor child was buried in the snow. Are you loading the gun? It is already loaded. The cart is too heavily laden. The minister of war has invited all [the] officers to (zum) dinner. In the beginning God created heaven and earth.

2. Why do you beat the child? I beat it, because it
²was ¹naughty. (The) dogs *are* often beaten. Cain (Kain)
slew (160) his brother Abel. Our music-master ²always ¹wears
a grey hat. Two soldiers carried the officer out of the battle
and washed his wound. »One hand washes the other«, says a
German proverb. Henry, wash your face, you are dirty. Are
my handkerchiefs washed? No, Sir, not yet, they will *be*
washed to-morrow. The oak grows very slowly. These violets *have* grown in my garden.

## Conversation.
### (*Comprising the four Conjugations.*)

Was essen Sie da?　　　　Ich esse Fleisch und Brot; es ist
　　　　　　　　　　　　mein Frühstück.

Wer hat es Ihnen gegeben?　Ich habe es (mir) gekauft.
Gaben Sie meinem Bedienten　Ja, ich gab sie ihm vor (—ago)
die Kleiderbürste (brush)?　　einer Stunde.
Haben Sie heute schon die Zei-　Ja, ich habe sie gelesen.
tung (news-paper) gelesen?
Giebt es (is there) etwas Neues?　Ich habe nichts Neues darin ge-
　　　　　　　　　　　　funden.

Wer ist zum Balle eingeladen?　Viele junge Herren und Damen.
Kennen Sie einige von ihnen?　Ja, ich kenne die meisten von ihnen.
Ist Ihr Vater von seiner langen　Gott sei Dank! er ist ganz (quite)
Krankheit genesen (8)?　　　genesen.
Wo ist der Wirt (landlord)? ich　Er ist ausgegangen; aber er wird
muß ihm etwas sagen.　　　bald wieder zurückkommen.
Was ist geschehen, daß das Volk　Ein Maurer (bricklayer) ist vom
so zusammen (together) läuft?　Dache gefallen.
Hat er sich verletzt (hurt)?　Ja, er hat ein Bein gebrochen.
Wer hat Ihnen befohlen, meine　Niemand befahl es mir; ich trug
Stiefel zum Schuhmacher zu　sie dahin, weil sie zerrissen sind.
tragen?
Hat man Ihren Ring wieder　Er lag auf dem Boden, hinter dem
gefunden? Wo lag er?　　　Schranke (press) verborgen (18).
Wer fand ihn?　　　　　　Die Magd fand ihn, als sie das
　　　　　　　　　　　　Zimmer putzte (cleaned).

Haben Sie Ihre Uhr nicht mehr?　Nein, sie ist mir gestohlen worden.
Wovon spricht dieser Mann?　Er spricht vom Kriege.
Hat der Krieg schon begonnen?　Nein, aber er wird bald beginnen.
Bist du verwundet? Hat je-　Eine Biene hat mich in die Wange
mand dir etwas (any harm)　(cheek) gestochen und jetzt ist
gethan?　　　　　　　　diese geschwollen.
Steckt der Stachel (the sting)　Nein, man hat ihn gleich (im-
noch darin?　　　　　　mediately) herausgezogen (127).
Was thut dieser Mann hier?　Er fängt Vögel.
Hat er schon einige gefangen?　Ich glaube, er hat erst (only)
　　　　　　　　　　　　wenige gefangen.

Ist der Dieb ergriffen (caught) worden?

Wer hat diese Feder geschnitten? In was sind Sie gefahren?

Wann hat Gott die Welt erschaffen?

Warum sind die Flüsse und Bäche (brooks) so angeschwollen?

Wer hat den Brief auf die Post getragen?

Was that der Knabe am Brunnen (spring)?

Wo haben Sie diese schöne Lilie gefunden?

Warum haben Sie das Wasser ausgegossen (119)?

Hatten Sie schönes Wetter zu (for) Ihrem Spaziergang auf den „Königstuhl"?

Ja, man ergriff ihn, als er aus dem Hause schlich.

Ich selbst habe sie geschnitten. Ich fuhr in einem Wagen

Die Bibel sagt: „Im Anfang schuf Gott Himmel und Erde."

Weil der Schnee auf den Bergen geschmolzen (146) ist.

Der Bediente trug ihn vor einer halben Stunde dahin (there).

Er wusch seine Hände und trank Wasser.

Sie ist in meinem Garten gewachsen.

Es war nicht rein (clean). Ich begoß Ihre Blumen damit.

Die Sonne schien herrlich, als wir anfingen (began), den Berg zu ersteigen; aber bald kam ein Gewitter (a thunder-storm), und wir waren gezwungen, wieder herab (down) zu gehen.

---

## Additional Remarks to the irregular verbs.

As the learner has already observed, some of the irregular verbs also change their radical *consonants* either in the *Present*, *Imperfect* or *Participle*. We subjoin here those little irregularities.

1) In the *present tense.*

> Ich nehme, du nimmst, er nimmt (double m).
>
> ich schelte, er schilt
> ich halte, er hält
> ich rate, er rät
> ich gelte, er gilt
> instead of schelltet, haltet, ratet ꝛc. (lose the termination t).

2) There is further an old form of the third person singular of some verbs, with the diphthong **eu**, which still occurs in poetry, viz:

> Er fleugt, kreucht, beut, fleußt, geußt for fliegt (flies), kriecht (crawls), bietet (offers), fließt (flows), gießt (pours)

3) In the *Imperfect tense:*

> Ich bieb, gehauen from hauen (takes a final b) *)
> ich traf, getroffen from treffen
> ich schuf, geschaffen from schaffen } (lose one f in the *Imp.*).
> ich kam, gekommen from kommen (loses one m in the *Imp.*).

---

*) This **b** is hardened out of *v* = u becoming a consonant.

13*

4) In the *Imperfect* and *Participle*:

Jch bat,    gebeten from bitten (loses one t).
ich faß,    gefeffen from fißen (changes ß into ff)
ich ſtanb    geſtanben from ſtehen (changes h into nb).
ich litt,    gelitten from leiben      ⎫ (change b into
ich ſchnitt, gefchnitten from ſchneiben   ⎭      double t).
ich pfiff,   gepfiffen from pfeifen      ⎫
ich ſchliff, gefchliffen from ſchleifen   ⎬ (double their f)
ich griff,   gegriffen from greifen     ⎭
ich jog,    gejogen from jiehen (changes h into g).
ich ſott,   gefotten from ſieben (changes b into double t).

5) There exist some older forms of the *Subjunctive* mood of the *Imperfect*, which still occur now and then, viz..

Jch beföhle instead of befühle; verbürge for verbärge.
ich ſtünbe for ich ſtänbe; ich ſtürbe for ich ſtärbe
ich verbürbe for verbärbe, ich gewönne for gewänne.

6) The regular verb fragen, *to ask*, has for the *Imperfect tense*, besides the regular form ich fragte, an old form ich frug; *Subj.* ich früge; thus also: — ſchallen *resound:* ſcholl and ſchnauben snort: ſchnob.

7) Some regular verbs have a second participle of the ancient form which is commonly used as an adjective. Such are:

Verworren confused, from verwirren *(reg. v.)* to confuse.
gefpalten split,       - ſpalten *(reg. v)* to split.
gefaljen salt, salted   - ſaljen *(reg. v.)* to salt
gemahlen ground ,    - mahlen *(reg. v.)* to grind.
verwogen dared      - ſich verwegen to dare (comp *irr. v.*133).
gerochen avenged    - rächen *(reg. v.)* to revenge.

### An alphabetical list of all the irregular verbs.

*NB*   Simple verbs which are not found in this list, are to be considered *regular*. Compound verbs must be sought for under their primitives.

| Infinitive. | Imperfect. | Part. Past. | Nr. |
|---|---|---|---|
| Baden to bake | but (badte) | gebaden | 155[1] |
| * bebürfen[2] to need, like bülfen   *Pres.* ich bebarf | beburfte | beburſt | — |
| befehlen to order, to command | befahl | befohlen | 17 |
| befleißen, ſich, to apply one's self | befliß | befliffen | 62 |
| beginnen to begin | begann | begonnen | 36 |
| beißen to bite | biß | gebiffen | 61 |
| beflemmen to press | beflomm | beflommen | 134 |
| bergen to hide, to conceal | barg | geborgen | 18 |

1) These figures indicate the number of each of the irregular verbs from p. 163 to 192
2) The verbs marked * are *partly* irregular (see p. 126, § 6), verbs marked with † are *neuter* and take ſein as auxiliary (see p. 164 *)

| Infinitive. | Imperfect. | Part. Past. | Nr. |
|---|---|---|---|
| †berſten to burst, to crack | barſt | geborſten | 19 |
| beſinnen, ſich, to meditate | beſann | beſonnen | 39 |
| beſitzen to possess | beſaß | beſeſſen | 13 |
| betrügen to cheat, to deceive | betrog | betrogen | 113 |
| bewegen to induce | bewog | bewogen | 133 |
| biegen to bend | bog | gebogen | 111 |
| bieten to offer | bot | geboten | 112 |
| binden to bind, to tie | band | gebunden | 43 |
| bitten to beg, to request | bat | gebeten | 11 |
| blaſen to blow | blies | geblaſen | 97 |
| †bleiben to stay, to remain | blieb | geblieben | 80 |
| braten to roast | briet | gebraten | 98 |
| brechen to break | brach | gebrochen | 20 |
| *brennen¹) to burn | brannte | gebrannt | — |
| *bringen to bring | brachte | gebracht | — |
| *Denken to think | dachte | gedacht | — |
| dingen to hire (a servant) | (dingte) | gedungen | 58 |
| dreſchen to thrash | draſch | gedroſchen | 21 |
| †dringen to press forward, to urge | drang | gedrungen | 47 |
| Empfangen to receive | empfing | empfangen | 100 |
| empfehlen to recommend | empfahl | empfohlen | 16 |
| empfinden to feel | empfand | empfunden | 44 |
| †entrinnen to escape | entrann | entronnen | 38 |
| †erbleichen to turn pale | erblich | erblichen | 63 |
| erkieſen to choose | erkor | erkoren | 150 |
| †erlöſchen to become extinct | erloſch | erloſchen | 135 |
| *erſchallen to resound | erſcholl (erſchallte) | erſchollen | 136 |
| †erſchrecken to become frightened | erſchrak | erſchrocken | 22 |
| erwägen to consider | erwog | erwogen | 126 |
| eſſen to eat | aß | gegeſſen | 2 |
| †Fahren to drive | fuhr | gefahren | 156 |
| †fallen to fall | fiel | gefallen | 99 |
| fangen to catch | fieng | gefangen | 100 |
| fechten to fight | focht | gefochten | 137 |
| finden to find | fand | gefunden | 44 |
| flechten to twist | flocht | geflochten | 138 |
| †fliegen to fly | flog | geflogen | 114 |
| †fliehen to flee | floh | geflohen | 115 |
| †fließen to flow | floß | gefloſſen | 116 |
| freſſen to eat = to devour | fraß | gefreſſen | 3 |
| frieren to freeze | fror | gefroren | 117 |
| Gären to ferment | gor (gärte) | gegoren | 139 |
| gebären to bring forth | gebar | geboren | 24 |
| geben to give | gab | gegeben | 1 |
| gebieten to order, to command | gebot | geboten | 113 |
| †gedeihen to thrive | gedieh | gediehen | 86 |
| gefallen to please | gefiel | gefallen | 99 |
| †gehen to go | gieng | gegangen | 108 |
| †gelingen to succeed | gelang | gelungen | 48 |
| gelten to be worth | galt | gegolten | 23 |

1) See the foot-note 2) p. 196.

| Infinitive. | Imperfect. | Part. Past | Nr |
|---|---|---|---|
| †genefen to recover | genaß | genefen | 8 |
| genießen to enjoy | genoß | genoſſen | 118 |
| †geraten to fall or get into | geriet | geraten | 104 |
| †geſchehen to happen | geſchah | geſcheben | 9 |
| gewinnen to win, to gain | gewann | gewonnen | 37 |
| gießen to pour | goß | gegoſſen | 119 |
| gleichen to resemble | glich | geglichen | 65 |
| †gleiten to glide, slide, slip | glitt | geglitten | 66 |
| †glimmen to burn faintly | glomm | geglommen | 140 |
| graben to dig | grub | gegraben | 157 |
| greifen to gripe, to grasp | griff | gegriffen | 64 |
| Halten to hold | hielt | gebalten | 101 |
| †hangen to hang | hieng | gehangen | 102 |
| hauen to hew | hieb | gehauen | 107 |
| heben to lift | hob | gebeben | 141 |
| heißen to be called, to bid | hieß | gebeißen | 96 |
| helfen to help | half | geholfen | 25 |
| *Kennen to know | kannte | gekannt | — |
| †klimmen to climb | klomm | geklommen | 140a |
| klingen to tingle, to sound | klang | geklungen | 49 |
| kneifen to pinch | kniff | gekniffen | 67 |
| kreiſchen to scream | kriſch | gekriſchen | 88 |
| †kommen to come | kam | gekommen | 42 |
| †kriechen to crawl, to creep | kroch | gekrochen | 120 |
| Laden to load | lub | geladen | 158 |
| laſſen to let, to leave | ließ | gelaſſen | 103 |
| †laufen to run | lief | gelaufen | 106 |
| leiden to suffer | litt | gelitten | 68 |
| leihen to lend | lieh | geliehen | 87 |
| leſen to read | las | geleſen | 5 |
| †liegen to lie | lag | gelegen | 12 |
| lügen to tell a lie | log | gelogen | 142 |
| Meiden to shun, to avoid | mied | gemieden | 84 |
| melken to milk | molk (melkte) | gemolken | 143 |
| meſſen to measure | maß | gemeſſen | 4 |
| mißfallen to displease | mißfiel | mißfallen | 99 |
| Nehmen to take | nahm | genommen | 28 |
| *nennen to call | nannte | genannt | — |
| Pfeifen to whistle | pfiff | gepfiffen | 69 |
| pflegen to entertain, treat (with) | pflog | gepflogen | 151 |
| preiſen to praise, to extol | pries | geprieſen | 91 |
| Quellen to spring forth | quoll | gequollen | 152 |
| Raten to advise | riet | geraten | 104 |
| reiben to rub | rieb | gerieben | 81 |
| reißen to rend, to tear | riß | geriſſen | 70 |
| †reiten to ride (on horseback) | ritt | geritten | 71 |
| *rennen to run, to race | rannte | gerannt | — |
| riechen to smell | roch | gerochen | 121 |
| ringen to wrestle, to wring | rang | gerungen | 50 |
| rinnen to leak, to flow | rann | geronnen | 38 |
| rufen to call | rief | gerufen | 110 |

| Infinitive. | Imperfect. | Part. Past. | Nr. |
|---|---|---|---|
| ſaufen to drink (of animals) | ſoff | geſoffen | 153 |
| ſaugen to suck (also regular, | ſog | geſogen | 144 |
| ſchaffen to create | ſchuf | geſchaffen | 159 |
| ſcheiben to separate | ſchieb | geſchieben | 85 |
| ſcheinen to seem, to shine | ſchien | geſchienen | 93 |
| ſchelten to scold, to chide | ſchalt | geſcholten | 27 |
| ſcheren to shear | ſchor | geſchoren | 145 |
| ſchieben to shove, to push gently | ſchob | geſchoben | 128 |
| ſchießen to shoot | ſchoß | geſchoſſen | 122 |
| ſchinben to flay | — (ſchanb | geſchunden | 59 |
| ſchlaſen to sleep | ſchlief | geſchlaſen | 105 |
| ſchlagen to beat, to strike | ſchlug | geſchlagen | 160 |
| †ſchleichen to sneak, to steal into | ſchlich | geſchlichen | 73 |
| ſchleiſen to sharpen, to grind | ſchliff | geſchliffen | 72 |
| ſchließen to lock, to close | ſchloß | geſchloſſen | 123 |
| ſchlingen to wind, to twist | ſchlang | geſchlungen | 51 |
| ſchmeißen to fling, smite | ſchmiß | geſchmiſſen | 75 |
| ſchmelzen to melt, to smelt | ſchmolz | geſchmolzen | 146 |
| ſchnauben to breathe, to snort | ſchnob | geſchnoben | 154 |
| ſchneiben to cut | ſchnitt | geſchnitten | 76 |
| ſchreiben to write | ſchrieb | geſchrieben | 82 |
| ſchreien to scream, to cry | ſchrie | geſchrieen | 88 |
| †ſchreiten to stride, to step | ſchritt | geſchritten | 77 |
| ſchweigen to be silent | ſchwieg | geſchwiegen | 94 |
| ſchwellen to swell | ſchwoll | geſchwollen | 147 |
| †ſchwimmen to swim | ſchwamm | geſchwommen | 41 |
| †ſchwinben to vanish | ſchwanb | geſchwunden | 45 |
| ſchwingen to swing, to brandish | ſchwang | geſchwungen | 52 |
| ſchwören to swear | ſchwor | geſchworen | 148 |
| ſehen to see | ſah | geſehen | 6 |
| *ſenben to send | ſanbte | geſanbt | — |
| ſieben to boil | ſott | geſotten | 129 |
| ſingen to sing | ſang | geſungen | 53 |
| †ſinken to sink | ſank | geſunken | 55 |
| ſinnen to meditate | ſann | geſonnen | 39 |
| †ſitzen to sit | ſaß | geſeſſen | 13 |
| ſpeien to spit | ſpie | geſpieen | 89 |
| ſpinnen to spin | ſpann | geſponnen | 40 |
| ſprechen to speak | ſprach | geſprochen | 28 |
| ſprießen to sprout | ſproß | geſproſſen | 130 |
| †ſpringen to spring | ſprang | geſprungen | 54 |
| ſtechen to sting | ſtach | geſtochen | 29 |
| *ſtecken to stick | ſtak | geſteckt | 14 |
| †ſtehen to stand | ſtanb | geſtanden | 15 |
| ſtehlen to steal | ſtahl | geſtohlen | 30 |
| †ſteigen to mount | ſtieg | geſtiegen | 95 |
| †ſterben to die | ſtarb | geſtorben | 31 |
| †ſtieben to fly off | ſtob | geſtoben | 131 |
| ſtinken to stink | ſtank | geſtunken | 60 |
| ſtoßen to push hard | ſtieß | geſtoßen | 109 |
| ſtreichen to rub | ſtrich | geſtrichen | 74 |
| ſtreiten to quarrel | ſtritt | geſtritten | 78 |

| Infinitive. | Imperfect. | Part. Past. | Nr. |
|---|---|---|---|
| Thun to do | that | gethan | 16 |
| tragen to carry, to wear | trug | getragen | 161 |
| treffen to hit, to meet | traf | getroffen | 35 |
| treiben to drive | trieb | getrieben | 83 |
| †treten to tread | trat | getreten | 7 |
| triefen to drop, drip | troff | getrieft | 132 |
| trinken to drink | trank | getrunken | 56 |
| trügen to deceive | (trog) | (getrogen) | 113 |
| Verbergen to hide, conceal | verbarg | verborgen | 17 |
| verbieten to forbid | verbot | verboten | 112 |
| verberben to spoil, to ruin | vertarb | verborben | 32 |
| verbrießen to vex | verdroß | verdrossen | 124 |
| vergessen to forget | vergaß | vergessen | 10 |
| verlieren to lose | verlor | verloren | 125 |
| *vermögen (Pres. ich vermag) to be able | ich vermochte | vermocht | — |
| †verschwinden to disappear | verschwand | verschwunden | 45 |
| verzeihen to pardon | verzieh | verziehen | 90 |
| Wachsen to grow | wuchs | gewachsen | 162 |
| wägen to weigh | wog | gewogen | 126 |
| waschen to wash | wusch | gewaschen | 163 |
| weben to weave | wob | gewoben | 149 |
| †weichen to yield | wich | gewichen | 79 |
| weisen to show | wies | gewiesen | 92 |
| *wenden to turn | wandte | gewandt | — |
| werben to sue | warb | geworben | 33 |
| *werden (aux. verb) to become | (warb) wurde | geworden | — |
| werfen to throw | warf | geworfen | 34 |
| wiegen to weigh | wog | gewogen | 126 |
| winden to wind | wand | gewunden | 46 |
| *wissen to know (Pres. ich weiß) | wußte | gewußt | — |
| Zeihen to accuse | zieh | geziehen | 90 |
| ziehen to draw, to pull | zog | gezogen | 127 |
| zwingen to force, to compel | zwang | gezwungen | 57 |

---

# Thirtieth Lesson.

## INSEPARABLE VERBS.

### (Untrennbare Zeitwörter.)

Most German verbs allow of certain prefixes or prepositions to be placed before them. Unaccented particles or prefixes assimilate themselves with the simple verb so as to form one inseparable combination, such as:

bezahlen to pay; ich bezahle I pay; ich bezahlte I paid.

Verbs of this kind are called *inseparable verbs*. Their particular character is as follows:

1) The prefixes remain attached to the verb through its whole conjugation.

2) The prefixes are always unaccented.

3) They do not admit of the syllable ge in the Past Participle, as: bejaȟlt' paid (not gebejaȟlt).

4) The sign of the infinitive, ju, is put before the combination, as in English: ju bejaȟlen to pay.

Their conjugation depends on their being regular or irregular. — There are eleven inseparable prefixes·

be, emp, er,     ge, miß, voll,
ent, ver, ȝer,     ȟinter and wiber.*)

---

## 1. Conjugation of a regular inseparable verb.

### Bebecfen to cover.

| Present | Imperfect. |
|---|---|
| Ȝd) bebecfe I cover | Ȝd) bebecfte I covered |
| bu bebecfȝt thou coverest | bu bebecfteȝt ꝛc. |
| er bebecft he covers | er bebecfte ꝛc. |
| wir bebecfen we cover | wir bebecften ꝛc. |
| Sie bebecfen you cover | Sie bebecften ꝛc. |
| ȝie bebecfen they cover. | ȝie bebecften ꝛc. |

#### Perfect.
Ȝd) ȟabe bebecft I have covered; bu ȟaȝt bebecft ꝛc.

| Future. | Conditional. |
|---|---|
| Ȝd) werbe bebecfen I shall cover. | Ȝd) würbe bebecfen. |

| Imperative. | Part. past. | P. pres. |
|---|---|---|
| Bebecfen Sie cover. | bebecft covered. | bebecfenb. |

Infinitive: bebecfen or ju bebecfen to cover.

---

*) When the four last prefixes serve to compound a *noun* or an adjective, they are accented, as: ber Miß'mut ill-humour; miß'günȝtig envious; tie Vollmacȟt authority, vollfommen perfect; ber Wi'berȝprud) contradiction; tie Ȟin'terlȝt cunning, artifice.

## 2. Conjugation of an irregular inseparable.

Infinitive: Verlaſſen to leave (a place).

| *Present.* | *Imperfect.* |
|---|---|
| Ich verlaſſe I leave | Ich verließ I left |
| du verläſſeſt thou leavest | du verließeſt thou leftest |
| er verläßt he leaves | er verließ he left |
| wir verlaſſen we leave | wir verließen we left |
| Sie verlaſſen you leave | Sie verließen you left |
| ſie verlaſſen they leave. | ſie verließen they left. |

*Perfect.*

Ich habe verlaſſen I have left; du haſt verlaſſen ꝛc.

*Future.*

Ich werde verlaſſen I shall leave; du wirſt verlaſſen ꝛc.

| *Imperative.* | *Part. past.* |
|---|---|
| Verlaſſen Sie leave etc. | verlaſſen left. |

Such are:

| | *Infinitive.* | *Present.* | *Perf. tense.* |
|---|---|---|---|
| be: | beloh'nen *reg.* to reward | ich belohne | ich habe belohnt |
| | behalten *ir.* to keep | ” behalte | ” behalten. |
| emp: | empfinden *ir.* to feel | ” empfinde | ” empfunden. |
| | empfangen *ir.* to receive | ” empfange | ” empfangen. |
| er: | erhalten *ir.* to receive | ” erhalte | ” erhalten. |
| | erfahren *ir.* to learn | ” erfahre | ” erfahren. |
| ent: | †entgehen *ir.* to escape | ” entgehe | ich bin entgangen. |
| | entfernen *reg.* remove | ” entferne | ich habe entfernt. |
| ver: | vergeſſen *ir.* to forget | ” vergeſſe | ” vergeſſen. |
| | verlieren *ir.* to lose | ” verliere | ” verloren. |
| zer: | zerſtören *reg.* to destroy | ” zerſtöre | ” zerſtört |
| | zerreißen *ir.* to tear up | ” zerreiße | ” zerriſſen. |
| ge: | gehorchen *(Dat.) reg.* to obey | ” gehorche | ” gehorcht. |
| | gefallen *(Dat.) ir.* to please | ” gefalle | ” gefallen. |
| miß: | mißfal'len *ir.* to displease | ” mißfalle | ” mißfallen |
| | mißbrauchen *reg.* to misuse | ” mißbrauche | ” mißbraucht. |
| voll: | vollbringen to accomplish | ” vollbringe | ” vollbracht. |
| | vollziehen *ir.* to execute | ” vollziehe | ” vollzogen. |
| hinter: | hinterlaſſen to leave behind | ” hinterlaſſe | ” hinterlaſſen. |
| | hintergeh'en *ir.* to deceive | ” hintergehe | ” hintergangen. |
| wider: | widerſteh'en *ir.* to resist | ” widerſtehe | ” widerſtanden. |
| | widerſprechen to contradict | ” widerſpreche | ” widerſprochen. |

*NB.* We advise every learner always to form, as a repetition, also the *Imperf.* tense of these verbs

*NB.* The force of these particles can only be clearly defined for a few of them, *viz.*:

　　ent denotes *removal* or *separation;*

　　zer means *apart, asunder* or to pieces;

　　miß is the English *mis-* or *dis-;*

**voll** indicates *accomplishment;*
**wider** means *against, with* (in *withstand*).

*Note.* For the prefixes **burch**, **über**, **unter** and **um**, which are sometimes separable and sometimes inseparable, see p. 213—216.

## 3. Derivative inseparables.

Some of the above particles are prefixed to nouns, to form a verb of them, or to verbs already compounded with other prefixes. The accent is then on the second syllable, and such verbs are treated as inseparbles:[1])

| *Infinitive* | *Pres.* | *Part. past.* |
|---|---|---|
| beab': beab'sichtigen *reg.* to intend | ich beabsichtige | beabsichtigt |
| bean': bean'tragen *reg* to propose | ich beantrage | beantragt. |
| beant': beant'worten *reg.* to answer | ich beantworte | beantwortet. |
| benach': benach'richtigen *reg.* to inform | ich benachrichtige | benachrichtigt |
| be•un': beun'ruhigen *reg* to disturb | ich beunruhige | beunruhigt. |
| be•ur': beur'teilen to criticise, judge | ich beurteile | beurteilt |
| verab'•: verab'scheuen *reg.* to detest | ich verabscheue | verabscheut. |
| vernach': vernach'lässigen *reg.* to neglect | ich vernachlässige | vernachlässigt. |
| mißver: miß'verstehen misunderstand | ich mißverstehe[2]) | mißverstanden. |
| verun': verun'reinigen *reg* to soil | ich verunreinige | verunreinigt. |
| verur': verur'sachen *reg.* to cause | ich verursache | verursacht. |
| „   „   verur'teilen *reg.* to condemn | ich verurteile | verurteilt |

## 4. Some other inseparables.

The following verbs compounded with an adjective or substantive are also inseparable, but having both the syllables accented, they must take the prefix **ge** in the Participle past:

| *Infinitive.* | *Present.* | *Perfect tense.* |
|---|---|---|
| Früh'stücken *reg* to breakfast | ich frühstücke | ich habe gefrüh'stückt. |
| ant'worten *r.* to answer | • antworte | • geant'wortet. |
| ur'teilen *r.* to judge, criticise | • urteile | • geur'teilt |

Further:

| | | |
|---|---|---|
| Lieb'losen to caress | • liebkose | • gelieb'lost. |
| lustwandeln *reg.* to walk | • lustwandle | • gelustwandelt. |
| arg'wöhnen to suspect | • argwöhne | • geargwöhnt. |
| recht'fertigen to justify | • rechtfertige | • gerechtfertigt |
| mut'maßen to presume, guess | • mutmaße | • gemutmaßt. |
| wett'eifern to emulate | • wetteifere | • gewetteifert. |
| hand'haben to handle, maintain | • handhabe | • gehandhabt |
| wett'terleuchten to sheet-lighten | es wetterleuchtet | es hat gewetterleuchtet |
| weis'sagen to prophesy | ich weissage | ich habe geweissagt. |

1) Bevor'stehen is separable: ich stehe bevor, because bevor is a word used by itself and therefore *separable* (see p. 209).

2 Here miß is followed by a second *unaccented* prefix; it takes therefore the accent; miß'verstehen, miß'verstanden, whilst *all* the other inseparable prefixes do *not*, even in the same case.

*Note.* The two verbs willfah'ren *(to comply with)* and froh=
lo'cken *(to exult, to shout),* may either take or omit the prefix ge
in the participle, which may be willfahrt' or gewill'fahrt; frohlo'ckt
or gefroh'lockt. The former is best, will and froh being unaccented.

---

## Words.

| | |
|---|---|
| Das Land the land. | versprechen *(ir.* 28) to promise. |
| das Glück fortune. | entsagen *reg.* to abdicate, resign. |
| das Laster vice. | günstig favorable, *adv.* —ly. |
| die Studien *pl.* the studies. | begünstigen *reg.* to favour. |
| der Aufseher the overseer. | berauben *reg.* to rob, to deprive. |
| der Weg the road, way. | bewohnen to inhabit. |
| der Bauer *(pl.* —n) the peasant. | befolgen *reg.* to follow. |
| bebauen to cultivate. | bessern *reg.* to amend. |
| das Gepäck the luggage. | beschmutzen *reg.* to soil. |
| der Gedanke the thought. | zerstreuen *reg.* to disperse, scatter. |
| das Betragen the behaviour. | die Kette the chain. |
| erraten *(ir. v.* 104) to guess. | die Scheibe the pane of glass. |
| das Vertrauen (the) confidence. | der Räuber the robber. |
| erobern *reg.* to conquer, take. | ganz, gänzlich entirely, quite. |
| behalten *(ir.* 101) to keep. | nachher *adv* afterwards. |

## Reading Exercise. 75.

1. Der Schnee bedeckt die Erde im Winter. Die fleißigen
Schüler werden belohnt. Diese Bücher gefallen mir nicht. Die
Feinde eroberten die Stadt. Ich erkannte Sie nicht gleich
(at once), weil es dunkel war. Behalten Sie, was Sie haben.
Haben Sie mich verstanden? Ja, ich verspreche Ihnen. Ihren
Rat zu befolgen. Widersprechen Sie mir, so lange als Sie
wollen (like); am Ende werden Sie sagen, daß ich recht habe.
Dieses Schloß wird von der Gräfin F. bewohnt. Der Gärtner
hat vergessen, meine jungen Pflanzen zu begießen.

2. Der König hat zu gunsten (in favour of) seines Sohnes
dem Throne entsagt. Der Sohn des Lord K. hat seine Studien
ganz vernachlässigt. Herr Walker hat mein Buch sehr günstig
beurteilt. Die guten Menschen verabscheuen das Laster. Die
Nachricht von dem Siege (victory) der Feinde hat einen großen
Schrecken (panic) verursacht. Der Aufseher hatte sein Geschäft
(business) ganz vernachlässigt. Der junge Mann rechtfertigte das
Vertrauen, das wir in ihn setzten.

## Aufgabe. 76.

1. Water covered the land. You lose your friends. I
had not received your letter. Good children obey their *(Dat.)*
parents. This young man *was* much (sehr) favoured by (the)
fortune. The peasants cultivate their land. The road is planted

(bepflanzt) with walnut-(Nuß=)trees  A robber has robbed me
(*Acc.*) of my luggage (*Gen.*).  You have guessed (104) my
thoughts.  The boy promised me (*Dat.*) to amend his behaviour.
We have lost our money.  The child has soiled its dress.  I
will keep this book  Have you executed the orders (Befehle)
of the king?

2.  I *was*\*) deceived (113) by my neighbour; he deceives
everybody.  Carthage (Karthago) *was* destroyed by the Romans.
I have received several letters from America.  Do not contradict your teacher (*Dat*.).  Have you breakfasted?  I breakfast every morning at nine o'clock.  The dog broke (tore, 70)
his chain and ran off (fort).  Your boots are torn, shall I
take (tragen) them to (zu) the shoemaker?  A bird flew (114)
against the window and broke a pane of glass  Afterwards
₂nobody ₁knew (,) who ₃had ₂broken ₁it.  I *was*\*) not (or
*have* not *been*) informed of (von) the death of Mr. Graham.
The robber *was* condemned ₂to ₁*be* ₁hanged (*Pass. voice*).

## Conversation.

| | |
|---|---|
| Was thaten die Feinde? | Sie eroberten die Stadt. |
| Wer bewohnt jenes Schloß? | Der österreichische Graf F. |
| Ist er reich? | Man sagt, daß er sehr große Reichtümer besitzt. |
| Warum hat der Gärtner die Blumen nicht begossen? | Er hatte keine Zeit; er wird sie diesen Abend begießen. |
| Was versprach der Knabe? | Er versprach, sich zu bessern. |
| Wer von Ihnen hat mir wider= sprochen? | Niemand von uns hat Ihnen widersprochen. |
| Hat dieser Mann sein Geschäft besorgt (attended to)? | Nein, er hat es gänzlich vernach= lässigt. |
| Haben Sie einen Brief von Ihrem Freunde erhalten? | Ich erhalte oft Briefe von ihm. |
| Haben Sie viele Freunde? | Der Tod hat mich aller meiner Freunde beraubt. |
| Was thun die Bauern? | Sie bebauen die Felder. |
| Können Sie meine Gedanken erraten? | Ich habe sie oft erraten, aber nicht immer. |
| Hat der Feind die Stadt zerstört? | Nein, er hat sie nicht zerstört. |
| Hat der König dem Throne entsagt? | Ja, zu gunsten seines Sohnes. |
| Wissen Sie, wer dieses Glas zerbrochen hat? | Nein, mein Herr, ich weiß es nicht; ich habe es nicht zerbrochen. |

---

\*) *was* = wurde or bin..worden, see the foot-note 2) p. 174.

# Thirty-first Lesson.

## SEPARABLE VERBS.

(Trennbare Zeitwörter.)

*Separable verbs* aıe such as consist of a verb and of a separable prefix which may be detached from it The prefixes employed with the separable verbs are also employed as independent parts of speech, mostly prepositions or adverbs, as. aus=gehen to go out; weg=gehen to go away; an=fangen to begin.

When conjugated in the *Present* and *Imperfect* of the Indicative, and in the *Imperative*, these prepositions are detached from the verb, and placed at the end of the clause, as:

*Present:* ich gehe diesen Abend aus;
*Imperfect:* ich ging gestern nicht aus;
*Imperf.:* Gehen Sie mit mir aus. Fangen Sie jetzt an.

The prefix remains with the verb in the *Infinitive*, in those tenses formed with the Infinitive (1st *Future* and 1st *Conditional*), and in both *Participles*. Ex.: anfangen to begin; *Fut.* ich werde anfangen; *Part. pres.* anfangend.

In the *Past participle* the syllable ge is placed between the particle and the verb, as: an=ge=fangen, ausgegangen. The same rule applies to the word „zu", when this is required in the Infinitive, as: an=zu=fangen, auszugehen ıc. The accent of the *separable* verbs is double, one on the separable particle, the other on the verb, as. an'fan'gen, but the *principal* stress or accent of the two is on the *separable particle*. You can therefore simply retain as a rule· Whenever the *prefix* of a compound verb is *accentuated,* then the compound verb is *separable,* when *not,* the verb is *inseparable.* The only exception makes miß, in case that a *second* prefix be following, compare p. 203, note 2. —

## Conjugation of a separable verb.

Abschreiben (ich schrieb . . ab, — abgeschrieben) to copy.

*Present.*

Ich schreibe . . ab I copy      wir schreiben . . ab we copy
du schreibst . ab thou copiest      (ihr schreibt . . ab) ye copy
er schreibt . . ab he copies      Sie schreiben . . ab you copy
sie schreibt . . ab she copies.      sie schreiben . . ab they copy.

*Imperfect.*

Ich schrieb . . . ab I copied    wir schrieben . . . ab we copied
du schriebst . . . ab     ꝛc.    (ihr schriebet . . . ab)    ꝛc.
er schrieb . . . ab      ꝛc.    Sie schrieben . . . ab     ꝛc.
sie schrieb . . . ab     ꝛc.    sie schrieben . . . ab     ꝛc.

*Perfect*     Ich habe . . abgeschrieben I have copied etc.
*Pluperfect.*  Ich hatte . . abgeschrieben I had copied etc.
*1st Fut.*     Ich werde . . abschreiben I shall copy etc.
*2nd Fut.*    Ich werde abgeschrieben haben I shall have copied.
*1st Cond.*   Ich würde . . abschreiben I should copy etc.
*2nd Cond.*  Ich würde abgeschrieben haben I should have copied.

I m p e r a t i v e.

Schreibe . . . ab   ⎱      schreiben wir . . . ab  ⎱ let us
schreiben Sie . . . ab ⎰ copy.   wir wollen abschreiben ⎰ copy.

I n f i n i t i v e.

Abschreiben and abzuschreiben to copy.

P a r t i c i p l e s.

*Pres.* Abschreibend copying. | *Past.* abgeschrieben copied.

---

## 1. Simple separable particles.*)

1) **ab:** †ab'reisen *reg.* to set out, *Pres.* ich reise . . ab; *Imp.* ich
reiste . . ab; *Perf.* ich bin abgereist. Thus: ab'nehmen to
take off, ab'schlagen to refuse; †ab'weichen to deviate.

2) **an:** †an'kommen to arrive; *Pres.* ich komme an; *Imp.* ich
kam . . an; *Perf.* ich bin angekommen. Thus: an'fangen
to begin; an'nehmen to accept; an'ziehen to put on;
an'kleiden *reg.* to dress  *P. p.* angekleidet.

3) **auf:** †auf'stehen to get up; *Pres.* ich stehe . . auf; *Imp.* ich
stand . . auf; *Perf.* ich bin aufgestanden. Thus: auf'halten
to detain; auf'hören *reg.* to cease; auf'machen to open.

4) **aus:** †aus'gehen to go out; *Pres.* ich gehe . . aus; *Imp.* ich
ging . . aus; *Perf.* ich bin ausgegangen. Thus: aus'lassen
to leave out; aus'geben to spend (money); aus'sprechen
to pronounce.

5) **bei:** †bei'stehen (*Dat.*) to assist; beitragen to contribute.

6) **dar:** dar'stellen *reg.* to represent; darbringen to offer; dar-
thun to evince, to state.

7) **ein:** ein'führen *reg.* (with the prep. bei or in) to introduce;
ein'laden to invite. *P. p.* eingeladen.

---

*) We advise the student, as a very useful repetition, always
to form of *all* these verbs, even where the book does not give
them, the *Pres.*, *Imperf.* and *Perf.* tenses, just as from 1, to 4,
the above list has given them.

8) **fort:** fort'fahren to go on, to proceed; fort'tragen to carry off; fortdauern *reg.* to last; fortſetzen *reg.* to continue; fort'begleiten to see off.
9) **her:** her'bringen to bring here (hither).
10) **heim:** †heim'kommen *reg.* to come *or* return home.
11) **hin:** hin'ſtellen *reg.* to put down; †hingehen to go there.
12) **los:** los'laſſen to let loose; losreißen to tear off.
13) **mit:** mit'teilen *reg.* to communicate, to impart, to tell; mitwirken to co-operate; mitnehmen to take with (you).
14) **nach:** nach'laſſen to subside, to abate; †nachfolgen *reg.* to follow (after); †nachlaufen to run after.
15) **nieder:** nieder'legen *reg.* to lay down.
16) **vor:** vor'ſtellen *reg.* (*Dat.*) to introduce, to present; vorleſen to read to somebody; †vorkommen to occur, to appear.
17) **weg:** weg'nehmen to take away; †wegbleiben to stay away.
18) **wieder:** wieder'leſen to read again (see p. 216, Note 1).
19) **zu:** zu'machen to shut; zu'ſchließen to close, to lock; zu'* laſſen to admit; zu'bringen to spend (time), *Perf.* ich habe . . zu'gebracht (spent).
20) For **durch, um, über'** and **unter** see p. 214. Ob as prefix is obsolete and occurs only in ob'liegen and ob'ſiegen.

## Words.

| | |
|---|---|
| Das Anerbieten the offer. | der Abend the evening. |
| das Konzert' the concert. | ab'brennen to burn down. |
| die Not the distress, need. | †auf'gehen (*of the sun*) to rise. |
| die Zeichnung the drawing. | ſchlecht badly.  ſchon already. |
| die Sonne the sun. | morgens *adv.* in the morning. |

## Reading Exercise. 77.

Ich ſchreibe die Aufgabe ab. Wer ſchrieb dieſen Brief ab? Karl hat ihn abgeſchrieben. Wann fingen Sie an, ihn abzuſchreiben? Ich habe geſtern Abend angefangen und fahre dieſen Morgen fort. Wir kamen um halb ſechs Uhr hier an. Das Mädchen ſchloß die Thüre zu. Ich nehme Ihr gü= tiges (kind) Anerbieten mit Vergnügen an. Stehet auf, Kinder, es iſt Zeit. Die Kinder ſind (have) dem Eſel nachgelaufen. Das ganze Dorf iſt abgebrannt. Ich ging nicht aus, weil ich krank war. Haben Sie Ihren Freund fortbegleitet (seen . . home)? Fürchten Sie nichts, ich ſtehe Ihnen bei!

## Aufgabe. 78.

I copy all my letters. *Are* you *going* (go you) out? Yes, I *am going* out. My brother *has* set out (1) for (nach) London this morning. The concert begins (2) at 7 o'clock. Assist (5) your neighbour in his distress. Pray (Bitte), introduce (16) me to your friend. In summer ▸the ▸sun ▸rises at three o'clock in the morning. The sun has (iſt) risen beautifully. Leave out (4) this page (Seite). Have you copied the letter? It is already copied Take your drawing away Our friends went away from (von) here at six o'clock Do you not take me with [you]? I accept (2) your offer with great pleasure. The young man has spent (19) his time very badly. The doctor imparted (13) this news [to] me (Dat). Do not detain (3) him [any] longer Put on (2) your shoes. How have you spent your evening yesterday? I was (gone) out. He was not yet dressed (2).

## 2. Compound separable particles.*)

1. Bevor': †bevor'ſtehen to impend. *Pres.* ich ſtehe . . bevor.
2. Dabei': dabei'ſtehen to stand close by. *Pres* ich ſtehe dabei.
3. Daher'· †daher'kommen to come along. *Pr.* ich komme daher.
4. Dahin': †dahin'eilen to hasten away. *Pres.* ich eile dahin.
5. Darnieder': darnieder'liegen to lie down. *Pr.* ich liege d.
6. Darauf': darauf' beſtehen to insist on. *Pr.* ich beſtehe darauf
7. Davon': davonlaufen to run off. *Pres.* ich laufe davon.
8. Davor': davorſtellen to put before. *Pres* ich ſtelle . . davor.
9. Dazu' or hinzu'· dazu'thun to add. *Pres.* ich thue . . dazu.
10. Dazwiſchen': dazwiſchenlegen to put *or* lay between.
11. empor': empor'halten to hold up; emporheben to lift up.
12. entge'gen (towards). entgegengehen to go to meet.
13. entzwei'· entzwei'ſchlagen to striike asunder (in two).
14. herab'. herab'ſteigen } to get down. *Pres* ich ſteige herab.
15. hinab': hinab'ſteigen } to descend ⸗ ⸗ ⸗ hinab.
16. herauf': heraufſteigen } to ascend. ⸗ ich ſteige herauf.
17. hinauf'. hinaufſteigen } to mount (up). ⸗ ich ſteige hinauf.
18. heraus'. } herausrufen to call out. ⸗ ich rufe heraus.
19. hinaus': } hinaus⸗ or heraustragen to carry out.
20. herein': herein'kommen to come in *Pres* ich komme herein.
21. hinein' hinein'gehen to go in. *Pres.* ich gehe hinein.
22. herü'ber. } herüber'kommen to come over.
23. hinü'ber } herüber'⸗ or hinüber'werfen to throw over.
24. herun'ter: herunter'fließen } to flow down.
25. hinun'ter. hinunter'fließen }
26. heran': heran'kommen to approach. *Pres.* ich komme heran.
27. herbei': herbei'rufen } to call ⸗ ich rufe herbei.
28. herzu': herzu'rufen } (towards you). ⸗ ich rufe herzu.
29. herum': herum'tragen to carry about. ⸗ ich trage herum.
30. hervor': hervor⸗bringen to produce (to bring forth).
31. hinweg': hinwegnehmen to take away.
32. hinzu': †hinzu'eilen to hasten thither.
33. überein'· †überein'kommen to agree *Pres.* ich komme überein.

---

*) *NB.* When learning these verbs, always form, as a repetition, also their *Imperf.* and their *Perf. tenses*

34. um̡er': um̡er'= or ̡erum'ſd)weiſen to ramble about.
35. voran': voran'ge̡en to precede. *Pres.* id) ge̡e voran.
36. voraus':\ voraus'= or voi̡er'ſagen to foretell.
37. vor̡er':∫ vor̡er'wiſſen to foreknow; vor̡er'ſe̡en to foresee.
38. vorbei': \ vorbei= or vorüberge̡en to pass by; vorbeiſa̡ren
39. vorü'ber:∫  to drive by; vorübeiziē̡en to pass *or* march by.
40. ʒurüd': ʒurüd'̕ommen to come back; ʒurüd'̕e̡ren *reg.* to
      return; ʒurüd'ſd)iden *reg.* to send back, to return.
41. ʒuſam'men: †ʒuſam'men̕ommen or †ʒuſam'mentreſſen mit
      to meet with; ʒuſammenbiingen to collect; ʒuſammen=
      ſē̡en *reg.* to compose.

*Note 1.* Most of these compound particles serve to attach to
the verbs the idea of *peculiar locality*, whereas the simple ones
give the verbs a more *general* meaning. For instance:
An̕ommen means *to arrive;* but ̡eran̕ommen *to draw near you.*
auf̕egen *to impose, to inflict;* but barauf=, ̡erauf= or ̡inauf=
      ̕egen means *to lay on* (upon *or* in) certain place.
aus ge̡en *to go out* (for a walk); — ̡eraus= or ̡inausge̡en *to
      go out* (of a room, a house where you are etc.).
ausruſen means *to exclaim, to proclaim;* but ̡erausruſen *to call
      out* (of a certain place).
unter̕aſſen *to omit;* but ̡erunter̕aſſen *to let down.*
vorʒie̡en *to prefer,* but ̡ervorʒie̡en *to draw* or *pull forth* etc

*Note 2.* Some of these particles, simple or compound, may also
be prefixed to inseparable verbs, as: an'vertrauen to intrust; an'=
beſe̡len to recommend; aus'vertauſen to sell off, voraus'beʒa̡len to
pay in advance. — In this case the separable particles are transposed
in the above mentioned tenses, the inseparable ones remain. In
the infinitive the ʒu goes between the two prefixes.

Such inseparable verbs, when compounded with a *separable*
prefix, are thus conjugated:
*Pres.* Jd) vertraue .. an  *Part.* an'vertraut.  *Inf.* an'ʒuvertrauen.
 •  Jd) beſe̡le .. an  *Fut.* id) werde anbeſe̡len. *P.* id) ̡abe an'beſe̡len.
 •  Jd) beʒa̡le .. voraus.  *P.* vorausbeʒa̡lt.  *Inf.* vorausʒ u beʒa̡len.

*Note 3.* The following verbs which were formerly written
as two separate words, must be treated as separables:

| *Infinitive.* | *Pres.* | *Part. past.* |
|---|---|---|
| †Ge̡l'ſd)lagen *) fail, miscarry | id) ſd)lage .. ſe̡l | ſe̡l g eſd)lagen |
| frei'ſpred)en to acquit | id) ſpred)e .. frei | frei ge ſprod)en. |
| †gleid)'̕ommen to equal | id) ̕omme .. gleid) | gleid) ge̕ommen, |
| feſt'ſē̡en to fix, appoint | id) ſē̡e . feſt | feſt g e ſē̡t |
| lieb'̡aben to love | id) ̡abe .. lieb | lieb g e̡abt. |
| ſtill'ſd)weigen to be silent | id) ſd)weige .. ſtill | ſtill ge ſd)wiegen. |
| ſtatt'finden to take place | id) finde . ſtatt | ſtatt g e funden |
| wa̡r'ne̡men to perceive | id) ne̡me .. wa̡r | wa̡r ge nommen. |

---

*) When spelled separately, the three first verbs have a dif-
ferent meaning, viz.: ſe̡l ſd)lagen *to strike false, to miss one's blow;*
frei ſpred)en *to speak frankly;* gleid) ̕ommen *to come directly.*

# Observations.

1. The separation of the preposition from the verb can only take place in *principal* sentences, as: Ich schreibe einen Brief ab ꝛc. In sentences, beginning with a *relative pronoun* or a *subordinative conjunction,*\*) requiring the verb to be at the end, the prefix remains before Ex :

Der Brief, welchen ich jetzt abschreibe.
The letter which I am copying now.

Ich wünsche, daß Sie heute nicht ausgehen.
I wish you would not go out to-day.

Als ich in Paris ankam ꝛc.
When I arrived in Paris etc.

Wenn Sie zuviel Geld ausgeben.
If you spend too much money.

2. Particles compounded with her (such as herab, herein, herunter ꝛc.) denote motion *towards* the person who is speaking, while those compounded with hin (hinab, hinein, hinunter ꝛc.) denote the contrary motion or direction *away* from the speaker. Ex.:

Kommen Sie herein come in (here, *lit.* here in).
*(Come towards me who am in the room.)*

Gehen Sie hinein walk in (there).
*(The speaker is outside.)*

Gehen Sie hinauf go up stairs.
*(The speaker is below; motion away from him.)*

Kommen Sie herauf come up (here).
*(The speaker is up stairs — motion towards him)*

---

## Words.

†Um'kommen *ir. v.* to perish
die Kugel the ball.
†hinab'rollen *reg* to roll down.
der Hügel the hill.
der Thurm the tower
der Arzt the physician, doctor.
die Veränderung the change.
die Gesundheit health.
der Buchhändler the bookseller.
die Grammatik the grammar.
der Plan the plan.

der Bischof the bishop.
an'streichen *ir.* to paint.
frisch freshly, newly.
ab'tragen *ir.* to carry off.
wieder her'stellen *reg.* to restore.
erkennen to recognise.
vortreff'lich excellent.
un'zufrieden discontented.
gänzlich completely.
ab'schlagen to refuse.
vermutlich probably.

---

\*) Such as wenn if; weil because; als when, da as, daß that ꝛc. (See the 36th lesson p 248.)

14\*

### Reading Exercise. 79.

Lesen Sie mir dieses schöne Gedicht vor. Geben Sie acht (take care), die Thüre ist frisch angestrichen. Sind die Speisen (dishes) schon abgetragen? Der Bediente trägt sie eben (just now) ab. Sind die Kinder angekleidet? Das Kinds= mädchen (nurse) kleidet sie eben an. Weiche nie von der Wahrheit ab. Der Sturm hat nachgelassen (or aufgehört). Das Schiff ist gesunken; zwanzig Personen sind (have) umge= kommen. Der Dieb ist davon'gelaufen. Der Kaufmann reiste im ganzen (whole) Lande umher' (or herum'). Das habe ich Ihnen vorausgesagt Der Arzt ist eben vorbeigegangen.

### Aufgabe. 79a.

The ball rolled ₂down ₁the ₂hill (acc.). The luggage *was* carried out. We have (sind) ascended (on auf, acc.) the tower. Much rain produces weeds (Unkraut, *sing.*). The hunter rambles about (in) the forest. Captain R. has (ist) just ridden past. I had no time to carry the child about. The messenger brought the letter back. Great changes have taken place (Note 3) in the administration (Staats=Verwaltung). Mr. Murray is an excellent physician, he has entirely restored my health. I agreed (33) with the bookseller for (wegen) a new grammar We met (41) with some friends in Paris. The plan which we had made, *has* completely miscarried. I have just (eben) sent back the books you had lent me. If you refuse*) him such a trifle (Kleinigkeit), ₂he ₁will be very discontented. If I in- troduce (1, 16) you [to] the count (*Dat.*), ₂you ₁will probably *be* invited to (zum) dinner. When**) Mr. Grove *was* introduced to the Bishop, ₂he ₁recognised an old friend in him.

### Conversation.

Haben Sie Ihre Übersetzung schon abgeschrieben?

Ich schreibe sie eben ab. Ich werde auch die von gestern abschreiben

Um wieviel Uhr gehen Sie die= sen Abend aus?

Heute gehe ich nicht aus.

Sind Sie gestern auch nicht (not—either) ausgegangen?

Nein, ich hatte keine Zeit, aus= zugehen.

Wann reisen Sie ab?

Ich gedenke (intend), morgen früh abzureisen.

Wer hat das Kind ausgekleidet?

Die Mutter hat es ausgekleidet.

Soll ich mich ankleiden?

Ja, kleiden Sie sich an.

Wer hat meine Stickerei (em- broidery) weggenommen?

Niemand nimmt hier etwas weg

Wann geht die Sonne auf?

Im Sommer geht sie um 3 Uhr des Morgens auf.

---

*) See p. 211. Observations, 1).
**) Als, see the foot-note *) p. 170. and p. 211, 3rd Ex.

Wird der Offizier heute hier vorbei'reiten? — Vermutlich, denn (for) er reitet jeden.Tag hier vorbei'.

Ist der Bediente schon zurück= gekommen? — Nein, er bleibt immer so lange aus.

Wer hat Ihnen diese Nachricht mitgeteilt? — Mein Neffe Ludwig teilte sie mir mit.

Wann fängt das Theater an? — Es fängt im Winter um sechs Uhr, im Sommer um sieben Uhr an.

Hat der Schneider meinen Rock mitgenommen? — Er hat ihn mitgenommen, aber nicht zurückgebracht.

Wie kommt dieser Hund hierher? — Er ist mir nachgelaufen.

Wer geht dem Oheim entgegen? — Karl und ich gehen ihm entgegen.

Hat das Konzert' gestern statt= gefunden (taken place)? — Nein, es findet erst (only) heute statt.

Konnte man dieses vorher'sehen? — Gewiß, es war leicht vorherzusehen.

Wollen Sie ein wenig herauf= kommen? — Ich habe jetzt keine Zeit, hinauf= zugehen.

Können Sie morgen herüber= kommen? — Ja, ich werde einen Augenblick hinüberkommen.

Ist es erlaubt, hinein zu gehen? — Ja, mein Herr, kommen Sie nur herein.

Bringt man meinen Koffer (port-manteau) herauf? — Er ist schon oben (up stairs). Ich habe ihn selbst hinaufgetragen.

---

## 3.  Separable and inseparable verbs.

In consequence of a different meaning, some verbs compounded with durch, über, unter and um, must be treated as separable, others as inseparable verbs.*)

A. When durch, über, unter and um are separable:

When such verbs have a double accent, one on the prefix — which is the principal and decisive one, comp. p. 206. — the other on the verb, they are *separable*, and treated like all separable verbs. Ex.:

Durch'rei'sen *reg.* to travel through, like ab'rei'sen. *Pres.* ich reise . . durch  *Perf.* ich bin durch'gereist.

In this case, the prepositions durch, über, unter, um, are taken in their full and natural sense; so that their meaning prevails over that of the verb. **Most of such verbs are intransitive and take the auxiliary sein.** Ex.:

*) In English a few examples of such verbs are still found, as: *I look over* and *I overlook; I set up* and *I upset; I undergo* and *I go under* etc.

Ich bin hier über'gesetzt *I have* crossed here.

Das Boot ist untergegangen the boat *has* sunk *or* gone down

### Such separable verbs are:

*a*) Compounded with durch.

Durch'schnei'den to cut through. | durch'streich'en to strike out, cross.
durch'zieh'en to pull through. | †durch'fah'ren to pass through.
durch'setz'en to attain, obtain |

*Part. p.* durch'geschnitten, durch'gezogen, durch'gestrichen.

*b*) Compounded with über.

†ü'bergeh'en to pass over. | †ü'berfahren | to ferry *or* carry
†ü'berlaufen to run over. | †ü'berfetzen | to cross. [over
u'bergießen to pour upon. | ü'berwerfen to throw over

*Part. p.* übergegangen, übergelaufen, übergefahren 2c

*Note 1.* These six verbs are the only *separables* with über

*Note 2.* Überfahren and überfetzen with the same meaning to cross are also used as inseparable and active verbs.

*c*) Compounded with unter.

†Un'tergehen to go down, to | un'terbringen to shelter.
set, sink. | †un'terstehen to go under shelter.

*d*) Compounded with um.

†Um'kehren *reg.* to turn round. | †um'sinken to sink down, to fall
†um'fallen to fall (over), upset. | um'drehen to turn. [over.
um'werfen to upset, overturn. | †um'gehen to have intercourse.
um'kleiden to dress anew. | †um'kommen to perish
um'bringen to kill. | um'stoßen to overthrow etc.

### Examples

Dieser Mann setzt alles durch (attains everything).
Wir haben unser Vorhaben durch'gesetzt.
We have succeeded in our design.
Die Milch ist über'gelaufen the milk has run over
Das Boot geht unter the boat is sinking.
Herkulanum und Pompeji sind unter'gegangen
Herculanum and Pompeji have perished (sunk).
Nach einer Stunde kehrte ich um (I returned).
Der Knabe hat den Stuhl umgeworfen.
The boy has upset the chair.

B. When durch, über, unter and um are inseparable:

When these prefixes, burch, über, unter and um, are taken in a figurative sense, and when therefore they do not lessen the actual meaning of the verb itself, they are used as *inseparables*. The difference, for instance, between burd'rei'fen (*sep.*) and burdrei'fen, (*insep.*) is this The first, being doubly accented, means to *travel right through*, *to pass through*, with the purpose of reaching another destination; whereas burdreif'en, whose prefix burd is unaccented [comp. p. 206.], means to travel *over* or *about* a country, not straight *through*, so as to leave to the verb reifen its full meaning, viz.· *travelling*.

**Most transitive verbs compounded with über and unter are inseparable,** have therefore no ge in the *Part. past* and take haben.

Such inseparable verbs (with haben) are:

*a*) Inseparables compounded with burd.

Durdrei'fen *r.* to travel over. | burdblät'tern to peruse, to turn
burdbre'den to break through. | over the leaves.
burdbring'en to penetrate. | burdfu'den *reg.* to search.
burdboh'ren *reg.* to pierce. | burdfte'den to dig through etc.

*Part.* burdreift', burdbroden, burdbrungen, burdbohrt 2c.

*b*) Inseparables compounded with über.

überge'ben *ir.* to hand. | übertreff'en *reg.* to excel, surpass.
überfet'en *reg.* to translate. | überbring'en to deliver, to bear.
übergeh'en to miss, omit, skip. | überneh'men *ir.* to undertake
überhäu'fen *r.* to heap, overload. | überzeu'gen *reg.* to convince etc.

*Part.* überge'ben, überfett', übergangen, übertroffen, überzeugt.

*c*) Inseparables compounded with unter.

Unterfu'den *reg.* to examine. | unterjod'en *reg.* to subjugate.
unterneh'men *ir.* to undertake. | unterbrü'den to subdue, oppress.
unterfdrei'ben *ir.* } to sign, to | unterhal'ten to entertain, amuse.
unterzeichnen *reg.* } subscribe | unterrid'ten *r.* to instruct, teach.

*Part.* unterfudt', unternommen, unterfdrieben, unterhalten 2c.

*d*) Inseparables compounded with um.

Umar'men *reg.* to embrace. | umgeh'en *ir.* to avoid.
umrin'gen *reg.* } to surround. | umfdif'fen to circumnavigate.
umge'ben *ir.* } to encircle. | umwölf'en *reg.* to cloud (over).

**Examples.**

Id burdrei'fe ganz Deutfdland I am travelling all over
Id habe ganz Deutfdland burdreift'. [Germany.
Id überfet'e Sdillers Wilhelm Tell.
I translate Schiller's William Tell.
Id habe fdon die Hälfte (the half) überfett'.
Bitte, unterfuden Sie jene Kifte pray, examine that box.

Ich habe sie schon unterfucht'.
I have already examined it.
Umarme mich, mein Sohn embrace me, my son.
Der Sohn hat den Vater umarmt'.

*Note 1.* There is also *one* inseparable verb compounded
with wieder, viz.: wiederholen to repeat, as:

Haben Sie Ihre Aufgabe wiederholt? have you repeated your l.?
Ich wiederhole sie jeden Tag I repeat it every day.

All other verbs compounded with wieder are separable,
and are mostly written as two words. Ex.:

Mein Bruder ist wiedergekommen or better wieder gekommen.

*NB.* The prefix spelled wider, is inseparable. See p. 201.

*Note 2.* Only a few verbs admit of both the separable
and inseparable form, such as: ü'berfetzen and überfetz'en;
ü'bergeh'en and übergeh'en :c.

---

### Words.

Die Stränge, *pl.* the traces.
der Polizeidiener the constable.
der Verstand understanding.
die Schrift the writing.
das Gefühl sentiment, feeling.
die Leitung the management.
die Einbildungskraft the imagi-
  nation.

die Schärfe acuteness, keenness.
die Geduld patience.
der Mantel the cloak.
der Satz the sentence.
der Kutscher the coachman.
der Sturm the storm.
dialektisches Denken logical rea-
  soning.

### Reading Exercise. 80.

1. Man hat die Stränge des Pferdes durchgeschnitten. Es
regnet stark, lassen Sie uns un'terstehen.*) Gestern sind wir auch
untergestanden, als es anfing, heftig zu regnen. Mit Geduld
setzt man alles durch. Nach einer Stunde sind wir umgekehrt.
Gestern ist jemand im Wald umgebracht worden. Ist dies der
Schiffer, welcher uns übergesetzt hat? Kennen Sie den Schriftsteller (author), welcher Lamartines Schriften ins Deutsche über-
setzt hat? Der Kaiser von Österreich hat die ganze Provinz
durchreist. Die Römer haben viele Völker unterjocht.

2. Der Polizeidiener hat das ganze Haus durchsucht. Mein
Sohn hat die Leitung des Geschäftes übernommen. Ihre Worte
haben mich von der Wahrheit der Sache überzeugt. In dieser
Schule werden die Knaben bis (till) zu ihrem 14ten Jahre unterrichtet. Wie konnten Sie [es] unternehmen, dies zu thun?

---

*) Obs. Un'terste'hen, ich stand unter, ich bin untergestanden
is only used in South-Germany, in the northern parts they say
either sich un'terste'llen or un'tertre'ten.

Schiller übertrifft alle deutschen Dichter (poets) an Tiefe des Gefühls, Lebhaftigkeit der Einbildungskraft und Schärfe des dialektischen Denkens; aber er wird von Göthe an Genauigkeit der Beobachtung (exactness of observation), an angebornem Reichtum poëtischer Anschauung (inborn richness of poetical intuition) und an praktischem Verstande übertroffen. Plötzlich sahen wir uns von dem Feinde umringt. Ich bitte Sie, bald wieder zu kommen.

### Aufgabe. 81.

1. When (Als) we came to (an, *acc.*) the river, ²we ¹crossed in a little boat. Can you tell me, who has translated Milton's Paradise Lost (verlornes Paradies)? I have no mind (keine Lust) to translate this book. You should (ought to) throw on (*or* over) your cloak. A whole regiment of infantry (Infanterie-Regiment) went (sing.) over to (zu) the enemy. Why have you skipped this sentence? I omitted it, because it seemed to me too difficult. Three vessels went down (perished) in the last storm.

2. The coachman has upset the carriage. Have (sind) you *had much intercourse* with Mr. Adam? I wish I were so happy [as] to have much intercourse with him. What business have you undertaken? Have you repeated your lesson? You must change your dress (sich umkleiden), or (sonst) ²you ¹can not go with us. This box (Kiste, *f*) must *be* examined. Our house is surrounded with a garden. Mr. F. has killed himself. Have you a wish to sign this paper? I have already signed it.

### Reading-lesson.

#### Der Sirokko. The Sirocco.

Eine der größten Plagen[1] für ganz Italien, besonders[2] für Neapel und Sicilien, ist der Sirokko. Er heißt auch Südostwind, in Afrika der Samum, in der Schweiz der Föhn. In Neapel und in andern Teilen Italiens weht[3] er nicht so heftig wie in Sicilien, welches näher bei Afrika liegt; aber er dauert[4] mehrere Wochen und läßt Mutlosigkeit[5] und Niedergeschlagenheit[6] zurück. In Neapel weht er im Juli so heiß, daß die Menschen ganz erschlafft[7] und entnervt[8] werden. Alle Thätigkeit[9] in dem Menschen erstirbt[10], und die gefährlichsten[11] Folgen[12] würden daraus entstehen (arise), wenn er in Sicilien länger als 30 bis 40 Stunden wehte, und nicht ein Nordwind ihm folgte (translate von einem Nordwind gefolgt[13] wäre), welcher die Menschen wieder stärkt.

1) plague. 2) especially. 3) to blow. 4) dauern to last. —
5) despondency. 6) dejection. 7) relaxed. 8) enervated. 9) energy.
10) ersterben to die away, cease. 11) dangerous. 12) consequence.
13) followed

Sobald (As soon as) der Sirokko zu wehen anfängt, zieht[14] sich jedermann in die Häuser zurück, macht Thüren und Fenster zu, oder behängt[15], in Ermangelung[16] von Fensterscheiben (panes), die Fenster und andre Öffnungen[17] mit nassen Tüchern und Matten[18]. In den Straßen sieht man keinen Menschen. Auch in den Feldern thut der Sirokko oft großen Schaden[19]; er ver= sengt[20] das Gras und die Pflanzen so, daß man sie zu Pulver zerreiben[21] kann, als wenn sie aus einem heißen Ofen kämen. Glücklicherweise[22] weht er nicht ganz nahe am Boden[23]. Die Leute, welche in dem Felde sind, werfen[24] sich deswegen auf den Boden nieder[24], und so thut er ihnen keinen Schaden (harm).

14) sich zurückziehen to retire.   15) to hang, cover with   16) in the absence.   17) openings   18) mats   19) much damage.   20) to singe, scorch.   21) to grind, rub to powder.   22) fortunately. 23) ground   24) to prostrate one's self

---

# Thirty-second Lesson.

## Neuter and intransitive verbs.

### (Neutrale Zeitwörter.)

*Neuter verbs* are those which ascribe to the subject a *state* or *condition*, which is neither *active* nor *passive*; and *intransitive verbs* are those which express an action that does not pass over to an object. Of the first kind are ich stehe I stand; ich sitze I sit; ich liege I lie etc. Of the second description are: ich gehe I walk; ich komme I come; ich fahre I drive *or* ride in a carriage.

Their conjugation does not differ from that of the active verb, except in the compound tenses where they are mostly*) conjugated with the auxiliary sein (to be).

*) The following *intransitive* verbs, some of which are occas-ionally used as active with an accusative, are conjugated with haben:

| | |
|---|---|
| antworten to answer. | leben to live. |
| arbeiten to work. | ringen to wrestle. |
| atmen to breathe. | pfeifen to whistle. |
| bellen to bark. | ruhen to rest. |
| blühen to bloom. | scheinen to shine, seem. |
| bluten to bleed. | schweigen to be silent. |
| dauern to last. | schlafen to sleep. |
| fechten to fight. | schreien to cry out. |
| glänzen to glitter. | siegen to conquer. |
| horchen to listen. | speien to spit. |
| kämpfen to fight. | weinen to weep, cry. |
| krähen to crow. | zögern to hesitate. |
| lachen to laugh | wohnen to reside, to dwell. |

We subjoin here an example of a regular and an irregular intransitive verb

## 1. Reiſen to travel.

| Indicative. | Subjunctive |
|---|---|
| | |

*Present.* Ich reiſe I travel | Ich reiſe
*Imperf.* Ich reiſte I travelled | Ich reiſte.
*Perfect.* Ich bin gereiſt I *have* tra- | Ich ſei gereiſt
du biſt gereiſt [velled | du ſeiſt gereiſt
er iſt gereiſt | er ſei gereiſt

wir ſind gereiſt | wir ſeien gereiſt
{ihr ſeid gereiſt | {ihr ſeiet gereiſt
{Sie ſind gereiſt | {Sie ſeien gereiſt
ſie ſind gereiſt. | ſie ſeien gereiſt.

*Pluperf.* Ich war gereiſt | Ich wäre gereiſt
du warſt gereiſt | du wäreſt gereiſt
er war gereiſt | er wäre gereiſt

wir waren gereiſt | wir wären gereiſt
Sie waren gereiſt | Sie wären gereiſt
ſie waren gereiſt. | ſie wären gereiſt.

1st *Fut.* Ich werde reiſen | Ich werde reiſen
2nd *Fut* Ich werde gereiſt ſein | Ich werde gereiſt ſein
du wirſt gereiſt ſein ꝛc. | du werdeſt gereiſt ſein ꝛc.

1st *Cond.* Ich würde reiſen I should travel.
2nd *Cond.* Ich würde gereiſt ſein or ich wäre gereiſt ꝛc.
*Infinitive.* Gereiſt ſein or zu ſein to *have* travelled

## 2. Gehen to go.

*Present.* Ich gehe I go | Ich gehe
*Imperf.* Ich ging I went | Ich ginge.
du gingſt, er ging ꝛc |
*Perfect.* Ich bin gegangen I *have* | Ich ſei gegangen
du biſt gegangen [gone | du ſeiſt gegangen
er iſt gegangen | er ſei gegangen

wir ſind gegangen | wir ſeien gegangen
Sie ſind gegangen | Sie ſeien gegangen
ſie ſind gegangen. | ſie ſeien gegangen.

---

*Perf.* Ich habe gearbeitet, ich habe geblutet, ich habe gelebt, ich habe geſchlafen, ich habe gelacht, ich habe gewohnt ꝛc

*NB.* Some verbs have a double auxiliary haben and ſein, as: abtreten *act.* to yield up, — †abtreten *neut.* to go away, beſtehen *act.* to stand the test; — ‡beſtehen *neut.* to consist of. fortfahren to continue; Ex : Er hat fortgefahren zu arbeiten ‡fortfahren to go away in a carriage. Ex:. Die Dame iſt f

*Pluperf.*  Ich war gegangen.          | Ich wäre gegangen.
1st *Fut.*  Ich werde gehen.           | Ich werde gehen.
1st *Cond.*  Ich würde gehen.          | —          —
2nd *Fut.*  Ich werde gegangen sein.   | Ich werde gegangen sein.
2nd *Cond.*  Ich würde gegangen sein or ich wäre gegangen ꝛc.
*Infinitive.*  Gegangen sein to *have* gone.

*Note.* From their nature, these verbs cannot have a passive voice. Some of them, however, occur as impersonal verbs in the third person singular of the passive form, as:

Es wird gesprochen, — gelacht, — gereist ꝛc.
There is talking, — laughing, — travelling etc.

## 3. A list of the neuter and intransitive verbs,
which (commonly) take in German the auxiliary
sein (to be), in English *to have.*

| | |
|---|---|
| Ab'laufen (Zeit) to expire. | nfolgen (*dat.*) to follow. |
| ab'weichen to deviate. | gedeihen to prosper, to thrive. |
| Rab'reifen*) to leave, set out, | gehen to go. |
| an'kommen to arrive.  [start. | gelingen ⎱ to succeed. |
| auf'stehen to get up, to rise. | geraten ⎰ |
| Rauf'wachen*) to awake. | genesen to recover. |
| Raus'arten to degenerate. | geraten (in or unter etwas) to |
| aus'gleiten to slip | get into, to fall among. |
| Rbegegnen**) to meet, happen. | geschehen to happen. |
| bleiben to remain, to stay. | hinaufgehen or =steigen to go up. |
| bersten to burst | hinuntergehen ⎱ to get down, |
| davonlaufen to run away. | hinabsteigen ⎰ to descend. |
| entlaufen to abscond. | nklettern ⎱ to climb. |
| Reilen to hasten. | klimmen ⎰ |
| eindringen to penetrate. | kommen to come |
| einschlafen to fall asleep. | nlanden to land, go on shore. |
| entkommen to escape. | laufen to run. |
| entfliehen to run away. | Rmarschieren to march |
| erbleichen to turn pale. | reiten to ride, to go on horse- |
| erscheinen to appear. | Rreisen to travel.  [back. |
| erschrecken to be frightened. | Rennen to run. |
| ertrinken to be drowned | Rrollen to roll. |
| fahren to drive. | Rrosten to rust. |
| fallen to fall. | nscheitern to be wrecked, to |
| Rfaulen to rot. | founder. |
| Rflattern to flutter | schleichen to sneak, slink. |
| fliegen to fly. | schmelzen to melt. |
| fliehen to flee | schwimmen to swim. |
| fließen to flow. | sinken to sink. |

*) Those preceded by R are regular, all others irregular.
**) Begegnen takes also haben with the acc.

| | |
|---|---|
| fpazieren gehen to walk. | verfcheiden to expire. |
| fpringen to leap, to burst. | fteigen to mount. |
| ftehen to stand. | verfchwinden to disappear |
| fterben to die. | vorbei=, vorüber'gehen to pass by. |
| uftürzen to fall, to rush. | wachfen to grow. |
| überein'fommen to agree. | uwandern to wander. |
| um'fommen } to perish, | weichen to yield. |
| unter'gehen } to set (of the sun). | werden to become, to get. |
| uverdorren } to dry, | uzurück'fehren } to return, |
| uverwelfen } to wither. | zurückommen } to come back. |

Besides these, most of the above verbs when compounded
with other prefixes, but not preceded by be. *)

4. By a change of the vowel or a consonant, *transitive* verbs with a *causative* signification have been formed
of the following *intransitives*. Whereas these latter are
mostly *irregular* and take fein, the former are all *regular*
and conjugated with haben.

| *Intransitive* (with fein) | *Transitive & regular* (with haben). |
|---|---|
| †Einfchlafen to fall asleep: | einfchläfern to put or lull asleep. |
| †ertrinfen to be drowned: | ertränfen to drown. |
| †fahren to drive | führen to guide, to lead. |
| †fallen to fall: | fällen to fell, to cut down. |
| †fliefgen to flow. | flöfgen to float. |
| †hangen to hang (suspended) | hängen to hang up |
| lauten to sound· | läuten to ring the bell. |
| †liegen to lie: **) | legen to lay, to put. |
| †fchwimmen to swim. | fchwemmen to (make) bathe, to water (horses). |
| †finfen to sink: | fenfen to (make) sink. |
| †fitzen to sit: **) | fetzen to place, to set. |
| †fpringen 1) to leap, to jump, 2) to burst, to crack. | fprengen or auffprengen to break open, to blow up |
| †ftehen to stand· **) | ftellen to put upright, to stand. |
| †fteigen to mount: | fteigern to raise, to enhance. |
| †verfchwinden to vanish, dis- | verfchwenden to waste. |
| trinfen to drink } [appear: | tränfen to water. |
| wiegen to weigh, } (take haben): | wägen to weigh = to ascertain |
| to be of weight } | weight (*Part.* gewogen). |

---

*) The prefix **be** gives an *active* sense to the verb, as ftei-
gen *intr.* to mount; befteigen *act* to ascend; befolgen to follow,
befommen to get etc All verbs with be take haben, except
begegnen, when construed with the dative.

**) See *) p. 165.

## Words.

Die Schildwache the sentinel,
das Thor the gate. [sentry.
der Knall the report, crack.
das Unternehmen the under-
taking, enterprise.
die Achtung esteem.
der Mitbürger fellow-citizen.
der Holzhauer the wood-cutter.
die Küste the coast, shore
die Ladung the cargo, load.
der Graben the ditch.
die Familie the family.

der Leuchter } the candlestick.
der Lichtstock }
der Boden the ground, floor.
die Gefahr the danger.
der Sklave the slave.
der Koffer the trunk.
zu Bett gehen to go to bed.
fürchterlich dreadful.
hierher hither.   müde tired.
vorsichtig cautious.
holländisch Dutch.
gewöhnlich generally.

### Reading-Exercise. 82.

1. Das Buch liegt auf dem Tisch(e). Ich schlief unter einem
Baum. Die Schildwache ist am Thore gestanden. Die Mädchen
sind in den Garten gegangen. Wir sind gestern vom Lande
zurückgekehrt, wo wir drei Wochen geblieben waren. Mein Freund
ist (was) in England geboren. Auf (upon) die Nachricht von der
Krankheit seines Sohnes ist der Vater hierher gereist. Der Krieg
zwischen diesen zwei Völkern (nations) hat noch nicht begonnen.
Wir sind alle über (at) diesen fürchterlichen Knall erschrocken. Was
ist ihm geschehen? Das große Unternehmen des Herrn Turner
ist nicht gelungen.

2. Dieser Mann ist in der Achtung seiner Mitbürger sehr
gesunken. Der Soldat ist an (of) seinen Wunden gestorben. Der
Schnee ist geschmolzen. Das Fleisch ist nicht genug gebraten
(roasted). Der Holzhauer hat die Eiche gefällt. Ein Raben-Nest
ist heruntergefallen. Viele Arten (kinds) von Tieren sind von
der Erde verschwunden, welche in früheren (former) Zeiten darauf
gelebt haben. Ein holländisches Schiff ist an der Küste Afrikas
gescheitert; die ganze Ladung ist untergegangen. Der größte Teil
der Mannschaft (crew) ist (have) umgekommen; nur einige Matrosen, welche ans Land geschwommen sind, haben sich gerettet.

### Aufgabe. 83.

1. I travelled in Spain. Our uncle (is) arrived yesterday.
The child *has* fallen into a deep ditch. We sat round (um)
the table  The candlestick stands on (auf, dat.) the table.
The little boy sits on the chair; his mother placed (setzte) him
on it (darauf). Many English families live[1] in Germany and
Italy. The books lie on the table; I laid them on it. How
did you (haben Sie) sleep last night? I slept pretty (ziemlich)

---

1) To live (in a country) means leben, to live in a house etc,
is translated wohnen.

well; I was tired *when* (als) I went to (ju) bed; I had worked
very hard (ſtark). At what o'clock *did* you (ſind Sie) fall
asleep? I fell asleep at half past eleven. The slave *has*
hardly (kaum) escaped.

2. The purse *has* fallen to (auf) the ground. The regiment *has* marched[1]) nine hours a (den) day. The peasants
*have* gone· to (in die) town. The servant *has* jumped out of
the window of the third story (Stock, m.). Nothing important
(Wichtiges) *has* happened. These plants *have* not thriven in
our garden. The glass *has* burst (cracked). They (man)
have broken open (p. 221) the door. The dog *has* *swum* over
the river. Did you water the horses? How many pounds
does the trunk weigh? We have not yet weighed it; I think
it weighs sixty pounds. Weigh it, if you please (gefälligſt).
A man was (iſt) drowned.

## Conversation.

Was iſt geſchehen?

Um wieviel Uhr ſind Sie von
Franffurt abgereiſt?

Wann ſind Sie hier ange-
kommen?

Wann ſtehen Sie des Morgens
auf (get up)?

Warum ſind Sie ſo erſchrocken?

Sind Sie allein nach Brüſſel
gereiſt?

Wollen Sie ein wenig mit uns
ſpazieren gehen?

Wann iſt Ihr Freund zurückgekehrt?

Wie kommt es, daß dieſer Baum
umgefallen iſt?

Warum iſt (has) dieſe Familie ſo
arm geworden?

Wo haben Sie dieſe Karte gefunden?

Wer hat ſie dahin geworfen?  .

Hat man die Pferde getränkt
(watered)?

Es iſt etwas Wichtiges geſchehcn.

Wir ſind um halb ſechs abgereiſt.

Gegen zehn Uhr.

Gewöhnlich um 6 Uhr; aber heute
bin ich um 7 Uhr aufgeſtanden.

Wir haben einen fürchterlichen
Knall gehört.

Nein, mein Bruder iſt mitge-
gangen.

Wir danken Ihnen, wir ſind dieſen
Morgen ſchon gegangen.

Vor drei Wochen (—ago): aber
er iſt nicht hier geblieben, er
iſt wieder abgereiſt.

Der Holzhauer hat ihn gefällt.

Weil der Vater nicht arbeiten
wollte.

Sie iſt auf dem Boden (floor) gelegen (or ſie lag auf dem B.).

Ich kann es nicht ſagen; vielleicht
(perhaps) iſt ſie hinuntergefallen.

Ja, der Stallknecht (hostler) hat
ſie eben (just now) getränkt.

---

1) See p. 126, 4).

# Thirty-third Lesson.

## IMPERSONAL VERBS.

(Unperjönliche Zeitwörter.)

True impersonal verbs have, as in English, besides the *Infinitive*, only the third person *singular* throughout. Most of them are the same in both languages, as:

| *Infinitive.* | *Present.* |
|---|---|
| Regnen to rain. | es regnet it rains. |
| ſchneien to snow. | es ſchneit it snows. |
| hageln to hail | es hagelt it hails. |
| donnern to thunder. | es donnert it thunders. |
| blitzen to lighten. | es blitzt it lightens. |
| gefrieren to freeze. | es gefriert (friert) it freezes. |
| reifen to be a hoar frost. | es reift it is a hoar frost. |
| tauen to thaw (and to dew). | es taut it thaws. |
| tagen to dawn. | es tagt it dawns. |
| geben (there .. to be). | es giebt there is. |

They are all regular verbs, except es friert; (*P.* gefroren, see p. 185. Nr. 117) and es giebt (*Part.* gegeben).

All are conjugated with the auxiliary haben. Ex.·
Es hat geregnet, es hat gedonnert, es hat geblitzt ꝛc.

## Table of conjugation.

### 1. Schneien to snow.

#### Indicative Mood.

| | |
|---|---|
| *Present.* | es ſchneit it snows. |
| *Imperfect.* | es ſchneite it snowed. |
| *Perfect.* | es hat geſchneit it has snowed. |
| *Pluperf.* | es hatte geſchneit it had snowed |
| 1st *Fut.* | es wird ſchneien it will snow. |
| 1st *Cond.* | es würde ſchneien it would snow. |
| 2nd *Fut.* | es wird geſchneit haben it will have snowed. |
| 2nd *Cond.* | es würde geſchneit haben ⎫ it would have snowed or es hätte geſchneit ⎭ |

#### Subjunctive Mood.

| | |
|---|---|
| *Present.* | daß es ſchneie. |
| *Imperfect.* | daß es ſchnei(e)te. |
| *Perfect.* | daß es geſchneit habe. |
| *Pluperf.* | daß es geſchneit hätte |
| 1st *Fut.* | daß es ſchneien werde. |

## 2. Es giebt (or gibt) there is, there are.

*Present.* es giebt there is, there are.
*Imperfect.* es gab there was, there were.
*Perfect.* es hat gegeben there has (have) been.
*Pluperf.* es hatte gegeben there had been.
1st *Fut.* es wird geben there will be.
1st *Cond.* es würde geben (es gäbe) there would be.
2nd *Fut.* es wird gegeben haben there will have been.
2nd *Cond.* es würde gegeben haben there would have been.
*(Potential.* es mag or kann geben there may (can) be.)

## Observations.

1) *There is, there are,* must be translated **es giebt,** when they express *indefinite existence* without mentioning a *distinct* (small) place. It always remains in the *singular,* and takes its object in the *accusative.* Ex.·

Es giebt gute und schlechte Bücher.
There are good books and bad ones.

Es giebt Leute, welche die Schönheit der Tugend vorziehen.
There are people who prefer beauty to virtue.

Es giebt Vogelnester,*) welche eßbar sind.
There are nests of birds which are eatable.

Was giebt es Neues? what (is the) news?

Es giebt nichts Neues there is no news.

*NB.* With es giebt, the es is never dropped

2) *There is* has also the meaning es ist, *there are* es sind; *there was* es war, pl. *there were* es waren. This is always the case, when a *definite existence,* in `a *distinct small place* or *space,* is expressed. With this, the noun is in the *nominative* case  Ex .

Es ist ein Vogel in dem Käfig.
There is a bird in the cage.

Es war kein Wasser in dem Glas.
There was no water in the glass.

Es sind zwei Vögel in dem Käfig
There are two birds in the cage.

Es ist kein Platz mehr auf dieser Bank.
There is no more room on this bench.

*NB.* When *there is etc.,* in the sense of es ist, are used in the *interrogative* or *inverted* form, the es is dropped. Ex :

---

*) It would be the same to say  Es giebt Vogelnest'er in Amerika or in Indien or in diesem Land, because America (*or* India etc ) is not a *small* (*narrowly* circumscribed) place

Ift Wein in jener Flaſche?
Is there any wine in that bottle?
Wie viele Vögel ſind in dem Käfig?
How many birds are (*there*) in the cage?

3) To indicate *weather* or *time*, impersonal sentences are
formed with es iſt, as in English:

| | |
|---|---|
| Es iſt kalt it is cold. | es iſt ſpät it is late. |
| es iſt warm it is warm. | es iſt Abend it is evening. |
| es iſt dunkel it is dark. | es iſt halb ſechs Uhr it is half |
| es iſt feucht it is damp. | past five etc. |

#### Other verbs used impersonally.

4) Further, there are some other verbs which are occasionally *used as impersonal verbs*, both in the singular and plural:

| | |
|---|---|
| Es ſcheint it seems, appears. | es läutet the bell rings. |
| es betrifft it concerns. | es fängt an it begins. |
| es folgt it follows. | es hört auf it ceases. |
| es fehlt (it) is wanting. | es erhellt it is evident. |
| es geſchieht it happens. | es nutzt nichts it is of no use. |
| es genügt it suffices. | es bedarf it requires. |
| es ſchlägt zehn Uhr it strikes ten | es kommt darauf an it depends. |
| o'clock. | es iſt kein Zweifel there is no doubt. |

#### Reflected impersonals.

5) Others occur impersonally used with a personal pronoun:

a) *In the accusative.*

| | |
|---|---|
| Es 'freut mich*) I am glad. | es wundert mich*) I wonder. |
| es reut mich I repent. | es hungert mich**) I am hungry. |
| es ſchmerzt mich I grieve. | es bürſtet mich**) I am thirsty. |
| es friert mich*) I am cold. | es langweilt mich it wearies |
| es ſchaudert mich*) I shudder. | (me). |
| es jammert mich I pity. | es ſchickt ſich it is proper. |
| es ekelt mich it disgusts (me). | es verſteht ſich of course, it is |
| es ärgert mich*) I am vexed. | a matter of course. |
| es verdrießt mich it vexes me. | es fragt ſich it is (a) question. |

b) *In the dative.*

Es iſt mir leid } I am sorry.　　es gefällt mir } I am pleased,
es thut mir leid }　　　　　　es beliebt mir } I like.

---

*) These five marked*) are used also personally, viz. Ich freue
mich, ich friere, ich wundre mich, ich ſchaudre, ich ärgre mich ꝛc.
**) Es hungert mich and es bürſtet mich are used especially in
poetry as well as ich hungere, ich burſte; the common prose expression
is: ich bin hungrig; ich bin durſtig; or ich habe Hunger, ich habe
Durſt.

es nüßt mir nichts it is of no use to me. [me.

es ahnt mir my heart misgives

es schwindelt mir I am giddy.

es dünkt mir methinks.

†es gelingt mir I succeed.

es begegnet mir it happens to me

es liegt mir viel daran it is very important for me.

es kommt mir vor } it seems to es scheint mir  } me.

es fällt mir ein it occurs to me.

es ist mir wohl I feel well.

es ist mir warm*) I am warm.

was fehlt Ihnen? what is the matter with you?

wie geht es Ihnen? how are you?

es geht mir gut I am well.

6) By a transposition of the subject after the verb, the latter takes sometimes an *impersonal* form both in the singular and plural, the (first) place of the subject being filled up by es (in English *there*). This however is rather poetical, as:

Es kam ein Wandrer die Straße entlang.
There came a wanderer along the road.

Es gingen drei Jäger auf die Jagd.
Three sportsmen went shooting.

Es fielen Hagelkörner so groß wie Tauben-Eier.
There fell hailstones as large as pigeons' eggs.

7) The *impersonal* form appears also in the Passive Voice of active and neuter verbs**) in the 3rd person as:

Es wird in Deutschland viel gesungen und getanzt.

or: Man singt und tanzt viel in Deutschland.
They sing and dance much in Germany.

or: There is much singing in Germany.

Es wurde viel gegessen, aber mehr getrunken.
Much was eaten, but more drunk.

Es wird viel von dem Krieg geredet (or gesprochen).
There is much talking about war.

---

## Words.

Das Holz the wood.

der Betrüger the cheat.

die Beharrlichkeit perseverance.

die Schwierigkeit the difficulty.

eine Brille a pair of spectacles.

das Tintenfaß the inkstand.

der Philosoph' the philosopher.

die Kleider *pl.* clothes.

die Gesellschaft the company.

das Schauspiel play, spectacle.

überwin'den to overcome.

hell clear. offen open.

dauern to last. noch still.

die Welt the world. doch yet.

ewig eternal, everlasting.

glauben to believe, to think.

heftig violent. handeln to act.

folglich consequently.

---

*) We cannot say: ich bin warm, we may say also · ich habe warm, the best way is . es ist mir warm. Likewise do not say ich bin kalt; but ich habe kalt or ich friere, or es friert mich.

**) Like the Latin *itur, venitur, ventum est* (see the Note p. 220).

15*

### Reading Exercise. 84.

1. Schneit es? Nein, es schneit nicht; es regnet. Es wird bald hageln. Es wäre gut, wenn es schnette. Es würde schneien, wenn es nicht so kalt wäre. Eben (just now) hat es gedonnert Es wird noch mehr donnern. Die Kälte ist vorbei (over), es taut. Ich glaube, daß es morgen tauen wird. Es reut mich, daß ich gestern nicht nach Mannheim gegangen bin. Es wird Sie reuen, wenn Sie das Pferd nicht kaufen. Wie gefällt es Ihnen in Paris? Es gefällt mir sehr wohl Es wundert mich, daß Sie noch hier sind. Es verdrießt mich, daß ich nicht dagewesen bin. Scheint es Ihnen nicht, als ob (as if) einiges von diesem Holze gestohlen worden wäre? Es fängt an, hell zu werden.

2. Es nützt Ihnen nichts, so viele Bücher zu kaufen, wenn Sie sie nicht lesen. Es folgt aus Ihrer Erzählung (from your report), daß der Kaufmann ein Betrüger ist. Es fehlt heute ein Schüler. Es reut mich, meine Uhr verkauft zu haben. Es giebt ein ewiges Leben. Wenn es kein ewiges Leben gäbe, so wären die Menschen unglücklicher als die Tiere Mit (by) Be=harrlichkeit gelingt es uns, alle Schwierigkeiten zu überwinden. Es gefiel mir sehr wohl in der Gesellschaft jener jungen Leute. Es giebt Brillen für alle Augen, folglich wird es auch eine (some) für die Ihrigen geben. Es stand ein Wagen vor dem Hause.

### Aufgabe. 85.

1. It rains, yesterday ²it ¹snowed Last (Letzten) winter ²it ¹snowed much. It will soon rain. It has rained all night (die ganze Nacht), and this morning (acc.) ²it ¹freezes. It thunders; do you hear it? How many times (mal) has it thundered? It has just (eben) lightened. I did not think that it would lighten. Is [there any] ink (Tinte) in your inkstand? There will be a great many (sehr viele) walnuts this year. There are streets in London which are two miles long There are people who believe nothing. There have been philosophers at (zu) all times. Is [there a] fire in my room? No, Sir, there is no fire in your room, but I will make [one] directly (gleich).

2. The boy is hungry and thirsty. It is very important to me to know what they do. I shudder when (wenn) I think how many [of the] poor ·have ¹no ²warm ³clothes, although (obschon) it ³freezes ¹so ²hard (stark). We wonder that he is silent (schweigt). It does not seem to me that you will succeed. Mr. Dean had company last night (gestern Abend); they played and danced much. It occurs to me that I have left my door open. It appears that he has not attended (sich . . . abgegeben hat) to (mit) that business. It is proper to act so There were already a great many people in the ball-room (im Ball=saal) when I arrived. There was no play yesterday. I do not think, that there can be a more beautiful old castle in the world than that of Heidelberg. Is there any news (any-thing new)? There is no news (nothing new) to-day.

## Conversation.

Donnert es?

Haben Sie den Blitz gesehen?

Glauben Sie, daß es heute Nacht gefrieren wird?

Wie gefällt es Ihnen in London?

Hat es Ihrem Bruder in Amerika gefallen?

Ist es kalt?

Fehlt etwas an diesem Gelde?

Glauben Sie, daß das Wetter sich ändern (change) wird?

Wird es dieses Jahr guten Wein geben?

Genügt es, meinen Namen zu unterschreiben?

Was fehlt ihm?

Was verdrießt Sie?

Was ist Ihnen geschehen?

Warum sind Sie so traurig?

Ist noch Platz für mich auf dieser Bank (bench)?

Giebt es etwas Neues?

Ich habe nichts gehört.

Ja, es hat sehr stark geblitzt.

Ich glaube nicht, daß es gefrieren wird; aber es wird schneien.

Es gefällt mir sehr wohl.

Es scheint, daß es ihm sehr gut gefallen hat.

Nein, es ist nicht mehr kalt.

Ja, es fehlen drei Mark.

Es scheint mir so; wenigstens fängt es an, warm zu werden.

Die Rebleute*) (vine-growers) sagen, daß es sehr viel Wein geben wird.

Nein, Sie müssen auch das Datum beifügen (add the date).

Es fehlen ihm Kleider und Geld.

Es verdrießt mich, daß ich zu Hause bleiben muß.

Es schwindelt mir.

Es schmerzt mich, daß ich meinen treuen Diener verloren habe.

Wir werden Ihnen (for you) Platz machen.

Ich weiß nichts, als (except) daß Herr B. gestern gestorben ist.

## Reading-lesson.

Die Biene und die Taube. The bee and the dove.

Ein Bienchen fiel in einen Bach[1].

Dies sah von oben[2] eine Taube;

Sie brach ein Blättchen von der Laube[3]

Und warf's ihr zu. Das Bienchen schwamm darnach[4]

Und half sich glücklich aus dem Bach. —

Nach kurzer Zeit dieselbe Taube

Saß wieder friedlich[5] auf der Laube.

Da[6] schlich ein Jäger leis[7] heran

Und legte seine Flinte an[8].

Schon hatte er den Hahn[9] gespannt:

Das Bienchen kam und stach ihm in die Hand;

Puff! ging der Schuß daneben (aside);

Die Taube flog davon. — Wem dankte[10] sie ihr Leben?

1) brook. 2) from above. 3) arbour 4) after or to it. 5) quietly. 6) then. 7) softly. 8) die Flinte anlegen to aim, or to take aim at. 9) den Hahn spannen to cock the gun. 10) danken (instead of verdanken) to owe.

*) or die Winzer.

230

# Thirty-fourth Lesson.
## REFLECTIVE VERBS.
### (Zurückbezügliche Zeitwörter.)

1) When the action of a verb returns upon the subject from which it proceeds, the verb is called *reflective* or *reflected*. Such verbs are therefore conjugated with *two* pronouns, one the subject and the other the object. The latter stands commonly in the *Accusative*, with a few verbs in the *Dative*, as:

Ich betrage mich I behave (*myself*).
Er zeichnete sich aus he distinguished *himself*.

All such verbs are conjugated with the auxiliary haben.*)

This reflective form is very extensively employed in German, whilst in English most of these verbs are used in the *neuter* sense, i. e. without an objective personal pronoun, as: I rejoice ich freue mich.

### Conjugation of a reflective regular verb.
### Sich freuen to rejoice, to be glad.
#### Indicative Mood.

| *Present.* | *Imperfect.* |
|---|---|
| Ich freue mich I rejoice | Ich freute mich I rejoiced |
| du freuest dich thou rejoicest | du freutest dich thou rejoicedst |
| er freut sich he rejoices | er freute sich he rejoiced |
| sie freut sich she rejoices | sie freute sich she rejoiced |
| man freut sich people rejoice | man freute sich people rejoiced |
| wir freuen uns we rejoice | wir freuten uns we rejoiced |
| ihr freuet euch } ye rejoice | ihr freutet euch } ye rejoiced |
| Sie freuen sich } you rejoice | Sie freuten sich } you rejoiced |
| sie freuen sich they rejoice. | sie freuten sich they rejoiced. |
| *Perfect.* | *Pluperfect.* |
| Ich habe mich gefreut | Ich hatte mich gefreut |
| du hast dich gefreut | du hattest dich gefreut |
| er hat sich gefreut ꝛc. | er hatte sich gefreut ꝛc. |
| *First Future.* | *Conditional.* |
| Ich werde mich freuen I shall | Ich würde mich freuen I should |
| du wirst dich freuen [rejoice | du würdest dich freuen [rejoice |
| er wird sich freuen ꝛc. | er würde sich freuen ꝛc. |

*) The only exception is sich bewußt sein to be conscious of, which has in the Present tense. ich bin mir bewußt, and in the compound tense: ich bin mir bewußt gewesen ꝛc.

*Second Conditional.*

Ich würde mich gefreut haben
du würdest dich gefreut haben ꝛc.

# Subjunctive.

| *Present.* | *Imperfect.* |
|---|---|
| Daß ich mich freue | Daß ich mich freuete |
| daß du dich freuest ꝛc. | daß du dich freuetest ꝛc. |

| *Perfect.* | *Pluperfect.* |
|---|---|
| Daß ich mich gefreut habe | Daß ich mich gefreut hätte |
| daß du dich gefreut habest ꝛc. | daß du dich gefreut hättest ꝛc |

# Imperative.

| *Singular.* | *Plural.* |
|---|---|
| Freue dich ⎱ rejoice. | Freuen wir uns let us rejoice. |
| freuen Sie sich ⎰ | freuet euch, freuen Sie sich rejoice. |

# Interrogative form.

| *Present.* | *Imperfect.* |
|---|---|
| Freue ich mich? do I rejoice? | Freute ich mich? did I rejoice? |
| freuest du dich?    ꝛc. | freutest du dich?    ꝛc. |

# Negative form.

*Present.*   Ich freue mich nicht I do not rejoice etc.

# Negative-Interrogative.

*Imperf.*   Freute ich mich nicht? did I not rejoice? etc.
*Perfect.*   Habe ich mich nicht gefreut? have I not rejoiced? etc.

2) Many German active verbs may take the reflective form by adding the corresponding personal pronoun. Ex.:

| active. | reflective. |
|---|---|
| Ich kleide das Kind an. | Ich kleide mich an. |
| I dress the child. | I dress (myself). |
| Ich rühme den Freund. | Ich rühme mich. |
| I praise the friend. | I boast. |
| Er verwundete den Knaben. | Er verwundete sich. |
| He wounded the boy. | He wounded himself. |

3) There are however a great many true reflective verbs, which are always employed with the reflective pronoun, having no meaning without it, whilst others have a different sense when the reflective pronoun is omitted.

We subjoin in alphabetic order those most in use: Those marked with an asterisk* should be learnt first.

Sich aufhalten to make a stay.
sich beeilen to make haste.
*sich befinden to be (in health).
sich befleißigen to apply one's self.
sich behelfen to make shift.
*sich beklagen (über *acc.*) to complain of.
*sich bekümmern (um) to care for.
sich belaufen (auf) to amount.
sich bemächtigen to seize, to take possession of.
*sich bemühen to endeavour, to take the trouble.
sich benehmen ) to behave.
*sich betragen )
sich besinnen (über) to reflect.
sich bewerben (um) to apply for.
*sich bücken to stoop.
sich einlassen (in) to enter upon.
sich enthalten (*Gen.*) to abstain.
*sich entschließen to resolve, to make up one's mind.
*sich erbarmen (*Gen.* or über) to have mercy on.
sich ereignen to happen.
*sich erfreuen (*Gen.*) to enjoy.
*sich ergeben to surrender.
sich erholen (von) to recover from illness.
*sich erinnern (*Gen.*) *) to recollect, to remember.

*sich erkälten to catch cold.
sich erkundigen to inquire.
*sich fürchten (vor) to be afraid.
sich gedulden to have patience.
*sich gewöhnen (an) (*with the acc.*) to accustom one's self to.
sich grämen to grieve.
*sich irren †) *r. v.* to be mistaken.
sich kümmern (um) to care for.††)
sich nähern (*Dat.*) to approach.
sich nähren (von) to feed on.
sich rächen (an) to take revenge.
*sich schämen (über or *Gen.*) to be ashamed.
sich sehnen (nach) to long for.
*sich setzen to sit down.
sich stellen (als ob) to feign, pretend.
sich unterstehen en to dare, venture.
*sich unterhalten (über) to converse, to amuse.
sich verirren to go astray.
*sich verlassen (auf) (*with the acc.*) to rely (depend) on. †††)
sich versehen (in) to mistake.
sich verspäten to be (too) late.
sich verstellen to dissemble.
sich vorbereiten to prepare.
*sich weigern to refuse.
sich widersetzen (*Dat.*) to oppose.
*sich wundern (über) to wonder.
sich zutragen to happen.

*Remark.* Reflective verbs are sometimes employed to express the passive voice, as:

Der Schlüssel hat sich gefunden the key has been found.
Die Thüre öffnete sich the door (was) opened.

4) The following eleven require the pronoun in the Dative:

Sich anmaßen to usurp.
sich ausbitten to request, ask.
*sich einbilden to imagine, fancy.

sich die Freiheit nehmen to take the liberty.
sich getrauen to dare.

---

*) **Sich erinnern** takes also the preposition **an** with the Accusative, when *things* are spoken of, as: Ich erinnere mich mit Vergnügen an jenen Tag (or jenes Tages).
†) I am mistaken ich irre mich. *Perf.* ich habe mich geirrt.
††) sich Kummer machen um to grieve for.
†††) Verlassen, without sich, means *to leave.*

ſich verſchaffen to procure.
ſich vornehmen to take the resolution, make up one's mind.
*ſich ſchmeicheln to flatter one's self.

ſich vorſtellen to imagine.
ſich wehe thun to hurt one's self.
ſich zuziehen to incur.

Examples.

S. Ich ſchmeichle mir
du ſchmeichelſt dir
er ſchmeichelt ſich.

Pl. wir ſchmeicheln uns
Sie ſchmeicheln ſich
ſie ſchmeicheln ſich.

Ich bilde mir ein I imagine.

5) Some phrases with reflective verbs:

Wie befinden Sie ſich? how do you do?
Bemühen Sie ſich nicht do not take the trouble.
Geben Sie ſich Mühe take pains.
Er erholt ſich langſam he recovers slowly.
Ich erinnre mich ſeines Namens I recollect his name.
Sie irren ſich, mein Herr you are mistaken, Sir.
Er hat ſich ganz verändert he is quite altered.
Das Wetter ändert ſich the weather changes.
Ich begebe mich nach Frankfurt I go to Frankfort.
Er beruft ſich auf mich he appeals or refers to me.
Ich enthalte mich des Weines I abstain from wine.
Es ereignete ſich it happened.
Wir fühlen uns glücklich we feel happy.
Die Thüre öffnete ſich the door opened.
Nehmen Sie ſich in acht take care, be careful.
Setzen Sie ſich sit down, take a seat.
Die Sache verhält ſich ſo the matter is so.
Sie zerſtreuten ſich they dispersed.
Wenden Sie ſich an den König.
Apply (address yourself) to the king.
Sie rächten ſich an ihren Feinden.
They revenged themselves on their enemies.

---

### Words.

Der Mut the courage.
ſich auszeichnen to excel.
auf'ſtehen to get up.
beweiſen to prove.
überzeugen to convince.
das Urteil the sentence.
das Vorhaben the design.
die Ruhe rest.
die Zufriedenheit satisfaction.
verwunden to wound.
die Nation', pl. —en, nation.

die Rechnung the account, bill.
der Vorgeſetzte the superior.
das Betragen the behaviour.
häufig frequently.
unſchuldig innocent.
vertheidigen to defend.
auf'geben to give up.
urteilen to judge.
betreffen, angehen to concern.
vermeiden to avoid.
verletzen to hurt.

*

## Reading Exercise. 86.

1 Sie irren sich, mein Herr; ich bin nicht der (the one), den Sie suchen. Verzeihen Sie, ich habe mich wirklich (really) geirrt. Miltiades zeichnete sich in der Schlacht bei Marathon aus. Gewöhnen Sie sich, früh aufzustehen. Der Wolf näherte sich mir auf (within) zehn Schritte (paces). Mithridates ver= teidigte sich mit großem Mute gegen die Römer. Wenn Sie sich über (at) das Glück andrer freuen, so beweist dieses, daß Sie ein gutes Herz haben.

2. Wir haben uns bemüht, ihn von' seinem Unrecht (of his being wrong) zu überzeugen, aber er konnte sich nicht entschließen, sein Vorhaben aufzugeben. Der König weigerte sich, das Urteil zu unterschreiben. Sie würden sich besser befinden, wenn Sie sich gewöhnten, häufiger in der frischen Luft spazieren zu gehen. Ich sehne mich nach Ruhe. Ich werde mich bemühen, alles zu Ihrer Zufriedenheit zu vollbringen. Ich würde mich schämen, so etwas (such a thing) zu thun. Der junge Mann hat sich immer gut betragen.

### Aufgabe. 87.

1 We rejoice greatly (sehr) to see you. I *am* mistaken. You have also been mistaken. I wash myself every (*acc.*) day with cold water. Charles has wounded himself with his pen-knife. All nations long for (nach) liberty. The enemies have surrendered (themselves) [1]. If they had not surrendered (them-selves), 2they 1would *have* all *been* killed [2]. Dear Sir, have mercy on me (meiner). Nobody must imagine himself to be without faults. That man was a bad father, he did not care for (um) his children. I recollect to have seen that lady, but I cannot remember her name (*Gen.*). As (wie) I see, 2you 1enjoy (a) good health (*Gen.*).

2. The bill of my tailor amounted to a hundred and fifty marcs. I hastened to pay it, as soon as (sobald als) I 2got (bekam) 1money. Young people must not take the liberty (,) to judge of (über, *Acc*) things which do not concern them. A good Christian does not revenge himself on his enemy. We *were* mistaken in (in) the name of the street. Do not feign [to be] [1] so innocent; be ashamed of [3] your behaviour and resolve to avoid 2such 1a 3fault 4for the future (künftig). He who is conscious (sich bewußt ist) of having (to have) done his duty, (Pflicht, *f.*) may quietly await (entgegensehen) the judgment (dem Urteil) of his superiors.

---

1) Remember that words enclosed in a *parenthesis* (. . .) are to be translated, and words in *brackets* [. . .] are to be *left out*.

2) Second Conditional, see p. 131.

3) sich schämen (*to be ashamed*) governs either the *genitive case* or the preposition über with the *Accusative*.

## Conversation.

Ich freue mich, Sie zu sehen, mein Herr; wie befinden Sie sich?

Ich danke Ihnen, ich befinde mich, Gott sei Dank! sehr wohl.

Wie befindet sich Ihr Bruder, der (Herr) Kapitän?

Er befindet sich nicht wohl, er hat sich erkältet.

Haben Sie sich entschlossen, die Reise zu machen (or zu unternehmen)?

Ich habe mich noch nicht entschlossen; aber ich werde mich bald entschließen.

Auf wen verlassen (rely) Sie sich?

Ich verlasse mich auf die Güte des Fürsten.

Werden Sie Ihr Haus verkaufen?

Sie irren sich, ich werde es nicht verkaufen.

Glauben Sie, daß ich mich verspäten (be late) werde?

Wenn Sie schnell gehen, werden Sie sich nicht verspäten

Vor wem fürchten Sie sich?

Ich fürchte mich vor diesem Hund

Bilden Sie sich ein, allein weise zu sein?

Nein, aber ich glaube, die Sache besser zu verstehen, als andre.

Schämt sich dieser Jüngling nicht über sein Betragen?

Doch[1] es scheint, daß er sich schämt; er kommt nicht mehr zu uns.

Haben Sie Lust (a mind), mit mir ins Theater zu gehen?

O ja, wenn Sie warten wollen, bis ich mich angekleidet habe.

Haben Sie sich verletzt (or wehe gethan) (hurt)?

Ja, meine Hand blutet; ich habe mich an einem Nagel verletzt.

Wie hoch belief sich die Rechnung Ihres Wirtes (landlord)?

Sie belief sich auf dreiundachtzig Mark

Womit beschäftigen (occupy)*) Sie sich jetzt?

Ich lese Schillers „Lied von der Glocke" (song of the bell).

Wird Ihre Mutter bald hierher kommen?

Ich weiß nicht, wann sie kommt, aber ich sehne mich, sie zu sehen.

Warum sind Sie nicht früher gekommen?

Wir haben uns im Walde verirrt.

Werden Sie sich um eine Stelle (appointment) bewerben (to apply)?

Ich habe mich schon um mehrere beworben, aber bis jetzt (as yet) habe ich keine erhalten.

Soll der Christ sich an seinem Feinde rächen?

Nein, Christus hat gelehrt, daß man seine Feinde lieben soll.

Über was (worüber) beklagt sich Ihre Mutter?

Sie beklagt sich über das Betragen ihres Vetters.

---

*) oder: What do you *busy* yourself *about* now?

# Thirty-fifth Lesson.

## ON THE ADVERBS.

(Von den Umſtandswörtern.)

1) Adverbs are words destined to modify verbs, adjectives or other adverbs. They therefore denote *manner, place, time, order, motion, relation, comparison, number, quantity, quality, affirmation, doubt, negation, interrogation.* Adverbs are not variable, except that those of manner, quality and time, are subject to the degrees of comparison. Almost all *adjectives* are used as *qualifying adverbs* without .changing their form; not only in the positive but also in the comparative and superlative degrees. Ex.:

Der Diener wurde reich belohnt.
The servant was *richly* rewarded.

Dieſer Brief iſt ſchön geſchrieben.
This letter is *beautifully* written.

Mein Brief iſt ſchöner geſchrieben als Ihrer.
My letter is *better* written than yours.

*Note 1.* In the Superlative however they cannot take the article as in English, but are preceded by am or aufs, as: am höchſten or aufs höchſte; am ſchönſten, aufs ſchönſte; am ſtärkſten, aufs ſtärkſte ꝛc.

*Note 2.* A few words take also the termination ens, as: höchſtens, beſtens, ſchönſtens, ſpäteſtens ꝛc.

2) Adverbs of *manner* or of *time* are sometimes placed in English *before* the verb; in German they must always *follow* it. Ex.:

My friend *gladly* accepted the offer.
Mein Freund nahm das Anerbieten gern an.

I *never* go out ich gehe nie aus.

The adverbs of *quality*, being adjectives, cannot therefore be enumerated. Those of *place, time, quantity, comparison, affirmation* and *negation* are the following:

## 1. Adverbs of place.

| | |
|---|---|
| Wo where? | hier here. |
| †wohin*) where, whither. | †hieher here, hither, this way. |
| †woher where .from, whence? | hieraus hence. |

---

*) Those marked † are used with verbs of *motion* or direction; those with †† both for *rest* and *motion*; the others not marked, are used only with verbs denoting *rest*

da, dort } there,
daselbst } yonder.
†dahin } there, thither,
†dorthin } that way.
darin therein, within
außen } outside,
draußen } out of doors.
von außen from outside.
aus'wendig outside.
innen } within.
drinnen }
von innen from within
in'wendig inside.
oben } up stairs,
droben } (there) above.
†hinauf*) } up, up stairs.
†herauf }
unten } down stairs,
drunten } below
†herunter*) } down.
†herab }
vorn before, in the front
hinten behind.
†aufwärts upwards.
†abwärts downwards.
†vorwärts forwards.

†rück'wärts } backwards
†rück'lings }
auswärts abroad, outward
††rechts right, to the right.
††links left, to the left.
††diesseits on this side.
††jenseits on that side.
daneben close by, near by.
gegenü'ber opposite.
anderswo } elsewhere,
†anderswohin } somewhere else.
irgendwo } somewhere,
†irgendwohin } anywhere.
nirgends nowhere.
ü'berall(hin) } everywhere,
allenthalben } anywhere.
ringsum all around
††rund herum round about
†zusam'men } together.
beisammen }
††auseinander asunder, apart.
††weit } far, far off
fern } off, at a distance.
unterwegs' on the way.
†nach Hause (or heim) home.
zu Hause (daheim) at home.

## 2. Adverbs of time.

Wann? when?
eben just.
eben jetzt just now
jetzt or nun now.
gegenwärtig at present.
jemals or je ever (before).
niemals or nie never.
meistens mostly.
sonst, ehedem } formerly
ehemals, vormals }
früher, eher sooner, earlier
hernach' } afterwards,
nach'her } after (adv.).
später later.

einst, einstmals once.
einmal once, one day.
neulich the other day
kürzlich } lately, of late.
jüngst }
unlängst } a little while ago,
vor kurzem } not long ago.
vorher } before. **)
zuvor }
künftig, in Zukunft for the future.
manchmal }
zuweilen } sometimes.
bisweilen }
dann und wann now and then

---

*) The adverbs hinauf, hinein, herein, heraus ꝛc are to be considered as *separable prefixes*, and are frequently preceded by a substantive with the *prep* zu, as Er kam zur (zu der) Thüre herein Der Vogel flog zum Fenster hinaus through the window etc. Concerning the difference between her= and hin= See p. 211, Obs 2.

**) The English *before* is *adverb* when found *after* its noun. Ex. An hour *before* eine Stunde vorher or zuvor. When it

oft, oftmals often.\
häufig frequently.\
selten seldom.\
von nun an from this time forth.\
von jetzt an henceforth.\
seitdem since then.\
gleich ⎱ directly,\
sogleich ⎰ immediately.\
bald soon.\
bald—bald sometimes — sometimes.\
anfangs, zuerst at first.\
zuletzt at last.\
bisher hitherto, till now.\
bis jetzt as yet, till now.\
wieder again.\
erst only, not — till.\
endlich at last, at length.\
dann ⎱\
damals ⎰ then, at that time.\
immer, allezeit always.\
auf or für immer for ever.\
einstweilen ⎱\
unterdessen ⎰ meanwhile.

schon, bereits already, ever.\
noch still, yet.\
noch einmal once again, once more.\
noch nicht not yet.\
noch nie never before, never yet.\
heute to-day.\
gestern yesterday.\
vorgestern the day before yester-\
morgen to-morrow    [day.\
morgen früh to-morrow morning.\
übermorgen the day after to-morrow.\
lange, lange Zeit long (time).\
stündlich hourly. täglich daily.\
monatlich monthly.\
jährlich yearly.\
allmälig ⎱ by degrees,\
nach und nach ⎰ gradually.\
gewöhnlich usually.\
plötzlich suddenly.\
gleich or gleich nachher presently.\
augenblicklich instantly.\
spornstreichs at full speed.

### 3. Adverbial expressions of time.

Im Jahr in the year.\
im Sommer in summer.\
am Morgen, des Morgens*),\
  or morgens in the morning.\
mittags or um Mittag at noon.\
vormittags in the forenoon.\
nachmittags in the afternoon.\
am Abend, des Abends or\
  abends in the evening.\
zur rechten Zeit ⎱ in time,\
beizeiten ⎰ betimes.\
am Tag or bei Tag by day.\
bei Nacht, nachts by night.\
am Dienstag on Tuesday.

Sonntags on Sundays.\
zum ersten Male ⎱ for the first\
zum erstenmal ⎰ time.\
das nächste Mal the next time.\
zum letztenmal for the last time.\
um 1 (ein) Uhr at one o'clock.\
im Anfang in the beginning.\
am Ende at the end.\
am zehnten Mai ⎱ on the 10th\
am 10ten Mai ⎰ of May.\
diesen**) Morgen this morning.\
eines Tages*) one day.\
eines Abends one evening.\
heut zu Tage now-a-days.

---

precedes the noun, it is preposition and means vor. Ex.· Before an hour vor einer Stunde. When before begins a sentence, it is *conjunction* and translated. bevor or ehe. (See p. 218, a.)

*) The *Genitive* of nouns is used for *adverbs of time*, when the time is *indefinite*.

**) The *Accusative* of nouns is used for *adverbial expressions of time*, when the time is *distinctly* expressed.

nächster Tage one of these days. | einen Tag um den ) every
um Ostern about Easter | andern, alle 2 Tage} other day.
gegen 11 Uhr about 11 o'clock. | alle Tage )
ein wenig vor 10 Uhr ) by ten | jeden*) Tag } every day.
bis zehn Uhr } o'clock. | den ganzen Tag all day.
bei Sonnenaufgang at sunrise. | heute über 8 Tage this day week.
bei Tagesanbruch at day-break. | heute über 14 Tage this day fort-
vor 8 Tagen a week ago | Tag für Tag day by day. [night.
vor 14 Tagen a fortnight ago. | auf einige Zeit for a while.
zur Zeit in the time. | eine zeitlang for a time.
bis jetzt noch nicht not as yet. | von Zeit zu Zeit from time to time.
erst morgen not till to-morrow. | vor zeiten in old times.
drei Tage lang for three days. | an einem schönen Morgen on a
seit drei Tagen these three days. |   fine morning. [night.
zweimal des Tages twice a day. | in einer kalten Nacht on a cold

## Words.

Der Kaufmann the merchant.
der Löffel the spoon.
die Arznei the medicine.
der Zeuge the witness.
die Handlung the action.
das Lager the camp.
die Ecke the corner.
der Pfarrer the clergyman.
der Bettler the beggar.
suchen to search
hoffen to hope.

der Dienst the service.
übel gelaunt ill humored, cross.
großmütig magnanimous, generous.
allein alone.
willkommen welcome.
gefälligst if you please.
einwilligen to consent.
belästigen to annoy, to trouble.
unaufhörlich incessantly.
also, folglich consequently.

### Reading Exercise. 88.

1. Woher kommen Sie? Ich komme von Wien. Der Mann, welchen Sie suchen, wohnt nicht hier; er wohnt weit von hier. Der Knabe fiel rückwärts in den Fluß. Ich saß auswendig bei (with) dem Kutscher; die Damen saßen inwendig im Omnibus. Ringsum waren Feinde. Man sieht diese zwei jungen Herren immer beisammen. Mein Haus steht rechts, das Ihrige links. Der Herr ist nicht zu Hause; suchen Sie ihn anderswo. Das Dorf liegt seitwärts. Ist Ihre Mutter unten? Nein, sie ist oben. Soll ich hinaufgehen und es ihr sagen? Wenn Sie so gut sein wollen. Ich begegnete dem Kaufmann unterwegs.

2. Der Kranke muß stündlich einen Löffel voll Arznei nehmen. Anfangs wollte er nicht, aber zuletzt willigte er ein. Von jetzt an werde ich fleißiger sein; bisher habe ich nicht viel gearbeitet. Niemals werde ich jene Stunde vergessen. Mein Diener erhält

*) See the foot-note p 238.

monatlich zehn Mark, also jährlich zusammen hundertundzwanzig Mark. Neulich war ich Zeuge einer großmütigen Handlung. Vormittags arbeite ich, nachmittags gehe ich spazieren. Unser Arzt ist manchmal übel gelaunt. Sie müssen gleich nachher die Stadt verlassen. Der Offizier ritt spornstreichs ins Lager der Feinde.

### Aufgabe. 89.

1. Where is my stick? You will find *it* there in the corner. I beg your pardon (ich bitte um Verzeihung), it is not there; it must be elsewhere. You are welcome everywhere. Where (whence) does the letter come from? It comes from America. Come down, if you please. I could find him no-where. Where is my dog? It is out of doors. The house of the clergyman is very far off. I was not at home. You may go home. I have heard it somewhere. Have you searched everywhere? The one came hither, the other went thither. I could open the door neither (weder) from within nor (noch) from without. Do as if (als wenn) you ₁were (*Subj.*) ₁at ₂home.

2. *Did* you know him formerly? Yes, I have known him long. I shall be ₂at (zu) your service ₁directly.*) He was not often happy, because (weil) he ₂was ₁idle. He is more frequently at (in) the coffee-house, than at home. She has arrived sooner than I. She is ₂better ₁to-day*) than she was yesterday. Go ₂away ₁instantly. My uncle will al-ways be satisfied. Could you not come earlier? The next *time* ₂I ₁shall**) be ₂here ₁betimes.*) I am seldom alone. Have you seen our friend lately? Yes, I saw him *the other day*, and I hope I shall see him ₃again ₁very ₂soon. At present ₂we ₁are incessantly annoyed by beggars. I am in the habit (ich pflege) of seeing him (to see him) now and then.

---

## 4. Adverbs of quantity and comparison.

| | |
|---|---|
| Wie? how? | beinahe, fast almost, nearly. |
| wieviel, wie sehr? how much? | nur, blos', allein only. |
| viel much. | meistens mostly. |
| mehr more. | höchstens at the highest, at most. |
| noch ⎫ some more, | wenigstens at least. |
| noch mehr ⎭ any more. | spätestens at the latest. |
| noch zwei two more. | anders otherwise. |
| am meisten most. | sonst etwas anything else. |

---

*) Adverbs of *time* precede all other adverbs or adverbial expressions. *Time before place.*

**) Observe that when an *adverb* or *adverbial expression* (see p. 238) begins the sentence, the verb *precedes* the subject (see p. 80, 3).

ſehr, recht very or much.
zu, zu ſehr too or too much.
zu viel too much.
nichts nothing.
gar nichts nothing at all.
kein — mehr no more —.
etwas something.
ein wenig a little.
hinlänglich sufficiently.
genug enough.
kaum scarcely.
einigermaßen ⎱ somewhat
gewiſſermaßen ⎰
ziemlich tolerably, pretty.
ungefähr, etwa about.
um viel ⎱ by far,
bei weitem ⎰ by a great deal.
um die Hälfte by one half.
noch einmal ſo ⎱ twice as.
zweimal ſo ⎰ as . . . again.

gerade precisely, exactly, just.
ſonſt nichts nothing else.
ſo, ebenſo so, as, thus.
ebenſoſehr as much.
ebenſowenig — als no more —
   than.
ebenfalls, gleichfalls likewise.
gleichſam as it were.
um ſo mehr the more.
um ſo weniger the less.
ſogar', ſelbſt even. ganz quite.
gänzlich wholly, entirely.
vollends completely, quite.
ganz und gar thoroughly.
teilweiſe, teils partly.
beſonders ⎱ especially,
insbeſondere ⎰ particularly.
hauptſächlich chiefly.
überhaupt at all, generally.
im allgemeinen in general.

## 5. Adverbs of affirmation, doubt and negation.

Ja, ja doch, doch yes.
ja wohl o yes, certainly.
allerdings by all means.
jedenfalls at all events.
gewiß surely, certainly.
ſicherlich ⎱ to be sure,
freilich ⎰ of course.
fürwahr', wahrlich truly.
wirklich ⎱ really,
in der That ⎰ indeed.
gern or gerne*) willingly.
ungern unwillingly.
nein no.
nicht not.
gar nicht not at all.
keineswegs ⎱ by no means.
durchaus nicht ⎰

wahrſcheinlich ⎱ probably.
vermutlich ⎰
wahrhaftig truly.
zufällig by chance.
vielleicht, etwa perhaps.
ſchwerlich hardly, scarcely.
ohne Zweifel without or no doubt.
vergebens, umſonſt ⎱ in vain.
vergeblich ⎰
durchaus' absolutely, quite.
auch nicht nor — either, nor.
nicht einmal not even.
niemals or nie never.
nicht mehr no more.
nimmermehr never more.
im Gegenteil on the contrary.
vielmehr rather.

## 6. Adverbs of interrogation.

Wann (wenn) when?
warum why?
weshalb' ⎱ wherefore?
weswe'gen ⎰
wie how?
wieſo how so?
wieviel(e) how much (many)?

wieviel. noch how much more?
wieviele noch how many more?
wie lang(e) how long?
wo where?
wohin' whither, where?
woher' whence?
wodurch by what means? etc.

---

*) See the foot-note **) p. 242 and *Conversation*, p 244.

# 7. Adverbs of order.

Erſtens, fürs erſte first(ly).     dreimal three times.
zweitens secondly.     viermal four times.   [more.
drittens thirdly.     noch einmal once again, once
viertens fourthly etc.     noch zweimal twice again.
ferner further.     zuerſt' at first.
hernach hereafter, afterwards.     zuletzt at last.
dann, ſodann then.     einerlei of one kind, the same.
einmal once.     zweierlei of two kinds.
zweimal twice.     allerlei of all kinds.

*Note.* In German there is also another way of forming adverbs; namely by adding the word „weiſe" to various substantives and adjectives, as:

Teilweiſe partly. *)     herdenweiſe in flocks.
ſtückweiſe piece-meal.     tropfenweiſe by drops etc.
haufenweiſe by heaps, in crowds.     möglicherweiſe possibly.
maſſenweiſe in masses.     glücklicherweiſe fortunately.
ſtromweiſe by streams     unglücklicherweiſe unfortunately

# 8. Degrees of comparison.

Besides the *adjectives* used as adverbs, which admit of a comparison, the following true adverbs are also subject to the degrees of comparison.

| | *Comp.* | *Superl.* |
|---|---|---|
| Wohl well. | beſſer better. | am beſten or aufs beſte the best. |
| bald soon. | {früher} sooner, {eher} ere. | {am eheſten (am früheſten) the soonest. baldigſt very soon. |
| gern **) (I like) willingly. | lieber (I like better). | am liebſten (I like best). |
| oft often. | öfter oftener. | am häufigſten (am öfteſten) the oftenest. |
| ſehr very. | — | höchſt, äußerſt extremely. |
| übel, arg evil. | ärger (übler) worse. | am ärgſten (am übelſten) the worst. |
| viel much. | mehr more. | am meiſten most. |
| wenig little. | {weniger} {(minder)} less. | {am wenigſten} {(am mindeſten)} the least. |

*) The Latin *partim, frustatim, gregatim etc.*

**) Gern, lieber, am liebſten correspond with the English *I like, I like better, I like best,* and are mostly connected with a verb, as:

Ich ſpiele gern I like to play or playing
Ich tanze lieber I like better to dance or dancing.
Ich gehe am liebſten ſpazieren I like best walking.

## Words.

Das Sprichwort the proverb.    geschickt skilful. kosten to cost.
der Nebel the mist, fog.    von neuem anew.
das Zusammentreffen meeting.    angreifen to attack.
das Gesicht the face, counte-    stillen to appease, to quiet.
klug wise, prudent.    [nance. verpflichten to engage.
das Versprechen the promise.    gehorchen to obey.
das Murren the murmurs.    die Meile the mile.
der Vorschlag the proposal.    treulich faithfully.
verderben to spoil.    entkommen to escape.
erstaunt surprised, astonished.    verwerfen to reject.
thöricht } stupid, foolish.    richtig correctly.
dumm }    aussehen to look.
unvorsichtig improvident, heedless.

### Reading Exercise. 90.

1. Wie haben Sie geschlafen, mein Herr? Sehr gut, ich danke Ihnen. Wieviel Geld haben Sie? Ich habe nicht viel, ich habe sehr wenig. Ein deutsches Sprichwort sagt: „Zu wenig und zu viel verdirbt alles Spiel." Weiß der Knabe genug? Er weiß gar nichts. Derjenige wird den Preis erhalten, welcher am besten lesen und schreiben kann. Der Nebel ist nach und nach verschwunden. Man hat mir nicht einmal geantwortet. Kein Mensch kann immer glücklich sein. Werden Sie morgen mit uns (zu Mittag) speisen? Morgen kann ich nicht, aber übermorgen werde ich kommen.

2. Gehen Sie rechts, ich werde links gehen. Der kluge Mann irrt sich (is mistaken) selten; der unvorsichtige irrt sich am häufigsten. Der Geschickteste wird am meisten gelobt werden. Wir haben lange gewartet. Sie hätten (ought to have) noch länger warten sollen. Wenn der Fuchs die wilden Bienen angreift, [so] werfen sie sich haufenweise auf ihn. Mehr als einmal gelang es (dem) Kolumbus, das Murren seiner Schiffsmannschaft (crew) zu stillen; aber bald nachher begannen sie von neuem zu murren; endlich verpflichteten sie sich, noch drei Tage zu gehorchen. Am dritten Tage sahen sie wirklich Land.

### Aufgabe. 91.

1. When will you set out? To-morrow or the day after to-morrow. He has been here at least*) three times. Charles is improving (macht Fortschritte), especially in (im) German. That is ²beautiful ¹indeed. We *were* attacked unawares (unversehens), and *have* scarcely escaped. We went there by turns*) (abwechselnd). He will (Es wird ihm) by no means succeed. Our meeting was quite by chance (zufällig). I am not at all surprised at your saying so (daß Sie zc). How much do you charge (fordern) *for it?* It will cost you twenty marcs at most (at the highest). It is about thirty miles off (weit).

---

*) See the foot-note *) p. 240.

2. It is not otherwise. At present ₂I ₁want nothing else. At first ₂I ₁thought I knew his face. If we have given a promise, let us faithfully keep (halten) it; ₂lse (sonst) ₂we ₁shall certainly lose our good name. We dine precisely (pünktlich) at four o'clock. I think he will not willingly do it. Perhaps ₂you ₁would do better not to reject his proposal. He writes less correctly than his cousin. Miss Mary is less happy than you think. It is quite in vain to talk to (mit) this man; he will never listen to you (auf Sie hören).

### Conversation.

| | |
|---|---|
| Woher kommen Sie, mein Freund? | Ich komme von Köln (Cologne). |
| Haben Sie diese Reise zu (on) Fuß oder zu Wagen gemacht? | Nein, zu (by) Wasser; ich reise lieber zu Wasser als zu Land. |
| Ist Ihre Schwester zu Hause? | Nein, sie ist ausgegangen. |
| Wo ist Ihr Bruder? | Er ist heute wahrscheinlich in unserm Garten. |
| Wann kommt er nach Hause? | Er wird gegen acht Uhr kommen. |
| Ich habe Sie lange nicht gesehen; wo waren Sie? | Ich war meistens zu Hause; ich war nicht ganz wohl. |
| Wie viele Wörter soll ich lernen? | Wenigstens zwei Seiten (pages). |
| Wie finden (like) Sie das Haus des Herrn B.? | Es ist inwendig sehr schön; aber auswendig sieht es alt aus. |
| Wollen Sie auf mich warten (wait for me)? | Ein wenig, aber nicht lange. |
| Dieser Brief ist nicht schön geschrieben. Wie kommt das? | Ich habe ihn zu schnell geschrieben. |
| Spricht dieser Mann Englisch? | Er spricht sehr gut. |
| Wann erwarten Sie Ihren Freund? | Ich erwarte ihn diesen Nachmittag. |
| Wird er allein kommen? | Er wird vielleicht seinen Sohn mitbringen. |
| Geht der Knabe gern (does he like) in die Schule? | (Des) Morgens geht er gern in die Schule; aber nachmittags spielt er lieber. |
| Essen Sie gern(e) Schinken (ham)? | Ja, aber ich esse lieber Braten (roast-meat). |

### Reading-lesson.
### Der dankbare Löwe. The grateful lion.

Ein armer Sklave, der aus dem Hause seines Herrn entflohen war, wurde zum Tode verurteilt (condemned). Man führte ihn auf einen großen Platz¹, welcher mit einer Mauer umgeben war, und ließ einen furchtbaren Löwen auf ihn los (loose).

Tausende von Menschen waren Zeugen (witnessed) dieses Schauspiels (scene).

1) square.

Der Löwe sprang grimmig[2] auf den armen Menschen los; aber plötzlich blieb er stehen, wedelte[3] mit dem Schweife, hüpfte[4] voll Freude um ihn herum und leckte ihm freundlich die Hände. Jedermann verwunderte sich[5] und fragte, wie das komme[6].

Der Sklave erzählte folgendes: „Als ich meinem Herrn entlaufen war, verbarg ich mich in einer Höhle[7] mitten in einer Wüste[8]. Da kam auf einmal dieser Löwe herein, winselte[9] und zeigte mir seine Tatze[10], in welcher ein großer Dorn stak. Ich zog ihm[11] den Dorn heraus, und von der Zeit an (forth) versorgte[12] mich der Löwe mit Wildpret[13], und wir lebten in der Höhle friedlich beisammen. Bei der letzten Jagd wurden wir gefangen und von einander getrennt[14]. Nun freut sich das gute Tier, mich wieder gefunden zu haben.

Alles Volk war über (at) die Dankbarkeit dieses wilden Tieres entzückt[15] und bat laut um Gnade[16] für den Sklaven und den Löwen. Der Sklave wurde freigelassen[17] und reichlich beschenkt[18]. Der Löwe folgte ihm wie ein treuer Hund und blieb immer bei ihm, ohne jemand ein Leid (harm) zu thun[19].

2) fiercely, furiously. 3) to wag (with) his tail. 4) to jump. 5) to be astonished. 6) to come to pass. 7) cavern, cave. 8) desert. 9) to whine. 10) paw. 11) for him. 12) to supply. 13) game. 14) separated. 15) delighted, enraptured. 16) pardon. 17) set free. 18) rewarded. 19) see the 24th lesson.

---

# Thirty-sixth Lesson.
## On the Conjunctions.
### (Von den Bindewörtern.)

Conjunctions are particles which serve to connect words with words, and sentences with sentences, in order to bring them into a certain relation with one another. This relation can be very different; it may express either a mere connection, or an opposition, a condition, comparison, cause, consecution of time, just as in English.

They have a great influence upon the *position of the verb*; we therefore divide them into three classes according to their governing the construction.

### 1. Class: Co-ordinative Conjunctions.

The following seven conjunctions do not alter the construction.

| | |
|---|---|
| und and. | aber *or* allein but. |
| oder or. | sondern but (after the neg. *not*). |
| denn for, since. | sowohl — als both — and. |

Examples.

Ich muß zu Hause bleiben, denn ich bin krank.
I must stay at home, for I am ill

Der Strauß hat Flügel, aber er kann nicht fliegen
The ostrich has wings, but he cannot fly.

*Note.* Aber is sometimes placed after the subject or even after the verb, without altering the sense. Ex.:

Der Vater aber sprach but the father said.
Der Strauß hat Flügel, er kann aber nicht fliegen

## Observations.

1) Sondern contradicts one of the members of the previous negative clause, it can only be used, if the antecedent clause contains the negation *not*, and in a clause which has not its own subject and verb, completing only the first. Ex.:

Nicht ich bin krank, sondern mein Vater
I am not ill, but my father.

Ich halte ihn nicht für boshaft, sondern für närrisch.
I do not think him malicious, but foolish.

Ich liebe nicht seine Tochter, sondern seine Nichte.
I do not love his daughter, but his niece.

2) But when the second clause has its own *subject* and *verb*, aber must be used, even after a negation Ex.:

Ich habe ihn nicht selbst gesehen, aber ich habe ihm ge‑
schrieben
I did not see him myself, but I wrote to him.

Er ist noch nicht angekommen, aber wir erwarten ihn
jeden Augenblick.
He has not yet arrived, but we expect him every moment.

3) If the antecedent contains *no* negation, *but* must always be translated aber or allein, both of which are indifferently used. Ex.:

Er wollte aufstehen, aber (or allein) er konnte nicht.

## 2. Class: Adverbial Conjunctions.

Like all other *adverbial expressions*, the following *adverbial conjunctions* require the *inversion*, that is an exchange of place between the *subject* and the *verb*, when they begin the sentence or clause.

| | |
|---|---|
| Also so, thus, therefore. | dann, da then. |
| auch also, too (auch nicht nor). | dagegen \| on the contrary. |
| außerdem besides, moreover. | hingegen ∫ on the other hand. |
| bald — bald now — now; | daher', deswegen\| therefore, on |
| sometimes — sometimes. | darum, deshalb ∫ that account. |

demnach accordingly.
dennoch and yet, still.
dessen=un'geachtet neverthe-
desgleichen likewise.   [less.
desto ⎰ the — (with a follow-
um so ⎱   ing comparative).
doch, jedoch, ⎱ yet, still,
gleichwohl   ⎰ however.
entweder—(oder)either—(or).
ferner further.
folglich ⎱ consequently,
mithin  ⎰ accordingly.
indessen, unterdessen mean-
kaum scarcely.     [while.

nicht nur ⎱       ⎧not only
nicht allein ⎬-**sondern auch**⎨ — but
nicht blos ⎰       ⎩ also
nichts=desto=weniger nevertheless.
noch nor.   auch — nicht nor.
jetzt, nun now, then.
so so, thus.
sonst else, or else, otherwise.
teils — teils partly — partly.
überdies besides, moreover.
übrigens as for the rest, how-
vielmehr rather     [ever.
weder — noch neither — nor.
zwar indeed, it is true.

**Examples.**

Meine Schwester ist krank, also (or deshalb', des'wegen,
    da'rum, da'her, mit'hin, folglich) kann sie nicht abreisen.
Kaum hatte er dieses Wort gesprochen . .
Doch (jedoch, indessen) war es schon spät geworden.
Ferner hatte es viel geregnet.          *
Zwar konnten wir nicht sehen, wer es war; aber (allein)
    wir erkannten seine Stimme (voice).

---

**Words.**

Die Schwägerin the sister-in-
schaden to injure, hurt.  [law.
die Nahrung the food.
der Gipfel the top, summit.
das Rohr the reed, cane.
sich biegen to bend.
ruhig quietly.  naß wet.
ermahnen (*Acc.*) to speak to.

verteidigen to defend, protect.
erwarten to await.
verschwenden to waste.
der Mitschüler the school-fellow.
die Regel the rule.
fort'fahren *intr.* to continue.
das gemeine Volk the populace.
begegnen to meet.    ˘

**Reading Exercise. 92.**

Ich habe den Brief geschrieben, und mein Bruder hat ihn
abgeschrieben. Sie müssen mir das Buch zurückgeben, oder ich
werde es dem Lehrer sagen. Die Kinder konnten die Kirschen nicht
essen, denn sie waren nicht reif. Sie können jetzt ausgehen; aber
Sie müssen um vier Uhr wieder zurück sein. Meine Schwägerin
hat mir versprochen, mich in London zu besuchen: aber sie hat ihr
Wort nicht gehalten; auch hat sie mir gar nicht geschrieben; des=
wegen (demnach) werde ich sie nicht mehr erwarten. Entweder
müssen Sie fleißig arbeiten oder die Schule verlassen, sonst werden
Sie fortgeschickt (expelled) werden. Weder sein Oheim noch
seine Tante werden dieses erlauben. Sowohl der Vater als die
Mutter haben den Sohn gesucht. Der gerechte Mann schadet
weder dem Reichen noch dem Armen.

### Aufgabe. 93a.

You and I. He or she. We have written a long exercise, but we have not learnt it. (The) gold and silver are metals. You must go home directly, or you will become wet; *for* it will soon rain. The reed bends, but (it) does not break. We shall defend our country with courage, and we shall quietly await the enemy. You ought to speak *to* your children; for they are very naughty I do not know him by sight (von Gesicht), but I know him by reputation (dem Namen nach). Did you see Mr Long to-day? Yes, but I could not speak to him (mit ihm sprechen). I must stay at home, *for* I am not quite well. Do not waste your time, for (the) life is made of it (daraus). I do not know the man, for I have never seen him.

### Aufgabe. 93b.

Some of my school-fellows are ill; consequently they cannot come to (in die) school. Some one has done it, either you or your brother. This horse may be very strong, nevertheless ʒit ʋdoes not please me. I have shown him the rule, yet he has not understood it. He was very tired, nevertheless he continued working (to work). Scarcely had he pronounced these words, when (als, see below, 3. Cl.) the populace threw (*sing*.) themselves on him. He has not only promised him something but also given it I know neither him nor his wife. I did not expect, to see you here; the (desto) greater is my pleasure to meet you. I can neither read nor write. Not only the king was expected, but also the queen and the princess

## 3. Class: Subordinative Conjunctions.

1) All *subordinative* conjunctions, simple as well as compound, throw the verb to the end of the clause, which is indicated by a ··mma, semicolon or full-stop.

### a) *Simple subordinative Conjunctions.*

| | |
|---|---|
| Als[1]) when, as, than. | nachdem' after. |
| bevor', ehe before. | ob if, whether. |
| bis until. | obgleich', obschon' } though, |
| da as, since (*reason*). | obwohl', wiewohl } although. |
| daß that. | seit or seitdem since (*time*). |
| damit' that, in order that. | so oft (als) as often as. |
| falls (im Fall) in case that. | sobald (als) as soon as. |
| indem' as, while. | solange (als) as long as (while). |
| je — the — (*with the comp*.)[2]). | ungeachtet notwithstanding. |

---

1) *When* with the verb in the **Imperfect tense.**
2) For instance: Je größer . . . See p. 109, 10; & 255, 4. Observe that the second *the* is desto and belongs to the 2nd class.

während[1] while, whilst. | wie as, how.
wenn if, when (with present). | wofern' in as much as, provided.
weil because.

Examples.

Es war vier Uhr, als die Sonne aufging.
It was four o'clock when the sun rose.
Warten Sie, bis ich meinen Brief vollendet habe.
Wait till I have finished my letter.
Sprechen Sie laut, damit' ich Sie verstehen kann.
Speak aloud that I may understand you.

2) When the first *clause* of the sentence begins with
one of the foregoing *subordinate* conjunctions, then the
second clause or part *begins with the verb,* and the
subject follows it. If the verb in the first clause is a
separable one, the *separation does not take place*
(see also p. 211, Obs. 1). Ex.:

Als die Sonne aufging, war es vier Uhr.
Nachdem' wir miteinander (together) gefrühstückt hatten,
  gingen wir (not wir gingen) spazieren.
Während wir Karten spielten, lasen unsre Freunde (not
unsre Freunde lasen) die Zeitungen (newspapers).

## Observations on some of these Conjunctions.

### Als when, as, than.

1) This conjunction has different meanings. When beginning a sentence, or clause of a sentence, it denotes *time* and
signifies *when* or *as.* The English *when,* followed by an
Imperfect or Pluperfect Tense, [*] is therefore always rendered
by the German als with the Imperfect or Pluperfect, as:

Als der Prinz die Thüre geschlossen fand, klopfte er ꝛc.
When the prince found the door locked, *he* knocked.
Als er seine Rede geendigt hatte, —
When (as) he had finished his speech —.

2) After a comparative, or after so or ebenso before an
adjective, als answers to the English *than* and *as,* for instance:
Karl ist größer als Ludwig Charles is taller than Lewis.
Ich bin nicht so gelehrt als (or wie) Sie glauben.
I am not so learned as you think.

---

1) instead of während (*while*) people sometimes use indessen as
a *subordinate* conjunction, as: Wir gingen im Garten spazieren, indessen er zu Mittag speiste. This is however not to be recommended.

*) except only in such phrases in which *when* means *as often
as,* ex · When he went out, he was always followed by a great
suite. Wenn er ausging, begleitete ihn immer ein großes Gefolge. Wenn
(When) er gespeist hatte, pflegte er ein wenig zu ruhen (have a little nap).

3) After the adverbs of negation: *nothing* and *nowhere*, *but* is translated alß:

Nothing *but* truth nichtß alß (die) Wahrheit.
Nirgendß alß in England nowhere *but* in England.

4) Alß denotes also quality or condition, as:
Er handelte alß Vater he acted as a father.

### Da as, since.

Da denotes a *reason* or *motive*, and corresponds with the English *as* or *since*. Ex.:

Da der Knabe so fleißig ist, (so) muß man ihn belohnen.
As the boy is so industrious, we must reward him.

Da ich ihn nicht kenne, (so) kann ich ihm nicht trauen.
As (*or* since) I do not know him, I cannot trust him.

### Indem' as (in the moment when); the subject remaining the same.*)

Indem' denotes a short simultaneous action and is often translated with the English *Participle present*. Ex.:

Indem ich in das Zimmer trat.
As I entered the room *or* On (my) *entering* the room.

Indem er mir die Hand drückte, sagte er zu mir:
Shaking hands with me, he said to me etc.

Indem er seinen Arm ausstreckte stretching out his arm...

### Obgleich, obschon, obwohl though, although.

1) These conjunctions should not be divided. A separation however sometimes takes place, when two or more mono-syllables follow, as:

Obschon ich ihn achte though I esteem him.
Obgleich ich arm bin or ob ich gleich arm bin.
Although I be poor.
Obgleich er mich nicht kennt though he does not know me.

2) The first of the above three is most used; all however have the same meaning. When a sentence begins with one of them, the second member corresponds to it by means of doch or dennoch (yet) in the 3rd place.

Obschon er noch jung ist, hat er (doch) schon graue Haare.
Although he is still young, *he has* already grey hair.

### So so, if, as.

1) The *conjunction* so is not to be confounded with the *adverb* so which modifies the adjectives following it (so groß,

---

*) When the subj. changes, „während" must be used.

ſo ſchön ꝛc.) or signifies »in this manner.« — So, as a conjunction, stands before a verb and at the beginning of the *second* clause of a compound sentence, when the first member begins with wenn, da, obgleich, obſchon or obwohl, but it has no particular meaning (like *then*).

Wenn es regnet, ſo geht man nicht ſpazieren.
When it rains, (*then*) people do not go to walk.

Wenn Sie früher gekommen wären (or Wären Sie früher gekommen), ſo hätten Sie mich noch zu Hauſe angetroffen.
Had you come earlier, you would have found me at home.

Obgleich er ſelbſt arm war, ſo unterſtützte er doch die Armen.
Though he was poor himself, he assisted the poor.

It appears from these examples that this ſo cannot be translated into English except perhaps with *then*. The purpose of its being used in German is easily understood. Those members of the above sentences which begin with ſo, are the chief members, and should, properly speaking, stand before the other clause which begins with a conjunction. The strict arrangement of those sentences would be:

Man geht nicht ſpazieren, wenn es regnet.
Sie hätten mich noch zu Hauſe angetroffen, wenn Sie früher
gekommen wären.
Er unterſtützte doch die Armen, obgleich er ſelbſt arm war.

Hence we see that in the above sentences a transmutation of both clauses has taken place, which is indicated by ſo. It is however not at all necessary to express it; we may just as well say:

Wenn es regnet, geht (instead of ſo geht) man nicht ſpazieren ꝛc.

2) So, denoting *if*, is antiquated, and found in a few old phrases only: So Gott will if God please.

3) So before an adjective, followed by auch = *however*, is a compound conjunction and found p. 254, b) and 255, 7).

### Wann? wenn, als.

The English conjunction *when* corresponds with three German words, viz.: wann? wenn, als.

#### a) wann?

1) Wann is interrogative in direct and indirect questions:

Wann werden Sie kommen? when will you come?
Sagen Sie mir, wann Sie kommen wollen.
Tell me when you will come.

2) Wann answers also to the English *when* = *whenever*, or *every time when*, as:

Sie können es ſchicken, wann Sie wollen.
You may send it when (whenever) you like.

b) **wenn.**

1) 𝔚enn corresponds with the English *when* used with a present tense, and is therefore peculiarly fitted to convey general ideas, whereas alß relates to a particular event. As often therefore as *when* is connected with a Present, it is to be translated in German wenn.[1] Ex.:

Wenn ich an der Arbeit bin, liebe ich keine Besuche.
When I *am* at work, I do not like visitors (company).

Wenn die Leidenschaften heftig sind, ist die Tugend in Gefahr.
When the passions are violent, virtue is in danger.

2) Wenn in a conditional sense is *if*.
Wenn Sie nicht kommen können if you cannot come.

3) When *if* is used with an Imperfect or Pluperf. tense, this must be in German in the Subjunctive mood. Ex :

Es wäre mir lieb, wenn er käme or gekommen wäre.
I should be glad if he *came* or *had come*.

c) **alß.**

Alß refers to a particular event which is *past*, and requires the verb in the Imperfect or Pluperfect (Obs. 1, p. 249).

Alß ich krank wurde, schickte ich nach dem Arzte.
When I *became* (fell) ill, I sent for the physician.

Alß Cäsar von Brutus ermordet wurde . .
When Cæsar was slain by Brutus etc.

### Words.

| | |
|---|---|
| Das Gefängniß the prison. | die Ganß the goose. |
| der Stern the star. | außweichen avoid. |
| der Gipfel the top. | überfallen to overtake, attack |
| das Gewitter the thunderstorm. | unawares. |
| der Kauf the bargain. | die Gefahr the danger. |
| dienen to serve. | sicherlich surely. |
| dunkel dark. | stören to disturb. |
| herannahen to approach. | loßbrechen to break loose. |
| anziehen to put on. | plündern to pillage, plunder. |
| gesund in good health. | gegenwärtig present. |

### Reading Exercise. 94.

1. Alß ich nach Hause kam, ging ich zu Bett. Ich schlief noch, alß mein Bedienter inß Zimmer trat. Sobald (alß) *) ich den Brief empfangen hatte, reiste ich ab. Die Soldaten plünderten die Stadt, biß der General ein Ziel (stop) setzte. Warten Sie,

---

1) In this sense wann is also used. Compare p. 249 *).
*) with or without alß.

bis ich angekleidet bin. Da der Arbeiter sehr fleißig war, (so) wurde er gut bezahlt. Die Diebe werden in die Gefängnisse gebracht, damit sie nicht mehr stehlen. Ehe (or bevor) das Kind sein neues Kleid anzieht, muß es sich die Hände rein waschen. So lange die Menschen gesund sind, denken sie selten [daran], daß sie auch krank werden können.

2. Man weiß nicht, ob die Sterne bewohnt sind, oder nicht. Ich sprach mit ihm, obgleich (or obschon) ich ihn nicht kannte. Kaum hatten wir den Gipfel des Berges bestiegen, als das Gewitter losbrach. Es ist ein leichter Kauf, wenn Freunde durch Güte gewonnen werden. Die gegenwärtige Zeit ist die beste, weil sie unsre eigne (own) ist. Die wilden Gänse sind schwer zu schießen, weil sie schnell und sehr hoch fliegen. Wenn man die Gefahr herannahen sieht, so kann man ihr ausweichen; aber wenn sie uns schlafend überfällt, wird sie uns sicherlich verderben.

## Words.

| | |
|---|---|
| Alone allein. | to inform benachrichtigen. |
| to put out auslöschen. | the language die Sprache. |
| the candle das Licht. | the war der Krieg. |
| the business das Geschäft. | ambitious ehrgeizig. |
| to hesitate zögern. | in future künftig, in Zukunft. |
| the truth die Wahrheit. | punctual pünktlich. |
| astonished erstaunt. | to mend verbessern. |
| possible möglich. | tranquillity die Ruhe. |
| to take a walk einen Spazier- | in the country auf dem Land. |
| gang machen (not nehmen). | |

### Aufgabe. 95.

When I arrived here, ₂it ₁was quite dark. As (since) he does not work, ₂I ₁shall give him nothing. Put out the candle before you go to (zu) bed. I wish you (ich bitte Sie) to wait till I have done my exercise. Since I have lost my friend, ₂I ₁am quite alone. He told me that the child was dead. I see that you have not yet finished your business. She has been very well, since she has been in (auf) the country. I am astonished, that you *have* not yet departed. Since (da) you are my friend, you will not hesitate to tell me the truth. Is it possible that he is arrived yet (schon)? After I had breakfasted, I took a walk, although it rained a little. The city [of] Paris *has* become much more beautiful, since (seit) you saw (have seen) it. *As soon as* the general arrives (will arrive), you will inform us of it. Has he not asked you *if*[1]) you had [a] mind (Lust) to go out with him? No, Sir.

### 96.

I was scarcely ten years old *when* I lost my father. *The* more I study German, *the*[2]) more ₂I ₁like this language.

---

1) When *if* means *whether*, it must be translated ob. 2) besto.

When you are ready, we will go for a walk (fpazieren gehen).
There will always be (geben) wars among men (unter ben Men=
fchen), as long as they are ambitious. I do not know, whether
he is rich or poor. Pardon your enemies (Dat.), since (as)
God pardons you also. Ask him if[1]) he will sell his horse.
Why did you sleep so long? I slept so long, because I was
very tired. I will go with you, if you promise me (Dat.),
to be more punctual in future. Though we did not make
the world, we may help [to] mend it. If you be (are) poor,
do not wish to seem rich. The master will not pardon him,
until he improves (fich beffert). He will never learn, since he
is idle. While I was there, ꞌtranquillity ꞌprevailed (herrfchte)
in the country. I do not know how he will get (befommen) it.

### b) Compound subordinative Conjunctions.

Compound conjunctions are those consisting of two
separate words of the kind. We present them independ-
ently of the simple ones, merely that they may be more
easily understood, and the memory aided.

| | |
|---|---|
| Als bis until, before. | felbft wenn even if. |
| als wenn ⎱ as if, as though | fo baß so that. |
| als ob ⎰ (with the Imperf | wie -- auch ⎱ however ... (with |
| wie wenn ⎰ Subj.). | fo -- auch ⎰ an adj. between). |
| als baß but that, but. | fo fehr -- auch much as |
| anftatt baß instead of. | †wenn -- nicht ⎱ unless[3]). |
| bis (baß) till, until. | †wofern -- nicht ⎰ |
| †bamit -- nicht lest (Subj.). | †wenn -- auch ⎱ |
| im Fall (baß) in case. | †wenn -- gleich ⎰ even if, |
| je -- --, befto the Ꞌ-- --, the | †wenn -- fchon ⎰ although. |
| (with a comparative). | vorausgefetzt,baß⎱supposing, |
| je nachbem' according as. | †wenn -- nur ⎰provided(that). |
| gleichwie, fowie just as. | †wenn -- auch noch fo though |
| ohne baß without.., unless, | or if ever so .. |
| but that.[2]) | um..zu (with theInf.) inorderto. |

Note. Besides these, notice the expressions: ba'von baß,
baburch baß, bamit baß, barin baß ꞇc. which have no equivalent
in good English. See less. 45, § 7.

### Observations.

1) Lest in the sense: for fear of, after a negative clause, is
sometimes translated aus Furcht (baß):

---

1) See the foot-note 1) p. 253.
2) The French sans que.
3) Unless means also: es fei benn baß, but this is ratherantiquated;
it occurs often in the Lutheran translation of the holy Bible.

I did not go there, lest I should disturb him.
Ich ging nicht dahin aus Furcht, ihn zu stören.

*Lest* after the verb *to fear* (fürchten) is rendered simply by daß:
I feared lest he should die ich fürchtete, daß er sterben möchte.

2) Those of the above conjunctions marked † require the
second component to be placed after the subject, and if there
are personal pronouns, also after these, as:

Gehen Sie schnell, damit Sie nicht überrascht werden.
Go quick, lest you be surprised. ⋅

Wenn er mich nicht bezahlt ꝛc. unless he pay me etc.

Wenn er auch noch so viele Bücher hätte ꝛc.
Though he had ever so many books etc.

3) Als daß is used after a negative clause with the word
anders, when it answers to the English *but* or *but that*, before which *otherwise* is understood. Ex.:
I don't know *but* (*that*) he is alive still.
Ich weiß nicht anders, als daß er noch lebt.

Als daß is further used to render the English Infinitive
after *too . . . for . . .*[1] Ex.:
This news is *too* good *for me* to believe it.
Diese Nachricht ist zu gut, als daß ich sie glauben könnte.

4) The *dashes* after je — indicate that the whole first
clause is to follow before desto. Ex.:
Je mehr Sie lernen, desto mehr wissen Sie.
The more you learn, the more you know.

5) Sowie is equivalent to gleichwie, as:
Sowie die Sonne ihre Strahlen auf die Erde sendet.
As the sun darts his beams to the earth etc.
Der Neid, sowie jede andre Leidenschaft ꝛc.
Envy as well as every other passion etc.

6) Ohne daß corresponds with the English *but* after an
excluding negation, as:
Not an hour passes *but* I see him.
Es vergeht keine Stunde, ohne daß[2] ich ihn sehe.

7) Wie . . . auch, so . . . auch, take the adjective and the
pronoun between them, as:
Wie reich auch (*or* so reich auch) Ihr Vater sein mag.
However rich your father may be.
So schön es auch sein mag, so kann es mir doch nichts nützen.
However handsome it may be, it cannot be of any use
to me.

---

1) The French *pour que*. — 2) The French *sans que*.

8) The *dash* between ſo ſeɦr — aud indicates the place
for the personal pronouns. With this no adjective is used.

So ſeɦr ich iɦn aud gebeten ɦabe.
Much as I have begged him.

If the subject is a noun, ſo ſeɦr aud need not be separated.

So ſeɦr aud mein Vater iɦn gebeten ɦat.
Much as my father has begged him.

## c) *Relative Conjunctions.*

All adverbs of interrogation have in *indirect questions*
(see p. 145, *Note*) the value of *relative conjunctions ;* therefore they require the verb at the end of the clause, as:

| | | |
|---|---|---|
| Wann when. | wie lange how long. | worin wherein |
| warum why. | wo where. | woran whereat. |
| weshalb ⎱ wherefore. | woɦer whence | wobei wherewith |
| weswegen ⎰ | woɦin whereto. | wovon whereof. |
| wie how. | wodurd whereby. | worauf whereon |
| wieviel how much. | womit with which. | worunter where- |
| ꞌauf welche Weiſe in what manner etc. | | [under |

### Examples.

Ich ɦabe iɦn gefragt, wann ich iɦn zu Hauſe finden werde.*)
Ich weiß nicht, warum er meinen Brief nicht erɦalten ɦat.
Darf ich fragen, wie lange Sie da geblieben ſind?
Sie können bleiben, wo Sie ſind.
Wiſſen Sie, woɦer er kommt?
ꞏDieſes iſt das Haus, wovon Sie geſtern geſprochen ɦaben

*Note.* Observe that the whole verb of the first clause
must precede the relative conjunction. It would be wrong
to say: Darf ich, wieviel Sie bezaɦlt ɦaben, fragen? Ex.:

I have not been told where he has gone.
Man ɦat mir nicht geſagt, woɦin er gegangen iſt.
not Man ɦat mir nicht, woɦin er gegangen iſt, geſagt.

### Words.

| | |
|---|---|
| Die Beleidigung the insult. | die Luft the air. |
| die Unruɦe uneasiness. | geɦorchen to obey. |
| laſterɦaft vicious | erlangen to obtain. |
| ungeſchidt awkward. | das Löſegeld the ransom. |
| droɦen to threaten. | der Ruɦm fame, renown |

### Reading Exercise. 97.

1. Es ſcheint mir, als wenn (or als ob) ich dieſen Herrn
ſchon geſeɦen ɦätte. Dieſe Beleidigung iſt zu groß, als daß ich

---

*) The *direct* questions are Wann werde ich iɦn zu Hauſe finden?
— Warum ɦat er meinen Brief nicht erɦalten? etc.

ſchweigen könnte. Ich weiß nicht anders, als daß ſein Geſchäft gut geht. Mein Feind hat mich zu ſehr beleidigt, als daß ich ihm verzeihen könnte Karl ſpielt, anſtatt daß er ſeine Aufgabe lernt. Warten Sie, bis (daß) ich fertig bin. Nehmen Sie einen Regen= ſchirm, damit Sie nicht naß werden. Ich werde ihm die Erlaub= nis nicht geben, wenn er auch noch ſo ſehr bittet Je laſter= hafter die Menſchen ſind, deſto mehr Unruhe haben ſie.

2. Je kälter die Luft iſt, deſto mehr wiegt ſie; je wärmer ſie iſt, deſto leichter iſt ſie. Sie werden belohnt werden, je nach= dem Sie fleißig ſind Dieſer junge Menſch iſt ſehr ungeſchickt, er nimmt nie etwas in die Hand, ohne daß er es zerbricht. Wir können dieſe Aufgabe nicht machen, wenn Sie uns nicht helfen. Je mehr Sie mir drohen, deſto weniger werde ich Ihnen gehorchen Der Gefangene wird ſeine Freiheit nicht erlangen, wenn er nicht ein hohes Löſegeld bezahlt. Wie groß auch der Ruhm dieſes Fürſten ſein mag, der ſeines Vaters war noch größer

### Words.

| | |
|---|---|
| To marry heiraten. | to practise üben. |
| the assistance der Beiſtand. | to hurt ſchaden, wehe thun. |
| careful vorſichtig. | to disappear verſchwinden. |
| the price der Preis. low nieder. | to perish †um'kommen. |
| frequently häufig. | somewhere irgendwo. |

### Aufgabe. 98.

It seems to me as *if* I had seen you somewhere Give me your letter *that* (in order that) I [may] send it to the (auf die) post-office. He says he will not marry *until* he has a profession (einen Beruf). *In case* you want (need) my assistance, call me. Read it twice, *lest* you forget it. The lady must be careful *lest* she fall (*Pres Subj.*). The merchant will sell much or little, *according as* the price is high or ˉlow. *The* more frequently you practise what you had in your music-lesson, *the* better ₂you ₁will play it. He cannot play *but* (*transl.* without that) he hurts himself (ſich). Go in *without* his seeing you (*transl.* without that he ₂sees ₁you). The plebeians (die Plebejer) intended to leave Rome, *in case* the patricians (die Patrizier) did not keep (hielten) their word. We shall not go, *unless* she invites us. Romulus disappeared *without* any one's knowing (*knew*) how he *had* perished.

### Words.

| | |
|---|---|
| To consent einwilligen. | security die Sicherheit. |
| to retire (*refl. v.*) ſich zurückziehen | admirable bewundernswührdig |
| learned *adj.* gelehrt. | the act die That. |
| vain eitel, ſtolz. | to liberate befreien. |
| to trust trauen, vertrauen. | doubtful, dubious zweifelhaft. |

dominant herrſchend.
the passion die Leidenſchaft.
to approve (of) billigen.

the advice der Rat.
victory der Sieg.
to attribute zuſchreiben.

## Aufgabe. 99.

1. Who shall not go into the (auf das) country, *unless* he consents to come with us. The night came, *so that* I was obliged to retire. Though he is very learned, nevertheless he is not vain. Nobody can trust you (*Dat.*), unless you bring good security. My friend said he would lend me a hundred pounds, provided I would give them back to him within (in) three months. However admirable the act of William Tell may (mag) have been (,) by (durch) which he liberated his country from a cruel tyrant, — its morality (ihr ſittlicher Wert) is dubious. I cannot do it, unless you help me. *Provided* you know the dominant passion of some one, you are sure to please him.

2. Unless the Lord build the house, they labour (ſo arbeiten diejenigen) in vain, who build it *Though* you [should] have the best teacher in England, *if* you do not learn your grammar well, *you* will never speak good German. Tell me, if you please (gefälligſt), where I may (kann) find your umbrella. I do not know why he has not yet written to me. Ask him when he will come. *Although* Antiochus approved [of] Hannibal's advice, *yet* he would not act according to it (darnach), *lest* (aus Furcht) the victory should (möchte) *be* attributed to Hannibal, and not to him.

### Conversation.

| | |
|---|---|
| Können Sie dieſe Arbeit thun? | Nicht ohne daß Sie mir helfen. |
| Wird der Arbeiter belohnt werden? | Ja, wenn er fleißig iſt |
| Kennen Sie mich? | Nein, aber es ſcheint mir, als ob ich Sie ſchon geſehen hätte. |
| Wurde der Gefangene freigelaſſen? | Ja, nachdem er ein hohes Löſegeld bezahlt hatte. |
| Wer hat dieſen Knaben gelobt? | Sowohl der Vater als die Mutter. |
| Sind Sie geſtern ſpazieren gegangen? | Ja, obſchon es geregnet hat. |
| Iſt Lord M. ein gelehrter Mann? | Er iſt ſehr gelehrt; deſſenungeachtet iſt er nicht ſtolz. |
| Warum ſoll ich dieſe Aufgabe noch einmal ſchreiben? | Damit Sie ſie beſſer lernen. |
| Was halten (think) Sie von Herrn Weiß? | Ich glaube, daß er ein rechtſchaffener Mann iſt. |
| Iſt es geſund (wholesome) lange zu ſchlafen? | Nein, je länger man ſchläft, deſto träger wird man. |
| Wird der Lehrer ihm verzeihen? | Nicht eher, als bis er ſich beſſert. |

Haben Sie mich hier erwartet? Keineswegs; desto mehr freue ich
mich, Sie hier zu finden.
Wird der Fürst hier bleiben? Ich zweifle, ob er hier bleiben wird.
Soll ich Ihnen Ihr Buch zu- Je eher Sie es thun, desto an-
rückschicken? genehmer wird es mir fein.
Ist der Kranke aufgestanden? Ja, obgleich der Arzt es ihm verboten hat.
Wissen Sie, warum er nicht Nein, er hat es mir nicht gesagt.
kommt?

# Thirty-seventh Lesson.
## ON THE PREPOSITIONS.
(Von den Vorwörtern.)

Prepositions are particles. which serve to show the
relation which exists between a verb and a noun. This
relation being of different kinds, the prepositions destined
to indicate it, govern different cases, namely the *Accu-*
*sative, Dative* or *Genitive case.*

### 1. Prepositions with the Accusative case.

Durch through, by. | ohne without, but for.
für for | um about, round, at.
gegen *) towards, against, to. | wider against
Further four compounds which *follow* their substantives:
hinauf up **) | hindurch through.
hinab, hinunter down | entlang along. um..herum round.

Examples

Durch das Thor through the gate.
Durch welche Mittel? by what means?
Für Ihre Schwester for your sister.
Gegen mich against me.
Gegen das Gebirge towards the mountain.
Ohne einen Pfennig without a penny.
Um die Stadt (herum) about the down.
Um den Tisch round the table.
Wider seinen Willen against his will.
Die Stiege hinauf, — hinunter up stairs, down stairs.
Den Fluß entlang along the river. — Den Winter hindurch
[through (the) winter.

---

*) There is also an old expression· gen Himmel up to heaven,
for gegen den Himmel.
**) These words are only considered prepositions when an
Accusative is joined to a neuter verb. Ex.:
Gehen Sie die Stiege hinauf.

17*

## 2. Prepositions with the Dative case.

| | |
|---|---|
| Aus out of, from. | nächst, zunächst next to. |
| außer except, besides. | nebst, samt together with. |
| bei near, with, by, at. | seit since, for. |
| binnen within (*for time*). | von from, of, by. |
| mit with. | von — an from, since. |
| nach*) after, to, according to. | zu to, at. — bis zu as far as. |

Further the compounds, which follow their nouns:

| | |
|---|---|
| entgegen against (to meet). | zufolge**) according to. |
| gegenüber †opposite. | zuwider { in opposition, |
| gemäß according to. |           contrary to. |

### Examples.

Aus dem Hause (Garten) out of the house, from the garden.
Außer einem Koffer besides a portmanteau.
Bei meinem Freund at my friend's (with my friend).
Bei unsrer Ankunft on our arrival.
Binnen wenigen Minuten within a few minutes.
Bis zu dem nächsten Dorfe as far as the next village.
Nach der Schlacht after the battle.
Nach dieser Regel according to this rule.
Nach meiner Meinung in (according to) my opinion.
Nächst (zunächst) dem Hügel next the hill.
Nebst (samt) meinen Kindern together with my children.
Seit jener Zeit since (from) that time.
Von meinen Eltern by (from) my parents.
Von Kindheit an from childhood.
Er kam zu mir he came to me (to my house).
Meinen Befehlen entgegen against my orders.
Dem Rathause gegenüber opposite the town-hall.
Ihrem Wunsche gemäß (zufolge) according to your wish.
Dem Befehl des Königs zuwider contrary to the king's order.

---

### Words.

| | |
|---|---|
| Der Hirsch the stag. | die Eiche the oak-tree. |
| ruhen to rest. rollen to roll. | die Brücke the bridge. |
| der Zugvogel the bird of pas- | der Beutel the purse. |
|     sage. der Bote messenger. | der Strom the stream. |
| der Frühling spring. | spazieren gehen to walk. |
| der Pfau the peacock. | der Hügel the hill. |

---

*) Nach is sometimes placed *after* the noun, when no time
is denoted and it means *according* or *by*, Latin *secundum*. Ex.
    Dem Namen nach by the name.
    Dem Alter nach according to age.

**) zufolge is generally employed with the Genitive case, but
when placed *after* the substantive, it governs the Dative. Ex.·
    Zufolge Ihres Auftrags (Befehls) }
    or: Ihrem Auftrage zufolge   } according to your order (p. 261).

## Reading Exercise. 100.

Ein Kanarienvogel flog durch das Fenster und setzte sich auf einen Baum. Der Knabe hat gegen den Baum geschossen. Sei höflich gegen jedermann. Der Hund lief mehreremal um das Haus (herum) und suchte seinen Herrn. Der Hirsch ruhete im Schatten einer Eiche. Die Zugvögel verlassen uns im Herbst (autumn) und kehren im Frühling zu uns zurück. Joseph war während einiger Zeit Sklave bei Potiphar. Die Familie des Lord B. wohnt auf dem Lande. Der Pfau ist der schönste unter den Vögeln.

## Aufgabe. 100a.

1. I went through the forest. This book is for your brother. Go round the garden. I got this packet (Päckchen) by a messenger, it is for you. Let us walk through the town. Nobody can swim a long time against the stream. The ball rolled ₂down ₁the ₂hill.

2. Somebody has taken my purse out of my pocket. Lord E. wishes to go to France. He will depart within the next week. I shall go out after (the) dinner. Where does that gentleman live? He lives near the bridge, opposite the church. Contrary to the order of the queen ₂the ₂lady ₁left the palace.

---

## 3. Prepositions with the Genitive case.

| | |
|---|---|
| Anstatt or statt instead of. | um — willen for the sake of. |
| außerhalb without, outside. | unbeschadet without prejudice. |
| innerhalb within (*place*). | ungeachtet notwithstanding. |
| oberhalb above (*higher up*) | unweit (unfern) not far from. |
| unterhalb below (*lower down*). | vermöge by means of. |
| diesseits on this side of | vermittelst (mittelst) by means of. |
| jenseits on the other side of, | während*) during. |
| längs*) along.        [beyond | wegen**) on account of. |
| trotz*) in spite of. | zufolge according to. |

Examples.

Anstatt eines Briefes instead of a letter.
Außerhalb der Stadt without (outside) the town.
Diesseits des Flusses on this side of the river.
Jenseits des Meeres beyond the sea.
Innerhalb der Mauer within the wall.
Oberhalb der Brücke above the bridge.
Unterhalb des Dorfes below the village etc.

---

*) längs, trotz and während are sometimes used with the dative, the latter especially with words (for inst. *numerals*; that admit of no Genitive form, as. trotz meinem Befehl in spite of my order; während sechzig Jahren

**) wegen may be placed after its noun, as wegen meiner Ehre or meiner Ehre wegen on account of my honour

Besides these, there are some antiquated prepositions, viz.:
halber or halben on account of, for the sake of; kraft by power
of; laut according to.    Ex.:

Ihrer Ehre halber or halben for the sake of your honour.
Laut des königlichen Befehls according to the king's command.

## 4. Prepositions with the Dative and Accusative.

There are nine prepositions, which govern sometimes
the *dative*, sometimes the *accusative*.  The *dative* is required, when the ruling verb signifies a *state of repose;*
— the *accusative*, when it denotes a *motion from one
place to another*, or *direction towards a place*. This distinction may be rendered more evident by applying the
questions *where?* or **in** *what place?* and *whither* or **to**
what place? Take for instance the sentence: *The book
lies on the table.* You ask· *Where* or **in** *what place does
it lie?* The answer is in the *dative*:  Das Buch liegt auf
bem Tisch; auf governs the dative here, because the
verb *to lie* indicates *repose* or *rest*.

But: *Put the book upon the table* is translated: Legen
Sie das Buch auf den Tisch. The question is here· *whereto
(whither)* or **to** *what place?* — The answer is· auf den
Tisch, with the *accusative*, because the verb legen (*to lay*
or *to put*) implies a motion from some other place to the
table; the book is *to be moved* to the table.

These nine prepositions are as follows:

| | |
|---|---|
| An at, on, close to. | über over, above, across.  · |
| auf upon, on. | unter under, among. |
| hinter behind. | vor before, ago, outside. |
| in in, into, to. | zwischen between. |
| neben by the side of, near. | |

### Examples.

Wir stehen an dem Fuß (*Dat.*) des Berges.
We stand at the foot of the mountain.

Wir stellten uns an das (*Acc.*) Thor.
We placed ourselves at the gate.

Er hatte einen Hut auf dem Kopf (*Dat.*).
He had a hat on his head.

Setzen Sie sich auf diesen Stuhl (*Acc.*).
Sit down (place yourself) on this chair.

Die Fische leben in dem (im) Wasser.
The fish live in the water.

Das Kind ist in das (ins) Wasser gefallen.
The child has fallen into the water.

Der Hof ist neben dem Hause.
The yard is near (or by) the house.

Ich legte das Buch neben mich.
I laid the book beside me.

Wir setzten über den Fluß we crossed the river.

Der Hund liegt (spielt)*) unter dem Tisch.
The dog lies (plays) under the table.

Die Katze kroch unter das Bett.
The cat crept under the bed.

Ich stand vor dem Aufgang**) der Sonne auf.
I got up before sunrise.

Die Truppen rückten vor die Stadt.
The troops marched to the town.

Zwischen dem Hügel und dem Bach steht ein Haus.
Between the hill and the brook stands a house.

Hängen Sie das Bild zwischen die zwei Fenster
Hang the picture between the two windows

*Note.* To fix a distance, the prepositions. nach, zu, an, auf, hinter, in, vor may be preceded by bis, answering to the English *as far as* or *to,* as bis nach Rom as far as Rome, bis an die or bis zur Grenze to the frontier, bis auf den Berg to the top of the mountain.

## Observations.

The chapter on the *prepositions* is no doubt one of the most difficult of the German Grammar, and the proper use of them requires an intimate acquaintance with the character of the German language. The peculiar nature of every expression, particularly of the verb, is to be considered, and the prepositions therefore cannot always be rendered literally. Reserving further »Remarks« for the Second Part, we give here some hints which may direct the pupil, how to translate properly the English prepositions most in use.

**at** before a *Proper name* is rendered by in when the place is on the same level with the speaker, and by auf, if it is higher up, as: *at* Paris in Paris; he arrived *at* the village er kam in dem Dorfe an; *at* the hotel im Gasthause; *at* the castle auf dem Schloß.

---

*) There is no motion meant from one place to another or towards a certain place, but a motion remaining in the same place; therefore dative case. So, as well Er reitet auf dem Pferd, but Er reitet das Pferd. (He rides on the horse, he rides the horse.)
**) Vor, in and an used for *time,* always take the *dative*

Observe the following locutions with **at** and **to:**

| With to be *(dat.)* | With to go *(acc.)* |
|---|---|
| at the market auf bem Marft. | to the market auf ben Marft. |
| at the ball auf bem Ball. | to the ball auf ben Ball |
| at the post-office auf ber Poft. | to the post-office auf bie Poft. |
| at the chase auf ber Jagb. | to go hunting auf bie Jagb gehen. |

Denoting the hour of the day· or night, **at** is um, as: at three o'clock um brei Uhr. — *at the beginning* is im An= fang; *at* the end am Enbe; *at* the age of sixty years im Al= ter von 60 Jahren; *at* home zu Haufe.

**by** with the *Passive voice* is translated von, as: I am loved *by* my father ich werbe von meinem Bater geliebt. — *by* with a *place* is bei or neben: by the bridge neben or bei ber Brüde. — Denoting a *means*, it is burch, as: *by* force burch Gewalt; *by* practice burch Übung. — *By* land or water is translated: zu Lanb ober zu Waffer.

**in** answers to the German in with the dative, denoting rest: I found it *in* my pocket in meiner Tafche; I was *in* Heidelberg ich war in Heibelberg. Further: *in* German auf Deutfch or im Deutfchen (not in Deutfch).

*in* the country is auf bem Lanbe, whereas 'to go *into* the country' signifies auf bas Lanb gehen.

**into** is the German in with the *accusative* denoting motion: Put it *in* or *into* your pocket fteden Sie es in Ihre Tafche.

**on** meaning *upon*, is the German auf, as: *on* the table auf bem Tifch, or when motion is understood: auf ben Tifch. Meaning *close to*, it is an, as: Frankfort on the Main Frank= furt am Main. Denoting *time*, it is also rendered by an: *on* what day an welchem Tage? *on* Tuesday am Dienstag. Other expressions are: *on* my arrival bei meiner Ankunft; *on* this occasion bei biefer Gelegenheit; *on* horseback zu Pferb; *on* that condition unter biefer Bebingung.

**to,** denoting a direction to a place bearing a Proper name is nach: I go *to* Paris, *to* America etc. ich gehe nach Paris, nach Amerika ic. To go *to* a person or a person's house is zu: I go *to* him or *to* his house ich gehe zu ihm; *to* my aunt's zu meiner Tante. *To*, denoting a direction to a place higher up than the speaker, means auf, as: *to* the castle auf bas Schloß. Denoting a direction to a place (common name) *to* is translated an with the *accusative*, as: *to* the railway an bie Eifenbahn; *to* the bridge an bie Brüde. When synonymous with *into* (inside), *to* is translated in with the *accusative:* I go *to* church ich gehe in bie Kirche; let us go *to* the hotel wir wollen in ben Gafthof gehen.

**with** is commonly mit, when used with verbs of motion as: I go *with* my friend ich gehe mit meinem Freunbe. But

when it means *at* somebody's house, shop, country etc., it is
bei: he lives *with* me er wohnt bei mir; *with us* (in our
country) bei uns; does he dine with you? speist er bei Ihnen?
(Further examples on the use of the Prepositions are found
in the II. Part. Less. 49.)

## Words.

| | |
|---|---|
| Die weiße Rübe the turnip. | die Erlaubnis permission. |
| der Befehl the order, command. | vollkommen perfect. |
| der Schriftsteller the writer. | die Festung the fortress. |
| die Vorstellung remonstrance. | die Kapelle the chapel. |
| seit wann how long? | der Verlust the loss. |
| das Landgut the estate. | das Sopha the sofa. |
| der Topf pot. klettern to climb. | der Fußpfad the foot-path. |
| auslaufen to set sail. | betrachten to look at. |
| der Einfluß the influence. | erfahren to learn, to hear. |
| sich versammeln to assemble. | scharenweise by troops. |

## Reading Exercise. 101. .

Die Köchin hat gelbe Rüben (carrots) gekocht anstatt weißer
Rüben. Die Damen sind längs des Flusses spazieren gegangen.
Vor sechs Uhr werde ich nicht nach Hause gehen; warten Sie bis
morgen. Wegen des widrigen (contrary) Windes konnte das Schiff
nicht auslaufen. Seit wann (how long) wohnen Sie in diesem
Hause? Seit zwei Monaten. Bei Tagesanbruch gingen Kolumbus
und seine Gefährten ans Land und nahmen Besitz (possession)
von der Insel im Namen des Königs von Spanien. Während
dieser Zeremonie versammelten sich die Indianer scharenweise um
die Spanier und betrachteten bald die fremden weißen Männer,
bald die schwimmenden Häuser, auf welchen sie über das Meer
gekommen waren.

## Aufgabe. 102.

1. I shall take my umbrella instead of my stick. May
I send my daughter instead of my wife? Why did you go to
Baden? I went there on account of my health. There are a
great many foreigners (sehr viele Fremde) at Baden during the
summer. During winter there are fewer. The Royal garden
is outside the town. Mr. R. lives on the other side of the
river. According to an order of the Emperor Napoleon, *several French writers *were *obliged (mußten) to leave France,
notwithstanding their remonstrances. We obtained the permission by means of the influence of our aunt. Richmond
lies 12 miles above, and Greenwich 5 miles below London
bridge (der Londoner Brücke). Nothing is perfect *on this side*
the grave. *Not far* from the hill stands the chapel. He takes
a walk notwithstanding the bad weather. The garden is situ-
ated (liegt) outside the town.

2. He is a rich man in spite of his great loss. Who knocks at the door? Put the flower-pot before my window. To (an) whom (*Acc.*) did you write a letter? I wrote to (an *acc.*) the Duke of Wellington. I found this ring before the sofa. Who laid this book on my table? The servant stood at (an) the door of the house and looked (faŋ) after the birds. This old man is above (über) ninety years old. The enemy lay six months before the fortress which was built on the mountain. Men do much for the sake of (des) money. The prisoner looked up to Heaven. According to the king's command the troops must march. The castle of the duke is *on the other side* of the river. Along the river [-*side*] there is a foot-path (Fußpfad).

## Conversation.

| | |
|---|---|
| Wo wohnen (live) Sie? | Ich wohne bei dem Schlosse. |
| Welches ist der schönste unter den Vögeln? | Der Pfau gilt (is considered) für den schönsten unter den Vögeln. |
| Wo leben die Affen? | In heißen Ländern. |
| Wohin flog der Kanarienvogel? | Er flog auf einen Baum. |
| Wo saß er nachher? | Er saß auf dem Dach. |
| Wann verlassen die Zugvögel Europa? | Im Herbst (autumn), vor dem Anfang des Winters. |
| Wohin fliegen sie? | In südliche (southern) Länder, meistens nach Afrika |
| Was hat die Köchin gekocht? | Gelbe Rüben statt Kartoffeln. |
| Haben Sie meinen Hund nicht gesehen? | Doch, er ist eben um das Haus gelaufen. |
| Wo sind Sie diesen Morgen gewesen? | Ich habe einen Spaziergang längs des Flusses gemacht. |
| Warum sind Sie so traurig? | Wegen eines großen Verlustes, der mich betroffen hat. |
| Wo sind Sie dem Herrn N. begegnet (met)? | Außerhalb der Stadt, dem Bahnhof (railway-station) gegenüber. |
| Wohin geht der Koch? | Er geht auf den Markt. |
| Wohin reist der Graf? | Er reist auf das Land. |
| Wo lebt Ihre Tante? | Sie lebt im Sommer auf dem Lande, im Winter in der Stadt. |

## Reading - lesson.

### Das zerbrochene Hufeisen. The broken horse-shoe.

Ein Bauer ging mit seinem Sohn, dem kleinen Thomas, in die nächste Stadt. „Sieh", sagte er unterwegs zu ihm, „da liegt ein Stück von einem Hufeisen auf der Erde[1], hebe[2] es auf und stecke es in deine Tasche." — „Ah!" versetzte[3] Thomas, „es ist nicht der Mühe wert[4], daß man sich dafür bückt[5]." Der Vater

1) ground.   2) aufheben to pick up.   3) replied.   4) worth the trouble.   5) to stoop.

erwiberte³ nichts, nahm das Eiſen und ſteckte es in ſeine Taſche.
Im nächſten Dorfe verkaufte er es dem Schmied⁶ für drei Pfennig
(farthings)*) und kaufte Kirſchen dafür.

Hierauf ſetzten⁷ ſie ihren Weg fort. Die Hitze⁸ war ſehr groß.
Man ſah weit und breit⁹ weder Haus, noch Wald, noch Quelle¹⁰.
Thomas ſtarb beinahe¹¹ vor Durſt¹² und konnte ſeinem Vater
kaum folgen.

Dann ließ der letztere, wie durch Zufall¹³, eine Kirſche fallen.
Thomas hob² ſie gierig¹⁴ auf und ſteckte ſie in den Mund.
Einige Schritte¹⁵ weiter ließ der Vater eine zweite Kirſche fallen,
welche Thomas mit derſelben Gierigkeit¹⁶ ergriff. Dies dauerte
fort¹⁷, bis er ſie alle aufgehoben hatte.

Als er die letzte gegeſſen hatte, wandte der Vater ſich zu ihm
hin und ſagte: „Sieh', wenn du dich ein einziges¹⁸ Mal hätteſt¹⁹
bücken wollen (wished), um das Hufeiſen aufzuheben, würdeſt du nicht
nötig²⁰ gehabt haben, dich hundertmal für die Kirſchen zu bücken."

6) the smith. 7) continue. 8) the heat. 9) far and wide.
10) spring. 11) was near dying. 12) thirst. 13) by chance.
14) greedily, eagerly. 15) steps. 16) greediness. 17) continued,
lasted. 18) single. 19) see p. 94, 5 — 20) needed.

## On the Interjections.

The interjections are mostly original sounds, which
serve to express a sudden emotion of the soul, and are
produced by the impulse of the moment. Other words
however are employed also as *interjections*, and uttered
as such. Interjections admit of no change.

| | |
|---|---|
| Ah! ach! ei! ah! oh! | potz tauſend! what the deuce! |
| ach! ah! alas! o dear! | ſt! ſtill! hush! hist! |
| he! he da! oh! I say! | leider! alas! unhappily! |
| au! oh! hu! ugh! | heiſa! huzzah! hurrah! |
| oh! ho! oh! ho! | juchhe! hurrah! |
| o wehe! o dear! alas! | hm! humph! hum! |
| patſch! pat! | ſo! indeed! wohlan! well then! |
| piff! paff! bang! | auf! auf denn! on! forwards! |
| pfui! fie! psh! | Achtung! take care! attention! |
| halt! halt! stop! | o Wunder! o dear! |
| holla! holla! hollo! .holloa! | Sieh da! look! behold! |
| ſachte! gently! [halloo! | Heil! hail! |
| weg da! out of the way! | Wehe! woe! |
| fort! be gone! be off! | Feuer! fire! |

*) A *farthing*, properly speaking, is the fourth part of an
English penny (= about 8 German Pfennige), therefore = to 2
German Pfennige, but as smallest English coin it corresponds with
our 'Pfennig' of now a days, or with our Heller (= ½ Pfennig)
of former times.

Gottlob! God be praised!    vorwärts! forwards!
recht fo! 'tis well! all right!    zu Hilfe! help!
gut! good!    Wer da! who's there!

## Promiscuous Exercises for Translation and Conversation.*)

### 1.

Have you a pair [of] gloves? Yes, Sir, I have two pairs. — What has the merchant? He has different (or many) kinds[1] [of] wares (Waren). — Have you [any] friends? I have some friends. — How many friends have you? I have six faithful[2] friends. — Have your friends [any] wine or beer? They have [some] wine. — Has the shoemaker good shoes? He has always good shoes and good boots. — What have the Englishmen? They have fine horses. — Has the captain[3] any good sailors[4]? He has some good and some bad [ones][5]. Have you much bread and cheese? I have a good deal (viel). Have you enough? I have quite[6] enough. — What day of the month is it[7]? It is the twelfth. — Is it not the thirteenth? No, Sir, it is the eleventh or twelfth. — Which horses have you? We have our own[8] horses.

1) vielerlei. 2) treue, see p. 101. 3) Kapitän. 4) Matrose, m., 2nd decl. 5) see p. 113, Obs. 2. 6) ganz. 7) see p. 116, Obs. 3. 8) eigen (pl. —en).

### 2.

Had you much salt? I had only (nur) a little, but I had enough. — Has the woman much silk (Seide)? She has not much, she has not enough. — Have you any more[1] wine? I have some more[1] wine — Have you any more money? I have no more money (kein Geld mehr). — Which volume[2] of my work[3] have you? I have the second. — Have you as much[4] gold as silver? I have neither[5] gold nor silver. — Have you as many[4] stockings[6] as shoes? I have more stockings than (als) shoes — Has this soldier as much courage[7] as I [have]? He has quite as much. — Has the foreigner[8] [a] mind[9] to buy this house? He has [a] mind to buy it. — Have you [a] mind to make (zu schneiden) my pen? I have a mind to make it, but I have no time. Has your cousin [a] mind to sell his horse? No, he has no mind to sell it, he will keep[10] it.

1) any more = noch, see p. 306, 13. 2) acc. Band, m. 3) Werk, n. — 4) ebensoviel. 5) neither . . . nor weder . . . noch. 6) Strümpfe. — 7) Mut, m. 8) der Fremde. 9) Lust, f. 10) behalten.

*) These Exercises may be translated either orally or by writing between the other Exercises, as soon as the pupil has gone through the 25th lesson or even sooner.

## 3.

*Am* I (§abe idƷ) right to take[1] a walk? You *are* quite right. — *Is* he wrong to spend[2] his money? He *is* wrong to spend too much money. — To (Ʒu) whom *do* you wish to go? I wish to go to my uncle's. — Is your brother at home? He is not yet at home, but he will soon come home. *Do* you wish to speak *to* (mit) some one? Yes, I wish *to* speak to some one. — *To* whom do you wish to speak? I wish to speak *to* your aunt. — Do you wish to drink (some) red wine? I shall drink white wine. — What *does* the little girl wish to drink? She wishes to drink *some* milk. — *Are you going*[3] home[4]? Not yet, but in an hour. — Do your boys go to (in bie) school? No, they have private lessons (ƷЗrivat'ƒtunben). — Who wishes to write a letter? My daughter wishes to write several letters. — *To* (an) whom (*Acc.*) will she write? She will write *to* her [female] friends. — Who shall take[5] these letters to the post-office (auf bie ƷЗoƒt)? The servant must take them there[6].

1) einen ©paƷier'gang Ʒu madƷen or ƒpaƷieren Ʒu gebzen. 2) aus'Ʒu* geben 3) ©ebzen ©ie? 4) nadƷ §aus. 5) tragen. 6) babzin'.

## 4.

What have you to do (tbzun)? I have to write a French exercise[1]. — What has your brother to do? He has to do[2] his German exercise for to-morrow. — What did the English-man answer you (*Dat.*)? He answered nothing. — *Did* (bzat) he not say, he would come to (Ʒu) me? No, Sir, he said nothing at all[3]. — Where is the child of my neighbour? It is in your garden. — Have you many flowers in your garden? We have all kinds[4] *of* flowers. — *Are you in want of* (braudƷen ©ie) my knife? I am not in want of it, but I want a pen-knife. — What o'clock is it? It is four o'clock or half past four. — *Did* your friend not say, it was (es ‌märe) a quarter past four?[5] No, Sir, he said, it was a quarter to five. At (um) what o'clock do you go out? I go out at six o'clock this (*Acc.*) evening.

1) Ʒlufgabe f. 2) Ʒu madƷen. 3) gar nidƷts 4) aſlerſei ƗЗl. (p. 113, 8). 5) See p. 113, 5.

## 5.

Will you stay here? I cannot stay here, I am engaged[1]. Is it late? It is not late, it is but (erƒt) eight o'clock. — Can you lend me a pen or two? Here, Sir, here are four good [ones] — What have you to say [to] me? I have a word to say *to* you. — About (über) what? It concerns (be* trifft) your man-servant. — Do you love your uncle? Yes,

1) idƷ bin abgebzalten or verbzinbert or beƒdƷäftigt

I *do* love him — Does your sister love you? She *does* love me — Do the Americans like (the) tobacco[2]? They like *it* very [much]. — Do you know my cousin (*f.*)? I know her very well[3]. — Does she know your grandfather? She does not know him. — *Did* your uncle send you [any] money? He sent me seventy marks[4]. — What do you buy at (auf) (*Dat.*) the market? I buy potatoes. — Are you afraid[5] to go out in the night? I am not afraid at all[6]. — Does the father work as much as the son? The son works much more, because[7] he is young and strong.

2) ben Tabaf.   3) wohl or gut.   4) Marf.   5) Fürchten Sie sich? see 34 Less., p. 232.   6) gar nicht.   7) weil.

## 6.

Do you find what you are looking[1] [for]? I find what I *look for.* — Who was looking *for* me? Your master looked for you. — Can the cook find (,) what he looks for? He cannot find it — What is he doing? He is killing a chicken[2]. — Aie you going for[3] anything? Yes, I am going for something. — Tell me what you are *going for.* I am going for [some] meat. — *For*[4] whom does your mother send[5]? She sends for the cook (*f.*). — Do you learn German? I do learn it. — When (wann) *did* you begin[6] to learn it? I began it two months ago. — Do you speak French? No, Sir, not yet[7], but I am learning it. — How many lessons have you a (in ber) week? I have a lesson every other day. — Are these gentlemen English[8]? No, they are Scotchmen[9]. — Do they study German? I do not know, but I believe [they do]. — What does your pupil need? He needs a new book. Does he need anything else[10]? Yes, he needs a new coat and a pair of boots.

1) to look for = suchen   2) ein Hähnchen.   3) to go for = holen.   4) nach wem?   5) schicken.   6) angefangen.   7) noch nicht. 8) *subst.* (not *adj.*) Engländer, see p. 68, 8. — 9) Schottländer. 10) sonst etwas.

## 7.

Does the foreigner intend[1] to stay here? No, he intends to depart. — When do you intend to sell your house? I intend .to sell it to-day. Whose cloak is this[2]? It is mine. — Whose hats are these[2]? They belong[3] to the Englishmen. — What book do you read? I read a novel[4] by Sir Walter Scott. — Do you know that man? I do not know him. — Have you seen him already? I have seen him somewhere[5]. — Where *have* you been? I *have* been at (the) church. — Whcie has your mother been? She has been

1) to intend = gebenfen, vor'haben, gesonnen sein. 2) see p. 72, *Note 1.* 3) gehören (*Dat.*). 4) Roman', m. 5) irgenbwo

also at church. — *Has* your sister ever (ſdjon) been in France? She has never been there. — Does she intend to go there? She intends to go ▸there⁶ ▸next ▸year. — Were you at the ball last night⁷? I was not there. — Will there be a ball this evening? It will not take place⁸. — When were you at (in) the theatre? I was ▸there ▸yesterday.

6) bahin = thither. 7) geſtern abenb. 8) ſtattfinben.

**8.**

Can you swim as well (gut), as a sailor¹? I cannot swim so well as a sailor. — Can this boy swim better than I? He can swim better than you. — At what o'clock *did* Mr Green breakfast? He (has) breakfasted at nine o'clock. — *Did* he dine² before (ehe) he left³? No, Sir, he left before (vor, *prep.*) (the) dinner. — Have you told it [to] me (*dat.*)? I told it you the day before yesterday. — Which words have you written? I have written these three words. — Which book have you read? I have read the book .. you have lent me. — Are your shoes mended⁴? They are not yet mended. — Are your handkerchiefs and your stockings washed⁵? Neither the one (bie einen, *pl.*) nor the others are washed. — Why do you not eat? I do not eat because I am⁶ not hungry. — Why are you not hungry? Because I have eaten some bread and ham⁷. — Are you thirsty⁸? I am not thirsty, I have drunk some beer.

1) ein Matroſe. 2) ſpeiſen, reg. v. 3) to leave = ab'rei'ſen. 4) geſlidt. 5) gewaſchen 6) *verb last*, see p. 248, 3. 7) Sdjinten. 8) burſtig.

**9.**

Is your servant a good one? He is a good one. — Is he as good as mine? I think he is better than yours. — Are you satisfied with him? I am quite satisfied. — Do you like¹ fish? Yes, I like fish, but I like fowl² better. — Does your aunt like mutton³? She likes roast mutton and roast veal⁴. — Do the pupils *like*⁵ to learn by heart⁵? They do not like learning˙ by heart, they like⁶ writing better⁶. — To (an, *Acc.*) whom do you address⁷ your letters? I address them to a friend. — Do you admire this work⁸? I do admire *it*. — How do you amuse the ladies? I play [on the] piano (Klabier). — Have you helped your sister (*Dat.*)? I could not help *her*. — Have you asked⁹ [for] wine? No, I have ordered¹⁰ tea. — Have you bought this map¹¹? I have borrowed¹² *it*. — Have you satisfied your relations¹³? They

1) Eſſen Sie gern .. 2) eſſe lieber Geflügel 3) Hammelfleiſch. 4) Kalbfleiſch. 5) Lernen . gern auswendig? 6) ſie ſchreiben lieber — 7) abreſſieren. 8) Arbeit, f. 9) to ask for = verlangen, *reg. v.* (*Acc.*) — 10) beſtellen, *reg. v.* 11) Landkarte, f. 12) entlehnen, *r. v.* 13) Berwanbten.

ask⁹ nothing. — Has the boy fed¹⁴ his birds? He feeds
them every morning. — Did you guess (ɧabeu Sie . . erraten)
the riddle¹⁵? I could not guess it. — Have you sold your
field¹⁶? I do not intend to sell it.

14) to feed füttern, *reg v*  15) baß Rätſel  16) baß Felb.

### 10.

Have you lost (the) hope¹? I ₂never ₁lose hope. —
Has the gardener planted some trees? He has planted many
trees. — Has the soldier cleaned² his gun³? He *is* just (eben)
*cleaning*⁴ it. — Why has the tailor not cleaned the coat?
Because I have not sent it [to] him. — Has the cook roasted
the hare? He will roast it to-morrow. — Has the maid washed
her gloves? She has washed them — Where are my boots?
They are at (bei) the shoemaker's. — Why does Mary open the
window? She likes fresh air⁴. — Why does she shut the
door? She will (will) not⁵ have a draught⁶. — *Has* (iſt)
the man got up early? He *has* got up late, because he
is ill. — Will he not put out⁷ the fire? No, he wants it
still (noch). — What does he boil? He boils potatoes and
carrots. — Did you empty⁸ the bottles? All [the] bottles
are emptied. — Are they clean? They are very clean; you
may put in⁹ what you like (wollen).

1) bie Hoffnung  2) reinigen  3) Gewehr, n.  4) = he cleans.
5) Luft, f.  6) not a = feinen Zug, m.  7) ausّlöſchen.  8) leeren,
*reg. v.*  9) hineinthun.

### 11.

Is the little boy dressed? He is dressed. — Has he
dressed himself (ſich ſelbſt)⁹ Yes, he dressed himself. — Were
his shoes cleaned? The servant has cleaned them. — Did
he wash his hands? He has washed his face and his hands.
When did (iſt) the ship set¹ sail? The ship (*has*) set sail
the 'day before yesterday. — Do your friends travel by (zu)
land or by sea?ᐧ They travel by land. — *For* (auf) whom
(*Acc.*) do you wait? I wait *for* my coachman. — Have you
spoken about the mattei²? We had no time to speak about
it³. — Have you learnt reading of (von) him? I learnt it
of his brother. — Do you know your lesson? I think I
know it; I have taken⁴ pains — Does the pupil read well
(gut)? He reads pretty (ziemlich) well. — How many pages⁵
does he write every day? He writes only one page, and
that is enough. — Have the boys done⁶ their exercises?
They are doing them still⁷. — Which verb⁸ have they learnt?
They have learnt an irregular⁹ verb. — Have they written
it? No, they must not write it.

1) to set sail = ┼ab'ſegeln, *reg v.*  2) über bie Sache.  3) about
it, see p 142, § 7.  4) I take pains ich gebe mir Mühe.  5) Seite, f.
6) gemacht.  7) noch  8) baß Zeitwort.  9) unregelmäßig.

## 12.

Which[1] is the best place? The first place is the best. —
At what o'clock do we dine? We dine at one o'clock. —
What kind of meat is that? This is mutton. — How much
do you charge[2] for (the) dinner[3]? One shilling — Is dinner
ready? Yes. — Where is my dog? It is before the door. —
To whom (*dat.*) does that house belong? It belongs to
Mr. Lion. — Is that true? That is quite true. — Did you
understand me? Yes, Sir [I did]. — Is the carriage come?
The carriage is not yet come, but the horses are come —
What (wie) do you call[4] this country? It is Bavaria[5] —
Will you come with me? I have no time. — *Have* you been
at (auf, *dat.*) the post-office? I shall go »there ‹directly
(gleich). — Are *there* [any] letters for me? Not to-day. —
What do you think of (von) this letter? I cannot understand
it. — When shall we set off[6]? In a few days. — Will you
take a walk[7] in the garden? With great pleasure, if you
will go with me.

1) See p. 146, 2 — 2) forbern, verlangen. 3) das Mittageſſen.
4) nennen. 5) Bayern. 6) abreiſen. 7) einen Spazier'gang machen.

## 13.

Did[1] you tell him to come (daß er kommen ſoll)? Yes,
Sir [I did]. — Did (tſt) she get up early? She got up very
late. — Why has this boy no handkerchief? He has lost it. —
What is the price of that cloth[2]? This cloth is very cheap
(wohlfeil), it costs four marcs — Can you not take less[3]
I cannot give it cheaper[3]. — Have you no better[4]? I have
[some] better, but it is dearer. — How is the weather to-day?
It is very fine — Shall we have fine weather to-morrow?
I am afraid it will rain — Is (the) dinner served[5]? The servant
is serving it. — Shall I give you some soup? Yes, Madam,
if you please — Do you like fruit[6]? I like it very [much]. —
Will you have some potatoes? I shall take some. — Do
you breakfast, before[7] you take a walk? No, I take a walk
before I breakfast. — How long were you ill? I was ill [for]
a fortnight (14 Tage). — *Have* you been at (auf) the market?
I have not been there. — *Has* your aunt been in (auf) the
country? She has not yet been there, but she will go soon.
Has she been anywhere? She has been with (bei) her cousin[8].

1) Transl. *have you told.* 2) Tuch, n. 3) wohlfeiler. 4) fein beſſeres.
5) to serve = auf'tragen, ir. v. 6) das Obſt. 7) Conjunction ehe
or bevor'. 8) Couſine

## 14.

Who has burnt[1] my letters? The servant has burnt
them — Has Charles torn his coat? His brother has torn

1) verbrennen, see p. 126.

Lesson 37.

it. — Has the boy broken a chair? He has broken a table
and a chair. — Is your neighbour as poor as he says? He
is not so poor. — Does your tailor make good coats? He
makes good and bad [ones]. — Have you consulted² your
friends? They were not at home, when (als) I called³ on
them. — Have you paid [for] the wine? I have paid [for]
the dinner, but not [for] the wine. — Did (Hat) the servant
light⁴ the (dem) professor down stairs? Yes, [he did]. — Where
were (sind) you born? I was born in Italy. — In which
of (von) these streets does he live? He lives in (the) Frederick-
Street. — How will you spend⁵ this evening? I ²hardly
¹know it myself. — Will you go to⁶ the play with me? I thank
you; I shall be ready at seven o'clock. — Is tea ready? It
will be ready in a moment. — When *may I* send you this
letter? Whenever⁷ you please. — Where shall (soll) I send
it *to*? I will give you my direction⁸.

2) befragen, *reg.* 3) I call on or upon them ich befuche fie.
4) hinunter leuchten, *reg.* 5) zu'bringen. 6) ins Theater. 7) wann
es Ihnen gefällt (or wann Sie wollen). 8) die Adreffe.

## 15.

When will you set out for (nach) Paris? The day after
to-morrow. — *May I* trouble¹ you with a letter? I shall
take² it with great pleasure. — Will you sup³ with me? I
thank you, I am engaged⁴, it is impossible for me. — When
shall I see you again? I will call upon you this evening after
(the) supper. — Will you play [at] cards?⁵ I play very in-
differently⁶. — Do you *like*⁷ to play [at] whist?⁸ Yes, I *like*
it. — How high do you play? As high as you please. —
How many points⁹ have you? I have only seven points. —
Any news (Etwas Neues) of (von) your brother? I have not
heard from him [for a] long time. — Were many spectators¹⁰
there? There were a great many [there]. — Will you soon
go into (auf, *acc.*) the country? I intend setting out¹¹ in a week.

1) beläftigen, bemühen. 2) mitnehmen. 3) zu Abend effen. 4) ab-
gehalten. 5) Karten, *pl.* 6) gleichgültig, mittelmäßig. 7) I like to play
ich fpiele gern. 8) Whift. 9) der Punkt, Stich. 10) Zufchauer.
11) abzureifen.

## 16.

Will you help me [to] work? I am sorry, I have no
time. — Will you have the goodness to pass¹ that plate to
me? With much pleasure. — When shall we go [to] bathe?
This evening, if you like. — How *is* your grand-mother?
She is not quite well, she has caught² a cold. — How does
Mr. Gray look³? He looks very well; he is in very good

1) reichen. 2) to catch a cold = sich erfälten or den Schnupfen
bekommen. 3) ausfehen.

health. — Why did he send for the physician? His daughter
is ill. — Of (an) what illness did (ift) your neighbour die?
He died of apoplexy⁴. — Why does this little girl cry? What
*has* happened [to] her? She cries because her mother died
yesterday. — Why do you laugh at (über, *acc.*) this man?
I do not laugh at him, I laugh at his dress⁵. — Do you
know this professor? Yes, I know him very well. — Is
this bread sufficient for you? It is quite sufficient for me;
but not for the children.

4) am Schlagfluß. 5) Kleidung, f.

## 17.

Will you ask your nephew whether he is satisfied with
the cloth I have sent him? When I see him, ₂I ₁will ask
him — May I ask you for¹ a little water to wash² my
hands? I will *go for* it directly. — Have they (man) served
up³ the soup? It was served up some minutes ago. — Do
the windows look⁴ into the street? No, they look on the
yard. — Which is the shortest way to the library⁵? Go down
this street, and when you come to the bottom (ans Ende),
turn to the right, and you will see it in (auf) the great square.
— Did you forget your books, when (als) you went to school?
We never forget anything. — How many times have you
been at Paris? Only three times. — How many birds has
the hunter shot? He has killed about⁶ thirty. — Does this
merchant sell on credit⁷? He does not sell on credit —
Have you seen the fine rifle⁸ (which) I have won? I should
like to see it. — Has the prince bought the beautiful carriage
of which I spoke to (mit) you? No, Sir, the man asked⁹ a
great deal (viel) too much. — Whom have you seen at the
ball? A great many young ladies and gentlemen.

1) to ask *for* = um etwas bitten. 2) see Less. 44, p. 325, § 10.
3) aufgetragen. 4) Gehen . . auf die Str. 5) die Bibliothek 6) un=
gefähr. 7) auf Krebit'. 8) die Büchse. 9) to ask verlangen.

—————————

# Part II.

# SYNTAX.

# Thirty-eighth Lesson.

## Special use of the Article.

The use of the German article offers a great many deviations from the English practice. In general, the article is more frequently employed than in English, and as a perfect knowledge of these peculiarities is of great importance, the pupil must be careful to observe the following rules.

### I. The definite article is used in all its cases:

1) Before abstract nouns, when taken in their whole extent, as:

| | |
|---|---|
| Der Fleiß industry. | die Güte goodness, kindness |
| die Trägheit idleness. | die Beschäftigung employment. |
| die Bildung learning. | die Geduld patience. |
| die Liebe love. | die Ungeduld impatience. |
| der Haß hatred. | die Zufriedenheit contentment. |
| die Freundschaft friendship. | die Schönheit beauty. |
| die Feindschaft enmity. | die Jugend youth. |
| die Undankbarkeit ingratitude. | das Alter old age. |

*Gen.* of industry des Fleißes, of youth der Jugend 2c.

Examples

Die Tugend ist das höchste Gut virtue is the highest good.
Das menschliche Leben ist kurz human life is short.

*Note.* Of course, this is not only the case in the nominative, but in all the other cases, thus: *Gen.* of virtue der Tugend, *Dat.* to virtue der Tugend, of human life des menschlichen Lebens 2c.

2) Before collective names of corporations, bodies, governments, sciences or religious creeds, as:

| | |
|---|---|
| Der Adel nobility. | die Geschichte history. |
| die Regierung government. | das Christentum Christianity, |
| die Monarchie monarchy. | das Judentum Judaism. |

ancient history die alte Geschichte.

3) Before concrete ideas which represent a whole genus or species, as:

Der Mensch ist sterblich man (*viz.* every one) is mortal.
Die Stimmen der Tiere sind sehr verschieden the voices of animals are very different.

4) Before names of streets and mountains:

Wir wohnen in der Friedrichstraße (Frederick-street).

5) Before common names immediately followed by a proper name. Ex..

King Henry the Eighth ber König Heinrich ber Achte.
Queen Victoria bie Königin Viktoria.
Admiral Nelson ber Admiral Nelson.

Except in the *Gen* of masc. names, when in an inversion. Ex..
Admiral Nelsons Sieg (see p. 64).

6) When an adjective precedes the proper name, as:

Poor Frederick ber arme Friedrich.
Saint Paul ber heilige Paulus.

7) Before the names of metals, seasons, months, days and parts of the day. Ex.:

Gold is dearer than silver.
Das Gold ift teuerer als bas Silber.
Iron is the most useful metal.
Das Eifen ift bas nühlichfte Metall.
Summer is lovely and warm.
Der Sommer ift lieblich und warm.
April was wet and cold ber April war naß und falt.

8) Before the following and a few similar substantives

| | |
|---|---|
| Der Menfch man, mankind. | bas Glück fortune, happiness |
| bie Menfchen men. | bas Unglück adversity, misfor- |
| bie Leute people. | bas Schickfal fate.    [tune. |
| bas Frühftück breakfast. | bie Zeit time. |
| bas Mittageffen dinner | bas Gefeh law. |
| bas Abendeffen supper. | bie Natur nature. |
| ber Thee tea | ber Himmel heaven. |
| ber Durft thirst. | bas Leben life. |
| ber Hunger hunger. | ber Tod death. |
| bie Sitte custom. | ber Krieg war. |

Hence. *after dinner* nach bem Mittageffen.

9) In the following phrases:

Die meiften Menfchen most men.
. Er wohnt in ber Stabt he lives in town.
Das Kind ift in ber Schule the child is at school
Der Knabe geht in bie Schule the boy goes to school.
In ber Kirche at church. | In bie Kirche *to* church.

10) In German the definite article replaces the English indefinite article when the price of wares is indicated:

Drei Schillinge bas Kilo three shillings *a* Kilo.
Sechs (engl.) Pfennige*) ber Meter sixpence *a* meter or metre.

---

*) In German currency = 50 ₰ (sixpence = ½ a shilling cr about ½ a German marc).

11) The definite article is also employed instead of the *possessive adjective* in sentences like the following:

Karl hat das Bein gebrochen Charles has broken *his* leg.
Ich habe mir (mich) in den Finger geschnitten.
I have cut *my* finger.
Ich hatte mein Schwert in der Hand.
I had my sword in *my* hand (see Less. 41, II.).

## Repetition of the article.

12) The definite as well as the indefinite article must be repeated before each substantive in the singular, when several of them follow in succession; if they are in the plural, one article *may* serve for all. Ex.:

Das Messer und die Gabel, der Löffel und der Teller.
The knife and fork, the spoon and plate.
Ein Schuhmacher, ein Schneider und ein Hutmacher saßen in einem Wirtshause.
A shoemaker, tailor and hatter sat in a tavern.
Die Brüder und Schwestern the brothers and sisters.
Die Wiesen und (die) Felder the meadows and fields.

## Position of the article.

13) The article always precedes not only the substantives, but also the adjectives and adverbs before them. The exceptional position in English after *both, half, double, quite, too, so, as* and *how,* is not admitted in German. We say:

Both the pupils die beiden Schüler.
Half an hour eine halbe Stunde.
Double the sum die doppelte Summe.
So good a father ein so guter Vater.
Quite an old hat ein ganz alter Hut.

### Reading Exercise. 103.

1. Die Trägheit ist eine böse Eigenschaft[1]. Die Schönheit und die Sanftmut[2] sind nicht immer vereinigt[3]. Mars war bei den Römern der Gott des Krieges Der Graf Derby ist verreist[4]. Die Fürsten sind Menschen und können nicht immer helfen. In Italien ist der Winter nicht kalt; dagegen ist der Sommer sehr heiß. Das Abendessen und der Thee sind bereit[5]. Die Erde und der Himmel sind das Werk Gottes. Die Natur ist ein offenes Buch. Kommen Sie nach dem Frühstück zu mir, oder wenn Sie lieber[6] wollen, nach dem Mittagessen.

1) quality. 2) meekness *or* gentleness. 3) united. 4) from home. 5) ready. 6) like better.

1. Wieviel koſtet die Flaſche? Die Flaſche koſtet eine
halbe Mark. Wieviel koſtet der Meter von dieſem Tuche? Ich
verkaufe es zu (für) ſieben Mark den Meter. Dieſer Knabe hat
den Arm gebrochen; ſeine Schweſter hat ſich aus Unachtſamkeit[7]
in die Hand geſchnitten. Ich habe einen Stock, einen Regenſchirm und ein Raſiermeſſer[8] gekauft. Der Schüler hat eine halbe
Seite[9] auswendig (by heart) gelernt. Ich habe ihm die doppelte
Summe bezahlt.

    7) from carelessness. 8) razor. 9) page.

### Aufgabe. 104.

1. Time is precious. Fortune is changeable[1]. Spring is a
fine season[2]. Horses are useful animals. Iron and copper[3] are
more useful than gold and silver. Adversity borrows[4] its (his)
sharpest sting (Stachel, m.) from our impatience. Ingratitude
dries up (vertrocknet) the fountain[5] of all goodness. Concealed[6]
hatred is more dangerous[7] than open enmity. Learning is an
ornament (Zierde) to youth (Gen.) and a comfort (Troſt, m.)
to (of) old age[8].

2. Employment is necessary[9] to man; if agreeable, »it ꞁis
a pleasure, if useful, »it ꞁis a happiness. Industry is the
true[10] philosophers' stone (Stein der Weiſen), which turns[11] all
metals into gold. The sweetest salve (Salbe, f.) for misery[12]
is patience, and the only (einzige) medicine[13] for want (die Not)
is contentment. Tea is ready. Nature is contented with little,
but the cravings of luxury (die Bedürfniſſe des Luxus) are
boundless[14]. Those who wish to study history, ought to begin
with ancient history.

    1) veränderlich 2) Jahreszeit, f. 3) das Kupfer 4) borgen, ent-
lehnen. 5) die Quelle. 6) verborgen (Part p.). 7) gefährlich. 8) old
age das Alter. 9) nötig. 10) wahr. 11) welcher . . . verwandelt.
12) das Elend. 13) Arznei, f. 14) grenzenlos.

---

## II. The article is omitted:

1) Before names of materials when taken in an indefinite sense, no particular kind, measure or quality
being meant This form is called in French »sens par-
titif«, the substantive not being taken in its whole extent.
When we say: Ich habe Gold und Silber I have (some)
gold and silver; er hat Fleiſch und Brot he has (some)
meat and bread, we do not mean all the gold and silver,
all the meat and bread, but *some of it.* This relation
is often expressed in English by the word *some* (or *any*)
preceding; in which case the substantive is used without the article in German, as:

Wein wine *or* some wine.    Papier (some) paper.
Waſſer some water.    Tinte some ink.
    Brot und Butter (some) bread and butter.

2) After the word *all* alle (in the plural), and sometimes after *both* beide. Ex..

All the boys alle Knaben.
Both the sisters beide Schwestern.

*Note.* When the article is expressed with beide, it must precede, and beide takes n, as:
Both the sisters die beiden Schwestern.

3) The indefinite article is omitted in the expressions *many a* (mancher, e, 8) and *no less a* (fein geringerer). Examples:

Many *a* flower manche Blume.
He was *no less a* man than the bishop.
Er war fein geringerer Mann als der Bischof.

4) In the plural all kinds of substantives may be used without the article, as in English, when understood in an *indistinct* and *general sense*. Ex..

Federn, *pl.*, pens. | Eier eggs.
Männer und Frauen (or Weiber) men and women.
Knaben und Mädchen boys and girls.
Schafe, Kühe, Ochsen sheep, cows, oxen.

*Note.* *Some* before a noun in the *plural* is generally translated einige, as: Some friends einige Freunde; some papers einige Zeitungen ic.

5) The article is sometimes omitted before the names of the cardinal points of the compass. Norden (Mitternacht) the north; Süden (Mittag) the south, Osten (Morgen) the east, Westen (Abend) the west, when these words are preceded by the preposition gegen or nach, as:-
Rußland liegt gegen Osten Russia lies towards the east.

Without the preposition gegen, the article is used
Die Sonne geht im Westen unter the sun sets in the west.

6) As in English, it is usually omitted in proverbs·
Armut ist feine Schande poverty is no disgrace.
Zufriedenheit geht über Reichtum.
Contentment is better than wealth.

7) In such questions as: *Is the river a deep one?* the article *a* as well as *one* is omitted. We simply say:
Ist der Fluß tief?

8) In the inversion of the Saxon Genitive, when it precedes the substantive by which it is governed·

Eduards Mutter und Karls Tante.
Edward's mother and Charles's aunt.
In meines Oheims (or Onkels) Haus in my uncle's house.
Ihres Nachbars Garten your neighbour's garden

*Note.* This Saxon Genitive can only be used when the word in the Genitive expresses a person; and it should not be made use of after a preposition that governs the genitive case, nor after another Genitive. Ex.: By means of my uncle's influence — cannot be translated. vermittelst meines Oheims Einflusses, but: vermittelst des Einflusses meines Oheims.

9) After the Genitive of the relative pronoun in the singular and plural. Ex.:

Der Knabe, dessen Vater krank liegt.
The boy whose father lies ill.
Die Blume, deren Schönheit so sehr bewundert wird.
The flower, *the* beauty of which is so much admired.

10) No article in the following expressions:

Zu Land by land.
zu Wasser by water.
zu Pferd on horseback.
zu Fuß on foot.
zu Wagen in a carriage.
zu Schiff on board ship.
vor Hunger of (with) hunger.
vor Durst of thirst.
bei Tag by day.
bei Nacht by night.
mit Vergnügen with pleasure.
aus Verdruß from vexation.
aus Haß from hatred.
recht haben to be right.
unrecht haben to be wrong
Hunger haben*) to be hungry.
Durst haben*) to be thirsty.
zu Mittag essen (speisen) to dine.
zu Teil werden (*dat.*) to fall to one's lot.
zu Nacht (Abend) essen to sup.
(sein) Wort halten to keep *one's* word.
Lust haben to have a mind.
Rechenschaft geben or ablegen to render account, account for.

in Ohnmacht fallen to faint, swoon.
Schrecken einjagen to terrify.
Teil nehmen (an) to take part.
Abschied nehmen to take leave.
Gefahr laufen to run a risk.
achthaben or geben ⎱ to take
sich in acht nehmen ⎰ care.
Geduld haben to have patience.
Mitleid haben to have compassion.
um Verzeihung bitten to beg *one's* pardon.
Glauben schenken or beimessen to give credit.
Hilfe leisten to render assistance.
Gesellschaft leisten keep company.
zu Hilfe kommen to come to one's assistance or help.
zu Bett gehen to go to bed.
Trotz bieten to bid defiance.
zu Grunde gehen to perish.
zustande kommen to succeed.
zustande bringen to accomplish.
Erwähnung thun to mention.
um Rat fragen to ask for advice.

---

*) or hungrig sein; durstig sein.

## Reading Exercise. 105.

**1.** Ich habe Fleisch und Brot gegessen. Gehen Sie auf den Markt und kaufen Sie Butter und Eier. Leihen Sie mir einige Federn, ich muß einige Briefe schreiben. Amerika liegt gegen Westen. Ende gut, alles gut. Gewalt[1] geht vor Recht. In meines Großvaters Garten steht ein alter Nußbaum, dessen Stamm (trunk) ganz hohl[2] ist. Hier ist das Buch, dessen Verfasser Sie so sehr bewundern. Wollen Sie schon Abschied nehmen? Reisen Sie zu Pferd oder zu Wagen? Ich reise zu Fuß

**2.** Sie müssen Geduld haben. Haben diese Herren Wein oder Bier getrunken? Sie haben sechs Flaschen Wein und einige Gläser Bier getrunken. Reisen Sie zu Wasser oder zu Land? Ich reise zu Land. Zu Wasser läuft man Gefahr, zu ertrinken[3] Sie haben recht. Haben Sie schon von Ihren Freunden Abschied genommen? Noch nicht, aber ich werde es morgen thun. Fräulein Elisabeth ist in Ohnmacht gefallen. Jedermann hatte Mitleid(en) mit ihr.

1) power. 2) hollow. 3) to be drowned.

### Aufgabe. 106.

**1.** We had some cheese, bread and butter. Do you want anything? Yes, I want some sugar and coffee. America lies towards the west Contentment goes before (über) wealth. Henry's cousin is very ill. The boy whose books *were*[1] found under the table. *has been*[1] punished for his carelessness[2]. Charles has gone to bed. I have read all the letters which your brother wrote (has written) to (an) my sister My uncle (*has*) travelled a great deal (viel) by water and by land. *Am* I right to take a walk? Yes, you *are* quite right

**2.** *Is* he wrong to spend[3] his money? He *is* wrong to spend too much money. At what o'clock to you dine? We dine at five. Dinner is ready Are you hungry? I am hungry and thirsty. I do not like to go out by night. This gentleman has German lessons[4], but I believe[5], only twice a (in der) week. I beg your pardon, he has a lesson every other day[6] I must take leave of (von) you. What[7] a mistake[8]! What beautiful peaches[9]! How much do they cost a piece (costs the piece)? She is ₂so ₃kind ₁a ₄lady. Macbeth was not willing[10] to commit[11] so great a crime[12]

1) Passive voice. 2) Nachlässigkeit, Unachtsamkeit. 3) ausgeben 4) Stunden. 5) glauben 6) see p. 239. 7) was für ein 8) Fehler, m 9) Pfirsich, m. 10) to be willing = wollen. 11) begehen. 12) Verbrechen, m

### Reading-lesson.

**Das doppelte Verbrechen. The double crime.**

Drei Einwohner von Balk reisten miteinander; sie fanden einen Schatz[1] und teilten ihn. Sie setzten dann ihren Weg fort,

indem[2] sie sich über den Gebrauch (use) unterhielten[2], welchen sie
von ihren Reichtümern machen wollten. Die Lebensmittel[3], welche
sie mit sich genommen hatten, waren aufgezehrt[4], sie kamen überein[5], daß einer von ihnen in die Stadt gehen sollte, um welche
(some) zu kaufen, und daß der jüngste diesen Auftrag[6] über-
nehmen[7] sollte; er ging fort.

Unterwegs sagte er zu sich selbst: „Nun bin ich reich; aber
ich würde viel reicher sein, wenn ich allein gewesen wäre, als der
Schatz gefunden wurde... Diese zwei Menschen haben mir meine
Reichtümer entrissen. Könnte ich sie nicht wieder bekommen (get)?
Das würde mir leicht sein: ich dürfte (need) nur die Lebensmittel
vergiften[8], die ich kaufen soll; bei (upon) meiner Rückkehr würde
ich sagen, daß ich in der Stadt (zu Mittag) gespeist habe; meine
Gefährten[9] würden ohne Mißtrauen davon essen, und sie würden
sterben. Ich habe jetzt nur den dritten Teil des Schatzes, und
dann würde ich alles bekommen" (get).

Indessen[10] sagten die beiden andern Reisenden zu einander:
„Wir brauchen die Gesellschaft dieses jungen Menschen nicht; wir
haben den Schatz mit ihm teilen müssen; sein Teil würde die
unsrigen vermehrt[11] haben, und wir würden sehr reich sein. Er wird
bald wieder kommen, wir haben gute Dolche, wir wollen ihn töten."

Der junge Mensch kam mit vergifteten Lebensmitteln zurück;
seine Gefährten[9] ermordeten ihn; sie aßen, sie starben, und der
Schatz gehörte[12] niemand.

So fanden alle drei ihren verdienten Lohn[13].

1) treasure  2) conversing (see p 248, the conj indem).
3) provisions  4) to consume, eat up.  5) to agree.  6) commission
or task  7) undertake.  8) to poison.  9) companions. 10) meanwhile. 11) to increase. 12) belong. 13) reward.

## Conversation.

| | |
|---|---|
| Wer reiste mit einander? | Drei Einwohner der Stadt Balk. |
| Was fanden sie auf dem Wege? | Einen Schatz. |
| Was thaten sie mit demselben? | Sie teilten ihn unter sich. |
| Wovon sprachen sie unterwegs? | Sie unterhielten sich über den Gebrauch, den sie von dem Gelde machen wollten. |
| Als ihre Lebensmittel aufgezehrt waren, was beschlossen (determine) sie, zu thun? | Sie kamen überein, daß einer von ihnen in die Stadt gehen sollte, welche zu kaufen. |
| Wer mußte gehen? | Der jüngste von ihnen. |
| Welchen Plan faßte (made) dieser unterwegs? | Er beschloß, die Lebensmittel zu vergiften. |
| Warum wollte er dieses thun? | Um den Schatz für sich allein zu bekommen. |
| Was wollte er bei seiner Rückkehr zu seinen Gefährten sagen? | Daß er schon in der Stadt gespeist habe. |

Welchen Erfolg (result) hoffte er von diesen Worten?

Er hoffte, seine Gefährten würden dann ohne Mißtrauen die vergifteten Speisen essen.

Was hatten die beiden andern während seiner Abwesenheit verabredet (agreed)?

Sie wollten ihn ermorden, wenn er zurückkäme

Zu welchem Zwecke (purpose)?

Um seinen Teil des Schatzes für sich behalten zu können.

Führten sie ihren Entschluß aus (carry out)?

Ja, sie töteten ihren Kameraden

Was thaten sie dann?

Sie aßen von den Speisen.

Was war die Folge davon?

Sie starben an dem Gifte.

Wem gehörte dann der Schatz?

Er gehörte niemand.

---

# Thirty-ninth Lesson.

## Remarks on the Genitive of substantives.

1) The pupil knows already, that one substantive governed by another, is generally expressed by the *genitive*, as: Der Hund (whose wessen?) des Gärtners, die Blätter des Apfelbaumes; das Dach des Hauses 2c.; or expressed by the *Saxon* genitive, in which the article of the nominative is omitted, as ·

Des Gärtners Hund, des Knaben Fleiß, des Fürsten Wunsch.
Wallenstein drückte des Kaisers Länder mit des Kaisers Heer.
(Schiller.)

2) A great number of substantives connected with another noun by means of the preposition *of*, are rendered in German by *compound* substantives. Such are.

Die Wahrheitsliebe*) the love of truth.
die Dichtkunst the art of poetry.
ein Blumenkranz a wreath of flowers.
das Schlachtfeld the battle-field.
ein Blutstropfen a drop of blood.
die Thatsache the matter of fact.
ein Geschäftsmann a man of business.

3) The genitive case of substantives is sometimes employed to form *adverbs*, either alone or with adjectives ·

Des Morgens**) (or am Morgen) in the morning.

---

*) For euphony's sake sometimes an ß, e or n is inserted.
**) When such expressions of time are accompanied by an adjective, the prep. an is mostly used. Ex:
On a hot day an einem heißen Tage.

Des Abends (or am Abend) in the evening.
Dreimal des Jahres three times a year
Eines Tages one day. Meines Wissens to my knowledge.
Gerades (geraden) Weges straightway.
Langsamen Schrittes with tardy step, at a slow pace.

*Note 1.* Feminine nouns require a preposition, as:
Zweimal in der Woche twice a week.

*Note 2* However, when the time is *distinctly* expressed,
the *accusative* is required, as:
Diesen Morgen this morning. | Jeben Abend every evening.
Den (or am) zehnten Juli on the tenth of July.
Letzten (nächsten c.) Sonntag last (next etc.) Sunday.
Ich erwarte meinen Freund jeden Augenblick.
I expect my friend every moment.
Sie hat zwei Stunden (*Acc.*) geschlafen
She has slept (for) two hours

4) But the English preposition *of* does not always
denote a real genitive When the names of *countries,
towns, villages* and *places,* also of *months* are connected
with their generic names, they stand in the nominative,
being considered as apposition to them. Ex.:

Die Stadt London (not Londons) the city *of* London
Das Königreich England the kingdom of England
Die Universität Heidelberg the university of Heidelberg
Der Monat Mai the month of May
Der achte März (not von März) the eighth *of* March.

5) This is also the case after words importing *measure,
weight, number, quantity;* the preposition *of* is not to be
translated:

Ein Glas Wasser a glass *of water.*
Ein Kilo Butter a Kilogram (or Kilo) *of butter.*
Zwei Kilo Fleisch (not Fleisches) two Kilograms (or Kiloes)
Eine Flasche Wein a bottle *of wine.*     [*of meat.*
Zehn Meter Tuch ten meters *of cloth.*
Hundert Malter Weizen a hundred bushels *of wheat.*
Ein Regiment' Soldaten a regiment *of soldiers.*
Eine Herde Schafe a flock *of sheep.*

*Note 1.* When such substantives are taken in a *particular* or
*definite* sense, *of* must be translated von, as:
Zwei Kilo von diesem Fleisch.
ein Stück von diesem Brot
ein Buch von dem Papier, welches Sie empfohlen haben.

*Note 2* When preceded by an adjective, the *Genitive* must be
used, as Eine Flasche guten Weines

## Reading Exercise. 107.

Des Kaisers Wille muß geschehen (be done). Des Knaben Fleiß ist belohnt worden. Wir erwarten jeden Tag einen Brief von Herrn P. Der Arzt riet mir, des Morgens und des Abends einen Löffel voll von dieser Arznei[1] zu nehmen. Meines Wissens ist London die größte Stadt in Europa. Langsamen Schrittes fuhr der Wagen des königlichen Prinzen durch den Park. Diesen Abend habe ich nicht Zeit, meine Stunde (lesson) zu nehmen. Die Universität Heidelberg ist berühmt[2]. Den zwölften April 1852 besuchte ich das Schlachtfeld von Waterloo.

1) medicine. 2) renowned.

### Aufgabe. 107a.

This is my (*Gen.*) father's house. The city *of* Rome is very old. The city of St. Petersburgh *was* built by Peter the Great (*Dat.*). When do you wish to have your lessons, *in* the evening or in the morning? I am engaged (beschäftigt or verhindert) in the morning; it would be most convenient[1] for me, to take them in the afternoon between two and four. The kingdom of Saxony (Sachsen) has an extent[2] of only 280 German square miles[3]. Bring me a glass of beer[4]. The streets of (von) Paris are more beautiful than those[5] of London. The month of July was very hot.

1) am bequemsten or am passendsten. 2) eine Ausdehnung von. 3) Quadrat'meilen. 4) Bier. 5) See p. 145, 3.

---

6) The sign of the genitive, **of**, must be translated **von**, in the following cases:

*a*) With substantives expressing *rank* or *title:*

Die Königin von Spanien the queen *of* Spain.
Der Herzog von Wellington the duke *of* Wellington.

*b*) Before cardinal numbers·

Ein Mann von dreißig Jahren a man *of* thirty years.
In einer Entfernung von sechs Meilen.
At a distance *of* six miles.
Er starb im Alter von siebzig Jahren.
He died at the age of seventy years.

*c*) Before the names of *metals* and other *materials,* if the adjective be not preferred:

Ein Schiff von Eisen*) a ship of iron.
Ein Becher von Gold a cup (goblet) of gold.
Eine Bildsäule (or ein Standbild) von Marmor a statue of marble.

---

*) Or: ein eisernes Schiff, ein goldner Becher, eine marmorne Bildsäule.

*d*) Before nouns in the *partitive* sense not expressing measure:

Der Verlauf von Büchern the sale *of* books.
Die Nähe von Städten the vicinity *of* towns
Eine Sache von geringem Wert a matter *of* little value.

*e*) After the demonstrative, relative and indefinite pronouns, after the cardinal and ordinal numerals, and the superlative degree, *of* is mostly rendered by von, though the Genitive may also be used.*) Ex.:

Derjenige von Ihren Schülern, welcher ꝛc. (that *of* your p.).
Welcher von diesen Männern? which of these men?
Einige von meinen Freunden*) some of my friends.
Der zehnte von dreißig Schülern of 30 scholars the tenth.
Die schönste aller Frauen or   } the handsomest of all
Die schönste von allen Frauen }    women (ladies).

7) The English genitive of the participle present, replacing a substantive, when governed by another, is expressed in German by the Infinitive with zu:

Die Kunst zu tanzen the art *of dancing*
Das Geheimnis reich zu werden the secret of becoming rich.

8) *Of* preceded by a substantive formed from a verb requiring a preposition, is translated in different ways according to the meaning of that preposition; no certain rule can be given for such case:

Der Gedanke an Gott the thought *of* God (denken an).
Die Furcht vor dem Tode the fear *of* death (sich fürchten vor).
Die Liebe zum Leben the love *of* life (Liebe haben zu).
Aus Mangel an Geld from want *of* money (Mangel haben an).

### Reading Exercise. 108.

Die Königin von England ist stolz auf ihre Marine (navy). Man baut jetzt ganze Schiffe von Eisen. Ist dieser Ring von Gold oder von Silber? Er ist von Gold. Welcher von diesen Knaben hat den ersten Preis erhalten? Es war Julius; er war der Erste von fünfzig Schülern Die Kunst zu ringen[1] ist sehr alt; sie blühte[2] am meisten bei (with) den alten Griechen. Das Verlangen (desire) nach Reichtum veranlaßt (induces) diesen Mann, so großartige[3] Unternehmungen zu machen. Die Liebe

1) to wrestle. 2) flourished. 3) grand, great

---

*) This is a matter of *euphony* We may say as well: Einige meiner Freunde, die meisten Ihrer Schüler, but it would be less harsh to say die meisten von Ihren Schülern Welcher Ihrer Schüler would be intolerably harsh

zum Leben ift allen Menſchen angeboren [4], dagegen die Furcht vor dem Tode iſt ihnen anerzogen [5].

4) innate   5) imbibed by education.

**Aufgabe. 108a.**

1  Two of (von) my brother's children *have* died. The queen of England has married[1] Prince Albert. We saw a large fire at (in) a distance *of* about (ungefähr) seven miles. Grateful nations[2] erect[3] statues of bronze (Erz) or stone [to] their great men. Emily was the handsomest of all the young ladies [present] at the ball. No one[4] of my friends has written to me. On the tenth of July, ₂I ₁shall make a journey of fifty miles, to see (um . . . zu beſuchen) a friend. This gentleman is of high rank (Rang). This Frenchman is the father of nine children.

2.  Most of the pupils were not prepared[5] for the lesson. Which of the (man-) servants is[6] to go? Some of the finest houses of the town are burnt down[7] My friend has discovered[8] a new way[9] of catching fish[10] The habit[11] of taking snuff (zu ſchnupfen) is very common in many countries. The traveller *was obliged to* return for (aus) want *of* money. When nothing but (als) the fear of (the) punishment[12] ₂prevents[13] ₁us, from acting wrong (unrecht zu thun), ₂we ₁are guilty[14] in the eye[15] of God.

1) geheiratet. 2) die Nation. 3) errichten. 4) keiner, *sing.* 5) vor-bereitet  6) is to ſoll  7) abgebrannt. 8) entdeckt. 9) Methode, f. 10) Fiſche, *pl* 11) die Gewohnheit. — 12) Strafe, f. 13) uns verhin-dert  14) ſchuldig  15) in den Augen Gottes.

### Reading-lesson.
### Alphons der Fünfte.

Alphons V., König von Arragonien, genannt der Groß-mütige[1], war der Held (hero) ſeines Jahrhunderts. Er dachte nur [daran], andre glücklich zu machen (of making) Dieſer Fürſt ging gern[2] ohne Gefolge (suite) und zu Fuß durch die Straßen ſeiner Hauptſtadt. Als man ihm einſt Vorſtellungen[3] machte über[4] die Gefahr, welcher (*Dat.*) er ſeine Perſon ausſetzte[5], antwortete er: „Ein Vater, welcher mitten unter ſeinen Kindern umher'geht[6], hat nichts zu fürchten.

Man kennt folgenden Zug[7] von ſeiner Freigebigkeit[8]: Als einer von ſeinen Schatzmeiſtern[9] ihm eine Summe von tauſend Dukaten brachte, ſagte ein Offizier, welcher eben zugegen[10] war, ganz leiſe[11] zu jemand: „Wenn ich nur dieſe Summe hätte, würde ich glücklich ſein“ — „Du ſollſt es (so) ſein!“ ſprach der König, welcher es gehört hatte, und ließ ihn dieſe tauſend Dukaten mit ſich nehmen.

1) generous. 2) liked. 3) to remonstrate. 4) concerning the danger. 5) to expose. 6) walks about. 7) trait, instance. 8) muni-ficence. 9) treasurer  10) present. 11) low.

Auch der folgende Zug zeugt¹² von seinem edlen Charakter:
Eine mit Matrosen und Soldaten beladene Galeere¹³ ging unter;
er befahl, ihnen Hilfe zu bringen; man zögerte¹⁴. Da sprang
Alphons selbst in ein Boot, indem¹⁵ er zu denen, welche sich vor
der Gefahr fürchteten, sagte: „Ich will lieber ihr Gefährte¹⁶, als
der Zuschauer¹⁷ ihres Todes sein."

12) proves, gives witness. 13) galley. 14) to hesitate. —
15) saying. 16) companion. 17) the spectator.

### Conversation.

| | |
|---|---|
| Wer war Alphons V.? | Er war König von Arragonien. |
| Wie wurde er genannt? | Er hieß „der Großmütige". |
| An was dachte er immer? | Andre glücklich zu machen. |
| Wie ging er gern durch die Stadt? | Ohne Gefolge und zu Fuß. |
| Welche Vorstellung machte man ihm deshalb? | Daß er seine Person einer Gefahr aussetze. |
| Was antwortete er darauf? | „Ein Vater hat unter seinen Kindern nichts zu fürchten." |
| Was brachte ihm eines Tages sein Schatzmeister? | Eine Summe von tausend Dukaten. |
| Wer war gerade (just) zugegen? | Ein Offizier. |
| Was sagte dieser Offizier leise in seiner Gegenwart? | „Ich würde glücklich sein, wenn ich dieses Geld hätte." |
| Was sagte darauf der König? | „Wenn diese Summe Sie glücklich macht, so sollen Sie sie haben." |
| Wie bewährte (showed) er ein andres Mal seine Nächstenliebe (humanity)? | Als eine mit Soldaten beladene Galeere untersank, befahl er sogleich, ihnen zu Hilfe zu kommen. |
| Und als niemand helfen wollte, was that er? | Er sprang selbst in ein Boot und ruderte (rowed) ihnen zu Hilfe. |
| Welche edlen Worte sprach er bei dieser Gelegenheit? | Er sagte: „Ich will lieber der Gefährte als der Zuschauer ihres Todes sein." |

---

# Fortieth Lesson.

### Remarks on the Auxiliaries of mood.
(See the 17th lesson p. 88.)

From the great deficiency of forms possessed by the
English *auxiliaries of mood*, their translation into German
requires much attention. Observe the following remarks:

## I. On the auxiliary können.

1) Können denotes in the first place *physical* possibility, *the being able* to do something, and is in this
sense sometimes replaced by imstande sein.

Ein Lahmer kann nicht gehen (ist nicht imstande, zu gehen).
A lame man *cannot* walk.

Diefe Leute fönnen uns nicht fchaden.
These people are not able to injure us.

2) Können answers to the English *may*, when it means a possibility *granted by the speaker*:

Sie können herein kommen you *may* come in.
Er kann ein Betrüger fein he *may* be a cheat.

3) If *could* refers to a past tense, it is the Imperfect Indicative (= *was able*) and is translated konnte:

Ich war in feinem Haufe, aber ich konnte ihn nicht fehen.
I was in his house, but I *could* not see him.

4) When the English *could* is conditional, meaning: *would be able*, then it is translated könnte:

Er könnte, wenn er wollte.
He *could* (*he would be able*) if he would (liked).

5) If *could* depends on a preceding verb of *affirmation* fagte etc., i. e. in the "*oblique narration*", it is rendered by könne or könnte (see lesson 43, III). Ex:

Er fagte, er könne (or könnte) nicht kommen.
He said he *could* not come.

6) In speaking of languages, können signifies *to know* or *to be able to speak*:

Können Sie Französisch?
Do you know (*or* speak) French?

Nein, ich kann nicht Französisch, aber ich kann Englisch.
No, I cannot speak French but English.

*Note. I cannot help* or *forbear* means ich kann nicht umhin Ex.:
I could not forbear laughing.
Ich konnte nicht umhin', zu lachen,
or: Ich konnte mich des Lachens nicht enthalten

## II. On mögen, wollen, im Begriff fein.

1) Mögen expresses that the *speaker* has no objection to another person's doing anything:

Er mag den Stock behalten he *may* keep the stick.
Sie mögen den Brief lefen you may read the letter.

*Note.* In this sense the Germans often use können:
Du kannst den Stock behalten.
Sie können b.n Brief lefen 2c.

2) It denotes a *possibility granted* by the speaker:

Er mag ein ehrlicher Mann fein he may be an honest man.
Es mag wahr fein it may be true.

3) It denotes an inclination of a person spoken of (similar to *to like* gern wollen). Ex :

Er mag keinen Wein trinken he does not like to drink wine.
Mag sie nicht tanzen? does she not like to dance?
Ich hätte ihn sehen mögen I should have liked to see him.

4) When *may* expresses a *wish*, it is translated in singular möchte (not mag) and in plur. mögen Sie or möchten Sie. Ex.:

Mögen (or möchten) Sie glücklich sein! may you be happy'

5) *To be going* or *about* to do something is translated in various ways, commonly by eben wollen, im Begriff sein, or auf dem Punkt stehen (to be on the point of). Ex.:

Er will eben abreisen or er steht auf dem Punkte, abzureisen.
He is just going to set out.

Ich wollte eben antworten. | Er war im Begriff zu sprechen.
I was about to reply.      | He was going to speak

6) Wollen denotes sometimes an assertion. Ex.:

Karl will es gehört haben.
Charles affirms that he has heard it

### Reading Exercise. 109.

Kannst du mir sagen, warum dein Bruder morgen nicht zu mir kommen kann? Der Knabe kann das Buch behalten, ich brauche es nicht mehr. Wenn unsre Soldaten die Stadt behaupten[1] könnten, so wäre der Sieg[2] nicht zweifelhaft[3]. Können Sie Deutsch? Nein, ich kann es noch nicht; aber ich lerne es. Ich hätte dort sein mögen. Als ich im Begriff war, das Fenster zu öffnen, war alles still. Ich wollte eben in das Bad gehen. Ich bin im Begriff, nach England zu reisen. Man wollte sich eben zu Tisch setzen, als der General ins Zimmer trat

1) hold. 2) the victory. 3) dubious.

### Aufgabe. 109a.

Can you come to-morrow instead of to-day? No, Sir, I cannot. You may stay[1] where you are. Have you learnt your lesson? I could not learn it, I had no book. I would learn it, if I had a book. The man could not lift (aufheben) the stone. Do you intend[2] to go to America? I was just about correcting your exercise, when your father came[3] to see me. I had [a] mind (Lust) to call[3] upon him (ihn zu besuchen), but my mother did not wish it.

1) See p. 256, *Note.* — 2) *to intend* means gedenken, vor'haben, beabsichtigen and gesonnen sein — 3) *to come* or *go to see* and *to call upon* (on) *a person* both mean Jemand besuchen.

## III. Laſſen.

The verb laſſen is often used as auxiliary verb, when joined to another verb, and requires the following Infinitive without zu.

1) It signifies, *to let, to suffer, to permit.*

Ich laſſe ihn*) ſchlafen I let him sleep.
Laſſen Sie mich gehen let me go.
Ich habe ihn gehen laſſen I have suffered him to go.

2) It signifies *to leave:*

Laſſen Sie das bleiben leave that alone.

3) It signifies *to make, to get ·*

Er ließ mich eine ganze Stunde warten.
He made me wait a whole hour.
Er ließ ihn ſeinen Zorn fühlen.
He made him feel his anger.

4) When in English the verbs *to have* or *to get* have an accusative *after* them, followed by a past participle, = 'to have (or get) a thing done', they are rendered by laſſen with the following verb in the Infinitive

Ich will mein Holz ſägen laſſen.
I will *have* my wood *sawn* (or *sawed*).
Wo laſſen Sie Ihre Bücher binden (or einbinden)?
Where do you *get* your books *bound?*
Man ließ ihn hereinrufen they *had* him *called* in.
Ich habe ein Paar Schuhe machen laſſen.
I have *got (had)* a pair of shoes made

5) It corresponds with the verb *to cause, to order;* but in German the following *Infinitive* must always be in *the active.* Examples:

Wir ließen ſeinen Freund kommen.
We caused his friend to come.
Der Richter ließ den Dieb verhaften (or arretieren).
The judge caused the thief *to be arrested.*

6) It signifies *to bid* (heißen), *to tell:*

Laſſen Sie die Dame hereintreten bid the lady walk in.
Er ließ (or hieß) den Boten draußen warten
He told the messenger to wait without

7) As an auxiliary to the Imperative mood, laſſen is used only for the *first person plural* of that mood:

---

*) The object of laſſen is mostly in the acc. When there are *two* objects, the *person* is in the dative, the *thing* in the acc. Ex.: Laſſen Sie mir (*dat.*) das Buch.

Laſſen Sie uns eine Taſſe Kaffee trinken.
Let us take (drink) a cup of coffee.

Laßt uns ſingen und tanzen let us sing and dance.

8) With the reflective pronoun ſich, it involves the idea of: *it can be* or *may be:*

Es läßt ſich nicht begreifen it cannot be understood.
Darüber läßt ſich vieles ſagen of that, much might be said.

### Reading Exercise. 110.

Wir ließen die Kinder bis acht Uhr ſchlafen. Ich werde es von dem Schreiner[1] machen laſſen. Wer hat dieſes Haus bauen laſſen? Mein Nachbar hat es für ſeinen Sohn bauen laſſen. Laß den Kutſcher[2] anſpannen[3]. Der Richter ließ die Gefangenen vor ſich kommen. Mein Herr, Sie haben uns lange warten laſſen. Laſſen Sie mir den Schneider rufen[4]. Wer ſich betrügen[5] läßt, verdient betrogen zu werden. Der Lehrer hat ſeine Schüler eine engliſche Überſetzung machen laſſen. Laſſen Sie uns einen Spaziergang machen. Der Vater ließ das Kind taufen[6] und ihm den Namen Marie geben. Laſſet die Kinder hereinkommen. Das läßt ſich (§ 8) nicht hoffen. Da läßt ſich nichts thun.

1) the joiner. 2) coachman 3) to put to. 4) to send for. 5) to deceive (here *to be deceived*). 6) to be christened.

### Aufgabe. 111.

Let me do it. I let him work six hours every day. Let me go Let us take a walk. Let the old man sit (down). Her father *allowed* her to marry. The governor[1] *caused* the murderer *to be arrested* (§ 5). The admiral *caused* the crew[2] to disembark (ausſchiffen). You must *have* a new house *built* (§ 4). The mother *made* her child pray[3] every morning and evening. Where do you *have* (*get*) your books *bound?* I *get* them *bound* by Mr. Long. Bid the gentleman come in. Who shall (ſoll) pluck[4] the cherries? I will *have* them *plucked* by John. Have you *had* the general *invited?* Yes, I have sent him an invitation[5]. This cannot be proved[6] (§ 8). That (Da) cannot be helped.

1) Der Statthalter. 2) die Mannſchaft. 3) beten 4) pflücken. 5) eine Einladung. 6) beweiſen.

---

## IV. On ſollen (müſſen).

The employment of this verb differs also in many respects from the English·

1) It signifies a moral necessity, equivalent to the English *shall* in the 2nd and 3rd person, or to *I am to* ich ſoll:

Du ſollſt nicht ſtehlen thou shalt not steal.

Du sollst deinen Nächsten lieben, wie dich selbst.
Thou shalt love thy neighbour as thyself.
Wer soll es thun, er oder ich? who *is to* do it, he or I?
Mein Sohn soll (or muß) Französisch und Deutsch lernen.
My son *is to* learn French and German.
Ich sollte um vier Uhr abreisen; aber es war nicht möglich.
I *was to* leave at four o'clock, but it was not possible.

2) In the Imperfect and Pluperfect it denotes a duty
= *I ought to:*
Er sollte seine Schulden bezahlen.
He ought to pay his debts.
Er hätte seine Schulden bezahlen sollen.
He *ought to have* paid his debts (see p. 94, § 5).
Sie hätten Ihre Lektion lernen sollen.
You ought to have learnt your lesson.
Ich hätte gehen sollen I should (ought to) have gone.

3) The Imperfect sollte is used after wenn, to express
a chance or an event which is not quite certain:
Wenn er kommen sollte, so sagen Sie ihm dieses.
If he should (were to) come, tell him this.
Wenn es regnen sollte (or Sollte es regnen), so werden
wir zu Hause bleiben.
Should it rain, we shall stay at home.
Wenn ich ihn sehen sollte, so werde ich ihm die Wahrheit sagen.
If I should see him, I shall tell him the truth.

4) Soll, *pl.* sollen, means sometimes *is* or *are said*\*),
*supposed* or *reported*, but only in the Present tense. The
other verb may be in the Past.  Ex.:
Das Testament soll falsch sein the will *is said* to be false.
Er soll in Amerika gestorben sein.
He *is said* to have died in America.

5) Sollen is sometimes used elliptically, an Infinitive
being understood·
Hier ist Karl, was soll er (i. e. thun)?
Here is Charles, what is he to do?
Was sollen diese Worte (i. e. heißen or bedeuten)?
What is the meaning of these words?
Was sollen diese Klagen (i. e. helfen, nützen)?
Of what use are these complaints?

_____

\*) in Latin *dicitur traditur* etc.

**Reading Exercise. 112.**

Wir sollen Gott fürchten und lieben. Du sollst nichts Böses von deinem Nächsten reden. Sie sollten Gott danken, daß Sie aus dieser Gefahr gerettet[1] worden sind. Wir sollen durch Andrer Fehler lernen, unsre eignen zu verbessern. Du hättest diesem Manne nicht trauen[2] sollen. Caligula befahl, daß die Römer ihm göttliche Ehre erweisen[3] sollten. Die Menschen sollten sich nicht über die Vorsehung[4] beklagen, wenn sie durch ihre eignen Fehler leiden. Der Kranke hätte[5] noch (more) viel Arznei nehmen müssen, wenn er nicht gestorben wäre. Der Graf soll auf der Jagd sein. Er soll sich in die Gunst[6] des alten Königs eingeschlichen[7] haben. Morgen soll (§ 4) der König in die Stadt kommen. Was soll diese ernsthafte[8] Miene? Was sollen diese Komplimente[9]?

1) to rescue. 2) to trust. 3) render. 4) Providence. 5) See p. 94, 5. — 6) favour. 7) to insinuate. 8) serious. 9) ceremonies.

**Aufgabe. 113.**

We *are to* be there at ten o'clock. Thou shalt not tell[1] lies. You shall not do what you like (wünschen), but what you ought. Which of your servants *is to* go, John or James (Jakob)? James *is to* go. You *should have invited*[2] also the old judge. She ought to be silent[3]. Should the weather be fine to-morrow, you may expect me at eight o'clock. If the merchant should *ask*[4] *[for]* money, tell him that I have none. You ought to rise earlier. The boy *ought to have written* his exercise. He *is said* to *have* gone to America. Mr Taylor *is said* to have taken poison[5]. These ladies *are supposed* to be very rich. You ought to *have learnt* the whole page by heart (auswendig). If *we were to* (should we) call on you, should you be at home? I see you are crying; what is the meaning (§ 5) of these tears[6]? What shall we do with this robber[7]?

1) *to tell lies* lügen. 2) einladen. 3) to be silent = schweigen 4) *to ask for* verlangen (*Acc.*). 5) Gift. 6) Thränen. 7) Räuber.

---

# V. On dürfen.

1) The usual meaning of dürfen is *to be allowed* or *may;* when negative *must not;* it denotes permission conceded by the law or by some person. Ex.:

Heinrich darf dieses Buch nicht behalten.
Henry is not allowed to keep this book.

Die Kinder dürfen diesen Nachmittag spazieren gehen.
The children are allowed to take a walk this afternoon.

Sie dürfen wissen, was er mir gesagt hat.
You *may* know what he told me.

2) It signifies sometimes *to dare, to venture:*
Man darf nicht alles sagen, was man denkt
People dare not say all they think

3) It answers to the English *need* (= brauchen):
Sie dürfen nicht darüber klagen (or brauchen nicht...zu klagen).
You need not complain of it.
Wir durften*) für nichts sorgen; alles war bereit.
We had no need to care for anything: all was ready.

4) The conditional dürfte can be used to denote what the speaker thinks probable or possible:
Diese Frage dürfte wohl überflüssig sein.
This question may (*or* might) (possibly) be superfluous.

### Reading Exercise. 114.

Kranke Personen dürfen diese Speise[1] nicht essen. Ich darf keinen Wein trinken. Sie dürfen diesen Brief lesen, wenn Sie wollen (like). Der Gefangene durfte sein Weib und seine Kinder nicht mehr sehen, bevor er auf das Schiff gebracht wurde. Darf ich Sie morgen besuchen? Diese Mädchen werden heute nicht auf den Ball gehen dürfen, wenn ihre Mutter nicht besser wird. Man darf ihm[2] nur ins Gesicht sehen, so erkennt man den Dieb. Darf man in den königlichen Garten hineingehen? Jedermann darf hineingehen. Darf man fragen, an was Sie denken? Er dürfte dieses wohl nicht wagen (dare). Der Kranke hat keine Arznei nehmen wollen, aber er hat gemußt. Sie dürfen nicht in dieses Zimmer gehen. Niemand darf hineingehen.

1) food, dish. 2) See p. 301, 2.

### Aufgabe. 115.

Charles may play. We dare not invite him. May I see, what you are writing? The pupils *have not been allowed to* go out. May I ask, why not? He dares not look[1] in my face[2]. How could he undertake[3] this, without[4] mentioning it to his father? We shall probably[5] not *be allowed to* buy these books. You need not pay the waiter[6]. The children *are not allowed to* play in this room. He might (dürfte) have been mistaken (sich geirrt haben). Have you *been allowed to* read the letter of your aunt? Yes, I have been allowed to read it.

1) sehen. 2) Gesicht, n. 3) unternehmen. 4) ohne es...zu sagen. 5) wahrscheinlich. 6) Kellner.

---

*) It would be better to say: Wir brauchten für nichts zu sorgen or wir hatten für nichts zu sorgen.

### Reading-lesson.
### Die ſechs Wörtlein.

Sechs Wörtlein nehmen mich in Anſpruch[1] jeden Tag:
Ich ſoll, ich muß, ich kann, ich will, ich darf, ich mag.
Ich ſoll, iſt das Geſetz, von Gott ins Herz geſchrieben,
Das Ziel[2], nach[3] welchem ich bin von mir ſelbſt getrieben.
Ich muß, das iſt die Schrank'[4], in[5] welcher mich die Welt
Von einer —, die Natur von andrer — Seite hält.
Ich kann, das iſt das Maß der mir verlieh'nen[6] Kraft,
Der That, der Fertigkeit[7], der Kunſt und Wiſſenſchaft.
Ich will, die höchſte Kron' iſt dieſes, die mich ſchmückt[8],
Das iſt der Freiheit Siegel, dem Geiſte aufgedrückt[9].
Ich darf, das iſt zugleich die Inſchrift[10] bei[11] dem Siegel,
Beim[12] aufgethanen Thor der Freiheit auch ein Riegel[13].
Ich mag, das endlich iſt, was zwiſchen allen ſchwimmt.
Ein unbeſtimmtes[14], das der Augenblick beſtimmt.
Ich ſoll, ich muß, ich kann, ich will, ich darf, ich mag,
Die ſechſe nehmen mich in Anſpruch jeden Tag.
Nur wenn Du[15] ſelbſt mich lehrſt, weiß ich, was jeden Tag
Ich ſoll, ich muß, ich kann, ich will, ich darf, ich mag.

1) claim me. 2) the goal, aim. 3) towards 4) the bounds, limits, constraint. 5) within. 6) granted. 7) dexterity. 8) adorns. 9) impressed, stamped. 10) inscription. 11) round *or* upon — 12) on the open door. 13) bolt. 14) something vague, undefined. 15) thou, o God.

---

# Forty-first Lesson.
## Remarks on the use of the Pronouns.
### (See the 23rd, 24th and 25th lessons.)
### I. On the Personal pronouns.

1) After a personal pronoun of the 1st or 2nd person, singular as well as plural, the same pronoun is repeated after the relative der, die, das (see p. 150, *Note*). Ex.:

Ich, der ich ihn kenne I who know him.
Du, der du ihn nicht kennſt you who do not know him.
Wir, die wir jung ſind we who are young.

2) The genitive case of the personal pronouns occurs mostly after verbs governing the genitive, and in connection with numerals:

Er ſpottete meiner he mocked me.
Ich erinnere mich ſeiner I remember him.
Unſrer zehn ten of us. | ihrer zwanzig twenty of them.

*Note.* This genitive is likewise joined with the prepositions wegen, halben and willen, in which case the r is changed into t, as: meinetwegen on my account, Jhretwegen on your account. Er : Jch that es um seinetwillen (ihretwillen). I did it for his (her) sake etc.

3) The dative and accusative plural of the reflective pronoun (sich) may take a *mutual* signification, meaning *one another.* Ex.:

Die zwei Schwestern gleichen sich (or einander). The two sisters resemble one another. Diese Leute beschimpfen sich (or einander). These people abuse one another.

---

## II. On the Possessive pronouns.

1) The *possessive* adjectives mein, dein, sein rc. are not so often used in German as in English; they are commonly replaced by the article, when there is no doubt of the person meant by the speaker, especially when parts of the body are spoken of. Ex.: .

I have broken *my* leg. Jch habe das (not mein) Bein gebrochen. The king held the sceptre in *his* hand. Der König hielt das Scepter in der Hand. She put *her* handkerchief before *her* eyes. Sie hielt ihr Taschentuch vor die (or ihre) Augen.

2) When not only possession is implied, but when a strong reference to the subject is expressed, the *possessive adjective* is replaced by the *personal* or *reflective pronoun* and by the definite article before the substantive. Ex.:

Jch habe mich in den Finger geschnitten. (*Lit.* I have cut myself into the finger.) I have cut *my* finger. Der Knabe muß sich die Hände waschen. The boy must wash *his* hands. Sie hat es ihm in die Hand gegeben. She has given it into *his* hand.

3) The four possessive pronouns, *mine, thine, his* and *ours,* when predicàte, are treated as adjectives and translated mein, dein, sein and unser, instead of meiner or der meinige etc. This takes place when they are joined to the preceding noun by the auxiliary *to be:*

Dieſer Garten iſt mein*) this garden is mine.
Jene Feder iſt ſein that pen is his.

4) Observe the following expressions:

A horse of ours eines von unſern Pferden or unſrer Pferde.
A friend of mine einer von meinen Freunden or ein Freund von mir.
A relation of ours — of yours einer von unſern (Ihren) Ver=
wandten or ein Verwandter von uns — von Ihnen.

### Reading-Exercise. 116.

Ich, der ich alles mit meinen eigenen Augen geſehen habe, kann das beſte Zeugnis[1] geben. Süßer Friede, der du vom Himmel kommſt, erfülle mein Herz. Erbarmen Sie ſich meiner. Ich bin um ſeinetwillen geſtraft worden. Die jungen Leute ver= zeihen ſich leicht ihre Thorheiten (follies). Iſt es wahr, daß Karl den Arm gebrochen hat? Ja, er hat nicht nur den Arm, ſondern auch das Bein gebrochen. Das Mädchen fiel auf die Kniee und betete. Einer meiner Vettern iſt geſtern geſtorben. Dieſer Stock iſt mein. Ich ſtand an dem Fenſter und hatte ein Buch in der Hand. Ihr Finger blutet[2]; haben Sie ſich geſchnitten? Ich habe mich (or..mir) mit einer Nadel[3] in den Finger geſtochen[4]. Kennen Sie dieſen jungen Mann? Ja, er iſt ein Vetter von mir.

1) evidence.   2) to bleed.   3) needle.   4) to sting, prick.

### Aufgabe. 117.

We who are old, cannot enjoy[1] these pleasures. He who wished to injure me (dat.), has served me (dat.). They laughed (lachten) at us.**) We left England for her sake. Don't these two girls love one another tenderly[2]? The boy had a cap[3] on *his* head. He has lost *his* senses (Verſtand, *sing.*). The queen had a crown[4] on *her* head and a sceptre[5] in her hand. *My* heart beats with (vor) joy. The prisoner has cut†) *his* throat (Hals). I am wounded in (an) *my* shoulder[6]. In firing (Beim Losſchießen) the gun (*Gen.*), I have wounded *my* hand. This hat is not mine, it belongs to my brother. This lead-pencil is mine, the other is his. A relation of ours has gone to America. A cousin of yours came yesterday to see us. The naughty boy threw a snow-ball[7] at (an) the man's head (*transl.* threw to the man (*Dat.*) a snow-ball at the head).

1) genießen.   2) zärtlich.   3) eine Kappe or Mütze.   4) Krone, f.
5) Scepter or Zepter, n.   6) Schulter, f.   7) Schneeball, m.

---

*) mein is used here as an adjective.
**) at us may be translated either with the *Genitive* unſrer or better with the preposition über with the *Accusative.*
†) See II, 2, first Ex.

### III. On the Relative pronouns.

1) The relative pronoun weld)er or ber must take the first place in the accessory sentence, and can only be preceded by prepositions; therefore, when in English a *noun* precedes the genitive of the relative pronoun, the former takes its place in German after the pronoun, losing at the same time the article.

I have some rings *the price of which* *) I do not know.
Jd) habe einige Ringe, beren Preis id) nid)t fenne.

We went to a house, from the windows *of which* (*from whose windows*) we saw it.
Wir gingen in ein Haus, aus beffen Fenftern wir es fahen.

A machine by means of which one can fly.
Eine Mafd)ine, vermittelft beren man fliegen fann.

2) The genitive of the relative pronoun preceded by *all* is translated in the nominative ·

He had five children *all of whom* died in their infancy.
Er hatte fünf Kinber, bie alle in ihrer Kinbheit ftarben.

3) This is also the case when *all* precedes a personal pronoun:

All of us wir alle.
all of you Sie alle. | all of them fie alle.

4) The correlatives *such as.* when equivalent to *those who* are rendered in German by biejenigen (or bie) weld)e.

Such as are poor bie, weld)e arm finb.

*Note.* The form fo. in the place of weld)e (*plur.*) is obsolete, as: Von allen fo (= bie) ba famen among all that came

5) When *such* is followed by a noun, it is considered as an adjective and translated fold); but then the following *as to* must be rendered by the conjunction baß:

I placed myself in *such a posture as to have* a view over all.
Jd) verfetzte mid) in eine fold)e Stellung, baß id) alle über= fehen fonnte.

### Reading Exercise. 118.

Der Engländer, beffen Sohn bei Ihnen wohnt, hat feine Brieftafd)e[1] verloren. Der alte Mann, mit beffen Sohn id) nach Englanb gereift bin, ift geftorben. Der Frembe, auf beffen Red)t= fd)affenheit[2] id) zählte[3], hat mid) betrogen. Diejenigen, weld)e

1) pocket-book. 2) honesty. 3) to rely, count.

---

*) If *of which* be changed into *whose*, the two languages perfectly agree *whose price* beren (*pl.*) Preis.

(such as) wir bis jetzt (as yet) gesehen haben, gefallen uns nicht. Werden Sie alle Bücher behalten, die ich Ihnen gestern geschickt habe? Ich kann noch nicht sagen, ob ich sie alle behalten werde; aber die beiden (zwei), welche ich bestellt (ordered) habe, werde ich gewiß behalten.

### Aufgabe. 118a.

That is the goal[1] for (nach)) which he strives[2]. A bird whose wings have been clipped[3], cannot fly. It is an illness against (gegen) [the] progress[4] of which (against whose progress) one cannot apply[5] remedies[6] too quickly. Charity[7], the practice[8] of which is our duty, makes us good and happy. We call that heavenly[9] body[9], by the brightness[10] of which our eyes *are* dazzled[11], the sun. Such as are good and industrious, may go home with me. I found myself in such a position[12] *as to* observe all that went on (vorging) around me.

1) das Ziel   2) streben   3) beschnitten or gestutzt.   4) Fortschritt, m. 5) anwenden   6) Heilmittel, n   7) die Barmherzigkeit   8) Ausübung, f. 9) Himmelskörper, m   10) Glanz, m   11) geblendet   12) Stellung, f.

## IV. On the Indefinite pronouns.

1) The German all, when in the singular of the *masc.* and *neuter* gender, and followed by a *possessive* adjective, is not declined:

All mein Geld all my money.

Ich bin all meines Geldes (*Gen.*) beraubt worden.
I have been robbed of all my money.

Mit all meinem Geld (*dat.*) with all my money.

But in the *feminine* gender and in the plural, it agrees with its noun:

Er hat alle seine Suppe verschüttet.
He has spilt all his soup.

Alle diese Bäume all these trees. | (*Gen.* aller dieser B.) ‹

2) The English *all* in the singular, when it denotes *the whole* of a thing or period must be translated ganz:

All the world die ganze Welt.
All the year das ganze Jahr.
All day den ganzen Tag. | All night die ganze Nacht.

3) In this signification, when placed before *names of countries and towns* ganz (*all*) remains unchanged in all the cases:

All England would rise ganz England würde aufstehen.
In all France in ganz Frankreich.
All Paris ganz Paris.

4) Alles means commonly *everything;* but it is sometimes applied to *persons* in an entirely general sense:
Alles freut sich everybody rejoices.
Alles fliehet everybody flees.

5) Alles was is in English *all that* or only *that:*
Alles, was ich gesehen habe all I have seen.

6) Jeder (*every*), when denoting time, may be as well rendered by the plural alle:
Every day jeden Tag or alle Tage.
Every year jedes Jahr or alle Jahre.
Every twenty-four hours alle vierundzwanzig Stunden.

7) Viel and wenig in the *singular* ought not to be declined, (except sometimes in the feminine) but it should always be done so before nouns in the plural:
Er hat viel Geld he has much money.
Ich habe wenig Zeit I have little time.
Haben Sie viele Freunde? have you many friends?
Ich habe nur wenige Freunde I have but few fiends.
Wenige (or wenige Leute) wissen das few people know that.

8) Ein wenig (*a little*) is indeclinable as in English:
Geben Sie mir ein wenig Salz give me a little salt

9) Beide (*both*) is sometimes used without a substantive, as · Beide sind tot both are dead. — It never admits of a genitive after it. Ex.:
Wir beide both of us.
Sie beide (or die beiden) both of them.
Mit uns beiden with both of us
In diesen beiden Häusern in both of these houses.

*Note.* The English *both — and* is a co-ordinative conjunction and is rendered by sowohl — als (see p 245, 1). Ex.:
*Both* silver *and* gold sowohl Silber als Gold

10) Either (einer von beiden) and neither (keiner von beiden). It must be observed, that in German „beide" is mostly dropped, and that *either of* must be translated „einer von", when two people are spoken of. Ex.:
Either of them einer (or *fem.* eine) von ihnen
Neither of my sons keiner von meinen (2) Söhnen.
On neither side auf keiner Seite.

11) The indefinite pronoun *either**) preceded by *not* is always keiner von beiden; *not any* is kein; *not anybody* niemand; *not anything* nichts. Ex.:

---
*) The negative adverb not (nor) — either is translated auch nicht Ex: I have *not* seen him either ich habe ihn auch nicht gesehen.

I do *not* know *either* of them ich fenne feinen von beiden.
We have *not* had *any* wir haben feinen (or e, ß) gehabt.
Have you *not* heard of *anybody* \*) haben Sie von niemand
I did *not* buy *anything* ich habe nichts gefauft. [gehört?

12) Other is commonly translated der andre; *another* ein andrer. But when it signifies *a second* or a *third thing* of the same kind, it is translated noch ein:

Take another glass of wine.
Nehmen Sie noch ein Glas Wein.
Will you have another cup of tea?
Wollen Sie noch eine Taffe Thee?

13) Something similar takes place with *more*; before a noun, not followed by *than*, it is translated noch:

Have you *any more* horses? haben Sie noch Pferde?
He has *two more* children er hat noch zwei Kinder.
Take some more cherries nehmen Sie noch einige Kirschen.
Give me a little (or some) more sugar.
Geben Sie mir noch ein wenig Zucker

14) When used negatively, *more* (or also *longer*) is rendered by mehr, but the German mehr *follows* the noun:

He has no *more* money er hat fein Geld mehr.
We have no more horses wir haben feine Pferde mehr.
The boy has no longer a father.
Der Knabe hat feinen Vater mehr.

### Reading Exercise 119.

Nehmen Sie das ganze Stück? Nein, ich brauche nur wenige Meter. Ganz Paris war erleuchtet[1]. Diese Pflanzen findet man in ganz Deutschland. Wir mußten den ganzen Tag arbeiten. Ich fann Ihnen nicht alles erzählen[2], was ich erlebt (experienced) habe. Wir sind alle reichlich beschenkt[3] worden. Wir alle waren hungrig und durstig. Eine Frau hatte eine Henne, welche alle Tage ein Ei legte. Herr Müller ist mit uns beiden nach Paris gereist. Einer von euch muß sterben, sagte der Räuber zu uns. Wollen Sie noch einen Apfel haben? Nein, ich danke, ich effe feinen mehr. Wie viele Schüler haben Sie noch? Ich habe noch zehn. Herr A. hat feinen Bedienten mehr.

1) illuminated.    2) relate.    3) rewarded.

### Aufgabe. 119a.

The travellers have been robbed[1] *of* all their luggage[2] (*Gen.*). We worked all day and all night, but we could not

---

\*) Except in questions like Haben Sie nicht etwas or jemand gesehen? Haben Sie nicht einen Freund in London?

finish our work. In all Europe such a man is not to be found
(ʒu finden). I will tell you all I know. All of you have been
warned (gewarnt) by the police-man[3]. I did not see anything.
They *were* every day entertained[4] with songs, *the* subject
(Gegenſtand) of which (*pl.*) was the happy valley. Take another cup of tea. Have you *any more* brothers[5] and sisters?
I have no ꞊more ꞊brothers, but two sisters. My father has
*no more* horses; he has sold them all.

1) berauben. 2) das Gepäck. 3) der Polizeidiener. 4) unterhalten.
5) brothers and sisters = Geſchwiſter.

## Reading-lesson.
### Epiktet'. Epictetus.

Der Philoſoph Epiktet' war ein Sklave des Epaphrodi'tus,
und hatte viel von ſeinem Herrn[1] ʒu erdulden[2]; aber er hatte eine
große und ſtarke Seele. Als einſt Epaphroditus ihm einen heftigen
Schlag[3] auf das Bein[4] gegeben hatte, warnte Epiktet ihn kalt
(coolly), daß er es ihm nicht brechen ſollte. Der Herr verdoppelte
ſeine Streiche[3], ſo daß er ihm den Knochen[5] ʒerſchlug'. Der
Weiſe antwortete ihm, ohne ſich ʒu entrüſten[6]: „Sagte ich es dir
nicht, daß du mir es ʒerſchlagen würdeſt!"

Epiktet war immer vergnügt, ſelbſt (even) in der Sklaverei.
„Ich bin," ſagte er, „an der Stelle, wo die Vorſehung[7] will, daß
ich ſein ſoll; mich darüber beklagen, hieße ſie beleidigen." Die
ʒwei Grundlehren[8] ſeiner Moral waren: „Wiſſe ʒu dulden
und dich ʒu enthalten[9]." Er fand in ſich ſelbſt die nötigen
Hilfsmittel[10], um den erſten dieſer Grundſätze[8] in Ausübung[11] ʒu
bringen.

„Wir haben ſehr unrecht," ſagte er bisweilen, „die Armut
anʒuklagen[12], daß ſie uns unglücklich mache; es iſt der Ehrgeiz[13],
es ſind unſre unerſättlichen[14] Begierden, welche uns wahrhaft
elend machen. Wären wir Herren der ganʒen Welt, ſo könnte uns
ihr Beſitz nicht von Furcht und Kummer (grief) frei machen; die
Vernunft[15] allein hat dieſe Gewalt."

Epiktet ſtarb in einem ſehr hohen Alter unter der Regierung
des Kaiſers Markus Aurelius. Die irdene[16] Lampe, womit er ſeine
philoſophiſchen Nachtwachen[17] erleuchtete[18], wurde einige Zeit nach
ſeinem Tode für 3000 Drachmen (2700 Franken) verkauft.

1) master. 2) endure. 3) blow. 4) leg. 5) the bone 6) to
grow angry. 7) Providence. 8) principal doctrines. 9) to forbear, to abstain. 10) resource. 11) to practise, to carry out. —
12) to accuse. 13) ambition. 14) insatiable desires. 15) reason.
16) earthen. 17) night-watch. 18) enlighten.

## Conversation.

Wer war Epiktet?　　　　Ein Philoſoph' und ein Sklave
　　　　　　　　　　　　des Epaphroditus.

20*

War sein Herr gütig gegen ihn?

Als dieser ihm einst heftig auf das Bein schlug, was sagte er?

Was that aber Epaphroditus?

Wurde Epiktet darüber entrüstet?

Beklagte er sich darüber, daß er ein Sklave war?

Was sagte er?

Welches waren seine zwei Grund-lehren?

Ist es die Armut, die uns un-glücklich macht?

Wann starb Epiktet?

Wie teuer wurde seine irdene Lampe verkauft?

Nein, er war hartherzig und grausam.

Er warnte ihn, daß er ihm das Bein nicht zerbrechen sollte.

Er verdoppelte seine Streiche und zerschlug ihm wirklich das Bein.

Nein, er antwortete ganz ruhig, daß er es ihm vorausgesagt habe.

Nein, er unterwarf (submitted) sich ruhig seinem Schicksal.

Er sagte: „Ich bin an der Stelle, wohin die Vorsehung mich ge-setzt hat."

„Wisse zu dulden und dich zu enthalten."

Nicht die Armut, sondern unsre Begierden.

Unter Markus Aurelius, in einem sehr hohen Alter.

Für 3000 Drachmen.

# Forty-second Lesson.
## Use of the Tenses of the Indicative Mood.

The use of the German tenses differs very little from that of the English. It presents therefore few difficulties.

### I. Present Tense.

1) For the *Present tense* we have only one form, viz..

Ich lese I read, I do read, I am reading.
Ich schreibe I (do) write, I am writing.
Ich esse nicht I do not eat etc.

The English form *I am reading, writing, eating etc.* must always be translated in the same manner: ich lese, ich schreibe ꝛc. Sometimes when the continuance of the action is desired to be stated, the adverbs eben or ge-rade or jetzt (just, now) are added. Ex.:

Ich frühstücke eben I am breakfasting.
Er schläft (jetzt) he is sleeping.

2) The same is to be observed through all the tenses:

*Imp.* Ich frühstückte (gerade od. eben) I was breakfasting.
*Perf.* Ich habe den ganzen Tag gelesen.
I have been reading all day.

3) The *Present tense* is sometimes employed for the Future, if near at hand, and the time indicated by another adverbial expression:

Ich reise diesen Abend ab I shall depart *this evening*.
In drei Tagen komme ich wieder zurück.
In three days I shall be back.

4) The *Present tense* is used in German in connection with the word schon or seit, for the English *Perfect* or *Compound tense*, when the latter expresses that the action or state still continues, especially in the question *how long* and the answer to it:

Wie lange sind Sie schon hier?
How long *have* you *been* here?
Wie lange lernen Sie schon Deutsch?
How long *have* you *been* learning German?
Ich lerne es seit acht Monaten.
I *have been* learning it *these* eight months.
Haben Sie diesen Bedienten schon lange? (not gehabt.)
*Have* you *had* this servant long?
Ich habe ihn schon zwei Jahre (or seit zwei Jahren).
I have *had* him *these* two years.

## II. Imperfect Tense.

This is the *narrative* tense, and its use does not differ at all from the English. Ex.:

Jesus sprach zu seinen Jüngern ꝛc.
Jesus spoke to his disciples etc.

It is always used after the conjunction als (*when, as*). Ex.:

Als ich ihn kommen sah when I saw him come (coming).
Wir gingen spazieren, während unsre Freunde Karten spielten.
We took a walk, whilst our friends *were playing* at cards.

## III. Perfect Tense.

1) The *Perfect tense* or *Compound of the Present tense* is used to express an action or event *perfectly* ended, without any reference to another event happening at the same time  It often corresponds with the English *Imperfect*:

Ich habe Ihren Brief richtig empfangen.
I have duly received your letter.
Der Arbeiter ist reichlich belohnt worden.
The workman has been (*was*) amply rewarded.

Wie lange ſind Sie in Deutſchland geweſen?*)
How long *were* you in Germany?

2) It is further employed for the English *Imperfect* in those cases where the time of the action is recent, and sometimes in accessory sentences:

Ich bin geſtern auf dem Balle geweſen (or ich war...).
I *was* at the ball yesterday.

Ich habe Sie lange nicht mehr geſehen.
It is long *since I saw you.*

3) In most short questions and answers:

Haben Sie ſchon (zu Mittag) geſpeiſt (dined)?
Ich habe um 4 Uhr geſpeiſt (I dined etc.).
Wann ſind Sie angekommen? (when did you arrive?)
Ich bin um 10 Uhr angekommen (I arrived at 10).

## IV. The Pluperfect Tense

is employed as in English:

Als (Nachdem) ich die Zeitung geleſen hatte, ging ich aus.
When (or after) I had read the newspaper, I went out.

Er hatte während des Gewitters geſchlafen.
He had slept during the thunderstorm.

*Note.* In subordinate sentences, the auxiliary hatte or war is sometimes left out, particularly in poetry. Ex.:

Und als er kaum das Wort geſprochen (i. e. hatte).
Scarcely *had* he spoken the word.
Und eh' ihm noch das Wort entfallen (i. e. war).          (Schiller)
And before the word *had* escaped (his lips).

### Reading Exercise. 120.

1. Die Stadt Rom liegt auf ſieben Hügeln. Nach dem Winter kommt der Frühling. Der Knabe ſchneidet (makes) ſeine Federn ſelbſt. Die Armut[1] wohnt oft neben dem Überfluſſe[2]. Morgen abend reiſe ich nach Straßburg; wollen Sie mich begleiten? Diogenes wohnte in einem Faſſe[3]. Ich kenne (I, 4) ihn ſeit ſeiner Kindheit. Durch wen wurde Abel getötet? Die Juden wohnten zuerſt im Lande Goſen; hernach zogen[4] ſie in das Land Kanaan. Vor drei Wochen hat der Jäger einen Hirſch[5] geſchoſſen.

1) Poverty. 2) abundance. 3) tub. 4) went, moved. 5) stag.

---

*) Or waren Sie. Your stay in Germany is *perfectly ended;* you are no more in Germany, when the question is asked, just as in French: Avez-vous été or étiez-vous? — Wie lange ſind Sie da geweſen answers to the English: *How long were you there?* (see III, 2).

2. Wir werden das Mehl von einem andern Bäcker kaufen.
Haben Sie Ihre Arbeit geendigt? Wir haben sie noch nicht ge=
endigt. Man hat alle Offiziere bestraft, welche die Fahnen ver=
lassen haben. Die Tyrier hatten durch ihren Stolz⁶ den König
Sesostris gegen sich aufgebracht⁷, der in Ägypten herrschte und
so viele Reiche⁸ erobert hatte. Ich hatte meine Geschäfte⁹ schon
beendigt, als ich Ihren Brief erhielt. Als er mir die Geschichte
erzählt hatte, schlief er ein. Es hat dieses Jahr nicht viele Trauben
gegeben. Sobald ich mein Geld erhalten habe, werde ich diese
Stadt verlassen.

6) pride. 7) irritated. 8) kingdoms. 9) business.

### Aufgabe. 121.

1. What are you doing? I am reading a very amusing[1]
book; you must read it also, to-morrow I shall send it [to]
you. Napoleon the First died in the year 1821. My friend has
published[2] a new English grammar. The servant has killed
his master[3]. Were you ever in France? No, Sir, I intend[4]
to go there next year. After I have read the book, you
shall have it. We waited [a] long time for you (auf Sie).
I have *been writing* letters all day. When shall I have the
pleasure of seeing you? I have always received[5] him kindly.
These two men will have done their work when you return.

2. To-day we shall have our dinner at six. He *has
lived* (lives, I, 4) long in Switzerland. I *lived* long in Switzerland. Is it long since you breakfasted? It is an hour and
a half. I *perceived* (III, 2) it the other day[6]. I *have perceived*
it for (*since*) several days. I *wore*[7] that coat two years. I
*have worn* this coat nearly two years. How long did you
wear these boots? They are worn out (abgetragen). How
long *have* you *lived* in this house? I have lived in it these
(seit) three years. *Have* you *known* these people long? I *have
known* them [for] many years.

1) unterhaltend. 2) herausgegeben. 3) Herr. 4) beabsichtige. —
5) empfangen. 6) neulich. 7) tragen.

### Reading-lesson.
### Einige Züge[1] aus dem Leben Heinrichs des Vierten.

Die berühmte Schlacht von Jvry allein könnte den Namen
Heinrichs des Vierten unsterblich machen. Als Heerführer[2] und
als Soldat zeigte er ebensoviel Geschicklichkeit[3] als Tapferkeit.
Vor dem Beginn des Treffens[4] durchschritt er die Reihen[5] mit einer
heitern Miene, welche den Sieg vorher verkündete, und sagte zu
seinen Truppen: „Kinder, wenn die Standarten euch fehlen[6], so
versammelt euch um meinen weißen Federbusch[7]; ihr werdet ihn
immer auf dem Wege der (to) Ehre und des Ruhmes finden; Gott

1) trait. 2) as a commander, general. 3) skill. 4) battle.
5) ranks. 6) fail. 7) plume.

ist für uns " — Nach einiger Zeit glaubte man, er wäre im
Schlachtgetümmel[8] umgekommen. Als er wieder zum Vorschein[9]
kam, mit dem Blute der Feinde bedeckt, so wurden seine Soldaten
Helden Die Verbündeten[10] wurden in Stücke gehauen. Der Marschall von Biron kommandierte das Reservekorps und hatte, ohne
eben in der Hitze des Gefechtes zu sein, einen großen Anteil[11] am
Siege. Er wünschte[12] dem König mit diesen Worten Glück[12].
„Sire, Sie haben heute gethan, was Biron thun sollte, und Biron,
was der König thun sollte."

Die Milde des Siegers erhöhte[13] den Ruhm des Triumphs.
„Rettet die Franzosen," schrie er, indem er die Flüchtlinge[14] ver-
folgte. Alle diese Züge malen[15] den großen Mann, welcher die
Kunst besaß, die Herzen zu gewinnen.

Man muß besonders die Genugthuung[16] bewundern, welche
er dem Herrn von Schomberg gab. Dieser General der deutschen
Hilfstruppen verlangte einige Tage vor der Schlacht die Löhnung[17]
seiner Truppen. Das Geld mangelte[18]; eine Bewegung des Un-
willens[19] reißt den König hin: „Nie," antwortete er, „hat ein
Mann von Mut am Tage vor einer Schlacht Geld verlangt."
Voll Reue[20] über diese kränkende[21] Lebhaftigkeit ergriff er, um
sie wieder gut zu machen[22], den Augenblick, wo[23] man kämpfen
wollte[24]. „Herr v Schomberg," sagte er, „ich habe Sie vor einigen
Tagen beleidigt. Dieser Tag ist vielleicht der letzte meines Lebens;
ich will nicht die Ehre eines Edelmannes mit mir nehmen; ich
kenne Ihr Verdienst[25] und Ihren Mut; ich bitte Sie um Verzeihung; umarmen Sie mich."

Schomberg antwortete ihm: „Es ist wahr, daß Ihre Majestät
mich letzthin[26] verwundete; heute töten Sie mich, denn die Ehre,
die Sie mir anthun[27], zwingt mich, bei dieser Gelegenheit für
Sie zu sterben." Der brave Deutsche zeichnete sich auch wirklich[28]
durch seine Tapferkeit[29] aus und wurde an der Seite des Königs
getötet.

8) din of battle. 9) to re-appear. 10) the leaguers 11) share.
12) to congratulate. 13) to enhance. 14) fugitives. 15) to paint,
describe. 16) satisfaction. 17) pay 18) failed, was wanting. —
19) anger. 20) repentance. 21) offending rashness. 22) to repair,
make up for. 23) when. 24) they were going to fight 25) merit.
26) the other day. 27) show, do. 28) indeed, really. 29) bravery.

## Conversation.

Welche Schlacht hat den Namen    Die Schlacht bei Jvry.
   Heinrichs IV. unsterblich ge-
   macht?

Was zeigte er dabei?             Ebensoviel Geschicklichkeit als Mut
                            und Tapferkeit.

Welche Worte sprach er vor der    Wenn sie ihre Fahnen verlieren,
   Schlacht zu seinen Soldaten?      sollten sie sich um seinen weißen
                            Federbusch scharen (collect).

Was für ein Führer (guide) würde dieser ihnen sein?

Wer kommandirte das Reserve-korps?

Mit welchen Worten wünschte dieser dem König Glück zu seinem Siege?

Wie war er als Sieger?

Wie zeigte er dieses?

Wie benahm (behaved) er sich gegen den General v. Schomberg?

Hatte er ihn beleidigt?

Bei welchem Anlaß (occasion)?

Wann suchte er sein Unrecht wieder gut zu machen?

Was sagte er zu ihm?

War von Schomberg dadurch befriedigt?

Was für ein Schicksal (fate) hatte er dann?

War v. Schomberg ein Franzose?

Der Führer zu Ruhm und Ehre.

Der Marschall Biron.

„Sire," sprach er, „Sie haben heute gethan, was Biron hätte thun sollen."

Er war sehr milde.

Er rief den Soldaten zu, daß sie die Franzosen retten sollten.

Er gab ihm eine glänzende Genugthuung.

Ja, der König hatte ihm einen unverdienten Vorwurf gemacht.

Als der General einige Tage vor der Schlacht die Löhnung für seine Truppen verlangte.

Im Augenblick vor dem Beginn der Schlacht.

„Ich will die Ehre eines Edelmanns nicht mit mir ins Grab nehmen; verzeihen Sie mir, General."

Gewiß, er sagte, diese Auszeich-nung (distinction) zwinge ihn, für seinen König zu sterben.

Er wurde an der Seite des Kö-nigs getötet.

Nein, er war ein Deutscher.

---

# Forty-third Lesson.

## On the Subjunctive Mood.

The subjunctive mood is employed when the speaker wishes to express *uncertainty* or *doubt* of the reality of an action or a statement. It is used in German.

1) after some of the conjunctions;
2) after certain verbs;
3) in the oblique narration.

### I. Subjunctive after conjunctions.

§ 1. Only a few of the *conjunctions* require the verb in the subjunctive; viz.:

*a)* bamit' (*that, in order that*) and bamit' ... nicht (*lest*):
Sagen Sie es ihm, bamit er es wiſſe.
Tell him, that he *may know* it.
Verſtecken Sie ſich, bamit man Sie nicht hier finbe.
Hide yourself, lest they find you here

*b)* wenn (*if*), and ob *if* or *whether*, but only when used
with an *Imperfect* or *Pluperfect:*
Wenn er mehr Gelb hätte if he *had* more money.
Wenn er nicht krank wäre if he *were* not ill.
Wenn ich ihn geſehen hätte, ſo würde ich es ihm geſagt haben.
If I had seen him, I should have told him.
Ich fragte ihn, ob er zufrieden wäre
I asked him *if* he was contented.

*c)* als wenn, wie wenn or als ob (*as if*):
Er ſieht aus, als wenn (or wie wenn) er krank wäre
He looks as if he were sick.
Es hat ben Anſchein, als ob es kalt werben würde.
It seems as though it would become cold

§ 2  If the *conjunction* wenn is understood, the verb
remains in the Subjunctive, but is placed at the beginning
of the sentence, as in English.  Ex.:
Hätte ich Gelb, ſo würde ich ein Pferb kaufen.
Had I money, I should buy a horse.
Wäre ich nicht krank, ſo würde ich mit Ihnen gehen
Were I not ill, I should go with you.
Wüßte er, baß ich' hier bin, ..
If he knew, that I were here etc.
Aufſtehen würde Englands ganze Jugend,
Sähe ber Britte ſeine Königin.  (Schillers Maria Stuart.)
All England's youth would rise,         .
If the Briton saw his queen.

### Reading Exercise. 122.

Schicke ber armen Frau ben Flachs, bamit ſie ihn gleich
ſpinne. Wenn er früher käme, würde er mich zu Hauſe finben
Wenn man Sie hier fänbe, ſo wären Sie verloren. Wenn er
fleißig wäre, ſo würde ich ihn loben. Ich würde es thun, wenn
ich etwas babei gewänne  Wenn Cäſar nicht ermorbet worben
wäre, ſo hätte er, ebenſowohl als Auguſtus, bie Römer an ſeine
Herrſchaft gewöhnt. Der alte Mann geht, als ob er lahm wäre.
Der Knabe liegt ba, als wenn er ſchlieſe. Er ſprach, wie wenn
er wahnſinnig (mad) wäre. Hätte ich gewußt, baß Hr. Müller
hier iſt, ſo würde ich ihn beſucht (called upon) haben.

**Aufgabe. 122a.**

I take medicine *that* I [*may*] recover[1]. He speaks aloud (*in order*) that every one *may* hear him. Send him away lest he [should] be found here I should be happy if I had as many books as you [have]. If he were rich, he would buy a carriage and horses. The hypocrite[2] speaks as if he were religious[3]. I should go to Paris myself if I had time. He spoke as if he *were* commanding it. Many a man would live happier, if he were contented Your pupils would have made more progress (Fortſchritte gemacht haben), if you had adopted[4] another method[5].

1) geneſen. 2) der Heuchler. 3) fromm. 4) an'nehmen. 5) Methode, f.

## II. Subjunctive after certain verbs.

§ 3. After verbs of *advising, begging, commanding, wishing, permitting, hoping, fearing etc.*, the verb in the dependent sentence beginning with daß, stands or ought to stand in the *Subjunctive*. Ex.:

Bitten Sie Ihren Vater, daß er Ihnen Geld gebe.
Beg your father to give you some money.

Ich erlaube (or rate) nicht, daß er nach Paris gehe.
Ich erlaube ihm nicht, nach Paris zu gehen.
I do not permit (allow, advise) that he *should* go to P.

Wünſchen Sie, daß ich nach dem Arzte ſchicke?
Do you wish *me* to send for the physician?

§ 4. After befehlen (to command *or* to order) and ſagen (to tell) the auxiliary ſoll (if the verb is in the present tense), or ſollte (after the Impf.) often replaces the Subjunctive.

Ich befahl, daß die Schüler im Zimmer bleiben ſollten.
I ordered the pupils to remain in the room.

Der König befahl, daß man eine Brücke bauen ſollte.
The king commanded a bridge to be built.

After the verb *to tell* (ſagen), the Infinitive or *should* is also translated ſoll or ſollte. Ex.:

Sagen Sie ihm, daß er kommen ſoll.
Tell him to come.

§ 5. After the verbs: fürchten to fear, bitten to beg, and sometimes wünſchen to wish, when in a *past tense*, the Subjunctive is often replaced by the auxiliary möchte. The conjunction daß may be left out, when the preceding verb is not in the negative Ex.:

Wir fürchteten*), daß er uns tadeln möchte (or er möchte u. t.).
We feared *lest**) he should blame us.
Er bat mich, daß ich ihn besuchen möchte.
He requested that I should call on him.
Ich wünschte (wollte), daß er hier bleiben möchte (or bliebe).
I wish that he *may* remain here.

*Note.* After wünschte or wollte the verb may also stand in
the Imperf. Subj. with or without daß. Ex.:
Ich wollte (wünschte), daß er bald käme (or er käme bald).
I wish he would come soon.

§ 6. Such verbs, as: glauben, meinen, zweifeln,
sagen, hoffen ꝛc., when used in the *Present* or *Future
tense*, especially *interrogatively*, are sometimes followed
by the *Subjunctive*, sometimes by the *Indicative*. The
latter takes place when the object leaves no doubt *in the
person who asks the question*, however doubtful it may
appear to others. Ex.:
Ich glaube nicht, daß er kommt.
The *Subjunctive* should be used, when the speaker is
in doubt about its truth or reality. For instance the
sentence »*Do you think, he will come?*« may be translated ·
Glauben Sie, daß er kommen wird or werde?

The meaning of the first sentence is: »*I (myself)
think that he will come; do you think so too?*« The second
means: »*I have a doubt as to his coming. What do you
think about it?*« Other examples:
Sagt er, (*Present tense*) daß er krank ist (or sei)?
Er sagt, daß er krank sei (ist).
Ich hoffe, daß er nicht sterben wird (or werde).
Man zweifelt, ob er gehen wird (or werde).

### Reading Exercise. 124.

Bitten Sie Ihre Schwester, daß sie bald hierher komme. Es
wäre zu wünschen (desirable), daß jener hohe Baum hier stände.
Jedermann wünscht, daß der General die Schlacht gewinnen möchte
(gewinne). Es wäre zu wünschen, daß der General die Schlacht
gewänne. Wir fürchten, daß das Eis bersten möchte. Ich wünsche,

---

*) When fürchten stands in the *Present* tense, the following
verb may also stand in the *Future* of the *Subjunctive*:
Man fürchtet, daß er nicht kommen werde.
It is to be feared he won't come.
**) After the verb *to fear* lest is translated daß or left out.

baß er balb genese. Jch wünschte, baß meine Tochter balb käme. Jch befehle, baß er bas Zimmer verlasse. Glauben Sie, baß es morgen regnen werde (wird)?

### Aufgabe. 125.

Do you think he will come? I am afraid he *will* come. I will *order* him to retire[1] (that he retire). I *ordered* that he *should* retire. I fear the ice[2] *may* break. We fear [lest] he [*should*] come. I wish the work[3] weie done. I wished that he *might* win the prize[4]. I fear [lest] he *should* die of (an) his wounds. I feared he would dislocate[5] his arm, ᵗif he *were to*[6] lift that heavy weight[7]. »Turn[8] this wicked fellow away,« said the duke, »lest he [should] pervert[9] these honest people.« It would be [a] pity (Schabe), if that beautiful fruit[10] *were to spoil* (verbärbe or verberben würbe).

1) refl v. sich zurückziehen. 2) bas Eis. 3) bie Arbeit. 4) ben Preis. 5) verrenken. 6) *were to lift* = aufhöbe. 7) Gewicht, n. 8) to turn away sortjagen. 9) verberben. 10) Obst, n.

---

## III. Subjunctive in the oblique narration.

§ 7. When a person relates in the *Imperfect tense* what the himself or another person *said* or *thought*, and does not mention the *exact words used*, but states the substance of them in a subordinate clause, the narration is said to be *oblique*. This particularly takes place after the verbs: sagen, erklären to declare; antworten to answer; behaupten to maintain, state; glauben or benken to think; vermuten to suppose; erzählen to relate *or* tell etc., when used in the *Imperfect*. In such *quoted assertions* or *quotations*, the verb in the dependent clause is in the *Imperfect* or *Present Subjunctive,* whilst in English the *Imperfect Indicative* is used. Ex.:

Er sagte mir, baß seine Mutter krank wäre (or sei) (— baß sie Kopfweh hätte or habe).
He *told* me, (that) his mother *was* ill — had a headache.

Jch glaubte, baß sein Vater Deutsch spräche (or spreche).
I thought that his father *spoke* German.

Er erkläre, baß er es nicht machen könnte (or könne).
He declared that he *could* not do it.

Jch vermutete, baß er arm wäre (or sei).
I supposed him to be poor.

§ 8. This is also the case when an *indirect question* is asked in the *Imperfect* tense.

Er fragte, warum wir nicht gekommen wären or seien.
He asked why we *had* (*did*) not come.

Ich wurde gefragt, ob ich sie kenne (or kännte).
I was asked whether I *knew* her.

*Note 1.* When such assertions have not the nature of *quotations*, but are *statements* in the Present, Perfect or Future, the *Indicative* must be used. Ex.:

Er glaubt (er sagt 2c.), daß er unrecht hat (that he *is* wrong).
Er hat selbst gesagt, daß er gefehlt hat.
He has said himself that he has been in fault.
Ich frage dich zum letztenmal, ob du gehen willst oder nicht.
I ask you for the last time, whether you will go or not
Er will (or wird) nicht glauben, daß sein Bruder gestorben ist.
He will not believe that his brother *is* dead.

*Note 2.* Observe that with verbs of *knowing, seeing, showing, being convinced* etc., the subordinate clause of the sentence with daß is usually in the *Indicative*. Ex.:

Ich weiß, daß er kommt
Ich wußte, daß er Wort halten wird.
Ich war überzeugt (convinced), daß er es gethan hatte.

§ 9. As in English, the conjunction daß (that) can be omitted, but then the order of the words is the same as in English; the verb does n o t go last:

Ich glaubte, er wäre (or sei) abgereist (for daß er — wäre).
I thought he *had* set out (or left).
Der Kaufmann behauptete, das Geld sei (or wäre) falsch.
The merchant stated that the money *was* false.

§ 10. As has been shewn in the above examples, the *Present* and *Imperfect* of the *Subjunctive* are indifferently used. We may say, it is a matter of euphony. With regular verbs however, where the *Imperfect* tense of the *Indicative* does not differ from the *Imperfect* of the *Subjunctive*, the *Present* tense is preferred for the *third person sing.*, the *Imperfect* for the other persons. Ex.:

Er sagte, daß er mich suche (or suchte).
He said that he *was* looking for me.
Ich fragte den Kaufmann, wieviel das Kilo koste.
I asked the merchant how much a kilo cost.
Ich glaubte, Sie wollten (not wollen) mich betrügen.
I thought you would cheat me.
Er fragte mich, warum ich nicht nach dem Arzte schickte (not schicke).
He asked me why I *did* not send for the physician.

§ 11. The Subjunctive is sometimes used to express a *command* or *wish*, and replaces in some cases the third person of the *Imperative:*

Jeder thue seine Pflicht let everybody do his duty.
Lang lebe der König long live the king!
Gott segne Sie God bless you!
Die Liebe sei ohne Falsch.
Let love be without dissimulation.

O daß mein Freund käme!
Oh that my friend would come!

O wäre ich doch reich or daß ich doch reich wäre!
Oh, if I were rich! were I but rich!

Hätte ich ihn doch nie gesehen! (Daß ich ihn doch nie g. hätte!)
Would I had never seen him!

*Note.* The English *let* with the third person (*him, her, them*)
is rendered either by the third person of the *Pres. Subjunctive,*
as in the above sentences, or by sollen  We may say as well:
  Let him do his duty er soll seine Pflicht thun.
  Let love be without dissimulation die L. soll ohne Falsch sein.
  Let them be free sie seien frei or sie sollen frei sein.
  Let him be flogged er soll gepeitscht werden.
  Let him (her) take his (her) share
  Er (sie) soll seinen (ihren) Anteil nehmen

§ 12. As in English, the *Imperfect Subjunctive* is often
used instead of the Conditional (see p. 78 and 83). Ex.:
  Es wäre schimpflich zu fliehen
  It *were* or would be shameful to flee.

---

### The Imperative Mood.

This mood presents no difficulty; observe only that
in the second person plural, Sie must be added to the
verb on addressing a person politely, as: Geben Sie mir,
sagen Sie mir 2c.  Ex.:
  Johann, machen Sie mir Feuer (an) John, make my fire.
  Nehmen Sie Ihre Handschuhe weg.
  Take your gloves away.

The simple form gebet, saget, except in familiar
talk, occurs mostly in the poetical or didactic style. Ex.:
  Vergeltet nicht Böses mit Bösem.
  Do not render evil for evil.

The English form of the Imperative (*let us*) in the
first person plural is translated either with lassen Sie uns
(lasset uns), or with wir wollen, or with the *verb* and wir
after it:
  Lassen Sie uns (lasset uns) arbeiten, ⎫
  Wir wollen arbeiten or arbeiten wir, ⎬ so lange es Tag ist.
  Let us work as long as it is day

### Reading Exercise. 126.

1. Mein Sohn sagte mir, daß er Kopfweh hätte (or habe).
Man schrieb mir neulich, daß Herr C. krank wäre, und daß sein
Bruder nach Amerika gegangen wäre. Man sagte, der König hätte
(habe) dem General eine große Ungerechtigkeit[1] zugefügt (done).
Man sagte, der Graf sei (or wäre) gestorben; aber ich habe seitdem erfahren[2], daß diese Nachricht falsch ist. Ich fragte ihn, warum
er seine Aufgabe nicht geschrieben hätte. Er antwortete, er habe
(hätte) keine Zeit gehabt. Mentor erzählte mir oft, welchen Ruhm[3]
Ulysses unter den Griechen erlangt[4] habe. Der General behauptete,
daß der Friede geschlossen[5] sei (or der Friede wäre geschlossen).

2. Man hat mich oft versichert[6], daß die Glückseligkeiten[7]
dieser Welt nur von kurzer Dauer sind. Fürst, man wird dir
sagen, du seiest allmächtig; man wird dir sagen, du seiest von
deinem Volke angebetet[8]. Haltet immer, was ihr versprochen habt;
aber versprechet nichts unbedachtsam[9]. Soldaten, laßt uns vorwärts marschieren, laßt uns siegen oder sterben. Wir wollen ein
wenig spazieren gehen. Er ist der Herr[10], er thue[11], was ihm
gefällt. Gott sprach: „Es werde Licht", und es ward Licht. O
dächten doch alle wie du und ich! Wäre er doch (O that)
aufrichtig[12]! O daß die Königin noch lebte!

1) injustice.   2) learnt.   3) fame   4) obtained.   5) made. —
6) assured.   7) enjoyments   8) to adore   9) inconsiderately. —
10) the Lord   11) he may do.   12) sincere.

### Aufgabe. 127.

1. My brother told me that he *had* lost his purse He
pretended[1] to *be* right (that he *was* right) What did your
friend tell you? He told me that you should (§ 4) come to
see him[2] some day (einmal). The advocate declared that he
*could* not do it. I thought that he *was* mistaken. She told
me that the tree *was* in blossom[3] They (Man) said we *could*
not rely[4] upon him People said that the king *would* come
to-morrow to (in) this town. Did you believe that I *had*
advised him (dat.) to do so (das)? I knew (§ 8, Note 2) that
he was ill. We thought he *was* a clever physician. We all
hoped that our father might recover[5], but in vain[6].

2. Were but (doch) all men as honest as they ought to be!
I did not pretend[1] that your brother *was* (*had been*) at the
play[7] yesterday. He said that his brother had (a) great influence[8] with (bei) the duke. Were you not afraid[9], that he
might steal your money? The duke ordered that they *should*
(§ 4) help the poor man. May God preserve[10] us from (vor)
war! Form[11] your mind and (your) heart, while you are

1) behaupten   2) to come to see = besuchen.   3) Blüte   4) rely
uns . verlassen auf (Acc.).   5) genesen   6) umsonst.   7) im Theater.
8) Einfluß, m   9) to be afraid = fürchten.   10) bewahren   11) bilden

young. Mary told her maids, that she would have left[12] them this dress rather (lieber) than the plain garb[13] which she *wore* (*Perf. Subj.*)[14] the day before, but that it *was* necessary for her to appear at the ensuing solemnity (bei der bevorstehenden Feierlichkeit) in a decent habit[15].

12) hinterlaſſen. 13) das einfache Gewand. 14) getragen hätte. — 15) anſtändige Kleidung.

## Reading-lesson.
### Die geprüfte Treue. Fidelity tried.

Der Kalife Mutewekul hatte einen ausländiſchen[1] Arzt, Namens Honaʼin, welchen er wegen ſeiner großen Gelehrſamkeit[2] ſehr ehrte. Einige Hofleute machten ihm dieſen Mann verdächtig[3] und ſagten, er könnte ſich auf ſeine Treue nicht wohl verlaſſen (rely), weil er ein Ausländer[4] ſei. Der Kalife wurde unruhig[5] und wollte ihn prüfen[6], inwiefern dieſer Argwohn[7] begründet wäre. Er ließ ihn zu ſich kommen und ſagte: „Honain, ich habe unter meinen Emirn[8] einen gefährlichen Feind, gegen welchen ich wegen ſeines ſtarken Anhanges[9] keine Gewalt[10] gebrauchen kann. Daher befehle ich dir, daß du ein feines Gift bereiteſt, das an dem Toten keine Spur[11] von ſich zurücklaſſen wird. Ich will ihn morgen zu einem Gaſtmahl (banquet, dinner) einladen, und mich ſeiner auf (in) dieſe Weiſe entledigen[12].“

Honain antwortete mutig: „Meine Wiſſenſchaft erſtreckt[13] ſich nur auf Arzneien, die das Leben erhalten[14], andre kann ich nicht bereiten. Ich habe mich auch nie bemüht, es zu lernen, weil ich glaubte, daß der Beherrſcher der wahren Gläubigen[15] keine ſolchen Kenntniſſe von mir fordern (require) würde. Wenn ich hierin unrecht gethan habe, ſo erlaube mir, deinen Hof zu verlaſſen.“

Mutewekul erwiderte, das ſei nur eine leere Entſchuldigung[16], wer die heilſamen Mittel kenne, der kenne auch die ſchädlichen. Er bat, er drohte, er verſprach Geſchenke. Umſonſt, Honain blieb bei ſeiner Antwort. Endlich ſtellte ſich[17] der Kalife erzürnt, rief die Wache und befahl, dieſen widerſpänſtigen[18] Mann ins Gefängnis zu führen. Das geſchah; auch wurde ein Kundſchafter[19] unter dem Scheine[20] eines Gefangenen zu ihm geſetzt, der ihn ausforſchen und dem Kaliſen von allem, was Honain ſagen würde, Nachricht geben[21] ſollte. Aber Honain verriet[22] mit keinem Worte ſeinem Mitgefangenen[23], warum der Kalife auf ihn zürne[24]. Alles, was er ſagte, war, daß er unſchuldig[25] wäre. (*To be continued*).

1) foreign. 2) skill, learning. 3) made him suspicious. — 4) foreigner. 5) uneasy. 6) try. 7) suspicion. 8) governors. — 9) party. 10) use no force. 11) trace 12) get rid of him. 13) to extend. 14) preserve. 15) commander of the faithful. 16) excuse 17) to feign. 18) obstinate. 19) a spy. 20) appearance 21) to inform. 22) to reveal, betray. 23) fellow-prisoner. 24) to be angry. 25) innocent.

## Conversation.

| | |
|---|---|
| Was für einen Arzt hatte der Kalife Mutewekul an seinem Hofe? | Er hatte einen fremden Arzt Namens Honain. |
| Wer machte ihn verdächtig? | Einige neidische (envious) Hofleute. |
| Aus welchem Grunde? | Weil er ein Ausländer war. |
| Was beschloß deshalb der Kalife zu thun? | Er beschloß, ihn zu prüfen (or ihn auf die Probe zu stellen). |
| Was verlangte er von Honain? | Er solle ein feines Gift bereiten, um einen Emir zu vergiften. |
| Wann sollte die Vergiftung stattfinden? | Am nächsten Tage bei einem Gastmahle. |
| Was antwortete Honain? | Daß er dieses nicht verstehe, und daß es ein schlechter Gebrauch seiner Wissenschaft sein würde. |
| War der Kalife mit dieser Antwort zufrieden? | Nein, er bestand (insisted) auf seinem Befehle; er bat, er drohte und versprach ihm Geschenke. |
| Gab Honain zuletzt nach? (Did H. yield?) | Nein, er blieb standhaft (firmly) bei seiner Antwort. |
| Was that zuletzt Mutewekul? | Er ließ ihn ins Gefängnis setzen. |
| War Honain allein im Gefängnis? | Nein, ein Kundschafter wurde zu ihm gesetzt. |
| Was sollte dieser thun? | Er sollte dem Kalifen von allem Nachricht geben, was Honain sagen würde. |
| Klagte der Arzt über die Ungerechtigkeit des Kalifen? | Nein, er sagte nur, daß er unschuldig sei. |

# Forty-fourth Lesson.
## ON THE INFINITIVE.
### I. The Infinitive used as a Substantive.

§ 1. The Infinitive is sometimes used *substantively*, either with the *neuter* article das, or sometimes without it, whereas in English the participle present is met with:

Das Reiten ist eine angenehme Bewegung.
Riding is an agreeable exercise.

Das Lesen ermüdet die Augen reading fatigues the eyes.

Geben ist seliger als Nehmen.
It is more blessed to give, than to receive.

*Note.* Concerning the Participle present with *of* before it, see p 323, § 5 and p. 329, § 5.

## II. The Infinitive without zu.

§ 2. The Infinitive *without* zu is used after the auxiliaries of mood sollen, wollen, können, mögen, müssen, dürfen: Wir können Deutsch sprechen we can speak German.

§ 3. Further with the following verbs: sehen, hören, fühlen, heißen (to bid), machen, lassen, lernen, lehren and helfen. Ex.:

Ich sah die Frau vorbeigehen I saw the woman passing by.
Die Not lehrt beten need teaches *to* pray.
Mein Sohn lernt Englisch lesen.
My son learns *to* read English.
Man hieß den Knaben hinausgehen.
They bade the boy go out.
Ich hörte meinen Freund in einer Gesellschaft singen.
I heard my friend sing at a party.
Er ließ den Mann hereinrufen he had the man called in.

*Note.* The above verbs, with the exception of fühlen, lehren sometimes also lernen and hören, have the peculiarity that in the *compound tenses* they are used in the *Infinitive* instead of the Participle past, when they have another Infinitive before them. Ex.:

Haben Sie das Buch liegen sehen (instead of gesehen)?
Man hat mich rufen lassen.
Ich habe sie singen hören (or gehört).
Der Mann hat mir arbeiten helfen.
Wir haben Französisch sprechen lernen (or gelernt).
Wo haben Sie ihn kennen gelernt?
Where have you made his acquaintance?

§ 4. The Infinitive *without* zu is further used in some particular expressions with the following verbs:

Bleiben: liegen bleiben, sitzen bleiben, stehen bleiben.
legen: schlafen legen.
lehren: schreiben lehren, lesen lehren, zeichnen (to draw) lehren zc.
gehen, reiten und fahren: spazieren gehen, spazieren reiten,
    spazieren fahren (to take a ride, a drive); schlafen gehen,
    betteln gehen (to go begging), baden gehen (bathing).

*NB.* These verbs always retain the *Participle past* in the compound tenses. Ex.:

Ich habe das Kind schon schlafen gelegt.
Dieser Lehrer hat mich schreiben gelehrt.
Mein Heft ist auf dem Tische liegen geblieben.
Wir sind spazieren gefahren, — geritten, — gegangen.

## III. The Infinitive with zu.

§ 5. The Infinitive with zu is used, when it depends on a foregoing substantive; whereas in English they often

21*

use the *Part. pres.* with *of* before it, instead of the *Inf.* with *to* (for inst. the pleasure *of seeing* you etc.):

Haben Sie Luſt (a mind), ins Theater zu gehen?
Er hatte nicht den Mut, über den Fluß zu ſchwimmen.
Wann werde ich das Vergnügen haben, Sie wieder zu ſehen?

§ 6. After adjectives which are susceptible of a government (*régime*):

Dieſes Gedicht iſt leicht zu lernen.
Dieſer Brief iſt ſchwer zu leſen.
Ich bin begierig (anxious), zu erfahren, wer es gethan hat.

§ 7. After *all other* verbs except those mentioned in § 2—4, zu is used, whereas in English the dependent verb is sometimes in the *Participle present*.

Er fing an zu lachen he began *laughing.*
Ich fürchtete, zu ſpät zu kommen (to be too late).
Wann werden Sie aufhören zu ſchreiben?
When will you cease *writing?*
Der Sklave bemühte ſich, die Gunſt ſeines Herrn zu erlangen.
The slave endeavoured to obtain the favour of his master.
Der Kapitän überredete den Fremden, mit ihm zu gehen.
The captain persuaded the stranger to go with him.

§ 8. When the auxiliaries haben and ſein are followed by an Infinitive, it takes zu:

Ich habe nichts zu thun.
Haben Sie mir etwas zu ſagen?
Was iſt da zu thun, — zu glauben, — zu antworten?
Es iſt zu bedauern, daß dieſer Mann geſtorben iſt.
It is *to be regretted* that this man has died.

*Note.* The Infinitive after the verb *to be*, is in English commonly taken in the *passive voice*; in German it must be in the *active voice.* Ex·

It was not *to be avoided* es war nicht zu vermeiden
His death is *to be feared* ſein Tod iſt zu befürchten.
That book is not *to be had* jenes Buch iſt nicht zu haben.
A change is much *to be wished for.*
Eine Veränderung iſt ſehr zu wünſchen.

### Reading Exercise. 128.

Das Schnupfen[1] iſt eine ſchlechte Gewohnheit. Zu viel (too much) ſchlafen iſt eben ſo ungeſund, als zu viel eſſen. Ich habe das Buch noch nicht leſen können. Haben Sie leſen wollen? Nein, ich habe ſchreiben wollen. Helfen Sie mir meine Überſetzung machen. Wer hat dich gehen heißen? Er hat mich tanzen gelehrt. Ich habe ihm arbeiten helfen. Sind Sie geſtern ſpazieren gegangen?

1) taking snuff.

Nein, ich bin spazieren geritten. Der König hat mir die Erlaubnis gegeben, einen Degen² zu tragen. Kennen Sie ein sicheres³ Mittel, die Mäuse zu vertilgen⁴? Das sicherste Mittel, unser Leben zu verlängern, ist, jeden Augenblick⁵ des Tages gut anzuwenden⁶. Ich habe keine Hoffnung mehr, meinen verlornen Sohn wieder zu finden.

2) a sword. 3) safe. 4) to destroy. 5) moment. 6) employ.

#### Aufgabe. 129.

Eating and drinking make one (Einen) sleepy. To speak too much is dangerous. The laughing of these people is very unpleasant¹. I bade him do it. I saw him take it. They could not make me laugh. Learn *to do* good (Gutes). Have you seen the young girl dance? No, but I have heard her sing. When our friends help us *to* work, we ought to be grateful² to them. Let us take a walk. Shall we have the pleasure of seeing you to-morrow? I have no mind to make the bargain (den Handel einzugehen), for (aus) fear of losing it. The slaves had no desire (Lust, *f.*) to run off (fort), knowing (*as* (da) *they knew*) what³ the consequence⁴ would be. I am eager⁵ to learn music. He was near (nahe daran) dying. The pupil was tired⁶ of reading German (*to read G.*). What have you to do? I have a letter to write. A pardon⁷ is not *to be hoped* [for].

1) unangenehm 2) dankbar. 3) welches, see p 145, Note. — 4) die Folge. 5) eifrig. 6) müde. 7) Begnadigung, f.

---

### The Infinitive with zu after prepositions.

§ 9. The Infinitive with zu is further required after the prepositions anstatt (*instead*) and ohne (*without*):

Anstatt zu lachen, weinte er.

Er ging aus, ohne mich zu fragen (without asking me).

Manche Leute werden gehaßt (hated), ohne es zu verdienen.

### IV. The Infinitive with um — zu.

§ 10. It is required after substantives and verbs, when a *design* or *purpose* is expressed, answering to the English *for* or *in order to* (the French *pour*). Ex..

Haben Sie Geld erhalten, um ein Pferd zu kaufen?
Ich brauche Papier, um einen Brief zu schreiben.
Ich reise, um die Welt zu sehen.

§ 11. After *adjectives* preceded by zu (too), or followed by genug:

Sie ist zu jung, um diese Arbeit zu verrichten (to do).
Herr A. ist nicht reich genug, um dieses Landgut (estate) zu kaufen.

## V. The English Accusative and Infinitive.

§ 12. The Infinitive used in English with an *Accusative* after the verbs *to know*, *to desire*, *to wish*, *to mean etc.* must be changed in German into a subordinate clause with baß, in which the Accusative governed by such a verb appears as the Nominative. For instance •the following sentence. *We know him to be a bad general*, is translated in German, as if it were: *We know that he is a bad general* wir wiffen, baß er ein ſchlechter Ge= neral ist (*Indic. Pres.*). Ex.:

I knew the captain to be a good rider
Ich wußte, baß ber Hauptmann ein guter Reiter war.

I wish *her* to do the work
Ich wünſche, baß ſie bie Arbeit thue (or thun möchte).

We desired our *friends* to come in.
Wir wünſchten, baß unſre Freunbe hereinfommen möchten.

## VI. The elliptical Infinitive.

§ 13. The Infinitive after the words *how*, *what*, *where*, must be completed in German with a subject and an auxiliary: ſollen, müſſen or fönnen. Ex.:

I do not know where to go.
Ich weiß nicht, wohin ich geh:n ſoll.

Show him how to do it
Zeigen Sie ihm, wie er es machen ſoll.

### Reading Exercise. 130.

Anſtatt zu arbeiten, ging er ſpazieren. Es hat aufgehört zu regnen. Ich frene mich, zu höien, baß Ihr Sohn ſolche Chien= bezeugungen[1] empfangen hat. Der Böſe hat nichts zu heffen. Ich hatte nichts mit dieſem ſchlechten Menſchen zu ſchaffen (do). Dieſer Knabe hat viele Schmeizen zu erbulden[2]. Der Hauptmann war zu mübe, nm Sie ſo ſpät zu beſuchen. Der Richter hat ben Gefangenen ins Gefängnis führen laſſen. Du biſt nicht würbig[3] genug, um bieſe Belohnung zu empfangen. Mein Nachbar hatte bie Abſicht[4], ſein Haus zu verfaufen, nm ſeine Schulden[5] bezahlen zu fönnen.

1) honours.  2) endure.  3) worthy.  4) intention.  5) debts.

### Aufgaße. 131.

We lost our time without knowing it. The boy *is* continually[1] *playing*[2] instead of learning his lesson. We cannot betray[3] the truth without being (*or* rendering ourselves) guilty. He did so (es), in order to frighten[4] you. My children must

1) fortwährend.  2) See p 308, § 1.  3. verraten  4) erſchrecken.

learn *to* draw, in order to be able to draw landscapes[5]. At last I began to long[6] for my native country[7], that I might (*translate:* in order to) (§ 10) repose[8] after my travels and fatigues[9]. The early death of the hero was much to be regretted[10]. If he were not ashamed[11] of confessing[12] the truth, he would say that he did not begin to work before ten o'clock. The stream[13] is too rapid[14] *to be* often *frozen* (.. zu gefrieren). She knew *him to please* (§ 12) everybody. I wish *you to read* the history of England by (von) Macaulay. When you know *a poor man to be* honest and industrious, you ought to esteem him more highly (höher), than a rich man (*acc.*) who violates[15] the duties[16] of a Christian[17].

5) Landschaften. 6) mich nach.. zu sehnen (refl. v.). 7) das Vaterland. 8) auszuruhen. 9 Anstrengungen. 10) zu bedauern, *Inf. act.* — 11) to be ashamed = sich schämen. 12) gestehen. 13) der Strom — 14) reißend. 15) verletzen. 16) die Pflichten. 17) Christ (2nd decl).

## Reading-lesson.
### Die geprüfte Treue. (Schluß.)

Nach einigen Monaten ließ (had) der Kalife ihn wieder vor sich rufen. Auf einem Tisch lag ein Haufen Gold, Diamanten und köstliche Stoffe: aber daneben stand der Henker[1] mit einer Geißel[2] in der[3] Hand und einem Schwerte unter dem[3] Arme. „Du hast nun Zeit genug gehabt," fing Mutewekul an, „um dich zu bedenken[4] und das Unrecht (fault) deiner Widerspänstigkeit[5] einzusehen. Nun wähle: entweder nimm diese Reichtümer und thue meinen Willen, oder bereite dich zu einem schimpflichen[6] Tode!" Aber Honain antwortete, die Schande liege nicht in der Strafe, sondern in dem Verbrechen. Er könne sterben, ohne die Ehre seines Standes[7] und seiner Wissenschaft zu beflecken[8]. Der Kalife sei der Herr seines Lebens; er thue (möge thun)[9], was ihm gefalle.

„Geht hinaus!" sagte der Kalife zu den Umstehenden; und als er allein war, reichte er dem gewissenhaften[10] Honain die Hand und sprach: „Honain, ich bin mit dir zufrieden; du bist mein Freund und ich der deinige. Man hat mir deine Treue verdächtig gemacht: ich mußte (I thought I must) deine Ehrlichkeit prüfen[11], um gewiß zu werden, ob ich mich vollkommen auf dich verlassen könne. Nicht als eine Belohnung, sondern als ein Zeichen[12] meiner Freundschaft werde ich dir diese Geschenke senden, die deine Rechtschaffenheit nicht verführen[13] konnten."

So sprach der Kalife und befahl den Dienern, das Gold, die Edelsteine und die Stoffe in Honains Haus zu tragen.

1) the executioner. 2) scourge 3) *his.* (See p 301, 1.) 4) to consider. 5) obstinacy, stubbornness. 6) shameful. 7) profession. 8) to stain 9) See p. 319, § 11 — 10) conscientious, honest. — 11) to prove, put to a proof. 12) token. 13) to corrupt, bribe.

### Conversation.

Wie lange blieb Honain im Gefängnis? — Einige Monate (lang).

Als Mutewekul ihn wieder rufen ließ, was zeigte er ihm? — Auf der einen Seite einen Tisch mit Gold und Diamanten, auf der andern einen Henker.

Was hatte der Henker in der Hand? — Er hatte eine Geißel in der Hand.

Was hatte er unter dem Arm? — Ein Schwert.

Was verlangte nun der Kalife von seinem Arzte? — Honain sollte wählen zwischen Reichtum und dem Tode.

Was antwortete Honain? — Die Schande liege nicht in der Strafe, sondern im Verbrechen.

Was setzte er noch hinzu (add)? — „Der Kalife thue, was ihm gefällt."

Fügte (submit) er sich endlich in den Willen des Kalifen? — Nein, er blieb standhaft bei seiner Weigerung (refusal).

Wie belohnte Mutewekul ihn dafür? — Er sagte, daß er mit ihm zufrieden sei, und gestand ihm, daß er ihn nur habe prüfen wollen.

Wie nannte er ihn? — Er nannte ihn seinen Freund.

Und wie bezeigte (show) er ihm seine Dankbarkeit? — Er ließ das Gold, die Edelsteine und kostbaren Stoffe in Honains Wohnung bringen.

---

# Forty-fifth Lesson.

## On the Participle present.

The Participle present, which is formed of all verbs by adding the syllable **end** to the root, is much less used than in English, and is often very differently employed.

§ 1. It is used as an *adjective* qualifying a substantive. Ex.:

Ein weinendes Kind a weeping child.
Eine liebende Mutter a loving mother.
Die aufgehende Sonne the rising sun.
Die ermunternden Worte the encouraging words.

Several Participles therefore, by being constantly used in this manner, have quite lost the nature of a verb, and are used as true adjectives, taking also the degrees of comparison:

belehrend instructive.
betrübend afflicting.
dringend pressing.

drückend oppressive.
ermüdend fatiguing.
fließend fluent, flowing.

ḫinreißenb overpoweiing.                  verleßenb offensive.
reizenb charming                          unterhalteub amusing etc.
  *Comp* ermüdenber; *Sup* ber, bie, baß eimüdenbſte ꝛc.; as:
  Eine ermüdenbere Reiſe a more fatiguing journey.

§ 2. The German *Participle present* is seldom used
*as such*. *Neuter* verbs, however, may be employed so,
when joined *adverbially* to another verb, in order to
express *manner* or *state:*
  Lachenb ſagte er zu mir ꝛc. laughing he said to me etc.
  Sie gingen ſchweigenb fort they went off in silence.

*Note.* Poets also occasionally use an *active* verb in the Par-
ticiple piesent, with its government before or after it. Ex :
  Patroklus, bem lieben Freunde gehorchenb (obeying).
  Ihn umgürtenb (girding) mit bem Heldenſchwert.
  Mit ben Händen ſchwingenb (brandishing) bie Speere.

§ 3. When used in English as a *substantive*, either
as subject or as object, we ꝛender it by the Infinitive,
with or without the article baß, such as· baß Lernen leain-
ing, baß Baben bathing, baß Tanzen etc. (see p. 322, § 1)
  *Reading* good books is necessary for young people.
  Daß Leſen guter Bücher iſt jungen Leuten nötig.
  Card-playing and smoking are expensive habits.
  Daß Kartenſpielen unb Rauchen ſinb koſtſpielige Gewohnheiten.

§ 4. If the participle replaces a relative pronoun,
the latter is to be expressed in German, connected with
the verb in the corresponding tense:
  A man *doing* good to everybody.
  Ein Mann, ber (welcher) jedermann Gutes thut.
  I see a woman selling cherries.
  Ich ſehe eine Frau, welche Kirſchen verkauft.

§ 5. The English *Participle present*, when depending upon a noun and preceded by the preposition *of*, must
be translated with the Infinitive and zu: (See p. 324, top.)
  The art of *writing* bie Kunſt zu ſchreiben.
  The pleasure of seeing you baß Vergnügen Sie zu ſehen.

§ 5a. The same is the case when it depends on
another verb:
  It began raining eß fing an zu regnen.
  He ceased speaking er hörte auf, zu ſprechen.
  I risked *losing* my life.
  Ich lief Gefahr, mein Leben zu verlieien.

§ 6. This is also the case when the *Participle present*
is immediately preceded by the prepositions *on, upon, in,
with, without, instead of* and *near* (nahe baran):

I have decided *on doing* it (*to do it*).
Ich habe beschlossen, es zu thun.
He insisted *upon seeing me*.
Er bestand darauf, mich zu sehen.
He left *without paying* er ging fort, ohne zu bezahlen.
The boy is playing *instead of learning* his lesson.
Der Knabe spielt, anstatt seine Aufgabe zu lernen.

### Reading Exercise. 132.

Herr Müller war ein sorgender[1] Vater und ein liebender Gatte[2]. Das Bild stellt (represents) ein lachendes Kind vor. Die folgende Aufgabe ist zu übersetzen. Campes „Robinson Crusoe" ist ein sehr unterhaltendes und belehrendes Buch. Das Baden ist gesund. Das Zeichnen ist eine angenehme Beschäftigung[3]. Das Lachen mancher Leute ist unangenehm. Hatten Sie die Ehre, seine Be= kanntschaft[4] zu machen? Das Spazierengehen ist für mich sehr ermüdend. Lesen und Schreiben ist für alle Leute nötig[5]. Meine Frau liebt das Rauchen nicht. Ich fand eine Flasche, welche roten Wein enthielt[6]. Sie fing eben an, einen Brief zu schreiben. Ich war nahe daran, nach Amerika auszuwandern[7]. Sie müssen fort= fahren, Englisch zu lernen

1) caring, careful. 2) husband. 3) occupation 4) acquaintance. 5) necessary. 6) contain. 7) to emigrate.

### Aufgabe. 133.

I *am going* to Paris in a few days. I saw the dying old man You will find the word on (auf) the following page. That was a very fatiguing journey. My friend lives in a charming country[1]. *Riding* (§ 3) and *dancing* are good bodily[2] exercises. Is learning necessary for young people? The burden[3] is oppressive. Clouds[4] *are* formed[5] from the vapours[6] *arising*[7] (§ 4) from the earth. I have seen a book containing[8] beautiful poems. Alexander asked his friends standing (§ 4) about his death-bed[9], if (ob) they thought they could find a king, like him. She was near dying He told me trembling, that he had lost all his money. *Speaking thus, (§ 2) she stabbed*[10] herself. Eliza, *weeping bitterly*[11], threw herself into the arms of her mother. The father stood mourning[12] by the tomb[13] of his son. The surgeon[14] began dressing (zu verbinden) the wound[15]. The rising (§ 1) sun disperses[16] the fog[17].

1) Gegend, f. 2) körperliche Übungen. 3) die Last. 4) die Wolken. 5) gebildet. 6) Dünste. 7) aufsteigen. 8) enthalten. 9) sein Todbett or Totenbett. 10) erdolchen 11) bitterlich 12) trauernd. 13) an dem Grab. 14) der Wundarzt. 15) Wunde, f. 16) vertreiben. 17) Nebel, m.

---

§ 7. But when in English a *possessive adjective* pre-cedes the Participle, with or without a preposition, this participial substantive must be expanded into a clause in German, and translated with a *conjunction* corresponding to the preposition; *viz.* with *of* and *at* corresponds baß; with *without* ohne baß; with *before* ehe or bevor; with *against* bagegen baß; with *by* baburch baß; with *on* or *upon* barauf baß; with *from* bavon baß. The *possessive adjective* is changed into a *personal pronoun*.

We noticed *his looking* at her.

Wir bemerkten, baß er sie ansah.

We heard *of his becoming* a soldier.

Wir hörten, baß er Solbat geworden war*).

I spoke *of (my) going* to Paris.

Ich sprach bavon, baß ich nach Paris gehen wollte.

I have nothing *against your going* there.

Ich habe nichts bagegen, baß Sie bahin gehen.

The landlord insisted *on our taking horses.*

Der Wirt bestand barauf, baß wir Pferbe nehmen sollten.

§ 8. When a noun in the *Genitive* is joined to the possessive adjective, it becomes in German the *Nominative* or *subject* of the second clause:

I wrote *without my father's knowing* it.

Ich schrieb, ohne baß mein Vater es wußte.

He wished to copy the letter *before his uncle's seeing* it.

Er wollte ben Brief abschreiben, ehe sein Onkel ihn sähe.

§ 9. All other prepositions joined to a *Participle present,* must in any case be expressed by a *corresponding conjunction* with the *Indicative.* Ex.:

*Besides* her being rich außerbem, baß sie reich ist.

He saved himself *by* jumping through the window.

Er rettete sich baburch, baß er aus bem Fenster sprang.

The prisoner was hanged *for killing* a man.

Der Gefangene wurbe gehängt, weil (or bafür baß) er einen Mann getötet hatte.

You must have perceived it, *while speaking* with him.

Sie müssen es bemerkt haben, währenb Sie mit ihm sprachen.

*After having* (I had) gone over the bridge, I had a splendid view into the valley.

Nachbem ich bie Brücke passiert hatte, hatte ich eine herrliche Aussicht ins Thal.

After *having* received my money, I paid my creditors.

Nachbem ich mein Gelb erhalten hatte, bezahlte ich meine Gläubiger.

_____
*) Literally: *that he had become*

§ 10. When the *Participle present* is used by itself, i. e. without a preposition, to denote *cause*, *reason* or *time*, as in Latin and French, it must always be replaced by the corresponding *conjunction* with the finite verb. When the Participle expresses *cause* or *reason*, the corresponding conjunctions are: ba (as *or* since) and weil (because). — For *time:* als (when), nachdem (after) or indem (as) must be used.

*a*) Participles expressing *reason* and *cause:*

This being the case.

Da dieses der Fall ist (or war).

*Wishing* to see him, I went to his house.

Da ich ihn zu sehen wünschte, ging ich in sein Haus.

Not having found him, I went there a second time.

Da ich ihn nicht angetroffen hatte, ging ich noch einmal hin.

My mother *being* ill, she cannot go out.

Weil (da) meine Mutter krank ist, (so) kann sie nicht ausgehen.

*b*) Participles expressing *time:*

*Going* to the castle, I was overtaken by the rain.

Als (indem) ich auf das Schloß ging, wurde ich vom Regen überfallen.

*Having* spoken so long, he was tired.

Nachdem*) er so lange gesprochen hatte, war er müde.

The town *being taken*, the soldiers pillaged it.

Nachdem die Stadt erobert war, plünderten sie die Soldaten.

### Reading Exercise. 134.

Ich las die Zeitung, ohne daß er es bemerkte. Wir sprachen davon, daß wir nach Wien gehen wollten. Der Schüler wurde gestraft, weil er träge gewesen ist. Er war böse[1] über mich, daß ich ihn geweckt hatte. Ich war gestern in Ihrem Hause, ohne Sie zu sehen. Durch das Beobachten[2] dieser Regeln kann man viele Fehler vermeiden. Ich werde spazieren gehen, nachdem ich meine Geschäfte beendigt habe. Ich fand dieses Päckchen diesen Morgen, als (on) ich aus dem Hause ging. Da ich finde, daß es mir unmöglich sein wird, mein Versprechen zu halten, so nehme[3] ich mein Wort zurück[3].

1) angry with.   2) to observe.   3) to retract.

### Aufgabe. 135.

1. She noticed *my looking* at her. She cannot endure[1] *his* going away. I am sure (Ich weiß gewiß) *of* his having

---

*) The subordinative conjunction: nachdem, generally requires the *Pluperfect* of the *Indicative.*

done it. I am rejoiced *at* hearing of him. The overseer[2] re-
pented[3] having been so cruel with (gegen) the slaves and began
treating[4] them with more humanity[5]. Hearing the noise[6] of
the cannon, we started[7] up. Having seen him, I went to his
brother. We form our minds (*sing.*)[8] *by* reading (§ 9) good
books. We have obtained peace by making great sacrifices[9].
You will learn to speak French by writing it. The setting[10]
sun indicated[11] that it would be useless[12] pursuing[13] the fugitives[14]. Having\*) taken leave[15], *he* departed. Being poor, *he*
*had been* neglected[16]. Having no money, I could not (cannot)
depart. Having told his ridiculous[17] stories, ₂he ₁went ₄off (fort)
₃laughing. Mary and her brother Henry, perceiving a pretty
butterfly[18], endeavoured (ſuchten) to catch it. Conjecturing[19]
(§ 10, *a*) that I *was* (*Subj.*) rich and finding that I was ignorant,
*he* thought it would be easy to deceive me. The old man
having spoken thus, the assembly[20] dispersed[21].

1) ertragen. 2) Auffeher 3) bereute, daß. 4) behandeln. 5) Menſchlich-
keit. 6) der Donner 7) auf'ſpringen. 8) bilden unſern Geiſt. 9) to make
sacrifices Opfer bringen. 10) untergehen. 11) an'zeigen. 12) unnüß.
13) verfolgen. 14) Flüchtlinge. 15) Abſchied. 16) vernachläſſigt 17) lächer-
lich. 18) der Schmetterling. 19) vermuten 20) die Verſammlung.
21) to disperse auseinander gehen.

## Reading-lesson.
### Kindliche Liebe. Filial love.

Ein berühmter preußiſcher General' war in ſeiner Jugend Edelknabe[1] an dem Hofe Friedrichs des Großen. Er hatte keinen Vater
mehr, und ſeine Mutter nährte ſich[2] kümmerlich[3] in ihrem Witwen-
ſtande[4]. Als ein guter Sohn wünſchte er, ſie unterſtützen[5] zu können,
aber von ſeinem geringen Gehalte[6] konnte er nichts entbehren[7].

Doch fand er ein Mittel, etwas für ſie zu erwerben. Jede Nacht
mußte nämlich einer von den Edelknaben in dem Zimmer vor dem
Schlafkabinet des Königs wachen, um ihm aufzuwarten[8], wenn er
etwas verlangte. Das Wachen war manchen zu beſchwerlich, und
ſie übertrugen[9] daher, wenn ihre Reihe[10] kam, ihre Wachen anderen.
Der arme Edelknabe fing an, dieſe Wachen für andere zu über-
nehmen; er wurde dafür bezahlt, ſparte das Geld zuſammen[11]
und ſchickte es dann ſeiner Mutter.

Einmal konnte der König nicht ſchlafen und wollte ſich etwas
vorleſen laſſen[12] Er klingelte[13], er rief, aber niemand kam.
Endlich ſtand er ſelbſt auf und ging in das Nebenzimmer, um
zu ſehen, ob kein Page da wäre. Hier fand er den guten Jüngling, der die Wache übernommen hatte, am Tiſche ſitzend Vor
ihm lag ein angefangener Brief an ſeine Mutter; aber er war über

1) a page  2) support.  3) with difficulty.  4) widowhood.
5) succour.  6) small salary.  7) spare.  8) to wait upon.  9) handed
over, committed  10) turn  11) to collect, to save.  12) see p 295,
§ 4 — 13) to ring the bell.

\*) See the foot-note p 332

dem Schreiben eingeschlafen. Der König schlich herbei (stole near) und las den Anfang des Briefes, welcher so lautete (ran): „Meine beste, geliebte Mutter! Dieses ist schon die dritte Nacht, daß ich für Geld wache. Beinahe kann ich es nicht mehr aushalten[14]. Indessen freue ich mich, daß ich nun wieder zehn Thaler für Sie verdient[15] habe, welche ich Ihnen hierbei schicke."

Gerührt über das gute Herz des Jünglings läßt der König ihn schlafen, geht in sein Zimmer, holt zwei Rollen mit Dukaten, steckt ihm eine in jede Tasche und legt sich wieder schlafen.

Als der Edelknabe erwachte und das Geld in seinen Taschen fand, konnte er wohl denken, woher es gekommen war. Er freute sich zwar sehr darüber, weil er nun seine Mutter noch besser unterstützen konnte; aber er erschrak auch zugleich, weil der König ihn schlafend gefunden hatte. Am Morgen, sobald er zum König kam, bat er demütig[16] um Vergebung wegen seines Dienstfehlers[17] und dankte ihm für das gütige Geschenk. Der gute König lobte seine kindliche Liebe, ernannte[18] ihn sogleich zum[19] Offizier und schenkte ihm noch (besides) eine Summe Geld, um sich alles anschaffen[20] zu können, was er für seine neue Stelle brauchte.

Der treffliche Sohn stieg hernach immer höher[21] und diente unter mehreren preußischen Königen als ein tapferer General bis in sein hohes Alter.

14) to stand, to endure. 15) to earn 16) humbly. 17) fault in servico. 18) to name, to appoint. 19) see p. 345, § 3. — 20) to procure, to buy. 21) higher and higher

### Conversation.

Was war ein preußischer General in seiner Jugend?

Er war Edelknabe an dem Hofe Friedrichs des Großen.

Hatte er damals seine Eltern noch?

Sein Vater lebte nicht mehr; aber seine Mutter.

Was war.sie also (then)?

Sie war eine Witwe.

Konnte der Sohn sie unterstützen?

Von seinem Gehalte konnte er es nicht thun.

Welches Mittel fand er, etwas für sie zu erwerben (earn)?

Er wachte für Geld in dem Vorzimmer vor dem Schlafkabinet des Königs.

An (in) wessen Stelle wachte er?

An der Stelle andrer Edelknaben.

Warum wachten sie nicht selbst?

Es war ihnen zu beschwerlich.

Was machte er mit dem Gelde, das er auf diese Weise erwarb?

Er schickte es seiner Mutter, um sie zu unterstützen.

Als der König einmal nicht schlafen konnte, was that er?

Er klingelte und rief.

Als niemand kam, was that er?

Er stand auf, um zu sehen, ob kein Page im Vorzimmer wäre.

Was sah er hier?

Der gute Jüngling saß schlafend am Tische.

Was hatte er vor sich liegen?    Einen angefangenen Brief.

An wen war dieser Brief gerichtet?    An seine Mutter.

Wie lautete der Anfang?    „Dieses ist schon die dritte Nacht, die ich für Geld wache."

Wieviel hatte er schon erworben?    Zehn Thaler oder dreißig Mark.

Weckte der König ihn auf?    Nein, er ließ ihn schlafen.

Was that er überdies (besides)?    Er holte zwei Rollen Dukaten und steckte ihm eine in jede Tasche.

Als der Edelknabe erwachte, was empfand er?    Er war anfangs erschrocken, freute sich aber doch über das Gold.

Warum war er erschrocken?    Weil er einen Dienstfehler begangen (committed) hatte.

Was that er am Morgen?    Er bat den König um Vergebung und dankte ihm für das Geschenk.

Wie bewies ihm der König sein Wohlwollen (favour)?    Er machte ihn zum Offizier und schenkte ihm eine Summe Geld.

Was wurde später (afterwards) aus (of) ihm?    Er stieg nach und nach immer höher und wurde zuletzt General.

---

# Forty-sixth Lesson.
## ON THE PARTICIPLE PAST.

1) The *Participle past* is frequently used as an adjective, is declined as such, and even admits the degrees of comparison:

Der geliebte Vater the beloved father.

Ein gesegnetes Land a fertile (blessed) country.

Ein gedrücktes Volk a people more oppressed.

Der geehrteste Professor the most honored professor.

2) Sometimes it becomes a real adjective and allows the syllable u n to be prefixed, which renders it negative, as

| | |
|---|---|
| Bekannt known. | unbekannt unknown. |
| bemittelt wealthy. | unbemittelt without means. |
| berühmt renowned. | unberühmt unrenowned. |
| geschickt skilful, clever. | ungeschickt awkward. |
| gewohnt accustomed. | ungewohnt unaccustomed. |
| gelehrt learned. | ungelehrt unlearned etc. |

3) The *Participle past* of some *neuter* verbs which express motion, occurs together with the verbs k o m m e n and g e h e n instead of the Participle *present*, as:

Der Knabe kam gelaufen, geritten, gesprungen, gefahren. The boy came *running, riding* etc.

Thus further geflogen, geſchwommen, gekrochen ꝛc. kommen. In the same way is formed the expression verloren gehen to be (get) lost. Ex.:

Eine Brieftaſche iſt verloren gegangen (has been lost).

4) It is sometimes used absolutely, replacing a short sentence, as: geſetzt or angenommen suppose, ausgenommen excepted; abgeſehen von or .. abgerechnet not reckoned; zugegeben granted (for: wenn man annimmt, abſieht, zugiebt).

5) It ist also employed in a few expressions only instead of the Imperative mood. In English, the Participle present, with a negation, is sometimes used in a similar manner:

Umgekehrt[1] turn about! — aufgeſchaut! look out! ausgetrunken! empty your glass! nicht mehr geweint! no more crying now! nicht geplaudert! no talking!

## On the Future participle.

There is in German a *Gerundive* or *Future participle* of the Passive voice, answering to the Latin Participle in *-dus* (*laudandus, a, um*), which is formed of the Participle present (lobend) by placing zu before it = zu lobend. It is used adjectively and therefoie declined. Its place is always between the article and the noun. Ex.:

Das zu lobende Kind the child (*that is*) *to be praised*. Die zu hoffende Ernte the harvest (*that is*) to be hoped *for*. Der zu fürchtende Unfall the acci**d**ent (*that is or was*) to be feared.

### Reading Exercise. 136.

1. Meine geliebte Tante iſt geſtorben. Unſer verehrter Profeſſor iſt krank. Peter der Große war der gebildetſte[1] Mann in Rußland. Nero war der gefürchtetſte römiſche Kaiſer. Der heute gefallene Schnee iſt zwei Fuß tief. Demoſthenes war der berühmteſte griechiſche Redner[2] Der Greis ging gebückt (stooping) an einem Stabe und bettelte. Die zu erfüllende Pflicht war ſchwer. Schiden Sie mir den zu färbenden[3] Hut. Abgeſehen[4] von dem Erfolge[5], muß man dieſe Unternehmung billigen[6]. Die zu gebende Oper iſt von (by) Roſſini. Er iſt ein wirklich zu empfehlender Mann.

2. Die zu erwartende Ankunft[7] unſrer geliebten Königin erfüllt alle Herzen mit Freude. Nachbar, getrunken! Die lang genährte[8] Hoffnung iſt endlich erfüllt worden. Ein ſtarkes Gewitter mit

1) accomplished. 2) orator. 3) to dye. 4) with no regard to. 5) result. 6) approve. 7) arrival. 8) to foster.

Hagel⁹ hat die gehoffte Ernte vernichtet¹⁰. Das gepreßte Herz fühlt sich erleichtert am teilnehmenden¹¹ Busen eines geliebten Freundes. Gerührt¹² von den Worten des alten Mannes, öffnete er die Thüre und ließ ihn eintreten. Der arme Student, all seines Geldes beraubt, setzte betrübt¹³ seinen Weg fort, bis er, in einem Dorfe angekommen, ganz ermüdet sich auf eine Bank¹⁴ setzte.

9) hail. 10) destroy. 11) sympathising. 12) touched, moved. 13) sadly. 14) bench.

### Aufgabe. 137.

1. Mr. A. is a renowned painter. If you study much, you will become a learned man. He stood there quite puzzled[1]. This man died unknown and unrenowned. The knight[2] returned discouraged[3] and dejected[4]. The most honored man is not always the best man. The most learned people write often the worst hand[5]. Arrived at (in) the village, he proceeded (ging er) to (in) the inn[6] where nobody recognised[7] him; he was so changed[8] and sunburnt[9]. The life of every man is a continued[10] chain of incidents[11]. Beloved and esteemed by every one, ₂the ₁old man ₁died at the (im) age of ninety years.

2. The problem[12] *to be solved*[13] has been communicated [to] all the students. It is a fact[14] not *to be denied*[15], that no man has any claim[16] to perfection[17]. My neighbour came running to inform[18] me that the queen had arrived. The prince came driving in a coach with six horses. The danger *to be avoided*[19] is not yet over (vorüber). Do you understand the sentence[20] *to be learnt?* Where is the boy [*who is*] *to be punished?* Protected[21] by an almighty[22] God, ₂we ₁may go through this life without fear, if we do not deviate[23] from the right path. »Well begun, half done« (*won*), is a German proverb.

1) P. p. verlegen, verwirrt. 2) der Ritter. 3) entmutigt. 4) niedergeschlagen. 5) Handschrift, f. 6) Gasthaus, n. 7) erkennen. 8) verändert. 9) sonn verbrannt. 10) fortgesetzt. 11) von Vorfällen. 12) Aufgabe. 13) zu lösend. 14) Thatsache. 15) zu leugnend. 16) Anspruch auf. 17) Vollkommenheit. 18) benachrichtigen (acc.). 19) vermeiden. 20) der Satz. 21) beschützt. 22) allmächtig. 23) abweichen.

### Reading - lesson.
**Der Mann mit der eisernen Maske. The iron mask.**

Einige Monate nach dem Tode des Kardinals Mazarin ereignete sich in Frankreich eine Begebenheit¹, welche nicht ihres Gleichen² hat. Ein unbekannter Gefangener, der größer als gewöhnlich, jung und von der schönsten und edelsten Gestalt³ war, wurde mit dem größten Geheimnis⁴ in das Schloß der Sankt-Margareten-Insel im Provencer Meerbusen⁵ geschickt. Dieser Gefangene trug unterwegs eine Maske, deren Kinnstück⁶ Stahlfedern⁷ hatte, welche ihm die Freiheit ließen, mit der Maske auf

1) event, occurrence. 2) its equal. 3) form, figure, stature. 4) secrecy. 5) bay. 6) chin-piece. 7) spring.

feinem Gesichte zu essen. Der Befehl war gegeben worden, ihn zu töten, wenn er sich entdecte. Er blieb auf der Insel, bis ein Offizier, Namens Saint-Mars, im Jahre 1690 zum Oberaufseher[8] der Bastille ernannt wurde. Dieser Offizier holte ihn von der St. Margareten-Insel ab und führte ihn, immer verlarvt[9], in die Bastille. Kurz vor seiner Versetzung[10] besuchte ihn der Marquis von Louvois auf dieser Insel und sprach mit ihm stehend und mit einer Achtung[11], die an Ehrfurcht grenzte (came near to veneration).

Dieser Unbekannte wurde in die Bastille geführt, wo er eine so gute Wohnung wie in einem Palaste erhielt. Man versagte[12] ihm nichts von dem, was er verlangte; er fand sein größtes Vergnügen an sehr feinem Weißzeug[13] und an Spitzen[14]; er spielte auf der Guitarre. Man hielt ihm einen sehr guten Tisch, und der Oberaufseher setzte sich selten vor ihm. Ein alter Arzt aus der Bastille, der oft diesen Mann in seinen Krankheiten behandelt[15] hatte, sagte, daß er nie sein Gesicht gesehen habe, obschon er oft seine Zunge und den Rest seines Körpers untersucht hatte. Er war äußerst schön gewachsen (well made), sagte dieser Arzt; seine Haut war ein wenig gebräunt; er erregte[16] Interesse durch den bloßen[17] Ton seiner Stimme; nie beklagte er sich über seinen Zustand[18], und ließ niemand merken[19], wer er sein könnte.

(*To be continued.*)

8) overseer, governor. 9) masked. 10) removal. 11) respect. 12) to deny, to refuse. 13) linen. 14) lace. 15) to attend. — 16) to excite, cause, raise. 17) mere. 18) condition, state. — 19) to guess, to perceive.

## Questions.

*NB. The pupil is now requested to seek the answers to the following questions in the above Reading Exercise.*

Was begab sich bald nach dem Tode des Kardinals Mazarin?
Wer wurde auf das Schloß der St. Margareten-Insel geschickt?
Wo liegt diese Insel?
Was trug der Gefangene beständig?
Wie lange blieb er auf der Insel?
Wohin führte ihn Saint-Mars?
Wer hatte ihn vor seiner Versetzung besucht?
Wie hatte er sich gegen ihn benommen (behaved)?
Was erhielt der Unbekannte in der Bastille?
An was fand er sein größtes Vergnügen?
Wer behandelte ihn in seinen Krankheiten?
Was sagte dieser Arzt oft?
Wodurch erregte er Interesse?

# Forty-seventh Lesson.

## Remarks on the Adjectives.

1) The qualifying adjective which is placed before its substantive, as in English, agrees with its substantive in gender, number and case. In poetry however many exceptions to this rule are found. Such are:

Ein Röslein rot a little red rose.

Die Blicke frei und fessellos (free and unrestrained).

Klein Roland instead of der kleine Roland ꝛc.

2) A number of adjectives admitting *a government* (*object*) take it either in the *accusative*, in the *dative*, or in the *genitive*.

## I. Adjectives which govern the Accusative.

1) Adjectives implying *weight, measure, age, value*, generally with a numeral preceding, require the accusative and are placed *after* their case. Such are:

| | |
|---|---|
| Schwer heavy, weighing. | hoch high. |
| lang long. | tief deep. |
| breit broad, wide. | groß great, large, tall. |
| alt old. | wert worth etc. |

Examples.

Der Stein war zehn Kilo*) schwer.
The stone weighed ten kiloes.

Die Mauer ist zwanzig Meter*) lang.
The wall is twenty meters long.

Die Frau war sechzig Jahre alt.
The woman was sixty years old.

2) When qualifying, together with their government they precede the substantive and *agree* with it (see p. 342, V.). Ex.

Hier ist ein zehn Kilo schwerer Stein.
Here is a stone weighing ten kiloes.

Sie bauten eine hundert Meter lange Mauer.
They built a wall a hundred meters long.

## II. Adjectives which govern the Dative.

| | |
|---|---|
| Abgeneigt disinclined. | angemessen appropriate, suitable. |
| ähnlich like, resembling. | angenehm agreeable |
| angeboren innate. | anstößig offensive. |

---

*) Not in the plural (see p 54, § 15).

bekannt known.
begreiflich conceivable.
bequem ⎱ convenient,
behaglich ⎰ comfortable.
beſchwerlich troublesome.
dankbar grateful.
dienlich serviceable.
eigen ⎱ peculiar.
eigentümlich ⎰
fremd strange.
gehorſam obedient.
gewogen ⎱ favourable.
günſtig ⎰
geneigt inclined.
gewachſen equal to, a match to.
gleich like, equal.
gnädig gracious, kind.

heilſam salutary.
läſtig troublesome, burdensome.
lieb ⎱ dear.
teuer ⎰
möglich possible.
unmöglich impossible.
nachteilig ⎱ prejudicial, detri-
ſchädlich ⎰ mental, hurtful.
nahe near.
nötig necessary.
nützlich useful.
treu, getreu faithful.
überlegen superior.
verhaßt odious
vorteilhaft advantageous.
willkommen welcome.
zuträglich conducive, beneficial.

These adjectives as well as their contraries formed by prefixing u n , as: unähnlich, unbequem, untreu ꝛc. require the person or object in the *dative* which must *precede*.

Examples.

Der Sohn iſt (or ſieht) ſeinem Vater ähnlich.
The son is like (resembles) his father.

Die Liebe zu der Freiheit iſt dem Menſchen angeboren.
The love of liberty is innate *in* man.

Die Arbeit war den Soldaten läſtig (or beſchwerlich).
Working was troublesome to the soldiers.

Das Baden iſt der Geſundheit ſehr zuträglich.
Bathing is very conducive to health.

Es war mir unmöglich zu kommen.
It was impossible *for me* to come.

### Reading Exercise. 138.

Dieſe Kugel iſt mehr als zehn Kilo ſchwer. Wie lang iſt dieſe Straße? Sie iſt achthundertzwanzig Meter lang. Die Feinde gruben einen zwölf Meter breiten Graben. Auf dem Platze¹ ſteht eine ungefähr² vierzig Meter hohe Bildſäule³. Dieſe Geſchichte iſt allen Franzoſen wohl bekannt. Zu viel eſſen iſt der Geſundheit nachteilig. Der König war dieſem Hofmann⁴ ſehr gewogen. Seid euern Wohlthätern⁵ immer dankbar. Die lange Reiſe war dem alten Manne ſehr beſchwerlich; er konnte ſie nicht weiter fortſetzen⁶. Die Feinde waren uns an Zahl⁷ weit über-legen; deſto ſtolzer (the prouder) waren wir auf unſern Sieg⁸, während der feindliche General über ſeine Niederlage⁹ beſchämt war.

1) square.   2) about.   3) statue.   4) courtier.   5) benefactor.
6) continue.   7) number.   8) victory.   9) defeat.

### Aufgabe. 139.

My room is ten meters long and fifteen wide. The boy climbed[1] over ıa ₅wall[2] ₂five ₃meteıs ₄high. In the room we found ıa ₇man ₂about ₄sixty-₂five ₅years ₆old. London-bridge[3] is nine hundred and twenty (English) feet long, fifty-five high and fifty-six wide. The monument[4] of London is a round pillar, two hundred feet high; it stands on a pedestal[5] *twenty feet high*. Travelling is conducive to health Your horse is much superior to mine. Smoking is not conducive to health, at least for those who have feeble lungs[6].

1) klettern. 2) eine Mauer 3) Die Londoner Brücke. 4) das L.=Denkmal. 5) Fußgestell, n 6) eine schwache Lunge (*Sing.*).

## III. Adjectives which govern the Genitive.

| | |
|---|---|
| Bedürftig ⎫ in want of, | los rid of. |
| benötigt ⎬ in need of. | mächtig master of. |
| bewußt conscious | müde, satt tired of, weary. |
| eingedenk mindful. | schuldig guilty. |
| fähig capable, able. | teilhaftig participant. |
| gewärtig expectful of. | überdrüssig tired of, weary. |
| gewiß, sicher certain, sure. | verdächtig suspected. |
| habhaft getting possession of | verlustig having forfeited. |
| kundig acquainted with. | würdig, wert worthy, worth. |

and those of the above adjectives which admit the prefix un, denoting the contrary, as: unbewußt, uneingedenk (unmindful), unfähig, unkundig, unschuldig, unwürdig ꝛc.

*NB* Observe that here, also, the object *precedes the adjective*.

Examples.

Die Armen sind des Geldes bedürftig (benötigt).
The poor are in want of money.

Der Bote war des Weges nicht kundig (or unkundig).
The messenger was unacquainted with the way.

Der General war des Verrats verdächtig.
The general was suspected of treason

Ich bin des Arbeitens müde I am tired of working.

## IV. Adjectives with Prepositions.

| | |
|---|---|
| Achtsam auf (*acc.*) careful of. | empfindlich über(*acc.*)sensible of |
| bange vor (*dat*) afraid of. | eifersüchtig gegen (sometimes |
| beschämt über (*acc.*) ashamed of. | über)*) (*acc.*) jealous of. |
| begierig nach desirous of. | eitel auf (*acc.*) vain of. |
| befreit von ⎫ rid of, | ermüdet von fatigued with. |
| frei von ⎬ free from. | fähig zu able, capable of. |
| ehrgeizig nach ambitious of. | froh über (*acc.*) glad of. |
| empfänglich für susceptible of. | fruchtbar an productive of. |

*) gegen with *persons*, über with *things*

| | |
|---|---|
| gierig nach covetous of. | unbekannt mit unacquainted. |
| gleichgiltig gegen indifferent to. | unwissend in (dat.) ignorant of. |
| gefühllos gegen insensible of. | verschwenderisch mit prodigal of. |
| grausam gegen cruel to. | zweifelhaft über (acc.) dubious of. |
| höflich gegen civil, polite to. | zufrieden mit contented, pleased, |
| nachlässig in (dat.) careless of. | satisfied. |
| reich an (dat.) rich in. | unzufrieden mit discontented, |
| stolz auf (acc.) proud of. | displeased with. |
| überzeugt von convinced, sure of. | |

*NB.* With these, the adjective may *precede* or *follow* the object.

Examples.

Ägypten ist fruchtbar an Baumwolle.
Egypt is productive of cotton.

Der Jüngling war begierig nach Kenntnissen.
The youth was desirous of knowledge.

### V. Adjectives with a complement.

The *complement*, which in English *follows* an attributive adjective, is, together with the latter, placed before the substantive, immediately after the article:

Ein viel gelesenes Buch a book much read.
Ein mit Wein gefülltes Glas a glass filled with wine.
Der durch Ruhe gestärkte Körper.
The body strengthened by repose.
Ein nach Kenntnissen begieriger Jüngling.
Die dem Menschen angeborne Liebe zur Freiheit.

### Reading Exercise. 140.

Ich bin mir keiner Schuld[1] bewußt. Die Auswandrer blieben immer ihres Vaterlandes eingedenk und waren niemals gleichgiltig (indifferent) gegen das Schicksal desselben. Jeder Mensch muß stets des Todes gewärtig sein, denn der Tod verschont[2] niemand. Die Dame erschrak so sehr, daß sie der Sprache nicht mehr mächtig war. Man hielt ihn einer solchen That[3] nicht fähig. Ich bin des Lebens und des Herrschens müde, so sprach der Fürst zu seinen Söhnen. Der Schüler war gleichgiltig gegen alle Ermahnungen[4] seines Lehrers. Es ist nicht der Mühe wert (worth the trouble), diesen Brief noch einmal abzuschreiben. Die Frauen sollen nicht eifersüchtig sein gegen ihre Männer[5]. Ein mit seinem Schicksale[6] zufriedener Mensch ist immer glücklich.

1) guilt. 2) to spare. 3) deed. 4) warnings. 5) husband.
6) fate.

### Aufgabe. 141.

We are always mindful of our duty[1]. They were not quite sure of their advantage[2]. Oh tell us, how have you

become ₄master (mächtig) ₁of ₂the ₃castle? I am tired of
reading The young man was not capable of ₂such ₁a deed[3].
He who kills a man, is guilty of a great crime[4]. I am not
pleased[5] with your behaviour. I am quite convinced of his
innocence[6]. England is rich in coal[7]. The foreigner was
ignorant of the language of the country; he was therefore
soon tired of his stay[8].

1) Pflicht, f. 2) Vorteil, m 3) That, f 4) Verbrechen, n. 5) zufrieden. 6) Unschuld. 7) Kohlen, pl. 8) Aufenthalt, m

### 142.

Young people should be civil to every body. I am
satisfied with my pupils. The boy is fatigued with running.
Human life is never free from troubles[1]. Many men are dis-
satisfied with their condition[2]. Those who commit suicide[3]
must be very tired of their lives (*sing.*). Let us never do
anything in secret[4], of which (worüber) we should be ashamed,
if it became known. At last I feel myself rid of that tedious[5]
disease. It is my duty to tell you, that you are totally[6]
ignorant of (in) the most important[7] facts[8] of history. I do
not like persons who are cruel to (gegen) animals The tailor
showed me a letter (p. 342, V.) written by his son. A man well
instructed (unterrichtet . ) in (the) history, judges[9] the events[10]
with impartiality[11]. He who is unmindful of his domestic[12]
duties and not careful of his children, is an enemy to (*Gen.*)
his family[13] and his country; he is guilty of great sins[14] the
consequence[15] *of which* (*pl.*)[16] he cannot foresee[17].

1) Mühe, Beschwerde, f 2) die Lage. 3) einen Selbstmord begehen
4) im Geheimen. 5) langweilig 6) ganz. 7) wichtig 8) Thatsachen
9) to judge beurteilen. 10) die Ereignisse. 11) Unparteilichkeit.
12) häuslich. 13) Familie, f 14) Sünde, f. 15) deren Folgen, pl
16) see p. 303, § 1 — 17) vorhersehen.

### Reading-lesson.

#### Der Mann mit der eisernen Maske. (Schluß).

Dieser Unbekannte starb im Jahre 1703 und wurde bei Nacht
im Kirchhof[1] der Pauls-Pfarrei[2] begraben. Was das Erstaunen
verdoppelt, ist, daß zu der Zeit, als man ihn nach der St. Margareten-Insel schickte, kein angesehener[3] Mann in Europa ver-
schwand. Und doch war dieser Gefangene ohne Zweifel ein solcher;
denn Folgendes hatte sich in der ersten Zeit, als er auf der Insel
war, zugetragen[4]: Der Oberaufseher stellte selbst die Schüsseln auf
den Tisch, und nachdem er ihn eingeschlossen hatte, ging er weg.

Einst schrieb der Gefangene etwas auf einen silbernen Teller
und warf den Teller zum Fenster hinaus, gegen ein Schiff, welches
am Ufer lag, fast am Fuße des Turmes. Der Fischer, dem dieses
Schiff gehörte, fand den Teller, hob ihn auf und brachte ihn dem

1) churchyard 2) parish. 3) distinguished. 4) happened.

Oberaufſeher zurück. Erſtaunt fragte dieſer den Fiſcher: „Haben Sie geleſen, was auf dieſem Teller geſchrieben ſteht, und hat jemand ihn in Ihren Händen geſehen?" — Dieſer Mann wurde feſtgehalten[5], bis der Aufſeher ſich wohl verſichert hatte, daß er nicht leſen konnte, und daß der Teller von niemand geſehen wor= den war. „Gehen Sie," ſagte er, „Sie ſind ſehr glücklich, daß Sie nicht leſen können."

Herr von Chamillart war der letzte Miniſter, welcher dieſes ſonderbare[6] Geheimnis wußte. Der Marſchall La Feuillade, ſein Schwiegerſohn[7], bat ihn bei ſeinem Tode auf den Knieen, ihm anzuzeigen, wer der Mann wäre, den man nie anders kannte, als unter dem Namen: „Der Mann mit der eiſernen Maſke." Chamillart antwortete ihm, daß es ein Staatsgeheimnis ſei, und daß er einen Eid geleiſtet[8] habe, es nie zu entdecken.

      5) arrested.    6) strange    7) son-in-law.    8) taken an oath.

### Questions.

Wann ſtarb dieſer Unbekannte?
Wo wurde er begraben?
Was trug ſich einſt auf der Inſel zu?
Was ſagte der Oberaufſeher zu dem Fiſcher?
Was geſchah dann dieſem Manne?
Wie lange wurde er feſtgehalten?
Mit welchen Worten wurde er entlaſſen (dismissed)?
Wer war der letzte, der dieſes Geheimnis wußte?
Welche Antwort gab Chamillart dem Marſchall La Feuillade?

---

# Forty-eighth Lesson.
## On the Governments of Verbs.

The usual way in which the object is connected with active verbs is by the *accusative case*, as: Ich liebe den Vater, wir loben die Schüler, Sie leſen das Buch. But there are also some verbs, the government of which is connected either by means of the *nominative*, or the *genitive*, or *dative*, or by *prepositions* (see p. 351). As they differ most from the English, they must be separately mentioned.

### I. Verbs which in German govern the Nominative.

1) The nominative case is required by the following verbs:

| | |
|---|---|
| Sein to be. | ſcheinen to appear, to seem. |
| werden to become, to get. | heißen to be called, to bear a |
| bleiben to remain. | name. |

E x a m p l e s.

Napoleon war ein großer Feldherr (general).
Der junge Mensch ist Soldat geworden.
Das scheint ein guter Plan (zu sein).

2) By the *passive voice* of the following verbs, which, in the active, govern a double accusative·

Nennen ⎫ to call.
heißen  ⎭

schelten *ir*. *v.* to scold. [names
schimpfen *reg. v.* to abuse, call

3) The verbs: to appoint ernennen; to elect erwählen; to make machen, governing in English two nominatives in the *passive voice*, require in German the preposition zu with the article in the dative. Ex·:

Herr A. ist zum Hauptmann ernannt worden.
Mr. A. was appointed captain.

Er ist zum Doktor gemacht worden.
He was made a doctor.

*Note*. The verbs erklären (*to declare*) and halten (*to consider, to think*), require the preposition für. Ex·:

He was declared a thief er wurde für einen Dieb erklärt.
Palmer was *found* guilty Palmer wurde für schuldig erklärt.
I consider that day lost ich halte diesen Tag für verloren.

---

## II. Verbs which in German govern the Dative.

1) The following verbs, most of which govern in English the *accusative*, when, in German, they are followed by one object, require the person in the *dative:*

Abraten to dissuade.
antworten to answer.
anhangen to adhere.
anstehen to suit.
befehlen to command, order.
†begegnen*) *act. v.* to meet, occur, to encounter.
†es begegnet *impers. v.* it happens.
†ausweichen**) to evade, avoid
behagen to please.
†bekommen (wohl or gut) to agree with a person's health. ·

†bevorstehen to impend.***)
beistimmen ⎫ to agree with
beipflichten ⎭ some one.
†beistehen to assist.***)
danken to thank.
dienen†) to serve.
drohen†) threaten.
†einfallen to occur.
einleuchten. to be evident.
†entfliehen ⎫ to run away,
†entgehen ⎱ to avoid,
†entkommen ⎰ to escape,
†entrinnen ⎰ to abscond.
†entlaufen ⎭

---

*) begegnen is also used with the *acc.*, then it takes haben.
**) Those marked with † are conjugated with sein (*to be*).
***) also with haben, see p. 159.
†) bedienen, bedrohen and befolgen take the *acc*

entfpred)en to answer the purpose, to correspond .with,
  to accord.

erlauben to allow, permit.

fehlen, mangeln to be wanting.

fluchen to curse

†folgen *) to follow

frönen to indulge (passions).

gebühren to be due.

gefallen to please.

  mißfallen to displease.

gehorchen to obey.

gehören to belong.

†gelingen to succeed (*impers.*).

genügen to suffice.

gereichen to redound, conduce

geziemen or ziemen to become,
  to be seemly.

gleichen to be like, resemble

glauben to believe.

helfen to help

huldigen to do homage.

leuchten to light (down stairs).

mißtrauen to mistrust.

mitteilen to impart.

fich nähern to approach.

nützen to be of use ·

paffen to fit, suit

raten to advise.

fchaden to injure.

fcheinen to seem

fchmeicheln to flatter.

fteuern to check, to remedy.

trotzen to bid defiance, to face.

trauen (verhauen) to trust.

†unterliegen to succumb.

verbieten to forbid.

fich unterwerfen to submit.

†vorangehen to precede.

vorbeugen to obviate, prevent.

vorwerfen to reproach.

wehe thun to hurt, injure.

†weichen to give way, to yield.

†widerfahren to happen

†widerstehen } to withstand,

fich widerfetzen / to resist, oppose.

widerfprechen to contradict.

willfahren to comply, to indulge.

wohlwollen to favour, wish well.

zuhören to listen to

†zukommen to fall to one's share,
  to be due.

and many more of these verbs compounded with bei, entgegen,
nach, vor, wider, zu.

Examples

Diefes Kleid paßt mir nicht this dress does not suit me.

Ich bin ihm diefen Morgen begegnet (met).

Ich ftimme dem Redner vollkommen bei.

I entirely agree with the speaker.

Der Krieg droht diefem Lande war threatens this country.

Wollen Sie mir helfen? will you help me?

*Observations.* — As these verbs are not transitive, they
cannot be used in the passive voice, except sometimes in the
third person (see p. 135, § 7); the passive sentence is therefore, in German, to be changed into a corresponding active
sentence. Examples:

He was readily obeyed man gehorchte ihm bereitwillig.

We were displeased with their society.

Ihre Gesellschaft mißfiel uns.

---

*) See the foot-note †) p. 345. When folgen means to *obey*,
it is always conjugated with haben, but it keeps the *Dat.* case
Ex: Er folgt mir he obeys me.

2) The following verbs which have *two* governments, a *person* and a *thing*, require the *person* in the *dative*, the *thing* in the *accusative*. The *dative* precedes the *acc.*:

| | |
|---|---|
| Abſchlagen to refuse. | ſagen to tell. |
| anbieten to offer. | ſchenken to present with, give |
| ausſetzen to expose. | ſchicken to send. |
| bringen to bring. | ſchulden, ſchuldig ſein to owe |
| empfehlen to recommend. | (be indebted). |
| leihen to lend | ſtehlen to steal from. |
| entreißen to snatch away. | verdanken to owe (have to |
| erzählen to relate, to tell. | thank). |
| gewähren to grant. | verzeihen to pardon. |
| geben to give. | verſchaffen to procure. |
| erſparen to save (trouble). | vorleſen to read to a person. |
| leiſten to render, to loan. | widmen to devote, dedicate. |
| liefern to furnish, provide. | zeigen to show. |
| nehmen to take *from* a perſon. | zuſchreiben to ascribe, impute. |

Examples.

Geben Sie dem Knaben*) das Buch.
Ich entriß (snatched away from) dem Soldaten das Gewehr.
Sagen Sie mir die Wahrheit (truth).
Er ſchenkte dem Knaben eine Mark.

### Reading Exercise. 143.

1. Mein Bedienter iſt ein ehrlicher Mann. Ein Narr bleibt immer ein Narr. Das ſcheint ein glücklicher Gedanke[1]. Mein Neffe iſt Offizier geworden. Der Fremde wurde für einen Be= trüger[2] erklärt. Ich habe meinem Freunde abgeraten, dieſes Werk herauszugeben[3]. Was hat man Ihnen geantwortet? Man hat mir gar nichts geantwortet. Dieſe Wohnung ſteht mir nicht an; ſie iſt zu klein für mich. Als der Redner geendigt hatte, ſtimmte (pflichtete) ihm die ganze Verſammlung bei. Der Fürſt ahnte[4] das Unglück nicht, welches ihm bevorſtand. Trinken Sie gern Bier? Ich trinke es gern; aber es bekommt mir nicht gut; es ſchadet meiner Geſundheit.

2. Die Kinder, welche ihren Eltern nicht gehorchen, mißfallen Gott. Dieſer Kammerdiener diente dem Grafen von P dreißig Jahre lang mit der größten Treue und Anhänglichkeit[5]. Dieſe Stelle[6] iſt dem gelehrten Profeſſor entgangen, ſonſt würde er gewiß eine lange Abhandlung[7] darüber geſchrieben haben. Der Dieb iſt dem Gefängniswärter[8] entlaufen. Ich begegnete heute einem meiner alten Freunde, welcher geſonnen iſt, in einiger Zeit nach Italien zu reiſen. Ich riet ihm ſehr, ſeine Reiſe nicht lange zu verſchieben[9]. Er zeigte ſeinem Freunde*) die Bilder.

1) idea. 2) a cheat. 3) from publishing 4. to anticipate. 5) attachment 6) passage 7) treatise, essay 8) jailor. 9) to put off.

---

*) Observe that in German the dative precedes the accusative.

### Aufgabe. 144.

1. Henry is a little boy. John has become [a] soldier.
Aristides was called »the Just«. My neighbour was abused [as]
a cheat (Betrüger). Is it true that your cousin has been
appointed *a* judge? I will make him my (zu meinem) friend.
What has happened to you? What did you answer your
master? The captain threatened the soldiers. Nobody has
ordered the man to open the gate[1]. It was impossible *for
me* to resist his requests[2]. This circumstance[3] must displease
the merchant. We should always assist our neighbours when
they are in want of[4] assistance. To whom does this hat
belong? It belongs to the hatter; he brought it to me *that
I might buy it.* Why do you not answer your master (teacher)
when he questions[5] you? He always bids defiance to his
enemies.

2. To (Um . . zu) escape (the) death, he seized a plank[6].
Let us follow this example[7]. I met him at the town gate[8].
Why did you not thank your teacher? I *have* not met him
these (seit) several weeks. The beggar approached me in a
suspicious manner (auf eine verdächtige Weise). Children must
obey their parents. The slave hardly escaped his pursuers[9].
How is your uncle pleased†) *with* (in) Frankfort? He is very
well pleased†). If you will listen to me, I will read you a
chapter (ein Kapitel) of Macaulay's »History of England«. Show
me your paintings[10], and I will show you my drawings[11]. Could
you lend me a dollar[12] or two? I will lend you them, if you
will give me them back to-morrow. Show the stranger the
way. Do not believe this liar[13].

1) bas Thor. 2) die Bitte 3) Umstand, m. 4) to be in want = brauchen
(acc.). 5) fragen (acc.). 6) ein Brett, n. 7, Beispiel, n. 8) bas Stabtthor
9) ber Verfolger — 10) bie Malerei, bas Gemälde. 11) Zeichnung.
12) about *dollar* and *thaler*, (Germ. dollar) see p. 165. 13) ber Lügner

## III. Verbs which in German govern the Genitive.

1) The following verbs take their *object* in the genitive; some of them may also take a preposition:

| | |
|---|---|
| Bedürfen *) (ich bedarf) to need, to be in want. | harren ††) to wait patiently for. |
| ermangeln to be void. [of. | lachen **) to laugh. |
| gedenken to remember, think | schonen *) to spare. |
| | spotten **) to mock. |

†) See p. 226, b, and p. 229, Conversation.
*) bedürfen takes sometimes, and schonen mostly, the accusative.
**) Lachen, spotten and sich schämen prefer the preposition über
with the accusative.
††) Harren may take the prep. auf with the acc.

2) The following verbs require the *person* in the *accusative*, and the *object* in the *genitive*, which follows:

| | |
|---|---|
| Anklagen ⎱ to accuse of. | entſetzen to dismiss, remove. |
| beſchuldigen ⎰ to charge with. | überheben to disburden, spare, |
| berauben to rob, to bereave. |   to dispense. |
| entbinden to release, absolve. | überführen to convict. |
| entkleiden to deprive, divest. | verſichern to assure. |
| entheben to exempt from. | würdigen to favour. |

3) The following reflective verbs govern the *object* in the *genitive*:

| | |
|---|---|
| Sich annehmen to interest one's self for, take care of. | ſich erinnern *) to remember. |
| ſich bedienen to make use of.†) | ſich entwöhnen to disaccustom one's self. |
| ſich befleißigen or befleißen to apply one's self. | ſich erbarmen to have mercy. |
| ſich bemächtigen to seize, to take possession of. | ſich erwehren to ward off, keep away. |
| ſich enthalten to abstain from, to forbear. | ſich erfreuen to enjoy. |
| ſich entledigen to get rid of. | ſich rühmen to boast of. |
| ſich entſchlagen to part with. | ſich ſchämen**) to be ashamed. |
| ſich entſinnen to recollect. | ſich verſehen to await. |
| | ſich verſichern to make sure of, to secure. |

4) Observe also the following peculiar expressions with the *genitive*.

Hungers ſterben to die of hunger.
Eines plötzlichen Todes ſterben to die a sudden death.
Seines Weges gehen to go one's way.
Sie ſind des Todes! you are a dead man!
Gutes Mutes ſein to be of good cheer.
Der Ruhe pflegen to take one's ease, to rest.
Der Meinung (or Anſicht) ſein to be of the opinion.
Willens ſein to purpose, to intend, to be willing.
Des Zieles verfehlen to miss one's aim.
Es iſt nicht der Mühe wert ⎱ it is not worth the trouble.
Es verlohnt ſich nicht der Mühe ⎰
Einen des Landes verweiſen to exile some one.
Seines Amtes warten to attend to one's office *or* business.

### Reading Exercise. 145.

1. Ich bedarf Ihres Beiſtandes jetzt nicht mehr. Wir wollen des empfangenen Böſen nicht gedenken. Wir harren noch der Entſcheidung[1]. Was für eines Verbrechens iſt dieſer Mann angeklagt? Man klagt ihn eines Mordes[2] an. Wilhelm iſt einer Unwahrheit überführt worden. Ich ging an ihr vorbei, und würdigte ſie keines

1) decision  2) murder.

---

†) 'to make use of' is often translated: gebrauchen with the *acc*.
*) Sich erinnern takes also an with the *acc*. — **) See p. 349.

Blickes   Die Frau hat sich des armen Kindes angenommen und ihm einige Kleidungsstücke (clothes) geschenkt (gegeben). Warum bedient sich dieser Mann einer Krücke[3][2] Weil er einen lahmen Fuß hat. Die Räuber bemächtigten sich meines Koffers. Meine Großmutter erfreut sich in ihrem hohen Alter noch einer guten Gesundheit. Enthaltet euch des Branntweins[4], denn er zerstört eure Gesundheit.

2. Ich glaube Sie zu kennen, mein Herr; aber ich kann mich Ihrer nicht erinnern. Entschlagen Sie sich dieser trüben Gedanken; Sie werden Ihr Unglück nur vergrößern. Erbarmet euch der Armen und Unglücklichen. Gehen Sie ruhig Ihres Weges. Harret des Herrn (or auf den Herrn), er wird euch nicht verlassen[5]. Es verlohnt sich der Mühe, diese Reise zu unternehmen Ich bin nicht dieser Ansicht; ich glaube vielmehr, man sollte sich aller weiteren Schritte[6] enthalten. Nachdem ich mehrere Nächte gewacht hatte, konnte ich mich des Schlafes nicht mehr erwehren. Mein Hausherr[7] ist heute eines plötzlichen Todes gestorben; gestern war er noch ganz gesund und munter[8]. Der Kranke muß der Ruhe pflegen, sonst (or) kann er nicht genesen[9].

3) crutch.   4) whisky.   5) forsake.   6) steps.   7) landlord. 8) lively.   9) recover.

## Aufgabe. 146.

1. I need a sharp knife to cut[1] this meat. She derided my threats[2]. ₂Never ₁mock the unfortunate. Are you still in want of my assistance? The prisoner has been accused of a murder. They accused me of a falsehood[3], because they did not understand what I said. The trees are deprived of their leaves. The soldiers were absolved *from* their oath[4]. The prince assured them of his favour. The captain released him from his promise. Some authors say that Belisarius was deprived of all his dignities[5] and cast into prison. Why have you abstained from smoking? Because it did not agree[6] [*with*] me.

2. The old man remembered the days of his youth. Having no scissors at hand (bei der Hand), I made use of a knife. The Jews abstain from pork[7], according to the law of Moses. We did not await such an answer[8]. Did anybody make sure of his pocket-book? This lady has disaccustomed herself *to* coffee   Remember always your benefactors[9]. The king had mercy on the poor prisoner and set him free[10]. Be ashamed of your behaviour   Are you obliged to *make use of* spectacles (einer Brille, *G sing*)? I have made[11] use of them from (since) my sixteenth year. Do you remember your absent friends? I ₂always ₁remember ₂them.

1) See p. 325, § 10. — 2) Drohung   3) die Lüge.   4) der Eid 5) die Würde.   6) gut bekommen (see p 345, II). — 7) das Schweine- fleisch   8) die Antwort   9) der Wohlthäter.   10) to set free = die Freiheit schenken.   11) *Pres* (see p. 309, § 4).

# IV. Verbs governing certain prepositions.

1) The preposition **an** is required by the following verbs:

| | | | | | |
|---|---|---|---|---|---|
| Adreſſiren an *acc.* | to direct to. | ſchreiben an *acc.* | to write to. |
| denken | „ „ think of | Teil nehmen *dat* | „ take part in. |
| ſich gewöhnen | „ „ accustom. | zweifeln | „ „ doubt of. |
| ſich wenden | „ „ apply to. | verzweifeln | „ „ despair of. |
| übertreffen *dat* | „ excel in. | erinnern | *acc.* „ remind of. |
| ſterben | „ „ die of. | ſich erinnern | |
| ſich anlehnen | | „ „ lean | gedenken | „ „ recollect. |
| „ lehnen | *acc.* | „ against. | hindern *dat.* | „ hinder from. |
| glauben | „ „ believe in. | ſich rächen | „ „ revenge on. |

2) The preposition **auf** is required by:

| | | | |
|---|---|---|---|
| Acht geben *acc.* | pay attention. | ſich belaufen *acc.* | to amount to |
| ſich verlaſſen | „ to rely on. | zählen | „ „ count upon. |
| antworten | „ „ answer. | beharren *dat.* | to insist. |
| vertrauen | „ „ trust upon. | beſtehen „ | |
| warten | „ „ wait for | | |

3) **aus** is required by·

| | | | |
|---|---|---|---|
| Trinken | to drink. | überſetzen | to translate from. |
| werden | „ become of. | beſtehen | „ consist of. |

4) **bei** is required by·

| | | | |
|---|---|---|---|
| Beſchwören | to conjure. | bei Seite legen | to lay aside. |
| wohnen | „ live at. | bleiben bei | „ stay with. |

5) **für** is required by.

| | | | |
|---|---|---|---|
| Bürgen | to bail, answer for, | ſorgen | to take care of. |
| gut ſtehen | „ warrant. | beſtrafen | „ punish for. |
| danken | „ thank for. | halten | „ consider |

6) **in** is required by:

| | | | |
|---|---|---|---|
| Sich miſchen | to meddle with. | einwilligen | to consent to. |
| beſtehen | „ consist in. | | |

7) **mit** is required by:

| | | | |
|---|---|---|---|
| Anfangen | to begin with | ſprechen | to speak to. |
| ſich abgeben | „ attend to. | vergleichen | „ compare with. |
| ſich beſchäftigen | to be occupied w. | verſehen | „ provide „ |
| bedecken | to cover with. | beehren | „ honour „ |
| beladen | „ load „ | Mitleid haben | „ have pity on. |
| vereinigen | „ join „ | belohnen | „ reward |

8) **nach** is required by:

| | | | |
|---|---|---|---|
| Abreiſen | to set out for. | ſtreben | to aspire to. |
| gehen | „ go to. | fragen | „ ask for. |
| ſich begeben | „ repair to. | ſich ſehnen | „ long „ |
| zielen | „ aim at. | ſchicken | „ send „ |

9) **über** with the *acc.* is required by:

| | | | |
|---|---|---|---|
| Urteilen | to judge of. | ſich wundern | to wonder at. |
| klagen, ſich beklagen | to complain | ſich freuen | „ rejoice „ |
| erröten | to blush at. [of. | nachdenken | } „ reflect on. |
| lachen | „ laugh „ | ſich beſinnen | |
| ſpotten | „ mock „ | ſich unterhalten | „ converse. |
| verfügen | „ dispose of. | herrſchen | „ reign over. |
| ſich erkundigen | enquire about. | ſich ſchämen | „ be ashamed of. |
| herfallen | to pounce upon. | ſich ärgern | „ be vexed at. |

10) **um** is required by:

| | | | |
|---|---|---|---|
| Spielen | to play for. | ſich ſtreiten | to dispute. |
| ſich (be)kümmern | „ care „ | ſich bewerben | „ apply for. |
| bitten | „ ask „ | | |

11) **von** is required by:

| | | | |
|---|---|---|---|
| Sprechen | to speak of. | befreien | to liberate |
| herkommen | „ come from. | abweichen | „ deviate from. |
| leben | „ live on. | ſich nähren | „ feed on. |

12) **vor** (*dat.*) is required by:

| | | | |
|---|---|---|---|
| Sich fürchten | to be afraid of. | ſich hüten | to beware of. |
| zittern | „ tremble. | warnen | „ caution. |

13) **zu** is required by:

Gehen to go to (a person). | machen to make.

### Reading-lesson.

**Edelmütige Freundſchaft des deutſchen Kaiſers, Karl V.**

Als Karl V., welcher ſpäter deutſcher Kaiſer wurde, nach dem Tode ſeines Großvaters, des Königs Ferdinand, nach Madrid reiſte, um von dem Königreich Spanien Beſitz zu nehmen, hatte er einen franzöſiſchen Grafen, de Boſſu, in ſeinem Gefolge. Die ungewöhnliche Größe[1] dieſes jungen Mannes, ſeine körperliche Ge-wandtheit (dexterity), welche ihn zum trefflichen Reiter machte, ſeine zuvorkommende[2] Dienſtbefliſſenheit[3] und ſeine übrigen (other) liebenswürdigen Eigenſchaften hatten ihn dem Kaiſer ſo lieb gemacht, daß er immer bei ihm bleiben mußte.

Einſt hatte Karl eine große Jagdpartie[4] veranſtaltet[5] und ſetzte[6] einem Eber (boar) tief in den Wald hinein mit ſolcher Hitze nach, daß er den Weg verfehlte (lost), und niemand ihm zu folgen wagte, als[7] de Boſſu. Aber dieſer Mann hatte das Unglück, ſich an einem vergifteten Dolche zu verwunden, welchen er nach da-maliger[8] Gewohnheit der ſpaniſchen Jäger bei ſich trug. Sobald Karl das Blut bemerkte, welches ſein Liebling[9] verlor (lost), fragte er ihn erſchrocken, ob der Eber ihn verwundet habe. Der Graf erzählte, was ihm begegnet wäre, und fügte bei, daß er niemand als[7] ſich ſelbſt Vorwürfe zu machen[10] habe.

Der König kannte sehr wohl die tötliche Wirkung[11] des Giftes, sobald es ins Blut übergegangen wäre Um seinen Liebling zu retten, dachte er nicht an die eigene Lebensgefahr; er sprang vom Pferde, befahl auch dem Grafen, abzusteigen[12] und sich ganz seinem Willen zu unterwerfen[13]. Der Graf machte zwar Einwendungen[14]; aber der König beharrte[15] auf dem edeln Entschlusse, seinem Freund das Leben zu retten, oder mit ihm zu sterben. Er riß die Kleidung von der Wunde weg, sog das Blut zu wiederholten Malen[16] aus und spie es weg. Diese entschlossene und hochherzige Handlung belohnte den königlichen Freund mit der Freude, seinem Freunde das Leben gerettet zu haben, ohne nachteilige Folgen für das seinige.

Wer sollte nicht diese wahre, aufopfernde[17] Freundschaft eines der mächtigsten Herrscher[18] der Erde bewundern?!

1) uncommon tallnes, size. 2) obliging. 3) readiness in service. 4) a hunting party. 5) to arrange. 6) nachsetzen to pursue. 7) but. 8) in use at that time 9) favourite 10) to reproach, to blame. 11) effect. 12) to dismount. 13) submit. 14) objections. 15) to insist. 16) repeatedly 17) self-sacrificing. 18, ruler, monarch.

### Questions.

Als der König Ferdinand von Spanien starb, wer erbte (inherited) das Königreich?
Warum reiste Karl nach Madrid?
Wer war in dem Gefolge Karls des Fünften?
Welche Eigenschaften zeichneten den Grafen de Bossu aus?
Was geschah einmal bei einer großen Jagd?
Was für ein Unglück hatte de Bossu?
Als der König das Blut bemerkte, was fragte er?
Als Karl erfuhr, was dem Grafen begegnet war, was beschloß er zu thun?
Was that er alsdann?
Was befahl er dem Grafen zu thun?
Wollte de Bossu es dulden?
Auf was beharrte (or bestand) der König?
Auf welche Weise rettete Karl dem Grafen das Leben?
Was muß man in diesem Falle bewundern?

---

# Forty-ninth Lesson.
## REMARKS ON THE PREPOSITIONS.

The use of the prepositions is of too various a nature to allow of its being determined by definite rules Their departure from the original signification can only be shown by examples, and by observing certain ex-

pressions. We accordingly add the following supplementary examples to Lesson 37 and L. 48, IV.

## I. On the use of some **German** prepositions.

### An.

This preposition signifies commonly *at*. Ex.:

Jemand klopft an die Thüre somebody knocks at the door.

An translated otherwise than by *at*:

Er starb an der Cholera he died *of* the cholera.
Sich anlehnen an (*acc.*) to lean *against*.
Wir glauben an Gott we believe *in* God.
An jemand (*acc.*) denken to think *of* some one.
Zweifeln an (*dat.*) to doubt (*of*).
Sich rächen an (*dat.*) to take revenge *on*.
Es ist an mir zu spielen it is my turn to play.
Ein Brief an mich (or für mich) a letter *for* me.
An den Ufern des Rheins *on* the banks of the Rhine.
Ich habe an ihn geschrieben I have written *to* him.
Frankfurt am (an dem) Main Frankfort *on* the Main.
Teil an einer Sache nehmen to take part *in* something.
Aus Mangel an Geld for want *of* money.
Reich an Verstand rich *in* wit (sense).
An dem Arm ergreifen to seize *by* the arm.
An der Hand verwunden to wound *in* the hand.

Auf (generally *on* or *upon*), as:

Das Buch liegt auf dem Tisch the book lies on (or *upon*)
Es kommt auf Sie an it depends *upon* you.    [the table.

Auf transl. otherw. than by *on* or *upon*:

Auf das Land gehen to go *into* the country.
Auf die Post gehen to go *to* the post-office.
Auf der Jagd sein to be out hunting.
Auf meine Kosten *at* my expense or cost.
Auf der Straße *in* the street. | Auf Reisen abroad.
Sich auf den Weg machen to set out.
Auf etwas (*acc.*) acht geben to pay attention *to* something.
Auf alle Fälle } *at* all events, at any rate.
Auf jeden Fall }
Auf morgen *for* to morrow.
Auf kurze Zeit *for* a short time.
Auf dem Lande *in* the country. ◄
Auf Befehl des Königs by the king's command.
Auf diese Weise *in* this manner.
Auf wie lange? *for* how long?
Auf immer, auf ewig *for* ever.

Auf der Welt *in* the world. Auf der Reise — travelling.
Das heißt auf Deutsch . . . that is *in* German.
Es ist dreiviertel auf sechs Uhr it is a quarter *to* six.

**Aus** (generally *out of* or *from*), as:
Aus dem Zimmer out of the room.
Aus Schwäche *from* weakness.
Aus Furcht sterben to die *from* or *with* fear.
Aus Erfahrung *from* experience.
Aus der Mode out *of* fashion.
Aus dem Deutschen ins Französische übersetzen.
To translate *from* German *into* French.

Other meanings:
Was wird aus mir werden? what will become *of* me?
Aus Versehen by mistake, through inadvertence.

**Bei** (generally. *at, near, by*):
Bei diesen Worten *at* these words.
Bei Nacht *by* night.
Bei Hofe sein to be *at* court.
In der Schlacht bei Marengo *at* the battle *of* Marengo.
Bei Tages-Anbruch *at* day-break.
Bei Tag und bei Nacht by day and by night.
Bei Licht arbeiten to work by candle-light.
Bei der Hand führen to lead by the hand.
Beim Spiel at play.
Ich rief ihn bei seinem Namen I called him by his name.
Bei Tische sein to be *at* dinner. | Bei uns with us.

Other meanings:
Bei meiner Ankunft *on* my arrival.
Bei Zeit in (*good*) time, betimes.
Bleiben Sie bei mir stay *with* me.
Bei guter Gesundheit sein to be *in* good health.
Bei hellem Tage in broad day-light.
Dieses steht bei Ihnen that depends upon you.
Ich habe kein Geld bei mir I have no money *about* me.
Bei den Römern *with* or *among* the Romans.

**Durch** (generally *through*):
Ich bin durch den Wald gegangen.
I have gone *through* the forest.
Durch ein Brett *through* a plank.

Other meanings:
Durch welches Mittel? *by* what means?
Ich wurde durch einen Pfeil verwundet.
I was wounded *by* an arrow.
Die ganze Zeit hindurch *during* all the time.

23*

Für (generally *for*).
 Wort für Wort word *for* word.
 Bürgen für etwas to answer *for*.
Other meanings:
 Ein Mittel für (or gegen) das Zahnweh.
 A remedy *against* the tooth-ache.
 Stück für Stück piece *by* piece.
 Sie sorgt für alles she takes care *of* everything, she sees
  to everything.

Gegen (generally *against, towards*).
 Gegen die Mauer *against* the wall.
Other meanings:
 Gegen sechs Uhr *by* six o'clock.
 Mildthätig gegen die Armen charitable *to* the poor.
 Unempfindlich gegen insensible *to*.
 Gegen bare Bezahlung *for* cash.
 Es sind gegen zwei Stunden it is *about* two hours.
 Taub gegen alle Bitten deaf *to* all entreaties.
 Ihr Übel ist nichts gegen das seinige (or seines).
 Your illness is nothing *compared* with his.

In (generally *in* or *into*).
 In Frankreich *in* France. | In Paris *in* Paris.
 Im Frühling *in* spring. | In das Wasser into the water.
 In Verzweiflung sein to be *in* despair.
Other meanings:
 In einem Ton *with* a tone.
 In der Schule sein to be *at* school.
 Im Ernst seriously, in earnest.
 Sich in den Finger schneiden to cut one's finger.
 Im Begriff sein or stehen to be *on* the point.
 In die Flucht jagen or schlagen to put *to* flight.

Nach (generally *after*).
 Nach Verlauf von zwei Monaten *after* two months.
Other meanings:
 Nach Hause gehen to go home.
 Der Weg nach der Stadt the way *to* the town.
 Ich gehe nach Wien I go *to* Vienna.
 Nach Belieben as you like.
 Nach meinen Befehlen according to my orders.
 Nach (or in) alphabetischer Ordnung *in* alphabetical order.
 Jemand fragt nach Ihnen somebody asks *for* you.

**Über** (generally *over*).

Über ben hohen Bergen *over* the high mountains.

Das Dorf liegt über bem Fluſſe.

The village lies *over* (*above* or *beyond*) the river.

### Other meanings:

Über ben Fluß ſetzen to cross the river.

Verfügen Sie über meinen Beutel dispose *of* my purse.

Es iſt über ein halbes Jahr it is *above* six months.

Heute über acht Tage this day week.

Den Sommer über *during* the summer.

Sich über etwas (ver)wundern to be astonished *at*.

Sich freuen über to rejoice *at*.

Lachen über to laugh *at*.

Das geht über meine Kräfte that is *above* (beyond) my strength.

**Um** (generally *round* or *about*).

Ums Feuer herum *about* the fire-place.

### Other meanings:

Ich will ihn um Rat fragen I will consult him.

Ich bitte Sie um Verzeihung I beg your pardon.

Um Geld ſpielen to play *for* money.

Um wieviel Uhr? *at* what o'clock?

Um ein Uhr *at* one o'clock.

Es iſt um ihn geſchehen it is over *with* him.

Bekümmern Sie ſich nicht um mich don't care *for* me.

Er hat ſich ſehr um mich verdient gemacht.

He has had a great deal of trouble with me

Dieſer Weg iſt um zwei Stunden (Meilen) kürzer.

This road is shorter *by* two leagues (miles).

**Unter** (generally *under*).

Unter zwölf Jahren *under* twelve years.

### Other meanings:

Unter ber Regierung Karls bes Großen.

*In* the reign of Charlemagne.

Was für ein Unterſchied unter (zwiſchen) . . .

What difference *between* . . .

Unter bieſer Bedingung *on* that condition.

Unter Segel gehen to set sail.

Unter bieſen Männern among these men.

Sie bekommen es nicht unter zehn Mark.

You will not get it for *less than* ten marcs.

Unter bem Tiſch hervor from under the table.

Bon (generally *of, from*).

Herkommen von einem to come from some one.
Bon = von Seiten jemandes from.
Bom Morgen bis zum Abend.
From morning till evening.
Bon Paris bis London from Paris *to* London

### Other meanings:

Bom erſten Februar an beginning with the 1st of February.
Bon ganzem Herzen with all my heart
Dieſes Buch iſt von Göthe geſchrieben worden.
This book has been written by Gœthe.

Bor (generally *before*).

Bor zehn Uhr before ten o'clock.

### Other meanings:

Bor drei Tagen three days ago.
Sich fürchten vor to be afraid of.
Schritt vor Schritt step by step.
Sich vor etwas hüten to beware of.
Bor der Stadt wohnen to live outside the town.
Bor Freude weinen to weep with joy.
Bor Anker liegen to be at anchor.

Zu (generally *to*).

Ich begab mich zu ihm I went *to* him.
Zu Bette gehen to go *to* bed (to sleep).

### Other meanings·

Zu jener Zeit *at* that time.
Die Liebe zum Ruhm the love *of* glory.
Zur Zeit des Auguſtus *at* the time of Augustus.
Zu Hauſe ſein to be *at* home
Zu Wagen in a carriage. | Zu Pferd on horseback.
Zu Fuß on foot. | Zu gleicher Zeit *at* the same time.
Zu Ehren der Königin *in* honour of the queen.
Zu Land und zu Waſſer by land and by water
Zum Glück fortunately. | Zum Beiſpiel for example.
Zu dieſem Gebrauch (Zweck) for this purpose.
Zum Gefangenen machen to make prisoner.
Das Maß zu einem Kleide nehmen to take one's measure.

### Reading Exercise. 147.

Ich denke oft an Sie. Ich konnte meine Reiſe nicht fortſetzen
aus Mangel an Geld. Die Schiffe ſind bereits auf hoher See.
Die Vögel, welche uns im Herbſte verlaſſen, kehren im Frühling
zurück. Es war im Sommer von 1840. Iſt der Herr zu Hauſe?

Nein, er ist ausgegangen. Er speist heute in der Stadt. Ich bin auf offener Straße beschimpft[1] worden. Die kleine Schar machte sich Bahn[2] durch die Feinde. Mein Schwager wird spätestens in drei Tagen ankommen. Während dieses ganzen Monats hat es nicht ein einziges Mal geregnet. Der Hund sprang unter dem Tisch hervor. Vom Ersten bis zum Letzten. Seit wann ist Julie eine Waise? Sie ist es seit ihrer Kindheit. Anfangs hatten die Römer keine Festungen[3]; sie setzten ihr ganzes Vertrauen auf ihre Heere[4], welche sie längs der Flüsse legten, wo sie von Entfernung[5] zu Entfernung Türme errichteten[6], um die Soldaten darin unterzubringen[7].

1) to insult. 2) way. 3) fortress. 4) army. 5) distance. 6) to erect. 7) to shelter.

### 148.

Alexander der Große starb in der Blüte des Lebens. Äsop blühte zur Zeit Solons. Vor drei Tagen haben wir einen Wolf erlegt[1]. Ich werde vor acht Tagen nicht ausgehen; der Arzt hat es mir verboten. Ich werde Sie nach den Marktpreisen bezahlen. Franz der Erste wurde in Italien gefangen und nach Spanien abgeführt. Gegen Abend sah man am Himmel eine feurige Kugel[2]. Mein Vater ist um zwei Uhr abgereist. Bei seiner Abreise war die ganze Familie versammelt[3]. Er wird in Paris von seinem Bruder mit offenen Armen empfangen werden. Sind Sie zu Land hierher gekommen? Ja, ich bin mit der Eisenbahn gekommen. Man muß nicht aus Eigennutz[4] das Gute thun. Reisen Sie zu Pferd oder zu Wagen? Keines von beiden; ich reise zu Schiffe. Ich band ein Taschentuch um seinen Arm. Das Kind weinte vor Freuden[5]. Heidelberg liegt an den Ufern[6] des Neckars.

1) killed. 2) glove. 3) assembled 4) selfishness. 5) joy. 6) banks.

---

## II. How to express some **English** prepositions.

### above.

*Above*, when it expresses *time* or *number*, so as to signify *more than* or *longer than*, is rendered in German by über or mehr als. Ex.:

The fight lasted *above* four hours.

Das Gefecht dauerte über (or mehr als) vier Stunden.

It is *above* (over) twenty miles from here

Es ist über (mehr als) zwanzig Meilen von hier.

### about.

*About:* 1) in the sense of *round* is to be rendered by um; 2) in the signification *concerning*, it is über with the accus.; 3) in speaking of things which people carry about them, it is translated bei with the dat. Ex.:

1) All thronged *about* the prince.
   Alle drängten sich um den Fürsten.
2) I will speak to him *about* this affair.
   Ich werde über diese Angelegenheit mit ihm sprechen.
   We shall consider *about* this matter.
   Wir werden über diese Sache nachdenken.
3) I have no money *about* me.
   Ich habe kein Geld bei mir.

## at.

*At:* 1) is most commonly rendered by bei or an without or with an article; 2) after nouns or verbs denoting *derision, anger, surprise, joy, sorrow* etc. *at* is rendered by über with the *accusative*; 3) *at* is translated bei, when, in English, it precedes the words *house* etc., either expressed or understood. Ex :

1) We were *at* dinner.
   Wir waren beim (or am) Mittagessen (bei Tisch).
2) She laughed *at* him sie lachte über ihn.
   I am surprised *at* what you say.
   Ich bin erstaunt über das, was Sie sagen.
3) We were *at* your aunt's wir waren bei Ihrer Tante.

## by.

*By:* 1) denoting the *agent* or *cause* is translated von:
   Mr. Bell is respected *by* everybody.
   Herr Bell wird von jedermann geachtet.
   Troy was destroyed *by* the Greeks.
   Troja wurde von den Griechen zerstört.

2) In oaths and asseverations *by* is translated bei:
   He swears *by* his honour er schwört bei seiner Ehre.

3) *By*, after the verbs *to sell, to buy, to work* etc., preceding a noun of *weight* or *measure, a day, week, month* or *year* is rendered in German by nach (either after or before its noun), or by adding weise to the noun, such as: pfundweise, tageweise, wochenweise 2c. Ex.:

   I sell the tea *by* the pound.
   Ich verkaufe den Thee nach dem Pfund or dem Pfunde nach or pfundweise.
   We work *by* the hour or *by* the day.
   Wir arbeiten nach der Stunde oder nach dem Tage.

4) When preceding a numeral immediately followed by an adjective of *dimension by* is rendered in German by und. Ex.:

This room is five meters long *by* three wide.
Dieſes Zimmer iſt fünf Meter lang und drei breit.

5) *By*, meaning '*by means of*', e. g. after *to kill, to wound etc.*, is translated durch. Ex.:

The officer was wounded *by* a musket ball.
Der Offizier wurde durch einen Flintenſchuß verwundet.

Achilles was killed at the siege of Troy *by* an arrow.
Achilles wurde bei der Belagerung von Troja durch einen Pfeil getötet

## from.

1) *From* and *to*, used in the same sentence, are rendered by von — zu. Ex.:

He went *from* street *to* street, from town to town etc.
Er ging von Straße zu Straße, von Stadt zu Stadt ꝛc.

2) When two names of towns or villages are mentioned, *from — to* is rendered by von — nach. Ex.:

From Paris *to* Rouen von Paris nach (or bis) Rouen.

3) *From* is rendered by von, and *to* by bis, when speaking of *extent* or *time*. Ex.:

From Easter to Christmas von Oſtern bis Weihnacht.

4) So also when extent of space is indicated. Ex.:

It rained violently from Strasburg to Berlin.
Es regnete heftig von Straßburg bis Berlin.

It would be too far from here to Paris.
Es wäre zu weit von hier bis Paris.

5) *From under* is unter . . . hervor. Ex.:

*From under* the bed unter dem Bett hervor

## in.

1) To have *a pain in* is translated with a compound word, such as: Kopfweh, Halsweh, Zahnweh haben ꝛc. Ex.:

I have constantly a pain *in* my head.
Ich habe immer Kopfweh.

2) *In* after words denoting *hurting, wounding etc.* and preceding a possessive adjective with any part of the body, is to be rendered by an with the definite article.

The child fell down and was hurt (injured) *in* his shoulder.\*)
Das Kind fiel und verwundete sich an der Schulter.

3) In adverbial expressions of *day-time, in* is expressed
in German either by am or by the Genitive case with or
without the article. Ex.:

*In* the morning am Morgen, morgens or des Morgens.
*In* the evening am Abend or abends or des Abends.

### on or upon.

1) *On* or *upon* is most generally auf. Ex.:

    He climbed *upon* (*up*) the tree er kletterte auf den Baum.

2) *On* or *upon* after the verb *to live* is rendered von:

    The prisoner lives *on* bread and water.
    Der Gefangene lebt von Brot und Wasser.

3) After *to play, on* is not translated at all. Ex.:

    You play *on* the violin, and I play *on* the piano
    Sie spielen Violine und ich spiele Klavier.

4) The preposition *on* before the days of the week
and with dates is translated am. Ex.:

    Come *on* Sunday kommen Sie am Sonntag
    *On* the twelfth of May am (or den) zwölften Mai.

### over.

    This preposition is commonly rendered in German by
über, but it must be expressed by vorüber or vorbei
(seldom aus), when it denotes an action ended. Ex.:

    As soon as the rain will be over.
    Sobald (als) der Regen vorüber sein wird.
    Is dinner over? ist das Mittagessen vorüber?
    Church is over (out) die Kirche ist aus.

### with.

1) *With* or *from* are rendered by vor after the verbs
*to starve, to die, to perish* etc. Ex.:

    He died *with* (from) cold er starb vor Kälte.

*Note. To die of* is translated sterben an. Ex.:

    He died *of* his wounds er starb an seinen Wunden.

---

\*) It would be indeed simpler and better in English to say,
. . . . and hurt his shoulder, but you will often hear also, he was
hurt (injured, wounded) *in* his shoulder, arm, hand etc.

2) *With* must not be translated after the following
verbs: *to meet with* begegnen (*Acc.*); *to trust with* anver=
trauen; *to reproach with* vorwerfen, *to agree with* wohl oder
gut bekommen. These German verbs govern the person
in the dative, and the object in the *accusative* without a
preposition. Ex..

He trusted me *with* his son.
Er vertraute mir feinen Sohn an.
I reproached him *with* his ingratitude.
Ich warf ihm feine Undankbarkeit vor.

### Remark.
Prepositions are placed in German *before* the interrogative
and relative pronouns which they govern; in English they
are sometimes placed after:

Whom do you speak *to*? mit wem fprechen Sie?
What's that for? zu was ift das?
The man whom you are interested *for*.
Der Mann, für den Sie fich intereffieren.

### Aufgabe. 149.
1. Where are you going? I am going into the country.
Gœthe died at Weimar in the year (im Jahre) 1832. My
friend arrived in the beginning of summer. Is this book to
(nach) your taste[1]? No, I do not like it (*It does not please me*).
I met that gentleman on my journey in Italy. The poor man
had to choose between slavery[2] and death. Why has she
been so injust towards her parents? Did you arrive before
or after four o'clock? Before the church there are three high
poplars[3]. I found this letter among my papers. Whisky[4] is
the source of great evils[5] among that people. They (man)
told me amongst other [things] that the ship had been taken
by the enemy (*pl.*).
2. He has sold all his horses except one or two. I went
from Hamburgh to Altona. Now we turn to (towards) [the]
south. Among the German merchants in London, there are
many beneficent[6] men. He lives *with* his brother. The tailor
will come to your house to-morrow. Where do you come
from? I come *from* my aunt's. The wooden horse was outside
the walls[7] of Troy[8]. The patient is at present out of (außer)
danger. Nobody besides myself was present[9]. Out of (von) sitxty
soldiers who tried the attack[10], twenty-five fell into the hands of
the enemy The dog sprang [out] from under the table.

1) Geschmack 2) Sklaverei. 3) Pappelbäume. 4) der Branntwein.
5) Übel. 6) wohlthätig. 7) Mauern. 8) Troja. 9) gegenwärtig.
10) Angriff, m.

## 150.

**1.** My father was not above twenty-two years old, when he was married[1] My uncle's country-house[2] is very handsome, but it cost him above eighty thousand marcs. It is above a year since my friend set off for[3] America. Rome *was* built by Romulus. The poor man was driven[4] out of his house by his creditors[5]. I will get up to-morrow at six o'clock Were you at Mrs. D.'s ball last night? I will pay you at the end of this month. I rejoice greatly *at* your good luck[6]. She always smiles[7] at everything which *is* said. Where was your sister this morning? She was at her aunt's. My box[8] is one foot and a half deep [*by*] two wide and four long. Harold was wounded *by* an arrow[9].

**2.** William the Second was killed *by* an arrow in the New-forest. Charles was wounded *in his* arm and not *in his* leg. I have very often [a] tooth-ache [*Upon*] *what* instrument does your sister play? She plays *on* the piano Men (man) do not live only *on* bread and meat, but *on* the grace[10] of God. That happened *on* the 12th [of] March. I am in the habit[11] of taking a cup of coffee, as soon as (the) dinner is *over* When you meet *with* a poor man, never reproach him [with] his poverty[12]. France extends[13] from the Vosges[14] to (bis zu) the Atlantic Ocean What does he complain[15] *of*?

1) to be married = ſich verheiraten. 2) Landhaus. 3) nach 4) treiben. 5) Gläubiger. 6) Glück. 7) lächeln. 8) die Kiſte. 9) der Pfeil. 10) die Gnade. 11) to be in the habit gewohnt ſein or pflegen 12) Armut 13) ſich erſtrecken. 14) den Vogeſen. 15) klagen über (*Acc.*) or ſich beklagen.

### Reading-lesson.
### Lukas Kranach.

Lukas Kranach war nicht nur der größte Maler ſeiner Zeit, ſondern auch ein Mann von edlem Herzen und großem Verſtand. Schon in ſeiner Jugend wendete er ſeine Zeit ſehr gut an, und daher kam es, daß er viel früher ein nützlicher Menſch wurde als andre. Im neunzehnten Jahre ſeines Alters lernte[1] ihn der Kurfürſt (Elector) von Sachſen, Johann Friedrich, als einen geſchickten[2] Jüngling kennen[1] und nahm ihn auf ſeiner Reiſe ins Gelobte Land[3] mit ſich. Nach ſeiner Rückkehr ins Vaterland berief er ihn an ſeinen Hof nach Wittenberg und machte ihn daſelbſt zum Bürgermeiſter[4].

Ein einziger Zug (trait) ſeiner ſchönen Seele iſt hinreichend[5], ſeinen Charakter zu ſchildern[6]. Als ſein Herr, der unglückliche Kurfürſt Johann Friedrich, bei Mühlberg in Sachſen in die Gefangenſchaft[7] Kaiſer Karls V. (des Fünften) geraten war, erinnerte

1) kennen lernen to become acquainted with, to know  2) clever. 3) Holy Land.  4) mayor (see p. 345, 3).  5) sufficient  6) to describe, paint.  7) to fall into captivity.

fich der Kaiſer, daß Kranach ihn als (when a) Knabe gemalt hatte,
und ließ dieſen edlen Maler in ſein Lager kommen.

„Wie alt war ich damals (then), als du mich malteſt?“ fragte
der Kaiſer. — „Eure Majeſtät,“ antwortete Kranach, „war acht
Jahre alt. Es gelang mir nicht eher[8], Eure Majeſtät ſtillſitzen zu
machen, als bis[8] Ihr Hofmeiſter[9] verſchiedene Waffen an die Wand
hängen ließ. Während Sie dieſe kriegeriſchen Inſtrumente mit un-
verwandten (fixed, staring) Augen betrachteten, hatte ich Zeit, Ihr
Bild zu entwerfen[10].“ — „Bitte (ask) dir eine Gnade von mir
aus, Maler!“ ſagte der Kaiſer.

Demütig fiel ihm Kranach zu Füßen und bat, mit Thränen
in den Augen, nicht um eine Summe Geld oder um einen Titel,
ſondern um die Freiheit ſeines Kurfürſten. Der Monarch kam in
die größte Verlegenheit; ſein Herz war durch dieſen gerechten Wunſch
eines treuen Unterthanen[11] ſehr getroffen; und doch glaubte er,
den rechtſchaffenen Kranach fürs erſte[12] abweiſen[13] zu müſſen. „Du
biſt ein braver Mann,“ ſagte er zu ihm; „aber es wäre mir lieber
(preferred) geweſen, wenn du um etwas andres gebeten hätteſt.“
Als nach einiger Zeit der Kurfürſt ſeine Freiheit erlangte, ließ er
dieſen ſeinen treuen Diener nie von ſeiner Seite; er mußte in ſeinem Schloſſe wohnen und ſelbſt bei ehrenvollen[14] Gelegenheiten
neben ihm im Wagen ſitzen.

8) nicht eher als bis = not before. 9) the governor, tutor.
10) to sketch, draw 11) subject. 12) for the present 13) to
refuse. 14) ceremonial.

## Questions.

Was war Lukas Kranach?
Wie kam es, daß er früher als andre ein nützlicher Menſch
Wann lernte ihn der Kurfürſt von Sachſen kennen? [wurde?
Wie hieß der Kurfürſt?
Wohin nahm er ihn mit ſich?
Was that er nach ſeiner Rückkehr?
Welcher ſchöne Charakterzug wird von ihm erzählt?
Welche Frage richtete der Kaiſer an den Maler?
Was antwortete ihm Kranach?
Welche Gnade bat ſich der Maler von dem Kaiſer aus?
Gewährte ihm der Kaiſer ſeine Bitte?
Was ſagte er zu ihm?
Wie ehrte der Kurfürſt den Maler, nachdem er ſeine Freiheit
   wieder erlangt hatte?

# Fiftieth Lesson.

## On Construction (Wortfolge).

German construction differs very much from English, and requires great attention. Every trifling deviation cannot be explained, but the principal rules must be stated here.

### I. On the principal or simple sentence.
#### A. The common construction.

As in other languages, the essential components of a principal sentence are the *subject* and *predicate* or *verb*:

Das Kind schläft. | Das Kind ist krank.

Further there are the *objects* or *governments*, and the *adverbial enlargements*. The *object* is twofold, viz. the *direct* one i. e. the *Accusative, Dative* or *Genitive*, and the *indirect* (with prepositions). The *adverbial enlargement* is of different kinds, viz. : *of time, of place, of manner etc.* Ex.:

Das Kind ist krank gewesen. | Der Knabe schlägt den Hund.
Der Bote brachte meinem Vater einen Brief.
Der Fremde wohnt in einem Gasthof (hotel).
Der Fremde reiste gestern nach Paris
Der Gärtner schickte mir heute die ersten Blumen aus meinem
Am Rande des Baches steht ein kleines Haus. [Garten.

### Rules.

1) In the regular order, the *subject*, which may be a substantive or a pronoun, begins a sentence and therefore stands in the *first* place, then *the verb* (*predicate*) or its substitute (*the auxiliary*) follows in the *second*, and the *object* in the *third* place. Ex.·

Der Knabe suchte seinen Ring.

2) The *adverbial of place* comes last of all. If the sentence contains also an adverbial of *time*, this must precede the accusative (object). Ex.:

Der Knabe suchte gestern seinen Ring überall.

3) With compound tenses the complement of the auxiliary, be it a *Participle* or an *Infinitive*, comes after the predicate, object and adverb, generally in the *last* place of the sentence. Ex.:

Ich bin lange krank gewesen.

Der Knabe hat den Hund auf den Kopf geschlagen.
Der Vater wird in einigen Tagen von Paris zurückkommen

4) When there are *two objects* in a sentence, generally that of the *person* precedes the *thing*. Ex.:

Der Lehrer hat dem Schüler (*Dat.*) ein Buch (*Acc.*) geliehen.
The master has lent the pupil a book.

Sie haben den armen Mann (*Acc.*) seinem Schicksale (*Dat.*)
They have left the poor man to his fate.    [überlassen

5) When the two cases are both *persons*, the accusative generally precedes the dative. Ex.:

Ich habe Ihren Sohn dem Fürsten empfohlen.
I have recommended your son to the prince.

6) When *one* of the two objects is expressed by a personal pronoun, it must precede the noun. Ex.

Herr Peter hat mir ein Geschenk gemacht.
Mr. Peter has made me a present.

Er hat dir (Ihnen, ihm, ihr 2c.) einen guten Rat gegeben.
He has given you (him, her etc ) good advice.

Haben Sie es Ihrem Freunde erzählt?
Have you told (it) your friend?

Der Briefbote hat uns (Ihnen, ihnen) einen Brief gebracht.
The postman brought us (you, them) a letter.

7) When both objects are personal pronouns, the smallest comes first; when both of them are monosyllabic, the *accusative* comes first.

Er hat sie (or es) ihnen (euch, Ihnen) gezeigt.
He has shown it to them (to you).

Ich kann mich seiner (ihrer) nicht erinnern.
I cannot remember him (her).

Ich habe sie ihm (not ihm sie) gezeigt.
I have shown them to him.    -

Er hat sich (*Acc.*) mir vorgestellt    (See 5.)
He has introduced himself to me.

*Note.* Mir and dir, however, may occur indifferently *before* or *after* the accusatives es, ihn, sie.

Robert hat es mir (or mir es or mir ihn) geliehen.
Robert has lent it to me.

8) The adverbial expressions of *time*, viz.: true adverbs as well as substantives with prepositions denoting a time, generally precede the object (*unless it is a pronoun without a preposition*, see 9), and take the third place, immediately after the predicate or auxiliary:

Ich habe gestern einen Brief an ihn (see 14) geschrieben
Mein Bruder kam diesen Morgen von Hamburg zurück
Der General wird eiligst einen Brief an den Fürsten senden.
Ich habe neulich meinen Freund A. gesehen.
Wir werden in drei Tagen nach Hamburg reisen.
Herr Müller wird in einer Stunde das Packet erhalten.

9) Adverbs of *time* cannot precede personal pronouns *without a preposition*. These always come first. Ex.:

Ich habe ihn (or sie) heute nicht gesehen
Er wird uns (euch, Sie) morgen besuchen.

10) Adverbs of *manner* follow the direct object (acc.):

Sie haben Ihren Brief schön geschrieben.
Der Knabe hat seine Aufgabe sehr schön geschrieben.
Wir haben unsre Pflichten mit Freuden erfüllt.

11) Of all *adverbs* and *adverbial expressions* those *of place* are the last and should be placed close to the Participle, when the verb stands in a compound tense:

Der Mann hat heute das Kind überall gesucht
Die Feinde haben das Haus auf allen Seiten umstellt.
The enemies have surrounded the house on all sides.

12) But when the verb is in the Present or Imperfect, such adverbs must come last

Der Mann suchte sein Kind überall.
Wir erfüllten unsre Pflicht mit Freuden.
Die Feinde umstellten das Haus auf allen Seiten.

*Note.* Adverbs *never* precede the verb standing in the Present or Imperfect, as I *always* say ich sage immer.

13) Adverbs of *place* and *manner* (not *time*) are therefore generally placed after the negation nicht. Ex.:

Der König ist nicht hier gewesen.
Der König ist heute nicht hier gewesen.
Der Bote hat nicht lang genug gewartet
Das Schiff ist nicht schnell gefahren (or gesegelt).
Ihr Brief ist nicht schön geschrieben.

14) Pronouns with a preposition *follow* the adverb and the object.

Ich habe gestern dieses Buch bei Ihnen gesehen.

15) Of two adverbial expressions of *time* the true *adverb* precedes the other formed with a substantive:

Ich werde morgen um zehn Uhr abreisen.
Herr A. geht immer des Abends spazieren.

16) The negation nid)t always *follows the direct object* (*Accus.*). Ex.:

Id) finde mein Federmeffer nid)t.
Id) kann mein Federmeffer nid)t finden.
Id) habe mein Federmeffer nid)t gefunden.
Friedrid) lernte feine Aufgabe nid)t gut.
Der Minifter hat die Deputation nod) nid)t empfangen.
The minister has *not yet* received the deputation.

*Note.* In questions however nid)t sometimes precedes the object. We say:

Haben Sie das Bud) nid)t gelefen? but
Habe id) nid)t das Red)t, fo zu handeln?

17) But when the object is preceded by a preposition, which is called *indirect* object, the negation nid)t *goes before* it. Ex.:

Wir fpred)en nid)t von diefem Bud).
Spiele nid)t mit dem Meffer. | Gehen Sie nid)t in das Haus.
Man hat den Dieb nid)t im Keller gefunden.

### Reading-lesson.
### Der edle Offizier.

In dem letzten Kriege, den Frankreid) gegen Spanien führte, hatten die deutfd)en Hilfstruppen ein Städtd)en an den Ufern des fpanifd)en Fluffes Tajo befetzt, aber nur eine fd)wad)e Befatzung (garrison) von 22 Mann darin gelaffen. Diefe wurden auf Zureden[1] fpanifd)er Soldaten von den Einwohnern ermordet. Nur einer entkam[2] und brad)te die Nad)rid)t von der blutigen That in das franzöfifd)e Lager. Hier forderte man, des Beifpiels wegen, blutige Rad)e[3]. Sogleid) erhielt der badifd)e Hauptmann H. den Befehl, mit einer Abteilung[4] feiner Truppen die Stadt zu umringen, niederzubrennen und in einen Steinhaufen zu verwandeln[5]; die Bewohner follten eingefd)loffen (shut in) bleiben und in unthätiger Verzweiflung[6] ihre Habe[7] von den Flammen verzehren fehen. Von diefer Maßregel erwartete der franzöfifd)e General den beften Erfolg. Denn Deutfd)e waren ausgefd)ickt, den fd)mählid)ften Tod ihrer Brüder zu räd)en, und ihr Anführer war im ganzen Heer als einer der tapferften, entfd)loffenften[8] und mutigften Offiziere bekannt.

Aber er war nod) mehr als das. Sein edles, menfd)enfreundlid)es Herz wurde mit Graufen[9] erfüllt, als er den Auftrag[10] vernahm. Dod) konnte und wollte er ihn nid)t ablehnen[11]. Das nahe fd)reckliche Schickfal fo vieler unglücklid)er Menfd)en, die an dem Morde größtenteils unfd)uldig waren, ergreift feine edle Seele. Schon fieht er im Geifte die Stadt auflodern[12], hört das Klagegefd)rei der Frauen, das Jammergefd)rei[13] der Kinder und Greife,

1) persuasion. 2) to escape. 3) vengeance. 4) company. — 5) to turn. 6) despair. 7) goods. 8) resolute. 9) horror. 10) order. 11) to decline, to refuse. 12) to blaze up. 13) lamentation.

das Röcheln[14] der Sterbenden; und entworfen[15] ist schon sein Plan, fest sein Entschluß. Noch[16] in später Nacht giebt er seinen Leuten den Befehl zum Aufbruch[17]. Der Weg führte[18] an einem Kloster vorüber, das unweit der bedrohten Stadt lag. Das kluge und menschenfreundliche Benehmen des Vorstehers[19] und aller Bewohner desselben gegen Freund und Feind hatte ihnen den Schutz und die Liebe beider Teile erworben und dieses wahre Gotteshaus zur Freistätte[20] für jeden Flüchtigen gemacht. Der Hauptmann H. verlangt Einlaß und eine Unterredung[21] mit dem Prior. Beides wurde ihm gewährt (granted). Der Vertrauteste[22] seiner Leute begleitete ihn.                                    (*To be continued.*)

14) the groans of the dying. 15) projected. 16) in the very night. 17) to set out. 18) vorüberführen to pass. 19) prior. — 20) asylum. 21) interview. 22) trusty, confident.

## Questions.

Wer hatte im letzten spanischen Kriege ein Städtchen besetzt?
Was ereignete sich damals?
Auf wessen Zureden geschah die blutige That?
Wurden Alle getötet?
Wie erfuhr man die Nachricht im französischen Lager?
Was verlangte man hier?
Welchen Befehl erhielt der badische Hauptmann H.?
Warum versprach sich der französische General den besten Erfolg?
Was für ein Mann war jener Hauptmann?
Was sah er schon im Geiste?
Was hörte er im Geiste?
Wohin führte ihn sein Weg?
Wie hatten sich die Vorsteher und die Bewohner jenes Klosters immer benommen?
Was begehrte daselbst der Hauptmann?
Wer begleitete ihn?

---

## B.  On the Inversion.

The foregoing rules refer to the regular and common construction. This regular arrangement of words, however, may be frequently *inverted*, by removing one of the parts of speech from its usual place to the beginning of the sentence.

1) *The inversion of the subject and predicate* (*verb*) appears as in English:

*a*) In interrogative and exclamatory sentences:

Glauben Sie diesem Manne? do you believe this man?

Hat der Polizeidiener den Dieb gefangen?
Has the constable caught the thief?

Sollte der Mann es gehört haben?
Should the man have heard it?
Warum hat das Kind geweint? why did the child cry?

*b*) In imperative sentences, where however in the singular
the pronoun-subject is seldom expressed
Fange (du) an zu lesen begin (thou) to read.
Lesen Sie diese Seite ganz laut read this page quite loud.

*c*) In conditional sentences, when the conjunction wenn (*if*)
is omitted, as in English:
Hätte ich es gestern gewußt (instead of wenn ich es 2c.).
Had I known it yesterday.
Wäre ich zehn Jahre älter were I ten years older.

*d*) After all *adverbs* and *adverbial conjunctions* (see p. 246):
Gestern war ich im Theater yesterday I was at the theatre.
Kaum hatte ich das Messer in die Hand genommen
Scarcely had I taken the knife in *my* hand.
Indessen war der Winter herangekommen.
Meanwhile winter *had* drawn near.

2) *The inversion of the object* takes place, when more
stress is laid upon it. One consequence of this change is,
that the subject assumes its place after the verb. The
regular sentence. Ich nehme diesen Vorschlag gerne an, ap-
pears inverted in the following shape:
Diesen Vorschlag nehme ich gerne an.
This proposal I accept willingly.
Den Beutel hat er gefunden, aber nicht das Geld.
The purse he has found, but not the money.
Dieses Mannes kann ich mich durchaus nicht erinnern.
This man I cannot remember at all.
Nicht Reichtum, nur Zufriedenheit wünsche ich Ihnen.
Not riches, only contentment I wish you.

3) *Personal* pronouns, especially monosyllables, often
precede the subject, when the latter is of two or more
syllables or accompanied by an adjective:
Da ihn (es) niemand gesehen hatte (for niemand ihn or es).
Wenn Ihnen ein schlechter Rat gegeben wird. —

4) *The inversion of the adverbial* expressions. Adverbial expressions of all kinds, especially those of time,
very frequently begin the sentence, when much stress
is to be laid on them. Here, too, the verb goes before
the subject. Ex.:

Diesen Morgen ging Herr Grün an meinem Hause vorbei.
This morning Mr. Green passed my house.
Freundlich drückte sie mir die Hand.
In a friendly manner, she shook *my* hand
Überall findet man die Spuren der Weisheit Gottes.
Everywhere man finds the traces of the wisdom of God.
Unter dem großen Steine lag eine Schlange.
Under the large stone, [there] lay a snake.

5) According to the stress laid upon the words, the following and similar sentences may be expressed in various ways:

Wir können dieses Buch in London nicht bekommen.
Dieses Buch können wir in London nicht bekommen.
In London können wir dieses Buch nicht bekommen.
Mein Freund hat gestern nach langem Harren den ersehnten Brief von seinem Vater erhalten
After waiting long, my friend received yesterday the wished for letter from his father.
Gestern hat mein Freund nach langem Harren den ersehnten Brief von seinem Vater erhalten.
Nach langem Harren hat gestern mein Freund den ersehnten Brief von seinem Vater erhalten.
Den ersehnten Brief von seinem Vater hat mein Freund gestern nach langem Harren erhalten.

## II. Accessory sentences.

1) An accessory sentence is a *completing addition* to one member of the principal sentence in form of a clause,*) and always begins either with a *relative pronoun* or a *relative adverb*. The order of the subject, object and adverbial undergoes no change in accessory sentences; only the *verb (predicate)* leaves its usual place for the *end* of the sentence. When compound, the participle or infinitive precedes the auxiliary. Ex.:

Der Wein, welchen ich von Ihnen kaufte, ist nicht gut.
The wine which I bought of you, is not good.
Das Buch, das ich verloren hatte, ist wieder gefunden.
The book I had lost, has been found again.

---

*) For instance, in the sentence *I found a bottle containing poison*, the two latter words *containing poison* are a completing addition to *bottle*. If you give them the form of a *clause = which contained poison* welche Gift enthielt, you have an *accessory sentence*.

Der Stock, womit ich ihn schlug, ist zerbrochen.
The stick with which I struck him, is broken.
Ich fragte ihn, warum er so ernst wäre.
I asked him why he was so serious.

2) When there are two Infinitives (one Infinitive for
the Participle), the auxiliary haben precedes the two:

Das Taschentuch, welches ich habe waschen laſſen.
Der Bach, in welchem (wo) ich ihn hatte baden ſehen.  ·
Nachdem ich ihn hatte rufen hören.

### Aufgabe. 151.

London is a very large town. I have bought a beautiful
garden for my children. We have had clear days but dark
nights. We cannot see all the numberless (zahlloſen) stars.
Henry was to-day more industrious than yesterday; he will
be the most industrious to-morrow. They went away from
here at four o'clock. He often visited us formerly. They
entered[1] (in) the wood and ‹soon ‹perceived the habitations[2]
of men. I do not know the man whom you are speaking of.
The first battle (which) they fought[3] was with the Saracens[4].
I did not know who it was. To be sure (Gewiß), I have told
it (to) him. I am infinitely obliged[5] [to] you. I was wander-
ing[6] through the street with a heavy heart. Finally (Endlich)
we discovered[7] the truth. I have not been anywhere (nowhere). — Prosperity[8] gains friends, and adversity tries (prüft)
them. Without a friend the world is but (nur) a wilderness[9]. —
What does this man teach your children? He teaches them
[to] read and write. The tempest[10] increased[11], and the ships
lost sight of each other (verloren .. aus dem Geſicht).

1) to enter eintreten. 2) Wohnung. 3) liefern. 4) Sarazenen.
5) unendlich verbunden. 6) wandern. 7) entdecken. 8) das Glück.
9) Wildnis, f. 10) der Sturm. 11) to increase zu'nehmen.

### Reading-lesson.
### Der edle Offizier. (Fortſetzung.)

Nach einer halben Stunde kehrte er zu den Seinigen zurück,
aber allein; — ſein Begleiter[1] iſt unbemerkt und vermummt[2] durch
eine andre Thüre hinausgeſchlüpft[3] und hat bald auf einem näheren
Wege die zum Verderben beſtimmte[4] Stadt erreicht, welcher (Dat.)
er mit einem Briefe des Priors als ein Himmelsbote erſcheint.
Die Weiber und Kinder, kranke Männer und Greiſe ſind eingeladen,
ſich und ihre Habe auf dem nächſten Wege nach dem Kloſter zu
flüchten. Der Zug[5] beginnt, durch den Mondſchein begünſtigt,
Mütter, ihre Säuglinge[6] an der Bruſt oder auf dem Rücken, er-
öffnen den Zug; dankbare Söhne tragen die Mütter. So gelangen

1) companion. 2) disguised. 3) slipped out. 4) destined, see
p. 342, V. 5, procession, march 6) baby.

(reach) fie an das Klofter, wo der Prior fie mit feinen Mönchen
gaftfreundlich[7] aufnimmt. Während deffen hat der wactere Hauptmann feine Leute auf einem andern Wege gegen die Stadt geführt.
Er läßt[8] fie umringen, doch fo, daß jener Weg zum Klofter offen
blieb; er befiehlt den zurückgebliebenen Männern, außerhalb der
Stadt Stroh und Holz aufzutürmen[9]. Es gefchieht[10], und bald
lodern auf allen Seiten helle, hohe Flammen in der Morgenröte
auf; aber hinter dem Feuer ruhten ficher die verfchonten (spared)
Häufer und Hütten und — an Plünderung wird nicht gedacht.

Nach zweiftündigem Brande wird ein Eilbote[11] an den General
gefchickt, um Nachlaß[12] zu erbitten. Diefer kehrte mit dem Befehle
zurück, daß die Stadt bis Mittag brennen müffe[13]. Sogleich wird
der übrige Vorrat[14] von Holz und Stroh zur Unterhaltung[15]
des Feuers herbeigefchafft und das Gebälke[16] einiger öffentlichen
Häufer, die man, um doch etwas zu zerftören, niedergeriffen[17]
hatte, wird zu gleichem Zwecke verbraucht. Endlich fchlägt die
zwölfte Stunde und giebt das Zeichen zum Abzuge[18], der einem
wahren Triumphzuge gleicht; denn unter den Taufenden ift nicht
Einer, der nicht Freudenthränen weint. Begleitet von den männ-
lichen Bewohnern der Stadt, welche den Soldaten die Gewehre
und Tornifter[19] tragen, fie mit ihren Dankfagungen und Segens-
wünfchen[20] überfchütten[21], gelangt der bunte[22] Haufe zum Klofter.
Die von dem feinen Feuer erfchreckten Greife, Weiber und Kinder
eilen den Kommenden mit ängftlichen Fragen entgegen. Aber bald
wird der fürchterliche Zweifel[23] zur fröhlichen[24] Gewißheit, als fie
erfuhren[25], daß der edle Hauptmann nicht nur ihr Leben, fondern
auch ihre Häufer und Güter gerettet habe. Sie fallen vor ihm
nieder, fie küffen ihm die Hände, er kann fich der lebhafteften
Äußerungen[26] des Dankes kaum erwehren[27].

7) hospitably. 8) causes, see p. 295, 5. — 9) to heap or pile
up. 10) they do so. 11) courier. 12 pardon. 13) see p. 315,
§ 3 and p. 317, § 7. — 14) store. 15) to support. 16) timber.
17) pull down, demolish. 18) departure. 19) knapsack. 20) bless-
ings 21) load. 22) the mingled troop. 23) doubt. 24) joyful.
25) learn. 26) manifestations. 27) to keep off.

## Questions.

Wann kehrte der Hauptmann zurück?
Was wurde aus feinem Begleiter?
Welche Einladung enthielt das Schreiben des Priors?
Wie war der Zug der Flüchtlinge befchaffen?
Wie ließ der Hauptmann die bedrohte Stadt umringen?
Von was läßt er ein Feuer anmachen?
Brannten die Häufer?
An was wird nicht gedacht?
Was gefchieht nach zweiftündigem Brande?
Welche Antwort brachte der Eilbote?
Was gefchieht nun ferner?

Wem gleicht der Abzug der Truppen?
Als die Soldaten abzogen, was thaten die Männer?
Was thaten die Greise und Frauen, als man beim Kloster an=
Was hatte ihnen der edle Hauptmann gerettet? [langte?
(*To be continued.*)

---

# Fifty-first Lesson.

## On the compound sentence.

After having explained the simple sentence with its components and enlargements, we proceed to a short exposition of the *compound sentence*.

The compound sentence is formed:

I. by co-ordination,
II. by subordination

### I. Co-ordinate compound sentences.

(Satzverbindungen )

There are three ways of co-ordinating sentences:

*a*) They can be placed simply beside each other without any connection. Ex.:

Die Rosse wieherten, es schmetterten Trompeten;
Die Fahnen flatterten, die Fahrt ward angetreten.
Ich erzählte ihm alles; er wußte noch nichts davon
Gehen Sie rechts, ich werde links gehen.

*b*) They are connected by a demonstrative pronoun:

Karl der Große und Napoleon waren zwei mächtige Krieger;
jener verband (joined) die größte Weisheit mit der
größten Tapferkeit; dieser eroberte fast ganz Europa.

Das Glück und die Tugend sind nicht immer verbunden; dies
wird durch die Geschichte aller Zeiten bestätigt.

*Note.* Sentences joined by a relative pronoun are not considered as compound, but as *accessory* sentences (see p. 372).

Ich habe das Buch gelesen, welches Sie mir geliehen haben.

*c*) By means of the *co-ordinative conjunctions* (see p. 245): und, oder, aber, allein, sondern, denn, sowohl — als. Ex.:

Der Winter verging, und der Frühling kam.
Winter passed and spring came.

Ich verlasse Sie jetzt, aber ich werde bald zurückkehren.
I leave you now, but I shall soon return.

Karl wurde Soldat; denn er war der Mißhandlung überdrüssig.
Charles turned soldier; for he was tired of ill treatment.

Ich wollte nach England reisen; aber ich hatte nicht Geld genug.

Er konnte nicht kommen, denn er war krank.

Vergnügungen sind für den Menschen notwendig; allein sie
dürfen nicht mit Unmäßigkeit genossen werden.

Die armen Reisenden hatten nicht nur kein Geld mehr, sondern, was noch schlimmer war, die Lebensmittel waren
ihnen auch ausgegangen.

d) By means of the *adverbial conjunctions* (see p. 246):

Ich erwarte einen Gast; deswegen muß ich zu Hause bleiben.

Diese Feder ist zu hart; deshalb taugt sie nicht zum Schreiben.

Er hat mich zwar schwer beleidigt; dessen ungeachtet will ich
ihm verzeihen.

Vergnügungen sind für den Menschen notwendig; jedoch
dürfen sie nicht mit Unmäßigkeit genossen werden.

Der Mensch muß sich selbst beherrschen können, sonst wird
er beherrscht.

## II. Compound sentences with subordinate clauses.

(Satzgefüge.)

1) These consist of two essential parts, the *principal
sentence* and *subordinate sentences*. Their connection is
effected by the *subordinative conjunctions* (see p. 248—256).
All the *subordinate clauses* are characterised by the following particulars:

a) The verb is removed to the end:

Es war Nacht, als ich in London ankam.

b) In compound *tenses* the auxiliary follows the participle:

Er wurde freigelassen, nachdem er seinen Paß vorge-
zeigt hatte.

c) In *separable verbs* the particle is not separated:

Er erfuhr es nicht, weil er nicht ausging.

d) All the depending cases are placed between the subject
and the verb:

Du würdest ihm zürnen, wenn er jetzt diesen Brief Karls
deinem Vater zeigte.

2) The *subordinate* sentence may be the first member
as well as the second; if it is the first, the subject of
the second, which is the *principal* one, is removed after
the verb. This change is often indicated by the little
word ſo, which must not be translated:

Er gab den Armen nichts, weil er geizig war.

or: Weil er geizig war, gab er den Armen nichts.

Because he was avaricious, *he gave* nothing to the poor.

Obſchon der Angeklagte ſeine Unſchuld beteuerte, (ſo) wurde
er doch zum Tode verurteilt.
Although the accused man asserted his innocence, yet he
was condemned to death.

Als man ihn fragte, wodurch (durch was *relat.*) dies ge=
ſchehen ſei, antwortete er nichts.
When they asked him, how this had happened, he answered nothing.

Mein Oheim iſt aus Amerika gekommen, um ſeine Familie
zu holen.
My uncle has come from A. in order to fetch his family.

{ Ich kann keine Bücher kaufen, da ich kein Geld habe, or
{ Da ich kein Geld habe, kann ich keine Bücher kaufen

Dadurch, daß wir das Laſter haſſen (by hating vice),
beſtärken (strengthen) wir uns in der Liebe zur Tugend.

3) When the pronoun of the subordinate sentence represents a person or inanimate object, or abstract idea
of the principal sentence, it is carried to the principal
and the substantive to the subordinate.

Obſchon der Mann ſehr arm iſt, iſt er doch recht glücklich.
Seitdem Ihr Bruder bei mir war, habe ich ihn nicht wie=
der geſehen.

In the latter two sentences the words „der Mann‟ and
„Ihr Bruder‟ should, properly speaking, have their place in
the principal sentences, and „er‟ in the subordinate, as

Der Mann iſt doch recht glücklich, obſchon er ſehr arm iſt.
Ich habe Ihren Bruder nicht wieder geſehen, ſeitdem er bei mir war.

4) The subordinate sentence may also be inserted
between the words of the principal sentence, without
affecting the order of the latter. Ex.

Ich erfuhr ſogleich, als ich in München ankam, das Un=
glück meines Freundes.

5) The two conjunctions wenn and daß may be omitted;
in this case the verb is not removed to the end.

Hätte ich es geſehen, ſo würde ich es verboten haben.
Er ſagte, er habe Kopfweh (instead daß er Kopfweh habe).

6) Very often two or more subordinate and accessory
clauses appear in a compound sentence; but this makes
no other change in the arrangement of words than if only
one were there. Each of them takes its proper place. We
subjoin here some *enlarged compound sentences*, the words
forming the principal sentence being indicated by italics.

## Examples.

### I.

1. Ich behaupte, daß dieser Feldherr, welchen alle bewundern, sein Vaterland hätte retten können, wenn nicht die Menge (the numbers) der Feinde jeden Widerstand unmöglich gemacht hätte. — 2. Heinrich der Löwe wurde in die Acht erklärt (declared in outlawery), weil er seinen Kaiser verlassen hatte, als dieser mit den Lombardischen Städten kämpfte, welche sich der kaiserlichen Oberherrschaft zu entziehen (withdraw) strebten. — 3. Eine Mailändische Gesandtschaft von sechzehn adeligen Männern, an deren Spitze (head) die Konsuln der Stadt standen, begab sich nach Lodi, um mit dem Kaiser über die Unterwerfung zu unterhandeln. — 4. Was mir zu wissen frommt (profits); woran ich ohne Gefahr meiner Seele nicht zweifeln darf; das ist mit leserlicher (legible) Schrift in mein Gewissen eingegraben. — 5. Die Kluft (cleft) zwischen Gott und dem Menschen ist so groß, daß der Mensch zweifeln müßte, je zu dem Aufschauen des Höchsten zu gelangen, wenn ihm Gott nicht selbst entgegen käme.

### II.

1. Diejenigen, welche sich um ein Amt bewarben (solicited), kannte Philipp der Zweite, auch ehe sie sich vorstellen ließen, so gut wie von Person. — 2. Es giebt Gegenden der Erde, sowie Zeiten in der Geschichte des einzelnen (private) Menschen und ganzer Völker, in denen die Fülle der Lebenskräfte gleichsam (as it were) über ihre Dämme getreten ist, und wo mit jeder That das Vermögen zum Thun, mit dem Genuß das Sehnen (desire) sich steigert. — 3. Plato erzählt, daß Sokrates auf einem Feldzuge, den er mit Alcibiades gemeinschaftlich machte, von dem athenienschischen Heere gesehen worden sei, wie er einst einen ganzen Tag und eine Nacht lang bis an den anbrechenden Morgen unbeweglich auf einer Stelle stand, mit einem Blicke (countenance), welcher anzeigte, daß er sehr angestrengt über einen Gegenstand nachdachte. — 4. Wenn auch (though) einige Tiere an Gestalt dem Menschen ähnlich sind; wenn andre ihn an Körperkraft, an Schärfe einzelner Sinne übertreffen (excel); wenn noch andre merkwürdige Beweise von Klugheit geben: [so] bleibt doch zwischen ihnen und dem Menschen eine unübersteigliche Kluft, über welche die Tiere sich auf keine Weise anzunähern vermögen, weil ihnen die Vernunft, und deren (its) Ausdruck, die Sprache, fehlt.

### Aufgabe. 152.

This being resolved[1], my wife undertook to manage[2] the business herself. The horse was unfit[3] for the road, as wanting an eye. Leaving my cloak behind me, I set out[4] to view[5] the town a little. As I was going across[6] one of

1) beschlossen. 2) aus'führen. 3) untanglich. 4) machte ich mich auf den Weg, um. 5) betrachten, besehen. 6) über.

the principal squares[7], I was followed by[8] a little boy, who insisted on cleaning[9] my boots.　He was provided[10] with a footstool[11] and with brushes; and I do not doubt [but] that he would have polished[12] my boots admirably.　However I had neither time nor inclination[13], and as (ba) this was the case, I declined[14] the honour.　The boy followed me through several streets, and I never stopped[15] but (ohne baß) he put down (nieber ſtellte) his stool and wanted (wollte) to begin.　When he had exhausted[16] his powers of persuasion[17] and found me deaf[18] to entreaty[18] ʌhe ₂departed in search of[19] a less obstinate[20] subject[21].

7) Haupt=Pläße.　8) transl: ₃a ₄little ₅boy ₁followed ₂me ... See p. 346, Obs — 9) pußen, wichſen　10) verſehen.　11) Fuß= Schemel, m　12) wichſen.　13) noch Luſt.　14) ab'lehnen.　15) ſtehen bleiben.　16) erſchöpft.　17) ſeine Überrebungskunſt.　18) taub gegen alle Bitten.　19) um ... zu ſuchen　20) eigenſinnig.　21) einen .. Menſchen.

## Reading - lesson.
### Der eble Offizier.　(Schluß.)

Dann tritt[1] der Prior, ein ehrwürbiger Greis in Silberhaaren, mit Thränen in den Augen ihm entgegen[1], und alle weichen ehrfurchtsvoll zurück[2].　„Ebler Jüngling," ſpricht er, indem er ihn mit zitternden Armen an ſein Herz brückt, „für deine That iſt jeder Lohn zu klein; nur in deiner Bruſt findeſt du den würdigen.　Auch ſind wir arm und beſißen nichts, was wir dir anbieten könnten.　Ich ſelbſt habe nur dieſes Kreuz[3] mit Ebelſteinen, das ich als Zeichen meiner Würde[4] trage; nimm es, laß mich es dir umhängen, nicht als ein Geſchenk, ſondern als ein Andenken an die vergangene Nacht.　Zwar zieren ſchon zwei andre Ehrenzeichen[5] deine Bruſt; doch ſei das dritte, das die Menſchheit dir weiht[6], dir nicht minder (less) wert!　Wehe[7] dem Tapfern, der nicht menſchlich iſt; aber Segen über jeden Krieger, der ſo fortfährt, Menſch zu ſein.　Darum ſegnen dich die Geretteten, darum ſegne ich dich, darum ſegne[8] dich Gott! —"

Der Hauptmann riß ſich tief erſchüttert[9] los und kehrte mit ſeiner braven Schar[10] in das Lager zurück.　Aber wie ward ihm zu Mute[11], als er am andern Morgen von einem ſeiner Freunde erfuhr, daß der franzöſiſche General von dem Vorfall[12] unterrichtet ſei!　Alle Offiziere waren von dieſem zur Tafel eingeladen; der Hauptmann durfte nicht fehlen.　Mit männlicher Faſſung[13] und geſtärkt von dem Bewußtſein[14] ſeiner hochherzigen That, ging er einer vielleicht entehrenden[15] Strafe entgegen, weil er den Befehl ſeines Vorgeſetzten[16] nicht befolgt hatte.　Der General empfing

1) came to met.　2) make room for him respectfully.　3) cross. 4) dignity.　5) decoration, badge of an order.　6) to dedicate, to devote. 7) Woe!　8) see p. 319, § 11.　9) moved.　10) troop.　11) how did he feel?　12) event. — 13) countenance, resignation.　14) consciousness.　15) dishonouring, infamous.　16) superior.

ihn mit hohem Ernste und winkte[17] ihm in ein Nebenzimmer. Mit klopfendem Herzen folgt der Hauptmann. Sie sind allein. Jetzt ergreift der General seine Hand, blickt ihn mit feuchtem[18] Auge eine Weile an, reißt ihn an sich, umarmt ihn mit Heftigkeit[19] und spricht: „Sie verstehen mich!“ Dann kehrte er mit ihm zur Ge= sellschaft zurück.

Wer möchte[20] nicht so gefehlt, wer möchte nicht so gestraft haben! Der Hauptmann schickte das Kreuz seinen Verwandten[21] und schrieb dabei. „Das ist die einzige Beute[22], die ich in Spa= nien gemacht habe und machen werde. Ungern trenne ich mich davon. Verkauft es und bezahlt davon meine Schulden, die ich hinterlassen habe." — Die Verwandten hatten aber schon längst die Schulden bezahlt und bewahren das Kreuz nun als einen Familienschatz[23].

17) to beckon.   18) moist   19) violence.  2)) would not like.
21) relations.  22) booty, spoil   23) heir-loom.

### Questions.

Wer trat dem Hauptmann entgegen?
Wie redete der Prior den Hauptmann an (address)?
Welches Andenken (token) gab er ihm?
Was geschah am andern Morgen im Lager?
Wie ging der Hauptmann zu seinem General?
Was hatte er zu fürchten?
Wie empfing ihn der General?
Welches waren seine Worte?
Was schrieb der Hauptmann an seine Verwandten, als er das Kreuz nach Hause schickte?
Was hatten die Verwandten schon vorher gethan?
Was ist aus dem Kreuze geworden?

---

# Promiscuous Exercises for Translation and Conversation.
(Continuation from page 375.)
### 18.

Are you acquainted with the French captain M.? Yes, Sir, I made his acquaintance last year at Baden. — Has the servant cleaned my spurs[1]? He is still cleaning them. — Has the butcher bought fat[2] oxen? He has bought fat oxen and cows, but no calves, nor[3] sheep. — Is this the coach-office[4]? Yes, Madam, here it is. — When does the stage-coach[5] start[6]? There is one in the morning at seven o'clock, and one in the evening at six. — How many places have you left (übrig) in the evening coach[7]? There are only two left. —

1) Spor(n)en. 2) fett 3) und keine 4) die Fahrpost. 5) der Eil= wagen or Postwagen 6) abgehen. 7) der Abendwagen

I want three, can I have them for to-morrow? Yes, you can have them. — How much do you charge[8] for a place? Three marcs and a half. — Do (the) children pay full[9] price? No, children pay only the half price. — When must I send the luggage[10]? An hour before the coach starts[6]. — At what o'clock shall we arrive at B.? In the afternoon between three and four. — Shall we pass[11] through S.? No, you leave the town to your left.

8) verlangen. 9) ben ganzen or vollen Preis. 10) bas Gepäck. 11) kommen, passieren.

## 19.

What is his manner of life[1]? He lives very retired[2]. — What services does he render[3] his fellow-citizens[4]? None, that (soviel) I know [of]. — Is he resolved to sell his estate[5]? He will sell it, if he finds a purchaser[6]. — How much does he ask for it? He asks 5000 pounds. — How long *have* you *been* in Germany? I have been here these three months. — How much do you pay a month[7] for your lodgings[8]? I pay a hundred marcs a month. — How many rooms have you? I have five rooms, viz.: a parlour (Besuchzimmer), a dining-room, and three bed-rooms — What curtains[9] have you? I have white and red curtains. — Have you your own furniture (Möbel, *pl.*)? No, I have hired it (*pl.*). — How much do you pay for it? A hundred and twenty marcs for six months. — How many English miles[10] make one German mile? Six English miles are equal[11] to one German mile. — How far is it from Heidelberg to Frankfort? It is ten German miles or sixty English miles. — Were your parents in Switzerland last year? They were not there last year, but they intend going there this year.

1) bie Lebensweise. 2) zurückgezogen. 3) leisten. 4) ber Mitbürger. 5) bas Gut or Landgut. 6) Käufer. 7) monatlich. 8) Wohnung, *sing.* 9) Borhang, m. 10) bie Meile. 11) gleich (*Dat.*).

## 20.

To whom have you presented[1] your flowers? To the lady who came to see my sister. — What wine is that? Good old Rhine wine[2]. — Where can I buy good ink? The stationer[3] in William-Street sells very good ink. — Which do you prefer, veal or mutton? I like both, but I prefer ham. — What have you bought in this·shop[4]? I bought steel-pens and pencils. — Where have you seen the finest horses? In England. — Is there an English physician in this town? Yes, there are two English physicians and a French one here. — Is [there] good wine to be had[5] here?

1) überreichen or schenken. 2) Rheinwein. 3) ber Papierhändler or Schreibmaterialienhändler. 4) Laden. 5) zu haben.

Yes, but bad beer. — How much richer are you than your
neighbour? I need⁶ not tell you — Which flowers are finer
than mine? The flowers of my (female-) neighbour are much
prettier. — Which edifice⁷ is the highest in the town? The
church is the highest. — Why do you not let him alone
(gehen)? I want to speak to him.

'    6) id) braudje. 7 Gebäube. n.

### 21.

Has the coachman put the horses to¹ [the coach]? Nobody has ordered it — Have you sent for the music-master?
Yes [I have], but he is not at home. — Is it allowed to
speak to (mit) the prisoners? That cannot be allowed. —
May the tailor come in? He may come in. — Does this
young man smoke cigars? Yes, he smokes every day five
or six. — Have you already spoken to the advocate²? I spoke
to him, but he would (wollte) not hear me — Who can
judge³ a person⁴ without knowing him? Nobody should do
so (das). — Are you not allowed to play in this room? No,
we must play in the yard. — Did (hat) the lady allow the
children (dat.) to play in her room? Yes, she did, but only
[for] an hour. — What shall I say of such behaviour⁵? You
must blame⁶ it. — What am I to do? You are to work instead
of playing. — Ought⁷ I to have gone to Baden? Either to
Baden or to Ems — Are these men really so selfish⁸?
They (es) are the most selfish men I ever have known. —
Is anybody knocking⁹? Yes, some one has knocked at (an)
the door. — Who is there? It is I, your friend B. — How
do you do? I thank you, I am quite well.

    1) an'fpannen. 2) ber Abvofat'. 3) beurteilen. 4) einen Menfchen.
5) bas Benehmen or Betragen. 6) tabeln. 7) See p 94, 5. —
8) eigennützig. 9) Klopfen.

### 22.
(On verbs governing the dative: see p. 345.)

Why did you not thank your master? I have not seen
him since last week. — What is the matter with you (was
fehlt Ihnen)? I am not quite well. — The father would no
more believe his son, because he had told a falsehood —
Do not wish him anything bad. — This cloak belongs not
to you, it belongs to the doctor. — What did the baron
present (fchenfen) to his niece? He presented her [with] a
new bonnet. — I wish you [a] good morning. — To which
physician did you send your card? I sent it to Dr. Murray. —
Have you anything to tell me? Yes, I have a word to say
to you. — What is it? I must tell you alone. — Do you
understand what I say? I understand you well. — Why
don't you answer me (dat.)? I do not know what I am to

answer you. — What do you mean by that (bamit)? Nothing
that (was) concerns[1] you. — What is your age (How old
are you)? I am fifteen years old. — How old is your brother?
He is near[2] eighteen. — I thought he *was*[3] older.

1) betreffen (*acc* ). 2) beinahe. 3) wäre (see p. 317, § 7).

## 23.

' (ON MEETING.) Good morning, Sir. — I have the
honour to wish you [a] good day — How do you do[1] to-
day? I hope you are in good health. — I am very well. —
How does your father do? He is not quite well. — How
do all the family do? (*or* How do they all do at home?) I
thank you, all are in good health. — How is Mrs. R., your
aunt? She is a good deal (viel) better. She is tolerably[2]
well. — She is rather[2] unwell. She is very ill. — What
ails her (fehlt ihr)? (What is the matter with her?) She has
got a cold (sich erkältet) I am very sorry to hear it. — How
long[3] has[4] she *been* (schon) ill (unwell)? I did not know
that she was ill. — What is her illness? She has a fever[5]. —
Does she take anything for it? The doctor attends[6] her every
day. He says that it will not be of any consequence (von
Bedeutung) So much the (Desto) better. I am[7] very glad to
hear it.

1) sich befinden. 2) ziemlich. 3) seit wann. 4) see p. 309, 4. —
5) das Fieber 6, besuchen. 7) Es freut mich sehr.

## 24.

(NEWS.) Is there any news[1] to-day? Do you know
anything new? What news can you tell us? I know nothing
new. There is no (nichts) news. I have not heard of anything. —
*Did* you read the news-papers? What do the papers say?
I have read no paper to-day. Did you see that in a paper?
It is only mentioned[2] in a private (Privat'=) letter. This
news[3] wants[4] confirmation[4]. I have that news[4] from (aus)
a good authority[5]. I have it from the first hand. — *Has* that
news *been* confirmed? That news has proved (sich als . . gezeigt)
false[6]. — Is war still spoken of (do *people* still talk of war)?
No, people speak no longer of it. — Have you heard anything of (von) your brother? I have not[7] heard from him
these[8] two months. He has not written for (seit) three months.
I expect a letter from him every day.

1) etwas Neues. 2) erwähnt. 3) Nachricht, f. 4) bedarf der Be-
stätigung 5) Quelle, f 6) falsch. 7) nichts. 8) seit

## 25.

(BREAKFAST AND DINNER.) Have you breakfasted?
Not yet. You come just in time (gerade recht); you will
breakfast with us. — Breakfast is ready. — Do you drink

tea or coffee? I prefer coffee. — Which shall I offer you?
Here are rolls[1] and toast[2]. — What do you like best?
I will take (of) both. — How do you like (finden Sie) the
coffee? Is it strong enough? It is excellent. — Is it sweet
enough? I find it quite sweet — At what time do we dine
to-day? Do we dine at five o'clock? No, we shall not dine
before six o'clock. — Shall we have anybody at dinner to-
day? We expect Mr. Black and Miss White. — What have
we [got] for our (zum)- dinner? Shall we have any fish?
There was not a fish in the market. — What shall I help[3]
you to[3]? Will you have some soup? I thank you, I will
trouble you for (bitten um) a little beef. It looks so very
nice. — Which way (Wie) shall I cut it? Any way (Wie Sie
wollen). — Will you have it well done (weich) or underdone[4]?
Rather well done, if you please. I do not like it underdone.
I hope this piece is to your liking[5]. It is excellent. Now I
am going to send you a piece of (von) this pie[6]. I had
rather take a little piece of that pudding[7]. Try[8] both. —
Shall I send you a slice[9] of this leg of mutton (Hammels-
keule)? Give me but very little of it. You eat nothing. I beg
your pardon, I am eating very heartily (mit gutem Appetit).

1) Milchbrote 2) geröstete Brotschnitten. 3) vorlegen. 4) wenig
gekocht, halbweich. 5) nach Ihrem Geschmack 6) Pastete, f. 7) der
Pudding, Kloß. 8) versuchen. 9) eine Schnitte

## 26.

### (TRAVELLING BY RAIL-ROAD) (mit der Eisenbahn).

I intend to set off to-morrow for Paris. At what o'clock does
the first train[1] start[2]? Here is the time-table[3] for the
summer with the fares (Preisen). — The first is a mixed
(gemischt) train and goes very slowly. — Does it stop often?
It stops at every intermediate station (Zwischenstation), and
is liable[4] to all sorts of delays[5]. — The next train goes much
faster. — Where is the railway-station[6] (depot)? Near[7] the
gate on the right hand. — Where do you get the tickets
(Billete)? The first opening[8] on the left hand is for the
second and first classes, and the next for the third. — How
are the second class carriages made? They are covered in
(gedeckt), and have windows or slides[9] on (an) the sides. —
Are the seats[10] stuffed[11]? No, only in the first class carriages
you find stuffed seats. — What have I to pay? Fifty francs
for yourself and five francs for your luggage[12]. — Where is
my luggage? The porter is just taking it from the scales[13]
and bringing it out (heraus).. — Will he place it on the top

1) der Zug 2) ab'gehen. 3) der Fahrplan. 4) unterworfen —
5) Verzögerung 6) Bahnhof, m. 7) bei. 8) Schalter, m 9) Schieb-
fenster. 10) Sitz, m. (or Bank, f). 11) gepolstert. 12) Gepäck, n. —
13) die Wage, sing.

of (oben auf) the carriage in which I have taken my seat?
No, Sir, all [the] luggage is put into the luggage-van[14].
Now, farewell[15]!

14) ber Gepäckwagen. 15) Leben Sie wohl!

---

# Anecdotes for Translation into German.

## 1.

A sick man being asked[1], why he did[2] not send for
(nach) a physician, answered[3]: »It is, because I have no mind
(Lust), *to *die *yet« (schon).

1) Als ein . . . gefragt wurbe, see p. 332. 2) verb last 3) In
German, the pronoun er (he) must be added, when a sentence
begins with a subordinative conjunction.

## - 2.

Milton being asked by (von) a friend, whether (ob) he
would instruct[1] his daughters in the different[2] languages[3],
replied[4]. »No, Sir, one tongue[5] is sufficient[6] for a woman.«

1) unterrichten 2) verschieben. 3) Sprachen. 4) see 1, Note 3.
5) bie Zunge, bie Sprache 6) genug

## 3.

An Irishman meeting[1] another (Dat.) asked him: »What
has (ist) become[2] of (aus) our old friend John?« »Alas, (ach)!
my dear,« replied the other, »poor John[3] was[4] condemned[5]
to be[6] hanged, but he saved his life by dying[7] in (im
prison[8]«

1) Als ein Irländer begegnete 2) geworben 3) put the definite article. 4) Passive voice 5) P. p. verurteilt 6) gehängt zu
werben. 7) ba'burch, baß er . . starb 2c (see p. 331, § 7). 8) Ge=
fängnis, n.

## 4.

Socrates being asked by one of his friends, which (welches)
*was[1] *the *way, to gain[2] a good reputation[3], replied[4]: »You
will gain it, if you endeavour[5] to be, what you desire to
appear[6].«

1) wäre, see p. 146, Obs. 2. — 2) zu erwerben. 3) einen guten
Namen, m. 4) see above 1, Note 3. — 5) sich bemühen 6) scheinen

## 5.

An Alderman[1] of London *once *requested[2] an author[3]
to write a speech[4] for him to speak[5] at Guildhall »I must
first dine with you«, replied he, »and see, how you open your
mouth[6], in order to know, what sort of[7] words [will] fit it[8].«

1) Ratsherr 2) bitten, irreg. v. see p. 164. — 3) Schriftsteller.
4) eine Rede. 5) welche er in G. halten wollte. 6) Munb, m. 7) was
für Wörter, s. p. 73, 2 8) für ihn passen.

### 6.

An old philosopher[1] observing a young man, who[2] had
₂to ₃great ₁a ₄volubility[3] of tongue[4], spoke thus to him:
»Take notice[5], my friend, that nature[6] has given us two
ears, and but (nur) one mouth, that[7] we [may] ₂listen ₁much,
and ₂speak ₁little.«

1) Philosoph'. 2) relat. pron, see p. 149. — 3) Geläufigkeit, f.
4) put the article 5) Bedenken Sie 6) bie Natur. 7) bamit'.

### 7.

The celebrated Molière, who[1] was at one time prohibited[1]
from representing[2] Tartuffe, revenged[3] himself (on the) next
day, by saying[4] to the spectators[5] after the play[6]: »I am
very sorry, gentlemen. You should have had (bekommen) to-
day the Tartuffe, but the first president will[7] not have *him*
to be played«[7].

1) welchem.. verboten wurbe. 2) aufzuführen 3) sich rächen, reg v.
4) baburch, baß (or inbem) er zu.. 5) Zuschauer. 6) Schauspiel, n.
7) will nicht haben, baß man ihn (*himself*) spiele.

### 8.

A certain professor, lecturing[1] a young man on (wegen)
his ₁rregular[2] conduct[3], added[4] with great pathos[5]: »The
report[6] of your vices[7] will bring your (*Gen.*) father's grey
hair (*pl.*) with sorrow[8] to (in) the grave[9].« — »I beg[10] your
pardon, Sir,« replied the pupil, »my father wears[11] a wig[12].«

1) tabeln 2) unorbentlich 3) Betragen, n. 4) bei-fügen, reg
5) Pathos, m, Salbung, f 6) bie Nachricht von 7) Laster, n.
6) Kummer. 9) bas Grab. 10) Ich bitte um Verzeihung. 11) tragen,
ir. v. 12) Perücke, f.

### 9.

A nobleman of N. standing at a window, and seeing (*saw
how*) an ass-driver[1] beat his ass unmercifully[2], cried to him[3]:
»Have done[4], have done, rascal[5], else (sonst) ₂I ₁shall have you
whipped[6].« The ass-driver answered: »Pardon, good Sir, I
did not know, that my ass had friends (relations)[7] at court
(bei Hofe).«

1) Eseltreiber. 2) unbarmherzig. 3) rief er ihm zu. 4) hören Sie
auf 5) Schlingel. 6) peitschen lassen (see p. 295, § 4. 7) Verwandte

### 10.

When (Als) Cortez returned[1] to Spain, ₂he ₁was coolly[2]
received[3] by the emperor Charles V. One day[4], he suddenly
presented[5] himself to the monarch[6]. »Who are you?« said
the emperor haughtily[7]. »The man,« said Cortez, as[8] haught-

1) zurückkehren 2) kalt. 3) empfangen 4) Eines Tages 5) stellte
er sich... vor. 6) ber Monarch', König. 7) stolz. 8) ebenso.

ily, »who has given you (*Dat.*) more provinces⁹, than your
ancestors¹⁰ left¹¹ you cities «

9) bie Proviṅʒ'. 10) Borfaḣren, pl. 11) .. ḣinterlaffen ḣaben

## 11.

A Persian¹ philosopher² being asked by³ what method he
had acquired so much knowledge⁴, answered: »I was never⁵
ashamed to ask⁶ questions when I was ignorant«⁷.

1) perfifḣ. 2) Pḣilofopḣ', m. 3) auf welḣe Weife. 4) Renntniffe, *pl.*
5) Iḣ fḣämte miḣ nie — 6) to ask questions = fragen, or Fragen
ſtellen 7) unwiffenb.

## 12.

A traveller came into the kitchen¹ of an inn² on (in) a
very cold night, and stood so close³ to the fire, that he burnt⁴
his boots. A man who sat in the chimney-corner⁵, cried to
him, »Sir you'll burn your spurs⁶ presently⁷.« — »My boots,
²you ¹mean, I suppose (vermutliḣ) ⁹« said the gentleman
»No, Sir,« replied the other, »they (biefe) are burnt already.«

1) bie Küḣe 2) Wirtsḣauß 3) naḣe bei (*Dat*). 4) an'brennen
see p 126, 6. 5) Ramin'=Ede, f 6) Spor(n)en. 7) gleiḣ

## 13.

A blacksmith¹ of a village murdered a man, and *was*
condemned to *be*² hanged. The chief peasants³ of the place
joined together⁴ and begged the judge that the blacksmith
might not suffer⁵, because he was⁶ necessary to the place
which could not miss⁷ a blacksmith, to shoe⁸ horses, mend⁹
wheels etc.¹⁰ But the judge said: »How ³then ¹can ²I fulfil¹¹
justice?« A labourer answered. »Sir, there are two weavers¹²
in the village, and for so small a place ²one¹³ ¹is enough,
hang the other.«

1) Sḣmieb 2) See Nr. 8, Note 6. — 3) bie vornehmſten Bauern.
4) traten ʒuſammen. 5) ben Tob niḣt leiben möḣte. 6) *Subjunctive.*
7) entbehren (*Acc*.). 8) um . ʒu beſḣlagen. 9) Räber außbeffern.
10) unb ſo weiter. 11 vollſtreden. 12) Weber. 13) *Nom masc.* see
p. 112, 1

## 14.

A gentleman who had lent a guinea for two or three
days to a man whose¹ promises he had not much faith in¹,
was very much surprised to find, that he very punctually
kept² his word [with] him. The same gentleman being some
time after³ desirous⁴ of borrowing⁵ a larger sum⁶, »»No,«
¹said ²the ³other, »you have deceived⁷ me once, and I am
resolved⁸ that you shall not do it a second time (Mal, n.) «

1) beffen Berfpreḣungen er niḣt traute. 2) to keep = ḣalten.
3) *adv.* naḣḣer'. 4) I was desirous of, iḣ wünſḣte 5) ʒu borgen.
6) Summe, f. 7) getäuſḣt. 8) entſḣloffen.

**15.**

A young fellow[1], having been very extravagant[2], wrote
to his father for (um) more money, and used[3] all means; but
nothing would prevail (helfen). At length he very ingeniously[4]
wrote to his father, that he was[5] dead, and desired (bat) him
to send [up] money to (um . . zu) pay [for] his burial[6].

1) Mensch or Mann. 2) verschwenderisch. 3) gebrauchen 4) witzig
or sinnreich 5) *Subj.* 6) Begräbnis, n.

**16.**

A very poor inhabitant of N. finding one night[1] thieves
in his house, said to them, without being concerned[2] at it:
»I do not know, what you look [for] in my house by night[3],
as[4] for me[4], I cannot find anything in it[5] in broad day-light[6].«

1) einmal nachts. 2) ohne darüber zu erschrecken 3) bei Nacht
4) was mich betrifft. 5) See p 142, 7. — 6) bei hellem Tage.

**17.**

A rich farmer[1] in Devonshire made a will[2] in which[3]
the following[4] article was found (stand): »I bequeath[5] to John
Wilkes, late[6] member of Parliament for Aylesbury, five thousand pound sterling, as (als) a grateful return[7] for the courage with which[3] he defended[8] the liberty of his country, and
opposed[9] the (*Dat.*) dangerous progress[10] of arbitrary power[11].«

1) Pächter. 2) Testament, n  3 see p 150, 5 (worin). — 4) der
folgende Artikel 5) vermachen 6) vormaligem Parlaments-Mitglied. —
7) Vergeltung 8) verteidigen. 9) sich . . . widersetzte. 10) Fortschritt, m.
11) Willkür-Herrschaft, f.

**18.**

The Emperors Theodosius, Arcadius and Honorius wrote
ı to (an) ıRufinus ıthe ıPrætor· »If anybody speaks ill (Böses)
of ourselves or of our administration[1], ıwe ıwill not *have*[2]
him *punished*. If he spoke through levity[3], he ought to *be*
despised[4]. If it be[5] through madness, he ought to *be* pitied[6]:
if it be (is) an injury[7], he ought to be pardoned[8] (ıone
ıshould pardon him) (*Dat.*).«

1) Regie'rung  2) lassen; see p 295, 4. — 3) aus Leichtsinn. —
4) verachtet werden. 5) wenn es aus Wahnsinn geschieht. 6) bedauert
werden 7) Beleidigung. 8) see p. 135, § 7.

**19.**

A countryman, who was passing[1] over the Pont-au Change[2]
at Paris, perceived no wares[3] in several [of the] shops[4].
Prompted[5] by curiosity, ıhe ıwent near (zu) a broker's[6] shop
»Sir,« asked he, with a silly[7] look[8], »tell me what goods[3] you
sell.« The merchant who wished, to amuse himself at the

1) ging. 2) die Change-Brücke. 3) Waren, *pl* 4) Laden, *pl.*
Läden. 5) Angetrieben von Neugier 6) Mäkler. 7) einfaltig. 8) Blick, m.

man's expense[9], answered: »I sell asses' heads«[10]. — »Faith
(wahrlich)«, replied the countryman, »you must have a great
demand[11] for[12] them, for (denn) I see but[13] one left (übrig) in
your shop.«

9) auf Koſten des Mannes 10) Eſelsköpfe 11) Nachfrage (f.).
12) barnach. 13) nur.

## 20.

Some courtiers made reproaches[1] to the emperor Sigis-
mond, because[2], instead of *having*[3] his vanquished enemies
put to death (töten), he[2] loaded[4] them with favours[5], and
put them in a situation[6] to hurt[7] him: »*Do I not destroy*[8] *my
enemies,*« said he, »*by making*[9] *them my friends*«[10]?

1) Vorwürfe. 2) weil er 3) laſſen (see p. 295, 4. — 4) über=
häuſen 5) Gunſtbezeigungen. 6) Lage, f. 7) ſchaben (Dat.). — 8) zer=
ſtören 9) see p. 331, § 7 and 9. — 10) zu; see p. 345, 3.

## 21.

Malec, vizir (Vezier) of the Caliph[1] Mostadi, had just
obtained[2] a victory[3] over the Greeks (acc.), and had taken[4]
their emperor in a battle. Having[5] *had* this prince brought[5]
into his tent (Zelt, n.) he asked him, what treatment[6] he
expected from the conqueror. »If you make war[7] like (wie)
a king,« answered the emperor, »send me back again: if you
wage[7] it like a merchant, sell me · if you make[7] it like a
butcher[8], slaughter[9] me « The Turkish General sent him back
without a ransom[10].

1) ber Kaliſe (2nd decl.) 2) erringen, gewinnen. 3) Sieg, m
4) gefangen genommen. 5) Nachbem er .. hatte bringen laſſen (see
p. 373, 2. — 6) eine Behandlung 7) Krieg führen. 8) ber Metzger
9) ſchlachten. 10) ein Löſegelb, n

## 22.

Some Frenchmen, who had landed on the coast[1] of Guinea,
found a negro[2]-prince seated[3] under a tree, on a block[4] of
wood for[5] his throne; three or four negroes[2], armed[6] with
wooden pikes[7] served for[8] his body-guard[9]. His sable[10] majesty
:anxiously[11] inquired[12] »Do they[13] talk much of me in
France?«

1) Küſte, f. 2) Neger. 3) ſitzend 4) Holzblock 5) ſtatt ſeines
Thrones 6) bewaffnet 7) Pike, Lanze, f. 8) als 9) Leibwache.
10) ſchwarz. 11) neugierig 12) fragte. 13) man.

## 23.

The Duke of Ossona, Viceroy[1] of Naples, *had* gone on
board[2] the gallies of the King of Spain, on (an) a great holiday, to indulge[3] himself in a right which he had to set a
slave at (in) liberty. He questioned several of them, who

1) Vizekönig von Neapel 2) auf bie Galeeren 3) um ein Recht
aus-zu-üben, welches.

all endeavoured to excuse themselves, and convince him of
(von) their innocence. One alone ₂ingenuously[4] ₁confessed[5]
his crimes[6], and said that he was deserving[7] [of] a still greater
punishment. *»Turn[8] this wicked fellow away«* said the Duke,
*»lest he* (bamit er nicht) *[should] pervert[9] these honest people.«*
  4) freimütig  5) gestehen, ir. v.  6) Verbrechen, n.  7) verdienen.
8) Jagen Sie . . . fort  9) verderbe.

## 24.

An apothecary[1] having refused[2], to resign[3] his seat at
the theatre to an officer's lady, the officer felt himself insulted
and sent him a challenge[4]. The apothecary was punctual at
(bei) the meeting (Zusammenkunft, *f.*); but he observed that he
was not accustomed to fire[5], and that he had to propose[6] a
way[7] of settling[8] the dispute. He ₂then ₁drew from (aus)
his pocket a pill-box[9], took from it two pills, and ₄thus ₁ad-
dressed[10] ₂his ₃antagonist[11]: »As (als) a man of honour, Sir,
₂you ₃certainly ₁would not wish to fight me[12] but on (nut)
equal terms (Waffen); here are two pills, one composed of
(aus) the most deadly poison[13], the other perfectly harmless[14]:
we are therefore on equal ground[15], if we each swallow[16]
one. You shall take your choice (die Wahl haben), and I
promise faithfully, to take that (*f.*) which you leave[17].« —
It is needless to say, that the affair (Sache) was settled[18] by
(durch) a heartly laugh.
  1) Ein Apotheker.  2) to refuse sich weigern    3) abzutreten
4) Herausforderung.  5) zu schießen.  6 vorzuschlagen.  7) Mittel, n
8) den Streit bei'zulegen  9) eine Pillen=Schachtel.  10) anreden.
11) Gegner.  12) = with me mit mir anders zu fechten als
13) Gift, n.  14) unschädlich  15) auf gleichem Boden.  16) verschlucken
17) übrig lassen  18) beigelegt.

## 25.

A beggar[1] soliciting[2] ₂alms (um ein Almosen) [of] ₁Dr.
Smollet, he gave him, through inadvertence[3], a guinea[4]
instead of a shilling. The poor fellow, who was lame, hobbled[5]
after him, and pointed out[6] the mistake[7]. »My God,« remarked
Smollet to a friend, who was with (bei) him, »what a wretched[8]
lodging has honesty[9] taken [up with]!« Thus saying[10] and
adding[11] another to it, he returned[12] the guinea to the over-
joyed (überglücklichen) and grateful beggar.
  1) Bettler. 2) bitten  3) aus Versehen. 4) Guinee', f. 5 hinkte
ihm nach. 6) erklärte  7) den Irrtum  8) elend  9) die Ehrlichkeit.
10) Indem er ꝛc. 11) und noch eine dazu fügte  12) zurück'geben

## 26.

A little girl, five years old, was equally[1] fond of[1] her
mother and grandmother. On (An) the birth-day of the latter,
  1) liebte gleich sehr.

₂her ₂mother ₁said to her   »My dear, you must pray[2] to God
to bless[3] your grandmamma, and that she may live[4] to be
very old.«   The child looked[5] with surprise *at* her mother,
who perceiving it, said. »Well[6]! will you not pray to God to
bless your grandmamma, and that she may become very old?«
»Ah, mamma!« said the child, »she is very old already, I
will rather[7] pray that she may become young.«

2) to pray to God = either Gott bitten or zu Gott beten.
3) baß er . . segne (*Subj.*). 4) sehr alt werbe. 5) to look *at* = an-
sehen, sep. v. 6) Ei! 7) lieber.

## 27.

The late[1] General Schott, so celebrated for his success[2]
in gaming[2], *was* one evening *playing* very high with the Count
d'Artois and the Duke de Chartres, at Paris, when a petition[3]
was brought up[4] from the widow[5] of a French officer, stating[6]
her various[7] misfortunes[8], and praying relief[9]. A plate *was*
handed[10] round, and each put in (hinein) one, two, or three
louisd'or, but when it *was* held[11] to the general, who was
going[12] to throw for a stake (Satz, m.) of five hundred louis-
d'or, he said: »Stop[13] a moment, if you please, Sir, here
goes[14] for the widow!« The throw[15] was successful[16]; and
he ₂instantly[17] ₁swept (schob) the whole into the plate, and
sent it down [to] her.

1) verstorben   2) wegen seines Glücks im Spiel. 3) eine Bittschrift
4) herauf   5) Witwe   6) to state barlegen (see p. 329, § 4) —
7) mannigfach   8) Unglücksfälle.   9) um Unterstützung   10) herum-
gereicht   11) vorgehalten   12) im Begriff war (see p. 294, 5) —
13) Halten Sie . .!   14) dieses gilt.   15) der Wurf.   16) glücklich, er-
folgreich.   17) sogleich

## 28.

Dr. Radcliffe ₂once ₁refused[1] to take a fee[2] for[3] attending
a friend during a dangerous illness. Upon (nach) his recovery,
however, the patient presented the proper[4] amount in a purse,
saying: »Sir, in this purse I have put every day's fee[5], and
your goodness must not get[6] the better of my gratitude.«
The doctor eyed[7] the purse, counted the number[8] of days,
and holding out[9] his hand, replied: »Well, I can hold out[10] no
longer; singly[11] I could have refused them for[12] a twelve-
month[12], but altogether they are irresistible«[13].

1) to refuse = sich weigern   2) ein Honorar.   3) dafür . . baß er
4) entsprechend.   5) das Honorar für jeden Tag   6) to get the better
of = übersteigen (*acc.*), or größer sein als.   7) betrachtete   8) Zahl, f
9) ausstrecken.   10) standhaft bleiben.   11) einzeln.   12) ein ganzes Jahr
lang   13) unwiderstehlich

## 29.

Sir Isaac Newton's temper[1] is said (soll) to have been so
equal[2] and mild, that no accident could disturb[3] it; a remark-
able instance[4] of which (davon) *is* related as (wie) follows.

1) das Gemüt   2) gleichmütig.   3) stören   4) Beispiel, n.

Sir Isaac had a favourite[5] little dog, which he called Diamond.
Being one evening called out of his study[6] into the next
room, Diamond remained behind (blieb D. zurück) When Sir
Isaac returned, having[7] been absent but a few minutes, ₂he
₁had the mortification[5] to find that Diamond had overturned[9]
a lighted[10] candle among some papers, which were the nearly
finished[11] labour of many years. The papers soon were
₁(ſtanden) in flames, and (were) almost consumed[12] to ashes.
This loss[13], ₂from[14] Newton's advanced age, ₁was irrepar-
able[15]; but, without punishing the dog, ₂he ₁exclaimed: »O,
Diamond! you (du) don't know what mischief[16] you have done!«

5) ein Lieblings-Hündchen  6) Studier'zimmer, n.  7) nachdem er nur.
8) den Verbruß  9) umgeworfen.  10) brennend  11) vollendet  12) zu
Aſche verbrannt  13) der Verluſt.  14) wegen N.'s hohen Alters. —
15) unerſetzlich.  16) das Unheil.

### 30.

The prince of Conti being[1] highly pleased with[1] the in-
trepid behaviour of a grenadier at the siege of Philipsburgh,
in 1734, threw him a purse, excusing[2] the smallness of the
sum[2] it contained[3], as[4] [being] ₂too ₃poor ₁a ₄reward for
such courage. Next morning, the grenadier went to the prince
with two diamond rings and other jewels[5] of considerable[6]
value. »Sir,« said he, »the gold I found in your purse I
suppose[7] you intended[7] for me; but these ₂I ₁bring back to
you, having[8] no claim to them (Anſpruch darauf).« — »You
have doubly deserved them by your bravery, and by your
honesty,« said the prince, »therefore you may keep them.«

1) welchem das unerſchrockene Benehmen .  ſehr gefiel.  2) indem
er ſich wegen der geringen Summe entſchuldigte.  3) die er enthielt
4) als eine.  5) Juwe'len.  6) beträchtlich, bedeutend  7) beſtimmten Sie
vermutlich  8) see p. 332, § 10, a.

### 31.

Casimir II, King of Poland[1], received a blow from a
Polish[2] gentleman, named[3] Konarsky, who had lost all his
money while playing[4] with the prince. Scarcely was the
blow given, when[5], sensible[5] of the enormity of his crime.
he betook[6] himself to flight; but he was soon apprehended[7]
by the king's guards, and condemned to lose his head. Casimir, who waited for (auf, Acc.) him in silence (silently) amid
his courtiers, as soon as he saw him appear, said: »I am not
surprised at (über) the conduct[8] of this gentleman. Not being
able[9] to revenge himself on (an dem) fortune, it is not to be
wondered[10] [at], that he has ill-treated[11] his friend. I am

1) Polen.  2) polniſch.  3) Namens  4) see p 331, § 9, 3rd Ex.
5) als er, im Bewußtſein der Größe .  .  6) ſich auf die Flucht begab
7) ergriffen  8) das Betragen  9) Da er ſich nicht ... konnte.  10) see
p 324, § 8, Note  11) mißhandeln, insep. v.

the only one (der einzige) to blame in this affair [12], for I ought not, by my example, to encourage [13] a pernicious practice [14], which may be the ruin of my nobility« [15] Then turning [16] to the criminal [17], he said: »I perceive, you are [18] sorry for your fault [18] — that is sufficient (*enough*); take your money again, and let us renounce gaming [19] for ever.«

12) Sache 13) ermutigen 14) eine verderbliche Gewohnheit — 15) Abel, m. 16) indem er sich . . wandte. 17) Verbrecher. 18) Ihr Fehler ist Ihnen leid. 19) auf das Spiel verzichten

## 32.

On [1] the morning of the day on [1] which Molière died, his wife and his friends, seeing how weak he was, tried to prevent his [2] going down to play that night — but in vain »A man,« he said, »suffers long ere (ehe) he dies: I feel that, with me [3], the end is at hand [3]; but there are fifty poor workmen, who have only their day's wages [4] to live on [5], — and who *is to* give them bread to-night, if I play not?« So he went down, and played the *Malade Imaginaire* [6]; then home to bed, and died.

1) An. 2) see p 330, § 7 — 3) daß es mit mir zu Ende geht. 4) Tagelohn, m. 5) wovon sie leben müssen 6) den eingebildeten Kranken

## 33.

It happened at Athens, during the public representation [1] of a play exhibited [2] in honour of the commonwealth [2], that an old gentleman came too late, to get [3] a place suitable [4] to his age and quality [5]. Many of the young gentlemen who observed the difficulty and confusion [6] he was in, made signs to him that they would accommodate [7] him, if he came (dahin käme) where they sat. The good man bustled [8] »through the crowd accordingly (daher); but when he came to the seats [9] to (zu) which he was invited, they sat close [10] and exposed him, as he stood out of countenance [11], to the whole audience [12]. The frolic [13] went round (durch) all the Athenian benches. But on (bei) those occasions [there] were also particular places assigned [14] for foreigners: when the good man skulked [15] towards the seats appointed [14] for the Lacedæmonians [16], these honest people rose all up, and with the greatest respect received him among them. The Athenians (Athener) being suddenly touched [17] with a sense of the Spartan virtue and their own degeneracy [18] gave a thundering applause [19]; and the

1) Aufführung 2) welches zu Ehren der Republik or des Freistaats gegeben wurde 3) see p 325, § 10 — 4) passend 5) Stand. 6) Verlegenheit, worin 7) ihm Platz machen 8) drängte sich 9) zu den Bänken 10) gedrängt 11) außer Fassung 12) dem Gelächter des ganzen Publikums 13) der Spaß, Scherz 14) bestimmt 15) schlich, sich drängte. 16) Lacedämonier 17) ergriffen von 18, Entartung 19) Beifall, m.

old man cried out· »The Athenians understand what is good,
but the Lacedæmonians practise[20] it «
·    20) üben es aus.

---

## DIONYSIUS, PYTHIAS and DAMON.*)
### (A DIALOGUE.)

*Dionysius.* Amazing[1]! what do I see? Pythias is arrived
— it is indeed Pythias. I did not think[2] it possible. He is
come to[3] die, and to redeem (erlöfen) his friend!

*Pythias.* Yes, it is Pythias. I had left the place (Ort,
*m.*) of my confinement[4] with no other views[5] than to pay
to Heaven the vows I had made, to settle[6] my family[6] concerns according (nach) to the rules of justice; and to bid
adieu[7] to my children, that (damit) I might die tranquil and
satisfied.

*Dionysius.* But why dost thou return? Hast thou no fear
of (vor dem) death? is it ₂not ₃mad ₁then, to seek it?

*Pythias.* I return to suffer[8], though I do not deserve
death. Honour forbids me to let my friend die for me.

*Dionysius.* Dost thou, then, love him better[9] than
thyself?

*Pythias.* No, I love him as[10] myself; but I know I ought
to suffer death rather than my friend, since (da) ₂it ₂was ₁I
whom thou hadst decreed to die (zum Tode verurteilt). It
were not just that Damon should suffer, to[11] free me from
that death which was not for him, but for me only.

*Dionysius.* But thou sayest that it is as unjust to inflict[12]
death [upon] thy friend.

*Pythias.* Very true, we are both innocent, and it is
equally[13] unjust to make (laffen) either of us suffer[8].

*Dionysius.* Why dost thou, then, say that it were wrong
to put[14] him to death instead of thee?

*Pythias.* It is equally unjust to inflict death either on
Damon or on myself; but I should be highly culpable to let
Damon suffer that death which the tyrant had prepared for me.

*Dionysius.* Dost thou return hither to-day with no other
view than to save the life of thy friend, by losing thy own?

1) Seltjam! 2) ich halte es nicht für möglich. 3) see p 325, § 10.
4) Gefangenschaft. 5) Absicht. 6) Familien-Angelegenheiten zu ordnen.
7) Lebewohl zu jagen 8 to suffer = den Tod erleiden. 9) mehr. —
10) wie 11; see p 325, § 10. — 12) dem Fr. den Tod aufzuerlegen
or ben Fr . . hinzurichten. 13) ebenfo. 14) to put somebody to
death = Einen .tec) hinrichten laffen

---

*) This piece may be translated more freely.

*Pythias.* I return, in regard to[1] thee, to suffer a death which it is common[2] for tyrants to inflict; and with respect to Damon, to perform my duty by freeing him from the danger which he incurred[3] by his kindness to (gegen) me

*Dionysius.* And now, Damon let me speak to thee  Didst thou really not fear that Pythias would never return, and that thou wouldst be put to death for him?

*Damon*  I was but (nur) too well assured, that Pythias would return· and that he would be more anxious[4] to keep (halten) his promise than to save his life.  Would to Heaven (wollte Gott) that his relations and friends had detained him by force.[5]  He would then have lived for the comfort and benefit[6] of good men; and I should then have had the satisfaction[7] of dying for him.

### Continuation.

*Dionysius.* What[9] art thou not fond of (liebst du — nicht) life?

*Damon.* No; I am not, when I see and feel the power of a tyrant.

*Dionysius.* It is well!  Thou shalt see him no more·  I will order thee to be put[8] to death (hinrichten lassen).

*Pythias.* Pardon the feelings of Damon, of a man who feels for his dying friend; but remember that it was I, who was devoted (geweiht) by thee to (dem) death.  I come to submit to it (mich ihm zu unterwerfen), that I may (um — zu) redeem my friend.  Do not refuse me this comfort in my last hour

*Dionysius*  I cannot endure (leiden) men who despise death and defy[9] my power

*Damon.* Thou canst not endure virtue.

*Dionysius.* No, I cannot endure that proud, disdainful (hochmütige) virtue, which contemns life, which dreads not pain, and which feels not the charms[10] of riches[11] and pleasure·

*Damon.* Thou seest, however, that it is a virtue which feels the dictates (Gebote) of honour, justice, and friendship

*Dionysius.* Guards, take (führet) Pythias to execution[12]  We shall see whether Damon will still despise my authority.

*Damon.* Pythias, by returning to submit[13] himself to thy pleasure[14] has merited his life, and [deserved] thy favour, but I have excited[15] thy indignation[16], by placing myself in

1) In Bezug auf   2; *turn: which* tyrants commonly inflict (auferlegen). 3) in welche er . . . geraten ist. 4) daß ihm mehr daran gelegen wäre. 5) mit Gewalt. 6) zum Troste und zum Wohle   7) Befriedigung  8) see p 326, § 12. — 9) trotzen (*Dat*)  10) Reize. — 11) Reichtum, m sing  12) zum Tode  13) sich unterwerfen (*refl v.*). 14) Willkür, f, Willen, m.  15) erregen  16) Unwillen, m.

thy power, in order to save him. Be ²satisfied, ¹then (alfo), with this sacrifice¹, and put me to death.

*Pythias.* Hold, Dionysius; remember, it was I alone that offended thee; Damon could not.

*Dionysius* Alas, what do I see and hear? — Where am I? How miserable, and how worthy to be so (eŝ)! I have hitheɪto known nothing of (von) true virtue. I have spent my life in daɪkness and error². Not all my power and honours are sufficient to produce love. I cannot boast³ of having⁴ gained a single friend in the course⁵ of a reign of thirty years, and yet these two persons⁶, in priɪate life⁷, love one another tenderly, ²fully ¹confide⁸ in (auf) each other, are mutually happy, and ready to die for each other.

*Pythias.* How couldst thou, who⁹ hast never loved any person, expect to have friends? If thou hadst loɪed and respected men, thou wouldst have secured¹⁰ their love and respect. Thou hast feared and oppressed¹¹ mankind (ɒie Menſчen), and they [both] fear and detest¹² thee

*Dionysius.* Damon, Pythias, condescend¹³ to admit me as a third friend in a ²connection¹⁴ ¹so ²perfect¹⁵. I give (ſ陆enfe) you ɟour liɪes (*Sing.*), and I will load¹⁶ you with ɪiches.

*Damon.* We have no desire to be enriched¹⁷ by thee: and as to¹⁸ thy friendship, we cannot accept or enjoy it, till thou become good and just. Without these qualities, ²thou ¹canst be connected with none · but (mit niemanɒ alŝ mit) trembling slaves and base flatterers¹⁹ To be loɪed and esteemed by men²⁰ of free and generous minds²⁰, thou must be virtuous, kind, just, and know²¹ [how] to liɪe on a soɪt of equality (auf gleiчem Fuſⓔe) with those who share²² and deserve thy friendship

1) Opfer, n. 2) Ɉɪɪtum, m. 3) to boaɪt = ſiч rühmen *refl. v.*). 4) see p. 329, § 5. — 5¹ Lauf. 6) Perſonen 7ɪ im Priɪat'leben — 8) vertɪanen 9) bu, ber bɪ, see p 300, I. — 10) ſiчeɪliч erworben. 11 unterbrücɪt 12ɪ verabſчenen 13) ſeib ſɔ gut or gewährt mir ɒie Bitte. 14) Bunb, m. 15) vollfɪmmen 16) überhäuſen 17 bɪeɪчern 18ɪ aɪ to waŝ .. betɪifft 19) Schmeiчler 20ɪ von freiſinnigen unb ebelmütigen Männeɪn. 21) verſtehen 22ɪ teilen

More such pieces will be found iɪ the little volume. **Materials for translating Fnglish into German by Dr. Emil Otto**, (5th Edit) which is to be considered as a continuation of this grammar.

## Materials for German conversation.

**1.**

| | |
|---|---|
| Was haben Sie da? | What have you there? |
| Was wollen Sie kaufen? | What do you wish to buy? |
| Haben Sie etwas gekauft? | Did you buy anything? |
| Wieviel (was) kostet das Kilo? | How much a kilo? |
| Das Kilo kostet zwei Mark | Two marcs a kilo |
| Ich finde das sehr teuer. | I find this very dear. |
| Das ist sehr wohlfeil (or billig). | This is very cheap. |
| Haben Sie Ihr Pferd verkauft? | Have you sold your horse? |
| Ich habe es noch nicht verkauft. | I have not yet sold it. |
| Wollen Sie es nicht verkaufen? | Will you not sell it? |
| Ja, ich will es verkaufen | Yes, I will sell it. |
| Warum wollen Sie es verkaufen? | Why will you sell it? |
| Ich brauche Geld | I want some money |
| Bringen Sie mir Brot und Butter | Bring me some bread and butter |
| Ich habe genug gegessen (bin satt | I have eaten enough. |
| Haben Sie ein Glas Wein getrunken? | Did you drink a glass of wine? |
| Hier ist frisches Wasser | Here is some fresh water. |
| Tragen Sie diesen Brief auf die Post | Take this letter to the post-office. |
| Was sagen Sie? | What do you say? |
| Ich sage nichts (gar nichts). | I say nothing (at all). |
| Mit wem sprechen Sie? | To whom do you speak? |
| Verstehen Sie, was ich sage? | Do you understand what I say? |
| Ich verstehe nicht alles | I do not understand all. |

**2**

| | |
|---|---|
| Was verlangen Sie? | What do you ask for? |
| Was wünschen Sie? | What do you wish for? |
| Ich verlange nichts | I (require) ask for nothing |
| Haben Sie die Güte. | Have the goodness. Be so kind. |
| Sie würden mich sehr verbinden. | You would oblige me very much. |
| Sie sind sehr gütig. | You are very kind. |
| Was suchen Sie da? | What are you looking for? |
| Ich suche meine Uhr. | I am looking for my watch. |
| Was wollen Sie thun? | What are you about to do? |
| Was machen or thun Sie da? | What are you doing there? |
| Ich lerne meine Aufgabe. | I am learning my lesson. |
| Ich werde es mit Vergnügen thun. | I shall do it with pleasure. |
| Wissen Sie, ob er kommen wird? | Do you know, if he will come? |
| Ich weiß es nicht. | I do not know — (it). |
| Ich weiß nichts davon | I know nothing about it |
| Kennen Sie diesen Mann? | Do you know this man? |
| Ich kenne ihn sehr gut. | I know him very well |
| Ich kenne ihn von Gesicht | I know him by sight. |
| Ich kenne ihn nicht. | I do not know him |

### 3.

| | |
|---|---|
| Glauben Sie das? | Do you believe this (so)? |
| Glauben Sie das (doch) nicht. | Do not believe that. |
| Ich glaube es nicht | I do not believe it. |
| Das ist wahr. Das ist Wahrheit. | That is true. That is truth. |
| Ich bin Ihrer Meinung (Ansicht). | I am of your opinion. |
| Sie spaßen, Sie scherzen | You joke. |
| Sind Sie mit ihm zufrieden? | Are you contented with him? |
| Sind Sie befriedigt? | Are you satisfied? |
| Wir sind damit zufrieden | We are contented (with it) |
| Ich bin Ihr Diener | I am your servant. |
| Das ist allerliebst. | That is charming. |
| Welches Vergnügen! | What pleasure! |
| Welche Freude! | What joy! |

### 4.

| | |
|---|---|
| Wer ist da? | Who is there? |
| Es ist mein Bruder Karl. | It is my brother Charles. |
| Wohin' gehen Sie? | Where are you going? |
| Wir gehen ins Theater | We are going to the theatre. |
| Wohin' geht die Köchin? | Where does the cook go? |
| Sie geht auf den Markt. | She goes (is going) to the market. |
| Woher' kommen Sie? or | Whence do you come? |
| Wo kommen Sie her? | Where do you come from? |
| Ich komme aus der Schule | I come from school. |
| Wir kommen aus dem Konzert'. | We come from the concert. |
| Sie kommt von dem Ball | She comes from the ball |
| Gehen Sie jetzt nach Hause? | Are you going home now? |
| Gehen Sie nicht so schnell. | Do not go so fast |
| Ruhen Sie ein wenig aus. | Rest a little. |
| Kommen Sie bald wieder | Come back soon |
| Gehen Sie hinauf — hinunter | Go up (stairs), go down (stairs). |
| Gehe fort! Gehen Sie fort! | Go away! Be off! (leave). |

### 5

| | |
|---|---|
| Guten Morgen (Tag), mein Herr. | Good morning, Sir. |
| Guten Abend, mein Herr. | Good evening, Sir. |
| Setzen Sie sich. | Sit down, be seated |
| Nehmen Sie Platz. | Take a seat. |
| Wie befinden Sie sich? | How do you do? |
| Sehr gut, ich danke Ihnen | Very well, I thank you. |
| Und Sie (selbst)? | And you (yourself)? |
| Wie geht es Ihnen? | How are you? |
| Nicht sehr gut. | Not very well. |
| Ziemlich gut. | Tolerably well (pretty well). |
| Zeigen Sie mir gefälligst. | Show me, if you please. |
| Ich bitte Sie or bitte, sagen Sie mir | Please tell me. |
| Geben Sie mir. Leihen Sie ihm | Give me. Lend him. |
| Machen Sie mir das Vergnügen | Do me the pleasure. |
| Ich bitte Sie darum | I beg you. |
| Ich danke Ihnen. | I thank you. |
| Sehr verbunden. | Very much obliged to you. |

| | |
|---|---|
| Iſt Herr N zu Hauſe? | Is Mr. N. at home? |
| Ja, er iſt zu Hauſe. | Yes, Sir, he is at home. |
| Sind Sie ein Deutſcher? | Are you a German? |
| Ich bin ein Engländer. | I am an Englishman. |
| Dieſe Dame iſt eine Engländerin. | This lady is an Englishwoman |

### 6.

| | |
|---|---|
| Wieviel Uhr iſt es? | What o'clock is it? |
| Es iſt ſpät, es iſt neun Uhr. | It is late, it is nine o'clock |
| Wann werden Sie ausgehen? | At what o'clock do you go out? |
| Ich werde um 10 Uhr ausgehen. | I shall go out at ten o'clock. |
| Um halb acht Uhr. | At half past seven. |
| Um breiviertel auf ſieben or ein Viertel vor ſieben | At a quarter to seven. |
| Um ein Viertel auf ſechs or Um ein Viertel nach fünf | At a quarter past five. |
| Punkt 7 Uhr. | At seven precisely. |
| Um Mittag.  Um zwölf Uhr. | At noon, at twelve. |
| Um Mitternacht | At midnight. |
| Geſtern morgen | Yesterday morning |
| Geſtern abend. | Yesterday evening, last night. |
| Vorgeſtern | The day before yesterday. |
| Heute  —  Morgen | To-day.  —  To-morrow. |
| Morgen früh. | To-morrow morning. |
| Übermorgen. | The day after to-morrow. |
| Vor acht, vierzehn Tagen. | A week ago, a fortnight ago. |
| In ſechs Wochen. | In six weeks. |
| In einigen Tagen | In a few days. |
| Von einem Tag zum andern. | From one day to another. |

### 7

| | |
|---|---|
| Was für Wetter iſt heute? | How is the weather to-day? |
| Es iſt ſchönes (ſchlechtes) Wetter. | It is fine (bad) weather |
| Was für herrliches Wetter! | What beautiful weather! |
| Es iſt ſehr heiß (warm) — (kalt) | It is very hot (warm) — (cold). |
| Es regnet. | It rains, it is raining. |
| Es iſt nur ein Schauer. | It is but a shower |
| Es iſt ſehr windig. | It is very windy. |
| Haben Sie (or Iſt Ihnen) warm? | Are you warm? |
| Frieren Sie (or haben Sie kalt)? | Are you cold? |
| Wir werden ein Gewitter bekommen. | We shall have a thunder-storm. |
| Es donnert — Es blitzt. | It thunders.  It lightens. |
| Haben Sie den Donner gehört? | Did you hear the thunder? |
| Welch ein ſchöner Regenbogen | What a beautiful rainbow! |
| Es geht ein kalter Wind. | It is a cold wind. |
| Der Winter kommt heran. | Winter draws near. |
| Es gefriert | It freezes. |
| Es hat dieſe Nacht gefroren. | It has frozen last night. |
| Es iſt glatt zu gehen. | It is very slippery. |
| Es ſchneit (es fällt Schnee). | It snows. |
| Die Sonne ſcheint. | The sun shines. |
| Im Sonnenſchein | In sunshine. |
| Die Sonne geht unter. | The sun sets. |
| Im Mondſchein | In the moonlight. |

| | |
|---|---|
| Die Sonne geht prächtig auf. | The sun rises beautifully. |
| Es ist dunkel (nacht). | It is dark (night). |
| Es ist heller, lichter Tag. | It is bright day-light. |

---

## Idiomatical Expressions.

### 1.

| | |
|---|---|
| Wer hat es Ihnen gesagt? | Who (has) told you? |
| Was soll das heißen? | What is the meaning of that? |
| Wie nennt man (wie heißt) dieses? | What do you call this? |
| Was ist zu thun? | What is to be done? |
| Was halten Sie davon? | What do you think about it? |
| Das freut mich sehr. | I am very glad (of it). |
| Es thut mir sehr leid. | I am very sorry. |
| Ich habe Langeweile. | I am weary. |
| Ich bin es. Wir sind es. | It is I. It is we (us). |
| Ich gehe meinem Freund entgegen. | I go to meet my friend. |
| Gehen Sie Ihres Weges. | Go your way. |
| Das geht Sie nichts an. | That does not concern you. |
| Was fehlt Ihnen? | { What ails you? <br> { What is the matter with you? |
| Ich habe Kopfweh. | I have a head-ache. |
| Ich habe einen bösen Finger. | I have a sore finger. |
| Es fehlt mir nichts. | Nothing is the matter with me. |
| Haben Sie Geld bei sich? | Have you any money about you? |
| Sie sehen gut aus. | You look well. |
| Wollen Sie mir Gesellschaft leisten? | Will you keep me company? |
| Es ist Zeit zum Essen. | It is time for dinner. |
| Ist der Tisch gedeckt? | Is the cloth laid? |
| Das Essen ist aufgetragen. | Dinner is served up. |
| Tragen (decken) Sie ab. | Take away the things. |

### 2.

| | |
|---|---|
| Im Anfang. | At the beginning. |
| Lassen Sie mich gehen. | Let me alone. |
| Lassen Sie meine Bücher liegen. | Let my books alone. |
| Diese Muster sind nicht übel. | These patterns are not amiss. |
| Mir ist alles einerlei. | It's all the same to me. |
| Sind Sie fertig? | Have you done (are you ready)? |
| Ich bin mit meiner Aufgabe fertig. | { I have done my exercise. <br> { I am through with my task. |
| Das wird Ihnen wohl bekommen. | That will agree with you. |
| Das Bier bekommt mir nicht gut. | Beer does not agree with me. |
| Ich habe mir das Bein gebrochen. | I have broken my leg. |
| Ich bin (wäre) beinahe gefallen. | I had nearly fallen. |
| Er verdient sein Brot. | He gets his living. |
| Wie gefällt es Ihnen hier? | } How are you pleased here? |
| Wie gefällt Ihnen diese Stadt? | } |
| Es gefällt mir sehr wohl hier. | { I am very much pleased with <br> { this town. <br> { I like this town very much. |
| Wo sind wir stehen geblieben? | Where did we stop? |

| | |
|---|---|
| Er spielt gerne | He likes playing (gambling). |
| Haben Sie Nachrichten von ihm? | Have you any news of him? |
| Ich habe lange nichts von ihm gehört | I have not heard of him for a long time. |
| Ich weiß nicht, was ich davon halten (or denken) soll | I do not know what to think of it |

**3.**

| | |
|---|---|
| Es fragt jemand n a ch Ihnen | Somebody asks for you. |
| Wer hat nach mir gefragt? | Who has asked for me? |
| Wer wartet a u f mich? | Who is waiting *for* me? |
| Warten Sie ein wenig auf mich | Wait a moment *for* me |
| Wer hat aus diesem Glas getrunken? | Who has drunk out of this glass? |
| Haben Sie Ihre Ansicht geändert? | Have you changed your opinion? |
| Haben Sie noch etwas zu sagen? | Have you any more to say? |
| Thun Sie, was Sie wollen | Do anything (or as) you please. |
| Auf jeden Fall | At any rate, at all events. |
| Was den Brief Ihres Sohnes betrifft — | As to the letter of your son — |
| Dem sei, wie ihm wolle | Be that as it may. |
| Er macht sich Gedanken darüber | He troubles his head about it |
| Das ist keine Kunst | Any one can do it. |
| Nehmen Sie sich in acht | Look about you. Take care. |
| Ich will es darauf ankommen lassen | I will take my chance of that. |
| Er ist der deutschen Sprache mächtig | He is master of the German language. |
| Ich kann ihm die Stirn bieten | I can face him. |
| Ich werde Sie nach Hause führen | I shall see you home. |

**4.**

| | |
|---|---|
| Ich kann mich nicht von ihm losmachen | I cannot get away from him |
| Bleiben Sie nicht zu lange aus | Do not stay beyond your time. |
| Ihnen allein kann es gelingen. | None but you can succeed. |
| Auf meiner Uhr ist es vier Uhr | It is four o'clock by my watch. |
| Er nahm es mit Gewalt. | He took it by force. |
| Er ist von Geburt ein Franzose. | He is a Frenchman by birth. |
| Sie ist viel hübscher als ihre Schwester | She is prettier by far than her sister |
| Sie mögen allein gehen. | You may go by yourself. |
| Er geht nächstes Jahr auf Reisen | He goes abroad next year. |
| Ich war im Begriff, wegzugehen. | I was about to go away |
| Vor allen Dingen vergessen Sie das nicht | Above all, don't forget this. |
| Sie ist über zwanzig | She is above twenty. |
| Gegen Einbruch der Nacht. | About the close of the evening |
| Wir wollen einen Gang um die Stadt machen. | Let us take a turn about the town. |
| Soll ich ihm davon benachrichtigen? | Shall I send him word about it? |
| Ich konnte mich des Lachens nicht enthalten | I could not forbear laughing. |
| Ich würde nichts dabei gewinnen. | It would be no advantage to me. |
| Das wird recht or gut sein. | That will do. |

### 5.

| | |
|---|---|
| Ich bin nicht reich genug, um eine solche Ausgabe zu machen. | I cannot afford to spend so much. |
| Was haben Sie am Auge? | What ails your eye? |
| Es fehlt ihr immer etwas. | She is ever ailing. |
| Lassen Sie sich von mir raten. | Be advised by me. |
| Sie würden nicht übel daran thun, dahin zu gehen. | It would not be amiss for you to go there (you had better go). |
| Dieses ist schwer zu erlangen. | That is hard to come at. |
| Mit leichter Mühe. | With no great ado. |
| Nach vieler Mühe. | After much ado (or trouble). |
| Er weiß sich in alles zu finden. | Nothing comes amiss to him. |
| Soviel ich weiß. | As far as I know. |
| Soviel ich mich erinnre. | To the best of my remembrance. |
| Ich werde so frei sein, Sie zu besuchen. | I shall take the liberty to call on you. |
| Heute über ein Jahr. | By this time twelve months. |
| Wann werden Sie wieder zurückkommen? | How long will it be before you come back? |
| Es ist mir um so lieber. | I like it all the better. |
| Ich kann ihn nicht ausstehen. | I can't abide (bear) him. |
| Wenn ich ihm je begegnen sollte. | If I ever chance to meet him. |
| Was liegt mir daran? | What care I? |
| Glauben Sie, so leicht davon zu kommen? | Do you think to come off so? |

### 6.

| | |
|---|---|
| Sie müssen es thun, Sie mögen wollen oder nicht. | Willing or unwilling, you must do it. |
| Ich bin dazu geneigt. | I am inclined that way. |
| Ich frage nichts darnach. | I do not care. |
| Kehren Sie sich nicht daran. | Never mind that. |
| Soll ich ihn holen lassen? | Shall I send for him? |
| Ist das Ihr Ernst? | Are you serious? |
| Wenn es Ihnen gefällt, so nehmen Sie es. | If you like it, take it. |
| Nun, was soll dieses alles bedeuten? | Well and what of all this? |
| Ich möchte wissen, was das ist. | I wonder what this is. |
| Da steckt etwas dahinter. | There is some mystery about it. |
| Ich halte (nehme) Sie beim Wort. | I take you at your word. |
| Ich kann nichts dafür. | That is not my fault. I cannot help it. |
| Man kann nicht dahinter kommen. | You cannot get at it. |
| Ich nehme es nicht so genau mit ihm. | I am not so strict with him. |
| Was wollte ich doch sagen? | What was I going to say? |
| Ich habe nichts daran auszusetzen. | I find no fault with it. |
| Wir müssen uns behelfen. | We must make shift. |
| Die Sache hat nicht viel auf sich. | It is of no great consequence. |
| Das geht nicht mit rechten Dingen zu. | It is not at all right about it. |
| Das hat nichts zu sagen. | That does not signify. |
| Das thut nichts. | No matter for that. |
| Es geschieht ihm recht. | It serves him right. |
| Das kann mir niemand verdenken. | No one can blame me for that. |

| | |
|---|---|
| Sich den Kopf zerbrechen | To split one's head with thinking. |
| Sie werden ausgelacht werden | You will be laughed at. |
| Er hat sich aus dem Staube gemacht. | He has taken himself off. |

## Some German proverbs.

### 1.

| | |
|---|---|
| Der Mensch denkt's, Gott lenkt's. | Man proposes, and God disposes. |
| Durch Schaden wird man klug | Experience makes a man wise. |
| Ehrlich währt am längsten | Honesty is the best policy. |
| Alles hat seine Zeit | All in good time. |
| Eile mit Weile. | The more haste, the worse speed. |
| Aufgeschoben ist nicht aufgehoben. | Delaying is not breaking off. |
| Müßiggang ist aller Laster Anfang | Idleness is the root of all evil. |
| Viele Händ' machen bald ein End'. | Many hands make quick work |
| Das Werk lobt den Meister. | The work recommends the master |
| Frisch gewagt ist halb gethan. <br> Frisch begonnen, halb gewonnen | Well begun is half done. |
| Armut ist keine Schande. | Poverty is no disgrace. |
| Wie gewonnen, so zerronnen. | Lightly come, lightly gone |
| Wie die Arbeit, so der Lohn. | As the labour, so the reward. |
| Wie der Herr, so der Diener. | Like master, like man |
| Not kennt kein Gebot. | Necessity has no law. |
| Eine Schwalbe macht keinen Sommer | One swallow makes no summer. |
| Ein Unglück kommt nie allein. | Misfortunes never come singly. |
| Allzuviel ist ungesund. | Too much of one thing is good for nothing. |
| Ein gebranntes Kind scheut das Feuer | A burnt child dreads the fire. |

### 2.

| | |
|---|---|
| Jeder weiß am besten, wo der Schuh ihn drückt. | None knows so well, where the shoe pinches, as he that wears it. |
| Gleich und gleich gesellt sich gern. | Birds of a feather flock together. |
| Wovon das Herz voll ist, geht der Mund über | What the heart thinks, the mouth speaks. |
| (Der) Hunger ist der beste Koch. | A good stomach is the best sauce. |
| Die Zeit bringt Rosen | Time and straw make medlars ripe. |
| Wer lügt, der stiehlt. | Show me a liar, and I'll show thee a thief |
| Wer zuerst kommt, mahlt zuerst | First come, first served. |
| Den Gelehrten ist gut predigen | A word to the wise. |
| Jeder ist sich selbst der Nächste | Charity begins at home. |
| Besser etwas, als nichts. | Better aught, than nought. |
| Kleine Töpfe laufen bald über | A little pot is soon hot. |
| Nach Regen folgt Sonnenschein. | After the storm comes a calm. |
| Morgenstund hat Gold im Mund. | Early to bed and early to rise makes a man healthy, wealthy and wise. |
| Es ist nicht alles Gold, was glänzt. | All is not gold that glitters. |
| Übung macht den Meister | Practice makes perfect. |
| Wie man's treibt, so geht's | Do well and have well. |

26*

| | |
|---|---|
| Unrecht Gut gebeiht nicht | Ill gotten wealth never prospers. |
| Unkraut verbirbt nicht | Ill weeds grow apace. |
| Neue Besen kehren gut. | A new broom sweeps clean. |
| Ende gut, alles gut | All's well that ends well |

## Easy conversations.

### 1.

| | |
|---|---|
| Wer klopft an die Thüre? | Who knocks at the door? |
| Wer ist da? | Who is there? |
| Machen Sie auf | Open the door. |
| Der Schlüssel steckt | The key is in the door |
| Sind Sie noch im Bett? | Are you in bed still? |
| Stehen Sie auf. | Get up (rise). |
| Es ist Zeit aufzustehen. | It is time to get up. |
| Es ist heller Tag. | 'Tis broad day. |
| Warum stehen Sie so spät auf? | Why do you rise so late? |
| Ich bin vorige Nacht lange aufgeblieben. | I sat up late last night. |
| Ich bin sehr spät ins Bett gegangen und habe schlecht geschlafen. | I went to bed very late, and I slept ill to-night. |
| Wann stehen Sie gewöhnlich auf? | What time do you generally get [up? |
| Um sieben Uhr | At seven o'clock. |
| Und um wieviel Uhr sind Sie heute aufgestanden? | And you, at what o'clock did you rise to-day? |
| Ich stand mit Sonnenaufgang auf. | I got up with sun-rise. |
| Ich schlafe nicht gern lange. | I don't like to sleep long. |

### 2.

| | |
|---|---|
| Lernen Sie Deutsch? | Do you learn German? |
| Ja, mein Herr, ich lerne es. | Yes, Sir, I learn it (I do). |
| Man sagt, Sie sprechen sehr gut Deutsch | It is said that you speak very well German. |
| Ich verstehe es besser, als ich es sprechen kann. | I understand better, than I can speak. |
| Verstehen Sie, was Sie lesen? | Do you understand what you read? |
| Ja, mein Herr, ich verstehe alle deutschen Bücher. | Yes, Sir; I understand all German books. |
| Sagen Sie mir einmal, wie nennen Sie dieses auf Englisch? | Tell me, what do you call that in English? |
| Ich glaube, man nennt es . . . | I believe they call it . . . |
| Spreche ich gut aus? | Do I pronounce well? |
| Ziemlich gut. | Pretty well. |
| Sie bedürfen nur noch ein wenig Übung. | You only want a little more practice. |
| Nichts wird ohne Mühe erlangt | There is nothing to be got without pains. |

3.

| | |
|---|---|
| Mein Herr, sind Sie ein Engländer? | Sir, are you an Englishman? |
| Ja, mein Herr, Ihnen zu dienen. | Yes, Sir, at your service |
| Sprechen Sie Deutsch? | Do you speak German? |
| Ich spreche es ein wenig. | I speak a little. |
| Wie lange sind Sie schon in Deutschland? | How long have you been in Germany? |
| Zehn Monate | Ten months. |
| Sie sprechen ziemlich gut Deutsch für diese kurze Zeit | You speak German pretty well for this short time. |
| Ich habe keine Fertigkeit im Sprechen | I have not the facility of speaking |
| Diese wird mit der Zeit kommen | That will come in time. |
| Sagt Ihnen Ihr Lehrer nicht, daß Sie immer Deutsch sprechen müssen? | Does not your master tell you, that you must always speak German? |
| Ja, mein Herr; er sagt es mir sehr oft, aber ich wage es nicht | Yes, Sir, he tells me so very often, but I dare not. |
| Glauben Sie mir, seien Sie kühn und sprechen Sie, ohne zu besorgen, ob Sie einige Fehler machen oder nicht. | Believe me, be confident, and speak without minding whether you make some mistakes or not. |
| Wenn ich so spreche, so wird mich jedermann auslachen | If I speak so, every body will laugh at me. |
| Dieses hat nichts zu sagen, aber ich glaube es nicht. | No matter for that, but I think not. |
| Wissen Sie nicht, daß, um gut sprechen zu lernen, man anfängt, schlecht zu sprechen? | Do you not know, that to learn to speak well, one begins by speaking badly? |

———❦———

# APPENDIX.

A FEW SPECIMENS OF GERMAN POETICAL LITERATURE.

# 1. Fabeln und Erzählungen.

## 1. Das Hühnchen und der Diamant.

Ein verhungert Hühnchen fand
Einen feinen Diamant[1]
Und verscharrt[1] ihn in den Sand.

„Möchte doch, mich zu erfreu'n,"
Sprach es, „dieser schöne Stein
Nur ein Weizenkörnchen fein!"

Fr. v. Hageborn (died 1794).

## 2. Das Bächlein.

Du Bächlein, silberhell und klar,
Du eilst vorüber immerdar,
Am Ufer steh' ich, sinn'[2] und sinn';
Wo kommst du her'? Wo gehst du hin'?

„Ich komm' aus dunkler Felsen Schooß;
Mein Lauf[3] geht über Blum' und Moos;
Auf meinem Spiegel[4] schwebt so mild
Des blauen Himmels freundlich Bild.

D'rum hab' ich frohen Kindersinn;
Es treibt mich fort, weiß nicht wohin.
Der[5] mich gerufen aus dem Stein,
Der, denk' ich, wird mein Führer sein."

Göthe. † 1832.

## 3. Der Ochse und der Esel.

Ochs und Esel zankten sich[6]
Beim Spaziergang um die Wette:
Wer am meisten Weisheit hätte;
Keiner siegte, Keiner wich. —

Endlich kam man überein[7]:
Daß der Löwe, wenn er wollte,
Diesen Streit entscheiden sollte, —
Und was konnte klüger sein?

Beide treten, tiefgebückt,
Vor des Tierbeherrschers Throne,
Der mit einem edlen Hohne[8]
Auf das Paar hernieder blickt.

---

1) to hide. 2) think. 3) course, way. 4) mirror. 5) he who.
6) quarrelled. 7) came to the agreement. agreed. 8) scorn.

Endlich spricht die Majestät
Zu dem Esel und dem Farren[1]:
„Ihr seid alle beide Narren." —
Jeder gafft ihn an[2] und geht.

Pfeffel  † 1809.

#### 4.  Der Knabe und die Datteln.

Ein Knabe aß, wie viele Knaben,
  Die Datteln für sein Leben gern[3],
Und um des Guten viel zu haben,
  So pflanzt er einen Dattelkern
  In seines Vaters Blumengarten. —
  Der Vater sah ihm lächelnd zu
Und fragte: „Datteln pflanzest du?
O Kind, da mußt du lange warten;
  Denn wisse! dieser edle Baum
  Trägt oft nach zwanzig Jahren kaum
Die ersten seiner süßen Früchte" —
  Karl, der sich dessen nicht versah[4],
  Stand anfangs ganz betroffen da;
Doch bald mit fröhlichem Gesichte
  Ruft er: „Das soll mich nicht verdrießen; —
Belohnt die Zeit nur[5] meinen Fleiß,
So kann ich ja dereinst als Greis,
  Was jetzt der Knabe pflanzt, genießen."    Pfeffel.

#### 5.  Der Fischer.

Saß ein Fischer an dem Bach, wollte Fischlein fangen;
Doch es blieb den ganzen Tag leer die Angel hangen.
Endlich zuckt[6] es, und er sah Fischlein zappelnd[7] schweben.
Goldenrötlich hing es da, fleht' ihn um sein Leben.

„Lieber Fischer, laß mich los," sprach's mit glatten Worten,
„Laß mich in der Wellen Schoß, bis ich groß geworden."
„Fischlein, das kann nicht gescheh'n, hier hilft kein Beklagen.
Ließ' ich jetzt dich wieder geh'n, möcht' zu viel ich wagen."

„Denke doch, wie klein ich bin; hast ja kaum drei Bissen[8].
Laß mich in die Flut dahin; wirst mich nicht vermissen."
„Weil du gar zu niedlich bist und so jung am Leben,
Sei dir eine kleine Frist[9] noch von mir gegeben.

Wirst du aber größer sein, denk' an deine Worte.
Stelle dich zum Fange ein hier an diesem Orte."
Fröhlich sprang das Fischlein hin in die Wellenkühle[10],
Trieb mit heiter'm, frohem Sinn seine lust'gen Spiele.

1) ox. 2) to gaze at. 3) liked very much, was fond of. —
4) to expect. 5) *instead of* wenn nur, provided. 6) to bob. —
7) wavering, trembling. 8) bite. 9) delay. 10) the cool waves

Als ein Jahr vorüber war, dacht' es seiner Worte,
Stellte sich dem Fischer dar an dem alten Orte.
Doch der sprach: „Weil du so treu an dem Wort gehangen,
Laß ich dich auf immer frei, will dich niemals fangen."

Besselbt

### 6. Der weiße Hirsch.

Es gingen drei Jäger wohl auf die Birsch[1],
Sie wollten erjagen den weißen Hirsch.

Sie legten sich unter den Tannenbaum,
Da hatten die Drei einen seltsamen Traum.

#### Der Erste.
Mir hat geträumt[2], ich klopf' auf den Busch[3],
Da rauschte der Hirsch heraus, husch, husch!

#### Der Zweite.
Und als er sprang mit der Hunde Geklaff[4],
Da brannt' ich[5] ihm auf das Fell, piff, paff!

#### Der Dritte.
Und als ich den Hirsch an der Erde sah,
Da stieß[6] ich lustig ins Horn, trara!

So lagen sie da und sprachen die Drei,
Da rannte der weiße Hirsch vorbei.

Und eh' die Jäger ihn recht geseh'n,
So war er davon (off) über Tiefe und Höh'n.
Husch, husch! piff, paff! trara!

L. Uhland. † 1862.

### 7. Äsop.

Äsop ging einst nach einem Städtchen hin.
Ein Wand'rer kam und grüßte ihn —
Und fragt': „Wie lange, Freund, hab' ich zu geh'n
Bis zu dem Flecken[7] dort, den wir von weitem seh'n?" —
„Geh!" spricht Äsop. — Und er: „Das weiß ich wohl,
Daß, wenn ich weiter kommen soll,
Ich gehen muß; allein du sollst mir sagen:
In wieviel Stunden?" — „Nun, so geh'!" — „Ich sehe wohl,"
Brummt hier der Fremde, „dieser Kerl[8] ist toll;
Ich werde nichts von ihm erfragen;"
Und dreht sich weg und geht. — „He," ruft Äsop, „ein Wort!
Zwei Stunden bringen dich an den bestimmten Ort."

1) hunting. 2) I dreamt. 3) to beat the bush. 4) barking.
5) I fired at him. 6) I blew. 7) town. 8) this fellow.

Der Wand'rer bleibt betroffen stehen.
„Ei," ruft er, „und wie weißt du's nun?"
„Und wie," versetzt Äsop, „konnt' ich den Ausspruch thun[1],
    Bevor ich deinen Gang[2] gesehen?" —

Nicolai. † 1811.

### 8. Der Blinde und der Lahme.

Von ungefähr muß einen Blinden
Ein Lahmer auf der Straße finden,
Und jeder hofft schon freudenvoll,
Daß ihn der and're leiten soll.

„Dir," spricht der Lahme, beizustehen? —
Ich armer Mann kann selbst nicht gehen.
Doch scheint's, daß du zu einer Last
Ein Paar gesunde Schultern hast.

Entschließe dich, mich fortzutragen,
So will ich dir die Wege[3] sagen;
So wird dein starker Fuß mein Bein,
Mein helles Auge deines sein."

Der Lahme hängt mit seinen Krücken
Sich auf des Blinden breiten Rücken. —
Vereint wirkt also dieses Paar,
Was einzeln keinem möglich war.

Du hast nicht das, was and're haben,
Und andern mangeln[4] deine Gaben.
Aus dieser Unvollkommenheit
Sprießt[5] Nutzen und Geselligkeit.

Gellert. † 1762.

### 9. Der Schatzgräber.[6]

Ein Winzer[7], der am Tode lag,
Rief seine Kinder an und sprach:
„In unserm Weinberg liegt ein Schatz;
Grabt nur darnach!" — „An welchem Platz?"
Schrie alles laut den Vater an. —
„Grabt nur!" — O weh', da starb der Mann.
Kaum war der Alte beigeschafft[8],
So grub man nach aus Leibeskraft[9].
Mit Hacke, Karst' und Spaten ward
Der Weinberg um und um gescharrt[10];

1) to give the decision. 2) pace, gait. 3) the ways, paths. 4) to be wanting. 5) comes forth, arises. 6) the treasure-digger. 7) a vine-dresser. 8) buried. 9) with all their strength. 10) dug up.

Da war kein Kloß, der ruhig blieb,
Man warf die Erde gar durchs Sieb
Und zog die Harken kreuz und quer
Nach jedem Steinchen hin und her.
Allein da ward kein Schatz verspürt
Und jeder hielt sich angeführt [1].
Doch, kaum erschien das nächste Jahr,
So nahm man mit Erstaunen wahr [2],
Daß jede Rebe dreifach trug.
Da wurden erst die Söhne klug,
Und gruben nun, Jahr ein, Jahr aus,
Des Schatzes immer mehr heraus.      Bürger. † 1794.

### 10. Der Reisende.

Ein Wand'rer bat den Gott der Götter,
Den Zeus, bei ungestümem [3] Wetter,
    Um stille Luft und Sonnenschein.
Umsonst! Zeus läßt sich nicht bewegen.
Der Himmel stürmt mit Wind und Regen;
    Denn stürmisch sollt' es heute sein.

Der Wand'rer setzt, mit bitt'rer Klage:
Daß Zeus mit Fleiß [4] die Menschen plage,
    Die sau're Reise mühsam fort
So oft ein neuer Sturmwind wütet [5]
Und schnell ihm stillzusteh'n gebietet,
    So oft ertönt ein Lästerwort [6].

Ein naher Wald soll ihn beschirmen,
Er eilt dem Regen und den Stürmen
    In diesem Holze zu entgeh'n:
Doch, eh' der Wald ihn aufgenommen,
Sieht fern er einen Räuber kommen
    Und bleibt vor Furcht im Regen steh'n.

Der Räuber greift nach seinem Bogen,
Den schon die Nässe schlaff gezogen [7];
    Er zielt [8] und faßt [8] den Pilger wohl;
Doch Wind und Regen sind zuwider;
Der Pfeil [9] fällt matt [10] vor dem darnieder,
    Dem er das Herz durchbohren soll.

„O Thor," läßt Zeus sich zornig hören, —
„Wird dich der matte Pfeil nun lehren,
    Ob ich dem Sturm zu viel erlaubt?

1) deceived. 2) they perceived. 3) stormy. 4) on purpose
5) rages. 6) a blasphemy. 7) relaxed, slacked. 8) he views and
aims. 9) arrow. 10) powerless.

Hätt' ich dir Sonnenschein gegeben,
So hätte dir der Pfeil das Leben,
Das dir der Sturm erhielt, geraubt."          Gellert.

## 11. Die Tabakspfeife.

„Gott grüß' Euch, Alter! Schmeckt[1] das Pfeifchen?
    Weißt her! — Ein Blumentopf
Von rotem Ton, mit gold'nen Reifchen:
    Was wollt Ihr für den Kopf?"

„Ach Herr, den Kopf kann ich nicht lassen!
    Er kommt vom bravsten Mann,
Der ihn, Gott weiß es, welchem Bassen[2]
    Bei Belgrad abgewann.

Da, Herr, da gab es rechte Beute!
    Es lebe Prinz Eugen'!
Wie Grummet[3] sah man unf're Leute
    Der Türken Glieder[4] mäh'n."

„Ein andermal von euern Thaten;
    Hier, Alter, seid kein Tropf!
Nehmt diesen doppelten Dukaten
    Für Euern Pfeifenkopf!"

„Ich bin ein armer Kerl und lebe
    Von meinem Gnadensold[5];
Doch, Herr, den Pfeifenkopf, den gebe
    Ich nicht um alles Gold.

Hört nur! Einst jagten wir Husaren
    Den Feind nach Herzenslust[6];
Da schoß ein Hund von Janitscharen
    Den Hauptmann in die Brust.

Ich hob ihn flugs auf meinen Schimmel[7] —
    Er hätt' es auch gethan —
Und trug ihn fort aus dem Getümmel[8]
    Zu einem Edelmann.

Ich pflegte sein. Vor seinem Ende
    Reicht' er mir all' sein Geld
Und diesen Kopf, drückt mir die Hände,
    Und blieb im Tod noch Held.

Das Gold mußt du dem Wirte schenken,
    Der dreimal Plünd'rung litt —

1) how do you like? 2) Turkish Pasha. 3) after-grass. 4) ranks.
5) pension, half-pay. 6) with pleasure. 7) grey horse. 8) din.

So dacht' ich, und zum Angedenken
 Nahm ich die Pfeife mit.

Ich trug auf allen meinen Zügen[1]
 Sie wie ein Heiligtum,
Wir mochten weichen oder siegen,
 Im Stiefel mit herum.

Vor Prag verlor ich auf der Streife
 Das Bein durch einen Schuß,
Da griff ich erst nach meiner Pfeife
 Und dann nach meinem Fuß." —

„Ihr rühret, Freund, mich bis zu Zähren;
 O sagt, wie hieß der Mann?
Damit auch mein Herz ihn verehren
 Und ihn beweinen kann."

„Man hieß ihn nur den tapfern Walther
 Dort lag sein Gut[2] am Rhein." —
„Das war mein Vater, lieber Alter,
 Und jenes Gut ist mein.

Kommt Freund, Ihr sollt nun bei mir leben!
 Vergesset Eu're Not!
Kommt, trinkt mit mir von Walthers Reben[3],
 Und eßt von Walthers Brot!"

„Nun, topp[4]! Ihr seid sein wack'rer Erbe,
 Ich ziehe morgen ein,
Und Euer Dank soll, wenn ich sterbe,
 Die Türkenpfeife sein!"   Pfeffel.

1) campaigns.  2) estate.  3) vines.  4) well.

---

## 2.  Lieder und Elegien.

### 1.  Der Schütze.[1]

Mit dem Pfeil und Bogen
 Durch Gebirg und Thal,
Kommt[2] der Schütz gezogen[2]
 Früh am Morgenstrahl.

Wie im Reich der Lüfte
 König ist der Weih[3],

1) the shooter, archer.  2) walks out.  3) as the hawk is a king in the air, &c.

Durch Gebirg und Lüfte
    Herrscht der Schütze frei.

Ihm gehört das Weite[1];
    Was sein Pfeil erreicht,
    Das ist seine Beute,
    Was da kreucht[2] und fleugt[2].

Fr. v. Schiller. † 1805.

## 2. Gefunden.

Ich ging im Walde so für mich hin,
Und nichts zu suchen, das war mein Sinn.

Im Schatten sah ich ein Blümchen steh'n,
Wie Sterne leuchtend[3], wie Äuglein schön.

Ich wollt' es brechen, da sagt es fein:
„Soll ich zum Welken[4] gebrochen sein?"

Ich grub's mit allen den Würzlein aus;
Zum Garten trug ich's am hübschen Haus.

Und pflanzt' es wieder am stillen Ort[5],
Nun wächst es wieder und blüht so fort.

Göthe † 1832.

## 3. Herbstlied.

Bald fällt von falben Zweigen
    Das letzte Blatt herab;
Die Büsch' und Wälder schweigen,
    Die Welt ist wie ein Grab.
Wo sind sie nun geblieben
    Die Vög'lein all', die lieben?
    Ach! sie sangen erst so schön! —
Der Reif[6] hat sie vertrieben
    Weg über Thal und Höh'n.

Und bange[7] wird's und bänger
    Und öd' in Fels und Hag;
Die Nächte werden länger
    Und kürzer wird der Tag.
Die Sanger sind verschwunden
    In diesen trüben Stunden,
    Suchen Frühling anderswo;
Und wo sie den gefunden,
    Da sind sie wieder froh.

1) space. 2) obsolete forms for kriecht and fliegt (creeps and flies). 3) shining, glittering. 4) to wither. 5) place. 6) the hoar frost. 7) sad, dull.

Und wenn von falben Zweigen
  Das letzte Blatt noch fällt,
Wenn Büsch' und Wälder schweigen,
  Als trauerte die Welt,
Dein Frühling kann nicht schwinden!
Bau' ihn in Herzensgründen [1],
  Sei du selber dir dein Glück!
So kannst du Frühling finden
  In jedem Augenblick.
                    Hoffmann v. Fallersleben.  † 1874

## 4. Winterlied.

Wie ruhest du so stille
In deiner weißen Hülle,
  Du mütterliches Land!
Wo sind die Frühlingslieder,
Des Sommers bunt Gefieder
  Und dein beblümtes Festgewand [2]?

Du schlummerst nun entkleidet;
Kein Lamm, kein Schäflein weidet
  Auf deinen Au'n [3] und Höh'n.
Der Vög'lein Lied verstummte;
Kein Bienlein mehr, das summte;
  Doch du bist auch im Winter schön.

Die Zweig' und Äste schimmern [4]
Und tausend Lichter flimmern [5],
  Wohin das Auge blickt.
Wer hat dein Bett bereitet,
Die Decke dir gebreitet [6]
  Und dich so schön mit Reif geschmückt?

Der gute Vater droben
Hat dir dein Kleid gewoben;
  Er schläft und schlummert nicht.
So schlumm're denn in Frieden!
Der Vater weckt die Müden
  Zu neuer Kraft und neuem Licht.

Bald bei des Lenzes Wehen
Wirst du verjüngt erstehen
  Zum Leben wunderbar.
Sein Odem [7] schwebt hernieder;
Dann Erde, prangst du wieder
  Mit einem Blumenkranz im Haar.
                    Krummacher  † 1845

1) at the bottom of thy heart.   2) blooming festival attire.
3) die Aue the field.   4) shine.   5) glitter.   6) spread.   7) Odem,
*poet.* for Atem breath.

OT.

## 5. Schweizer=Lied.

**Fischerknabe** (singt in dem Kahn).

Es lächelt der See, er ladet[1] zum Bade,
Der Knabe schlief ein am grünen Gestade;
Da hört er ein Klingen[2] wie Flöten so süß,
Wie Stimmen der Engel im Paradies.
Und wie er erwachet in seliger Lust,
Da spielen die Wasser ihm um die Brust.
Und es[3] ruft aus den Tiefen! Lieb' Knabe bist mein;
Ich locke den Schläfer, ich zieh' ihn herein.

**Hirte** (singt auf dem Berge).

Ihr Matten[4], lebt wohl,
Ihr sonnigen Weiden[5]!
Der Senne[6] muß scheiden,
Der Sommer ist hin.

Wir fahren zu Berg, wir kommen wieder,
Wenn der Kuckuck ruft, wenn erwachen die Lieder.
Wenn mit Blumen die Erde sich kleidet neu,
Wenn die Brünnlein fließen im lieblichen Mai.

Ihr Matten, lebt wohl,
Ihr sonnigen Weiden!
Der Senne muß scheiden,
Der Sommer ist hin.

**Jäger** (singt auf dem Felsen).

Es donnern die Höhen, es zittert der Steg[7],
Nicht grauet dem Schützen auf schwindlichem Weg;
Er schreitet verwegen auf Feldern von Eis,
Da pranget kein Frühling, da grünet kein Reis.
Und unter den Füßen, ein nebliges Meer,
Erkennt er die Städte der Menschen nicht mehr:
Durch den Riß nur der Wolken erblickt er die Welt,
Tief unter den Wassern das grünende Feld.

Schiller (Wilhelm Tell). † 1805

## 6. Schlaf' ein, mein Herz.

Schlaf' ein, mein Herz, in Frieden!
Den müden Augenliden[8]
Der Blumen hat gebracht
Erquickungstau[8] die Nacht.

---

1) for ladet ein invites. 2) a tone, sound. 3) es ruft = a voice,
a call is heard. 4) ye meadows! 5) pasture. 6) the herdsman,
cow-keeper. 7) wooden bridge. 8) the night has brought refre-
shing dew to the weary eyelids.

Schlaf' ein, mein Herz, in Frieden!
Das Leben schläft hienieden,
Der Mond in stiller Pracht,
Ein Auge Gottes, wacht.

Schlaf' ein, mein Herz, in Frieden!
Von Furcht und Gram geschieden[1];
Der[2] Welten hat bedacht,
Nimmt[3] auch ein Herz in acht[3].

Schlaf' ein, mein Herz, in Frieden!
Von bösem Traum gemieden,
Gestärkt von Glaubensmacht,
Von Hoffnung angelacht.

Schlaf' ein, mein Herz, in Frieden!
Und wenn dir ist beschieden
Der Tod hier in der Nacht,
So bist du dort[4] erwacht.                  Rückert. † 1866

### 7. Wächterruf.

Höret, was ich euch will sagen!
Die Glock' hat Zehn geschlagen.
Jetzt betet und dann geht zu Bett;
Doch löscht das Licht aus, eh' ihr geht;
Schlaft sanft und wohl! Im Himmel wacht
Ein klares Aug' die ganze Nacht.

Höret, was ich euch will sagen!
Die Glock' hat Elf geschlagen.
Und wer noch bei der Arbeit schwitzt[5],
Und wer beim Kartenspiel noch sitzt,
Dem sag' ich's laut und deutlich nun:
's ist hohe Zeit, nun auszuruh'n.

Höret, was ich euch will sagen!
Die Glock' hat Zwölf geschlagen.
Wo noch in stiller Mitternacht
Ein krankes Herz voll Kummer wacht,
Gott geb' ihm Trost[6], verleih' ihm Ruh'
Und führ's dem sanften Schlummer zu.

Höret, was ich euch will sagen!
Die Glock' hat Eins geschlagen.

1) separated.  2) he who.  3) takes also care.  4) in the
other world.  5) to sweat, *here:* to work hard.  6) comfort.

Und wo durch Satans List [1] und Rat
Ein Dieb hinschleicht [2] auf dunk'lem Pfad,
Ich will's nicht hoffen; doch geschieht's [3]!
So geh' er [4] heim, sein Richter sieht's.

Höret, was ich euch will sagen!
Die Glock' hat Zwei geschlagen.
Und wem die Sorg' [5], schon eh' es tagt [6],
Schwer an dem wachen Herzen nagt [7]:
Der arme Tropf [8]! sein Schlaf ist fort;
Gott sorgt, verlaß dich [9] auf sein Wort!

Höret, was ich euch will sagen!
Die Glock' hat Drei geschlagen.
Die Morgenstund' am Himmel schwebt [10];
Wer friedevoll den Tag erlebt [11];
Der danke Gott und fasse Mut,
Geh' ans Geschäft und halt' sich gut.

Nach Hebel  † 1828

### 8.  Des Deutschen Vaterland.  .

Was ist des Deutschen Vaterland?
Ist's Preußenland?  Ist's Schwabenland?
Ist's wo am Rhein die Rebe blüht?
Ist's wo am Belt die Möve [12] zieht?
  O nein! o nein! o nein!
  Sein Vaterland muß größer sein.

Was ist des Deutschen Vaterland?
Ist's Baierland?  Ist's Steierland [13]?
Ist's wo der Marsen Rind sich streckt?
Ist's wo der Marker Eisen reckt [14]?
  O nein! o nein! 2c. 2c.

Was ist des Deutschen Vaterland?
Ist's Pommerland?  Westfalenland?
Ist's wo der Sand der Dünen [15] weht?
Ist's wo die Donau brausend [16] geht?
  O nein! o nein! 2c. 2c.

Was ist des Deutschen Vaterland?
So nenne mir das große Land!
Gewiß, es ist das Österreich,
An Siegen und an Ehren reich.
  O nein! o nein! 2c. 2c.

1) cunning and advice. 2) sneaks. 3) yet, if it be so. 4) let
him go home. 5) care  6) dawns. 7) gnaws. 8) fellow, man
9) rely. 10) hovers. 11) lives to see  12) the sea-gull. 13) Styria.
14) forges. 15) downs. 16) foaming.

Was ist des Deutschen Vaterland?
So nenne mir das große Land!
Ist's Land der Schweizer, ist's Tyrol?
Das Land und Volk gefiel' mir wohl.
   Doch nein! doch nein! 2c. 2c.

Was ist des Deutschen Vaterland?
So nenne endlich mir das Land!
So weit die deutsche Zunge klingt
Und Gott im Himmel Lieder singt:
   Das soll es sein! das soll es sein!
Das, wack'rer Deutscher, nenne dein!

Das ist des Deutschen Vaterland:
Wo Eide[1] schwört der Druck der Hand,
Wo Treue hell vom Auge blitzt[2],
Und Liebe warm im Herzen sitzt:
   Das soll es sein! das soll es sein!
Das, wack'rer Deutscher, nenne dein!

Das ganze Deutschland soll es sein!
O Gott! vom Himmel sieh' darein;
Und gieb uns echten deutschen Mut;
Daß wir es lieben treu und gut!
   Das soll es sein! das soll es sein!
   Das ganze Deutschland soll es sein!
           E. M. Arndt. † 1860.

## 9. Gebet während der Schlacht.

Vater, ich rufe dich!
Brüllend umwölkt mich der Dampf der Geschütze[3],
Sprühend umzucken[4] mich rasselnde Blitze.
Lenker der Schlachten, ich rufe dich!
   Vater, du führe mich!

Vater, du führe mich!
Führ' mich zum Siege, führ' mich zum Tode;
Herr, ich erkenne deine Gebote;
Herr, wie du willst, so führe mich.
   Gott, ich erkenne dich!

Gott, ich erkenne dich!
Wie im herbstlichen Rauschen[5] der Blätter,
So in dem Schlachten-Donnerwetter,
Urquell[6] der Gnad' ich erkenne dich.
   Vater, du segne mich!

1) oaths. 2) flashes. 3) cannon. 4) flash round me. 5) autumnal rustling. 6) primitive source.

Vater, du segne mich!
In deine Hand befehl' ich[1] mein Leben,
Du kannst es nehmen, du hast es gegeben;
Zum Leben, zum Sterben segne mich.
Vater, ich preise dich!

Vater, ich preise dich!
's ist ja kein Kampf für die Güter der Erde:
Das Heiligste schützen wir mit dem Schwerte;
D'rum fallend und siegend preis' ich dich,
Gott, dir ergeb' ich mich!

Gott, dir ergeb' ich mich!
Wenn mich die Donner des Todes begrüßen,
Wenn meine Adern geöffnet fließen;
Dir, mein Gott, ergeb' ich mich!
Vater, ich rufe dich!          Körner. † 1813.

### 10. Elegie in den Ruinen des Heidelberger Schlosses.

Schweigend, in der Abenddämm'rung Schleier,
Ruht die Flur, das Lied der Haine[2] stirbt;
Nur daß hier im alternden Gemäuer
Melancholisch noch ein Heimchen[3] zirpt.
Stille sinkt aus unbewölkten Lüften,
Langsam zieh'n die Herden von den Triften[4],
Und der müde Landmann eilt der Ruh'
Seiner väterlichen Hütte zu.

Hier auf diesen wald-umkränzten Höhen,
Unter Trümmern der Vergangenheit,
Wo der Vorwelt Schauer[5] mich umwehen,
Sei dies Lied, o Wehmut, dir geweiht!
Trauernd denk' ich, was vor grauen Jahren
Diese morschen Überreste waren:
Ein betürmtes Schloß, voll Majestät,
Auf des Berges Felsenstirn'[6] erhöht!

Dort, wo um des Pfeilers dunkle Trümmer
Traurig lispelnd sich der Epheu schlingt,
Und der Abendröte trüber Schimmer
Durch den öden Raum der Fenster blinkt,
Segneten vielleicht des Vaters Thränen
Einst den edelsten von Deutschlands Söhnen,
Dessen Herz, der Ehrbegierde voll,
Heiß dem nahen Kampf entgegenschwoll.

1) I recommend.  2) grove, wood.  3) a cricket.  4) pasture.
5) awe.  6) rocky brow, forehead.

„Zieh' in Frieden," sprach der greise [1] Krieger
　　Ihn umgurtend mit dem Heldenschwert;
„Kehre nimmer, oder kehr' als Sieger;
　　Sei des Namens deiner Väter wert!"
Und des edlen Jünglings Auge sprühte [2]
Todesflammen; seine Wange glühte
　　Gleich dem aufgeblühten Rosenhain
　　In der Morgenröte Purpurschein.

Eine Donnerwolke flog der Ritter
　　Dann wie Richard Löwenherz zur Schlacht:
Gleich dem Tannenwald im Ungewitter
　　Beugte sich vor ihm des Feindes Macht.
Mild wie Bäche, die durch Blumen wallen,
Kehrt er zu des Felsenschlosses Hallen,
　　Zu des Vaters Freudenthränen-Blick,
　　In der teuern Mutter Arm zurück.

O der Wandlung [3]! Grau'n [4] und Nacht umdüstern
　　Nun den Schauplatz jener Herrlichkeit;
Schwermutsvolle [5] Abendwinde flüstern,
　　Wo die Starken sich des Mahls gefreut;
Disteln wanken einsam auf der Stätte,
Wo um Schild und Speer der Knabe flehte,
　　Wann der Kriegstrompete Ruf erklang
　　Und aufs Kampfroß sich der Vater schwang.

Asche sind der Mächtigen Gebeine
　　Tief im dunklen Erdenschoße nun!
Kaum, daß halbversunk'ne Leichensteine [6]
　　Noch die Stätte zeigen, wo sie ruh'n.
Viele wurden längst ein Spiel der Lüfte,
Ihr Gedächtnis sank wie ihre Grüfte [7];
　　Vor dem Thatenglanz der Heldenzeit
　　Schwebt die Wolke der Vergessenheit.

So vergeh'n des Lebens Herrlichkeiten,
　　So entflieht das Traumbild eitler Macht!
So versinkt im schnellen Lauf der Zeiten,
　　Was die Erde trägt, in öde Nacht!
Lorbeer'n, die des Siegers Stirn umkränzen,
Thaten, die in Erz [8] und Marmor glänzen,
　　Urnen, der Erinnerung geweiht,
　　Und Gesänge der Unsterblichkeit!

Matthisson. † 1831.

1) old, grey. 2) sparkled. 3) what a change! 4) awe. 5) melancholy. 6) tomb-stones. 7) graves, arched tombs, vaults. 8) ore, bronze.

## 3. Legenden, Romanzen und Balladen.

### 1. Barbarossa.

Der alte Barbarossa, der Kaiser Friederich,
Im unterirb'schen Schlosse hält er verzaubert[1] sich.

Er ist niemals gestorben, er lebt darin noch jetzt;
Er hat im Schloß verborgen zum Schlaf sich hingesetzt.

Er hat hinabgenommen des Reiches Herrlichkeit,
Und wird einst wieder kommen mit ihr zu seiner Zeit.

Der Stuhl ist elfenbeinern[2], worauf der Kaiser sitzt;
Der Tisch ist marmelsteinern, worauf sein Haupt er stützt[3].

Sein Bart ist nicht von Flachse, er ist von Feuersglut[4],
Ist durch den Tisch gewachsen, worauf sein Kinn ausruht.

Er nickt als wie im Traume, sein Aug' halb offen zwinkt;
Und je nach langem Raume er einem Knaben winkt.

Er spricht im Schlaf zum Knaben: Geh' hin vor's Schloß, o Zwerg,
Und sieh', ob noch die Raben herfliegen um den Berg.

Und wenn die alten Raben noch fliegen immerbar,
So muß ich auch noch schlafen verzaubert hundert Jahr.

Fr. Rückert.

### 2. Der Sänger.*)

„Was hör' ich draußen vor dem Thor,
    Was auf der Brücke schallen?
Laßt den Gesang vor unserm Ohr
    Im Saale wiederhallen!"
Der König sprach's, der Page lief;
Der Knabe kam, der König rief:
    „Laßt mir herein den Alten!"

„Gegrüßet[5] seid mir, edle Herrn,
    Gegrüßt ihr, schöne Damen!
Welch' reicher Himmel! Stern bei Stern!
    Wer kennet ihre Namen?
Im Saal voll Pracht und Herrlichkeit
Schließt Augen euch; hier ist nicht Zeit,
    Sich staunend zu ergötzen."

1) enchanted.  2) of ivory.  3) leans.  4) red like fire.  5) be
saluted.

---

*) The minstrel. *See the translation in the Key.*

Der Sänger drückt' die Augen ein,
  Und schlug[1] in vollen Tönen;
Die Ritter schauten[2] mutig drein,
  Und in den Schoß[3] die Schönen.
Der König, dem das Lied gefiel,
Ließ ihm zum Lohne für sein Spiel,
  Eine gold'ne Kette bringen.

„Die gold'ne Kette gieb mir nicht;
  Die Kette gieb den Rittern,
Vor deren kühnem Angesicht
  Der Feinde Lanzen splittern.
Gieb sie dem Kanzler, den du hast,
Und laß ihn noch die gold'ne Last[4]
  Zu andern Lasten tragen."

„Ich singe, wie der Vogel singt,
  Der in den Zweigen wohnet;
Das Lied, das aus der Kehle dringt,
  Ist Lohn, der reichlich lohnet.
Doch darf ich bitten, bitt' ich Eins:
Laßt mir den besten Becher Weins
  In purem Golde reichen."

Er setzt' ihn an, er trank ihn aus:
  „O Trank voll süßer Labe!
O wohl dem hochbeglückten Haus,
  Wo das ist[5] kleine Gabe!
Ergeht's euch wohl, so denkt an mich,
Und danket Gott so warm als ich
  Für diesen Trunk euch danke."          Göthe.

### 3. Der Erlkönig.[6]

Wer reitet so spät durch Nacht und Wind?
Es ist der Vater mit seinem Kind';
Er hat den Knaben wohl in dem Arm',
Er faßt ihn sicher, er hält ihn warm.

„Mein Sohn, was birgst du so bang dein Gesicht?"
— „Sieh'st Vater, du den Erlkonig nicht?
Den Erlenkönig mit Kron' und Schweif?" —
„Mein Sohn, es ist ein Nebelstreif[7]."

„Du liebes Kind, komm' geh' mit mir!
Gar schöne Spiele spiel' ich mit dir;
Manch' bunte Blumen sind an dem Strand';
Meine Mutter hat manch' gulden' Gewand."

1) played.  2) looked round.  3) lap.  4) burden.  5) where
this is considered a small gift.  6) The Fairy king.  7) a misty cloud.

„Mein Vater, mein Vater, und hörest du nicht,
Was Erlenkönig mir leise verspricht?" —
„Sei ruhig, bleibe ruhig, mein Kind!
In dürren Blättern säuselt der Wind."

„Willst, feiner Knabe, du mit mir gehn'?
Meine Töchter sollen dich warten[1] schön;
Meine Töchter führen den nächtlichen Reih'n
Und wiegen und tanzen und singen dich ein[2]."

— „Mein Vater, mein Vater, und siehst du nicht dort
Erlkönigs Töchter am düstern Ort'?" —
„Mein Sohn, mein Sohn, ich seh' es genau;
Es scheinen die alten Weiden so grau."

„„Ich lieb' dich, mich reizt deine schöne Gestalt;
Und bist du nicht willig, so brauch' ich Gewalt."" —
— „Mein Vater, mein Vater, jetzt faßt er mich an;
Erlkönig hat mir ein Leids[3] gethan."

Dem Vater grauset's (shudders), er reitet geschwind;
Er hält in den Armen das ächzende Kind,
Erreicht den Hof[4] mit Mühe und Not:
In seinen Armen das Kind war tot.        Göthe.

## 4. Der reichste Fürst.

„Herrlich," sprach der Fürst von Sachsen,
    „Ist mein Land und seine Macht.
Silber hegen[5] seine Berge
    Wohl in manchem tiefen Schacht[6]."

„Seht mein Land in üpp'ger Fülle,"
    Sprach der Kurfürst von dem Rhein.
„Gold'ne Saaten in den Thälern,
    Auf den Bergen edler Wein."

„Große Städte, reiche Klöster,"
    Ludwig, Herr zu Bayern, sprach,
„Schaffen[7], daß mein Land den eu'ren
    Wohl nicht steht an Schätzen nach[8]."

Eberhard, der mit dem Barte,
    Württembergs geliebter Herr,
Sprach: „Mein Land hat kleine Städte,
    Trägt nicht Berge, silberschwer;

1) wait upon. 2) sing into sleep. 3) injury. 4) farm, house.
5) to conceal, contain. 6) shaft, mine-pit. 7) cause. 8) steht nach
= is inferior.

Doch ein Kleinod[1] hält's verborgen:
  Daß in Wäldern, noch so groß,
Ich mein Haupt kann kühnlich legen
  Jedem Unterthan in Schoß."

Und es rief der Herr von Sachsen,
  Der von Bayern, der vom Rhein:
„Graf im Bart, Ihr seid der reichste,
  Euer Land trägt Edelstein."

J. Kerner. † 1862.

## 5. Andreas Hofer.

Zu Mantua in Banden
  Der treue Hofer war;
In Mantua zum Tode
  Führt ihn der Feinde Schar;
Es blutete der Brüder Herz,
Ganz Deutschland, ach! in Schmach und Schmerz!
  Mit ihm das Land Tirol.

Die Hände auf dem Rücken
  Andreas Hofer ging
Mit ruhig festen Schritten,
  Ihm schien der Tod gering;
Der Tod, den er so manches Mal
Vom Iselberg geschickt ins Thal
  Im heil'gen Land Tirol.

Doch als aus Kerkergittern[2]
  Im festen Mantua
Die treuen Waffenbrüder
  Die Hand' er strecken sah,
Da rief er laut: „Gott sei mit euch,
Mit dem verrat'nen deutschen Reich
  Und mit dem Land Tirol!"

Dem Tambour will der Wirbel[3]
  Nicht unter'm Schlegel[4] vor,
Als nun Andreas Hofer
  Schritt durch das finst're Thor;
Andreas noch in Banden frei,
Dort stand er fest auf der Bastei,
  Der Mann vom Land Tirol.

1) jewel  2) grated windows of prisons.  3) the tattoo, drum-
ming.  4) stick.

Dort soll er niederfnieen; .
　Er sprach: „Das thu' ich nit!
Will sterben, wie ich stehe,
　Will sterben, wie ich stritt.
So wie ich steh' auf dieser Schanz'[1],
Es leb' mein guter Kaiser Franz,
　Mit ihm sein Land Tirol!"

Und von der Hand die Binde
　Nimmt ihm der Korporal,
Andreas Hofer betet
　Allhier zum letztenmal;
Dann ruft er: „Nun, so trefft mich recht!
Gebt Feuer! — Ach! wie schießt ihr schlecht!
　Abe, mein Land Tirol!"

J. Mosen.

### 6. Das Lied vom braven Mann.

Der Tauwind[2] kam vom Mittagsmeer[3]
Und schnob[4] durch Welschland[5] trüb' und feucht;
Die Wolken flogen vor ihm her,
Wie wenn der Wolf die Herde scheucht[6],
　Er fegte die Felder, zerbrach den Forst;
　Auf Seen und Strömen das Grundeis borst[7].

Am Hochgebirge schmolz der Schnee;
Der Sturz von tausend Wassern scholl[8];
Das Wiesenthal begrub ein See,
Des Landes Heerstrom[9] wuchs und schwoll.
　Hoch rollten die Wogen, entlang ihr Gleis[10],
　Und rollten gewaltige Felsen Eis.

Auf Pfeilern und auf Bogen schwer,
Aus Quaderstein von unten auf
Lag eine Brücke drüber her,
Und mitten stand ein Häuschen d'rauf.
　Hier wohnte der Zöllner mit Weib und Kind. —
　„O Zöllner! o Zöllner! entfleuch geschwind!" —

Es dröhnt' und dröhnte[11] dumpf heran;
Laut heulten Sturm' und Wog' ums Haus.
Der Zöllner sprang zum Dach hinan
Und blickt in den Tumult hinaus. —
　„Barmherziger Himmel! erbarme dich!
　Verloren! Verloren! Wer rettet mich?"

1) redoubt.　2) the south wind.　3) the Mediterranean.　4) blew.
5) Italy.　6) to scare.　7) for barst, burst.　8) sounded, echoed.
9) mainstream.　10) bed.　11) to sound dully.

Die Schollen rollten Stoß auf Stoß [1]
An beiden Enden, hier und dort;
Zerborsten und zertrümmert schoß
Ein Pfeiler nach dem andern fort.
   Der bebende Zöllner mit Weib und Kind,
   Er heulte noch lauter als Sturm und Wind.

Hoch auf dem fernen Ufer stand
Ein Schwarm von Gaffern [2] groß und klein,
Und jeder schrie und rang die Hand;
Doch mochte niemand Retter sein.
   Der bebende Zöllner mit Weib und Kind,
   Durchheulte nach Rettung den Sturm und Wind.

Rasch galoppiert ein Graf hervor
Auf hohem Roß, ein edler Graf.
Was hielt des Grafen Hand empor?
Ein Beutel war es, voll und straff.
   „Zweihundert Pistolen [3] sind zugesagt
   Dem, welcher die Rettung der Armen wagt!"

Und immer höher schwoll die Flut,
Und immer lauter schnob der Wind;
Und immer tiefer sank der Mut. —
„O Retter! Retter! komm' geschwind!"
   Stets Pfeiler bei Pfeiler zerborst und brach;
   Laut krachten und stürzten die Bogen nach.

„Halloh! halloh! Frisch auf, gewagt!"
Hoch hielt der Graf den Preis empor.
Ein jeder hört's, doch jeder zagt;
Aus tausenden tritt keiner vor.
   Vergebens durchheulte mit Weib und Kind
   Der Zöllner nach Rettung den Sturm und Wind.

Sieh', schlicht [4] und recht ein Bauersmann
Am Wanderstabe schritt daher,
Mit grobem Kittel angethan [5],
An Wuchs und Antlitz hoch und hehr.
   Er hörte den Grafen, vernahm sein Wort
   Und schaute das nahe Verderben dort.

Und kühn, in Gottes Namen, sprang
Er in den nächsten Fischerkahn.
Trotz Wirbel [6], Sturm und Wogendrang
Kam der Erretter glücklich an.

1) one pushing another. 2) gaper. 3) guinea. 4) simply
and plainly. 5) dressed. 6) whirlpool.

Doch wehe! der Nachen war allzu klein,
Um Retter von allen zugleich zu fein.

Und dreimal zwang er seinen Kahn,
Trotz Wirbel, Sturm und Wogendrang;
Und dreimal kam er glücklich an,
Bis ihm die Rettung ganz gelang.
Kaum waren die Letzten in sichern Port,
So rollte das letzte Getrümmer fort.

„Hier," rief der Graf, „mein wack'rer Freund,
Hier ist der Preis! Komm her! Nimm hin!"
Sag an, war das nicht brav gemeint? —
Bei Gott! der Graf trug hohen Sinn;
Doch höher und himmlischer, wahrlich! schlug
Das Herz, das der Bauer im Kittel trug.

„Mein Leben ist für Gold nicht feil[1].
Arm bin ich zwar, doch hab' ich satt.
Dem Zöllner werd' Eu'r Geld zu teil,
Der Hab' und Gut verloren hat!"
So rief er mit herzlichem Biederton
Und wandte den Rücken und ging davon.

Bürger † 1794.

### 7. Die Bürgschaft.[2]

Zu Dionys, dem Tyrannen, schlich
Möros, den Dolch im Gewande;
Ihn schlugen die Häscher[3] in Bande.
„Was wolltest du mit dem Dolche? sprich!"
Entgegnet ihm finster der Wüterich. —
„Die Stadt vom Tyrannen befreien!"
„Das sollst du Kreuze bereuen."

„Ich bin," spricht jener, „zu sterben bereit
Und bitte nicht um mein Leben;
Doch willst du Gnade[4] mir geben,
Ich flehe dich um drei Tage Zeit,
Bis ich die Schwester dem Gatten gefreit[5].
Ich lasse den Freund dir als Bürgen,
Ihn magst du, entrinn' ich, erwürgen."

Da lächelt der König mit arger List[6]
Und spricht nach kurzem Bedenken:
„Drei Tage will ich dir schenken.

1) venal. 2) the hostage, security. 3) the guards. 4) a favour, grace. 5) wedded, married. 6) maliciously.

Doch wiſſe: wenn ſie verſtrichen die Friſt,
Eh' du zurück mir gegeben biſt,
So muß er ſtatt deiner erblaſſen [1],
Doch dir iſt die Strafe erlaſſen."

Und er kommt zum Freunde: „Der König gebeut [2],
Daß ich am Kreuz mit dem Leben
Bezahle das frevelnde Streben [3];
Doch will er mir gönnen drei Tage Zeit,
Bis ich die Schweſter dem Gatten gefreit:
So bleib' du dem König zum Pfande,
Bis ich komme, zu löſen die Bande."

Und ſchweigend umarmt ihn der treue Freund
Und liefert ſich aus dem Tyrannen;
Der andere ziehet von bannen.
Und ehe das dritte Morgenrot ſcheint,
Hat er ſchnell mit dem Gatten die Schweſter vereint;
Eilt heim mit ſorgender Seele,
Damit er die Friſt [4] nicht verfehle.

Da gießt unendlicher Regen herab;
Von den Bergen ſtürzen die Quellen,
Und die Bäche, die Ströme ſchwellen.
Und er kommt ans Ufer mit wanderndem Stab —
Da reißet die Brücke der Strudel hinab,
Und donnernd ſprengen die Wogen
Des Gewölbes krachenden Bogen.

Und troſtlos irrt er an Ufers Rand;
Wie weit er auch ſpähet und blicket
Und die Stimme, die rufende, ſchicket,
Da ſtößet kein Nachen vom ſichern Strand,
Der ihn ſetze an das gewünſchte Land;
Kein Schiffer lenket die Fähre [5],
Und der wilde Strom wird zum Meere [6].

Da ſinkt er ans Ufer und weint und fleht,
Die Hände zum Zeus [7] erhoben:
„O hemme des Stromes Toben!
Es eilen die Stunden, im Mittag ſteht
Die Sonne, und wenn ſie niedergeht,
Und ich kann die Stadt nicht erreichen,
So muß der Freund mir erbleichen [8]."

1) die. 2) orders. 3) attempt. 4) the appointed term or
day. 5) the ferry-boat. 6) like a sea. 7) Jupiter. 8) perish
for me.

Doch wachsend erneut sich des Stromes Wut,
Und Welle auf Welle zerrinnet,
Und Stunde an Stunde entrinnet.
Da treibt ihn die Angst, da faßt er sich Mut
Und wirft sich hinein in die brausende Flut [1]
Und teilt mit gewaltigen Armen
Den Strom, und ein Gott hat Erbarmen.

Und gewinnt das Ufer und eilet fort
Und danket dem rettenden Gotte;
Da stürzet die raubende Rotte [2]
Hervor aus des Waldes nächtlichem Ort,
Den Pfad ihm sperrend, und schnaubend Mord
Und hemmet des Wanderers Eile [3]
Mit drohend geschwungener Keule.

„Was wollt ihr?" ruft er vor Schrecken bleich,
„Ich habe nichts als mein Leben,
Das muß ich dem Könige geben."
Und entreißt die Keule dem nächsten gleich:
„Um des Freundes willen, erbarmet euch!"
Und drei, mit gewaltigen Streichen,
Erlegt er [4], die andern entweichen [5].

Und die Sonne versendet glühenden Brand,
Und von der unendlichen Mühe
Ermattet, sinken die Kniee:
„O hast du mich gnädig aus Räubers Hand,
Aus dem Strom mich gerettet ans heilige Land
Und soll hier verschmachtend verderben,
Und der Freund mir, der liebende, sterben!"

Und horch! da sprudelt [6] es silberhell
Ganz nahe, wie rieselndes Rauschen,
Und stille hält er, zu lauschen [7];
Und sieh', aus dem Felsen, geschwätzig, schnell,
Springt murmelnd hervor ein lebendiger Quell,
Und freudig bückt er sich nieder
Und erfrischet die brennenden Glieder [8].

Und die Sonne blickt [9] durch der Zweige Grün
Und malt auf den glänzenden Matten
Der Bäume gigantische Schatten;
Zwei Wanderer sieht er die Straße zieh'n,
Will eilenden Laufes vorüber flieh'n,

1) the roaring stream. 2) a band of robbers. 3) speed. 4) he
fells. 5) run away. 6) it bubbles. 7) to listen. 8) limbs. 9) peeps.

Da hört er die Worte sagen:
„Jetzt wird er ans Kreuz geschlagen[1]."

Und die Angst beflügelt[2] den eilenden Fuß,
Ihn jagen der Sorge Qualen:
Da schimmern[3] in Abendrots Strahlen
Von ferne die Zinnen[4] von Syrakus,
Und entgegen kommt ihm Philostratus,
Des Hauses redlicher Hüter,
Der erkennet entsetzt den Gebieter:

„Zurück! du rettest[5] den Freund nicht mehr,
So rette das eigene Leben:
Den Tod erleidet er eben.
Von Stunde zu Stunde gewartet' er
Mit hoffender Seele der Wiederkehr,
Ihm konnte den mutigen Glauben
Der Hohn des Tyrannen nicht rauben." —

„Und ist es zu spät, und kann ich ihm nicht
Ein Retter willkommen erscheinen,
So soll mich der Tod ihm vereinen.
Deß' rühme der blut'ge Tyrann sich nicht,
Daß der Freund dem Freunde gebrochen die Pflicht[6].
Er schlachte[7] der Opfer zweie
Und glaube an Liebe und Treue."

Und die Sonne geht unter — da steht er am Thor —
Und sieht das Kreuz schon erhöhet[8],
Das die Menge gaffend[9] umstehet;
An dem Seile schon zieht man den Freund empor;
Da zertrennt er gewaltig den dichten Chor[10]:
„Mich, Henker!" ruft er, erwürget!
Da bin ich, für den er gebürget[11]!"

Und Erstaunen ergreift das Volk umher,
In den Armen liegen sich beide
Und weinen vor Schmerzen und Freude.
Da sieht man kein Auge thränenleer,
Und zum Könige bringt man die Wundermär'[12];
Der fühlt ein menschliches Rühren,
Läßt schnell vor den Thron sie führen.

---

1) nailed. 2) to lend wings. 3) glitter. 4) roofs. 5) rescue.
6) word, promise. 7) let him slaughter. 8) raised up. 9) gazing.
10) crowd. 11) bailed. 12) the wonderful news.

Und blicket sie lange verwundert an,
D'rauf spricht er: „Es ist euch gelungen [1],
Ihr habt das Herz mir bezwungen;
Und die Treue, sie ist doch kein leerer Wahn [2],
So nehmet auch mich zum Genossen [3] an:
Ich sei, gewährt mir die Bitte,
In eu'rem Bunde der Dritte."

Fr. v. Schiller

## 8.  Der Ring des Polykrates.*)

Er stand auf seines Daches Zinnen,
Und schaute mit vergnügten Sinnen
Auf das beherrschte Samos hin.
„Dies alles ist mir unterthänig,"
Begann er zu Ägyptens König,
„Gestehe, daß ich glücklich bin."

„Du hast der Götter Gunst erfahren;
Die [4] vormals deinesgleichen waren,
Sie zwingt jetzt deines Zepters Macht.
Doch einer lebt noch, sie zu rächen;
Dich kann mein Mund nicht glücklich sprechen,
So lang' des Feindes Auge wacht."

Und eh' der König noch geendet,
Da stellt sich, von Milet gesendet
Ein Bote dem Tyrannen dar:
„Laß, Herr, des Opfers Düfte [5] steigen,
Und mit des Lorbeers muntern Zweigen
Bekränze dir dein fürstlich Haar.

Getroffen sank der Feind vom Speere.
Mich sendet mit der frohen Märe [6]
Dein treuer Feldherr Polydor;"
Und nimmt aus einem schwarzen Becken,
Noch blutig zu der beiden Schrecken,
Ein wohlbekanntes Haupt hervor.

Der König tritt zurück mit Grauen:
„Doch warn' ich dich, dem Glück zu trauen,"
Versetzt er mit besorgtem Blick;

1) you have succeeded. 2) idle dream. 3) into your fellow-
ship. 4) those who. 5) incense. 6) message.

---

*) See the translation in the Key.

„Bedenk', auf ungetreuen Wellen
— Wie leicht kann sie der Sturm zerschellen, —
Schwimmt deiner Flotte zweifelnd Glück."

Und eh' er noch das Wort gesprochen,
Hat ihn der Jubel[1] unterbrochen,
Der von der Rhede[2] jauchzend schallt.
Mit fremden Schätzen reich beladen,
Kehrt zu den heimischen Gestaden
Der Schiffe mastenreicher Wald.

Der königliche Gast erstaunet:
„Dein Glück ist heute gut gelaunet,
Doch fürchte seinen Unbestand.
Der Kreter[3] nie besiegte Scharen
Bedräuen[4] dich mit Kriegsgefahren,
Schon nahe sind sie diesem Strand."

Und eh' ihm noch das Wort entfallen,
Da sieht man's von den Schiffen wallen,
Und tausend Stimmen rufen: „Sieg!
Von Feindes Not sind wir befreiet,
Die Kreter hat der Sturm zerstreuet:
Vorbei, geendet ist der Krieg."

Das hört der Gastfreund mit Entsetzen:
„Fürwahr, ich muß dich glücklich schätzen;
Doch," spricht er, „zittr' ich für dein Heil.
Mir grauet[5] vor der Götter Neide
Des Lebens ungemischte Freude
Ward keinem Irdischen[6] zu teil[7]."

„Auch mir ist alles wohl geraten:
Bei allen meinen Herrscherthaten
Begleitet mich des Himmels Huld;
Doch hatt' ich einen teuern Erben,
Den nahm mir Gott, ich sah ihn sterben,
Dem Glück bezahlt' ich meine Schuld.

D'rum willst du dich vor Leid bewahren,
So flehe zu den Unsichtbaren,
Daß sie zum Glück den Schmerz verleih'n.
Noch keinen sah ich fröhlich enden,
Auf den mit immer vollen Händen
Die Götter ihre Gaben streu'n.

1) the shouts.  2) road, roadstead.  3) the Cretans.  4) old form
for bedrohen threaten.  5) I am afraid of, I fear.  6) mortal.  7) zu
teil werden to fall to one's lot.

Und wenn's die Götter nicht gewähren,
So acht' auf deines Freundes Lehren
Und rufe selbst das Unglück her;
Und was von allen deinen Schätzen
Dein Herz am höchsten mag ergötzen,
Das nimm und wirf's in dieses Meer."

Und jener spricht, von Furcht beweget:
„Von allem, was die Insel heget,
Ist dieser Ring mein höchstes Gut.
Ihn will ich den Errinnyen[1] weihen,
Ob sie mein Glück mir dann verzeihen," —
Und wirft das Kleinod in die Flut.

Und bei des nächsten Morgens Lichte,
Da tritt mit fröhlichem Gesichte
Ein Fischer vor den Fürsten hin:
„Herr, diesen Fisch hab' ich gefangen,
Wie keiner noch ins Netz gegangen,
Dir zum Geschenke bring' ich ihn."

Und als der Koch den Fisch zerteilet[2],
Kommt er bestürzt herbeigeeilet
Und ruft mit hocherstauntem Blick:
„Sieh, Herr, den Ring, den du getragen;
Ich fand ihn in des Fisches Magen[3],
O! ohne Grenzen[4] ist dein Glück."

Hier wendet sich der Gast mit Grausen[5]:
„So kann ich hier nicht länger hausen,
Mein Freund kannst du nicht weiter sein;
Die Götter wollen dein Verderben:
Fort eil' ich, nicht mit dir zu sterben."
Und sprach's und schiffte schnell sich ein.

Schiller

## 9. Kolumbus.

„Was willst du, Fernando, so trüb und bleich?
    Du bringst mir traurige Mär!" —
„Ach, edler Feldherr, bereitet euch;
    Nicht länger bezähm' ich das Heer!
Wenn jetzt nicht die Küste sich zeigen will,
    So seid ihr ein Opfer der Wut;
Sie fordern laut wie Sturmgebrüll[6]
    Des Feldherrn heiliges Blut."

1) the Avenging Goddesses, Eumenides. 2) dressed. 3) maw.
4) boundless. 5) terror. 6) like a howling storm.

Und eh' noch dem Ritter das Wort entfloh'n,
   Da drängte die Menge sich nach;
Da stürmten[1] die Krieger, die wütenden, schon
   Gleich Wogen ins stille Gemach,
Verzweiflung im wilden, verlöschenden[2] Blick,
   Auf bleichen Gesichtern den Tod:
„Verräter! wo ist nun dein gleißendes[3] Glück?
   Jetzt rett' uns vom Gipfel der Not!

„Du giebst uns nicht Speise, so gieb uns dein Blut!
   Blut!" riefen die Schrecklichen, „Blut!"
Sanft stellte der Große den Felsenmut
   Entgegen der stürmenden Flut:
„Befriedigt mein Blut euch, so nehmt es und lebt!
   Doch bis noch ein einziges mal
Die Sonne dem traurigen Osten entschwebt,
   Vergönnt mir den segnenden Strahl.

„Beleuchtet der Morgen kein rettend Gestad'[4],
   So biet' ich dem Tode mich gern.
Bis dahin verfolgt noch den mutigen Pfad
   Und trauet der Hilfe des Herrn!"
Die Würde des Helden, sein ruhiger Blick,
   Besiegte noch einmal die Wut.
Sie wichen vom Haupte des Helden zurück
   Und schonten sein heiliges Blut.

„Wohlan denn: es sei noch! Doch hebt sich der Strahl
   Und zeigt uns kein rettendes Land,
So siehst du die Sonne zum letztenmal!
   So zitt're der strafenden Hand!"
Geschlossen war also der eiserne Bund;
   Die Schrecklichen kehrten zurück.
Es thue[5] der leuchtende Morgen uns kund[5]
   Des herrlichen Dulders Geschick!

Die Sonne sank, der Schimmer[6] wich,
   Des Helden Brust ward schwer;
Der Kiel durchrauschte schauerlich
   Das weite, wüste Meer.
Die Sterne zogen still herauf,
   Doch ach! kein Hoffnungsstern!
Und von des Schiffes ödem Lauf
   Blieb Land und Rettung fern.

1) to rush in    2) dying, hopeless.    3) dissembling.    4) coast.
5) Let the . . . morning inform, tell us.    6) daylight.

Sein treues Fernrohr in der Hand,
  Die Brust voll Gram, durchwacht,
Nach Westen blickend unverwandt[1],
  Der Held die düst're Nacht.
„Nach Westen, o nach Westen hin
  Beflügle dich, mein Kiel!
Dich grüßt noch sterbend Herz und Sinn,
  Du, meiner Sehnsucht Ziel!

„Doch mild, o Gott, von Himmelshöh'n
  Blick' auf mein Volk herab,
Laß sie nicht trostlos untergeh'n
  Im wilden Flutengrab!"
So sprach der Held, von Mitleid weich[2].
  Da, horch! welch' eiliger Tritt!
„Noch einmal, Fernando, so trüb und bleich?
  Was bringt dein bebender Schritt?"

„Ach, edler Feldherr, es ist gescheh'n!
  Jetzt hebt sich der östliche Strahl!" —
„Sei ruhig, mein Lieber, auf himmlischen Höh'n
  Entspringt der belebende Strahl;
Es waltet[3] die Allmacht von Pol zu Pol,
  Mir lenkt sie zum Tode die Bahn." —
„Leb' wohl denn, mein Feldherr! Leb' ewig wohl!
  Ich höre die Schrecklichen nah'n!"

Und eh' noch dem Ritter das Wort entfloh'n,
  Da drängte die Menge sich nach;
Da strömten die Krieger, die wütenden, schon
  Gleich Wogen ins stille Gemach.
„Ich weiß, was ihr fordert, ich bin bereit:
  Ja, werft mich ins schäumende Meer!
Doch wisset, das rettende Ziel ist nicht weit.
  Gott schütze dich, irrendes Heer!"

Dumpf[4] klirrten die Schwerter; ein wüstes Geschrei
  Erfüllte mit Grauen[5] die Luft;
Der Edle bereitete still sich und frei
  Zum Wege der flutenden Gruft.
Gelöst[6] war nun jedes geheiligte Band;
  Schon sah sich zum schwindelnden Rand
Der treffliche Führer gerissen — und: Land!
  Land! rief es, und donnert' es: Land!

1) staringly, steadfastly gazing. 2) moved. 3) to rule.
4) dully. 5) fright. 6) loosened, broken.

Ein glänzender Streifen, mit Purpur gemalt,
Erschien dem beflügelten Blick;
Vom Golde der steigenden Sonne bestrahlt
Erhob sich das winkende[1] Glück:
Was kaum noch geahnet[2] der zagende Sinn,
Was mutvoll der Große gedacht, —
Sie stürzen zu Füßen dem Herrlichen hin,
Und preisen die göttliche Macht.

Luise Brachmann  † 1822.

1) beckoning.  2) to foresee, anticipate.

---

## 4. Lehr=Gedichte.

### 1. Die Hoffnung.

Es reden und träumen[1] die Menschen viel
Von bessern künft'gen Tagen;
Nach einem glücklichen, goldenen Ziel[2]
Sieht man sie rennen und jagen.
Die Welt wird alt und wird wieder jung,
Doch der Mensch hofft immer Verbesserung.

Die Hoffnung führt ihn ins Leben ein,
Sie umflattert[3] den fröhlichen Knaben,
Den Jüngling begeistert ihr Zauberschein[4],
Sie wird mit dem Greis nicht begraben:
Denn beschließt er im Grabe den müden Lauf,
Noch am Grabe pflanzt er die Hoffnung auf.

Es ist kein leerer, schmeichelnder Wahn,
Erzeugt[5] im Gehirne der Thoren;
Im Herzen kündet es laut sich an:
Zu was[6] Besser'm sind wir geboren.
Und was die innere Stimme spricht,
Das täuscht[7] die hoffende Seele nicht.

Schiller.

1) dream.  2) goal, object.  3) to hover around.  4) magic
light, charm.  5) arisen, produced.  6) etwas.  7) deceives.

## 2. Fragment aus dem „Lied von der Glocke".*)

Vivos voco.    Mortuos plango.    Fulgura frango.

Fest gemauert in der Erden
Steht die Form, aus Lehm gebrannt;
Heute muß die Glocke werden!
Frisch, Gesellen, seid zur Hand.
    Von der Stirne heiß
    Rinnen muß der Schweiß,
Soll das Werk den Meister loben;
Doch der Segen kommt von oben.

Zum Werke, das wir ernst bereiten,
Geziemt sich wohl ein ernstes Wort;
Wenn gute Reden sie begleiten,
Dann fließt die Arbeit munter fort.
So laßt uns jetzt mit Fleiß betrachten,
Was durch die schwache Kraft entspringt;
Den schlechten Mann muß man verachten,
Der nie bedacht, was er vollbringt;
Das ist's ja, was den Menschen zieret,
Und dazu ward ihm der Verstand,
Daß er im innern Herzen spüret,
Was er erschafft mit seiner Hand.

Nehmet Holz vom Fichtenstamme,
Doch recht trocken laßt es sein,
Daß die eingepreßte Flamme
Schlage zu dem Schwalch hinein!
    Kocht des Kupfers Brei!
    Schnell das Zinn herbei,
Daß die zähe Glockenspeise
Fließe nach der rechten Weise!

Was in des Dammes tiefer Grube
Die Hand mit Feuers Hilfe baut,
Hoch auf des Turmes Glockenstube,
Da wird es von uns zeugen laut.
Noch dauern wird's in späten Tagen
Und rühren vieler Menschen Ohr,
Und wird mit den Betrübten klagen,
Und stimmen zu der Andacht Chor.
Was unten tief dem Erdensohne
Das wechselnde Verhängnis bringt,
Das schlägt an die metall'ne Krone,
Die es erbaulich weiter klingt.

----

*) See the translation in the Key.

Weiße Blasen seh' ich springen;
Wohl! die Massen sind im Fluß.
Laßt's mit Aschensalz durchdringen,
Das befördert schnell den Guß.
　Auch vom Schaume rein
　Muß die Mischung sein,
Daß vom reinlichen Metalle
Rein und voll die Stimme schalle.

Denn mit der Freude Feierklange
Begrüßt sie das geliebte Kind
Auf seines Lebens erstem Gange,
Den es in Schlafes Arm beginnt;
Ihm ruhen noch im Zeitenschoße
Die schwarzen und die heitern Lose;
Der Mutterliebe zarte Sorgen
Bewachen seinen gold'nen Morgen. —
Die Jahre fliehen pfeilgeschwind.
Vom Mädchen reißt sich stolz der Knabe.
Er stürmt ins Leben wild hinaus,
Durchmißt die Welt am Wanderstabe,
Fremd kehrt er heim ins Vaterhaus.
Und herrlich, in der Jugend Prangen,
Wie ein Gebild aus Himmels-Höh'n,
Mit züchtigen, verschämten Wangen
Sieht er die Jungfrau vor sich steh'n.
Da faßt ein namenloses Sehnen
Des Jünglings Herz, er irrt allein;
Aus seinen Augen brechen Thränen,
Er flieht der Brüder wilden Reih'n;
Errötend folgt er ihren Spuren
Und ist von ihrem Gruß beglückt;
Das Schönste sucht er auf den Fluren,
Womit er seine Liebe schmückt.
O! zarte Sehnsucht, süßes Hoffen,
Der ersten Liebe gold'ne Zeit,
Das Auge sieht den Himmel offen,
Es schwelgt das Herz in Seligkeit.
O! daß sie ewig grünen bliebe,
Die schöne Zeit der jungen Liebe!

Denn wo das Strenge mit dem Zarten,
Wo Starkes sich und Mildes paarten,
Da gibt es einen guten Klang;
D'rum prüfe, wer sich ewig bindet,
Ob sich das Herz zum Herzen findet!
Der Wahn ist kurz, die Reu' ist lang.

—　　—　　—

Die Leidenschaft flieht,
Die Liebe muß bleiben;
Die Blume verblüht,
Die Frucht muß treiben;
Der Mann muß hinaus
Ins feindliche Leben,
Muß wirken und streben
Und pflanzen und schaffen,
Erlisten, erraffen,
Muß wetten und wagen,
Das Glück zu erjagen.

—   —

Wohl! Nun kann der Guß beginnen;
Schön gezacket ist der Bruch.
Doch, bevor wir's lassen rinnen,
Betet einen frommen Spruch!
    Stoßt' den Zapfen aus!
    Gott bewahr' das Haus!
Rauchend in des Henkels Bogen
Schießt's mit feuerbraunen Wogen.

Wohlthätig ist des Feuers Macht,
Wenn sie der Mensch bezähmt, bewacht,
Und was er bildet, was er schafft,
Das dankt er dieser Himmelskraft.
Doch furchtbar wird die Himmelskraft,
Wenn sie der Fessel sich entrafft,
Einhertritt auf der eig'nen Spur,
Die freie Tochter der Natur.
Wehe, wenn sie losgelassen,
Wachsend, ohne Widerstand,
Durch die volkbelebten Gassen
Wälzt den ungeheuren Brand!
Denn die Elemente hassen
Das Gebild der Menschenhand.
Aus den Wolken quillt der Segen,
Strömt der Regen;
Aus der Wolke, ohne Wahl,
Zuckt der Strahl!
Hört ihr's wimmern hoch vom Turm?
Das ist Sturm!
Rot, wie Blut,
Ist der Himmel;
Das ist nicht des Tages Glut!
Welch' Getümmel

Straßen auf!
Dampf wallt auf!
Flackernd steigt die Feuersäule,
Durch der Straße lange Zeile
Wächst es fort mit Windeseile;
Kochend wie aus Ofens Rachen
Glüh'n die Lüfte, Balken krachen,
Pfosten stürzen, Fenster klirren,
Kinder jammern, Mütter irren,
Tiere wimmern
Unter Trümmern:
Alles rennet, rettet, flüchtet,
Taghell ist die Nacht gelichtet;
Durch der Hände lange Kette,
Um die Wette,
Fliegt der Eimer, hoch im Bogen
Sprißen Quellen Wasserwogen.
Heulend kommt der Sturm geflogen,
Der die Flamme brausend sucht.
Prasselnd in die dürre Frucht
Fällt sie, in des Speichers Räume,
In der Sparren dürre Baume,
Und als wollte sie im Wehen
Mit sich fort der Erde Wucht
Reißen in gewalt'ger Flucht,
Wächst sie in des Himmels Höhen
Riesengroß!
Hoffnungslos
Weicht der Mensch der Götterstärke!
Müßig sieht er seine Werke
Und bewundernd untergehen.


   Leergebrannt
Ist die Stätte,
Wilder Stürme rauhes Bette.
In den öden Fensterhöhlen
Wohnt das Grauen,
Und des Himmels Wolken schauen
Hoch hinein.


   Einen Blick
Nach dem Grabe
Seiner Habe
Sendet noch der Mensch zurück;
Greift fröhlich dann zum Wanderstabe.

Was Feuers Wut ihm auch geraubt,
Ein süßer Trost ist ihm geblieben:
Er zählt die Häupter seiner Lieben,
Und sieh'! ihm fehlt kein teures Haupt.

— — — —

Nun zerbrecht mir das Gebäude,
Seine Absicht hat's erfüllt
Daß sich Herz und Auge weide
An dem wohlgelung'nen Bild.
  Schwingt den Hammer, schwingt,
  Bis der Mantel springt!
Wenn die Glock' soll auferstehen,
Muß die Form in Stücke gehen.

Der Meister kann die Form zerbrechen
Mit weiser Hand zur rechten Zeit;
Doch wehe, wenn in Flammenbächen
Das glüh'nde Erz sich selbst befreit!
Blindwütend mit des Donners Krachen
Zersprengt es das geborst'ne Haus,
Und wie aus off'nem Höllenrachen
Speit es Verderben zündend aus;
Wo rohe Kräfte sinnlos walten,
Da kann sich kein Gebild gestalten;
Wenn sich die Völker selbst befrei'n,
Da kann die Wohlfahrt nicht gedeih'n.

Weh', wenn sich in dem Schoß der Städte
Der Feuerzunder still gehäuft,
Das Volk, zerreißend seine Kette,
Zur Eigenhilfe schrecklich greift!
Da zerret an der Glocke Strängen
Der Aufruhr, daß sie heulend schallt,
Und, nur geweiht zu Friedensklängen,
Die Losung anstimmt zur Gewalt.

Freiheit und Gleichheit! hört man schallen;
Der ruh'ge Bürger greift zur Wehr.
Die Straßen füllen sich, die Hallen,
Und Würgerbanden zieh'n umher.
Da werden Weiber zu Hyänen
Und treiben mit Entsetzen Scherz:
Noch zuckend, mit des Panthers Zähnen,
Zerreißen sie des Feindes Herz.
Nichts Heiliges ist mehr, es lösen
Sich alle Bande frommer Scheu;

Der Gute räumt den Platz dem Bösen,
Und alle Laster walten frei.
Gefährlich ist's, den Leu zu wecken,
Verderblich ist des Tigers Zahn;
Jedoch der schrecklichste der Schrecken,
Das ist der Mensch in seinem Wahn.
Weh' denen, die dem Ewigblinden
Des Lichtes Himmelsfackel leih'n!
Sie strahlt ihm nicht, sie kann nur zünden
Und äschert Städt' und Länder ein.

Freude hat mir Gott gegeben!
Sehet! wie ein gold'ner Stern
Aus der Hülse, blank und eben,
Schält sich der metall'ne Kern.
Von dem Helm zum Kranz
Spielt's, wie Sonnenglanz.
Auch des Wappens nette Schilder
Loben den erfahr'nen Bilder.

Herein! herein!
Gesellen alle, schließt den Reih'n,
Daß wir die Glocke taufend weih'n,
Concordia soll ihr Name sein.
Zur Eintracht, zu herzinnigem Vereine
Versammle sie die liebende Gemeine.

Und dies sei fortan ihr Beruf,
Wozu der Meister sie erschuf!
Hoch über'm niedern Erdenleben
Soll sie im blauen Himmelszelt,
Die Nachbarin des Donners, schweben
Und grenzen an die Sternenwelt.
Soll eine Stimme sein von oben,
Wie der Gestirne helle Schar,
Die ihren Schöpfer wandelnd loben
Und führen das bekränzte Jahr.
Nur ewigen und ernsten Dingen
Sei ihr metall'ner Mund geweiht,
Und stündlich mit den schnellen Schwingen
Berühr' im Fluge sie die Zeit.
Dem Schicksal leihe sie die Zunge;
Selbst herzlos, ohne Mitgefühl,
Begleite sie mit ihrem Schwunge
Des Lebens wechselvolles Spiel.

Und wie der Klang im Ohr vergehet,
Der mächtig tönend ihr entschallt,
So lehre sie, daß nichts bestehet,
Daß alles Irdische verhallt.

Jetzo mit der Kraft des Stranges
Wiegt die Glock' mir aus der Gruft,
Daß sie in das Reich des Klanges
Steige, in die Himmelsluft!
Ziehet, ziehet, hebt!
Sie bewegt sich, schwebt!
Freude dieser Stadt bedeute,
Friede sei ihr erst Geläute.

Schiller.

## 5. Dramatische Fragmente.

### 1. Aus Schillers „Maria Stuart".

(Dritter Aufzug. Erster Auftritt.)

Maria.  Hanna Kennedy.

#### Kennedy.

Ihr eilet ja, als wenn ihr Flügel hättet;
So kann ich euch nicht folgen, wartet doch!

#### Maria.

Laß mich der neuen Freiheit genießen,
Laß mich ein Kind sein, sei es mit!
Und auf dem grünen Teppich der Wiesen
Prüfen den leichten, geflügelten Schritt.
Bin ich dem finstern Gefangnis entstiegen?
Hält sie mich nicht mehr, die traurige Gruft?
Laß mich in vollen, in durstigen Zügen
Trinken die freie, die himmlische Luft.

#### Kennedy.

O meine teu're Lady! Euer Kerker
Ist nur um ein klein weniges erweitert;
Ihr seht nur nicht die Mauer, die uns einschließt,
Weil sie der Bäume dicht Gesträuch verstecht.

### Maria.

O Dank, Dank, diesen freundlich grünen Bäumen,
Die meines Kerkers Mauern mir verstecken!
Ich will mich frei und glücklich träumen,
Warum aus meinem süßen Wahn mich wecken?
Umfängt mich nicht der weite Himmelsschoß?
Die Blicke, frei und fessellos,
Ergehen sich in ungemeſſ'nen Räumen:
Dort, wo die grauen Nebelberge ragen,
Fängt meines Reiches Grenze an,
Und diese Wolken, die nach Mittag jagen,
Sie suchen Frankreichs fernen Ocean.
    Eilende Wolken! Segler der Lüfte!
    Wer mit euch wanderte, mit euch schiffte!
    Grüßet mir freundlich mein Jugendland!
    Ich bin gefangen, ich bin in Banden,
    Ach, ich hab' keinen andern Gesandten!
    Frei in den Lüften ist eu're Bahn,
    Ihr seid nicht dieser Königin unterthan.

### Kennedy.

Ach, teu're Lady! Ihr seid außer Euch,
Die lang entbehrte Freiheit macht Euch schwärmen.

### Maria.

Dort legt ein Fischer den Nachen an!
Dieses elende Fahrzeug könnte mich retten,
Brächte mich schnell zu befreundeten Städten;
Spärlich nährt es den dürftigen Mann.
Beladen wollt' ich ihn reich mit Schätzen;
Einen Zug sollt' er thun, wie er keinen gethan,
Das Glück sollt' er finden in seinen Netzen,
Nähm' er mich ein in den rettenden Kahn.

### Kennedy.

Verlor'ne Wünsche! Seht Ihr nicht, daß uns
Von ferne dort die Spähertritte folgen?
Ein finster grausames Verbot scheucht jedes
Mitleidige Geschöpf aus unserm Wege.

### Maria.

Nein, gute Hanna. Glaub' mir, nicht umsonst
Ist meines Kerkers Thor geöffnet worden;
Die kleine Gunst ist mir des größern Glücks
Verkünderin. Ich irre nicht. Es ist
Der Liebe thät'ge Hand, der ich sie danke.
Lord Lesters mächt'gen Arm erkenn' ich drin

Allmählich will man mein Gefängnis weiten,
Durch Kleineres zum Größern mich gewöhnen,
Bis ich das Antlitz dessen endlich schaue,
Der mir die Bande löst auf immerdar.

Kennedy.

Ach! ich kann diesen Widerspruch nicht reimen!
Noch gestern kündigt man den Tod Euch an,
Und heute wird Euch plötzlich solche Freiheit.
Auch denen, hört' ich sagen, wird die Kette
Gelöst, auf die die ew'ge Freiheit wartet.

Maria.

Hörst du das Hifthorn? Hörst du's klingen,
Mächtigen Rufes, durch Feld und Hain?
Ach, auf das mutige Roß mich zu schwingen,
An den fröhlichen Zug mich zu reih'n!
Noch mehr! o die bekannte Stimme,
Schmerzlich süßer Erinnerung voll!
Oft vernahm sie mein Ohr mit Freuden,
Auf des Hochlands bergigen Haiden,
Wann die tobende Jagd erscholl.

---

(Zweiter Auftritt.)
Paulet. Die Vorigen.

Paulet.

Nun! Hab' ich's endlich recht gemacht, Milady?
Verdien' ich einmal Euren Dank?

Maria.

           Wie, Ritter?
Seid Ihr's, der diese Gunst mir ausgewirkt?
Ihr seid's?

Paulet.

        Warum soll ich's nicht sein? Ich war
Am Hof, ich überbrachte Euer Schreiben. —

Maria.

Ihr übergabt es? Wirklich thatet Ihr's?
Und diese Freiheit, die ich jetzt genieße,
Ist eine Frucht des Brief's —

Paulet (mit Bedeutung.)

Macht Euch auf eine größ're noch gefaßt.

Maria.

Auf eine größ're, Sir? Was meint Ihr damit?

Paulet.

Ihr hörtet doch die Hörner —

Maria.

Ihr erschreckt mich.

Paulet.

Die Königin jagt in dieser Gegend.

Maria.

Was?

Paulet.

In wenigen Augenblicken steht sie vor Euch.

Kennedy

(auf Marien zueilend, welche zittert und hinzusinken droht).

Wie wird Euch, teure Lady! Ihr erblaßt.

Paulet.

Nun! Ist's nun nicht recht? War's nicht Eure Bitte?
Sie wird Euch früh'r gewährt, als Ihr gedacht.
Ihr war't sonst immer so geschwinder Zunge:
Jetzt bringet Eure Worte an, jetzt ist
Der Augenblick, zu reden!

Maria.

O, warum hat man mich nicht darauf vorbereitet!
Jetzt bin ich nicht darauf gefaßt, jetzt nicht.
Was ich mir als die höchste Gunst erbeten,
Dünkt mir jetzt schrecklich, fürchterlich. — Komm, Hanna,
Führ' mich ins Haus, daß ich mich fasse, mich
Erhole —

Paulet.

Bleibt. Ihr müßt sie hier erwarten.
Wohl, wohl mag's Euch beängstigen, ich glaub's,
Vor Eurem Richter zu erscheinen.

_____

(Dritter Auftritt.)

Graf Shrewsbury und die Vorigen.

Maria.

Es ist nicht darum! Gott, mir ist ganz anders
Zu Mut — Ach edler Shrewsbury, Ihr kommt

OTTO

Vom Himmel mir ein Engel zugesendet!
— Ich kann sie nicht seh'n! Rettet, rettet mich
Vor dem verhaßten Anblick —

### Shrewsbury.

Kommt zu Euch, Königin! Faßt Euren Mut
Zusammen. Das ist die entscheidungsvolle Stunde.

### Maria.

Ich habe d'rauf geharret — Jahre lang
Mich d'rauf bereitet, alles hab' ich mir
Gesagt und ins Gedächtnis eingeschrieben,
Wie ich sie rühren wollte und bewegen!
Vergessen plötzlich, ausgelöscht ist alles,
Nichts lebt in mir in diesem Augenblick,
Als meiner Leiden brennendes Gefühl.
In blut'gen Haß gewendet wider sie
Ist mir das Herz, es fliehen alle guten
Gedanken, und die Schlangenhaare schüttelnd
Umstehen mich die finstern Höllengeister.

### Shrewsbury.

Gebietet Eurem wild empörten Blut,
Bezwingt des Herzens Bitterkeit! Es bringt
Nicht gute Frucht, wenn Haß dem Haß begegnet.
Wie sehr auch Euer Inn'res widerstrebe,
Gehorcht der Zeit und dem Gesetz der Stunde!
Sie ist die Mächtige — demütigt Euch!

### Maria.

Vor ihr! Ich kann es nimmermehr!

### Shrewsbury.

                              Thut's dennoch!
Sprecht ehrerbietig, mit Gelassenheit!
Ruft ihre Großmut an, trotzt nicht, jetzt nicht
Auf Euer Recht, jetzo ist nicht die Stunde.

### Maria.

Ach, mein Verderben hab' ich mir erfleht,
Und mir zum Fluche wird mein Fleh'n erhört!
Nie hätten wir uns sehen sollen, niemals!
Daraus kann nimmer, nimmer Gutes kommen!
Eh'r mögen Feu'r und Wasser sich in Liebe
Begegnen, und das Lamm den Tiger küssen —
Ich bin zu schwer verletzt — sie hat zu schwer
Beleidigt — Nie ist zwischen uns Versöhnung!

### Shrewsbury.

Seht sie nur erst von Angesicht!
Ich sah es ja, wie sie von Eurem Brief
Erschüttert war, ihr Auge schwamm in Thränen.
Nein, sie ist nicht gefühllos, hegt ihr selbst
Nur besseres Vertrauen — Darum eben
Bin ich vorausgeeilt, damit ich Euch
In Fassung setzen und ermahnen möchte.

### Maria.

Ach, Talbot! Ihr war't stets mein Freund — Daß ich
In Eurer milden Haft geblieben wäre!
Es ward mir hart begegnet, Shrewsbury!

### Shrewsbury (ihre Hand ergreifend).

Vergeßt jetzt alles. Darauf denkt allein,
Wie Ihr sie unterwürfig wollt empfangen.

### Maria.

Ist Burleigh auch mit ihr, mein böser Engel?

### Shrewsbury.

Niemand begleitet sie, als Graf von Lester.

### Maria.

Lord Lester?

### Shrewsbury.

Fürchtet nichts von ihm. Nicht er
Will Euren Untergang — Sein Werk ist es,
Daß Euch die Königin die Zusammenkunft
Bewilligt.

### Paulet.

Die Königin kommt!

----

### 2. Monolog aus Schillers „Wilhelm Tell".*)

### (Vierter Aufzug. Dritte Scene.)

### Tell.

Durch diese hohle Gasse muß er kommen:
Es führt kein andrer Weg nach Küßnacht — Hier
Vollend' ich's — die Gelegenheit ist günstig.

----

*) The best and cheapest edition of „Wilhelm Tell" with copious
English notes is by Dr. **Emil Otto**. Stuttgart, **J. G. Cotta**.

Dort der Hollunderstrauch verbirgt mich ihm;
Von dort herab kann ihn mein Pfeil erlangen:
Des Weges Enge wehret den Verfolgern.
Mach' deine Rechnung mit dem Himmel, Vogt!
Fort mußt du, deine Uhr ist abgelaufen.


Ich lebte still und harmlos — das Geschoß
War auf des Waldes Tiere nur gerichtet,
Meine Gedanken waren rein von Mord, —
Du hast aus meinem Frieden mich heraus
Geschreckt; in gährend Drachengift hast du
Die Milch der frommen Denkart mir verwandelt;
Zum Ungeheuren hast du mich gewöhnt —
Wer sich des Kindes Haupt zum Ziele setzte,
Der kann auch treffen in das Herz des Feindes.


Die armen Kindlein, die unschuldigen,
Das treue Weib muß ich vor deiner Wut
Beschützen, Landvogt! — Da, als ich den Bogenstrang
Anzog — als mir die Hand erzitterte —
Als du mit grausam teuflischer Lust
Mich zwangst, aufs Haupt des Kindes anzulegen —
Als ich unmächtig flehend rang vor dir;
Damals gelobt' ich mir in meinem Innern
Mit furchtbar'm Eidschwur, den nur Gott gehört,
Daß meines nächsten Schusses erstes Ziel
Dein Herz sein sollte — Was ich mir gelobt
In jenes Augenblickes Höllenqualen,
Ist eine heil'ge Schuld; ich will sie zahlen.


Du bist mein Herr und meines Kaisers Vogt;
Doch nicht der Kaiser hätte sich erlaubt,
Was du. — Er sandte dich in diese Lande,
Um Recht zu sprechen — strenges, denn er zürnet —
Doch nicht, um mit der mörderischen Lust
Dich jedes Gräuels straflos zu erfrechen:
Es lebt ein Gott, zu strafen und zu rächen.


Komm du hervor, du Bringer bitt'rer Schmerzen,
Mein teures Kleinod jetzt, mein höchster Schatz —
Ein Ziel will ich dir geben, das bis jetzt
Der frommen Bitte undurchdringlich war —
Doch dir soll es nicht widersteh'n. — Und du,
Vertraute Bogensehne, die so oft
Mir treu gedient hat in der Freude Spielen,
Verlaß' mich nicht im fürchterlichen Ernst!

Nur jetzt noch halte fest, du treuer Strang,
Der mir so oft den herben Pfeil beflügelt;
Entränn' er jetzo kraftlos meinen Handen,
Ich habe keinen zweiten zu versenden.

Auf diese Bank von Stein will ich mich setzen,
Dem Wanderer zur kurzen Ruh bereitet —
Denn hier ist keine Heimat — Jeder treibt
Sich an dem andern rasch und fremd vorüber
Und fraget nicht nach seinem Schmerz. — Hier geht
Der sorgenvolle Kaufmann und der leicht
Geschürzte Pilger — der andächt'ge Mönch,
Der düst're Räuber und der heit're Spielmann,
Der Saumer mit dem schwer belad'nen Roß,
Der ferne herkommt von der Menschen Ländern,
Denn jede Straße führt ans End' der Welt.
Sie alle ziehen ihres Weges fort
An ihr Geschäft, und meines — ist der Mord!

Sonst, wenn der Vater auszog, liebe Kinder,
Da war ein Freuen, wenn er wieder kam:
Denn niemals kehrt er heim, er bracht' euch etwas,
War's eine schöne Alpenblume, war's
Ein seltner Vogel oder Ammonshorn,
Wie es der Wand'rer findet auf den Bergen —
Jetzt geht er einem andern Waidwerk nach:
Am wilden Weg sitzt er mit Mordgedanken;
Des Feindes Leben ist's, worauf er lauert.
— Und doch an euch nur denkt er, liebe Kinder
Auch jetzt — Euch zu verteidigen, eure Unschuld
Zu schützen vor der Rache des Tyrannen,
Will er zum Morde jetzt den Bogen spannen.

Ich lau're auf ein edles Wild. — Laßt sich's
Der Jager nicht verdrießen, Tage lang
Umherzustreifen in des Winters Strenge,
Von Fels zu Fels den Wagesprung zu thun,
Hinanzuklimmen an den glatten Wänden,
Wo er sich anleimt mit dem eig'nen Blut,
Um ein armselig Grattier zu erjagen.
Hier gilt es einen köstlicheren Preis,
Das Herz des Todfeinds, der mich will verderben.

Mein ganzes Leben lang hab' ich den Bogen
Gehandhabt, mich geübt nach Schützenregel;
Ich habe oft geschossen in das Schwarze
Un

Vom Freudenschießen — Aber heute will ich
Den Meisterschuß thun und das Beste mir
Im ganzen Umkreis des Gebirgs gewinnen.

— —

### 3. Monolog aus Schillers „Jungfrau von Orleans".
#### (Vierter Auftritt.)

Johanna (allein).

Lebt wohl, ihr Berge, ihr geliebten Triften,
Ihr traulich stillen Thäler, lebet wohl!
Johanna wird nun nicht mehr auf euch wandeln,
Johanna sagt euch ewig Lebewohl.
Ihr Wiesen, die ich wässerte! Ihr Bäume,
Die ich gepflanzet, grünet fröhlich fort!
Lebt wohl, ihr Grotten und ihr kühlen Brunnen!
Du Echo, holde Stimme dieses Thals,
Die oft mir Antwort gab auf meine Lieder,
Johanna geht und nimmer kehrt sie wieder!

Ihr Plätze aller meiner stillen Freuden,
Euch lass' ich hinter mir auf immerdar!
Zerstreuet euch, ihr Lammer, auf der Heiden,
Ihr seid jetzt eine hirtenlose Schar,
Denn eine andre Herde muß ich weiden
Dort auf dem blut'gen Felde der Gefahr.
So ist des Geistes Ruf an mich ergangen;
Mich treibt nicht eitles, irdisches Verlangen.

Denn der zu Mosen auf des Horebs Höhen
Im feu'rigen Busch sich flammend niederließ
Und ihm befahl, vor Pharao zu stehen,
Der einst den frommen Knaben Isai's,
Den Hirten, sich zum Streiter ausersehen,
Der stets den Hirten gnadig sich bewies,
Er sprach zu mir aus dieses Baumes Zweigen:
„Geh' hin! Du sollst auf Erden für mich zeugen.

„In rauhes Erz sollst du die Glieder schnüren.
Mit Stahl bedecken deine zarte Brust!
Nicht Männerliebe darf dein Herz berühren
Mit sünd'gen Flammen eitler Erdenlust;
Nie wird der Brautkranz deine Locke zieren,
Dir blüht kein lieblich Kind an deiner Brust;
Doch werde ich mit triegerischen Ehren,
Vor allen Erdenfrauen dich verklären.

„Denn wenn im Kampf die Mutigsten verzagen,
Wenn Frankreichs letztes Schicksal nun sich naht,
Dann wirst du meine Oriflamme tragen,
Und, wie die rasche Schnitterin die Saat,
Den stolzen Überwinder niederschlagen;
Umwälzen wirst du seines Glückes Rad,
Errettung bringen Frankreichs Heldensöhnen,
Und Rheims befrei'n und deinen König krönen!"

Ein Zeichen hat der Himmel mir verheißen,
Er sendet mir den Helm, er kommt von ihm;
Mit Götterkraft berühret mich sein Eisen,
Und mich durchflammt der Mut der Cherubim;
Ins Kriegsgewühl hinein will es mich reißen,
Es treibt mich fort mit Sturmes Ungestüm;
Den Feldruf hör' ich mächtig zu mir dringen,
Das Schlachtroß steigt, und die Trompeten klingen.

----

(Fünfter Aufzug.   Vierzehnter Auftritt.)

(Soldaten mit fliegenden Fahnen erfüllen den Hintergrund. Vor ihnen der König und der
Herzog von Burgund; in den Armen beider Fürsten liegt Johanna, tötlich verwundet,
ohne Zeichen des Lebens. Sie treten langsam vorwärts. Agnes Sorel stürzt herein.)

Sorel.
Ihr seid befreit — Ihr lebt. — Ich hab' Euch wieder!

König.
Ich bin befreit. — Ich bin's um diesen Preis!
(Zeigt auf Johanna.)

Sorel.
Johanna! Gott! sie stirbt!

Burgund.
Sie hat geendet!
Seht einen Engel scheiden! Seht, wie sie da liegt,
Schmerzlos und ruhig, wie ein schlafend Kind!
Des Himmels Friede spielt um ihre Züge;
Kein Atem hebt den Busen mehr, doch Leben
Ist noch zu spüren in der warmen Hand.

König.
Sie ist dahin. — Sie wird nicht mehr erwachen,
Ihr Auge wird das Ird'sche nicht mehr schauen.
Schon schwebt sie droben, ein verklärter Geist,
Sieht unsern Schmerz nicht mehr und uns're Reue.

Sorel.
Sie schlägt die Augen auf! sie lebt!

**Burgund** (erstaunt)

Kehrt sie
Uns aus dem Grab zurück?  Zwingt sie den Tod?
Sie richtet sich empor!  Sie steht!

**Johanna** (steht ganz aufgerichtet und schaut umher).

Wo bin ich?

**Burgund.**

Bei deinem Volk, Johanna!  Bei den Deinen!

**König.**

In deiner Freunde, deines Königs Armen.

**Johanna** (nachdem sie ihn lange starr angesehen).

Nein, ich bin keine Zauberin!  Gewiß,
Ich bin's nicht.

**König.**

Du bist heilig wie ein Engel;
Doch unser Auge war mit Nacht bedeckt.

**Johanna** (sieht heiter lächelnd umher).

Und ich bin wirklich unter meinem Volk?
Und bin nicht mehr verachtet und verstoßen?
Man flucht mir nicht, man sieht mich gütig an?
— Ja, jetzt erkenn' ich deutlich alles wieder!
Das ist mein König! Das sind Frankreichs Fahnen!
Doch meine Fahne seh' ich nicht. — Wo ist sie?
Nicht ohne meine Fahne darf ich kommen;
Von meinem Meister ward sie mir vertraut;
Vor seinem Thron muß ich sie niederlegen;
Ich darf sie zeigen, denn ich trug sie treu.

**König** (mit abgewandtem Gesicht).

Gebt ihr die Fahne!
(Man reicht sie ihr. Sie steht ganz frei aufgerichtet, die Fahne in der Hand; der Himmel
ist von einem rosigen Schein beleuchtet.)

---

Printed by Julius Groos at Heidelberg.

Milton Keynes UK
Ingram Content Group UK Ltd.
UKHW021028231024
2330UKWH00037B/204